HAIKU EAST AND WEST ...

BPX 1

BOCHUM PUBLICATIONS In
Evolutionary Cultural Semiotics

<u>Aim and Scope:</u> Transdisciplinary contributions to the analysis of sign processes and accompanying events from the perspective of the evolution of culture.

<u>Modes of Publication:</u> Irregular intervals, approximately 5 to 10 volumes per year. Monographs, collections of papers on topical issues, proceedings of colloquies etc.

<u>General Editor:</u> Walter A. Koch (Bochum).

<u>Advisory Editors:</u> Karl Eimermacher (Bochum), Achim Eschbach (Essen).

<u>Advisory Board:</u> Yoshihiko Ikegami (Tokyo), Rolf Kloepfer (Mannheim), Roland Posner (Berlin), Thomas A. Sebeok (Bloomington), Irene P. Winner (Cambridge, Mass.), Thomas G. Winner (Cambridge, Mass.).

<u>Editorial Staff:</u> Peter Grzybek, Peter L. W. Koch, Susan Vogel, Yoriko Yamada-Bochynek (all Bochum).

<u>Editorial Address:</u>   Englisches Seminar
Ruhr-Universität Bochum
Postfach 102148
D-4630 Bochum 1
Fed. Rep. Germany
Tel. (0234) 700-2590 or 2519

<u>Orders</u> for individual volumes or the entire series should be directed to:
Studienverlag Dr. Norbert Brockmeyer
Querenburger Höhe 281
D-4630 Bochum-Querenburg
Fed. Rep. Germany
Tel. (0234) 701360 or 701383

A <u>list of available and forthcoming volumes</u> of the series is printed towards the end of this volume.

HAIKU EAST AND WEST

A Semiogenetic Approach

Yoriko YAMADA - BOCHYNEK

BPX 1

Studienverlag Dr. Norbert Brockmeyer · Bochum · 1985

CIP-Kurztitelaufnahme der Deutschen Bibliothek

CIP-Kurztitelaufnahme der Deutschen Bibliothek
Yamada-Bochynek, Yoriko:
Haiku East and West: a semiogenet. approach /
Yoriko Yamada-Bochynek. – Bochum:
Studienverlag Brockmeyer, 1985.
  (BPX; 1)
  ISBN 3-88339-404-1

NE: GT

© 1985 by Studienverlag Dr. Norbert Brockmeyer,
Querenburger Höhe 281, D-4630 Bochum-Querenburg, Fed. Rep. Germany.
Printed in Germany by Druck Thiebes GmbH & Co. KG, Hagen.

ISBN 3-88339-404-1
Alle Rechte vorbehalten. All rights reserved.

To my parents

bochum publications in
Evolutionary Cultural Semiotics

EDITORIAL

BPX is a series of monographs or collections of papers (also resulting from pertinent colloquia) that are published at irregular intervals. The series is designed to bring into focus the interaction of nature and culture. Particular emphasis will be given to the overall ideas of <u>integration</u> and <u>focus</u>. Communicative processes will be considered to be integrated parts of cosmogenesis, biogenesis, psychogenesis etc. The fundamental processes underlying all levels of evolution are assumed to be identical. Not unlike most other sciences, <u>evolutionary semiotics</u> is considered to share in an ultimately unitary and indivisible reality. Its specificity is derived solely from its focus on a particular level of evolution: although seemingly obvious, the exact nature of this inevitable bias (human or proto-human predicament) continues to deserve concentrated attention. The prototypical structure for this is considered to be <u>culture</u>: a phenomenon whose true integrative potentialities have not yet been fully discovered or explored. For a semiotics thus conceived, structure and process are not different phases of reality and/or sciences but rather mere faces of a unitary field. In the view of this series, then, any fruitful attempt at semiotic analysis will be based on premises of macro-integration - or <u>evolution</u> - and of micro-integration - or <u>culture</u>.

While it is the ambitious goal of this series to encourage interdisciplinary work on the nature of culture as outlined above, BPX will have to be content - especially in its initial stages - with more modest attempts at elucidating semiogenesis. In addition, most contributions will presumably be relatively specific, covering all possible areas of culture or proto-culture, with the desired unity or homogeneity - regarding aim and scope - largely confined to the background.

Bochum, December 1984   W. A. K.

ACKNOWLEDGEMENTS

This book was submitted to the Ruhr-Universität Bochum as a doctoral dissertation in 1984. I am deeply indebted to Prof. Dr. Walter A. Koch, the semiotician, without whose warm encouragement and academic advice the book would not have been completed. My sincere gratitude is also due to Prof. Dr. Bruno Lewin, the Japanologist, for having motivated me to rediscover the precious tradition of Japanese literature. I also should like to acknowledge the illuminative criticism and stimulating suggestions offered by Viktôria Eschbach-Szabô, William Walker, Susan Vogel, Achim Eschbach, and my colleagues at the English Department.

My special thanks go to Mrs. Lorena Sattler in Lodi, California, who kindly sent me several collections of American Haiku in late 1980, with which the analysis presented in this book could be launched, and above all, to my husband Christian, whose tireless support had helped me through the difficulties of studying in Germany.

TABLE OF CONTENTS

0.0 INTRODUCTORY REMARKS: THE DOMAIN OF THE PRESENT STUDY 1

0. INTRODUCTION; SEMIOTICS: THE THEORETICAL BACKGROUND
0.1 The Semiogenetic Approach 12
0.2 Semiogenetic Interdisciplinarity and Evolution: Peirce's Phenomenology and Epistemology 15
0.3 A Semiogenetic Model 18
0.3.1 The History Model: The Diachrony of Semiogenesis 19
0.3.2 Situation - Communication Model: The Synchrony of Semiogenesis 22
0.3.3 Diachrony in the Si-Model: The Ontogenesis and Phylogenesis of Semiotic Competence 24
0.3.4 Three Foci in the Si-Model 25
0.3.5 The Simplified Si-Model and Meta-Analysis 26
0.3.5.1 Participants in Texts as a Plurality of Texts 29
0.3.5.2 Texts as Signs 30
0.3.5.3 Trifocal Selection 30
0.4 The Analytical Framework of the Present Study 32

CHAPTER 1: PARTICIPANTS IN TEXTS AS A PLURALITY OF TEXTS 35

1.1 Text Production and Text Reception 35
1.1.1 Writerly Texts 35
1.1.2 Intertextuality in "the Role of the Reader" ... 38
1.2 Jakobson and Semiogenesis 44
1.2.1 Genesis, Metagenesis, and Equilibration 49
1.2.2 The Metagenetic Fallacy 53
1.3 Biogenesis: The Biogenetic foundation of Semiogenesis 57
1.3.1 The Brain and Semiogenesis: Hemisphericity 59
1.3.2 Cultural Hemiphericty: The Japanese Brain? ... 65
1.4 The Biogenesis of Art 73
1.4.1 Symmetry, Asymmetry, Integration 79
1.4.2 Firstness, Secondness, Thirdness 83
1.5 Summary 86

CHAPTER 2: TEXTS AS SIGNS 87

2.1 The Semiotics of Zen and Haiku 87
2.1.1 The Triadic Relation of Signs 89
2.1.2 Unlimited Semiosis 91

2.2	The Metageneticity of Zen Buddhism: the Signified of Zen	94
2.2.1	The Metasemiosis of Zen	95
2.2.2	The Physiological Process of Metasemiosis	99
2.2.3	Right Hemisphericity: the "Peak Experience" of Satori	108
2.2.4	Zen Buddhism as a Motor Action of Problem-Solving	114
2.2.5	Zen as a *Paleologic* or *Abduction*	126
2.3	Zen Texts: the Signifier of Zen Culture	135
2.3.1	The Manifestation of Asymmetry	137
2.3.2	Homeorhetic Texts and Homeostatic Zen Texts ...	141
2.3.3	The Types of Signs in Zen Texts	151
2.3.4	Indexicality and Iconicity in Zen Texts	160
2.4	Summary	168

CHAPTER 3: THE SEMIOTICS OF HAIKU 171

3.1	The Corpus of Haiku	171
3.1.1	The Corpus of Japanese Haiku	171
3.1.2	The Corpus of Haiku in English	172
3.2	Haiku in the Poetic Continuum of Japan	174
3.3	The Traditional Analysis of Haiku vs. Semiotic Analysis	181
3.3.1	Japanese Poet-Analysts	183
3.3.2	American Haiku Analysts	189
3.3.3	Semioticians	196
3.3.4	The Poetics of Haiku and the Semiotics of Poetry	200
3.4	The Trimodal Poeticalness of Haiku	212
3.4.1	The Theory of Trimodal Poeticalness of Koch ...	212
3.4.1.1	Aesthetic Poeticalness	216
3.4.1.2	Stylistic Poeticalness	217
3.4.1.3	Informational Poeticalness	219
3.4.2	The Three Haikai-Elements of Bashō	222
3.4.2.1	Aesthetic Poeticalness and Prosodic Intention	226
3.4.2.2	Stylistic Poeticalness and Kotoba	227
3.4.2.3	Informational Poeticalness and Kokoro	229
3.5	Dyads in Classical Haiku	236
3.5.1	The Aesthetic Poeticalness of Classical Haiku..	236
3.5.1.1	Rhythm	236
3.5.1.2	Phonology	240
3.5.1.3	Onomatopoeic *Gion-go* and Mimetic *Gitai-go* ...	244
3.5.1.4	Orthography	248
3.5.1.5	Presentation	249
3.5.2	The Stylistic Poeticalness of Classical Haiku..	252
3.5.2.1	Synonymy: *Engo* or Verbal Associations	253
3.5.2.2	Synonymy: *Hiyu* or Comparison and *2-ku,1-shō* through *Kireji*	254

3.5.2.3	Polysemy: *Kigo* or Seasonal Words	264
3.5.2.4	Polysemy: *Kakekotoba* or Pivot Word	265
3.5.2.5	Polysemy: *Honka-dori* or Allusive Variations	269
3.5.3	The Informational Poeticalness of Classical Haiku	272
3.5.3.1	Projection	273
3.5.3.2	Fūkyō or Projection in Converting Social Conventions	276
3.5.3.3	Equijection	281
3.5.3.4	Introjection	286
3.6	Summary	299

CHAPTER 4: A TEXT-TYPOLOGY OF HAIKU ... 302

4.1	The Seven Text-Types	303
4.2	The Diachronic Diversification of Haiku	306
4.2.1	The Trajectory of Haiku Poetogenesis	307
4.2.2	The Pre-Bashō Period: Genesis	308
4.2.2.1	Argumentative Text-Types	309
4.2.2.2	The Narrative-Joke Text-Type	311
4.2.3	The Classical Haiku Period: Metagenesis	315
4.2.3.1	The Narrative Text-Type	315
4.2.3.2	The Descriptive Text-Type with Two Reflexive Texts	317
4.2.3.3	The First Metagenesis	319
4.2.3.4	The Second Genesis in Issa	324
4.2.4	The Haiku Reformation: The Second Metagenesis	326
4.2.5	New Haiku: The Third Metagenesis and the Second Genesis	333
4.2.5.1	Vers-Libre Haiku	333
4.2.5.2	Tanritsu or Short Haiku	337
4.2.6	Present-Day Haiku: The Age of Diversification	340
4.2.6.1	Classicism	341
4.2.6.2	Modernism	344
4.2.6.3	The Various Haiku Factions	346
4.3	The Diachrony of Condensation and Expansion	347
4.4	Summary	349

CHPATER 5: A TEXT-TYPOLOGY OF HAIKU IN ENGLISH ... 354

5.1	The Epitome of the Development of Haiku in English.	354
5.1.1	The Trajectory of the Poetogenesis of Haiku in English	364
5.2	Pound and Imagism: Genesis	365
5.2.1	Ezra Pound and His Metro Poem	365
5.2.2	Pound's Exploration of Stylistic Poeticalness	370
5.2.3	The Image of Imagism	372
5.2.4	The Expansion of the Form of Super-Position	373
5.2.5	From Stylistic Poeticalness to Informational Poeticalness	375

5.2.6	Post-Imagism and Informational Poeticalness	377
5.3	Lowell and Crapsey: Metagenesis	386
5.3.1	Lowell's Adaptation of Hokku	386
5.3.2	Crapsey and the Cinquain	388
5.4	Yasuda as a Poet-Analyst and His Contemporaries: The Second Genesis	390
5.4.1	Kenneth Yasuda and the Second Genesis	390
5.4.1.1	The Aesthetic Poeticalness of Yasuda	392
5.4.1.2	The Stylistic Poeticalness of Yasuda	395
5.4.1.3	The Informational Poeticalness of Yasuda	398
5.4.2	The Informational Poeticalness of the Beat Poets	400
5.4.2.1	Rexroth and Reflexive Texts	400
5.4.2.2	Snyder and Haiku Components	402
5.4.3	The Haiku of Two Black American Poets: Wright and Knight	405
5.5	American Haiku: Metagenesis	408
5.5.1	The Misunderstood Informational Poeticalness of the Classical Haiku of Japan	409
5.5.2	Hackett and Informational Poeticalness	415
5.5.3	Haiku contests	417
5.5.4	The Diversity of American Haiku: Metagenesis	423
5.5.4.1	A Search for Greater Brevity?	424
5.5.4.2	Can Haiku Deal with Other than the Nature-Human Relationship?	428
5.6	Towards the Definition of American Haiku	432
5.6.1	Debates on the Form of Haiku	432
5.6.2	Debates on the Content of Haiku	440
5.6.2.1	The Bashō School and Informational Poeticalness	441
5.6.2.2	The Buson School and Stylistic Poeticalness	442
5.6.2.3	The Problem of Kigo	444
5.6.3	The Definition of American Haiku	446
5.7	Summary	450
CHAPTER 6:	CONCLUSION: A COMPARISON OF JAPANESE AND AMERICAN HAIKU	452
6.1	The Poetical Foci of Haiku in Japanese and in English	453
6.1.1	The Trimodal Poeticalness of Japanese Haiku	453
6.1.2	The Trimodal Poeticalness of Haiku in English	456
6.2	The Text-Types of Haiku in Japanese and English	458
6.2.1	The Reflexive Text-Type	459
6.2.2	The Descriptive Text-Type	460
6.2.3	The Narrative Text-Type	461
6.2.4	The Argumentative Text-Type	462
6.2.5	The Frog Poem and its English Versions	464

6.3 The Poetogenesis of Haiku in Japanese and
    in English 465
6.4 Poetry as Problem-Solving 468
6.5 The Poetic Principles of Haiku 471

EXCURSUS: HAIKU AS ONE TYPE OF SIMPLE FORM: DIRECTIONS
          OF FURTHER RESEARCH 474
7.1 Haiku as a Simple Form 474
7.2 The Affinity of Haiku to Other Simple Forms 480
7.3 Haiku and Senryū 484
7.4 The Genealogy of Haiku as a Simple Form 488

NOTES 491
BIBLIOGRAPHY 542
INDEX OF NAMES 573

0.0 INTRODUCTORY REMARKS: THE DOMAIN OF THE PRESENT STUDY

Suppose we ask an average Japanese to cite one prototypical haiku: he will most likely offer the following haiku by Matsuo Bashō (1644-94):

(1) 古池や 蛙飛こむ水のをと
   Furuike ya / kawazu tobikomu / mizu no oto
   (The old pond:/ a frog jumps in/ a sound of water)[1]

The reasons for his selection would be first the fact that this is one of the most famous haiku (the landmark, in fact, in Bashō's establishment of this poetic genre [cf. 3.5.3.4]); second, its observance of three fundamental haiku rules; and third, its exemplification of the textual characteristic of haiku, i.e., a unison of nature and man.

Traditionally, haiku has been defined in terms of three normative rules: (i) it consists of 17 *jion* (Japanese "symbol-sound") divided into three segments of 5, 7, and 5 (cf. 3.5.1.1); (ii) it includes a *kigo* (season word)(cf. 3.5.2.3); and (iii) it "sunders" ("切れる") through either a *kireji* (cutting word) or its equivalent (cf. 3.5.2.2). As is seen in Roman transcription, Bashō's haiku consists of 17 syllables, or, more precisely, *morae*[2] (LEWIN 1959: 33), with the obligatory pattern of 5-7-5:

$$\underline{\text{Furuike}}_{1\ 2\ 3\ 4} \ \underline{\text{ya}}_{5} \ / \ \underline{\text{kawazu}}_{1\ 2\ 3} \ \underline{\text{tobikomu}}_{4\ 5\ 6\ 7} \ / \ \underline{\text{mizu}}_{1\ 2} \ \underline{\text{no}}_{3} \ \underline{\text{oto}}_{4\ 5}$$

It also includes a seasonal element, "kawazu" (frog), lending the decor of spring to the poem (HORI 1972: 103). Further, it is severed by a typical kireji, "ya", manifesting a caesura at the end of the first segment: "the old pond" on the one hand and "a frog jumping into the water" on the other. It thus exemplifies what is commonly termed *2-ku, 1-shō* (two-clauses, one-statement: cf. 3.5.2.2), the most frequent morphological structure of haiku (cf. 4.4).

While thus fulfilling the formal requirements of haiku

composition, Bashō's haiku, (1), also illustratively presents its contextual domain, the domain that has been termed *descriptive symbolism* by the two American Japanologists Robert BROWER and Earl Roy MINER (1957: 526). As these two scholars of Japanese literature explain, "descriptive symbolism" grows from "the Buddhist ideal of the oneness of the natural order which includes man", and it thus deals with nature as "symbolic of man - of the human experience of beauty, transience, loss, salvation, and so on" (ibid.: cf. 3.5.3ff.). As a matter of fact, this haiku, (1), has been regarded as the manifestation of Bashō's striving towards the Zen Buddhist ideal of the complete dissolution of human ego (SUZUKI 1959: 16ff.: cf. 2.2ff): as far as the text is concerned, the existence of the poet's ego is totally subdued, and only the description of nature is present. It has been asserted many times that haiku records a momentary experience of this "oneness of the natural order"[3]. R. H. BLYTH, one of the most significant American interpreters of Japanese classical haiku, e.g., elucidates thus (1949: vii):

> Haiku record what Wordsworth calls those "spots of time", those moments which for some quite mysterious reason have a peculiar significance.

BLYTH (ibid.) goes on to declare that haiku is "a kind of *satori*, or enlightenment, in which we see into the life of things". The most learned Zen master in the Western world, SUZUKI Daisetsu Teitarō (1959: 228), interprets this haiku, while characterizing it as "having too much of Zen in it" (ibid., 229), as follows (cf. 3.5.3.4):

> Not only was the totality of the environment absorbed in the sound and vanished into it, but Bashō himself was altogether effaced from his consciousness. Both the subject and the object, "en-soi" and "pour-soi". ceased to be something confronting and conditioning each other. And yet this could not be a state of

absolute annihilation. Bashō was there, the old pond
was there, with all the rest.

BLYTH's and SUZUKI's assertions most representatively show
that haiku is deeply embedded in the context of Zen Buddhism –
at least at the time of its origin (cf. 0.4). It will be
one of our major purposes to re-examine the significance
of these somewhat enigmatic assertions.

Let us again suppose that we ask our Japanese informant,
provided that he understands English, to respond to a page
from a certain book[4] with the following appearance:

(2)

We ask him whether he considers it to be a poem. Would
he answer positively? Most likely, only if he happens to
know something about the techniques of so-called "concrete-
poetry" (KOCH 1971: 43-59) and considers "tundra" an example
of it. We then ask if he considers it a haiku. Viewing
this one-word poem in the middle of an otherwise blank page,
his reaction to the question would most likely be simple
astonishment. He would observe that this cannot be called
haiku at all, for it does not conform to the rules that have

been developed for this poetic genre: it has too few syllables, and it neither contains any seasonal element nor "sunders". We then disclose to him that this is a "haiku" written by an American haiku poet, Cor VAN DEN HEUVEL, collected in *The Haiku Anthology*, the collection of "English language haiku by contermporary American and Canadian poets". We further reveal that V. D. HEUVEL is the editor of the anthology and that this poet-editor declares that the Imagists and their followers "had no real understanding of haiku" (cf. 5.2.ff.), for they "failed to see the spiritual depth" embodied in haiku, or "the unity of man and nature it reveals" (V. D. HEUVEL 1974: xxvii). Presumably, then, this American haiku poet possesses a real understanding of haiku, while being quite aware of its spiritual depth as well as its revelatory characteristics. V. D. HEUVEL is, by his own testimony, evidently not one of those American poets who have "abandoned" classical Japanese standards for haiku "without knowing anything about them", to borrow the words of Harold G. HENDERSON, another American haiku authority (1965: 29). In addition, we tell our Japanese informant, V. D. HEUVEL is certainly quite aware that "the layout of the page, the amount of white space within which the words may work, and the choice of the other haiku on the spread" play a crucial role in presenting haiku (V. D. HEUVEL, xxv). Having disclosed this much of the context of "tundra", we ask again whether or not he considers (2) a haiku.

Obviously there are two possible answers, positive or negative, and each depends on how this person defines haiku poetry. If he accepts only those specimens that conform to Bashō's sample as "real" haiku, he would discard, along with POUND's and the Imagists' attempts, V. D. HEUVEL's "tundra" in spite of the poet's supposed real understanding of this succinct poetic genre. He is then, we can deduce, a reader of so-called "Classical haiku" (cf. 4.2.3). On the other hand, if this Japanese happens to be a reader of "New haiku" (4.2.5.1), he might accept "tundra" as an extreme example of it. He might recall, e.g., one of the "haiku *vers libre*"[5] by Ozaki Hōsai (1885-1926):

(3) 墓のうらに廻る
　　 Haka no ura ni mawaru[6]
　　 (To the back of a tombstone, I go around)[7]

Similarly to (2), (3) does not observe the formal rules. The whole poem sounds more or less like an utterance of colloquial parlance rather than a poem. Yet the poet called it a haiku and it has obtained the position of a haiku vers libre (cf. 4.2.1). Our informant might recall that a strong tendency to brevity, as exemplified in (3), has always been evident in the Japanese haiku tradition, and so he might consider (2) as an extreme case of such brevity.

Or he might recall another stream which has run through the tradition of haiku: pictoriality (MASAOKA 1897). He would remember that as early as the Temmei Era (1781-1789: cf. ICHIKAWA et al. 1958: 39ff.), one century after Bashō, haiku could show such experimental specimens as the following two by Yosa Buson (1716-1783):

(4) 　〽️一つ埋み残して若葉かな
　　 Fuji hitotsu/ umi-nokoshi te/ wakaba kana
　　 (〽️alone/ remains uncovered/ young green leaves!)[8]

(5) 　日の光今朝や🐟の頭より
　　 Hino hikari/ kesa ya iwashi no/ atama yori
　　 (The light of day/ this morning! from the head of
　　 the 🐟 / it came)

Buson was a famous *haikai*[9] poet as well as a first-rate painter. Here, he replaced the linguistic *signifiant*[10] with an artistic one, an *icon*, to use the semiotic term (cf. 2.3.3). The signifier "〽️" *represents* "Mt. Fuji", while "🐟" *stands for* "the sardine" (BLYTH 1949: 98). Buson's haiku, though they remained experimental and never

flourished as such, nonetheless give eloquent evidence
of the potential interplay between two semiotic *manifesta*
(2.1.1), or sign-vehicles[11], linguistic and pictorial, presented in the poetry of haiku. Thus our Japanese informant
might consider (2) to be at the extremity of this trend,
i.e., "the amount of the white space" presumably replaces
a linguistic manifestum which might read something like
"the vast, snow-covered fields of Siberia".

In either case, our Japanese friend might endorse the
claim of "tundra" to be a haiku on the gounds that (2), like
(3), presumably presents the unison of nature and man, even
though it has discarded the normative rules of haiku.
Whether he decides positively or negatively, however, his
initial astonishment on encountering (2) as a sample of
American haiku would remain undiminished; it is indeed amazing how far apart the criteria represented by the two
poems, one by a haikai master of the late 17th century and
the other by a contemporary American, have drifted. Leaving our informant in his profound amazement, we may now
ask ourselves what our hypothetical dialogue implies.

There seem to be five points of paramount importance:
(i) the *focus* of the text-recipient, our Japanese informant,
in encountering a *text*, specifically called haiku; (ii)
Bashō's haiku, (1), as the realization of Zen ideals; (iii)
the definition of haiku, whose standards were set up through
(1); (iv) the transformational process from poem (1) through
(4) and (5) by Buson and (3) by Hōsai to (2), i.e., from
the origins of Japanese classical haiku through haiku vers
libre and on to American haiku; and (v) the position and
the characteristics of haiku in the larger context of poetry
in general.

The first point is concerned with the *text situation*,
which is equivalent to the *communication situation* (JAKOBSON
1960: 357, KOCH 1976: 22ff.: cf. 0.3.2). When confronted

with the text (2), our Japanese informant (addressee or
text-recipient) *focuses* his mind on it and *selects* what is
meaningful to him. What are the components or parameters
of such communication situations? What does this *"focus"*
mean? What happens when one *reads* a text? HENDERSON
(1934: 1ff.) emphasized once that not only the *writing* but
also the *reading of haiku* is itself an art (1.1.1). Does
reading haiku in any way differ from reading other texts?
What is the relation between reading and writing? Our hypothetical Japanese informant first denied that (2) could be
a haiku. He had never encountered such a specimen as a "haiku"
and thus could not *select* any clues from the given text,
(2), which would have indentified the genre, such as the
5-7-5 syllabic pattern, the existence of kireji (or a caesura),
or that of a kigo (season word). Once informed about V. D.
HEUVEL and his alleged understanding of haiku, however, this
addressee was channeled towards a different *focalization* than
he had applied before, i.e., instead of applying the three normative rules, he then selected or *structured* the brevity or pictoriality of this genre. Such procedures in the communication
involve, thus, the whole competence which the addressee as the
text-participant possesses. What is the nature of such competence? How is such competence acquired? These questions concerning the text-communication-situation are the major inquiries
which *semiotics*, the investigation of *sign behaviors* of animal
and man, investigates, and they are the first questions that
must be clarified in the present study as well.

  The second point of cardinal importance is the clarification of the question as to what (1) consists of. BLYTH assures us, as quoted above, that haiku is "a kind of satori".
"Satori" is, however, a *psychophysiological* occurrence
(AKISHIGE 1977, SCHÜTTLER 1974: cf. 2.2.1), which, in the
traditional dichotomy of body-mind, belongs to the realm of
"body", whereas the writing and reading of haiku belongs to
"mind". What are the mechanisms, then, that link satori as
a psychophysiological occurrence with "Zen culture" in general,
and haiku in particular, as mental or *semiotic* occurrences?

To put it another way: what are the common features among
haiku, flower arrangement, calligraphy, or gardening, which
govern the realization of Zen ideals in terms of *signs*?
One of the common assertions among Zen masters is that Zen
experience cannot be verbalized and that what has been
put into words is no longer Zen (SUZUKI 1958: 48ff.: cf.
2.2.1ff.). Now, recent investigations into *neurophysiology*
have revealed that the *"minor"*, or *right hemisphere of the
cerebral cortex*, is responsible for a particular mode of
perception, i.e., "non-verbal, pictorial, holistic, and
spatial" perception, as opposed to the *"dominant"*, *left
hemisphere*, which possesses the "verbal, conceptual, analytical" mode of perception (ECCLES 1977: 352: cf. 1.3.1).
Can these functional characteristics of "the other side
of the brain" (BOGEN 1969) be correlated with the *semiotics
of Zen culture* (cf. 2.2.3ff.)? However "mysterious" Zen
experiences may be, they result from brain activities, and
an approach towards the clarification of the nature of (1),
which is embedded in the context of Zen culture in general,
through neurophysiological investigations seems quite prom-
ising. To expound (1) involves, thus, the clarification
of Zen experience (Zen's *signifié*: cf. 2.2ff.), which ultimately is manifested in the fine arts of Zen (its *signifiant*:
cf. 2.3ff.), of which haiku is one.

The third point of importance raised by our hypothetical
dialogue is the question as to how we define the poetry
of haiku. While haiku shares a great number of characteristics
with other fine arts of Zen in terms of signs, it is a
verbal art which possesses its own standards. What are these
standards? Simply to list three normative rules is, as our
dialogue clearly showed, quite unsatisfactory, since the poetry
of haiku obviously involves more than that. As the discussion of the focalization on the part of the text-participants
made clear, writings (and readings) of a text are determined
by the *foci* which are activated in writings and readings of

haiku (cf. 3.5ff.). Needless to say, haiku consists of *aesthetic texts* which differ from *normal discourses* (cf. 3.3.4). What makes haiku, which includes (2), a one-word poem, or (3), a very colloquial utterance, *poetry*? We have already seen that (1) *juxtaposes* two semantically *disparate* elements, whose construction was pointed out by Bashō: "*Hokku*[12] is made by combining things" (cf. UEDA 1970: 165: also, 3.5.2.2). What kinds of "things" are "combined" by the poet, and are "selected" by the reader, or in other words, how *poetic structures* are selected by the foci, becomes our central question.

If the third point concerns the poetry of haiku in its proto-phase, the fourth point is related to its *diachronic diversification*: how the poetry of haiku, whose standards were set up by (1), has diversified in the course of three hundred years. Which poetic structures have been retained and why? Haiku has experienced wide diversification not only in its native country (4.2.1), but also in the country where it has been transplanted (5.1.1). The evolution of haiku, or the *poetogenesis* of haiku, can be followed accordingly in terms of the changes in poetic structures, i.e., changes in *poeticalness or poeticity*, which transcend the difference of languages (JAKOBSON 1960, KOCH 1978, 1983).

While the fourth point of paramount importance is concerned with diachrony, the fifth is concerned with *synchronic diversification*. Our example of "tundra", (2), seemingly presented us with a line of demarcation between haiku and concrete poetry. This point thus involves the question of what poetry is in general. Yet in contrast to the fourth point, this point inevitably inquires into the position of poetry in human semiotic activities, i.e., it touches upon the fundamental question as to why human beings write poetry (and haiku as one specific kind of poetry) in the first place? What is the meaning of Wordsworth's "spots of time", which, in BLYTH's words, "for some quite mysterious reason"

possess "a peculiar significance" for human beings? What is
the nature of such "spots of time"? Obviously the question involves the *phenomenology* of our *cognitive processes* (cf.
1.4.1). Such "spots of time" are in fact the moments in
which we *solve the problem* we have been confronted with.
Such moments have survival value in that they set us free
from *existential anxieties*: poetry, which "records" such
moments in this sense, is an inevitable consequence of
human evolution resulting from our endeavours at *problem-solving* (cf. 2.2.4, 3.5.3.ff., and 6.4). Poetry is on the
continuum of such endeavours of problem-solving, just as
the practice of Zen, one specific type of concentrative
meditation, is the product of endeavours by Orientals to
overcome *the* existential problem, *the dichotomy of life
and death*, or the *curse of cognition* (cf. 2.2.3). Haiku
(1) incarnated, in the setting of Oriental Zen culture,
one specific *mode of problem-solving* (cf. 3.5.3.4), which
in the course of haiku's poetogenesis, has been replaced
by other modes of problem-solving in accordance with changes
in the temporal and geographical environments. Synchronic
diversification can thus present us with the whole gamut
of possible variations of modes of problem-solving attained
through one genre of poetry called haiku (cf. 5.2.1, 5.4.2.2.,
and 5.5.1).

The five important points arising from our hypothetical
dialogue thus offer us rich fields for further scrutiny. In
the following, I shall attempt to clarify these questions
through the *analytical frameworks offered by semiotics* in
general and *semiogenetics* in particular. The questions
are, to repeat:

  (i) The text-situation as the communication situation.
 (ii) The semiotics of Zen culture, in which haiku in its
     original phase was embedded.

(iii) The semiotics of the poetry of haiku
(iv) The poetogenesis of haiku encompassing both Japanese and American haiku.
(v) The function of poetry as a type of problem-solving.

INTRODUCTION

0. SEMIOTICS: THE THEORETICAL BACKGROUND

0.1 The Semiogenetic Approach

The roots of contemporary semiotics can be traced back to antiquity[1]. But the modern founding fathers of this "science of signs" (cf. HAWKES 1977: 123-50)[2] are the American philosopher Charles Sanders PEIRCE (1839-1914) and the Swiss linguist Ferdinand de SAUSSURE (1857-1915)[3], to whom such studies as the present one owe an enormous debt. PEIRCE conceived of a "formal doctrine of signs" (2.227)[4] in terms of logic[5], a doctrine which would be capable of studying any scientific discipline[6] as well as any "quality of feeling" (8.332). While PEIRCE called the prospective science "semiotic" (2.227), SAUSSURE named it "semiology", in reference to the Greek "sēmeîon" ('sign') (1960: 16). In envisioning the birth of the science, he defined it as a discipline which "studies the life of signs within society... [as] a part of social psychology and consequently of general psychology" (ibid.). Ever since then this new science has endeavoured to clarify the process of signification in sign systems, i.e., semiosis[7], which occurs in communication[8].

Investigations into signs as a means of communication have recently taken a dramatic turn: some semioticians[9] have begun to integrate semiotics into a "system of all systems", combining, to cite the major representatives, systems theory[10], biology[11], neurophysiology[12], and developmental psychology[13]. The *semiogenetic approach* is the point at issue. This approach can be characterized as evolutionary in its diachronic investigation, biological in its foundation, and neurophysiological and psycho-physiological in its verification (cf. D'AQUILI et al. 1979). It differs from typical semiotic approaches offered by

such leading semioticians as ECO (1976, 1979), CULLER
(1975, 1981), and RIFFATERRE (1978)[14], whose works
seem to concentrate on the synchronic aspect of semiosis.
The German "semiogenetician" Walter A. KOCH (1982: 16)
characterizes the approach of semiogenesis as "[seeing]
the genesis of all systems of signs and supersigns [...]
in their genetic interrelationship", and it is precisely
this aspect of semiotics which is relevant to the present
study.

Haiku poetry, the type of aesthetic text[15] which is the
major subject of the present study, is a verbal *supersign*[16],
a composition of elementary signs that can be "sent out
as units, received, and stored" (MOLES 1977: 70). It usually consists of only 17 syllables[17] or several words:
a chronic complaint of haiku experts, however, is that
haiku defies verbal explanation (BLYTH 1949: viff.). The
dilemma of most haiku critics seems to have been caused
by the fact that they have attempted to "understand"
(KOCH 1971a: 23) haiku either by commenting on its religious background[18], describing the circumstances under
which a particular poem was written[19], listing all the
possible images and concepts associated with the words
used in the poem[20], or by some combination of these
approaches. This inevitably leads to an entanglement in
the verbosity which haiku avoids in the first place[21].
This discrepancy between the succinct original text and
its verbose commentary has resulted in the above-mentioned
sense of frustration on the part of the critics of haiku.

If these approaches in principle "comment" on each
poem, a semiotic investigation such as the present study
proceeds differently: it does not paraphrase these
succinct poems but attempts to elucidate why they are
so succinct : instead of interpreting the end product

it sheds light on the *creative process* (1.5)
which results in the brevity of the haiku form, i.e.,
it expounds the semiosis of haiku.

As has often been pointed out[22], the poetry of haiku
is in its origin one of the creative arts informed by
Zen Buddhism along with the tea ceremony, painting,
calligraphy, flower arrangement, gardening, pottery,
and Nō theatre (HISAMATSU 1971). Further, Zen Buddhism
"morally and philosophically" (SUZUKI 1959: 61)[23] ordained
the code of the martial class of feudal Japan (12th
century - 1868) as well as its swordsmanship (61-214).
In other words, Zen "has entered internally into every
phase of the cultural life of the [Japanese] people"
(21). We have here a whole spectrum of cultural phenomena which are governed by this "discipline in Enlightenment" (5): they are tantamount to various "languages of culture"[24]
imbued with Zen Buddhism that function interdependently (LOTMAN et al.
1975: 6.1.0) and reveal "structural isomorphism" (8.000).

Semiotically speaking, then, Zen as a *signifié* invigo-
rated the Japanese to be creative on the level of *signifiant* (SAUSSURE 1960:67ff.), i.e., Zen was not only "sung"
verbally, as in the case of the haiku, but also presented
scenically, as in painting, Nō theatre, gardening or flower
arrangement, which are *non-verbal languages*[25]. In order
for us to understand haiku poetry as embedded in the context of culture[26], what is needed is an analytical model
capable of accounting for such a wide range of cultural
phenomena - a model which is "unifying" (cf. MORRIS 1946:
223ff.) and "interdisciplinary" (cf. WINNER 1981: 22,
CULLER 1981: 34ff.), i.e. a *semiogenetic* model.

0.2 Semiogenetic Interdisciplinarity and Evolution: Peirce's Phenomenology and Epistemology

PEIRCE (HARDWICK 1977: 85) proclaimed, in his letter to Lady Welby of December 23, 1908, the interdisciplinarity of the prospective science of signs[27]:

> It has never been in my power to study anything - mathematics, ethics, metaphysics, gravitation, thermodynamics, optics, chemistry, comparative anatomy, astronomy, psychology, phonetics, economics, the history of science, whist, men and women, wine, metrology - except as a study of semeiotic.

PEIRCE's claim that semiotics is to be all-embracing is based on his conviction that "all this universe is perfused with signs, if it is not composed exclusively of signs" (5.448)[28]. His notion of signs[29] interpenetrates thus the whole experience of living organisms including man[30], i.e., the traditional dualism of "nature" on the one hand and "human" on the other is to be discarded[31]. In lieu of anthropocentric investigations which had treated each phenomenon observed in the universe independently, a new science - a "normative science" as it was also designated by PEIRCE (5.39) - which would study signs in terms of the encoding and decoding of messages by the organism[32] was launched[33]. What PEIRCE proposed is then a "science of phenomenology"[34] which "studies the kinds of elements universally present in the phenomenon: i.e., whatever is present at any time to the mind in any way" (1.186).

The study of phenomenology, PEIRCE further declared, leads to the investigation of epistemology, or *Erkenntnistheorie*[35], the study of the general conditions "to

which thought or signs of any kind must conform in
order to assert anything" (2.206). In dealing with
this problem of "knowledge", or how the process of
knowing takes place, PEIRCE argued from an evolutionist
perspective, as the following passages eloquently show:

> ... all human knowledge, up to the highest flights
> of science, is but the development of our inborn
> animal instincts. (2.754)
>
> The instinct of *feeding*, which brought with it elementary
> knowledge of mechanical forces, space, etc., and the
> instinct of *breeding*, which brought with it elementary
> knowledge of psychical motives, of time, etc.
> (1.118)
>
> Man has thus far not attained to any knowledge that
> is not in a wide sense either mechanical or anthro-
> pological in its nature, and it may be reasonably
> presumed that he never will. (2.753)
>
> Unless man has a natural bent in accordance with na-
> ture's, he has no chance of understanding nature at
> all. (6.477)

These are PEIRCEian versions of Goethe's saying: "Wär'
nicht das Auge sonnenhaft,/Die Sonne könnt' es nie er-
blicken" (If the eye were not sunlike, it could never
see the sun)[36]. PEIRCE thus adumbrated the existence
of what BRUNSWIK (1955) later termed "ratiomorphic"
apparatuses[37], i.e., those mechanisms which are "phylogenetic precursors as the functional prerequisites"
for the process of knowing (LORENZ 1973: 118ff., RIEDL
1979: 213-4). PEIRCE clarified his evolutionist ideas
still more emphatically in his essay titled "Guessing",
written in the spring of 1907 and narrating an episode
in which he worked as a detective equipped with *abduction*, or

"instinctive powers", to solve a mystery (1929: 282). In discussing the types of human reasoning, PEIRCE sets up three categories, namely, *"induction, deduction"* (scientific reasoning) and *"abduction"* ("mere preparatory" reasoning) (7.218). The last of these is correlated with man's possession of an "inward light tending to make his guesses" right, without which the "human race would long ago have been extirpated by its utter incapacity in the struggles for existence" (1929: 269). PEIRCE's view of the survival value of this human capacity has an exact counterpart in the work of contemporary ethologists such as LORENZ (1965, 1967, 1973) or RIEDL (1979). *Ratiomorphic* apparatuses were "a priori" in the writings of Kant but ought to be "a posteriori"[38] according to PEIRCE: perceptual judgements are "the result of a process, although of a process not sufficiently conscious to be controlled and therefore not fully conscious" (cf. SEBEOK/UMIKER-SEBEOK 1980: 27). I shall elaborate on PEIRCE's *abduction* in comparison with LORENZ's *Gestalt perception* in the next chapter in connection with the core notion of Zen Buddhism, *satori* (Enlightenment)[39]; suffice it here to emphasize that PEIRCE foretold the future of semiotics as a synthesis of the "humanities" and the "natural sciences" - a synthesis which only began taking place in the thirties (cf. MORRIS 1932). POPPER and ECCLES (1977: VII), e.g., title their book *The Self and Its Brain*. In it they explore "the link between brain structures and processes on the one hand and mental dispositions and events on the other"[40]. Similarly, "biogenetic structuralists" such as D'AQUILI et al. (1974, 1979) employ an approach which is an "amalgamation of evolutionary, biological, neurophysiological, and structuralist theories" (1979: 4), an approach very similar to that of the present study.

Modern semiotics is thus doubly in debt to PEIRCE
for its interdisciplinarity: first with regard to the phenomenological quest for signs, a well-established field
among semioticians[41], and second with regard to the biogenetic quest of epistemology, a hitherto rather overlooked aspect, as CHOMSKY (1979) points out[42]. In
CHOMSKY's view, there has been "almost no one [who] has
tried to develop these ideas further, although similar
notions have been developed independently on various
occasions" (71). Evidently CHOMSKY was not aware that precisely this endeavour was being conducted by the German
semiotician Walter A. KOCH (1971, 1974, 1976, 1978,
1981, 1981a, 1982, 1983, 1983a). Designating his
approach "Semiogenesis" (1982), KOCH presents a "unifying" model in which "all structures of the world"
(1974:XVIII) are integrated according to the principle
of ontogenetic and phylogenetic evolution (1982: 16-78,
1983a).

0.3 A Semiogenetic Model

NÖTH (1980) supports KOCH's interdisciplinary model for
two reasons: first, it integrates the all too diverse
directions of disciplines. (Think, e.g., of ECO's preface to *A Semiotic Landscape: Panorama Sémiotique: the
First Congress of the International Association for
Semiotic Studies*, in which he refers to this publication
as a "disconnected series of philosophical opinions
without any recognizable common terminology" [CHATMAN
et al. 1979: V] . Indeed, the compilers [CHATMAN, ECO,
KLINKENBERG] chose the title as an indication of diversity[43]). And second, it clarifies the position of semiotic
investigation within the framework of a model which has
the power to integrate these disciplines (NÖTH 1980:15).

KOCH's semiogenetic approach includes two main models:
the History Model (H-model) for the diachronic aspect
of semiogenesis and the Situation of Communication
Model (Si-model) für the synchronic aspect (cf. SAUSSURE
1960).

0.3.1 The History Model: The Diachrony of Semiogenesis

KOCH (1974) offers the following scheme^{44}, with six
evolutionary stages of the universe, to which he later
adds one more stage; for the sake of the discussion, however, we will begin with the six-stage model (H stands for
the spatio-temporal orientation of each stage which influences structures causing evolution):

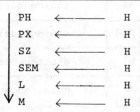

PH : physico-chemical structures, atomic, molecular,
     galactic, etc., processes
PX : biological, physiological-psychological processes
SZ : intra-phyletic organisation, sociological energy-
     flux, ecology, economy, biotope of the living in
     the sense of an inter-individual order, socio-
     logy
SEM: onset of memory, conditioned reflex, cognition,
     learning, symbol behaviour, "prelinguistic" en-
     coding, "animal languages"
L : human language
M : various forms of metalanguage, explicit model of
     L based on L, SEM, SZ, PX, and PH

Fig. 1: History Model (from KOCH 1974)

As is clear from the order of the stages, this model is conceived "genetically"[45]. Later KOCH (1982, 1982a) divides PX into two stages, the *biological* and the *psychological*, resulting in the seven-staged model (1982a: 449)[46], with the presentation of the corresponding sciences[47], as shown in the diagram below:

system		the science of ...
cosmos	PH	cosmogenesis
life	PX	biogenesis
human life	Px	psychogenesis
society	SZ	sociogenesis
language, art	SEM	semiogenesis
literature	L	glottogenesis
science	M	epistemogenesis

Fig. 2
System, Science and Evolution (from KOCH 1982)

Each stage presupposes the existence of the preceding one and foresees its successor, as KOCH (ibid.) explains: "[When] studying the semiogenesis of *language*, we also - at least implicitly - account for the origin of both its 'predecessors' (such as animal communication) and its successors (such as literature or sciences)".

KOCH's model of semiogenesis, i.e., the evolutionarily ordered systems of "language, art, and literature" (ibid.) can convincingly be supported by evidence from other scientific fields which developed independently. Biology is the point of departure. The German biologist RIEDL (1979) in his exposition of the "biology of epistemology", e.g., offers us a diagram of "the stratification of the real world" with further correspondences between "the age of levels and the complexity" and the "number of the representatives" (161). This exhibits a remarkable resemblance to KOCH's proposed model; except that the presentation of evolutions moves in the opposite direction to KOCH's and 'SEM, L, M' in KOCH's model are subsumed here under the category *Kultur-Wissenschaften* (sciences of culture):

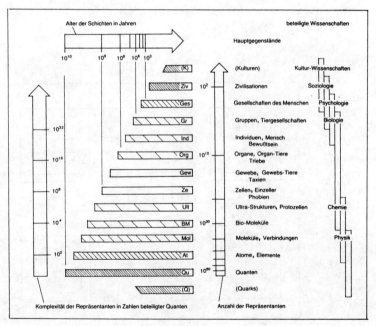

Fig. 3
Stratification of the Real World (from RIEDL 1979)

0.3.2 Situation Communication Model: The Synchrony of
      Semiogenesis

Semiotics sees signs as inherent in the process of
communication (PEIRCE 2.334, 2.92, 4.536; SHANNON/WEAVER
1949; MORRIS 1946, HULLET 1966, KLAUS 1966, BÜHLER 1934,
JAKOBSON 1960, KOCH 1971, 1976, ECO 1976, IVANOV 1977)[48].
Theories are numerous, and each theorist attempts to be
as inclusive as possible (cf. KROEPSCH 1976: 281-301).
KOCH's second major model, too, aims to integrate such
theories as the cybernetic biophysical model of brain
performance offered by KLAUS (1966: 175) and JAKOBSON's
(1960: 357) situation model of speech (and accordingly
BÜHLER's 'organon model' [1934: 28]). The situation of
communication model proposed by KOCH (1983: 55) is as
follows (cf. 1974: 241):

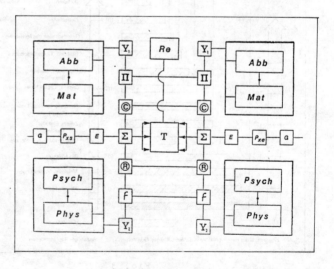

Fig. 4
Situation Model (from KOCH 1983)

KOCH (1982: 58ff.) correlates his model with JAKOBSON's (1960: 357), in the following respects:

a) P_{xs} (Sender) = addresser; producer of the text
b) P_{xe} (Empfänger) = addressee; recipient of the text
c) Y_1 = code
d) T (Text) = message
e) Re (Referem) = context
f) π (Playback) ⎫
   © (congruence) ⎪
   ® (reversibility) ⎬ = contact
   f (feedback) ⎪
   Σ (selection) ⎭

The five subdivisions corresponding to JAKOBSON's "contact" can be explained as follows:

a) playback: the situations and/or the texts evince specific structures for the stabilization of memory;
b) congruence: cortical and vegetative prerequisites of structuralization;
c) reversibility: relative capacity of P_{xe} and P_{xs} to reverse their roles of text-structuring;
d) feedback: relative impulses that P_{xe} imparts to P_{xs} for producing certain texts and certain structures;
e) selection: focalization according to the energy (E) available and the capacity and/or social structure (G), i.e., the *group* in which P_x (communication or text-situation) is embedded (ibid.; 56ff.). P_x (both P_{xs} and P_{xe}) structures the T with focal selection (Σ) which consists of 3 modes:

a) aesthetic focus
b) stylistic focus
c) informational focus[49]

The difference between the Si-model and comparable suggested models lies, KOCH (ibid., 58) ascertains, in the fact that "emphasis is laid on the idea that the T, the codes of mapped structures (Abb = Abbildung), and the codes of the linguistic matrix structures (Mat = Matrix) do *not* form a constellation *without mediation*" (1.3.2). Furthermore, the notion of "code" here implies not only the linguistic code (mapping and matrixing of Y_1) but also the paralinguistic code (Y_2) which is both psychological (Psych) and physical (Phys): as Fig. 2 suggests, Y_2 is onto-phylogenetically prior to the communicative competence (ibid., JAKOBSON/WAUGH 1979).

0.3.3 Diachrony in the Si-Model: The Ontogenesis and Phylogenesis of Semiotic Competence

Although the Si-Model introduced above is concerned with the synchronic aspect of communication, it implies that P_x (P_{xs} and P_{xe} = participants of the T) possesses communicative competence which has resulted from onto-genetic and phylogenetic development. This competence includes the whole gamut of evolutionary stages (from PH to, at least, SEM), or of "observation records", to borrow from the terminology of LORENZ (1973:118, and cf. PEIRCE's *induction, deduction, abduction*). In order for a sign to function as a sign, i.e., to be understood as such, it has to have been acquired (PEIRCE 2.231), otherwise there would be no way of conveying information. The apparatus to convey the information has developed from PH onwards, and it is for this reason that the semio-genetic approach is concerned with the exploration into this apparatus, i.e., the human brain, correlating psycho-physiological aspects with it, as will be seen in the second chapter of the present study.

0.3.4 Three Foci in the Si-Model

KROEPSCH (1976), in his detailed investigation of mass-communication, points out that *focal attention* is the "guarantee" for the P_{xe} to receive any kind of T in the first place. It is what KREITLER/KREITLER (1972: 23ff.) term "cognitive orientation", the physiological manifestation of linguistic equivalence, which amounts to the question "What-is-it?" (cf. SOKOLOV 1958). Neurophysiologically, such foci of attention can be located in the prefrontal lobe and its adjacent areas (MARCUS 1972: 494ff.).

The fact that focal attention is the prerequisite for any sort of T can be illustrated in innumerable daily experiences. When we come into an unknown town, e.g., everything seems new and strange, but we soon become habituated[50], and the excitation subsides and disappears: we await the new situation - entering a hitherto unknown town - with a great deal more energetic influx[51] than usual. To take another example: when we sit in a street-café and begin to scrutinize the passers-by, they are no longer background figures but suddenly turn out to be "objects" of interested observation[52]. This is the principle which "theater" maximally utilizes (HEIN 1976), and which is in fact closely related to the difference between normal language usage and "poetic language" (LOTMAN 1976a: 133, RIFFATERRE 1978: 53ff., SCHOLES 1982: 47ff.: also 3.3.4).

In confronting the T, P_x, equipped with the sum of onto-phylogenetic development (G), structures it with focal selection which is determined by the available energy (E) that P_x possesses. There are three foci which exert a definite influence on P_x in forming the respective *mediations* on which the codes of mapped structures

and those of matricized structures are based (1.3.2):
1) *aesthetic*[53] *focus*[54], 2) *stylistic focus*[55], and 3) *informational focus*[56]. *Aesthetic focus* detects any "non-trivial recurrences"[57] manifested in the matrix. Such recurrences are registered on the level of Y_2 (Fig. 4), i.e., the psycho-physical level, and thus are related to "intricate patterns" of recurrence such as those in the metre of poetry (metre being an instance of JAKOBSON's "poeticity" [cf. KOCH 1982: 54ff.]), or "in the metre and beauty of the peacock's fan" (ibid., 69). *Stylistic* focus registers any indication that suggests *deviation* from the ordinary world: the indicator is termed a *styleme* (KOCH 1983: 65)[58]. The stronger the deviation of the styleme, the higher is the grade of *semiotization*, i.e., the distortion that then appears as the manifestation of P_x's cognition (see *iconicity* in Ch. 2). The third, *informational*, focus "maps world structures" (ibid., 63), and *semioticizes*, or registers, the "thinking process" (239). Although such *mapped structures* are manifested in the semiotic means (i.e., matrix), of which language is the most effective (63), they are the least dependent on matrix: an "idea" can be conveyed by way of any natural language (English, French, German, Russian, Japanese, etc.), painting, gesture, etc. Informational focus detects what LEVI-STRAUSS (1958) terms "myth"[59], in which an opposition is *mediated* (cf. "magic synthesis" in ARIETI 1976).

0.3.5 The Simplified Si-Model and Meta-Analysis

Based on BÜHLER's organon-model (1934), KOCH et al. (1976) offer us the following simplified version of Fig. 4, Fig. 5a. In order to illustrate the Si-model, let us consider the following picture drawn in 1799 (Illustr. 1), depicting one of the most famous stone gardens in Kyōto, the ancient capital city of Japan (HENNIG 1980: 80; cf. HISAMATSU 1971: 286-9).

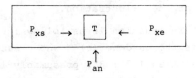

Fig. 5a: Simplified Model of Situation (Si-Model)
(from KOCH et al. 1976)

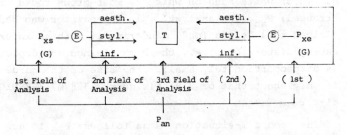

Fig. 5b: Three Fields of Analysis in Terms of
the Si-Model

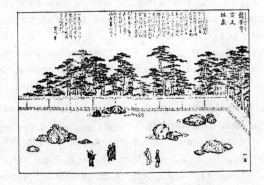

Illustr. 1: Stone Garden of Ryōan-ji

Actually the T-situation this illustration presents is twofold: 1) within the illustration and 2) outside of it, i.e., the situation in which the reader ("You!") = P_{xe} looks at the illustration.

The first T-situation is as follows: P_{xs}, the addresser, is the gardener(s)[60] who created this "empty garden" (HISAMATSU 1971: 88) presumably in awareness of the "Formless Self of Zen" (ibid.); P_{xe}, the addressee(s), is (are) the five people depicted in the foreground of the picture evidently appreciating the garden; T is the garden of white sand on which 15 moss-grown rocks are arranged; P_{an}, the analyst[61], is the painter who semioticized this "situation", rendering it with an interesting distortion, i.e., the human beings are depicted as disproportionately small - the size of the garden is only about that of a tennis court, 338 m^2 (HENNIG, 81-2).

The second T-situation is as follows: P_{xs} is now the painter[62] who drew the illustration with the miniature human figures; P_{xe}, "You", the observer or the T-recipient; P_{an}, "I", the author, who "knows everything that can be known from the viewpoint of the sum total of all the variant positions of P_x (P_{xs}, P_{xe})"[63]. As is clear, in a T-situation, P_{xs} does not have to be present[64]. We will be concerned here only with the second T-situation, since it is more relevant to the present topic.

In our T-situation, there are three main fields which deserve close attention (Fig. 5b): 1) in terms of *participants of T*, 2) of *T* itself, and 3) of *focal selection*. The first *analytical field* concerns the parameters of "G" and "P_x", (Fig. 4), i.e., the addresser/addressee's personal constitution in terms of the socio-cultural backgrounds (cf. 1.6.1) which P_x bring into the

situation. The second field, T, *the text*, concerns the
material aspects of the illustration such as the perspective, color, construction, presentation of the picture
and written text, types of lettering, etc., that is,
T as signs (cf. ECO 1979: 175-99). The third field,
focal selection concerns the Energy (E) with which P_x
confront T. There are three types of focal attention:
1) aesthetic, 2) stylistic, and 3) informational focus.

0.3.5.1 Participants in Texts as a Plurality of Texts

The first analytical field concerns the bio-socio-psycho-
cultural backgrounds of P_x, the participants in the T. Prior
to this T-situation, "you", the T-recipients (P_{xe}), are
already "a plurality of other texts" (BARTHES 1974: 10).
It is, e.g., crucial whether P_{xe} has ever seen the real
Ryōan-ji garden or not: should he have seen it before,
he would immediately notice the distortion of the figures.
Should he further be acquainted with Zen Buddhism, he
would immediately "recognize", i.e., *semioticize*, this
distortion as a semioticization on the part of P_{xs}, who
presumably realized the smallness of mankind in comparison with the magnificence of this rather tiny garden
(cf. HISAMATSU, 88-9). Should he be well versed in
other Zen manifestations, such as calligraphy, Zen
painting, or haiku, he would recognize that the same
principle of "asymmetry" (HISAMATSU 1971, SUZUKI 1959)
that governs Zen culture is valid here, etc. The investigation to pursue the prior experiences of P_x could
in fact continue endlessly, regressing from M to PH on
the evolutionary scale (Fig. 2). A recent debate among
semioticians, conducted mainly by KRISTEVA (1974,
1980), BARTHES (1974, 1975), and CULLER (1981) concerns
exactly this point, i.e., P_x as a sum of prior "texts".

These semioticians[65] can be said now to have cleared a
path into the domain of *metagenesis*, which goes in the
opposite direction to evolution. They seem, however,
not yet to have reached the position which the semiogenetic approach assumes: they have now arrived at the level
of "psychogenesis" but not "biogenesis" (Fig. 2). However,
this analysis cannot be dealt with in terms of *each* P_x:
it would require "many, many scientific books" (LORENZ
1959: 264). The principle operating in "G" can only be
expounded in terms of general ontogenesis and phylogenesis. The first chapter of this study thus concentrates
on this parameter of Si-Model, i.e., P_x as a plurality
of texts.

0.3.5.2 Texts as Signs

The second main analytical field resulting from the
Si-Model concerns the Text based on the theories of
signs. In observing the illustration, P_{xe} would notice
that this T is *iconic* in that it visualizes the scenery
fairly accurately, *indexical* in that it "points out" the
Weltanschauung of Zen Buddhism (reduced human 'ego'
[2.2.4]), and *symbolic* in that it has been semioticized
at all. Actually, such textual characters of things are,
as the Si-Model clearly shows, not immanent in signs themselves: they must be *selected* according to the P_{xe}'s
energy. It is, nonetheless, important for the further
discussion of this study to expound the notion of "signs" at
the outset. The second chapter thus concentrates on this
field, i.e., texts as signs, using the materials offered
by Zen culture in Japan.

0.3.5.3 Trifocal Selection

The third analytical field deals with focal selection on

the part of P_x. In observing the illustration of the Zen garden, P_{xe} would be forced to concentrate on the picture due to the T-situation[66]. Regardless of his previous experiences, he would register the visual stimuli of "recurrences" such as the distribution of five black stone groups. The repetition of wall and the pine trees in the background, the five human figures whose constellation somewhat mirrors the arrangement of the stones, etc. He would also notice the asymmetric character which is superimposed on such recurrences: 1) the 15 stones are arranged from the left to the right in five groups with the scheme 5-2-3-2-3, so that the first group of five confronts the rest with its mass; 2) a contrast is established between the pine trees and the white wall in terms of their color, contours, and forms; 3) the five observers are also arranged so that the left one, with his raised hand, draws our attention very much as do his black *garment* and the five massive stones; 4) the second group, while mirroring the second group of stones, is spatially opposed both to the stones and to the first figure; 5) the third group of stones and figures is diffusely arranged, opposing the first two groups; 6) there is further an opposition between the written text placed above the drawing and the drawing itself, etc. The illustration, however, would be taken as a whole, or "synthesized" at the end, so that P_{xe} receives a harmonious, integrated figure.

The process described above is due to aesthetic focus. I have deliberately omitted the other two foci in order to clarify that each focus goes through three phases: 1) symmetry, in which "recurrences" are registered; 2) asymmetry, in which "antinomy" is perceived; and 3) integration, in which mediation between the antagonistic forces occurs. Similarly to the process depicted above, stylistic focus would detect the *styleme* of the distortion, provided that P_{xe} has seen the real garden before, and asymmetry between "the real size" and "the distorted mini-figures" presents him with a "problem" which demands a solution. Should he obtain the "answer" - Buddhistic *Weltanschauung* - the antinomy is mediated. If P_{xe} has never seen the garden before, such a styleme would not be perceived. Similarly, the informational focus would vary greatly according to the "G" of P_{xe}. Whether P_{xe} attributes such a "harmony" between the semioticized presentation of the garden on the one hand and the non-proportionately miniaturized figures on the other to the illustration depends on how P_{xe} approaches the given T. If he knows that this garden has been traditionally considered "the sea of clouds with the towering summits", "the landscape of the sea", "the group of tigers crossing a mountain brook" (HENNING, 84), or the proportional harmony of potential cosmic power (ibid.), his informational focus would in fact dominate his focal selection, and not the other way around.

The focal modes subsequently encompass the preceding two analyses, which determine the T-situation, and it is for this reason that this study mostly concentrates on this subject: the trifocal approach of the T participants (P_x) in the case of verbal art, i.e., haiku, which is specifically termed the "*trimodal poeticalness*" of haiku.

0.4 The Analytical Framework of the Present Study

In order to define the creative process by which haiku are composed and are read, which is the ultimate analytical purpose of this study, I have set up the following analytical framework: This approach forms the bulk of chapter three through five of the present study.

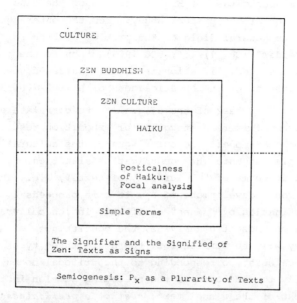

Fig. 6: The Analytical Framework of the Present Study

The merit of this configuration is three-fold: 1) it positions haiku in the wider context of culture; 2) it clarifies the general process of the present analysis, from the outer to the inner square; and it specifies the analytical focus in each field.

The first task of Fig. 6 is to establish the position of haiku in the context of its culture at the time of the formation of this poetic genre, namely, the mid-seventeenth century. Needless to say, this framework is not valid for the entire history of haiku (4.3.5), a history spanning at least 300 years and including all the haiku written in both Japanese and other languages. This positioning is justified, however, since Zen Buddhism played a decisive role in the genesis of haiku.

The second task of Fig. 6 is to show the general direction of the present study: from the outer square, the more general field of the problem of "the role of the reader" (Ch. 1) (cf. ECO 1979), then to the problem of "signs" (Ch. 2), which is in turn narrowed down to the question of the "poeticalness of haiku" (Ch. 3-6).

The third task of the diagram is to correlate each field with the three categories of exposition resulting from the Si-model. The outer square, the cultural context playing into the communication situation, is analysed in terms of "a plurality of texts", i.e., the diachronic development of P_x. It then proceeds to the investigation of "signs" manifested in Zen culture. Based on these two analyses, the poeticalness of haiku poetry will be scrutinized: there are three types of poeticalness, corresponding to the trifocal modes briefly touched upon in the preceding section in the context of the visual text: *aesthetic poeticalness, stylistic poeticalness*, and *informational poeticalness*.

CHAPTER 1

PARTICIPANTS IN TEXTS AS A PLURALITY OF TEXTS

P_x, the T-participant, is the sum of information that has been acquired phylogenetically and ontogenetically. Much neural processing of information - collection, evaluation, association, and storage - occurs "outside the bounds of normal awareness" (LAUGHLIN et al. 1979: 10). This informational processing, introspectively designated as "thought", "reason", etc. by human beings, is the result of "untold millenia of evolution" (ibid.). In confronting an event (T), humans, other mammals, and birds are forced to organize sensory inputs into a "systemic, cognitive whole" according to neural constraints, i.e., according to the *cognitive imperative* (ibid.). This chapter thus deals with the bio-sociopsychocultural aspects of P_x, the T-participant as the *plurality of T*.

1.1 Text Production and Text Reception

1.1.1 Writerly Texts

One of the most influential pioneers to contribute to the dissemination of haiku in the Western world is Harald HENDERSON (1934, 1965). In introducing haiku in his book *The Bamboo Broom* (1934: 1ff.), HENDERSON speaks of "the twin arts of reading and of writing haiku". In HENDERSON's view, haiku reading is "in itself an art, and [...] in order really to understand a good haiku one has to read it over many times" (5). The reason why one can talk about "the art of reading" in addition to that

of writing is because haiku readers have to disentangle
"so much suggestion ... put into so few words" by haiku
writers (5). Haiku writers in their turn "make great
use of what they call *renso* or association of ideas" (ibid.)
by employing a number of devices traditionally handed
down as well as individually discovered (cf. BARTHES 1970).

In HENDERSON's assertion, the reader may recognize
the same problem currently debated by semioticians, i.e.,
the "role of the reader" (cf. ECO 1979, CULLER 1981:
47ff.). What HENDERSON means by "the twin arts of reading
and of writing haiku" seems further to correspond to
what the French semiotician Roland BARTHES refers to by
designating certain type of texts as *scriptible*, translated into English as "writerly" (BARTHES 1974)[1].
For BARTHES, the "evaluation of all texts" is linked to
a "practice" which is that of "writing" (3-4). In his
opinion there are two types of texts: "readerly" and
"writerly" (4). The first, the readerly text, leaves
the reader only the "poor freedom" of reading it as a
"referendum" and accordingly this kind of text is of
little value (ibid.). In contrast, the writerly text
is of high value. Why? BARTHES answers (ibid.):

> Because the goal of literary work (of literature as
> work) is to make the reader no longer a consumer,
> but a producer of the text. Our literature is char-
> acterized by the pitiless divorce which the literary
> institution maintains between the producer of the
> text and its user, between its owner and its customer,
> between its author and its reader. This reader is
> thereby plunged into a kind of idleness - he is in-
> transitive ... instead of functioning himself, in-
> stead of gaining access to the magic of the signi-
> fier, to the pleasure of writing, he is left with
> no more than the poor freedom either to accept or
> reject the TEXT (ibid.).

BARTHES' writerly text, then, is that which motivates
the reader to "write" actively while reading. He further
specifies what happens in reading a text: "To read, in
fact, is a labor of language [...] To read is to find
meanings, and to find meanings is to name them [...]"
(ibid., 11). He then designates reading as a "tireless
approximation, a metonymic labor" (ibid.). What BARTHES
refers to then consists of two aspects: first, "naming",
and second, the succession of such "naming", i.e.,
"metonymic labor"[2].

BARTHES's discussion of reading concerns the fundamental nature of language, the nature JAKOBSON (1971: 51ff.) clarifies through the theory of two axes - the axis of metaphor and that of metonymy (cf. HOLENSTEIN 1975: 142-57). What BARTHES terms "naming" in each phase of reading corresponds to JAKOBSON's metaphor, while "metonymic labor", metonymy, is a succession of "naming"[3]. As HOLENSTEIN (1975: 145) clarifies, the principles of JAKOBSON's two axes are derived from SAUSSURE (1960: 123), who expounded two basic "relations" in a language-state: the *associative relation* which is *in absentia*, and the *syntagmatic relation*, which is *in praesentia*. Correlating BARTHE's "naming" and "metonymic labor" on the one hand and the JAKOBSONian/SAUSSUREian theory of language on the other, what happens in reading can be diagrammed as follows:

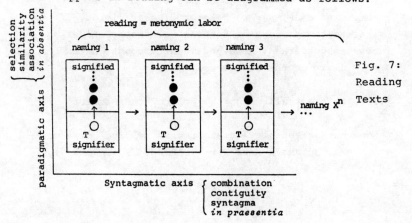

Fig. 7: Reading Texts

The reader (P_{xe}) "names, unnames, renames" (BARTHES ibid.) starting from the given T (signifier) and seeking a matching signified out of the innumerable possible signifieds. What he selects out of alternatives available to him ("... ● ● ...": Fig. 7) largely depends on his focal selection (cf. 0.3.5). The principle of *selection*, however, is valid in writing as well. The very same process occurs in writing: in producing a text (i.e., encoding messages) a writer (P_{xs}) starts out with his initial experience which he structures (not-yet-written T), selecting an appropriate signifier ("naming"!), and combines each selection (nomination) into a successive order with "metonymical labor". Thus the only difference between the writer and the reader is the starting point: P_{xs} begins with his signified (i.e., unwritten T) while P_{xe}, with his given signifier (i.e., written T). Whether or not P_{xe} reaches the same initial T that P_{xs} conceived is another matter. The main point here is to recognize that the process of reading, and for that matter, not only reading but viewing a moss-grown Zen garden, or a Chaplin film, is a "metaphorical labor", i.e., "naming". There surely is a difference between whether P_{xe} amuses himself, as in ECO's example with such texts as "the saga of Superman" or the "*acta sanctorum* of James Bond"- texts which are "open" to any "aberrant" decoding (ECO 1979:8) - or confronts such texts as *Finnegans Wake* or *Ulysses* (ibid., 9ff.). As far as the process of "naming" or "metaphorical labor" is concerned, however, T-participants (both P_{xs} and P_{xe}) are on the same level.

1.1.2 Intertextuality in "the Role of the Reader"

Three years after his "aristocratic" reading[4] of a writerly text, Balzac's *Sarrasine* (BARTHES 1974: 16-217),

BARTHES published *Le Plaisir du texte* to elucidate the difference between "the text of pleasure and the text of bliss: pleasure can be expressed in words, bliss[5] cannot" (English trans. 1975: 21). The unspeakability of bliss (*jouissance*)[5], contrary to "pleasure"[6] (*contentement*) (19) is also "asocial": "It is the abrupt loss of sociality, and yet there follows no recurrence to the subject (subjectivity), the person, solitude: *everything* is lost, integrally. Extremity of the clandestine, darkness of the motion-picture theatre" (39). His "phylacteries", as he calls this collection of disparate parts (vii), reveal to us that the *jouissance* of reading[7], especially with its physical connotation of "orgasm"[8], in fact resembles very much what we will later discuss in terms of "tension-relief", "homeostasis-pleasure", "illumination", or "satori": "bliss is unspeakable, inter-dicted"(21). In a very idiosyncratic way[9], what BARTHES preaches seems to suggest the semiotician's effort to converge with the procedures of the biologists. In KRISTEVA's opinion (1980: 93), BARTHES is the "precursor and founder of modern literary studies precisely because he located literary practice at the intersection of subject and history", i.e., the traditional distinction between subjectivity and objectivity seems to be more and more obliterated.

In this general trend of "positive subversion" (KRISTEVA, ibid.), semiotics has been currently dealing with *The Role of the Reader*, to cite the title of ECO's book (1979). Similarly, Jonathan CULLER (1981: 38) ascertains:

> Literary study experienced what Barthes called "the death of the author"[10] but almost simultaneously

it discovered the reader, for in an account of the
semiotics of literature someone like the reader is
needed to serve as center. The reader becomes the
name of the place where the various codes can be
located: a virtual site.

In dealing with "the role of the reader"[11], KRISTEVA
(1974) formulated the concept of "intertextuality",
stating that

> whatever the semantic context of a text, its
> condition as a signifying practice presupposes
> the existence of other discourses[...]This is to say
> that every text is from the outset under the juris-
> diction of other discourses which impose a universe
> on it. (ibid., 388-9)

As CULLER demonstrates (1981: 100ff.), intertextuality
at face value includes the whole "universe"[12]. BARTHES
(1974: 10), too, refers to it by calling the reader "a
non-innocent subject", for this subject that approaches
the text is "already itself a plurality of other texts,
of codes which are infinite or, more precisely, lost
(whose origin is lost)". In this respect, even such
an elaborated scheme as that offered by ECO (1979: 14)
to clarify the "intertextuality" the reader brings into
the communication situation is quite incomplete.

Actually, what is interesting in the debate about
intertextuality depends not so much on the state of
affairs - CULLER's "presupposition" (1981: 103), or
ECO's "inferences by intertextual frames" (1979: 21ff.)[13],
for example - but on the fact that such efforts as
BARTHES's to overthrow the distinction between subjectivity and objectivity (1974: 10ff.) converge with
the biologist's notion of the prerequisites for knowing,

which include "onto-phylogenetic precursors as the
functional prerequisites" for epistemology (cf. O.2).
While the semiotician BARTHES (1975: 33) speaks of the
"language's image-reservoirs" (cf. "L" in Fig. 2), or
KRISTEVA (1980: 133) of a *chora*[14] ("receptacle") for the
"semiotic disposition" ("SEM"), the ethologist LORENZ
(1973: 118) talks of "observation records", which permeate all the levels of the evolutionary scale:

BARTHES:
> To identify accurately language's image-reservoirs,
> to wit: the word as singular unit, magic monad;
> speech as instrument or expression of thought;
> writing as transliteration of speech; the sentence
> as a logical, closed, measure; the very deficiency
> or denial of language as a primary, spontaneous,
> pragmatic force ... [The] very definition of the
> image-reservoir [is] the unconsciousness of the
> unconscious.

KRISTEVA:
> We shall call this disposition *semiotic*[...]
> a *distinctiveness* admitting of an uncertain and
> indeterminate articulation because it does not
> yet refer (for young children) or no longer refers
> (in psychotic discourse) to a signified object for
> a thetic consciousness (this side of, or through,
> both object and consciousness). Plato's *Timaeaus* [sic]
> speaks of a *chora* (χώρα), receptacle, (ὑποδοχεῖον),
> unnamable, improbable, hybrid, [etc.].

LORENZ:
> We obviously possess a mechanism that is capable of
> absorbing almost incredible numbers of individual
> 'observation records', of retaining them over long
> periods, and on top of all that of evaluating them
> statistically.

What the two French semioticians refer to as "image-reservoir" or "chora" is the sum of collected "information" according to the ethologist.

LORENZ (1959: 264ff.) explicates what stored information contains: "We know two types in which an organism acquires information about its environment: first, [...] genetic-phylogenetic interaction of phyla with their environment, and second, the learning of an individual through accurate trial-and-error"[15]. About the information that is hereditarily acquired, i.e., the first type, LORENZ (264) writes:

> The genome, the system of the chromosomes, includes an incredibly tremendous stock of "information", which would fill many, many books of anatomy, physiology, and behavioral science, if we were ever able to transcribe it into human language[16].

The first type of stored information results from the adaptive activities of human beings and animals which have enabled them to survive (265) (cf. 0.2). The second type of collecting information is divided into two subtypes (255ff.): one that occurs on the subconscious level and the other on the conscious. The first method of information process is termed "Gestalt perception", which is the foundation of the second perception and results in "scientific knowledge" (255). Despite the "enormous difference" between these "lower and higher epistemological performances" (262), both are dependent on the "quantity" of information: the more information, the closer to the "truth" (268). LORENZ (1973:118) delineates how the crystallization of such stored Gestalt information into the consciousness can be cognized psychologically:

> Long before one can formulate reasons for it, one
> often notices that a particular complex of events
> appears interesting or fascinating. Only after a
> while does one begin to suspect that there is some-
> thing regular about them. Both circumstances lead
> one to repeat one's observation, and the result is
> then often attributed to 'intuition' or even 'in-
> spiration', although there is nothing supernatural
> about the process.

He calls the first method "ratiomorphous", following BRUNSWIK (119), and the second, "rational". Although both are closely analogous, in both "formal and functional respects", the ratiomorphous process takes place largely in our sensory and nervous systems, to which human consciousness has no access (ibid.). Despite the superiority of ratiomorphous functions in terms of the amount of stored information, they cannot be called up at will, as can the rationally stored information, and thus they remain independent of abstract thought (cf. ECCLES 1977). LORENZ's exposition of ratiomorphous functions and rational functions as well as PEIRCE's abduction will be of great use later when we discuss the nature of Zen.

The discussion of intertextuality has thus shown us the direction of "regressive analysis", as PIAGET (1970: 19) terms it, the analysis that can never reach an "absolute beginning" (cf. KOCH 1982: 55). Our next task is to explore the nature of the "stored information" which P_x is equipped with in communication situations, and the process - i.e., the "semiogenesis" - by which the information is stored.

1.2 Jakobson and Semiogenesis

In launching his investigation into semiogenesis, KOCH (1974: 280, 1983: 19) acknowledges his debt to JAKOBSON's (1941) "possibly stringent correlation of the ontogenesis and phylogenesis of language and their reverse: aphasia"[15]. Since these findings of JAKOBSON play a crucial role in the following discussion, a detailed survey of them is in order.

JAKOBSON correlated child language acquisition, especially in its phonological aspect, the loss of speech in aphasia, and the phonological universals observed in the various natural languages in the world[16]. In analyzing the child's acquisition of the different strata of the phoneme system (ontogeny), JAKOBSON proves that the relative chronological order of phonological acquisition "remains everywhere and at all times the same" regardless of the language type, whether "French or Scandinavian, English or Slavic, Indian or German, Estonian, Dutch or Japanese" (ibid., 46). His proof is based on the fundamental principle that he terms "the laws of unilateral solidarity" (51ff.). This principle maintains that the acquisition of "the secondary value presupposes the acquisition of the primary value" (59) and not vice versa, hence the foundations (JAKOBSON's term for them is "solidarity") of such processes are "irreversible" or "unilateral". Despite the risk of oversimplification, the gist of JAKOBSON's findings can be diagrammed as follows[17]:

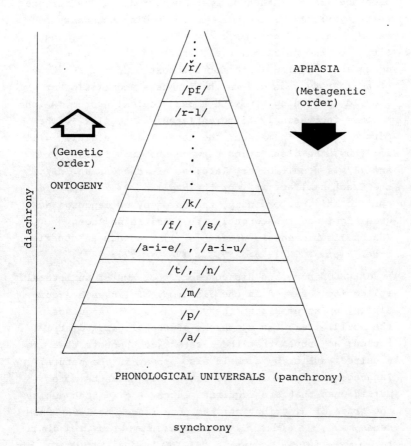

Fig. 8: Correlation of Ontogeny, Phylogeny, and Aphasia

As Fig. 8 shows, a child acquires /a/, a wide vowel, as the very first phoneme (primary value), followed by /p/, a stop consonant (secondary value). These two phonemes display the constitutive principle of linguistic systems, i.e., "maximal contrast"[18] (68). Once /p/ has been acquired, it then becomes the primary value for the next layer: /m/ is then its corresponding secondary value, i.e., /p/ becomes the prerequisite for the acquisition of the nasal bilabial, which in its turn becomes the prerequisite for the next phoneme. The laws of solidarity thus govern the language acquisition of a child, providing him with a phonological system, which becomes increasingly differentiated and complex[19]. The more a phoneme is marked, the later its acquisition will be: thus, the distinction between the two liquids, /r/ and /l/ is acquired very late; so are the German /pf/, the Czech sibilant /ř/, or the English /θ/. On the diachronic axis, accordingly, the ontogeny of language acquisition, and subsequently its possible phylogeny (Haeckel's biogenetic principle[20]), presents a "genetic order" (cf. KOCH 1974: 199ff., IVANOV 1977: 117).

JAKOBSON supports his concept, the laws of unilateral solidarity observed in the diachrony of language acquisition, by scrutinizing the varied natural languages of the world, i.e., the synchrony of phonological distribution. He proves that the less marked phonemes that are acquired earlier by a child also appear in the natural languages of the world more frequently than the more marked ones that are acquired later. Fig. 8 thus depicts the grade of distribution: the more fundamental the phonemes, i.e., the earlier they are acquired, the wider their distribution among natural languages[21]. JAKOBSON's final correlation concerns case studies of aphasic language impairment, which looks like a mirror image of ontogeny, i.e., an aphasic loses those phonemes first which he acquired last. Aphasia thus represents a "metagenetic order" (KOCH 1974: 200ff., cf. SARNO 1972, LENNEBERG/LENNEBERG 1975).

JAKOBSON's contribution[22] then is twofold: first, he advances the "biogenetic law" formulated by Haeckel in 1886: ontogeny recapitulates phylogeny[23], i.e., the gradual build-up of phonological systems by a child (ontogeny) can be corroborated by study of the synchronic evidence provided by the distribution of phonemes in natural languages, and second, he correlated this to the reverse process, gradual disintegration, clarifying the concept of "genetic and metagenetic order", to which references will be repeatedly made in the course of this discussion[24].

Concerning the first contribution, KOCH (1982: 19) points out that JAKOBSON's laws of solidarity, or even his more "elaborate 'semiogenesis of the phonemic system'" have been challenged as to their validity (cf. OKSAAR 1977) or "passed over in silence". JAKOBSON can find many supporters, though, if he leaves the linguists' circle and turns to more "interdisciplinary" evolutionary theorists. RIEDL (1979) claims, for example, in his impressive *Biologie der Erkenntnis* that the principle of "order-on-order" governs the entire evolution of organisms and that the uniformity of this "strategy of genesis" (RIEDL 1976) is today "uncontested"[25]. In accordance with this position, PIAGET (1945, 1969, 1970, 1972, 1976) established the developmental phases in children's cognitive as well as epistemological abilities (cf. KOCH 1982: 55). LENNEBERG (1967, 1975) and CHOMSKY (1970, 1973) investigated the biological prerequisites for language. KOENIG (1970) proved that such stratification can be observed in the continuation of cultural tradition.

LORENZ (1965, 1971, 1973) scrutinized "phylogenetic adaptation also by humans" to support his conviction that all that is animal is in the human, though not all that is human is in the animal[26]. MILNER (1967, 1976) expounds the developmental maturation of the central nervous system. The "order-on-order" principle of genesis thus can reasonably be assumed to operate in the acquisition of semiotic competence by the human child as well.

JAKOBSON's pioneer work on the acquisition of phonological systems by children has inspired studies not only of linguistic competence - syntax, semantics, pragmatics - in general (PIAGET 1945, 1974, LENNEBERG 1967, 1975, CHOMSKY 1970, GARDNER/GARDNER 1969, 1971, 1975, HEWES 1973, 1976, HELMERS 1967, BLACK/BOWER 1980, WINNER/ROSENSTIEL/GARDNER 1976), but also of narrative competence (CANISIUS 1982, UMIKER-SEBEOK 1979, MENIG-PETERSON/McCABE 1978, KLEIN 1980, KOCH 1982), poetic competence (WENZEL 1982, BILLOW 1975, KIRSHENBLATT-GIMBLETT 1976), artistic competence (KELLOG 1969; SCHENK 1982, RICHTER 1976), and communicative competence as a whole (HAHN/SIMMEL 1976, IVANOV 1977).

To return to haiku, I have already mentioned that haiku is a "succinct" form of poetry and that my purpose in this study is to "shed light on the creative process" which results in its brevity. In this connection, one of the recorded teachings of Bashō (HATTORI 1776: 548) may be cited here since it evinces the apparently regressive, i.e., metagenetic nature of haiku. Bashō is recorded to have preached, "Let haiku be composed by three-year-old children", or "The haiku by beginners are interesting". Elsewhere he praises "artlessness" (MUKAI 1776: 438, 456, 462). "Simpleness", "brevity", or "unartificialness" - characteristics which are observed at the beginning of onto-phylogeny[27] - are in fact the terms frequently used in characterizing not only haiku but also Zen culture in general (SUZUKI 1959, HISAMATSU 1971, MUNSTERBERG 1965, HENNIG 1980). Accordingly, the discussions of "strategies of genesis" will provide this study with a useful approach to a discussion of the creative process which results in haiku.

While one of JAKOBSON's contributions, the unilateral laws of solidarity in the acquisition of phonemic systems, has been validated by developmental investigations of semiotic competence, his second contribution, the notion of "genetic and metagenetic order" in the acquisition and loss of language, has been further developed by KOCH (1982, 1983, 1983a). The German semiotician extends this idea to the field of "biogenesis" and incorporates PIAGETian concepts of "accomodation, assimilation, and equilibration" (PIAGET 1959, 1969, 1976, 1977)[28], as will be discussed in the next section.

1.2.1 Genesis, Metagenesis, and Equilibration

In discussing "the biogenesis of knowledge", PIAGET (1972: 52-62) opts for the interactionist position which synthesizes "Lamarckian empiricism" ("behaviourists, logical positivists") on the one hand, and "maturationism" or "innatism" ("Chomsky's 'fixed innate kernel'") on the other (ibid.): "the *phenotype*[29] is the product of a continuous interaction between the synthetic activity of the genome during growth and external influences" (ibid., 53)[30].

This is also the position LORENZ (1965, 1971, 1973) upholds[31]. It seems quite plausible to KOCH (1974), therefore, to correlate JAKOBSON's findings with biogenetic epistemology, and in particular with the interactionist position. In the following KOCH (1974: 192ff., 1982: 26ff., 1983: 418ff.) postulates an overall scheme to explicate the growth of structure in general. It can be presented as follows:

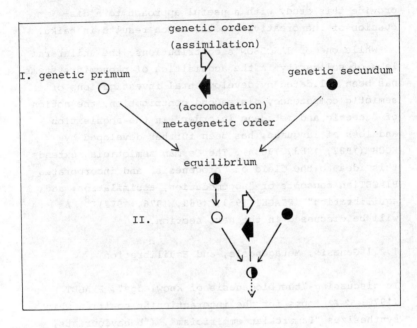

Fig. 9
Growth of Structure

As mentioned above, JAKOBSON formulated the "law of implication", i.e., if the secondary value is present, its corresponding primary value is already implied (JAKOBSON 1941: 59ff.). Of the two correlates, the genetic primum (◯)[32] possesses "geneticity, openness, dependence, impulse for order" (KOCH 1974: 199), i.e., "genetic order" (⇨). On the other hand the genetic secundum (●)

possesses "tendencies to counter-currence" in that it
proceeds opposite to "the higher, more completed, less
operational and more reflected" (ibid., 199-200). "metagenetic
order" (◉). The two, " ◯ " and " ● " then, interact,
or *equilibrate* (WADDINGTON 1957, PIAGET 1968, 1977), seeking the stabilization of the asymmetry (1983: 368ff.).
As the result of this interaction, "equilibrium" (◐),
or mediation[33], or homeostasis[34], is achieved, completing
the first phase (I) of the development of a structure.
The status of the secundum is, however, only "provi-
sional"[35], since in the next phase (II) the achieved
equilibrium in its turn becomes the primum, introducing
further development by the repetition of this "self-regu-
lating" process (cf. PIAGET 1972:57). Note that the newly
achieved homeostasis includes structural characteristics
of both the primum and the secundum, so that the form
of development is helicoidal (RIEDL 1979: 104)[36], or
homeorhetic[37]: the system has undergone "slight transformations of its structural organization" (KOCH 1982:
29). This model of structural growth integrates PIAGETian
adaptive behaviour ("assimilation", the subject's projection of acquired schemes into the environment) and
the subsequent "accommodation" (his adapting himself in
accordance with the environment). It is capable of
explicating systemic growth, since "regulations (with
their feedbacks, etc.) are found (after all) at all organic levels, from the genome onwards" (PIAGET 1972: 57).
Returning to JAKOBSON's example of the growth of phonological structures, we might apply the scheme to the
foregoing discussion as follows:

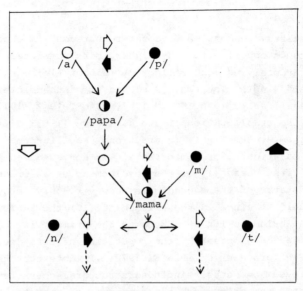

Fig. 10
Growth of Phonological structure

The genetic primum, /a/, introduces the secundum, /p/, they subsequently interact, and the first phase is completed by the stabilized mediation, /papa/ (JAKOBSON 1941: **49**)[38]. This equilibrium triggers the next development: the first consonantal contrast between the labial and nasal sounds, i.e., /papa/ vs. /mama/. This is followed by the contrast between labial and dental, /papa-tata/ on the one hand, and /mama-nana/ on the other, etc. This genesis observed in phonological acquisition is reversed in metagenesis, i.e., the loss of language, most representatively[39] observed in aphasics[40]. The applicability of the notion of genesis and metagenesis is, as mentioned above, far-reaching[41]: it operates on all the levels of evolution, i.e., from PH onwards (cf. Fig. 2). The formulation derived from the observation of the onto-

genesis of phonology will be repeatedly applied in
various contexts in the course of this study. Here is a
summary presentation: "○", genetic primum, "●", its
corresponding genetic secundum, and "◐", equilibrium
or mediation.

1.2.2 The Metagenetic Fallacy

Metagenesis is the opposite process to genesis. The
notion of metagenesis is useful in two ways: first, it
illustrates the evolutionary mechanisms which operate to
produce various levels of equilibrium, e.g., the equilibration between /a/ and /p/, as discussed above; and
second, it can be used to elucidate hitherto unexplained
phenomena or tendencies characteristic of the human
thinking process in general, such as mistaking "a posteriori"
argumentation for "a priori" reasoning, or attributing
superiority to the genetically late acquisition while
looking down on the genetic primata. These phenomena have
been termed "metagenetic fallacies" by KOCH (1974: 200)[42].

CHOMSKY uncovered an example of the metagenetic fallacy
when he pointed out that as late as 1979 the "biogenetic" side of PEIRCEian theories was totally neglected,
while the other side, the epistemological side had been
well investigated (see 0.2). The metagenetic fallacy operative in such neglect becomes even clearer if we also
consider CHOMSKY's delineation of two related problems in
scientific circles: first, a biologist's complaint,
and second, the difficulties encountered by scientists
who attempt to bridge "nature and man". LORENZ (1973: 4),
the biologist, had to justify his pursuit of "biological
and phylogenetic" studies to "many thinkers" who regarded
such a "venture" as "exceeding the competence of science"

and as partaking of too much "biologizing", if not as "an out-and
out blasphemy". LORENZ's (ibid., 1) point of departure
was "to investigate man as a physical entity that inter-
acts with an equally physical external world", and he
emphasized that this kind of attitude towards human
knowledge is "obvious to the biologist but is far from
universally accepted by philosophers and psychologists".
Similarly, scientists who endeavour to bridge "language
and brain" (SCHNELLE 1981), "the self and its brain"
(POPPER/ECCLES) or "neurophilology, ethology, psychology and anthropology" (D'AQUILI et al. 1979) must first
defend the inclusion of biological data^{43}. These examples
of the metagenetic fallacy thus concern philosophers,
psychologists, or linguists, who tend to overrate their
own fields while undervaluing biology, i.e., the sciences
which deal with the genetic secunda look down on the
science dealing with the genetic primum. This general
"overrating" of " ● " by human beings is "extremely natural", confirms RIEDL (1979: 51) since for us only "consciousness" (●) is conscious (cf. ratiomorphous perception
of LORENZ described in 1.1.2). As early as 1965, John
ECCLES, a neurophilologist, hypothesized that "conscious
experiences of the subject arise only in relationship to
neural activities in the dominant hemisphere (of the
brain)" (cf. POPPER/ECCLES 1977: 326). He now advances
this hypothesis more emphatically in supporting it
with the observations of commissurotomy, the so-called
"split-brain" operation (POPPER/ECCLES 1977: 325ff.)^{44},
to which we will presently return.

The metagenetic fallacy can, as said, be manifested in
two typical forms: one, the confusion in deciding the
genetic order, i.e., mistaking the secundum for the primum, and two, subordinating the latter to the former.

The human tendency to attribute priority to " ● "

thus explains, e.g., the tradition of logical positivism, in which language is considered prior to logic. PIAGET, however, (1970: 47ff.) has corrected the order in proving that the roots of mathematical and logical structures are to be found in the coordination of actions prior to the development of language (cf. PIAGET 1976), i.e., first logic (〇) and then language (●). Similarly, KOCH (1974: 341) criticizes ECO (1972) for his continuous commission of the metagenetic fallacy. ECO (1972: 47) is accused of considering the cybernetic mechanism of the *Stausee-Alarmvorrichtung* (Watergate alarm apparatus) as prior to natural language: ECO apparently thinks this because the former is "simpler". In KOCH's opinion, such a cybernetic system only "maps"[45] natural language, i.e., it results from human reflection on communication mechanisms, a case of "Meta-ierung" (metagizing). ECO (1976: 9-14) seems to repeat the same fallacy in placing "formalized languages" before "natural languages", or "visual communication" after "natural languages", in his summary of contemporary semiotic research: he starts from "the apparently more 'natural' and 'spontaneous' communicative process ... [and goes] on to more complex 'cultural' systems". "Formalized languages" are *metalanguages*, as KOCH has pointed out, while "visual communication" should be placed in the same position as "zoosemiotics", as the theory of "gestural language", accounting for the origin of human language, convincingly argues (cf. HEWES 1973, 1974, 1976, LINDEN 1980).

The metagenetic fallacy is seen not only in confusion in ordering genetic chronology but also when the genetic primum is undervalued. Precisely this kind of fallacious thinking is evident in the writings both of practitioners and theorists of haiku who have wanted to explain the genesis of this form as a process of eliminating "artificial" poetic devices. It is often said that haiku[46] prior to Bashō was nothing but "puns" and "wordplays" (cf. ULENBROOK 1979: 164). Then supposedly Bashō arrived and established a "poetry independent of rhyme and rhythm, of onomatopoeia and poetic brevity, of cadence and parallelism, of all form whatsoever", as the American haiku expert R. H. BLYTH (1949: 2-8) claims. Once established, the notion of the superiority of the poetry "independent of any form whatsoever" remained unchallenged. It exactly coincides with the traditional poetological dichotomy of *kotoba* (words, i.e., *matrix*: cf. Fig. 4) and *kokoro* (spirit, mind, feeling, i.e., *mapping*)[47]: the *kokoro* is superior to *kotoba* (4.1.3)[48].

In view of the ontogeny of poetic competence (WENZEL 1982), the metagenetic fallacy involved in such notions becomes more obvious. Peter WENZEL, a German semiotician, provides a corrective to this form of the fallacy by showing that children's poetic competence evolves from the phonological component of language, proceeds to simple tropes (metaphors and similes), and ends with "thinking about (the child's own) thought" (384), or *Meta-ierung* as Koch would call it. WENZEL (384-5) points out that traditional evaluations of various poetic devices regard "strict metric regularity and such techniques as wordplay and punning" as in general "rather poor"[49]. This is due to the natural human tendency - as exemplified by BLYTH - to assume that thought, or "spirit", is somehow superior and antecedent to "mere" language and its "effects".

The concept of the metagenetic fallacy warns us to be very careful about deciding the chronology of genesis and at the same time to beware of such biases as anthropocentrism (cf. the notion of *human ethology* in CRANACH et al. 1979).

1.3 Biogenesis: The Biogenetic Foundation of Semiogenesis

Human behavior, along with the "behavior of at least all higher vertebrates", is "a function of the interaction between the organism's central nervous system and the organism's environment" (D'AQUILI et al. 1979: 3)[50]. This premise of biogenetic structuralism[51], of which D'AQUILI is an exponent, is operative in the present study as well. Hitherto the problem for the discussion of haiku - or at least of the genesis of haiku - has been its total neglect of such a premise. This seems to have been responsible for the impasse of mere "verbosity", and the resulting frustration of the analysers of haiku. For one thing, in spite of their comments on the profound connection between haiku poetry and Zen Buddhism, they have never dared to explore the "biology of Zen" and have remained in the realm of religious considerations. For that matter, among the commentators on Zen Buddhism, the situation is the same: they either define Zen as "inexplicable", but then attempt to explain it (SUZUKI 1958, 1958a, 1959, 1982, OGATA 1959, SUZUKI S. 1970), or they define it by differentiating it from other, especially Western, religions (BENZ 1962, DÜRCKHEIM 1974, HERRIGEL 1959), or by delineating its methodology (SEKIGUCHI 1970, UCHIYAMA 1973).

Unique among the commentaries, however, is the work of Günter SCHÜTTLER (1974), a German psychologist, who went to Japan in order to analyse Zen experiences "medico-psychologically" (ibid., 83). His point of departure was that "religious experiences are after all psychological procedures"[52] (ibid.). His method was two-fold: the case study of each Zen master, i.e., conversations with the masters, followed by psychological analyses and the collection of neurphysiological data by electroencephalograms

(EEGs) taken during meditation in the hope of finding a correlation between psychological and physiological states[53]. In spite of such concrete data as the emission of alpha-waves "with the half-opened eyes" within "50 seconds after the start of Zen-meditation" (128), "rhythmical theta-waves with an amplitude-modulated alpha-background", or no "alpha-blocking habituation" (129)[54], SCHÜTTLER modestly concludes that what occurs in the mind, i.e., the "altered consciousness" (cf. SUGERMAN/ TARTER 1978), in experiencing Zen *satori* cannot be "psychologized"[55], for the question itself is "metaphysical"[56]. Instead of giving up, as SCHÜTTLER did, at this point of metagenetic reflection, i.e., at the level of "psychogenesis" (Fig. 2), I shall push the quest further to the level of "biogenesis", starting from a position very much similar to that of the biogenetic structuralists who analyse, e.g., human ritual behavior (D'AQUILI et al. 1979). LEX (1979), one of them, analyses "human trance" as a hitherto neglected "cultural universal" (118). She maintains that ritual trance functions as a "homeostatic mechanism for both individuals and groups" (ibid.): religious experiences are after all "neurophysiological" (119).

Although haiku and Zen are not synonymous, as SUZUKI (1959: 229, cf. BLYTH 1949: ivff.) rightly points out, haiku nonetheless "partakes of something of Zen, at the point where haiku gets related to Zen". While SUZUKI thus pursues the common ground for haiku and Zen through religious interpretation, I shall attempt to explore the neurophysiological process that results eventually in the poetry of haiku.

1.3.1 The Brain and Semiogenesis: Hemisphericity

One of the current issues in the neurosciences[57] specifically relevant to the present study concerns the two cerebral hemispheres, which are linked together most eminantly by a great commissural structure, the corpus callosum (MARCUS 1972: 534ff., ECCLES 1977: 229ff.). Anatomical evidence shows that these two hemispheres are "asymmetrical" (GESCHWIND/LEVITSKY 1968), and that this asymmetry can be correlated to functional asymmetries of the two hemispheres (BROWN 1977, JAKOBSON/WAUGH 1979, SCHNELLE 1981). The speech center is usually in the left hemisphere (PENFIELD/ROBERTS 1959: 201, KIMURA 1967, ECCLES 1977: 295-310). Hence, the left side is called the "dominant hemisphere"[58] (MARCUS 1972: 523ff.), as is shown in Fig. 11 (PENFIELD 1975: 32). This phenomenon of left-hemisphere-superiority in language perception was demonstrated by, above all, Doreen KIMURA (1967) who employed the so-called "dichotic hearing test" (1967: 174) and determined the "right ear dominance" (RED) (cf. ECCLES 1977: 302). Speech sound stimuli through the right ear result in better comprehension due to the contralateral auditory perception, as SPERRY's illustration below (Fig. 12a) shows. The lateralization of the speech center closely corresponds to "handedness", as MARCUS (1972: 524) writes: "Most individuals are right handed (93 % of the adult population), and such individuals are almost always left-hemisphere dominant". It has been estimated that "96 % of the adult population are left-hemisphere dominant for speech" (ibid.)[59] (the figure is arrived at by adding the proportion of left-handers who are also left-hemisphere dominant to the 93 %). SPERRY (1974: 7) diagrams clearly the essential functions of both hemispheres, as revealed through the investigations into commissurotomy, the operative transection of the corpus callosum. ECCLES (1977: 313) maintains that the findings of SPERRY and his colleagues[60] are of the utmost importance, but their "extraordinary implications for the self-brain problem have not yet been fully realized by philosophers and scientists" (cf. the metagenetic fallacy!). HARNAD (1977: xxviiff.) ascertains that functional asymmetries and a variety of motor asymmetry "wherein the organism turns all or part of its body toward one side of space" seem to be due to the phylogenetic primacy of the right hemisphere and to the "pervasive lateral synergism with which many other asymmetries of interest may be coupled".

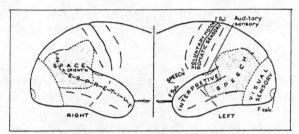

Fig. 11: The Functional Lateralization of the Brain (from PENFIELD 1975)

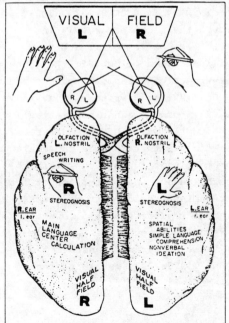

Fig. 12a: The Essential Functions of Two Cerebral Hemispheres (from SPERRY 1974)

While laying out the bilaterality of visual and auditory inputs[61] and the ipsilaterality of olfactory inputs, Fig. 12a shows that language is operated by the left hemisphere.

IVANOV (1977: 38-9) offers us, in this connection, a very stimulating illustration (Fig. 12b), which *maps* the linguistic functions of both cerebral hemispheres (cf. GRZYBEK 1983: 12):

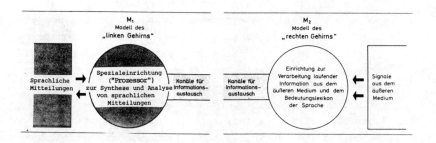

Fig. 12b: The Linguistic Functions of the Two Brain Hemispheres (from IVANOV 1977)

The recent investigations through "dichotic hearing tests"[62] have yielded a more differentiated picture of hemispheric superiority and of the linguistic aspect of language. Actually it is "distinctive features" constructing phonemes (JAKOBSON/WAUGH 1979) that operate in the left hemisphere, while all other components of speech, the "contoural, framing properties of the verbal messages" (ibid., 46), i.e., "the sentential prosody, emotive features, physiognomic properties", (ibid., 42ff.)[63] operate in the right hemisphere[64]. In considering the onto- and phylogeny of language, JAKOBSON/WAUGH (ibid., 47) thus agree with BALONOV and DEGLIN (1976: 194) who conclude that "the mechanisms of sound production and the auditory functions of the right hemisphere prove to be considerably older than the mechanisms of sound production and the auditory functions of the left hemisphere, which secure speech articulation and the discrimination of speech sounds on the basis of distinctive features". JAKOBSON/ WAUGH (ibid., 47) thus state their hypothesis: "asymmetric arrangement of the human brain and in particular the development of the left, dominant hemisphere have been apparently interconnected with the origin and growth of language" (cf. ECCLES [1977: 307]). In addition to the genetic priority of the right hemisphere (◯) in terms of speech articulation and discrimination, the two linguists emphasize the hierarchical order of speech sounds: "in the hierarchy of percepts the distinctive feature dominates all other features" (ibid.), i.e., the later acquired (●) dominates the primum. Their conclusion seems to be amply supported by the neuro-developmental study of MILNER (1967, 1976) who clarifies the "hierarchical-reduplicative phylogenetic-legacy pattern" of the central nervous systems (CNS) (1976: 48): MILNER confirms a basic assumption among biologists that the CNS are constructed so that the onto- and phylogenetically oldest parts (◯) are lower locally as well as functionally while the newer parts (●) are higher and dominant in the reduplicated forms[65] of their prima, which in turn confirms our previous discussion of the human tendency to the metagenetic fallacy.

The foregoing passage has clarified the two basic genetic orders with regard to the CNS[66]: one, from right (◯) to left (●), and the other, from below (○) to above (●)[67]. This genetic neural asymmetry seems of particular importance in researching the nature of "creativity" (KOCH 1981, 1982, KREITLER 1972) and subsequently Zen and haiku (cf. ORNSTEIN 1972). ORNSTEIN argues that interhemispheric communication results in creativity; syntheses occurring in the right hemisphere are interpreted and expressed semiotically by the left[68]. I shall return to this theme later (2.2.3); here it will suffice to present the following table showing the various functional differences between the two cerebral hemispheres summarized in ECCLES's (1977: 352) work (cf. GUR/GUR 1977: 262-3). The reader who is well versed in Zen as well as in haiku literature will have noticed that the functions of the right (minor) hemisphere are those most clearly reflected in Zen activities, including the composition of haiku:

Dominant hemisphere (●)	Minor hemisphere (○)
1) Liaison to consciousness	No such liaison
2) Verbal	Almost non-verbal
3) Linguistic description	Musical
4) Ideational, conceptual similarities	Pictorial and Pattern sense/visual similarities
5) Analysis of time	Synthesis of time
6) Analysis of detail	Holistic images
7) Arithmetical and computerlike	Geometrical and spatial

Fig. 13: Functional Differences between the Two Brain Hemispheres (from ECCLES 1977)

In addition, several other dichotomies offered by other

scientific fields and attributable to the modes peculiar to each half of the brain can be diagrammed as follows[69] (cf. IVANOV 1977: 27ff.):

Dominant Hemisphere	Minor Hemisphere	Researchers
Time-binding, verbal, linear mode	Timeless oceanic gestalt	LEX (1979)
Day-Yang-masculine	Night-Yin-feminine	ORNSTEIN (1972)
Propositional	Appositional	BOGEN (1969)
Discretism/digital	Syncretism/analogue	KOCH (1982)
Introspectionists/behaviorist's view of perception	Gestalt psychologists view of perception	DUSKIN (1973)
Analytic, fragmentary, abstract and symbolic, focal, sequential	Holistic and unitary, orientational, concrete perceptual insight	SPERRY (1974)
Speech	Space orientation	PENFIELD (1966)
Grammar	Semantics	IVANOV (1977)

Fig. 14: Two Modes of Consciousness

Of the seven characteristics ECCLES lists, the very first is of particular interest: only the left hemisphere possesses the liaison to consciousness (ibid., 310-333)[70], a conclusion which is based on the observation of commissurotomy: "the rigorous testing of the subjects who have been subjected to section of the corpus callosum has revealed that conscious experiences of the subject arise only in relationship to neural activities in the dominant hemisphere" (ibid., 326)[71]. In normal subjects activities in the minor hemisphere "reach consciousness only after transmission to the dominant hemisphere, which very effectively occurs via the immense impulse traffic in the corpus callosum" (ibid.), which consists of over 200 million fibres capable of carrying "a fantastic wealth of impulse traffic in both directions" (ibid.)[72]. ECCLES goes on to hypothesize that the location of the liaison area is restricted to the "linguistic areas in the widest sense"[73], i.e., the anterior speech cortex (Broca), superior speech cortex (Supplementary MOTOR), and posterior speech cortex (Wernicke) (ECCLES ibid., 297ff.), in addition to "polymodal sensory areas"[74], particularly of the prefrontal lobe and to "ideational areas"[75] (374). As will be shown later (2.1.1), the fact that the minor hemisphere has access only through the mediatory corpus callosum to the special language centers of the dominant hemisphere plays a crucial role in ritual trance.

1.3.2 Cultural Hemispherity: The Japanese Brain?

ORNSTEIN (1972) and BOGEN (1972) both hypothesize that there might exist a cultural bias for one or the other hemisphere, "hemisphericity". While the former analyzed ethnographic accounts of ritual trance and concluded that hemisphere alternation may be culturally influenced, the latter reported findings from tests administered to Hopi Indians and blacks, suggesting that "a tendency to rely more on one hemisphere than the other" may be culturally determined[76] (cf. IVANOV 1977: 191).

In this connection, one account - a best-seller in the meantime - authored by Tadanobu TSUNODA (1978), a Japanese speech therapist, ought to be discussed here briefly, since his book *The Brain of the Japanese* attempts to

elucidate the problem under discussion. In determining
the dominant hemisphere, TSUNODA introduces a "key-
tapping method" (1975) which utilizes the effect of
"delayed auditory feedback" (1978: 51ff.), an alternative method
to "the dichotic hearing test" or, in the case of neuro-
surgical purposes, "Wada-test", the injection of "sodium
amytal into the common or internal carotid arteries of
subjects" (ECCLES 1977:301). His preliminary hypothesis
states that the Japanese possess a unique brain (13ff.),
different from even their immediate neighbours, the Koreans
(128ff.), the Chinese, or the South-Western Asians (292).

TSUNODA presents the results of his examination of
experimentees from different nations - Japanese, white
Europeans, Bangladeshis, Koreans, etc., in addition to
a handful of foreigners of Japanese descent, in order
to "testify that the hemisphericity is cultural but not
hereditary" (58ff.). He assures us that the brain of the
Japanese possesses a "Japanese pattern", while all the
other nationalities he examined, including the Chinese
and Koreans, possess a "European pattern" (45ff.).
The difference between the two types of brain is twofold:
1) the Japanese brain handles vowels in the dominant
hemisphere, while the European brain does so in the minor
hemisphere, and 2) the Japanese brain handles with the
dominant hemisphere, contrary to the European brain,
various sounds in nature other than human speech sounds:
exclamatory voices, humming, cat's miaowing, bird's
singing, cricket's chirping, frog's croaking, cow's mooing
(73ff.), sounds of waves on the beach (356ff.), or (most
surprisingly!) musical sounds produced by the traditional
Japanese instruments, whereas musical sounds by European
instruments "enter" into the minor hemisphere[77].

Based on this observation, TSUNODA characterizes the
Japanese language as "a single-brained language" (71), for

both consonants and vowels are unilaterally handled, and
consequently Japanese culture, a "vocalic culture",
is opposed to "double-brained languages" and "consonantal
cultures" (132ff.).

TSUNODA then minutely analyses those auditory inputs
which "enter" into the dominant hemisphere, in contra-
distinction to the entrance of such inputs into the
minor hemisphere of the European brain, and concludes (79)
that

> the mechanism in which simple, continued vowels -
> all five Japanese vowels (/a/, /i/, /u/, /e/, /o/) -
> are operated in the dominant hemisphere lies in the
> formant construction[78] of vowels; furthermore, the
> minimal condition for it is that (a sound) must
> possess (at least) two formants.

In addition to this discovery, he also finds that 1) a
frequency-modulated sound (FM), a crucial component for
consonants and one normally received by the minor hemisphere, can be handled by the dominant hemisphere, if
1 KHz of pure tone[79] or short-band noise is added so that
the combinatory sound becomes similar to the formant
construction; and that 2) a combinatory sound in which
the "frequential proportion of two (or more) short-band
noises is *inharmonic*" can also be handled by the dominant
hemisphere (ibid.). TSUNODA then examined a handful of
Polynesians and discovered that these South Sea Islanders
show the Japanese-brain pattern: they, too, handle vowels
with the left hemisphere (292ff.)[80]. Comparing all the
results, he thus characterizes the respective halves of
each type of brain (84) that can be presented as follows:

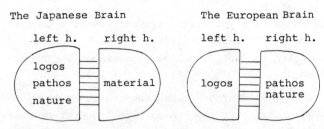

Although TSUNODA's analysis of the formant construction of vowels and consonantal combination is painstaking and convincing, his findings that both the Japanese and the Polynesians handle vowel sounds and their equivalences with the left hemisphere are not really surprising, since in these languages vowels function as distinctive features (JAKOBSON/WAUGH 1979), more so than in the European languages that TSUNODA examined. In the same way, in such "polytonic languages as Thai", the intonation contours, which function only as frame features in European languages, are used as the sense-discriminative features (JAKOBSON/WAUGH, 45). It seems thus very hasty of TSUNODA to categorize the natural languages in the world into just two, "single-brained" and "double-brained", solely on the ground that vowel sounds enter into the left hemisphere, especially in consideration of the fact that speech sound consists of both distinctive and framing features, as JAKOBSON and WAUGH pointed out. The auditory stimuli used in such cross-cultural texts should be selected in terms of the dichotomy of "distinctive features" vs. "framing features", but not in terms of simple vowel-consonant dichotomy. Similarly, TSUNODA's assertion that the Japanese "overwork" (139ff.) the dominant hemisphere because they make it handle both vowel sounds - natural and human - and consonants, while limiting the right hemispheric activities only to "musical sounds produced by Western instruments and machinery noises", seems extremely premature. His subsequent characterization

of the "Japanese brain", as opposed to the "European
brain", is also unconvincing, since one would logically
conclude that, if one side were so activated as to
be "overworked", the characteristic of that side would
be all the more clearly manifested, i.e., the "logical,
analytical, sequential" art of thought should have characterized the Japanese brain. The Japanese "are known",
however, "for their irrationality, emotionality, and
vagueness in logical thinking", as he himself points out
(89ff.). His hastiness in correlating such clichés with
his findings seems due to the confusion caused by his
diagram (84), in which the left hemisphere of the
Japanese-patterned brain is crammed with the examined
auditory stimuli, while the right hemisphere is spacious,
with only the two stimuli of "musical sounds (by European
instruments)" and "machinery noise" in it.

As a matter of fact, TSUNODA's assertion - that the
left hemisphere is "overworked" and the right is "underworked" (193) - contradicts his own notion that the Japanese
tend to think "divergently" (366, 369ff.), as opposed to "convergent
thinking", i.e., the Japanese tend to "overwork" the right hemisphere,
to use his own parlance. "The Japanese" are, he thus confusedly states,
"dependent more on the left hemisphere; however, how the brain works
cannot be easily determined" (371). Furthermore, his
findings and the characteristics of traditional Japanese
culture with its "highly creative nature" (360ff.) -
which is, in my opinion, evidence of right hemisphericity -
(2.2.3) seem incompatible. He emphasizes that a language
plays a decisive role in forming thought patterns (89), and
that therefore Japanese thought, conditioned by the Japanese
language, would be consistent throughout history - an assertion
we can heartily agree with[81].

It sounds quite implausible then that the Japanese, who
industriously activated the right hemisphere up until the

middle of the last century, have switched their hemisphericity - as his findings allegedly prove - in such a short time. For hemisphericity does not change that easily (LENNEBERG 1967).

The contradictions TSUNODA runs into seems to be largely due to the methodology he employs. His tests are weighted against the European examinees whose native languages handle vowel sounds "without consonantal environment" (73ff.) more as framing features and not necessarily as distinctive features.

In addition, it seems a gross mistake of TSUNODA to ignore totally the visual aspect of the Japanese language. Investigations into this language must, in my opinion, include the visual aspect of so-called ideograms, *kanji*, since cross-modal association plays a crucial role in language development (GESCHWIND 1974: 92ff.). Recent discussions of "graphemics" (BREKLE 1971, HALL 1960, KŌNO 1981, PIIRAINEN 1968) emphatically insist on the importance of such visuality (PIIRAINEN 1971: 81-2). The visual nature of the language is further evidenced in the experiments conducted on some Japanese aphasics. SASANUMA and FUJIMURA (1971) discovered the "selective impairment" of the Japanese aphasic patients by observing that ideographic *kanji* are the most resistant to this disorder while the partly visual *katakana* are less resistant and the phonetic *hiragana* are the least. Their further analysis of their experiments (1972) thus suggests that *kanji* processing seems *not* to involve phonological mediation, while *hiragana* processing does (cf. FENOLLOSA 1964). *Katakana* seems to be stored more or less ideographically, tending to be less impaired than *hiragana*. IVANOV (1977: 34ff.), referring to SASANUMA's further analysis of this observation (1975), ascertains that "in der rechten Hemisphäre der Sinn der Wörter (die 'bezeichnete Seite' der Zeichen oder ihre Bedeutung) in einer Form erhalten bleibt, die nicht von ihrer akustischen Verpackung abhängt", i.e., the "hieroglyphic" *kanji* are stored in the right hemisphere due to their pictorial nature (IVANOV ibid., 46ff.). Marc L. SCHNITZER (1976), using among other data those of SASANUMA/ FUJIMURA, also advocates the theory which states that phonological mediation is not always necessary for "mesotic", i.e., linguistic communication. In his analysis of aphasic impairment occurring in other than articulatory-auditory mesotics ("speaker-hearers"), such as "writing-reading", "finger spelling-finer reading", "articulatory-lip reading", or "braille writing-braille reading" mesotics (ibid., 141), SCHNITZER (157) points out that once "proficiency in non-articulatory-auditory mesotics is obtained, it is "sometimes possible to engage successfully in linguistic communication by means of these mesotics, *by-passing* phonological mediation".

Furthermore, TSUNODA's conclusion that the Japanese brain possesses left hemisphericity seems to be too inconsistent in social, historical, and cultural terms. For example, Yoshihiko IKEGAMI (1981), the leading Japanese semiotician, categorizes the Japanese language as a "BECOME-BE-language" as opposed to "DO-HAVE-languages"[82] to which English and German - the two European languages TSUNODA examined - belong. Basing his theoretical backgrounds on German "Lokalisten" such as Wüllner and Hartung (12), IKEGAMI analyses morpho-syntactical differences between Japanese and English/German. He then concludes that the cognitive faculty of Japanese can be characterized as a holistic perception of locality and state (280ff.), as opposed to the orientation of the individual, active agent and his subsequent goal-oriented activities (283ff.). IKEGAMI further suggests (284ff.) a correlation between a language typology and cultural typology, i.e., "BECOME-BE-languages", such as Japanese or Hopi, can be correlated with a pluralistic *Weltanschauung*, the syncretistic mode of perception, nature-oriented philosophy, or passivism, as opposed to individualism, analytic perception, human-orientation

and activism. IKEGAMI's analysis then points out the coincidence
between languages such as Japanese or Hopi and right-
hemisphericity[83]. In fact, it seems more plausible to me
to hypothesize that Asian people are more or less educated
to right hemisphericity, as ORNSTEIN (1972: 162ff.) assumes
(cf. IVANOV 1977: 191).

In spite of the criticisms expressed above, TSUNODA's
work offers interesting suggestions for the present study.
The mechanism that handles vowels or their equivalent
sounds as linguistic sounds, e.g., seems indeed responsible for so-called "onomatopoeic" expressions (ASANO/
KINDAICHI 1979) which are abundant in Japanese (LEWIN
1959: 89). Although I shall discuss onomatopoeic and mimetic
expressions - both *giongo* (sound-expressing words) and
gitaigo (state-expressing, or mimetic words) - in a later
chapter (3.3.1.3), it can be hypothesized here that "cross-
modal associations", or "intermediary zones"[84] as Flechsig,
the German neuroanatomist, termed them (KOCH, A., 1982: 154),
of the Japanese type of brain would be productive in onomatopoeic and mimetic expressions[85]. Haiku exploys them frequently (BLYTH 1949, SUZUKI 1959: 234ff.), and this "ono-
matopoeitization" might be one of the reasons why a "layman
can easily enter into haiku poetry", as TSUNODA suggests
(365). Another interesting thought presented by him concerns
what an American anthropologist, Ashley MONTAGU (1972), terms
"sociogenic brain damage", i.e.,

> social malnourishment, both structurally and func-
> tionally, can be just as brain/mind-damaging as
> physical malnourishment. Such sociogenic malnourish-
> ment affects the brains of millions of human beings
> not only in the United Stated but all over the world.
> It is a form of brain damage which has received
> far too little attention. Yet it constitutes an
> epidemic problem of major proportions [...]

TSUNODA points out the lack of any significant work on
artistic creativity over the last 100 years, despite the

cultural efflorescence of the Edo Period (from the seventeenth century till 1868), the source of what the contemporary Japanese export to the mostly Western world as "Japanese Culture" (361ff.). He concludes that this lack is due to our "over-orientation to the 'European framework of thought'" (365ff.), i.e., over-dependence on left hemisphericity. Whether or not this "sociogenic brain damage" à la Japan can be called an "epidemic problem" will have to be determined by further investigations. TSUNODA's warning against neglecting right hemisphericity is, however, certainly worth reconsideration.

The last point of interest to be mentioned here, though it does not fall within the scope of this study, is "bi-musicalism", an analogue of bilingualism (ibid., 148), which involves also the "plasticity" of the brain tissues in the sense of LENNEBERG (1967, ZANGWILL 1975). The difference between the traditional Japanese musical sounds and the European - "inharmonic" and "harmonic" sounds - on the one hand, and the lateralization in receiving these sounds, on the other, seems to be indeed an interesting field yet to be investigated cross-culturally.

1.4 The Biogenesis of Art

Anyone concerned with the theories of arts or creativity[86] would be surprised to find an equipotential procedure depicted in those theories. This procedure is tripartite: for the sake of abstraction, it can be stated as "first, then the second, and then the third". This syllogistic procedure seems extremely prominent in many disciplines. In terms of the ontogeny and phylogeny of phonology, ("L" in Fig. 2), we have already seen that the same principle is also operative: first, /a/(◯), and then /p/(●), and then their synthesis /papa/(◐). Or, in "genesis",

metagenesis and equilibrium, integration, or mediation"
(cf. 1.2.1). Such a tripartite process seems to have
been observed in Hegelian dialectical logic, viz., "thesis, antithesis, synthesis"; PEIRCE's "firstness, secondness, thirdness" (5.66: cf. 1.4.2); SAUSSURE's "signifier,
signified, sign" (1960: 114ff.); POPPER's "World I, World II,
World III" (1973: 137ff., 1977); and JAKOBSON's "sound,
sign, meaning" (1978, 1980), just to cite a few examples.
At first sight, these correspondences in such a wide
array of human activities seems to be overwhelming,
challenging us at the same time, however, to solve this
riddle. It can be hypothesized that this principle is a
manifestation of the endogenic information process (PH)
upon which the rest of the evolutionary stages are based (cf.
LORENZ 1959, RIEDL:1979:138ff.).

Assigning themselves the task of elucidating the creative process KREITLER/KREITLER (1972:12ff.) offer us "the
model of homeostasis", which is psycho-biological (ibid.,
13): the two psychologists presume that the process of
creating art is based on the mechanism of "tension and
relief" (16ff.), the latter inevitably accompanied by biological gratification, i.e., "pleasure" (12). This homeostatic model is valuable in explaining how organisms survive: it is "based on the assumption that there are optimal conditions for the existence and survival of organisms,
defined by a certain equilibrium between internal and external processes as well as among the various internal
processes themselves" (13). Organisms "strive to preserve"
the homeostasis, or equilibrium, whenever this balanced
state is disequilibrated: "any discernible stimulus (●),
external or internal, impinging on the organism can cause
a disruption of the homeostatic state (○) in the whole
system or in any of its subsystems, and can activate
mechanisms for the restoration of equilibrium (◐)" (ibid.).

The disequilibrium (○●) causes the organism to go into an "active state of energy mobilization", i.e., of "tension", activating the whole range of physiological processes ranging from "fast, low-amplitude EEG-waves to heightened muscular tonus, increased heart rate" (ibid.), etc. The relief from such a state of tension is tantamount to pleasure, as, for example, in "sexual or gastronomic pleasure" (ibid.), and it can also be defined in terms of both the reinstatement of the initial homeostasis and the "establishment of progressively new and more (○) stable states of balance"; mediation (◐) will be achieved. Actually, the final stage of KREITLER/KREITLER's model includes, as KOCH's model (see Fig.16) does, two different types of "gratification" which should be clearly differentiated - *homeorhesis* and *homeostasis*, which reinstate the initial balance with and without, respectively, the involved organs' transformation (1.4.1).

Still another hypothesis about creativity relevant to the present study is offered by Silvano ARIETI (1976), a psychiatrist, who elaborates on the Freudian "primary process" and "secondary process" (12ff.) as well as systems theory and neurophysiology.

ARIETI (401) argues that two kinds of evolution - one, biological evolution and the other, civilization - "may follow norms applicable to various systems", as general systems theory assumes (cf. BERTALANFFY 1955, 1968)[87]. Furthermore, he correlates the creative procedure and the neurophysiological procedure, localizing two "creative areas" on the neopallium, or neocortex (391ff.): one, the "TOP area", referring to the convergent areas of the temporal, occipital, and parietal lobes, and the latter, the "PF area", i.e., the prefrontal area[88].

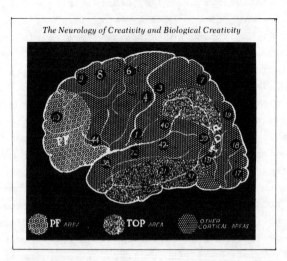

Fig. 15: The Creative Cortical Areas (from ARIETI 1976)

Localizing these "association areas" (391) bilaterally (392), ARIETI proceeds from the argumentation of PENFIELD (1966), who calls those cortical areas whose functions are still undetermined "committed"[89], while those which are still "mysterious" he terms "uncommitted" (391). ARIETI disagrees about the latter areas. In his opinion, through they might be considered "uncommitted" in the present state of investigation, they are "committed" to creativity: they are the areas where "the greatest number of associations and syntheses arise from inputs coming from all the other parts of the brain" (391-2), and accordingly they are the areas in which "the highest mental processes occur, such as symbolic activities, anticipations of the future, and abstractions of any kind" (392)[90]. Both the TOP and PF areas are thus "committed" to the "magic synthesis", as the title of his book suggests. In their

functions these areas are, ARIETI emphasizes, connected
with other important areas: both hemispheres are connected
with the TOP areas through the corpus callosum, with the
frontal lobes[91] through synaptic "cascade" connectives
(cf. ECCLES 1977:245), and with much lower structures
through the archipallium (392). The role of the PF areas
is four-fold according to ARIETI: 1) focal attention to
the object with the additional effect of "suppressing
secondary stimuli and delaying the response to them"
(392-3); 2) anticipation of the future; 3) permission for
"seriatim" (393) functions, i.e., for organizing acts
and thoughts in a given temporal sequence; and 4) transformation of the mental choice into a motor action (393).
MARCUS (1972:494) notes that the parts of the prefrontal cortex, including also the posterior orbital cortex and the poste-
riomedial orbital cortex, have "a common relationship
to the dorsomedial nucleus of the thalamus" (ibid., 494).
His report of clinical observation of patients with either
bilateral prefrontal lobotomy or prefrontal leucotomy
(disconnection of frontal lobe fiber connections to and
from other cortical and subcortical areas), seems to support ARIETI's assumption amply: these patients "often
were impulsive and distractable. Their emotional responses
often were uninhibited, with an apparent lack of concern
over the consequences of their actions" (496).

ARIETI's hypothesis is quite instructive in that
he points out the crucial role of two kinds of physical
connectives necessary for the "magic synthesis" to take
place: "fiber connections" on the one hand, and "neural
networks", transmitting the nervous impulse from neuron
to neuron through synapse (388ff.), on the other.

In the study of the ontogenesis of the CNS by MILNER
(1976), to which reference has already been made (1.4.1),

an wie ein Wunder: Sie aß
von dem Honig, dem Löwenzahn, aß
den gehorsamen Thymian, die Blaubeeren,
das Wachtelei, die sonnenschwangeren
Nektarinen, die Matisse-Kresse,
den frostwidrigen Steinpilz,
den heilshaften Wacholder.
Sie trank von dem Branntwein.
In des Spätsommers redseligem Laubwerk
wiegte mit weißem
Lied das Einhorn
sie in den Schlaf.
Das Raubtier war ihr Liebling.
Die Windrose folgte dem Hexengeruch,
dem Wink ihrer Hand,
die unter dem Distelstrauch, wo nichts ist,
wo die Keimkraft im Finstren
erstickt, wo Rabe und Schwan
einmütig west, Erde und Schlamm
zu Lehm sich verbünden,
sich weiter und weiter
ausdehnte, sich krümmte,
den Boden umpflügend;
die friedfertige Hindin
frönte der Hexe,
die im Traum Befehle ersann,
unentwegte Verheißungen,
dem Raubtier, dem von der Jagd heimkehrenden,
willkommene Labung.

                                             Es
                                     wachte auf. Es hatte
Jahre geschlafen. Jahrszeiten. Es hielt
der Hexe Versprechen. Vorsätzlich.
Es jagte die Menschenbrut, wo es sie sah,
zerriss mit der Herrin
ausgesprochenem Zorn
die brüchig gewordene Naht,
das aus dem Lot geratene
Neidgeschöpf, das missmutig
mit Gift das Haus bewarf.

Larissa, die Mondelbin

we find the conclusion that such connectives - "interconnecting tracts", as she calls them (ibid., 48) - are in fact present at all levels of the CNS: "each of the nine major CNS nerve centers - spinal cord, medulla, pons and cerebellum, midbrain, hypothalamus, thalamus, basal ganglia, old cortex, neocortex - may thus have anywhere from three to six of these categories of connecting tracts, not allowing for the two kinds of sensory and motor tracts, diffuse and specific" (ibid.), or "the pyramidal tract" as ECCLES calls it[92]. The fact that each level of the organ functions in a very similar way is, as MILNER makes clear, hardly surprising, because each new organ is "reduplicated" after its phylogenetic precursor, although the new reduplicated organ is needless to say functionally refined and more coordinating (KOCH, A. 1982: 151). It should also be noted that, upon the formation of the new reduplication, the older part is "reintegrated" into the new "homeostasis" ("homeorhesis") functionally as well as morphologically, as ARIETI (ibid., 402) argues. He thus explains the integration of the archipallium into the human CNS:

> "The archipallium, which is very important in lower mammals for the elaboration of olfactory perceptions, to a large extent loses this specific function in higher mammals, which depend less on the sense of smell [...] In a process of biological creativity, it becomes reintegrated with neopallial areas and comes to play an important role in the experiencing of emotions" (ibid.).

It is in fact fascinating to find the numerous correspondences that can be observed between the hitherto known psycho-physical activities and these neurophysiological findings. The fact that such "cascade"-transmission (ECCLES 1977: 235) takes time is, e.g., manifested in Walles's theory[93] of the experiences of the arts, in which a creative process is divided into four phases: "preparation, incubation, illumination, and verification". "Preparation" is the stage at which the subject collects the inputs (◯) with the "focal attention", specific to the PF area - a very important notion to which I shall return in the third chapter. It needs time, "incubation", before such electromagnetic neural "firing" (cf. ECCLES:229ff.) can be transmitted through "modular interactions". ECCLES (241) explains that each such module involves up to 10,000 neurons and that the whole human cerebral cortex is composed "perhaps of one to two million modules" (243). What information theorists measure in terms of a "higher" grade of information[94] can be ascribed to this immense potential[95] for combinations possessed by the brain (cf. ARIETI, 388ff.). "Illumination" occurs when the "solution" (◐) to the problem (◯ vs. ●) is achieved. Such a moment of "illumination" has been given different names: Karl BÜHLER termed it the "aha-experience" (cf. LORENZ 1959:299); PEIRCE, "abduction"; and Zen, though with some further modifications (2.1.1), *satori*, i.e., "enlightenment". The achieved integration is then in its turn to be verified for its appropriateness by the innovator (ARIETI, 15).

1.4.1 Symmetry, Asymmetry, Integration

KOCH (1983a) elaborates this three-phased principle, regarding it as being "of fundamental importance for any level of creation" (393) and thus as "the logic of nature" (411). This tripartite principle is diagrammed by KOCH as follows[96]:

Phase	Term	Symbol
1a	symmetry antisymmetry	○ ● ◐ ◑
2	asymmetry	○ ●
3	integration	◐

Fig. 16
General Phases in Creativity (from KOCH 1983)

KOCH (ibid.) ascertains that "symmetries are everywhere" manifesting themselves at any level of the evolutionary scale (Fig. 2),

"from atoms, molecules (PH), to macromolecules, bilateral organs of living beings (PX), social relations (SZ), patterns and figures of art (SEM), reduplication in child language (L), and metric arrangements in poetry and science (M)".

While symmetries "tend to be accepted as the beginning phase for the building-up of matter and mind", antisymmetries with their characteristics of "genesis-metagenesis" "permeate all parts of evolution" (394). The notion of antisymmetry as the initial phase introduces the "aspect of closure into an intrinsically open-ended symmetry" (KOCH 1983a:393). ECCLES (1977:243), e.g., states it thus: "Nowhere is there uncontrolled excitation: there is immense power excitation, and inhibition". LORENZ (1959:273ff.), too, offers the following two examples of such ratiomorphous apparatuses: first, the constant perception of color, and second, the "still object". LORENZ explains that the perception of one of two complementary colors (such as red vs. green) elicits simultaneously that of the other color, so that the result of

cognition is mediated as white. The second example is
what he terms the "reafference principle": at the moment
when the motoric impulse for eye-movement is sent out,
its corresponding input with the opposite mark will simultaneously be sent out into the cerebral cortex, which
compares it with the "perceived" information from the
retina. If both inputs are of the same intensity, then
both are erased as "Zero-input" (cf. RIEDL 1979:210), so
that still objects continue to be perceived as "still"
in spite of eye-movement.

The second phase, asymmetry, is "the strongest impulse
both for evolution and for its mirror-image: growing consciousness" (KOCH 1983a:394). It promotes the interaction between the two opposing forces - equilibration
(PIAGET) or self-regulation (LORENZ). It maps the evolutionary process, i.e., "reconstructing the genetic
order", and for this reason ("asymmetry is the ubiquitous
reminder of evolution": 397) it has the strongest manifestation in human consciousness. KOCH thus presents as an example
of such manifestations the "red square-black square" of
the paintings of the Russian suprematist Kasimir Malevič,
the "Janus-headed mask" of the Nigerian Ekoi, and the
"yin-yang" of ancient China (1981:158). It is what ROTHEN-
BERG (1971) terms "Janusian thinking", defined as "the capacity to conceive and utilize two or more opposite or
contradictory ideas, concepts, or images simultaneously".
The "bisociation" of Arthur KOESTLER (1964) - who advocated later the terminology "Janus principle" (1978:47) -
also belongs here. As we will presently see, it is exactly this principle that haiku is based on (3.3.3.6). Similarly, on the level of SZ there exist such dialectics as
"amity vs. enmity", "egoism vs. altruism", while on the
level of PX, there are "female vs. male", "life vs. death",
or "aggression vs. flight" (KOCH 1983a:395).

The third level reinstates the initial balanced state
either by integrating the opposition (○●), thus promoting *homeorhesis* (cf. /papa/ [◐]), or by returning to
the initial state without any transformation, i.e., by *homeostasis* (○), like most forms of neural excitement. The
first homeorhesis thus produces a mediation, or *tertium quid*
(◐), i.e., "neither black nor white". Discovering a
"deep-rooted and economical affinity between the phases
"of creation (PH) and the self-preserving cycle of
system" (PH-PX) (ibid., 396), KOCH diagrams (Fig. 16a)
five stages of homeostasis: 1) state of stability, 2) transition into instability, 3) state of instability, 4) transition to stability, and 5) state of stability regained.

Homeorhesis has the same first four stages, but its
last phase differs from that of homeostasis in that it
does not "regain" the initial balance but creates something new (396). According to KOCH (ibid.: cf. 1982c):

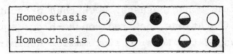

Fig. 16a
Homeostasis and Homeorhesis

Semiotically, this five-phased structure can be manifested as "pentads" occurring most typically in narrative
forms (KOCH 1982:63ff.). It then reduces itself metagenetically into the most reduced phase of "monads" where only "◐", the tertium quid, is present[97]. As mentioned
above, the verbal manifestation of Zen, the *kōan* (2.1.1.4),
and to a great extent haiku, utilize the pattern of the
"dyad".

1.4.2 Firstness, Secondness, Thirdness

The tripartite structure, ubiquitous at any level of evolutionary phases, can be expressed in the PEIRCEian terms of "firstness, secondness, and thirdness", PEIRCE's three ontological categories[98] (cf. CHOMSKY 1957:65, KOCH 1983:43). A summary presentation of his triad is as follows:

(a) firstness: "*Quality* of feeling" (5.66), or a "purely monadic state of feeling" (1.303), such as "to wake and in a slumberous condition to have a vague unobjectified, still less unsubjectified, sense of redness or of salt taste, or of an ache, or of grief or joy, or of a prolonged musical note" (ibid.)[99].

(b) secondness: "Reaction as an element of the Phenomenon" (5.66). "Second is the conception of being relative to, the conception of reaction with, something else". It is a dyad (1.326) which has "two sides according to which subject is considered as first"; thus firstness is independent of secondness, but secondness is dependent upon firstness to be the secondness (cf. FEIBLEMAN, 164).

(c) thirdness: "A Medium, between a Second and its First", i.e., it is representation as an element of the Phenomenon (5.66). It brings a first and second into relation (6.32), thus being the "process intervening between the causal act and effect" (1.328).

Note the similarity of the description of firstness and
the characterization of cognitive modes of the right-
minor hemisphere (1.3.1): non-separatedness, more intuitive perception, or Gestalt perception (cf. KÖHLER 1947,
KOFFKA 1935, WERTHEIMER 1967, ARNHEIM 1971, GLASS 1979)[100].
The main thesis of Gestalt psychology states that the
whole is more than the sum of its parts. Consequently it
establishes the genetic primacy (○) of the "whole" over
its "parts" in the form of "Laws of Primacy", which state that to
perceive and to react to the whole is more natural, primary and easier
than analytical, atomistic, or "discretistic"[101] perception (cf. JEKOSCH 1982). As LORENZ (1959) explains (1.1.2),
such ratiomorphous perception is, however, itself the method
of the information process, which takes place below the
conscious level but is superior in terms of the amount of
the information it can collect. PEIRCE's theory of *abduction*, which is opposed both to scientific or rational *induction* and to *deduction*, is thus another formulation of
this "firstness" (2.2.5). Furthermore, in terms of the
trifocal approach of T-reception, "firstness" corresponds
to the very first phase of aesthetic focus in which the
Gestalt of the illustration (illust. 1), i.e., its form,
figure, and pattern, is perceived as a whole, as an as yet non-
separate whole, as "symmetry" (cf. Fig. 12b).

PEIRCE's "secondness" corresponds to "asymmetry" in
which analytical perception, "the parts of the whole", is
reflected. It is a genetic secundum (●) which depends on
the primum. The secondness consists of a dyad in which
"two subjects [are brought] together" and which "imparts
a character to each of them" (1.326). Secondness thus is
characterized in terms of opposition: "it must have a
mode of being gained by its opposition to another" (1.456).
PEIRCEian secondness, or the asymmetrical phase, is,
according to IVANOV (1977: 38ff.), steered by the left

hemisphere of the brain.

The third category of PEIRCEian ontology concerns the "character of an object which embodies Betweenness or Mediation" (5.104). Thirdness is thus a "conception of complexity" (1.482), which involves the idea of "composition" (1.363). In addition to the aspect of synthesis, accordingly, what characterizes PEIRCE's "thirdness" is the notion of "relation", on which the semiotic function itself is based. Thirdness itself, however, is not monopolized by human beings. As the recent investigations into "zoosemiotics" (SEBEOK 1968, 1972, 1977, 1979, 1980)[102] have amply clarified, this thirdness is in fact ubiquitous in the universe. SEBEOK (1977a: ix) thus writes:

> [In] man, as in all other animals, semiosis has its source in the regulatory circuits that equilibrate and thus unify every living system (Cannon's principle of homeostasis), as well as establishes and maintains networks of stable relationships among diverse organisms (in Jacob's ascending hierarchy of integrons).

This thirdness manifests itself most effectively in human language (L in Fig. 2)[102], in which three factors are put into a relationship with each other: an *object* is related to its mental image, i.e., to the *interpretant* and this is in turn related to its mediatory sign, the *representamen* (2.418). Sciences are reflections (meta-analysis: M in Fig. 2) on this triadic relationship, and if the Moscow-Tartu School semioticians designate the semiotic model derived from reflection on language (meta-language) "the primary system" (LOTMAN et al. 1975), their designation can be justified[103] because of the effectivity natural languages possess in terms of communication (cf. SHUKMAN 1977: 23ff.). In the next chapter, it will be my task to analyse how this triadic structure

functions in communication situations, specifically in
T-receiving situations.

1.5 Summary

The present chapter has elucidated the role of the text (T)
recipient (P_{xe}) from the standpoint of *biogenetic semiotics*. P_{xe} structures, or "semioticizes", the text with
which he is confronted according to his "stored information" (1.1.2), which has been acquired through *ontogenetic*
and *phylogenetic development*. In semioticizing the given T,
he employs both *ratiomorphous* and *rational* reasoning,
subconscious and *conscious* cognition. In so doing, he
perceives first the whole, the *Gestalt*, second its parts,
the *asymmetrical* figures, and third, he *integrates* these parts,
which is cognized as a *relief from tension*. The *semiogenetic
approach* makes it clear that the semiotic faculties of P_{xe}
are based on a ubiquitous *triadic structure* which permeates
every phase of evolution (Fig. 2), as the main thesis of
systems theory states. Any system contains from its onset
two opposing forces, *genesis* and *metagenesis*: there can
be no *excitation* without corresponding *inhibition*. Any
disturbance of organs can be describes as the *five-phased
process*: 1) initial balanced state (*homeostasis*); 2) transition to the opposite; 3) the opposite state; 4) transition to the initial state; 5) initial balanced state either
by reinstatement of the initial *homeostasis* or creation of a
new factor, *tertium quid*, a *mediation* or *integration* of
the opposition (*homeorhesis*). Semiotics as a theory of
signs elucidates processes in which communication takes
place, i.e., how *messages* are *encoded* and *decoded*, a process which always involves three stages: the symmetric phase
(perception), the asymmetric phase (differentiation), and
integration (encodation).

CHAPTER 2

TEXTS AS SIGNS

In the T-situation, P_x as the plurality of T acquired phylogenetically and ontogenetically *structures* the T. T constructed according to semiotic systems exhibits, however, its own characteristics. The second chapter analyzes *texts as signs* exemplified specifically in the T of the fine arts of Zen.

2.1 The Semiotics of Zen and Haiku

The American haiku authority R. H. BLYTH (1949: v) remarks:

> I understand Zen and poetry to be practically synonymous, but as I said before, if there is ever imagined to be any conflict between Zen and the poetry of haiku, the Zen goes overboard; poetry is the ultimate standard.

I share his position: the ultimate concern of the present study is the poetical nature of haiku. Investigations into Zen Buddhism, however, will be very fruitful in clarifying our ultimate purpose, in that Zen reveals the *signified* of haiku in its original phase (the middle of the seventeenth century). The signified of Zen is experiences which are "intangible, indefinable, non-thing, non-abstract, non-moral, and non-rational" (ibid., iv). To this "nameless thing we call Life" (vi), BLYTH attributes two types of *signifiers*, or realization: one is "theoretical and abstract" and the other "practical and concrete" (v-vi)[1]. The first concerns the writings of Lao-tze, the *Diamond Sutra*, the verses of the *Hekiganroku* (cf. BLYTH 1960, 1964a, 1966) and *kōan*, while the second concerns the poetry of haiku. Actually not only haiku should belong to the "concrete" manifestations, as mentioned at the very beginning of the study (0.1): the tea ceremony, painting, calligraphy, flower arrangement, gardening, pottery, Nō theatre, and the code of the martial class belong as well. It seems, accordingly, to be of primary value to elucidate the nature of the signified of Zen in order for us to understand the poetry of haiku, the concretization of its signified.

This chapter thus deals first with the signified of Zen, which seemingly consists of the $world^2$ where "firstness", in PEIRCEian terms, or "ratiomorphous perception", in LORENZ's terms, dominates (cf. MÄLL 1964, 1965, 1968, 1968a, KRISTEVA 1980, BARTHES 1975). Similarly to the position maintained by the biogenetic structuralists (D'AQUILI et.al 1974, 1979), I propose that Zen, along with other techniques aimed at ritual trance[3], sensitizes the central nervous system by rendering *right-hemisphere dominance* and evoking simultaneous intense discharges both from the sympathetic and parasympathetic nervous systems in man (LEX 1979, D'AQUILI/LAUGHLIN 1979, KANELLAKOS/LUCAS 1974, AKISHIGE 1977). Furthermore, this biophysiological process of Zen as a form of "ritual behaviour" (cf. LEX 1979, FISCHER 1978) is embedded in a cultural context which offers the "semiotization" of the signified, i.e., the cognized antinomy (*myth!*)[4] and its solution through motor action, which is a phylogenetically older form of problem-solving (D'AQUILI/LAUGHLIN 1979:179ff.).

2.1.1 The Triadic Relation of Signs

Reference has already been made to the PEIRCEian theory of signs (1.4.2). Although it is the communication situation within which the text participants (P_x) structure the text, and thus any semiosis occurs in them, it nonetheless seems appropriate to sum up the triadic relation of signs independently, since the relation will play an important role in the course of further discussion.

The two founding fathers of semiotics, PEIRCE[5] and SAUSSURE[6], pioneered the notion of the triadic relation in signification[7]. In our example (Illust. 1) this triadic relation can be illustrated as follows (we will be considering the second situation, where P_{xs} = the painter, P_{xe} = "you", and T = the illustration): 1) there is the T which is printed on page 80 in the book *Japanische Gartenkunst* by HENNIG and which now appears in this study in connection with the discussion of focal attention (object); 2) there is the neutral image which the brain perceives and which thus is cognized by the perceiver (signified); and 3) there are the form, contours, color, perspective, construction, etc., of Illust. 1 (signifier). Following the now traditional way of presenting this triad according to OGDEN/RICHARDS (1923: II), but with the additional terminologies offered by PEIRCE and SAUSSURE, the above situation can be diagrammed thus (cf. FREGE 1892, ECO 1976: 59ff.):

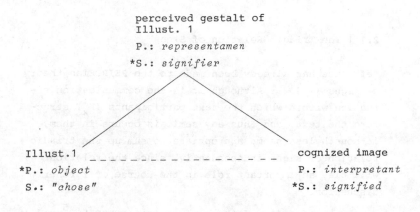

Fig. 17
The Triadic Relation of Signs
*=*terminologies employed in later discussion*

As discussed in the first chapter, the matrix of the illustration is in its Gestalt (signifier), while the matrix *maps* the cognized world, which is equivalent to the *information* of the T (signified). It should be emphasized that the signifier of the text is already a structured entity: in visual art like our example, the signifier is the drawing's Gestalt, and in verbal art like haiku, the signifier is the "acoustic image" (SAUSSURE, 66ff.) as well as the "written text", both of which we will presently discuss. Biogenetic structuralists (D'AQUILI et al. 1979: 12ff.) borrow the terminology of the anthropologist, R. A. RAPPAPORT (1967: 237-8) in order to differentiate two types of environment: "operational environment = E_o" and "cognized environment = E_c". *Object* or *chose* exists then in "E_o", whereas the other two of this trichotomy exist in "E_c".

In order for a sign to function as such, the signified must be presupposed to exist (PEIRCE 2.231). It is thus the signified which is capable of connecting the object and the signifier, and hence it is shown by a solid line, whereas the connection of the last two is only dependent on the signified, and hence is indicated by a broken line.

There have been many terminologies which describe the triadic relation of signs[8], and the concept has undergone further theoretical developments and refinements[9]. In what follows, however, I shall employ the terminologies offered by both PEIRCE and SAUSSURE: PEIRCE's *object*[10], operative in E_o, and SAUSSURE's *signified* and *signifier*, operative in E_c.

2.1.2 Unlimited Semiosis

In addition to the triadic relation, semiotic investigations (PEIRCE, ECO 1976: 121ff., HJELMSLEV 1959) have demonstrated that "the interpretant (i.e., the signified) of a sign is always itself a sign" (FEIBLEMAN, 130), i.e., the thought elicited by an initial sign becomes itself a sign which introduces another thought, and so on *ad infinitum* (cf. ECO 1976: 15)[11]. The PEIRCEian formulation of the notion of this possible infinity with regard to semiosis has been elaborated by ECO (1976: 55ff.). ECO clarifies the notion of "connotation", basing his argumentation on HJELMSLEV's *connotative semiotics* (1959): connotation is, in ECO's opinion, not "vague signification" or "emotional communication", as often falsely maintained, but is determined by a primary "denotation" (ibid., 55), i.e., the signified. ECO (ibid., 56) diagrams this *connotative semiotics* as follows (cf. HJELMSLEV 1943, 1959):

	Expression	Content	(connotation)
Expression	Content	(denotation)	

ECO (ibid.) maintains that there is a "connotative semiotics when there is a semiotics whose expression plane is another semiotics". As the diagram shows, the content of the former signification (denotation) becomes the expression of a further content (connotation). It follows that semiosis can be characterized as "infinite semantic recursivity" (ECO 1976:121ff.), that is, the primary denotation (the signified) of its expression (the signifier) itself becomes a sign ("expression" or the signifier) which in its turn signifies its content (connotation with regard to the primary denotation), and so forth.

Returning to our example (the second T-situation), the semiosis of Illustr.1, thus can be endlessly extended: the image cognized by "you" (denotation) elicits further in "your" mind another image or word (connotation), say, the day when "you" visited the Ryōan-ji Garden, how "you" felt, who "you" visited it with, etc., or such abstract words as "tranquility", "harmony", or "exoticism" according to previous experiences of P_{xe}, which in their turn elicit infinite connotations.

Both notions of semiotics, the triadic relation of signs (i.e., semiosis) on the one hand and its infinite extension on the other, consequently explain an intrinsic mental activity which operates in any T-situation. Furthermore, there is a built-in mechanism in human beings which reinforces semioses, i.e., the mechanism which the biogenetic structuralists term the "cognitive imperative" (D'AQUILI/ LAUGHLIN 1979:168). This mechanism itself is present in any organism[12]. An organism "organizes unknown or unexplained stimuli into some sort of cognitive framework", hence the difference between the E_o and E_c (2.1.1). Confronting such texts as Illust. 1, P_{xe} attempts to understand (organize) the picture according to his "known framework", i.e., in the case of human beings, the cognitive imperative triggers the semiosis of the picture. D'AQUILI and LAUGHLIN (ibid.) elucidate how a semiosis inevitably takes place, correlating the human's cognitive imperative with the function of the left hemisphere of the cerebral cortex: "[the] cognitive organization of external stimuli into a linear, causal, verbal mode of consciousness is an effect of the neural mechanisms[...] all operating primarily within the dominant hemisphere of the brain: [it] is this linear analytic and verbal form of cognition that precisely constitutes man's most efficient form of adaptation to certain environments". The very point of the discussion of the cognitive imperative is that "man is driven to understand the world around him" and he "cannot do otherwise" (ibid., 169). LENNEBERG (1975), similarly to JAKOBSON in developing the concept of phonological ontogeny, states that language development can be viewed as a "gradual increase in specializations and specificities" regarding semantics, syntax and phonology, whose ontogenetic development LENNEBERG terms "differentiation" (ibid., 32). Thus, in human cognition, to "understand" means to "differentiate" (cf. PIAGET 1959, LENNEBERG 1967, KOCH 1982:36ff.), or, semiosis is based on this cognized differentiation, going through the three stages of "symmetry-asymmetry-integration" (1.4.1, cf. IVANOV 1977: 38ff.).

When one considers this genetic manifestation of language-semiotic ability (LENNEBERG 1967), it is all the more surprising that Zen Buddhism consciously "inhibits"[13] the cerebral "computation", i.e., cognitive operations upon "potentially available data (various forms of physical energy)" (LENNEBERG 1975:19). One of the most typical Zen sayings on this point, the inhibition of computation,

is given by SUZUKI (1959:228) as follows: "Both the
subject and the object, *en-soi* and *pour-soi*, cease to
be something confronting and conditioning each other".
Differentiation, the very act which characterizes human
cognition, is rejected by Zen Buddhism. It can thus be
hypothesized that Zen Buddhism is a *conscious* effort at
metagenetic order, which attempts to return to the level
of PH on the evolutionary scale (Fig. 2). In order to
understand the cultural manifestations of Zen Buddhism,
then, our first task is to clarify the *signified* of Zen,
i.e., those Zen experiences characterized by *metageneticity*.

2.2 The Metageneticity of Zen Buddhism: the Signified of Zen

OGATA (1959: 13) offers a well-known statement, ascribed to
Bodhidharma, the founder of Zen in China, explaining that
in Zen no "dogma to accept" exists:

> A special transmission outside the scriptures;
> NO dependence upon words and letters;
> Direct pointing to the soul of man,
> Seeing into the nature and attainment of Buddhahood.

SUZUKI (1959:16ff.), too, emphasizes that "Zen does not
[...] indulge in abstraction or in conceptualization".
Further, *satori* is "emancipation, moral, spiritual, as
well as intellectual: when I am in my isness, thoroughly
purged of all intellectual sediments, I have my freedom
in its primary sense" (ibid.). It is of great interest
that SUZUKI speaks of "sediments" of intellectualism, since
the word eloquently describes the stratified structures
the human being has acquired. What both Zen masters are
referring to, then, seems to be exactly the opposite of
genetic development. The rejection of conceptualization,
verbalism, or intellectualism, all of which are functionally located in the analytical left hemisphere, points

up the *metageneticity* of Zen Buddhism. In the following, I shall discuss Zen's metageneticity with regard to five aspects: 1) metasemiosis; 2) the phyiological process of metasemiosis; 3) right hemisphericity; 4) *satori* as a motor action of problem-solving[14]; and 5) Zen as a *paleologic* or *abduction*.

2.2.1 The Metasemiosis of Zen

In a sort of manual for the practice of *zazen* (meditation in a sitting posture)[15] for Westerners, UCHIYAMA (1973), the *rōshi* (master) of Antaiji, a Sōtō Zen temple in Kyoto, uses the following illustration to show that a line ZZ´ presents "truly maintaining the posture of zazen" (33):

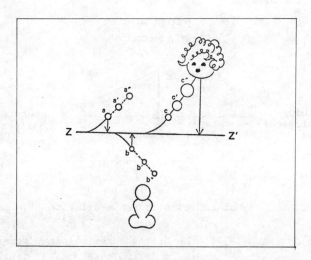

Fig. 18
Conscious Effort to Prevent Semioses from Taking Place (from UCHIYAMA 1973)

UCHIYAMA explains that the purpose of zazen is to concentrate on "the reality of life" (i.e., ZZ´), and it means that "chasing after thoughts (a, a', a", or c, c', c") [or] sleeping (b, b', b")" should be replaced by returning to zazen (34). From the Zen viewpoint, "all thought, delusions, and cravings are like bubbles and are nothing but empty comings and goings which have no real body when you wake up to zazen" (36). What UCHIYAMA refers to by depicting "a, a', a"" corresponds exactly to what PEIRCE termed "semiosis", and his explanation of zazen mediation thus describes the *inhibition* of *semiosis*. Utilizing the semiotic triangle, this metagenetic process can be diagrammed as follows, showing that the prerequisite for semiosis (i.e., differentiation in LENNEBERG's sense) is inverted:

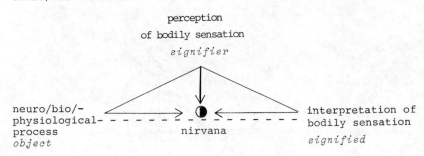

Fig. 19
Metasemiosis in Zen meditation

Ann SHUKMAN (1977), the British semiotician, comments on the Russian semiotician L. MÄLL (1968, 1968a, 1968b), who studies the Buddhist notions of *sarva-dharma-śūnyatā* (the emptiness of all signs). MÄLL concludes that the idea of *dharma* "might form the basis of semiotics and a way of overcoming the subject/object dichotomy" (cit. in SHUKMAN, 27).

MÄLL is referring thus to the state in which the "Void",
"nirvana" (*nehan*), or ku^{-16}, is experienced. "śūnyatā"
may be translated as void or emptiness, but is also means
"cypher or zero in Sanscrit, and hence *śūnyatā* implies a
philosophy of zero, which contains nothing in itself, but
as a mathematical concept and symbol stands for a great
many functions and possibilities" (FISCHER 1978:41-2,
cf. CHANG 1971, CHIHARA 1977:364, D. UEDA 1963:33-8).
Fig. 19 presents such conscious effort on the part of the
meditator to reach the Void: the object of zazen is the
neuro-bio-physiological process (2.2.2); the signifier
is the perception of bodily sensation; and the signified
is the interpretation of the bodily sensation. As the meditator
becomes more and more experienced, the triangle becomes
infinitely smaller, while "differentiation" is less and
less felt. The shrinking of the triangle explains differences existing among various forms of meditative techniques.
Zen Buddhism, especially of the Sōtō sect, does not necessarily aim at the total ahhihilation of this triangle,
while Indian yoga does go on to that extremity, or a final
converging point of Fig. 19 (cf. AKISHIGE 1977:52ff.).
Similarly, the "peak experience of *satori*" (FISCHER 1978:
40), which has become widely known especially through the
writings of SUZUKI (1953, 1958, 1958a, 1959), who belonged
to the Rinzai sect, very much resembles the yogic extremity,
as we will presently see. Needless to say this process of
metasemiosis is a cognitive phenomenon which is elicited
through biophysiological processes of meditation techniques,
as we will see in the next section. It is evident from various
Zen writings that Zen masters have viewed the process as
"unio Heimkehr" (HERRIGEL 1958:21), i.e., returning to the
"original but forlorn state" (ibid.). It is the state which
is phylogenetically as well as ontogenetically precedent.

Zen masters are well aware of the human capability of
abstraction which is realized through semioses[17]. SUZUKI
(1959:5) writes: "Zen is not necessarily against words,
but it is well aware of the fact that they are always
liable to detach themselves from reality and turn into
conceptions, [and] this conceptualization is what Zen is
against"[18]. EIBL-EIBESFELDT (1979:38), in his study of phylogenetic and cultural ritualization, points out that verbal communication has enabled human beings to "pass on factual information about the outer world in a detached, objective way", and that this represents an evolution from
"what animals perform in non-verbal engagements", which
is very often emotionladen and performed out of necessity
(cf. HEWES 1973). One example which EIBL-EIBESFELDT (ibid.)
gives for the type of speech that is "not detached from
emotions but is a ritualization of behaviors with a phylogenetic background" is man's verbal aggression, which
is "certainly the most elaborate ritualization of aggressive
behavior". The types of words Zen accepts are such as in
the example given by the human ethologist: "The word is not
to be detached from the thing or the fact or the experience"
(SUZUKI 1959:7). Or they are "the living word" (ibid.) which
has a phylogenetic background. The characteristic of Zen
verbalism is further clarified, when we consider PIAGET's
observations of language development in early childhood
(1945). The very first step of language towards a semiotic function[19], i.e., "representation"[20] (2.1.1), is observed in "deferred imitation"[21] which appears towards the
end of the sensorimotor phase (18-24 months). "Deferred
imitation, symbolic play, and the mental image" are, maintain PIAGET/INHELDER (1966:84), the "preliminary development of [the] individual forms of *semiosis*" for the acquisition of language. The legendary "Katsu!" (in Chinese
"hô"), an ejaculation used by Zen masters to chase dualistic,

egocentric thinking out of the human mind (KAPLEAU 1965: 174, 335), eloquently evidences Zen's metageneticity: instead of preaching through "representations" of language, Zen masters employ sounds which correspond to zoosemiotic communication[22] (cf. HEWES 1973, 1974, 1976), i.e., they use non-verbal sounds, "deren Wahrnehmung hauptsächlich durch die rechte (nicht-sprachliche) Hemisphäre besorgt [wird]" (IVANOV 1977: 36).

2.2.2 The Physiological Process of Metasemiosis

Physiological correlates of meditational states attained by Zen as well as other similar techniques (CARRINGTON 1978) seem to define a lowered metabolic state characterized by a drop in pulse rate, in the respiratory rate, in blood pressure, an increase in the galvanic skin response (GSR), and enhancement of the alpha density in electroencephalographic recordings (EEG) (AKISHIGE 1977, KANNELLAKOS/LUKAS 1974, ORME-JOHNSON 1971, WALLACE et al. 1971, HIRAI 1974).

AKISHIGE (1977: 37) maintains that as far as physiological processes are concerned, "Buddhist zazen and the zazen of other disciplines such as yoga are substantially the same": they all "enter the *samādhi* through *paryanka* sitting". The process of zazen is an "extremely compact 'feedback system'", in which "body regulation, breath regulation, and mind regulation" work reciprocally (32ff.). The posture taken in zazen is as follows (UCHIYAMA 1973: 22):

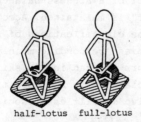

half-lotus full-lotus

Fig. 20: Zazen Posture

In this Zen posture, ideally "like an immovable mountain" (AKISHIGE 1977: 32), muscular activity is the least, outside of lying down (33): the muscular activity during a sitting of the master is about one-half that of the ordinary person (ibid.). Contrary to hypnotism and autosuggestion, where there is a reduction or disappearance of electric discharge in phasic muscular activity, the master continues to maintain the activity of the jaw muscles, though he is almost unconscious of this muscular activity (ibid., cf. MAKI 1972). NAKAMURA (1972) measured the EMG (electromyography) of the mentum muscle as an index of mental tension and relaxation along with the EEG and GSR, finding that the subjects with continuous appearance of alpha waves show moderate spontaneous responses of GSR, which shows clearly the trophotropic dominance, i.e., the dominance of the parasympathetic nervous system (GELLHORN/KIELY 1972). Similarly, SATŌ (1977) measured the microvibration of the fingertips as a guide for proving the stability of autonomic nervous function and emotion, thereby confirming mental and physiological stability and equilibrium during zazen. The "immovable" posture of zazen seemingly contributes to the trophotropic dominance in two ways: first, in its maintenance of hypoarousal (FISCHER 1978: 41ff.), and second, in its favorable position for abdominal breathing (ANDŌ 1977: 177).

AKISHIGE (1977: 33) states that "in cross-legged sitting there is considerable pressure on the thighs, and at times one feels numbness and pain" and through this sense stimulus "the moderate level of awareness balanced between activation and restraint" is maintained. According to NOBACK (1967), there are three classifications of afferent input: "exteroceptive modalities" responding mainly to external agents through receptors located in the skin; "proprioceptive modalities" associated with body position and movement; and "interoceptive modalities" associated with the visceral activities of digestion and circulation. Assuredly any meditation technique requires "a homogeneous space" in which exteroceptive inputs are kept minimal (AKISHIGE ibid., 32). LUDWIG (1966) lists "reduction of exteroceptive stimulation and/or motor activity" as the first in his exhaustive review of techniques that produce altered states of consciousness (ASC). Thus, in Zen meditation the reduction of exteroceptive inputs on the one hand ("sensory deprivation" cf. SUEDFELD/BORRIE 1978) and continuous proprio-interoceptive inputs on the other (the "immovable posture", muscle cramps, abdominal inspiration, etc.) form repetitive stimuli on the "electrocortical rhythms of the human brain" (cf. LEX 1979:122ff.). The significance of repetitive stimuli in ritual contexts has been well investigated (NEHER 1962:153ff., CHAPPEL 1970:38ff., LUCE 1971:121). This "stimulus bombardment" to alter biological rhythms, or "entrainment" (CHAPPEL 1970:27) through body regulation, reaches the brain stem reticular formation (AKISHIGE 1977:33). The reticular formation (the medulla, pons, and midbrain tegmentum) is responsible for the level of consciousness and the control of posture and orientation in space (JACOBSON 1972: 285ff.). Further, stimulation of the anterior hypothalamus excites the parasympathetic nervous system: "the heart beat and blood pressure decrease (vagal response), the visceral vessels dilate, peristalsis and secretion of digestive juices increase, the pupil constricts, salivation increases" (JACOBSON 1972a: 387ff.). The state thus induced, the "hypoaroused state" (FISCHER 1978:37), or trophotropic dominance "mediated by the serotonergic mechanisms in the raphe nucleus, turns the thalamic pacemaker on, thereby inducing an inhibitory cortical phasing of a 10/sec. frequency of alpha wave" (ibid.).

While the zazen posture thus contributes through repetitive stimuli on the brain stem to inducing the trophotropic arousal with its characteristic EEG pattern of alpha rhythm, it also makes abdominal respiration easier (AKISHIGE 1977:34). Zen respiration is "perfectly opposite" to natural respiration, in which inhalation is the more active phase. In Zen respiration, exhalation is the more active, and is sustained for a longer time (ANDŌ 1977:161). ANDŌ (ibid., 1979) points out that in the Orient, the importance of abdominal breathing instead of thoracic breathing has been suggested from ancient times, the breathing called *tanden* (abdominal) breathing (cf. UCHIYAMA 1973:23). ANDŌ assumes (1979) that in the *tanden* breathing with the concentration upon the *tanden* under the navel the diaphragmatic movement is very great and powerful in exhalation. This voluntary control of the diaphragm results on the one hand in the good ventilation of the residual air in the lungs and on the other in a change of intra-abdominal pressure which further induces the stimulation of the solar plexus and brings about the smoother functioning of the inner organs (ibid.). It should be also noted that this posture seems to be extremely favorable for the sacral plexus where the parasympathetic nervous system is also located. The respiratory rate during zazen decreases remarkably to 2-3 per minute as in an experiment with Zen monks (SUGI/AKUTSU 1964, 1968). The amount of ventilation per minute during zazen was about 80 % and the amount of oxygen consumption was reduced to 70-80 % of that during the time of rest (ibid.). SUGI and AKUTSU (ibid.), thus discovered the amazing fact that metabolism during zazen is approximately 20 % below that of basal metabolism (cf. NAGASHIMA/IKAWA/AKISHIGE 1977).

The lower metabolism during zazen is accompanied both by the decrease of the density of carbon dioxide in the

arterial blood and the decrease of the acid-base balance in the blood
(AKISHIGE 1977: 36). Referring to studies of the capilla-
ries, AKISHIGE explains blood pressure rises with mental excitement, parallelled by an expansion of brain
blood vessels causing a disequilibrium between extracellular fluid and intracellular fluid. The surrounding
water which envelopes the brain cells increases and the
brain cells are in an abnormal condition. According to
modern medicine, normality is gained through the decrease
of carbon dioxide (ibid.). NAGASHIMA et al. (1977) conclude that
the drop of CO_2 in the arterioles of vessels in the cerebral cortex ($PaCO_2$) is due to the hyperventilation induced by Zen respiration, which lowers hypertension by
"[inhibiting] cell excitation in the cerebral cortex"
and as a result "[activating a] sympathetic vasoconstriction
effect on arteriole[s]", which further induces a drop in
blood pressure (158). While the biochemical analysis of
venous blood thus evinces the decrease of $PaCO_2$ (NAGASHIMA/
IKAWA/AKISHIGE 1977 : 154, 155, cf. TAKEDA 1977: 217ff.),
AKISHIGE (1977: 36) further confirms that the blood which
tends toward alkalosis because of stress can be restored
to acid-base balance. The same tendency is observed,
AKISHIGE adds (ibid.) in urinalysis (cf. DOI 1977: 235ff.).

FISCHER (1978) offers us a quite interesting "cartography of conscious states [integrating] East and West"[23],
which can be presented here as a summary of the above discussion (cf. LEX 1979: 136). He charts for Western "tra-
velers" the perception-hallucination continuum of increasing
ergotropic arousal - an "inner excitation, called central
sympathetic or hyperarousal" (25). For the Eastern "tra-
velers", he charts the perception-meditation continuum of
increasing trophotropic arousal - a "tranquil relaxation, or
central hypoarousal on the subcortical level". The corresponding state
for Westerners is experienced cognitively as "normal, creative

hyperphrenic (including manic and schizophrenic as well as cataleptic and ecstatic)" states. In contrast, the voyage along the path of hypoarousal is a "succession of meditative experiences referred to by Easterners as *zazen, dhārnā, dhyān, savichār,* and *nirvichār samādhi"* (ibid., cf. AKISHIGE 1977:49). FISCHER's chart is reproduced below (1978:29):

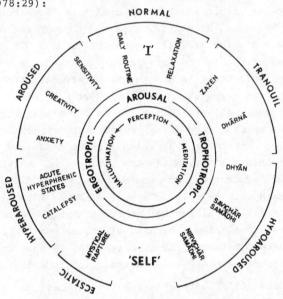

Fig. 21: Variety of Conscious States Due to Ergotropic Hyperarousal and Trophotropic Hypoarousal (from FISCHER 1978)

FISCHER explains the voyages on either side of "activation" leading to "arousal" (36ff.) in terms of a high "S/M ratio": The verification of voluntary motor activity (M), on which man's ability to cognize reality depends, becomes increasingly irrelevant as well as difficult (i.e., inhibition[24]), and "perceptions are transformed into intense 'inner sensations'" (28). Eventually M will be totally "blocked"[25] (ibid.), inducing the state that he terms "jammed computer state" (31). FISCHER explicates (28-45) that the extremity of both voyages is quite comparable: the "peak experience of raptus" (cf. BARTHES 1975) or the "ecstasy of St. Catherine of Siena"[27], on the one hand, and "*nirvichār* (without thought) *samādhi* (union, totality, absorption)" of the Indian Yogi or "unprovoked enstasis" in which the "lowest metabolic and arousal state" (Void) is achieved on the other. Thus, this enstasis belongs to the second category of trophotropic states described by FISCHER: the first class acquired through the Yogic technique of concentration (dhārmā) and the meditation (dhyān) to which zazen belongs[28], and the second class comprising a single state of raptus.

Returning to our metasemiosis presented in Fig. 19, it can thus be restated that the "voyage" of metagenesis in Zen meditation is the conscious effort of the meditator to inhibit the semiosis. Yet in Zen Buddhism the triangle which becomes ever smaller does not converge to a final point, differing from Indian Yoga, which aims to reach this extremity. This difference[29] is reflected within the Zen sects: while the Sōtō Sect considers that "the original enlightenment is training" (AKISHIGE 1977:59), the Rinzai sect states "without *satori* there is no Zen" (SUZUKI 1959:218). UCHIYAMA (1973:27), the rōshi of the Sōtō sect thus writes: "Doing zazen is to practice, put into effect, and actualize this *satori* here and now". He rejects the "sudden enlightenment" of the Rinzai sect: "*Satori* is not so-called 'enlightenment'. Nor is it some special experience which you strive for by doing zazen" (ibid.). Contrary to this Sōtō precept of more "gradual enlightenment" (cf. FISCHER 1978:40), the Rinzai sect emphasizes the attainment of *satori*, which is an "awakening" that "instantly brightens up the field of consciousness like a flash of lightning", though this does not mean

that "the consciousness thus once illuminated goes back
to its former drabness" (SUZUKI 1958:48). The experience
of this sudden satori is explicated by FISCHER in terms
of "peak experience", which involves a "hemispheric
switch" of the EEG pattern. It can thus be explained
best with regard to right hemisphericity, which is
the next topic in our discussion of the metageneticity
of Zen.

Before we leave the physiological process of metasemiosis, however, the metageneticity of zazen observed in the
EEG pattern should be commented on. According to the
neurolinguist Esther MILNER (1976:88ff.)[30], EEG patterns[31]
associated with the gradual postnatal maturation of the
central nervous system change in the following way:

Age Span	Associated EEG pattern
First several weeks after birth	Delta dominance
1 - 9 months	Emerging theta dominance
8 months - 4 years	Theta dominance
3 - 6 years	Shift towards alpha dominance begins
5 -12 years	Emergence of alpha dominance: development of adult alpha frequency
11-14 years	Greater EEG stability and organization
16-35 years	Systematized, mature EEG

Pioneer works investigating Zen meditation from the physiological angle were conducted more than 20 years ago.
KASAMATSU (1957), HIRAI (1960), KASAMATSU/HIRAI/IZAWA
(1962, 1963), and AKISHIGE/NAKAMURA/YAMAOKA (1962) demonstrated that the EEG pattern during Zen meditation is
characterized by alpha rhythms (8-13 cycles/second) with
occasional theta rhythms (4-8 cycles/sec.). Alpha waves
are associated with a "relaxed alert state of conscious-

ness" (LINDSLEY 1952), but theta waves with "creative imagery, reverie, day dreaming, and presleep stages of arousal" (FEHMI 1978:165). KASAMATSU/HIRAI (1966), HIRAI (1974), and SCHÜTTLER (1974) note that alpha waves in Zen meditation differ from those appearing in sleep in that Zen brain waves are more rhythmic and regular. Further, they point out that the concentration of the mind in zazen is superficially similar to the hypnotic trance but quite different in that there can be no habituation in alpha-blocking in Zen meditation (cf. TANIGUCHI 1977 : 296ff.). KASAMATSU/HIRAI (1966) also reported that Zen masters go through four stages during meditation: appearance of alpha waves with the beginning of meditation (Stage 1), increase in the amplitude of the alpha waves (Stage 2), decrease in the frequency of the alpha waves (Stage 3), and appearance of theta waves (Stage 4). Note that such stages, observed also in Yogi masters' meditation with "their more extensive lowering of the level of arousal" (FISCHER 1978: 41)^{32}, proceed in the exact direction of metagenesis, i.e., from the "mature EEG" which includes beta waves associated with "critical attitude, tense concentration, or mental effort" (FEHMI ibid.), through alpha dominance to theta dominance. "Unio Heimkehr" (2.2.1) can thus be evidenced in terms of EEG pattern. Incidentally, "delta waves", which are observed in the "first several weeks after birth", as MILNER points out, appear at the peak of sexual ecstasy or orgasm with the frequency of 4/sec. and a very high amplitude, 200 μV (COHEN / ROSEN/GOLDSTEIN 1976). FISCHER (1978:36) thus conceptualizes ecstasies as "phantom universe experiences": "Cut off - at the umbilical cord after birth - from a universal existence, the individual at the peak of ecstasy or orgasm incorporates again the universe into his body image as one indivisible gestalt". MILNER (1976: 88ff.), too, defines the age span from birth to four years as the period which is dominated by the "mammalian principle", while "the domination by the 'human principle'" sets in from five years onwards.

2.2.3 Right Hemisphericity: The "Peak Experience" of Satori

FISCHER (1978: 40) epitomizes zazen (of the Rinzai sect) thus:

> [Zazen] is a ritualized procedure using no words or letters but a right cerebral hemispheric gestalt-type perception-cognition with the aim of arriving at an Eastern "peak experience" or enlightenment: *satori*

Our previous discussion (1.3.1) has set forth the characteristics of the right hemisphere: "non-verbal, musical, pictorial and pattern sense, holistic-images, geometrical and spatial" (ECCLES 1977: 352). The genetic primacy of this nondominant sphere has been also assumed (KOCH 1981: 165ff., IVANOV, 1977: 37ff.). The preceding discussion has also explained the hypoaroused state (trophotropic dominance) as due to the activation of the brain stem reticular formation observed in zazen. It is, then, the task of this section to explain neurophysiologically the "peak experience" of satori which has been cognitively referred to as a "flash of lightning" (SUZUKI 1958: 48).

References have already been made to recent results obtained by COHEN et al. (1976): at the peak of sexual orgasm, a left to right hemispheric reversal of amplitude laterality takes place. GOLDSTEIN/STOLZFUS (1973) assure us that such reversal is also observed when, e.g., verbalization is followed by music or when NREM (non-rapid-eye-movement) sleep changes into REM sleep. FISCHER (1978: 36) ascertains that ecstatic experiences "may represent the ultimate interhemispheric integration with an ecstatic

(not yet epileptic) focus in the right hemisphere". This
"hemispheric switch" observed at the peak experience has
been explained by GELLHORN and KIELY (1972) as "mixed
discharges" of the ergotropic (sympathetic) system after
excessive "tuning", which is "the sensitization or faci-
litation of particular centers" (GELLHORN/LOOFBOURROW 1963:
91). The tuning, or "driving behaviors employed to facilitate ritual trance", as LEX (1979:136) characterizes them,
consist during zazen of three components. Two of them
have already been discussed: first, physiological "stimulus bombardment", comprising proprio-interoceptive rhythmical stimuli (respiratory rhythm, muscle cramps through
the static posture) and second, deliberate sensory deprivation. The third component for the tuning of zazen is
a psychoneurophysical "stimulus bombardment" which activates and eventually inhibits the ideational speech area
in the temporal lobe of, usually, the left hemisphere.
In Zen, this is brought about by the $k\bar{o}an$[33], a formulation, "in baffling language", (KAPLEAU 1966:335) which
is given to Zen students to "solve" (SEKIGUCHI 1970:104-
7). GLUECK and STROEBEL (1978:119ff.), in their investigation of the "synchronization-relaxation effect" produced
by Transcendental Meditation[34] techniques, hypothesize
that a "mantra"[35], used in yogic meditation practice and
employed in TM too, serves in two ways for the development of synchrony between the various cortical areas:
first, it bores and habituates the language-logic functions of the left temporal cortex, thus inhibiting beta
rhythm activation (desynchronization) and leading to
augmentation of alpha-theta synchrony (ibid., 120-1), and
second, it introduces a significant stimulus into the
left temporal lobe and "probably directly into the series
of cell clusters and fiber tracts that have come to be
known as the limbic system" (123, cf. MARCUS 1972:512ff.),

dampening the limbic system activity and producing thus
a relative quiescence in this critical subcortical
area (124).

ORNSTEIN (1972: 113) points out that there is a phonemic
similarity between such well known mantras as "Om"[36],
"$Om\ mani\ padme\ hum$", "Hum", and a kōan "Mu", which is
given to "freshmen" (OGATA 1959: 71). "Mu" is different
from mantras *per se*, however, in that it appears in the
context more or less of a riddle which "refuses to be
solved by mere thinking or logic" (OGATA, 72). The kōan
in question is as follows (ibid., 71):

(6) A monk once asked Master Jyōshū, "Has a dog Buddha-
nature or not?" Jyōshū said, "Mu" (No). "Now tell me,
what is 'Mu'?"

A marked characteristic of kōan is asymmetry: "Has a dog
Buddha-nature?" (○) vs. "Has it not?" (●)[37]. BLYTH
(1949: 206), an expert on haiku and Zen literature[38],
states that

> Zen is often conveyed by some intellectual *contradic-
> tion*, explicit or implicit, expressed in the form of
> paradox or dilemma, that is somehow resolved by a
> living experience.

When a kōan is given to the student, he is told to "stick"
to it (SUZUKI 1953: 92):

> Devote yourselves to it day and night, whether sitting
> or lying, walking or standing; devote yourselves to its
> solution throughout the twelve periods. Even when
> dressing, taking meals or attending to your natural
> wants, have your every thought fixed on the kōan.
> Make resolute efforts to keep it always before your
> mind. Days pass, years roll on.

There are 1,700 traditionally established kōan (SEKIGUCHI 1970:105). One may, however, spend five or ten years on a single problem (ibid.). The student has a private session (*dokusan*) with his master to report his "answer", being told time and time again "You are not yet ready" (ibid.), for presumably his answer still "relies on reason" (ibid.). FISCHER presumes that "the irrationality of the kōan" can be calculated to create an "artificial psychosis" (1978: 40), which can lead to the so-called "Zen madness" well known to Japanese doctors (JOHNSTON, 1971, SCHÜTTLER 1974). As mentioned (2.2.1), the very ideation executed through language (i.e., semiosis), which is normally actived for such problem-solving, is at the same time inhibited consciously.

This "dilemma", the paradox which defies intellectual solution together with its duration, forms a stimulous bombardment on the left temporal cortex. Significantly enough, the system of kōan - a method to create an "artificial psychosis" - was invented and developed, according to SUZUKI (1958: 37), to quicken Zen consciousness. SCHÜTTLER (1974:97) further counts as a "quickening" expedient sleep deprivation, especially during "*sesshin*" (a period of continuous meditation with a duration of usually one week)[39], which leads to exhaustion.

When the tuning of the central nervous system is augmented, its eventual outcome is "mixed discharges" (GELLHORN 1970, GELLHORN/KIELY 1972, GELLHORN/KIELY 1973). GELLHORN et al. recognize three stages of tuning: 1) activation of one of the sympathetic-parasympathetic subsystems while decreasing the reactivity of the other; 2) when activation continues, stimuli exceed a certain threshold, thereby completing the inhibition of the nonsensitized system and simultaneously eliciting a response in the sensitized system itself instead of in the nonsensitized system; and

3) if stimulation still continues, simultaneous discharges in both systems occur (cf. LEX 1979:137). It is "a state of stimulation of the median forebrain bundle, generating not only a pleasurable sensation but, under proper conditions, a sense of union or oneness with conspecifics" (D'AQUILI/LAUGHLIN 1979:157-8). GELLHORN and KIELY (1972) assume that the third stage of mixed discharges in the sympathetic-parasympathetic systems prevails as a product of chronic or intense excitation, as in prolonged or excessive stress and is characteristic of normal physiological states such as orgasm (cf. COHEN et al.1976), REM sleep (paradoxical sleep) (cf. GOLDSTEIN/ STOLZFUS 1973), learned behaviors, including Zen and Yogic meditation and ecstatic states, and of pathological states such as experimental and clinical neuroses, psychosomatic disorders, and psychoses (LEX 1979:137). Such "mixed discharges" of the autonomic systems are recorded on the EEG as the "hemispheric switch", which characterizes "peak experiences" (COHEN et al.1976). Although the satori moment has not been yet recorded on the EEG, as far as I know[40], the "suddenness" of the moment of satori has been well documented from ancient times[41]. How such a neurophysiological moment of "mixed discharges" and "hemispheric switch" can be cognized in the matrix of Zen Buddhism can best be illustrated by the following passage, taken from a letter of a Japanese executive who obtained satori under the guidance of Nakagawa rōshi of the Rinzai sect (KAPLEAU 1966:205):

> Then all at once I was struck as though by lightning, and the next instant heaven and earth crumbled and disappeared. Instantaneously, like surging waves, a tremendous delight welled up in me, a veritable hurricane of delight, as I laughed loudly and wildly: "Ha, ha, ha, ha, ha! There's no reasoning here, no reasoning

at all! Ha, ha, ha!" The empty sky split in two, then
opened its enormous mouth and began to laugh uproari-
ously: "Ha, ha, ha!"[42]

SUZUKI (1958: 48ff.) emphasizes that satori experiences
are characterized by "incommunicableness": "nothing that
enters into the very constitution of our being can be
transmitted to others - which means that what is at all
communicable is the result of intellection or conceptualization" (49). Language is, SUZUKI (ibid., 4) asserts,
a "treacherous instrument we invented when we desired to
communicate our experiences".

Such emphatic statements of "incommunicableness"[43] are,
as ORNSTEIN assumes (1972: 50ff.), due to the "right
hemisphericity" (1.3.1), i.e., the mode of right hemispheric perception is cognized while the left hemisphere is
totally inhibited. Jerry LEVI-AGRESTI and Roger SPERRY
(1968: 1151) suggest that human brains have evolved lateralization (with the spatial, simultaneous mode of information-processing to the right and language to the left)
because the sequential information-processing which must
underlie language, mathematics, and "rational" thought
is not readily compatible with the phylogenetic precursor,
the mode of the right hemisphere (cf. ORNSTEIN 1972: 63).
When the relational, orientational information-processing
is foregrounded, our verbal intellect can only term it as
"intuitive" understanding (LEVI-AGRESTI/SPERRY ibid.). Now
this corresponds exactly to how Zen masters describe satori
experiences: "mind of no-mind", or "*prajñā*-intuition"
(SUZUKI 1958: 2111, 218-9). The summing up of the "essence
of Zen Buddhism" cited earlier (2.2) can thus be well
understood: it is a "special transmission" independent
of any writings or verbalization, i.e., the right cerebral
hemisphere, which is "mute" when functioning all by itself,
as in the case of commissurotomy (ECCLES 1977: 324), has no

access to verbal, logical communication and therefore
it can only transmit through the specific, or "in-
coherent verbalism" of Zen (SUZUKI 1959:7). This is a
crucial point for the understanding of Zen culture in
general and haiku in particular, for this right hemisphericity exactly defines the nature of "sign" employed
in Zen culture (2.3.3).

2.2.4 Zen Buddhism as a Motor Action of Problem-Solving

GLUECK and STROEBEL (1978: 100) point out that the various
techniques used to produce relaxation "all have an impact
on the emergency response systems", which may be perceived by the individual as a "reduction in the subjective feelings of anxiety" (cf. "no fear of death" in Zen
Buddhism: AKISHIGE 1977:55ff.), or it may be measured by
the observer physiologically as a drop in respiratory
rate, pulse rate, oxgen consumption, blood pressure,
the level of CO_2 in the arterioles, as an increase in
galvanic skin response, alpha-theta synchronization, or
in terms of the change to acid-base blood, as we have
already seen (2.2.2). BENSON (1975), MAHARISHI MAHESH
YOGI (1966), and RADO (1969), all active in psychological
investigations, theorize that there is a natural tendency
within the organism to produce a more relaxed state (i.e.,
trophotropic-parasympathetic arousal) and avoid or escape
from painful situations (cf. GLUECK/STROEBEL:99-100).
Although there seems to exist a precisely opposite impulse
as well (e.g., curiosity or the inclination to adventure,
or a craving for science fiction, fantasy, and detective
stories), it seems uncontestable that Zen meditation in
general aims to dampen "the emergency response systems",
thereby using the "tuning-method" evoked by repetitive
stimuli (2.2.3).

Ethological investigations have established that such repetitive stimuli have, as their primary function", "signalling" or communication (cf.,e.g., CRANACH et al. 1979), but have also evolved the "equally important secondary tasks of controlling aggression and of forming a bond between certain individuals" (LORENZ 1966:72)[44]. "Ritual behavior", as ethologists term the utilization of repetitive stimuli, appears thus to be the "trigger for much of the cooperative behavior within species for which cooperation is essential for survival" (D'AQUILI/LAUGHLIN 1979:156)[45]. WALTER/WALTER (1949), and GELLHORN/KEILY (1972, 1973) have clarified that such repetitive auditory and visual stimuli can "tune" cortical rhythms and eventually produce an intensely pleasurable, ineffable experience in man (cf. ABRAHAMS 1976). The biogenetic structuralists thus maintain that it is clear that "a homologous affective state is produced by rhythmic repeated ritual behavior in other species" leading to the effect of "unifying the social group" (D'AQUILI/LAUGHLIN 1979:158). This "limbic coordination among conspecifics", they assume, is just as "present in human ritual behavior as it is among other animals" (ibid., 159).

Unlike other species, however, human beings most clearly manifest their ritual behavior in "religious, ceremonial ritual", which is always embedded in a "cognitive matrix" (ibid., 160), for members of the society are driven ("the cognitive imperative"!: 2.1.2) to "interpret the conceptual significance of certain behavior" (ibid.). This "cognitive matrix" generally takes the form of a "myth in nonindustrial societies" and a "blend of science and myth in western industrial societies" (ibid., 161). The structure of myth has been minutely analyzed by such structuralists as LÉVI-STRAUSS (1958,

1962, 1962a, 1964, 1967, 1968, 1971, 1973), MARANDA
(1974), KÖNGÄS-MARANDA/MARANDA (1971), and KÖNGÄS-
MARANDA (1972). The "mythical mind" establishes, according to LÉVI-STRAUSS (1958:364ff.), relationships among
socio-historically given elements, and it works on a
symbolic level "underlaid by the interplay of infra-
and super-structures" (cf. KÖNGÄS-MARANDA/MARANDA 1971:
24). The mythical mind "performs the specific task of
mediating irreducible opposites" (ibid.), or, in our
terms, *asymmetry*, the "Janus-principle" (KOESTLER 1978:
47), is integrated into a new homeorhetic *tertium quid*
(1.4.1). This mechanism of providing a *solution* (mediation!)
within the structure of a myth occurs, in the opinion of
the biogenetic structuralists (D'AQUILI/LAUGHLIN 1979:
162), at the *cognitive* level only, i.e., involves only
the ideational area of the neopallium. Such "cognitive
unification of antinomies" can "rarely, if ever", facilitate and sustain a psychologically fulfilling resolution
to problematic antinomies" (ibid.)[46]. The satisfactory solution can be obtained only when "affecting limbic and
autonomic functions" are simultaneously gratified, i.e.,
archipallium as well as homeostatic circuits must be involved, as D'AQUILI/LAUGHLIN maintain (ibid.). In attempting to overcome the antinomy in the form of a myth, "an
impossible achievement if, as it happens, the contradiction is real" (LÉVI-STRAUSS 1963:226), human beings thus
resort to motor behavior which "goes far back into their
phylogenetic past" (D'AQUILI/LAUGHLIN 1979:177, cf. LAUGHLIN/
McMANUS 1979). This motor behavior consists, as has been
mentioned, in repetitive driving stimuli, as in the case
of zazen. The "cognitive unification of antinomies" involves only the dominant left hemisphere, while a satisfactory solution must involve the nondominant right hemisphere as well.

In detecting the origin of the neurognostic substrata for "mythologizing", LAUGHLIN/D'AQUILI (1974) list three critical higher cortical functions: conceptualization, abstract causal thinking, and antinomous thinking. All myths are presented, they assure us, in terms of "named categories of objects that we call concepts or ideas", while involving, like all other rational thoughts, "causal sequences", and the orientation of the universe into "multiple dyads of polar opposites" (cf. D'AQUILI/LAUGHLIN 1979:162). The two biogenetic structuralists localize this "mythologizing" function of the brain in the area comprising the inferior parietal lobule, the anterior convexity of the frontal lobes, and the reciprocal interconnections (ibid., 164) of the dominant hemisphere. The importance of the inferior parietal lobule is stressed in the works of GESCHWIND (1965), LURIA (1966), and BASSO et al. (1973). GESCHWIND (1965, 1974:94-7) states that areas 39 and 40 of Brodmann's so-called cytoarchitectural map (cit. in MARCUS 1972: 458)[47] were developed to enhance the ability to make "cross-modal associations" (visual, tactile, and auditory) which underlies the learning of names of objects (cf. ECCLES 1977:305ff.). LURIA (1966) noted that the parieto-occipital area is intimately involved in the formulation of basic grammatical categories, while BASSO et al. (1973) point out that in this area several intellectual abilities are focally organized. Furthermore, mental activity involving causal sequencing has been localized in the frontal cortex by WALTER (1973), LIVANOV et al. (1973), LURIA (1973), and PRIBRAM (1973). Ontogenetically, these areas are the last to myelinate (MILNER 1967:167-239). Phylogenetically speaking, the two biogenetic structuralists (1979: 167) state, it was *Homo erectus*[48] about 750,000 years ago who was first capable of being both a "complex mythmaker and religious ritual practitioner". They base this conclusion on *homo erectus'* possession of inferior frontal convolutions, middle temporal convolutions, and the inferior parietal lobule. It seems on the other hand improbable that *Australopithecus*[49] was capable of being both, though he was "probably ordering his world in rudimentary conceptual opposites" (D'AQUILI/LAUGHLIN 1979:166).

Although these neural developments of higher cortical functions may be regarded as a "major adaptive advance, in so far as they allow man abstract problem solving" (ibid., 171), they can be also regarded as a "curse", for they make him "acutely aware of his own mortality and of the contingency of his existence in an unpredictable world" (ibid., cf. BECKER 1973), now that he can postulate, from experience, "probable events under given circumstances" (ibid.). This is the basis of the "existential anxiety that all men bear", and man seeks to relieve this "curse of cognition" by attempting to understand "reality" (ibid., cf. KUBOTA 1968:253ff.). The attempt results in the postulation of some kind of unknown supernatural power, such as gods or other entities, as agents responsible for "reality" (D'AQUILI/LAUGHLIN 1979:171). Thus, the *ultimate* aim of all human religious ritual is "the union of contingent and vulnerable man with a powerful, possibly omnipotent force" (ibid., 162), or "man vs. nature" (KOCH 1978:310ff.). The surface structures of myth thus manifest this polar opposition, which takes the dichotomy of "man" vs. "personified power(s)" along with such dichotomies as good/bad, heaven/hell, sky/earth, left/right, strong/weak, to cite a few of the most representative (IVANOV/TOPOROV 1982: 60ff.). Kōan, too, manifests a polar opposition, thus triggering Zen meditation to overcome the "curse of cognition".

Kōan, the "myth" of Zen, which was invented to "quicken" the satori process, as SUZUKI asserts (2.2.3), however, is

different from a typical myth structure in that in kōan
no mediation is offered in the surface structure (cf.
"zero mediator" in KÖNGÄS-MARANDA/MARANDA 1971:37-49).
Mediation, as understood in the structural analysis
of myth, implies "a permutation of roles or functions"
(ibid., 26), so that an initial opposition, i.e., problem
(○●) is "permuted" into the final outcome, i.e., solution (◐) of the process, i.e., "inversion takes place"
(cf. LÉVI-STRAUSS's 1958 *formula*: $f_x(a) : f_y(b) :: f_x(b) : f_a^{-1}(y)$). Thus the most typical myth can be characterized as "conciliation of opposites, *coincidentia oppo-
sitorum*, through a mediator" (KÖNGÄS-MARANDA/MARANDA
1971:24), or in our terms:

(*coincidentia oppositorum*) (problem)

asymmetry

(mediation)
tertium quid   (solution)

Decisive here is the fact that the *tertium quid* (mediation, or integration) is a *synthesis* containing some
characteristics of each half of initial opposites (cf.
KOCH 1983:83ff.), and that the process of *mentation* takes
place in the ideational areas in the dominant (left) cortical hemisphere. In contradiction to this type of myth,
kōan does not offer any mediation on the surface level.
Let us consider again our kōan example (6) stated above
(2.2.3). The *coincidentia oppositorum* of this kōan is:
"Has a dog Buddha-nature?" vs. "Has it not?" (problem!)
The given *solution* to this *riddle* is "Mu", which does
not contain any characteristics of the initial asymmetry:
"Mu" is not a mediation in the LÉVI-STRAUSS sense. The
difference between the myth structure described above
and the kōan structure lies in the *nature of the solution*.

If we use the sign "□" and the broken line to emphasize the "unrelatedness" to the initial problem (○ ●) of the solution and the process leading to the solution, respectively, then the process of kōan problem-solving can be presented as follows:

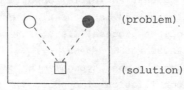

(problem)

(solution)

In order to illustrate this characteristic of kōan problem-solving, here are two examples (OGATA 1959:71):

(7) The Sixth Patriarch said to the monk Emyō, Think neither of the good nor the evil; but tell me what are [sic] your original features[50] before your parents gave birth to you?[51]

(8) The Master Haikuin said, 'What is the sound of one (clapping) hand?'[52]

In the kōan (7), the contradiction is expressed in the premise of "a face[53] before birth": for, in order to possess a face, one must have been born, and, conversely, if one is not born, one cannot have a face. The solution is to "show [the Zen master] the face before birth", or "Buddha-Nature" in Kōan (6). In (8), similarly to (7), a contradiction is posed: in order for a human to "clap", he needs both hands, and conversely, if he can only use one hand, he cannot possibly make a clapping sound. The solution is to tell the master what "the sound of one clapping hand" sounds like. It should be recalled that any "logical" answer is refused by the master, i.e., any answer that has the nature of the logical *tertium quid* is refuted by the master with the comment, "You are not

ready yet" (2.2.3). It seems that every possible neural
connection that can be made within the ideational areas
of the dominant hemisphere is explored and probed only
to be refused by the Zen master. What, then, can the
right solution be?

The solution is motor behavior[54], which is steered by the
right hemisphere (IVANOV 1977: 37) and is a phylogenetically primary way
to master the environment: "Like all other animals, man attempts to
master the environmental situation by means of motor behavior" (D'AQUILI/
LAUGHLIN 1979: 177, cf. LAUGHLIN/McMAGNUS 1979). OGATA (1959: 76-7) divulges the "satisfactory answers" to kōan ordinarily privy to
the masters alone. The basic tenor of problem-solving is
motor activity. Of the eight possible "forms" of answering,
the first two can be presented here to support our premise
(OGATA, 76):

> *Hosshin or Dharmakāya:* If a kōan is to be answered
> in this form, the student has to repeat the statement,
> gesture, action or silence with which the teacher
> raised the kōan.
>
> *Kikan or application:* When a student prefers to answer
> in this form, he has to illustrate or demonstrate it
> by acting some incident from daily life or by making
> use of something that happens to be within reach at
> the moment. Most irrational kōans are answered in this
> way.

The emphases on motor behavior in the Zen context have
been sufficiently described by Zen masters. SUZUKI (1959:
8ff.) thus speaks of "teaching by action, learning by
doing" or the "actional approach to enlightenment", and
gives several typical examples of this approach: when
Rinzai (Lin-chi, d. 867) was asked what the essence of
Buddhist teaching was, he came "right down from his seat
and, taking hold of the questioner by the front of his

robe, slapped his face, and let him go"; when one of the
Rinzai's students was challenged by another monk belonging
to another school with the question, "How deep is the
river of Zen", he "lost no time" in replying, "Find out
for yourself", by offering to throw the questioner from
the bridge, the reference to the river arising from the
fact that the encounter took place on a bridge (ibid., 5).

Now that the cognitive matrix of Zen Buddhism, i.e.,
the myth-problem as an "impossible" opposition and its
solution in motor behavior has been presented, the next
task in this section is to explain precisely how motor
behavior functions as a solution in Zen Buddhism.

I postulate that the "peak experience" of satori,
especially in the Rinzai sect, goes through four stages
which can be illustrated as follows (Fig. 22) (cf. D'AQUILI/
LAUGHLIN 1979:175-8):

STAGE 1: Man becomes aware of his mortality and the
contingency of his existence (▷). He
"accommodates" himself to this situation (◀)
by making a myth (an opposition: "man" vs.
"nature"). The dominant side (inferior parietal
lobule, the anterior convexity of the frontal
lobes, and their reciprocal interconnections)
is activated in this "mythologizing".

STAGE 2: He is instructed to practise zazen, which
consists in the "regulation of mind" (cognitive
matrix: seeking "Buddha-nature"), the "regulation of body" (repetitive stimuli) and the
"regulation of breath" (repetitive stimuli
+ trophotropic activation). At the same time,
through sermons and *dokusan* (private meetings
with the master), a Zen meditator is instructed
in the fundamental principle of problem-solving,
i.e., motor activity.

STAGE 3: Kōans are given to accelerate the "tuning" of the CNS: on the one hand the ergotrophic stimulation through mentation (left hemisphere) is highly activated in that every possible *tertium quid* will be probed, and, on the other, the trophotropic activation (the enhancement of the right hemisphere) is continued. During this period of "tuning", there will be some learning of the right hemisphere through corpus callosum, anterior commissure, posterior commissure, habular commissure, massa intermedia, and pons (cf. GLUECK/STROEBEL 1979: 127)

STAGE 4: The stimulation of the trophotropic system continues simultaneously with the stimulation of ergotrophic system of the left hemisphere due to the kōan as the driver for tuning. Then, the third stage of "mixed discharges" (GELLHORN/KIELY 1972) is reached, thereby eliciting a strong sense of "union" in which the initial opposition learned by the right hemisphere through the interhemispheric activities is *simultaneously perceived* and *resolved*. D'AQUILI/LAUGHLIN (1979:178) write:

> [Such states of peak experience] yield not only a feeling of union with a greater force or power but also an intense awareness that death is not to be feared, accompanied by a sense of harmony of the individual with the universe. This sense of universal harmony may be the human cognitive extrapolation from the more primitive sense of union with other conspecifics that ritual behavior excites in animals.

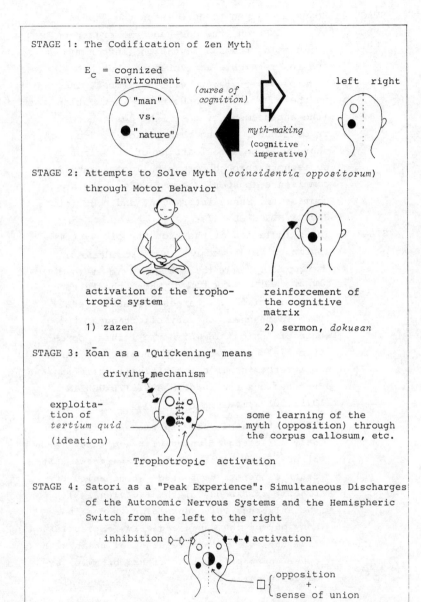

Fig.22: Four Stages Leading up to Satori

It should be also noted that the trigger of "mixed discharges" is allegedly some type of exteroceptive input, phonic[55], visual[56], or tactile[57], which directly enters into GESCHWIND's cross-modal transfer area without limbic mediation.

In the peak experience of simultaneous "spillover" (ibid., 176), the left hemisphere is more inhibited, while the right is highly aroused. The inability to communicate such "peak experiences" is well summarized in Arthur DEIKMAN's comment on "mystic" experiences in general: "Ordinary language is structured to follow the logical development of one idea at a time, and it might be quite inadequate to express an experience encompassing a large number of concepts simultaneously" (1966:339).

As a summary of this section, the following diagram can be presented, showing the two distinctive modes of problem-solving that can be attributed to either half of the cerebral cortex (cf. IVANOV 1977: 27-42):

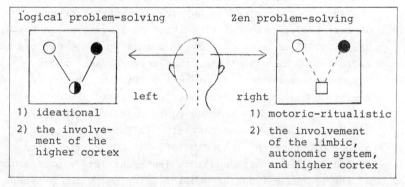

Fig. 23
The Two Modes of Problem-Solving and their Attribution to Either Cerebral Hemisphere

2.2.5 Zen as a *Paleologic* or *Abduction*

Neurophysiologically speaking, there seems, as the preceding discussion has stressed, a fundamental difference between the mythical mind that creates mediation in the ideational areas of the dominant hemisphere and *another* mythical mind that seeks the solution through motor behavior in which the *solution* is *nothing but the acceptance* of the original opposition as such. Or put another way, its *tertium quid* (solution!) is *not creating* any mediation in the sense of a permutation of the initial premises. The point is that in Zen the latter, right-hemispheric mode of problem-solving is *radically exploited* while the former, left-hemispheric, mode is totally subjugated. Usually, the two modes work complementarily, as D'AQUILI/LAUGHLIN (1979:161-2) suggest: that is, the mythical mind creates a mediation, and, at the same time, the mythic structure is "reinforced" by human religious ritual (ibid., 162). In the case of Zen, however, the right-hemispheric mode alone is approved. The total exhaustion of left-hemispheric thinking through a kōan, which takes, as SEKIGUCHI attests (2.2.3), as long as ten years, results in Zen's radical enhancement of the right cerebral hemisphere. Typical synonyms for "right-hemisphericity" in Zen writings are: "Buddha-nature", "suchness or is-ness" (SUZUKI 1958: 37), "completely homogeneous consciousness lacking discrimination and wisdom" (AKISHIGE 1977:51), "unself-conscious prostration" (KAPLEAU 1966:18). In this section I shall discuss this conscious (metagenetic!) exploitation of the right-hemispheric mode of thinking, which presents a strong affinity to what ARIETI (1976) terms "paleologic" and further to what PEIRCE referred to as "abduction", thereby bearing in mind the possible *genetic order* of types of problem-solving as well.

WALLACE/BENSON (1971: 131) point out that TM (Transcendental Meditation) can be viewed as the hypometabolic antithesis of the "defense-alarm reaction" ("fight or flight response") (cf. LEX 1979: 138). According to Niko TINBERGEN (1940), one of the founding fathers of modern ethology along with LORENZ, animals that are placed in situations in which they do not know whether to fight or flee exhibit a "third course"[58] in order to divert pent-up energy. TINBERGEN (1940, 1965) termed this type of animal behavior "Übersprung" ("displacement"). ARDREY (1966: 82ff.) elaborated TINBERGEN's notion of "care of body surface" ("preening"): "Were it not an instinct with a pattern of its own, then there would be no circuit into which frustrated energy could spark over". This "third course" of behavior is often manifested in body-care and ornamental arrangement[59] (the "bower of the satinbird" or the "bower of the orange-crested gardener" in FRISCH 1974: 235, Plate 97, and 236, Plate 99, cf. SEBEOK 1979: 30ff.). KOCH (1982: 457ff.) thus postulates that this diversion of pent-up energy, displacement, which often results in "new forms of attraction", is the major motor for the *genesis of art*[60], confirming the hypothesis offered by VYGOTSKY (1971: 246): "Apparently the possibility of releasing into art powerful passions which cannot find expression in normal every day life is the biological basis of art" (cf. SEBEOK 1979a). In KOCH's view (1981: 170) this triadic format, a "synthetic" (1982a: 454) structure with the initial opposition "fight vs. flight" displaced into "the third course", is omnipresent and is hence "the logic of nature" (1981: 169, 1982a: 454). The triadic logic is thus essential and phylogenetically primary, and the "mother of dyadic logic"; "consciousness is an extension of nature and not vice versa" (1982a, ibid.), or, in our terms, the left-hemispheric mode

is an "extension" of the former (1.3.1). It will be
noticed that this fundamental difference between the two
types of problem-solving seems to resemble the differentiation made by FREUD (1901: Ch. 7) between "primary process" and "secondary process" (cf. ARIETI 1976: 12ff.).
ARIETI, elaborating on the FREUDian distinction between
two types of information process, equates the "primary
process" with the way of thinking designated in various
terminologies as "primitive, immature, obsolete, archaic,
dedifferentiated, abnormal, defective, first-signalling,
concrete, mythic" (ibid., 66) (cf. the description of the
minor hemisphere in Figs. 12 and 13!), and with "paleologic"
(ibid., 67). He then opposes the "paleologic" type of
thinking to "the ordinary logic of the secondary process",
known as "Aristotelian logic" in Western civilization
(ibid., cf. IVANOV 1977: 55). In the Aristotelian law of
identity, ARIETI (ibid., 74) explains, "A is always A,
never B", or "A cannot both be and not be A at the same
time and place". But in paleological thinking, which
was first analysed by the psychiatrist Eilhard von DOMURUS
(1944) (ARIETI, 69) in his study of the logic of schizophrenic thinking, "A also becomes non-A - that is, B -
provided A and B have a predicate (or element) in common"
(ibid.) (cf. FROMM 1956: 85ff.).

As Erich FROMM (1956: 86), the German-born psychoanalyst,
in comparing two distinctive cultural modes, Eastern and
Western, points out, the "religious insight of the East"
(ibid., 85) manifests the paleological mode of thinking,
or "paradoxical logic" as FROMM terms it (ibid.). Zen exhibits it amply. One typical example of such paleological
thinking from the writings of Zen can be presented to illustrate the point under discussion (BLYTH 1949: ix) (cf.
"the One in the Many and the Many in the One" of SUZUKI
[1959: 28]):

(9) 差別即平等．平等即差別

Difference is identity; identity is difference

This paleological type of thinking takes place, ARIETI
(68ff.) assumes, not only in schizophrenics but also in
children, the mythical world of ancient peoples, the
cultural repertories of various aboriginal societies today,
and in the "large majority of creative processes" including "literature, art, and[...]science" (74). The notion of
paleological thinking thus clarifies the nature of kōan, explaining
that it drives Zen learners from the realm of Aristotelian,
"logical", left-hemispheric thinking to the more genetically primary mode of right-hemispheric paleological "thinking".
As is clear from the function of kōan, however, it should
be noted that Zen Buddhism with its superficial resemblance
to more "primitive" thinking, is the end product of *metagenesis*: the final state can only be attained after one
has exhausted the Aristotelian thought process (2.2.3).

ARIETI (ibid., 54ff.) further correlates the two modes
of thinking with two modes of perception; one is "amorphous
cognition", or *endoceptual* cognition, as he terms it, as
opposed to "a more mature form of cognition", i.e., *conceptual* cognition. *Endoceptual* cognition occurs "without being
expressed in images, words, thoughts, or actions of any
kind" and is referred to by other authors as "nonverbal,
unconscious, or preconscious" (ibid.). The *endocept* is,
ARIETI (ibid.) further explains, a "primitive organization of past experiences, perceptions, memory traces, and
images of things and movements", which are "repressed and
not brought back to consciousness, [but] continue to have
an indirect influence". The endocept does not "expand
into clearly felt emotion", and the content of an endocept
can only be communicated by being translated into expressions belonging to other levels, such as words, music,
drawings, etc. (54-5) (cf. the "image reservoir" of BARTHES
and the "chora" of KRISTEVA: 1.1.2). When a person refers to
his endocept, he could also term it a "global experience"

that cannot be "divided into parts or words" - something
similar to "what Freud called 'oceanic' feeling" (ARIETI,
55).

It should be recalled then that these two different
modes of perception and thinking correspond exactly to
what LORENZ (1959) referred to as unconscious, *ratiomorphous* perception on the one hand, and conscious, rational
perception on the other (1.1.2). Wilhelm KÖLLER (1980:
42ff.), the German semiotician, regards this correlation
as present in PEIRCEian semiotics as well: "Die PEIRCEsche
Deduktion und Induktion müßten [...] der linken Gehirnhälfte
zugeordnet werden, während die synthetisierenden Operatio-
nen der Abduktion, die sich weitgehend der expliziten Kon-
trolle entziehen, der ganzheitlich arbeitenden rechten Gehirnhälfte zuzuschreiben wären" (ibid., 46).

PEIRCE (1.65, 2.96, 2.266, 2.642, 7.97) categorizes
three types of *reasoning*: *deduction*, *induction*, and *abduction*. The three kinds[61] are related under "inference"
as follows (2.624):

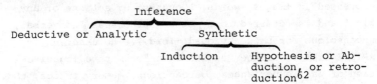

Deduction as PEIRCE defines (2.96) it, is an "argument representing facts in the Premiss, such that when we come
to represent them in a Diagram we find ourselves compelled
to represent the fact stated in the Conclusion", i.e.,
"the facts stated in the Premiss constitute an Index of
the fact which it is thus compelled to acknowledge". It
is the "only kind of argument which is compulsive" (ibid.)
(cf. FEIBLEMAN, 117ff.). Induction is "an Argument which
sets out from a hypothesis resulting from a previous Ab-

duction, and from virtual predictions, drawn by Deduction, of the results of possible experiments, and having performed the experiments, concludes that the hypothesis is true" (2.96). This conclusion is, however, held subject to "probable modifiction to suit future experiments" (ibid.). Deduction is thus analytic and explicative, while induction is experimental (cf. FEIBLEMAN, 116). Neither of them can, PEIRCE asserts (7.219), bring out any "matter of new truth": deduction "adds nothing to the premisses, but only out of the various facts represented in the premisses selects one and brings the attention down to it" (2.643), while induction is "mere processes for testing hypotheses already in hand" and thus "adds nothing to those hypotheses"(7.217) (cf. "induction by enumeration" by REICHENBACH 1951).

The "matter of new truth" can, PEIRCE emphasizes (7.219) "only come from abduction; and abduction is, after all, nothing but guessing" (cf. "induction by imagination" or "induction by guessing" by FRANK 1957). Abduction, "the originary Argument" (2.96) is the "first step of scientific reasoning, as induction is the concluding step", and therefore it is "merely preparatory" (7.218). Although abduction and induction share this characteristic, i.e., both lead to the "acceptance of a hypothesis" (ibid.), they are "the opposite poles of reason": abduction starts out with "facts, without, at the outset, having any particular theory in view, though it is motivated by the feeling that a theory is needed to explain the surprising facts", while induction starts out with a "hypothesis which seems to recommend itself, without at the outset having any particular facts in view" (ibid.), i.e., "abduction seeks a theory", while "induction seeks for facts" (ibid.).

By postulating the notion of abduction, PEIRCE established the status of "instinctive judgements" as the "initial propulsion" which has "insured" the "healthful life of modern science" (1.80) (cf. KÖLLER 1980: 43).

PEIRCE (ibid.) cites an example of such "inward power", which is not "sufficient to reach the truth by itself, but yet supplies an essential factor to the influences carrying [scientists'] minds to the truth": "Galileo appeals to *il lume naturale*[63] at the most critical stages of his reasoning. Kepler, Gilbert, and Harvey - not to speak of Copernicus - substantially rely upon an inward power ..." (ibid.)[64]. PEIRCE further clarifies why such *lume naturale*, or abductive reasoning, can lead to the discovery of ultimate truth:

> It is certain that the only hope of retroductive, i.e., abductive reasoning ever reaching the truth is that there may be some natural tendency toward an agreement between the ideas which suggest themselves to the human mind and those which are concerned in the laws of nature (1.80).

SEBEOK (1980) introduces PEIRCE's own detective episode in which PEIRCE let himself be guided solely by the "singular guessing instinct" (PEIRCE 1929:281, cf. SEBEOK 1980:22), whose characteristics are "its groundlessness, its ubiquity, and its trustworthiness" (PEIRCE Ms. 692, quoted in SEBEOK ibid., 23).

Abduction, or retroduction, or hypothesis is "pre-logical opinions" (2.122). "The essence of the opinion is that there is *something* that is SO, no matter if there be an overwhelming vote against it" (2.135). The verification of this hypothesis lies solely in "experience", which determines "belief and cognition" generally (2.138): "one may lie about [experience]; but one cannot escape the fact that some things *are* forced upon his cognition". There is the element of "brute force, existing whether you opine it exists or not" (ibid.). Now, recall LORENZ's (1973: 118) argument: "We obviously possess a mechanism that is capable of absorbing almost incredible numbers of individual 'observation records'"[65] (1.1.2). What LORENZ thus refers to as "ratiomorphous" vs. "rational" perception, or in ARIETI's terms "endocept" vs. "concept", is divided by PEIRCE (2.141-143) into "percepts" and "perceptual facts", respectively.

Fig. 24 presents the correspondences among the theories of LORENZ, ARIETI, and PEIRCE, all recognizing the right-hemispheric mode of thinking. The crystallization of "observation records" into an abductive "hypothesis" which takes place unconsciously, "ratiomorphously", "endoceptually", or on the level of "percepts" is illustrated in the first box; dots presenting each piece of information which is "stored" subconsciously, and thin arrows, the crystallization into "h" (abductive hypothesis = inspiration). Conversely, the identical process that takes place on the conscious level, i.e., induction, is illustrated with little circles, thick arrows, and "H" (inductive hypothesis):

	Right Hemisphericity		Left Hemisphericity	
	mode of perception	mode of logic	mode of perception	mode of logic
process	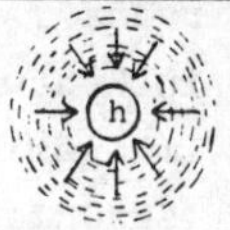 (dots → h)	 ○ ● □	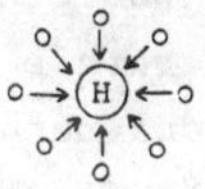 (circles → H)	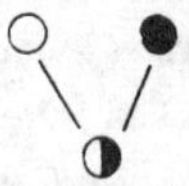 ○ ● ◐
LORENZ	ratiomorphous perception	'intuition' 'inspiration'	rational perception	scientific knowledge
ARIETI	endocept	paleologic	concept	Aristotelian logic
PEIRCE	percepts	abduction (retroduction, hypothesis)	perceptual facts	induction (deduction)

Fig. 24: Comparison among Lorenz, Arieti, and Peirce

Perceptual facts can, however, be "erroneous" (2.141), PEIRCE warns us (cf. LORENZ's notion of "epistemological monstrosity" [1973:195]). Whether or not the ancient Hindus, Zen's forerunners (SUZUKI 1958:3), were aware of man's proclivity for "epistemological monstrosity", which originates in "ideational areas" in the left hemispheric cerebral cortex, we cannot be certain. We are certain, however, of their having opted for *il lume naturale*, while subduing man's "cognitive imperative" - an extremely difficult task, indeed, since this metageneticity must return from "M" all the way back to "PH" (Fig. 2) in the case of Yoga and at least to "PX", or "biogenesis", in the case of Zen against the overpowering bias exerted by the dominant hemisphere.

SUZUKI (1958:4) affirms that, in our terms, right-hemisphericity emancipates the human being from analytical, causal left-hemisphericity, thus "transcending" the "curse of cognition" (2.2.4): "a life of emancipation [resulting from Zen] means that one is free from the bondage of karmic causation, or that one has crossed the stream of birth-and-death (*samsāra*) to the other side, to nirvana". What PEIRCE calls *il lume naturale* is designated in Zen writings as, along with the Buddha nature[66], "Prajñā Immovable", which is endowed with "infinite motilities" (SUZUKI 1959: 97): "it moves forward and backward, to the left and to the right, to every one of the ten quarters, and knows no hindrances in any direction" (ibid.). It is the axiom of Zen teaching to inhibit left-hemisphericity so that right-hemisphericity, or Prajñā Immovable, or *il lume naturale* can freely move about. When SUZUKI (1959:90-214) discusses "Swordsmanship" and HERRIGEL (1953), "the art of archery", it is precisely this principle of letting oneself be guided by *il lume naturale*, which is "possessed by all Buddhas and also by all sentient beings" (SUZUKI

1959:97), that they are referring to. Significantly
enough, PEIRCE employed the term "*retro*duction"[67], along
with abduction and hypothesis, which eloquently points
out the metageneticity of this principle, i.e., the return to the level of "biogenesis" as the mode of problem-solving[68].

The following diagram (Fig. 25) sums up the above
discussion. Ontogenetically and phylogenetically, the
problem-solving patten evolves through three phases: motor
action (I) (OH, PX, SZ), paleologic or abduction (II)
(SEM), and Aristotelian logic or induction and deduction
(III) (L, M). Zen exploits this genetic process *metagenetically*. Zazen is introduced as returning to "PH-PX" (the
physico-chemical-biological level of genesis), regulating
"breath and body". "Mind regulation" teaches the inhibition
of semiosis, i.e., metasemiosis, inducing *munen* or *mushin*,
or the state in which one lets oneself be guided through
il lume naturale (right-hemisphericity). A kōan is given
in order to exhaust Aristotelian logic, driving first and
possible "M" (epistemogenesis) to its extremity and subsequently forcing the meditator to become aware of the
existence of *il lume naturale*, or *Buddha-nature* through
concrete examples of paleologic and abduction (L, SEM),
i.e., kōan *precedes* satori, the final state of metagenesis.

2.3 Zen Texts: the Signifier of Zen Culture

The foregoing discussion has clarified the *metageneticity*
characterizing Zen Buddhism: "body-breath regulation" leads
the meditator to the level of the physico-chemical-biological genesis, while "mind regulation" subdues any occurrence of semiosis, i.e., it enhances the process of metasemiosis. This option of "mind regulation" has elicited a
quite unique type of "psychogenesis", which plays a decisive

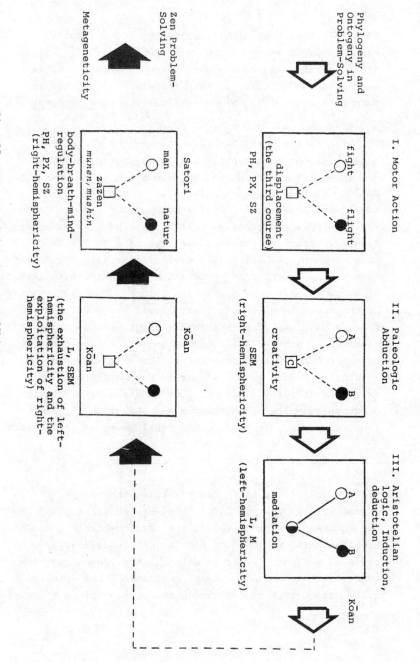

Fig. 25: Metageneticity in Zen Buddhism

role in the cultural manifestation of Zen. Zen's right-hemisphericity allows the semiotic manifestation to be "visual" instead of "verbal", "spatial" rather than "sequential"[69] (Fig. 12, 13), while "metasemiosis" is manifested as a simple "response" without any "semiotization", i.e., without any left-hemispheric *mediation*. If the "logic of nature" (KOCH 1981, 1983a) goes through the three phases "symmetry-asymmetry-integration" (1.4.1), the metagenetic Zen presents the process, "symmetry-asymmetry-symmetry". It is "homeostasis" (Fig.16a), but not "homeorhesis", which dominates the surface texts of Zen, and the signifier of Zen simply manifests the "asymmetrical phase" while implying the initial and final homeostatic phases. The following discussion concentrates first on this homeostatic nature of Zen manifestation, then proceeds to the creativity of the Zen-signified, and concludes with the spatio-visual nature of the Zen-signifier, i.e., "iconicity" as well as "indexicality".

2.3.1 The Manifestation of Asymmetry

The manifestation of Zen experience, i.e., semiotic realization, is characterized by the *dyadic structure* (1.4.1 and 2.2.4). As discussed in 2.2.5, Zen masters have obtained in the satori-experience the state in which object-subject dichotomy no longer exists, or in which the "third course" as the process of problem-solving is simply to *accept* antinomies as such. This state of awareness is termed in Zen writings *mushin* or *munen* (SUZUKI 1959: 111). SUZUKI elucidates this transcendental state of mind with examples from swordmanship, though the principle of *munen* seems to be applicable to any kind of Oriental sport[70]: "[*Munen* or *mushin*] is the original mind and not the delusive one that is chock-full of affects [...]. If the mind has something in it, it stops functioning, it cannot hear, it cannot see, even when a sound enters the ears or a light flashes before the eyes". There is no "stopping" or "abiding" in *mushin* (ibid., 95-6):

> Have no intention to counterattack him in response to his threatening move, cherish no calculating thought whatever. You simply perceive the opponent's move, you do not allow your mind to "stop" with it, you move on just as you are toward the opponent and make use of his attack by turning it on to himself. Then his sword meant to kill you will become your own and the weapon will fall on the opponent himself.

This cognitive-perceptive state of awareness has been the subject of psychological experiments. ONDA (1965), KASAMATSU/HIRAI (1966), and SCHÜTTLER (1974) among others have observed that Zen masters manifesting the characteristic EEG pattern of alpha waves during meditation do receive each external stimulus with the same intensity, but without any habituation: the stimuli may block the alpha waves for as long as 3 - 4 seconds, but thereafter the pattern of alpha waves will return. That is, there is no "habituation" to the "click" stimuli (cf. KANELLAKOS/ LUKAS 1974:10, ORNSTEIN 1972:30, 130-1).

"Habituation" is the psycho-physiological phenomena in which sensory systems primarily respond to changes in the external environment (ORNSTEIN 1972:130). When a person enters a room and hears a clock ticking, e.g., he hears it very clearly at first. This is the normal "orienting response" to a new stimulation. He fairly quickly tunes it out, however, "habituating" to the stimuli, although the slightest alteration of the stimuli (e.g., ticking louder or faster) would be responded to again (ibid., cf. the "Bowery El" effect in PRIBRAM 1969). On the psychological level, explains ORNSTEIN (ibid.), habituation can be described, in the example of the ticking of a clock, "as the construction of an internal model of the clock which then allows [the subject] to ignore it". If "consciousness were like a mirror", however, each time the clock ticked it would be "reflected" (ibid.), which is precisely what happens with Zen masters. The American psychologist thus considers the process of concentrative meditation as training for "deautomatization" (ibid., 132ff.), a condition in which one responds to each stimulus "anew" and "freshly". Referring to the same experiments, FISCHER (1978:39) characterizes the "mental state of Zen veterans" by stating that "it cannot be affected by either an external or an internal stimulus beyond the mere response to it".

This "psychogenesis" of Zen, or keeping one's awareness just like a "mirror", which reflects but does not linger (FISCHER 1978:39), has important consequences for the fine arts of Zen. In rendering this dynamic "motility" (SUZUKI 1959:97) or flexibility of the "Void", Zen semiotics selects precisely this S-R moment: the initial homeostasis (right-hemisphericity), which has already "transcended" asymmetry (☐) can develop into the asymmetrical phase (○●) *upon stimulation* (cf. Ch. 3). When the stimulation (afferent nervous input) is over, however, the initial homeostasis will be reinstated (☐). That is, instead of the left hemisphere being activated, *no semiosis* takes place, or semiosis is inhibited (*metasemiosis!*). Though it would be premature to undertake a detailed analysis of the first haiku mentioned in the introduction to the present study, "frog poem", (1), it can be pointed out that "a frog jumps in/ a sound of water" is simply *perceived*, just as the "click" stimuli in the experimental situation are precisely registered, without being followed by any "affection", "stopping", "abiding", or, in our terms, "semiotization" of the stimuli. On the surface text of (1), there are only *coincidentia oppositorum*: "the old pond" on the one hand and "a frog jumps in/ a sound of water" on the other. The pre-homeostasis and the post-homeostasis are implied through "the old pond". The "old pond" constitutes the "ground", while the "sound of water made by the frog", is the "figure" in terms of Gestalt psychology.

As in the psychological experiments mentioned above, the "stimulus" is precisely registered and reflected without any transformation in the surface structure of the text. After the stimulation is over, the initial homeostasis, which appears in the surface text as "ground", will be reinstated: there should be no semiotization, no mediation in the sense of Aristotelian logic. The signified of Zen fine arts, or their deep structure, is thus Zen experience in which no "abiding" or "semiotization" upon stimulation takes place. Semiotization is, as already mentioned (0.3.5), a "distortion" that the individual attributes to the E_c, the cognized world. When Zen masters who have trained themselves to transcend the "ego" that causes such "distortion" nonetheless attempt to communicate their experience, the result is a "direct reflex" of Stimulus-Response, i.e., they simply describe their capability to respond "im-mediately" (SUZUKI 1959:17). Fig. 26 presents this relationship of the signifier and the signified in Zen texts:

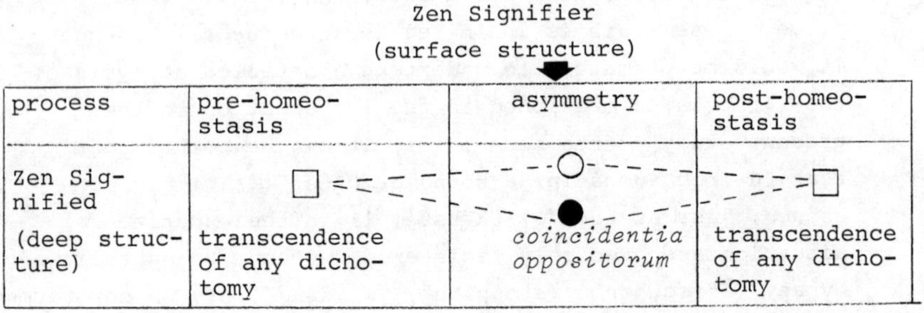

Zen Signifier
(surface structure)

process	pre-homeo-stasis	asymmetry	post-homeo-stasis
Zen Signified (deep structure)	transcendence of any dichotomy	*coincidentia oppositorum*	transcendence of any dichotomy

Fig. 26: The Relationship between the Zen Signified and the Zen signifier

2.3.2 Homeorhetic Texts and Homeostatic Zen Texts

ARIETI (1976: 68) elucidates the psycho-cognitive effect of problem-solving in the case of schizophrenia as follows:

The seriously ill schizophrenic, especially at the beginning of his illness, lives in a state of utter confusion. The world makes no sense; and this lack of understanding is often experienced as panic, anguish, turmoil, a desperate search for some meaning. At times some understanding does arrive, as a *sudden illumination*. Such an insight seems deceptive to us, but the patient feels extremely lucid and has at least a transitory feeling of exuberance, similar to that of a person who has made an important discovery. Now he "puts two and two together", now he is able to "solve the big jigsaw puzzle". (my italics)

As already discussed (1.4), such moments of problem-solving by a *sudden illumination*, to which Zen experiences also belong (2.2.2, 2.2.3), have a "survival value" in that the "disequilibration" resulting from "a disruption of the homeostatic state" is resolved, i.e., the initial equilibration is restored with the due "gratification" which resembles "sexual or gastronomic pleasure". It is thus the text-producer's task to present this moment of "illumination" or "aha-experience" (1.4). In what follows I shall explain the fundamental difference between *normal artistic texts*, which show some kind of "magic synthesis" (1.4.1), i.e., some sort of transformation on the level of surface structure and *Zen texts*, which simply present *coincidentia oppositorum* with very few such transformations.

First, let us consider Fig. 27, which presents the relationships between the signifier and the signified first when the signified is based on "the Logic of Nature", and then when the signified is based on "the Logic of Zen Semiotics"

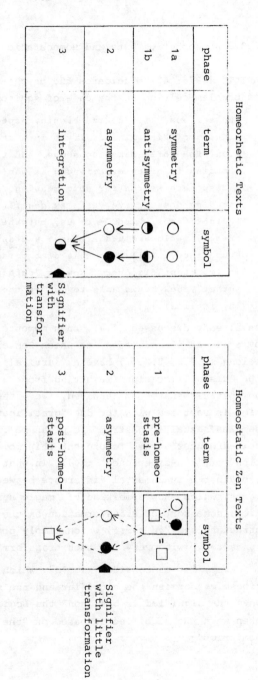

Fig. 27

Comparison between Homeorhetic Texts and Homeostatic Zen Texts

Homeorhetic Texts (T) exhibit the fundamental *triadic* structure, while homeostatic T demonstrate the *dyadic* structure (1.4.1). It is my contention that homeorhetic T fundamentally exhibit their "◐", *tertium quid*, while homeostatic Zen T exhibit the asymmetrical phase, suggesting that to "accept the antinomy" is *in itself mediation* (2.2.4): in Zen Texts, P_x unconsciously assume the moment of illumination to exist at the pre-homeostatic level.

Illustr. 2^{71} most typically and impressively shows the nature of homeorhetic texts: this is a drawing by a psychopath presenting "the technique of fusing numerous subjects" as ARIETI (1977: 214) analyses it, or in our terms, asymmetries being progressively integrated through *transformation*.

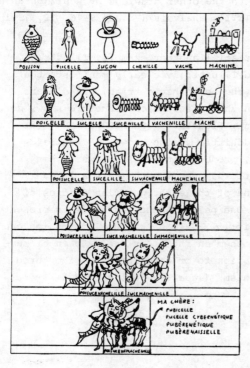

Illustr. 2:
A Homeorhetic Text
Presenting
Asymmetry and
Integration (from
BOBON/MACCAGNANI
1962)

There are originally six items: the fish, the girl, the
nipple, the caterpillar, the cow and the stram engine.
These items are given both verbally as well as pictorially.
The six items are then gradually integrated, two items at
a time. "Poisson" and "pucelle", e.g., are combined so
that "poicelle", a neologism (ARIETI ibid., 214) on the
linguistic level, and a mermaid figure, a "neomorphism"
(ibid.) on the pictorial level, are created: a transformation on the level of the surface structure has
occurred. Illustr. 2 is, however, unusual for homeorhetic T in so far as both Phase 2 and 3, asymmetry and
integration, appear on the surface T. Furthermore, it
presumably differs from artistic works *per se* in that
its surface structure presents a lack of convincing
power as visual art for such transformations (cf. ARIETI
ibid.), similarly to the other drawings by schizophrenics
exemplified in ARIETI's analysis (Figure 9-10, 12, 13 in
ARIETI ibid.).

Let us consider still another example, Illustr. 3,
which similarly to Illustr. 2, clearly manifests the
deep structure of the homeorhetic triad, but differs
from Illustr. 2 in that its surface structure shows more
artistic refinement. Illustr. 3 (YASHIRO/SWANN 1958:
Plate 20) is a Buddhistic statue known as "Ashura"
(Sanskrit: *Asura*), produced in 734 A.D., which has
survived with little damage, though it is a lacquer
work. Ashura is one of the eight guardian deities of
Buddhism (ibid.). One pair of Ashura's hands is presented
as *gasshō* (Sanskrit: *añjali*), a "gesture of joining one's
palms and putting them on the breast as a token of reverence for, salutation to or benediction of the three
treasures of Buddhism" (*Japanese-English Buddhist Dic-*

ASHURA – Detail

Künstler unbekannt. Nara-Periode, Entstehungsjahr 734
Trockenlack. Höhe 153,5 cm
Kōfuku-ji, Nara

Illustr. 3

Ashura (Kōfukuji, Nara)

tionary 1965: 70). The other two pairs are presented
as holding two crystal balls and swordhandles in each
hand (*Encyclopedia Japonica* 1967: 220-1). Though
Ashura came to be regarded as a devil, fond of fighting
by nature (*J.-E. Buddhist Dictionary*, 12), originally
asura was meant to be one of the divinities of good
nature (*E. Japonica*, 220). Ashura thus manifests the
juxtaposition of "good" and "bad". Ashura's attributes
are *realized* in the surface text by the three faces and
six arms, reminding us, due to the simultaneous presentation of paradigms (cf. KOCH 1983: 290ff.), of the
cubo-futurism of modern art[72], i.e., the syntagmatization of paradigms (ibid., 291). In Japan, early Buddhism
under the strong influence of India and China produced
innumerable similar works (cf. Plate 18, 33, 34, 52,
62, 64 in YASHIRO/SWANN), realizing thus the mediation
through surface-structural transformation.

While the homeorhetic T thus presents in a surface
T a "tertium quid", or "fusion", answering to the
initial conflicting position, the homeostatic Zen T
presents merely Phase 2, i.e., "asymmetry", with very
little transformation in the surface structure. Although examples are infinite, the following four will
suffice to clarify the point: two from Zen painting,
one from Zen gardening, and one from the Zen crafts
of pottery.

Illustr. 4 serves as a typical example of the
homeostatic T, in strong contrast to Illustr. 3
(SUZUKI 1959: Plate 12, cf. HISAMATSU, 29-30):

Illustr. 4
Śākyamuni Descending the Mountain
by Liang K'ai (early 13th century)

As opposed to Illustr. 3, in which Ashura is "transformed" into a multi-handed and -faced figure as a realization of the wishful thinking of the pious (mediation!), Illustr. 4 places Buddha - an extremely realistic figure without any of the grandioseness which normally accompanies Buddha figures - in a natural setting. There is no hierarchy linking Buddha and Nature: both are simply juxtaposed, suggesting *Zen mediation*, the acceptance of antinomy as such.

Similarly, Illustr. 5 (MUNSTERBERG 1965: 46-7) exemplifies typical Zen ink-painting: three human figures are totally embraced by the landscape, beautifully exhibiting Zen's notion of "All in One and One in All" (SUZUKI 1959: 35-7, cf. ex. [9] in 2.2.5): "no discrimination is to be exercised here, but one is just to accept it and abide with it, which is really no-abiding at all" (SUZUKI 1959: 35). Illustr. 6 and 7 represent the same principle as realized in the form of stepping-stones usually placed before the entrance of a temple (HENNIG, Figure 80), and in the form of pottery (HISAMATSU, 321).

Illustr. 5: *A Mountain Village* by Yü-chien (13th century)

Illustr. 6
The Stepping-stones of
the Shūon-an, Ikkyu-ji,
(17th century)

Illustr. 7
Red *Raku*-ware Teabowl,
called *Kaga-Kōetsu*

As SUZUKI (1959: 21) assures us (0.1), the creativity of Zen is manifested in "every phase of cultural life" in Japan. Before going into the type of signs characteristic of Zen T, the theme of the next section, I shall briefly discuss the source of creativity in Zen, since it decisively determines the signifier of Zen fine arts in general.

The signifier of Zen culture is produced by the signified of Zen experience, i.e., by *samādhi*, the "tranquil waking state" (FISCHER 1978: 47), coupled with the "cog-

nitive matrix" of selflessness, i.e., of "non-action",
"no art", "no technique", "relying on nothing", "no
rhythmicality", of the utter lack of anything resembling
what might be designated technique, to use the terms
in which seventeenth-century swordsman Odagiri Ichiun
characterized his Zen swordsmanship (SUZUKI 1959: 169).

As our physiological examination of Zen experience
has made clear (2.2.2), Zen masters seemingly have gained
control over the alpha-theta waves of the EEG pattern and
are able to emit them through meditative training. Psychologists have observed the correlation between such brain-wave patterns and cognitive states, especially in connection with "biofeedback" (DUSKIN 1973: 752-73, SCHWARTZ/
BEATTY 1977, ELMORE/TURSKY 1978, FEHMI 1978). A significant
number of such EEG biofeedback subjects started referring
to "alpha-theta brain-wave control" as "electric yoga",
"a short cut to nirvana", or "the magical mystery tour"
(DUSKIN, 767). The psychologist's explanation of alpha-
and theta-waves (DUSKIN 1973: 769) is as follows:

    Alpha: Deep relaxation, blank mind, time distortion
         (deep meditation)

    Theta: Out-of-body feelings, creativity in terms of
         vivid visual imagery

    Alpha-theta waves tend to occur during a state in which
    the individual is so unresponsive to "external" stimuli
    that "internal" events, perhaps from some "deeper" level
    of consciousness, may "pop" into the mind (such imagery
    is often referred to as "hypnagogic imagery"). In the
    relayed and open "Twilight" between sleep and wakeful-
    ness the individual is often not trying to think or do
    anything in particular ... The "let it happen" state of
    mind (as contrasted with the "make it happen" approach)

also has much in common with certain philosophical and
religious practices of Eastern wisdom. Studies of Zen
masters have shown that the best way to attain the
state of enlightenment may be to stop seeking it.
Therapeutic applications of biofeedback as "cultivated
low arousal" have thus been the concern of psychologists
in regard to "relaxation therapies" (BUDZYNSKI 1977: 436),
and Zen's suitability for such applications now seems to
be incontestable (SEKIGUCHI 1970: 20-2, AKISHIGE 1977:
56-62). AKISHIGE (1977: 52) apparently refers to this
"letting it happen" when he alludes to "a dragon which,
receiving water, rises to heaven" or to the "fierce
but imperturbed tiger against the background of mountains,
full of the power of life". The enhancement of "hypnagogic
imagery" in the hypoarousal state of $sam\bar{a}dhi$ seems thus to
be the source of Zen's creativity[73]. Significantly enough,
SUZUKI (1959: 31) refers to "a kind of automatic writing"
with regard to Zen painting: as a matter of fact, "a kind
of automatic writing" seems to dominate the signifier of
Zen T. Yet Zen T does not aspire to symmetry or balance
(again, metageneticity!): it is realized in "imbalance,
asymmetry, 'one-corner style' or 'thrifty brush'[74], *sabi*
or 'primitive uncouthness'[75], *wabi* or 'transcendental
aloofness', simplification, aloneness", as SUZUKI (1959:
21-8) characterizes the fine arts of Zen in general[76].

2.3.3 The Types of Signs in Zen Texts

In an earlier section (2.1.1), reference has been made to
the semiotic triangle: a sign is a triadic relation of the
signifier (*representamen*), its *object*, and its elicited
image in the mind of the observer, the signified (*interpretant*). PEIRCE further refines this triadic relation

(2.243), applying his notion of ontology, i.e., firstness,
secondness, and thirdness, or, "sensation, fact, and law"
(2.2.1). The three trichotomies of signs PEIRCE classifies are: 1) with regard to the signifier, *qualisign*,
sinsign, and *legisign*; 2) with regard to object, *icon*,
index, and *symbol*; and 3) with regard to the signified,
rheme, *dicent sign* (or *dicisign*), i.e., "a proposition or
quasi-proposition" (2.250), and *argument* (2.254-264).
PEIRCE recognizes the progressive complexity within the
three "Correlates", "the First Correlate", "the Second
Correlate", and "the Third Correlate" (2.235): "The First
Correlate is that one of the three which is regarded as
of the simplest nature" (ibid.), while "the Third Correlate is that one of the three which is regarded as of
the most complex nature" (2.236). Following FEIBLEMAN
(1946: 93), these three correlates can be diagrammed as
follows:

	signifier	object	signified
First	qualisign	icon	rheme
Second	sinsign	index	dicisign
Third	legisign	symbol	argument

Fig. 28
The Three Correlates in the Classification
of Signs

But one objection to this arrangement must be raised, as
NÖTH (1975: 18ff.) has rightly done: the order of "*icon,
index, symbol*" (2.299) should be corrected to "*index,
icon, and symbol*"[77] (NÖTH 1975: 20), thus resulting in the
"First Correlate"; "qualisign, *index*, and rheme" instead
of "qualisign, icon, and rheme". NÖTH's (ibid., 19)

reasons for this correction are that, first, ontogenetically index appears prior to icon (cf. PIAGET 1972: 163, 278, BRUNER 1979: 10ff.) and, second, phylogenetically index is the most frequent communication means[78]. Elaborating on BENSE's (1969: 23) delineation of the signs with regard to object, NÖTH, too, (ibid., 20) clarifies the progressive grade of arbitrariness among the three categories as shown below, by employing the concept of set theory:

Criterion	Diagram	The Type of Signs
Pars-pro-toto- Relation	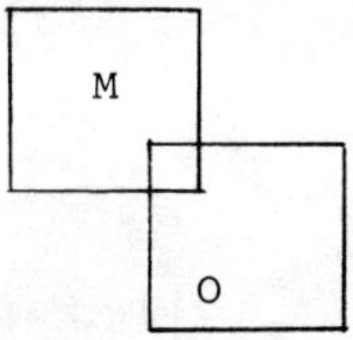 M, O (overlapping)	Index
Contiguity	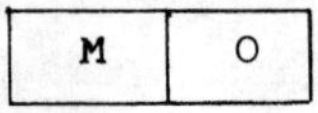 M | O	Index
Similarity	▨M▨ ▨O▨	Icon
Arbitrariness	▥M▥ O	Symbol

Fig. 29
The Progressive Grade of Arbitrariness among
Three Types of Signs with Respect to Object

With this correction at the outset, let us now consider the following diagram presenting the three trichotomies of signs (cf. BENSE/WALTHER [1973: 135]), showing again the "Correlates" for each component of signs (cf. Fig. 28):

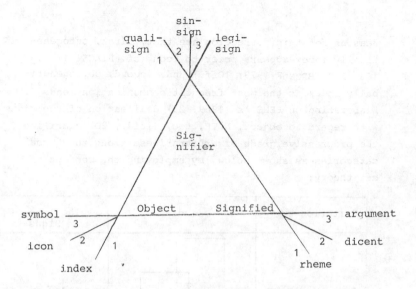

Fig. 30
The Scheme of Signs with Three Further
Trichotomies (after BENSE/WALTHER 1973)

Actually, PEIRCE's classification of signs is far more complicated[79] than Fig. 30. For the purpose of the present study, however, this scheme will serve us well enough. For the sake of the discussion, I shall first clarify the type of signs appearing in Zen T with regard to the signifier and the signified, leaving the signs with regard to the object to the last, a division which is most appropriate to this study, since as PEIRCE himself remarks, "The most fundamental division of sign is into *Icons*, *Indices*, and *symbols*" (2.275, also cf. 8. 368).

The earlier discussion of Zen's metasemiosis (2.2.1) has emphasized that Zen preaches the return to the state of firstness, i.e., the state in which "we attend to each part as it appears in itself, in its own suchness" while disregarding the connections (FEIBLEMAN, 147): "Red, sour, toothache, are each *sui generis* and indescribable" (ibid.). They are what PEIRCE calls "qualities" (1.419), occurring "perfectly individual[ly]" and "here and now" (ibid.). A Zen master, as a "plurality of texts", experiences the state of firstness. Although PEIRCE denies that such qualities depend on the subject (1.422), it seems undeniable that the Zen master is culturally conditioned and formed ("the cognitive matrix" in 2.2.4). He thus experiences his way of firstness in the state of satori. This experience then in its turn becomes the signified when he wishes to give these "qualities" a semiotic manifestation. It seems then very natural and logical of the Zen master to resort to the types of signs that are characterized as "firstness", i.e., "qualisign, index, and rheme", in bringing the deep structure into the surface structure. The employment of the signs that belong to the "First Correlate" is in fact the least degree of "conceptualization" of the firstness experienced by the meditator.

Qualisign is "a quality which is a sign" (2.244) or "the nature of an appearance" (8.334), as opposed to *sinsign*, "an individual object or event", and to *legisign*, "the nature of a general type" (ibid.). Consequently qualisign is, to put it another way, quite dependent on sinsign: it must be "embedded" (2.244) in a sinsign, which is a realization of its general "type". Later (8.347) PEIRCE designated qualisign as "Potisign", because it can be felt "positively possible" in spite of its mere possible existence (it must be perceived through sensory input!), sinsign as "Actisign", an object which is a sign as "experienced *hic et nunc*", and legisign as "Famisign", or a "familiar sign", which

occurs "many times with one and the same denotation".
PEIRCE's other designation for the trichotomy, "Mark,
Token, and Type", respectively, (8.362) is further elaborated by ECO (1976: 178-84). ECO applied this trichotomy in terms of sign production, while correcting
(ibíd., 178) the "naive notion of index and icon".
We will refer to his argumentation in connection
with the relation of the sign to object (2.3.4).

The assertion that Zen's metageneticity actually
attains firstness in terms of "quality" which is *sui
generis*, e.g., "a feeling of redness", to cite PEIRCE's
example (2.254), will become most clear when we consider such Zen texts as "Willows are green and flowers
red", "Bamboos are straight and pine trees are gnarled"
(SUZUKI 1959: 36), or "How big this rock and how small
that stone!" (SUZUKI 1958: 29): a plain fact, i.e., the
"greenness" of willows, the "redness" of flowers, the
"straightness" of bamboos, etc., which is normally not
stated because of its obviousness (the genetic primum ○)
becomes the center of the focalization of the Zen master
(metageneticity!) and is semiotically, here linguistically, expressed. SUZUKI (1959: 16, 36) emphasizes "a life
of *kono-mama* or *sono-mama*", or "isness", which he further
refers to as the Sanskrit *tathatā* ("suchness"). Significantly enough, the moments of satori seem to be triggered
by such sensory input as forms the firstness, or qualisign,
if it is perceived at the appropriate time, i.e., after
the "tuning" of the cerebral cortex has sufficiently matured (2.2.3). Illustr. 8 (SUZUKI 1958: 45) depicts one
such moment: "Tun-shan", the founder of the Sōtō school
of Zen Buddhism, comments SUZUKI, "attained enlightenment when, crossing a river one day, he chanced to see
his own reflection in the water". The qualisign of "his
own reflection" which is "embedded" in the sinsign of the

shape of the reflection on the shallow river was the
trigger of Tun-shan's satori.

Illustr. 8
"Tun-shan Crossing a River"; Zen's
Sinsign involving Qualisign

The relationships among this trichotomic division,
"qualisign, sinsign, and legisign" seem to be illustrated
most plausibly through the example of Zen calligraphy.
According to HISAMATSU (1971: 67), there are three general styles in calligraphy: 1) *kaisho*, the regular or
block style; 2) *gyōsho*, the semi-cursive or "running"
style; and 3) *sōsho*, the cursive or grass style.
HISAMATSU (ibid.) ascertains that Zen calligraphy may
generally be said to be of the grass style, for "the
overall feeling is never one of regularity". Now let us

consider Illustr. 9, one of the specimens collected by
HISAMATSU (ibid., 250):

Illustr. 9
The character "Buddha" by Jiun: Its Legisign "佛",
its Sinsign, "This Calligraphy" and its Qualisign,
"Non-Attachment" or "Freedom"

Illustr. 9 is a sinsign (token) of its legisign (type),
"佛", embedding Zen's qualisign of "mushin" or "munen"
(2.3.1), i.e., "no-abiding-ness" and "isness" in SUZUKI's
parlance or "Freedom from Attachment" in HISAMATSU's
(ibid., 68). The character "佛" as a legisign (deep structure) could have been written by Jiun in either of the
three styles HISAMATSU explained, each realization of
which would have been a sinsign (surface structure). Yet
Jiun realized the legisign or the type by choosing the
grass style as a necessary consequence of Zen's signified, i.e., its egolessness.

In terms of the trichotomy of the signified (Fig. 28, cf. BENSE 1967, 1971) Zen's sign consists, similarly to the "signifier relation", of the "First Correlate": it is "rheme" instead of dicisign or argument. Rheme or "term" (2.95) is "any sign that is not true nor false, like almost any single word except 'yes' and 'no'" (8.337). ZEMAN (1977: 35) assumes that PEIRCE uses the term "rheme" practically "synonymously with the way contemporary logicians use the term 'predicate'". For example, ZEMAN explains that the predicate "x is red", is a sign which "cannot be spoken of" as being true or false. Recall, e.g., Illustr. 5, the "Landscape": the sign (the painting by Yü-chien) is rhematic with regard to its interpretant (signified), for this ink-painting is a "Sign of Qualitative Possibility", i.e., "is understood as representing such and such a kind of possible Object" (PEIRCE 2.250). Yü-chien depicts the scenery as the signified of Zen, the transcendence of the dichotomy of 'nature' vs. "man" (2.2.4), i.e., "such and such a kind of possible Object". An example of dicisign, or "proposition", (2.95) can be seen in our Illustr. 1, which was discussed with regard to the simplified model of the Si-model. Illustr. 1 contains the proposition, "humans are small before the magnificience of the Zen garden of the Ryoan-ji Temple", i.e., the artist's (P_{xs}) statement (semiotization) about the "actual object", which is the garden with its five sightseers. PEIRCE (2.309) maintains that one characteristic of the dicisign is that is "conveys information", and "the readiest characteristic test" to decide whether a sign is a dicisign or not is that "a dicisign is either true or false, but does not directly furnish reasons for its being so" (2.310). Needless to say, dicisign "necessarily involves, as a part of it, a Rheme, to describe the fact which it is interpreted as

indicating" (2.251). As for the example of argument,
let us cite again one of Zen's famous texts, the above-
mentioned "Willows are green". This text represents
an instance of a "general class of Arguments,
which class on the whole will always tend to the truth"
(PEIRCE 2.253). Similar to the "Schlußfiguren, poetische
Formen (Sonett, Ode usw.) oder Axiomsysteme" (BENSE/
WALTHER 1973: 18), this text fragment "urges" (2.253) its
truthfulness, while representing its legisign or "type",
i.e., the general law that "willows are green" (2.263,
cf. FEIBLMAN, 110-6, also BENSE 1967).

2.3.4 Indexicality and Iconicity in Zen Texts

The "First Correlate" in terms of the two trichotomies
with regard to the signifier and the signified is valid
in the third trichotomy, i.e., with regard to "object".
As mentioned, the genetic order of this trichotomic
division should be "index, icon, and symbol"[80] due to
the progressive grade of arbitrariness. A sign and its
object have an indexical relation if they are in syntagmatic relation, i.e., in "contiguity" (2.306), an iconic
relation if they are in "association by resemblance" (ibid.),
and a symbolic relation if they are involved in "intellectual operations" (ibid.), i.e., the operations "of
the symbol-using mind, without which no such connection
would exist" (2.299)[81]. As might be expected, in Zen
signifiers what dominate are indexicality and iconicity,
though symbolic nature, as in the case of haiku or calligraphy is of course involved insofar as the language itself is, due to its triadic relation, a symbol.

Among the indices PEIRCE cites (2.285-290), the
following can be given by way of illustration: a man's
rolling gait is a probable indication that he is a

sailor; a sundial or a clock indicates the time of day; a low barometer reading indicates coming rain; a weathercock the direction of the wind; the pole star the direction north; the demonstrative pronouns "this" and "that" "call upon the hearer to use his powers of observation"; the relative pronouns "who" and "which" refer to their precedents; any "quantifier" such as "any, every, all, no none, whatever, etc." causes the hearer to "select" the object intended; the imperative or exclamatory "Look out!" calls attention to something.

Icon is based on the notion of a substitute for anything that should be "like" (2.276), and for this reason "images", "diagrams", and "metaphors" are icons: every picture, "however conventional its method" (2.279), every diagram, an algebraic formula, all primitive writing, "such as the Egyptian hieroglyphics", i.e., "ideographs", "mimicry" (2.280), "pictorial composition, architectural elevation" (2.281). In our haiku examples, we saw "the amount of the white space" in (2) as a possible substitution for the vast snow-covered landscape of "tundra", "/\" in (4) for Mt. Fuji, and in (5) " ⇡ " for the sardine. They are all obvious examples of iconic signs (O.O).

The term "symbol", which has acquired so many additional meanings in the course of time, is used in its "original meaning", PEIRCE assures us (2.297): "I do not think that the signification I attach to it, that of a conventional sign, or one depending upon habit (acquired or inborn), is so much a new meaning as a return to the original meaning". Any ordinary word such as "give", "bird", "marriage", is an example of a symbol (2.298): it does not, in itself, identify those things but "supposes that we are able to imagine those things, and have associated the word with them" (ibid.).

With this rather simplified survey of PEIRCE's
trichotomy of object relation in mind, let us now consider Illustr. 10 (HISAMATSU 1971: 119): an example of
Zen Ikebana, or *chabana* ("the floral art for the Way
of Tea") (ibid., 76). HISAMATSU maintains that the
three styles of calligraphy are also applicable to
the styles of ikebana: *rikka*, "standing flowers", is
a formal style, well-balanced and never unshapely
(ibid., 77), while *nageire*, "thrown in", characteristic
of Zen ikebana, manifests the "grass style" also observed
in Zen calligraphy (ibid., and cf. HAYASHIYA et al. 1974,
KOHEN 1935, NISHIKAWA 1964):

Illustr. 10
Chabana of clematis and Nanbu wall vase

Illustr. 10 is an index in that it "points out" its object, "a definite, singular, spatio-temporal-dependent
object" (BENSE/WALTHER 1973: 40), which is the experiencing

of the resolution of *coincidentia oppositorum*. In the
most reduced form the opposition is presented first in
"one white flower of clematis vs. five green leaves",
and, second, "the clematis vs. the vase". Although this
chabana is an iconic sign (PEIRCE 2.279) of its "substitution" for the parallel notion which is its object,
it is dominated by the function of deixis: in order for
the Zen master to indicate his Zen experience (the signified), which is "formless" (HISAMATSU, 52), he can only
"indicate" what is connected to his experience. In the
discussion of qualisign embedded in sinsign, it became
clear that for the Zen master any thing, when displaying
its "isness", becomes potentially the sinsign (token)
of the legisign (type) "selflessness". It follows that
in the eye of the Zen masters any object turns out to
be the incarnation of the Buddha-nature insofar as it
manifests "isness" or "suchness", or in SUZUKI's parlance (1959: 36), *śūnyatā* ("emptiness") or *tathatā*
("suchness"), which can be paraphrased as "the world of
the Absolute" and "the world of particulars", respectively.
Illustr. 10 can thus be characterized as "indexical" in relation to
its object, a "quali-sinsign" of "isness" in relation to
its signifier, and "rhematic" in relation to its signified in that it "predicates" the transcendence of antinomous thinking.

As mentioned, index is the ontogenetical as well as
phylogenetical primum. BRUNER (1979), in his minute
investigation of the transition from "communication to
language", clarifies that in children's language acquisition, deixis precedes the prelinguistic phase. BRUNER
(ibid., 30) recognizes three aspects in the beginning of
"reference": 1) "Hinweisen" ("indicating"), 2) "Deixis
or "das Benutzen von räumlichen, zeitlichen und interpersonalen Kontextmerkmalen in Situationen als Hilfsmittel

zur Herstellung gemeinsamer Referenzbezüge", and 3) "Benennen" ("naming"). A child is capable of following the *direction of sight* of adults when he is only four months old (ibid., 31), showing his focalization in his communication situation between him and his guardian, usually his mother. This "indicating" through glances occurs, it is clear, only in "situations" in which both the child and the mother (P_{xs} and P_{xe}, whose roles can be interchanged) are engaged together in such activities that the glances can be clearly understood (IVANOV 1977: 37). In the beginning, the child shows his volition, say to get hold of an object, by an "exaggerated signal" which is often accompanied by additional vocalization and gesture (ibid.). The child thus uses deixis, "exaggerated signals" in the very first phase, and the deixis then becomes more and more "decontextualized, conventionalized, and economical" (ibid.), i.e., abstractness increases. The child extends his hand toward the object with a pointing gesture (ibid., 35) at the age of eight months, or even earlier in the familial environment. After these learning processes begins holophrastic "naming" (ibid.), which eventually leads up to linguistic communication.

In the Zen masters' opinion, as mentioned, "language is a treacherous instrument we invented when we desired to communicate our experiences" (SUZUKI 1958: 4), and thus as soon as "we appeal to a medium the original experience is lost or at least loses its personal value" (ibid., 49). In communicating "the original experiences", accordingly, the Zen master simply "points out" what represents his experiences, i.e., his mode of sign production is deictic, similarly to a child's prelinguistic communication. Although any utterance, any sign production can be regarded as indexical insofar as it calls

the hearer's attention to something (PEIRCE 2.291),
what is characteristic in the T production of the Zen
master is that he employs the sign (token or sinsign)
which in its turn points out its type or legisign. Concerning this point ECO (1976: 179) speaks of "type/token-ratio"[82], which is quite useful in clarifying the
characteristics of the expression employed by the Zen
master.

In discussing "the replicability of sign vehicles"
(in our terms, the signifier), ECO (178ff.) first
differentiates the token, "doubles", "an absolutely duplicative replica" (180) from the token of "partial replicas"
(182), in which "the type is different from the token"
(ibid.). Every replica is a "token accorded to a type",
ECO further argues, whereby there are two distinctive
ratios that can be discerned (cf. MALTESE 1970): *ratio
facilis* and *ratio difficilis* (183). *Ratio facilis*
applies when an *expression-token* is accorded to an
expression-type, while *ratio difficilis* applies when
the expression-token is accorded to its content (ibid.).
Examples of the former are "road signs, strongly stylized pictorial entities", etc. (184), and of the latter
"footprints", "where the semantic analysis of the content has already been performed", or "paintings", where
"content is the result of the experience of 'inventing'
the expression" (219). In the case of Illustr. 10, the
representative of Zen T in general, the *chabana* is of a
ratio facilis in that "a pointing finger [...] can be indefinitely replicated" (185) with its syntactic markers
of "latitude, apicality, movement toward and dynamic
stress" as well as its semantic markers of "closeness,
direction, distance" (ibid.), i.e., the token and the
type are "pars-pro-toto" (Fig. 29). Furthermore, the

chabana (Illustr. 10) is of a *ratio difficilis* in that
it is "the result of the experience of 'inventing' the
expression", i.e., using the clematis and the vase in
order to express "the content of Zen experience" in
which *coincidentia oppositorum* is resolved. The token-
type relation manifested in the deixis of Zen T in
general is most clearly stated in the following passage
from SUZUKI (1959: 27): the "Zen way of looking [is to
look] at individual things as perfect in themselves and
at the same time as embodying the nature of totality
which belongs to the One". The clematis is thus
"indexical" or "deictic" in that it simply points out the object which has a pars-pro-toto-relation to "Nature". Furthermore,
this *chabana* is "iconic" insofar as the clematis and
the case "maps" the signified of Zen experience,
without mentioning that the material (the wild flower)
is a "partial replica" of the object.

Still another characteristic of Zen signs is "over-
coding" (ECO 1976: 129ff.), corresponding to the metageneticity of Zen, i.e., to the ontogenetically earlier
"holophrastic naming". In Zen T, the signifier is extremely economized, as our examples hitherto have made
clear (HISAMATSU, 28ff.). Yet, each signifier, while
"being sparse" (ibid., 30), is supported by *"genre rules"*,
which are what can be subsumed under such characteriza-
tions as "simplicity, austere sublimity, naturalness"
(ibid.). Thus, the audience, P_{xe}, must decode such "over-
coded rules". The failure of such decoding would result
either in missing the essence of Zen culture or in taking
the fine arts of Zen as "symbolic", not in the sense of
one of PEIRCE's trichotomic divisions but in the sense
that "Romantic poems are symbolic". In my opinion, the
economy in the signifier is not symbolic but perfectly

"concrete" in that each signifier is made perfectly
clear due to its indexicality. Let us consider, e.g.,
Illustr. 11, which presents one of the scenes from the
Nō play *Matsukaze*, in which the protagonist is scooping up
the sea water with a dipper (HISAMATSU, 361):

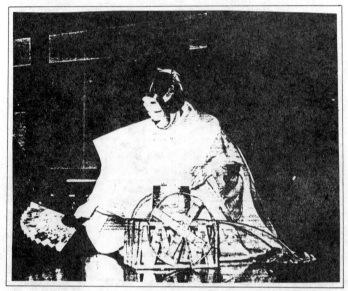

Illustr. 11: Scene from the Nō Play *Matsukaze*

A fan, the most indispensable stage property in the Nō
theatre, is used here as the dipper. Although the employment of a fan is itself symbolic (now in the PEIRCEian
sense) insofar as it is arbitrary, the context-situa-
tion makes its use perfectly clear ("concreteness")
due to the protagonist's "iconic" gestures and "indexical"
features including the plot, setting, costumes, etc. A
fan can be used in fact for anything (KEENE 1966: 219-26)[83],
yet its concreteness (*ratio facilis*) is perfectly maintained. The holophrastic tendency in Zen T is thus doubly
coded: symbolically as well as iconically.

2.4 Summary

Fig. 31 summarily presents the discussion of Chapter 2, showing the communication situation through deixis in Zen T:

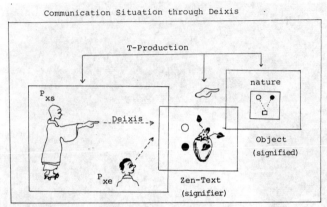

Fig. 31: T-Reception in the Fine Arts of Zen

In terms of T-production, the Zen master (P_{xs}) creates a T (the signifier) which is "indexical" with regard to its object, which coincides with the signified due to Zen's metasemiosis: the relation between the signifier and the signified is thus that of *pars-pro-toto*, for any sinsign embedding the qualisign of "isness", i.e., "nature", can become the Zen signifier. In terms of "type-token-ratio", it can be both of *ratio facilis* and *ratio difficilis*, resulting in its being both a "pointing finger" and the representation of "content nebula" (ECO 1976: 184). The signifier is also "iconic" insofar as it "maps" the signified, i.e., the *acceptance of coincidentia oppositorum* functions as the *mediation*, which is the solution of the initial "mythical" conflict, "man vs. nature" (2.2.4). Semiotic means for the signifier can be *chabana* as in the case of Illustr. 10, ink-painting as in Illustr. 4 and 5, Zen architecture as is represented by the arrangement of the stepping-stones, as in Illustr. 6, Zen artifacts as in Illustr. 7, and haiku as in Example (1). Regardless of the means of the surface structure, the Zen signifier presents thus the "isomorphism" of the asymmetrical phase (2.3.1), in contrast to such "homeorhetic" T as Illustr. 2 or 3, which are prototypical of the artistic "fusion" (2.3.2).

In terms of T-reception, the Zen T's dominant function is *deictic*, since, due to the nature of the signifier (indexicality and iconicity), P_{xe} is inevitably involved in the *situation*, i.e., P_{xs}, P_{xe}, and T are then all in spatio-temporal-communicative *contiguity* (2.3.4). In confronting the Zen T, P_{xe} thus follows the deixis of P_{xs}, similarly to the prelinguistic communication between the child and the mother: the glance being exchanged and the pointing finger simply suggest the existence of the object (again, the reconciliation of opposition!), in the *concrete context* created by the Zen *iconic* signs.

All the characteristics of the fine arts of Zen described above point out the right-hemisphericity of Zen. The Russian semiotician V. V. IVANOV (1977) in his study of *Die Asymmetrie des Gehirns und der Zeichensysteme* clarifies that the right hemisphere of the human brain operates in "Echtzeit" (37), i.e., it directs human body movement in the *concrete time* and *concrete space*, receiving and storing sensory inputs from the outer world. The left hemisphere, on the other hand, operates with *words*, and the resulting *logic*, independently of the concrete situation. This functional difference leads to the most astonishing fact evinced in the case studies of aphasia (41, cf. 1.3.2): for the right hemisphere, which is spatio-temporarily bound to *hic et nunc*, every statement *must be true*, whereas for the left hemisphere it is perfectly all right to *make a false statement* as far as the logical system permits it (cf. Fig. 12b). The peculiarity of *Zen's verbalism* (2.3.4), which in principle rejects *semiosis* or *representation*, becomes perfectly understandable in the light of IVANOV's elucidation.

Zen T are *homologous* in that they invariable present a common structural characteristic, i.e., the *immediate realization of the deep structure* depicting an *asymmetric perception (dyad)* in the surface structure. Accordingly, the fundamental *text-format* presented in Fig. 31a can be observed generally in any Zen T:

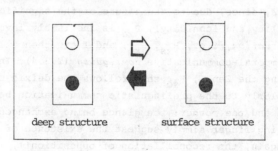

Fig. 31a: The Homologue of Zen Texts

CHAPTER 3

THE SEMIOTICS OF HAIKU

After the analyses of "the participants in texts" (P_{xs} and P_{xe}) as a "plurality of texts" in Chapter 1 and Zen texts as "signs" in Chapter 2, the following three chapters deal with the third analytical field presented in Fig. 5b: *focal selection* by P_x is now to be analysed. Chapter 3 deals with the *trimodal poeticalness* manifested in haiku poetry.

3.1 The Corpus of Haiku

3.1.1 The Corpus of Japanese Haiku (1530 - Present)

"Haiku Bungakukan", the Museum of Haiku Literature, located in Tōkyō, offers us the following statistics concerning the publication of haiku in contemporary Japan[1]:

- haiku-writers: approximately 1 million
- haiku-journals: approx. 700 titles
- haiku-books: approx. 1,000 yearly

While these numbers eloquently affirm the vitality of this short poetic form in contemporary Japanese society, they also leave haiku researchers in despair because of the incredible amount of new poetry, information, theories, etc., continually being published. It is, needless to say, of enormous interest to investigate contemporary haiku-phenomena in terms of their evolutionary processes; however, such investigation is beyond the scope of the present study, though some references to recent works will inevitably be made. The main focus

of this study, as has already been stated, is rather
on obtaining a clear conspectus of the synchronic diversification of haiku.

To narrow the scope of the research, the following
three haiku anthologies have been chosen:

A. *Matsuo Bashō-shū* (NKBZ 41: 1972)[2].
B. *Haiku Haibun-shū* (NKBZ 42: 1972)[3].
C. *Modern Japanese Haiku* (UEDA 1976)[4].

The first anthology collects the works of Bashō, starting
in 1662 when the master was 19, and ending in 1694, the year
of his death. It includes nearly 500 haiku. The second
anthology provides this study with some evolutionary
aspects of haiku history over three centuries (ca.
1550-1850) with over 1,000 poems by 138 poets. The last
volume collects the works of 20 major modern haiku poets,
all highly diverse. The spectrum ranges from classical
haiku to haiku in vers libre. The compiler, Makoto UEDA,
an authority on Japanese and comparative literature, has
selected 20 haiku by each poet. In addition, references
to other works such as BLYTH's four-volume *Haiku* (1949),
and the Japanese anthology *Gendai-Haikushū* (1958)[5], will
be made whenever necessary.

3.1.2 The Corpus of Haiku in English

Compared with the situation in Japan, the field of English-
language haiku publications is rather sparse: only six haiku
periodicals - as compared to 700 in Japan - are now being
published in the U.S., mostly as quarterlies[6]. Nonetheless, haiku in English seems to have taken root in American soil, not just, as YASUDA (1957) puts it, as "rest-
less experimenting" in the early decades of this century
by Imagists searching for better poetic values, but also

as a poetical form governed by the "aesthetic principles" which are "universal to all poetry" (YASUDA 1957: xx, and cf. NAKAGAWA 1976: 51-65).

For the corpus of haiku in English, the following six books and periodicals have been chosen:

D. Haiku or haiku-like poems by Ezra Pound, William Carlos Williams, Wallace Stevens, Richard Wright, Etheridge Knight, Kenneth Rexroth, and Gary Snyder in *The Norton Anthology of Modern Poetry* (ELLMANN/O'CLAIR 1973).
E. "Experiments in English" by Kenneth YASUDA in his own book *The Japanese Haiku* (1957)[7].
F. Thirty-one haiku by James William HACKETT in *A History of Haiku* (1964) by R. H. BLYTH[8].
G. *Borrowed Water: A Book of American Haiku* (1966)[9].
H. *The Haiku Anthology* (1974)[10].
I. *Haiku Journal* (1978, 79, 80)[11].

The reception of haiku by Western poets began with a group of poets called the Imagists, although their enthusiasm for this Oriental poetry did not last long. In addition to the poems of the Imagists compiled in *The Norton Anthology*, some references will be made to the book *The Japanese Tradition in British and American Literature* (1958) by Earl MINER, in which several interesting specimens by minor figures at that time are included. YASUDA, an American scholar of Japanese descent, pioneered the transfer of haiku into American literature. His profound knowledge of both English and Japanese poetry enabled him to explore the poetry of haiku both as a poet and as an analyst. Studying minutely the normative rules of haiku developed in Japan[12], he wrote classical haiku under the pseudonym of "Shōson". His 22 haiku in English exemplify an attempt to compose "authentic" English-language haiku. The third

book, which surveys the history of Japanese haiku,
covering five centuries of time, concludes with a section
on "World Haiku", in which HACKETT's haiku appear. If
YASUDA is an initiator of the transplantation of Japanese
haiku into American soil, HACKETT is a promotor, perfecting in the sense Bashō perfected *haikai poetry* (3.2)
three centuries before. The fourth book, *Borrowed Water*,
is an anthology whose title implies that "the concept
[is borrowed] from the Japanese"[13]. It includes more than
300 poems by a group of 13 poets who call themselves
"haiku composers of the Los Altos Writers Roundtable".
The fifth, *The Haiku Anthology*, is a compilation of
over 230 haiku by 38 poets including major figures such
as Nicholas VIRGILIO, Clement HOYT, HACKETT, and YASUDA,
to name but a few of them. This anthology is quite unique
in that it collects a wide spectrum of works, all of
which have been labelled "haiku in English", some of
them consisting of merely a few words. Two of them are
made of just one word, one of which has been quoted
in the introduction to the present study. The last
material is offered in the periodicals issued by the haiku
organization called "Yuki (有季) Teikei (定型) Haiku Society of U.S.A. and Canada", whose name clearly indicates
its guiding principles: "Yuki" means to "include seasons",
and "Teikei", "formal". They rigidly observe the standards
of classical haiku established by Bashō and his followers.
This organization of over 150 "haikuists" practices not only haiku composition but also the accompanying haiku-
culture - "Kukai" (句会), or haiku meetings, "Ginko" (吟行),
or haiku walks, and so on (TOKUTOMI 1979: 57ff.).

3.2 Haiku in the Poetic Continuum of Japan

The following discussion will briefly examine Japanese

poetic history in terms of its relevance to the genesis of haiku. It will demonstrate that this poetic form should be regarded as one of the forms within the poetic continuum nurtured in Japan, and hence as a manifestation of all the prosodic conventions found prior to its existence. Concerning this theme, there are two quite helpful analyses, one by BROWER and MINER (1961) entitled *Japanese Court Poetry*, which consists of the material considered to be the precursor of haiku, and the other by YASUDA in *The Japanese Haiku*. These two, among others, will be consulted in the following two sections.

The theory of the genesis of haiku varies greatly from one scholar to the next. Some[14] designate MASAOKA Shiki (1867-1902), a short-lived poet-critic of the Meiji Era (1868-1912), as a founding father of "haiku" as an independent literary genre. It is ture that Shiki[15] gave the term "haiku" to what had been called "hokku", meaning the first stanza of "haikai" and "renga"[16], both being long poems consisting of usually 36, 50, or 100 linked stanzas (MINER 1979). In this poetic practice, two or more poets would sit together and compose upper hemistichs (5-7-5 syllable pattern) and lower hemistichs (7-7) in turn (ibid.). Shiki declared that a haikai which was collectively composed by more than one poet was no art at all, for it involved intellectualism due to the consideration of an appropriate concatenation to a preceding line, whereas hokku, the opening upper hemistich, did not demand such considerations, enabling the poet to express his pure emotion, and thus could be regarded as artistic (MASAOKA 1893)[17]. The conception of haiku was thus clarified by Shiki in the last decade of the 19th century (MATSUI 1972: 17ff.); however, it is undeniable that he was a reformer and not a creator of haiku (BLYTH 1964: 21ff.). We have to go further back to locate the origin of haiku.

Other scholars (MASAOKA 1893: 156, ULENBROOK 1979:
171) agree in locating the starting point at the time
when Bashō propounded his Zen-informed style in his
later years, that is, after 1680. Still others (NGS
1958, BLYTH 1964, KOMIYA/YOKOZAWA/OGATA 1959, MINER
1979), seemingly the majority, recognize *haikai no
renga* (humorous poem in linked stanzas), as the immediate
precursor, which flourished from the 13th century to the
late 18th century. *Haikai no renga, haikai*, for short,
is, however, also a direct descendant of *renga*. *Renga*
in its turn is directly derived from *waka* (or *tanka*: the
2 terms refer to the same 31-syllable unit, but *waka* connotes the specifically Japanese character of the form,
whereas *tanka* merely means "short poem"), which flourished
during the Heian Period (794-1185). ICHIKAWA Sanki, a
prominent Japanese scholar of classical literature,
for instance, thus finds the origin of haiku in this
waka form (NGS 1958: ix).

While ICHIKAWA represents the scholars who observe
the haiku-genesis in the 31-syllable-form of waka, still
others, of whom Kenneth YASUDA is a representative, place
it in the prehistoric stage. YASUDA (ibid., 108ff.)
claims that haiku's origin must be sought in "the
primitive poems or songs" (歌謡 = *kayō*), which were recorded in Japan's first anthology *Man' yōshū* (ca. A. D.
759). In his very stimulating book *The Japanese Haiku*,
YASUDA states the following (108):

> Poetic experience seems to have sought this (haiku)
> form of expression from the earliest period, and an
> examination of the hustory of Japanese poetry will
> show that the haiku-like expression which gradually
> developed into a crystallized form is noticeable to
> an astonishing degree in all periods.

YASUDA thus traces "haiku-like tendencies" with regard
to the form and the content of haiku throughout history.
He reveals among the primitive songs and poems such
qualities as "ellipsis, condensation, spontaneity, and
nakedness of treatment" (111). In addition to such contextual elements, he also traces the "deep-rooted-ness"
of seventeen syllables, declaring that the "$katauta$[18]-
like rhythmic pattern (5-7-7, or 5-7-5) [...] seems to
show that the basic element of haiku lies deep within
the poetic instincts of Japan and foretell the future
poetic form we know today as haiku" (ibid.). This exposition of YASUDA, which relates the 17-syllable-poem
to the "poetic instinct", or to what T.S. ELIOT terms
"auditory imagination" (ELIOT 1933), is suggestive,
in that it eloquently supports Walter A. KOCH's (1978:
301) assumption about "aesthetic poeticalness", one of
the three modes of poeticalness constituting poetry in
general. According to KOCH, it is related to "Vorspiel,
Ritus, Droge, Einstimmung für 'peak experiences'" (ibid.).
$Kayō$ - primitive songs and poems, as they are customarily called in translation - are in their original meaning
"dance-songs", of which approximately 400 are extant
(NKBZ 1 1971: 372). KŌNOSU Hayao, a scholar of $kayō$,
maintains that they were meant for "vegetation rituals
and fertility rites of primitive culture" as well as
"mariners' working chants" (KŌNOSU in NKBZ 1 1971: 371),
quite understandable for a country which is surrounded
by the sea. YASUDA's otherwise convincing discussion
seems, however, to have lost its validity in regard
to form, for recent scholars no longer consider $kayō$ to
represent the original poems. BROWER and MINER (1961: 58)
for instance, state that they are "either of later composition or revisions" made by the compilers of $Man'yōshū$.

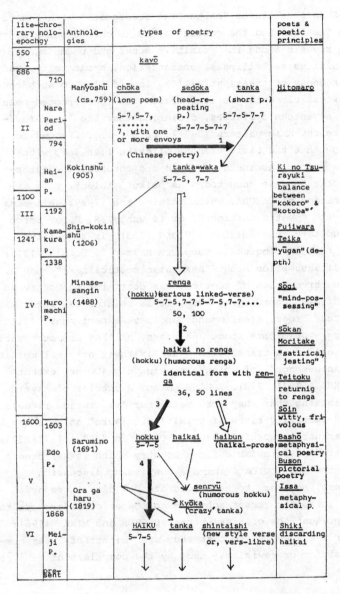

Fig. 32: The Continuum of the Japanese Poetic Tradition

Instead of a fixed form, these scholars recognize "two possible groups of lines": (i) an even number of lines of nearly equal length; and (ii) alternations of an odd number of longer (as many as 10 syllables) and shorter lines (as many as 3) (ibid.). Thus in locating the genesis of haiku, more modestly than YASUDA, in *waka*, we can observe the continuity of prosodical tradition in the form, that is, the alternation of 5- and 7-syllabled parts, of haiku.
Fig. 32 summarizes the discussion thus far with additional information about the major poets of each epoch and their poetic principles[19].

Explanation of Fig. 32

▬▶ = The process of condensation, or "shortening", as RIMER/MORRELL (1975: 16) put it. During the Nara Period *tanka* became more and more dominant, surviving as the sole poetic form out of the three initial forms. It represents, therefore, the horizontal direction (▬▶1). The second condensation is due to the reduction of the numbers of lines: the normal practice for *renga* was 100 lines, for *haikai*, 36 or 50 (▬▶2). In the course of the development of haikai, hokku acquired more and more independence. Bashō, for example, often composed hokku not as the first line of haikai but as a poem in its own right (YASUDA 1957: 107ff.), thus promoting the condensation from *haikai* to *haiku* (▬▶3). The way to the establishment of *haiku* was then completed by Shiki's so-called haiku-reformation (UEDA: 1976) (▬▶4). This condensing process appears once again during the Twenties and Thirties of

this century, when so-called "tanritsu" (short
haiku), a variation of haiku vers-libre, came
into vogue. This subject will, however, be discussed in Chapter 3.

⇒ = the process of expansion. The short form of 31-
syllabled *tanka* became more and more expanded as
renga began to assume the leading position (MINER
1979), reaching up to 1000 lines in its culmination
(⇒1). The second expansion of this kind took
place when haikai poetry was integrated into
prose writing, in the form of *haibun*, which was explored by
Bashō (NGS: 1958) (⇒2). Although for the sake
of simplification, we present only two periods
on our chart in which this phenomenon of expansion occurred, it in fact accompanied each
shortening process, as RIMER/MORRELL thus
elucidate (1975: 16-7):

> [...] we should also note that the shortening
> was accompanied by procedures for organizing
> these basic units into larger complexes ...
> In short, we seem to have another instance of
> the principle that for every action there is
> an equal and opposite reaction, although Newton
> certainly did not have Japanese poetry in mind
> when he came upon the notion. The shortening
> of the basic unit of poetry was compensated
> for by the integration of short units into
> longer forms.

3.3 The Traditional Analysis of Haiku vs. Semiotic Analysis

The Haiku Society of America, whose Honorary President is the above-mentioned Harold G. HENDERSON, was dissatisfied with the definition of haiku that appears in "those unabridged English dictionaries" and accordingly sent a letter to dictionary-publishers, offering "authoritative definitions" for the words related to haiku - namely, "haiku", "haikai", "hokku", and "senryū", the last of which is identical in form with haiku; i.e., it consists of 17 syllables in a 5-7-5 pattern. In this letter they assure the publishers that "to the Japanese and American haiku poets, it is the content and not the form alone that makes a haiku" (cit. in V.D. HEUVEL 1974: 248). Among the definitions, those for haiku and senryū are worth quoting here, not least because they exemplify a typical traditional approach (ibid., 249-50):

HAIKU:

(1) An unrhymed Japanese poem recording the essence of a moment keenly perceived, in which Nature is linked to human nature. It usually consists of seventeen *jion* (Japanese symbol-sounds).

(2) A foreign adaptation of (1). It is usually written in three lines of five, seven, and five syllables.

SENRYŪ:

(1) A Japanese poem structurally similar to the Japanese haiku, but primarily concerned with human nature. It is usually humorous or satiric.

(2) A foreign adaptation of (1).
(3) Loosely, a poem similar to haiku which does not meet the criteria for haiku.

According to the Haiku Society of America, then, the major difference between the content of haiku and that of senryū lies in the poetic subject of each: in the former, "Nature" is connected with human nature, whereas in the latter, "human nature" is observed humorously and satirically. Although the distinction between the two is a point that should be discussed in connection with haiku's affinity to other literary genres in a later chapter (7.2.), the emphatic statement of the Society that haiku should be defined by both its content and form is clear enough. As a matter of fact, the Society values the first part of its definition, the content of haiku, more than its form, thus encompassing those haiku (haiku vers-libre, e.g.) that would be excluded a priori by a normal definition such as that appearing in *Webster's New Collegiate Dictionary* (1973: 515): "An unrhymed Japanese verse form of three lines containing 5, 7, and 5 syllables respectively." These definitions thus attempt to be more descriptive; however, the explanation of the differences between the two types of closely related genres appears to be a bit careless, for there are enough examples of poems which should belong to one genre thematically but nonetheless are usually categorized into the other or vice versa (BLYTH 1949a). A differentiation on thematic grounds, as offered by the Haiku Society, is the traditional way to characterize the two: but this is only one way to describe them and it is indefinite. "The content of haiku" thus requires a different type of elucidation than a mere statement that haiku deals with Nature.

3.3.1 Japanese Poet-Analysts

Attempts to expound upon the "content of haiku" began with the incipient stages of this genre. This fact is quite understandable, since *haikai (no renga)* was differentiated from its precursor, *renga*, only through content, i.e., through the "humorous" attitude in dealing with the materials. KURIYAMA Riichi (1972 : 13), a leading haiku scholar, names Fujiware Kiyosuke (1104-1177) as an initiator of "hairon" (haikai poetics), which was to accompany the evolution of haiku. Kiyosuke equated the concept of "haikai" with that of "kokkei" (humour), adding that to compose haikai means "to analogize while being frolicsome" (ibid.: 14)[20] and that haikai is characterized by three phenomena (" 態様 "): (i) eloquence (" 弁説 "); (ii) clever parlance (" 利口 "); and (iii) oddity (" 狂 ")[21]. According to KURIYAMA (ibid.), these three phenomena can be glossed as follows: (i) eloquence: words coming out smoothly and fluently; (ii) clever parlance: discourse being witty and adroit; (iii) oddity: nonconformity as exemplarily presented in the phrase "fabricating even fire into water"[22]. Kiyosuke's trichotomy seems to have been indeed significant, for it found a corresponding idea in Bashō's haikai poetics, which followed 550 years later. This trichotomy also reappears, some 850 years later, but this time in Germany, not in Japan, in the general semiotic analyses of poetry discussed in 3.4 through 3.4.2.3.

KURIYAMA (ibid., 14) recognizes Kiyosuke's exposition as a prototype for haikai poetics, and it was, indeed, to be repeated in the succeeding centuries. Kiyosuke, however, was working within the frame of traditional Japanese poetics, in which the governing concept is the dichotomy of "kokoro" (mind, feeling, mood, heart)[23],

and "kotoba" (words, diction, vocabulary)[24].
These concepts can be traced further back to *Kokinshū*
(Fig. 32), Japan's first anthology of waka. Thus, the
conception of "kokoro no haikai" (haikai of mind) and
"kotoba no haikai" (haikai of words) was mentioned in
Azumamondō (1467), a renga anthology, compiled by
Iio Sōgi (1421-1502), which another haiku expert,
OGATA Tsutomu (1964: 202-17) designates as a direct
precursor of hairon. Interestingly enough, these two
frameworks can explain the genetic order of haikai: in
terms of Kiyosuke's trichotomy, haikai originated in
(i) eloquence (the Teimon School, in which *haigon*, or
haikai diction, was a dominant concern [1620-70]). This
was followed by (ii) clever parlance (the Danrin School,
in which *Gūgen-setsu*, the theory of allegory, metaphor,
analogy, by Okanishi Ichū [1639-1721] played a crucial
role [1670-80]), and finally by (iii) nonconformity
(the Bashō school, in which the then perfected philosophy of life, Zen Buddhism, was expressed [1868 on-
ward] (Fig. 32). This dichotomy of "mind" and "diction"
corresponds exactly to what KOCH (1978) refers to as
"mapping" on the one hand, and "matrix" on the other.
The genesis of haikai (and haiku) thus began with the
dominant orientation toward matrix - or surface texts -
conducted by the Teimon School, of whom Teitoku was a
leader. Through the transitional phase of the Danrin
School with its extravagant stylistic poeticalness,
haikai moved from the "haikai of diction" to the "haikai
of mind", i.e., to the dominant orientation toward mapping the world. Uejima Onitsura (1661-1738), realizing
the superiority of "haikai of mind" prior to Bashō,
asserted that "in composing verses, if someone crafts
only his style and words, there is very little *makoto*[25]
(truth, essence, sincerity) in his poetry: the most

desirable thing is just to deepen his feeling and be
careless about his style and words" and he concluded
that "haikai lies in nothing other than makoto" (quoted
in T. OGATA 1958: 205)[26]. As is clear in Onitsura's
assertion, kokoro is ranked above kotoba. The full implications of this assertion were developed in Bashō's
poetics.

Bashō's poetics was never written down as such; it
is rather a reconstruction of his occasional sayings
and teachings by his disciples, of whom MUKAI Kyorai
(1651-1704) and HATTORI Dohō (1656-1730) are reputedly
the most reliable (T. OGATA 1958: 207). Among the aesthetic
principles Bashō preached[27], those most relevant to our
study are his three "elements of haikai" (HATTORI 1776:
524). In referring to *haii* ("俳意") (the poeticalness
of haikai), Bashō cited (i) kotoba (diction), (ii) kokoro
(mind), and (iii) sakui (prosodic intention). It is noteworthy that in Bashō's exposition of haikai-poeticalness,
the two streams - Kiyosuke's trichotomy on the one hand
and the traditional dichotomy between mind and diction
on the other - are well-blended.

The establishment of haikai poetry by Bashō remained
by and large unquestioned, until Shiki challenged it
two centuries later (4.3.4). Shiki revolted against
the haikai-professionals who worshipped Bashō but were
not creative (UEDA 1976: 6). In such essays as "Bashō-
Zatsudan" (1893) (Colloquy on Bashō), "Haikai Taiyō"
(1895) (A Survey of Haikai), or "Haiku-Shinpa no Keikō"
(1899)[28] (New Trends in the New School of Haiku), Shiki clarified haiku poetry in terms of its diachronic as well as its
synchronic diversification. He employed the then newly

imported concept of "evolution"[29], expounding the view
that haiku evolved from the "simplicity" of Bashō through
the "complexity" of Yosa Buson, one of the so-called
"four pillars of classical haiku" (HENDERSON 1965), to
the "further complexity" as well as "pictorial construction" or "objective beauty" of his own group of poets,
"Nihonha" (the Nihon School) (Shiki 1899). In his elaboration of the categorization of haiku[30], Shiki inherited
the traditional dichotomy, which he termed *ishō* (the poet's
intention = kokoro) and *gengo* (language = kotoba) (MASAOKA
1894: 215), ranking the former above the latter. According
to Shiki, *ishō* denotes not only the poet's emotion but
also the poetic materials or phenomena that evoked the
emotion, or even the idea before it takes the form of
poetry (ibid.). Having thus defined *ishō*, Shiki declared
that it can be universally found (ibid.):

> Ishō is one and the same thing that is found throughout past and present, East and West, and every kind
> of art. Therefore, a good ishō for waka is a good
> one for haiku, for Chinese poems, for occidental
> poetry. Nay, it is not only good for literature,
> it is a good ishō for paintings - and for all other
> artistic genres.

In addition to Shiki's exposition of the universality
of ishō - he talks like a semiotician! -, we also find
another significant argument in this haiku reformer of
the Meiji Era. Shiki argued that literature possesses
"temporal nature", whereas painting is characterized by
"spatial nature". Because haiku is so brief, it is
forced to choose one of the two qualities, namely, the
spatial (1896a: 511). For this reason, Shiki affirms,
"haiku, though belonging to temporal literature, approximates very much to spatial painting"[31] (ibid., cf. KOCH
1982c). Shiki's proposition is indeed insightful in that

what he is referring to is what was later clarified in
terms of paradigm and syntagma by semioticians (KOCH
1982c). Unfortunately, however, his analytical methods
were rather undeveloped. Due to his immature methodology,
his haiku-typology, in which he subdivides haiku into
24 categories (1896), is said to have "no integratory
principles" (MATSUI 1972: 233).

This discovery of the spatial quality of haiku propounded by Shiki seems to be reflected by YAMAMOTO
Kenkichi (1946) in his essay "Aisatsu to Kokkei"
("Greeting and Humour"), which discusses haiku in terms
of its internal structure. YAMAMOTO, while giving Bashō's
frog poem as a prototype of haiku, affirms that "haiku is
a poem which lacks the duration of syllable counts: in
the course of the change from the 31-syllabled (that is,
tanka-wanka) to the 17-syllabled, a violent jump, namely,
the effacement of "temporal-ness" (" 時間性 "), was carried
out (quoted in MATSUI 1965: 555-7). This atemporalness
of haiku has three characteristic components, concludes
YAMAMOTO: (i) humour, (ii) greeting, and (iii) ad hoc-
ness (inid.). Accordingly, haiku is, YAMAMOTO assures us,
"the art of cognition" (ibid.).

Whereas Shiki and YAMAMOTO are thus concerned with
the non-temporalness of haiku poetry, Ōsuga Otsuji[32],
a poet-theorist, re-examined one of the three rules of
haiku, namely, the inclusion of *kireji* (the cutting
word), proclaiming "2-clauses, 1-statement" as the most
fundamental structure of haiku (cf. ASANO 1962: 9)[33].
The most typical haiku presents, according to Otsuji,
two clauses being sundered through kireji. Where kireji
appears, i.e., where a caesura is placed, the value of haiku
exists, asserts Otsuji. Moreover, of the two clauses, one
"must be seasonal", whereas the other may be "something
else", and the relationship of the two is nothing but

metaphorical ("暗示法"): Otsuji assures his contemporaries that "the method for the haiku of the new tendency is a kind of Suggestion" (MATSUI 1965: 179)[34]. As we will see in the next chapter, Otsuji's assertion is quite "suggestive" in that it points out the fact that two clauses of one haiku have a paradigmatic relationship to each other, i.e., "the poetic function of haiku projects the principle of equivalence from the axis of selection onto the axis of combination", to refer to JAKOBSON's (1960: 94) famous definition of the "poetic function" of language. It seems accordingly a bit surprising to hear that Yamaguchi Seishi, a leading 20th century poet-theorist was quite impressed by the then new theory of "montage", introduced to Japan around 1925, and employed it as a methodological basis for his haiku (MATSUI 1965: 397ff.). As a haiku expert, he could have found the same idea, though not in such fancy terminology as "montāju"[35], in the sayings of Bashō: "you should know that haiku is made out of 'toriawase'", i.e., out of combination, assortment (HATTORI, 592).

To conclude this section a mention of IMOTO Nōichi is in order. IMOTO, not a poet-theorist like all those mentioned above but rather a literary critic, states that haiku can be characterized by its particular way of "grasping objects", which he terms "ironisch" ("イロ一二ッス") (quoted in OGATA, 387, cf. MATSUI, 556). In haiku IMOTO finds a specific Weltanschuung[36], i.e., the philosophy of an unconventional life: "to understand to be poor is to be rich", e.g., (MATSUI: 572). We may notice, then, that IMOTO's notion is directly related both to what BROWER/MINER (1957: 515ff.) refer to as the attempt to "achieve harmony between personalism and super-personalism", i.e., between man and nature, and to KOCH's (cf. Fig. 39) concept of *informational peoticalness*, "the urge to harmonize such opposition" (2.2.4). Further, one part of Kiyosuke's trichotomy, i.e., "unconventionality", seems to correspond exactly to IMOTO's idea.

3.3.2 American Haiku Analysts

If Ezra POUND failed "to see the spiritual depth haiku embodies", as VAN DEN HEUVEL claims (1974: xxvii), this multitalented poet at least perceived an important structural technique of haiku which he called "a form of super-position" (POUND: 1914). Earl MINER (1958) considers that POUND's discovery of this technique "in a poetic form written in a language he did not know" should be ranked as "one of the insights of Pound's genius" (115). Although his direct association with haiku - or rather hokku, since at the time of his introduction to the form, Shiki's new terminology, haiku, had not yet become current (SATŌ 1978: 31ff.) - diminished, as his interest moved from "image" to "Chinese ideogram" (cf. FENOLLOSA 1964), and then to "Japanese Noh" (POUND/ FENOLLOSA: 1916)[37], his super-positiory technique can be traced in his later poems, as has been often pointed out (MINER 1958: 156-213). Much has been also said about his Imagist poem "In a Station of the Metro", which he called a "hokku-like sentence" (POUND 1914: 89). Suffice it here to point out that POUND provides us with two major points of interest: first, he had learned from haiku "how to write concise, suggestive, imagistic poems", as MINER (1958: 140) puts it, and second, he also advocated "three ways to charge language with meaning" (cf. UEDA: 1965: 104), reminding us exactly of the trichotomy Kiyosuke and Bashō mentioned: (i) melopoeia, (ii) phanopoeia, and (iii) logopoeia (POUND 1928: 20ff.). UEDA elucidates that

(i) denotes that "the words are charged ... with some musical property"; (ii) means "a casting of images upon the visual imagination"; and (iii) is "the dance of the intellect among words" (1965: 104).

Through its discovery by the Imagists, then, haiku was absorbed into twentieth-century poetry, as MINER convincingly argues (ibid., 156-213). At the same time, however, haiku was being introduced to the Occidental world by another channel. While the Imagist group had no knowledge of the Japanese language, the scholars now translating haiku read them in the original and saw the spiritual depth haiku embodies. The first of these scholars, Harold G. HENDERSON (1934), made it clear that a haiku cannot be translated as "epigram", for it is a "poem" intending to "express and to evoke emotion" (ibid., vii). It is also this scholar who mentioned that haiku records "high moments", the suggestive notion found in the elucidation of almost all American haiku scholars that followed him (ibid., 2):

> Haiku may be many kinds, grave or gay, deep or shallow, religious, satirical, sad, humorous, or charming: but all haiku worthy of the name are records of high moments - higher at least than the surrounding plain. And in the hands of a master a haiku can be the concentrated essence of pure poetry.

The fact that haiku is so brief, HENDERSON explains, leads it to employ several devices which make great use of "the association of ideas": (i) season, as "one experience common to all men", forming thus "a background for the picture"; (ii) references to Buddhism as well as to Japanese history; (iii) internal comparison[38], a comparison "of two or more ideas expressed in the poem it-

self"; (iv) condensation of verbal expression; (v) kireji,
which have no translatable meaning but have "an elu-
sive force of their own" (10). In elucidating Bashō's
haiku, which are "primarily pictures", HENDERSON quotes
Ernest Dimnet (36):

> Abbé Dimnet suggests that we should all make notes
> of those experiences which we would like to remember.
> These notes, he says, should be brief enough to pre-
> clude the danger of what the Veda calls "putting
> words between the truth and ourselves", and at the
> same time full enough to be clear to future, i.e.,
> almost alien, re-reading.

Suggestively enough, HENDERSON (23) also comments on some
of the metaphysical qualities presented in Bashō's haiku
(3.5.3.3).

Kenneth YASUDA (1957) attempts not only to describe
Japanese haiku but also to establish the art of English-
language haiku, following Japanese classical samples.
The central theme of his study is the notion of a "haiku
moment", similar to HENDERSON's "high moments", and
BLYTH's "spots of time", but with an additional component,
namely, "the power of 'resonation'" (YASUDA 1957: 24ff.).
Because of the restricted number of syllables "the words
can occur as a simultaneous happening" in the form of
haiku, in a way impossible with a "novel, a sonnet, or
even a quatrain" (ibid.). Thus, YASUDA also emphasizes
that a haiku moment is "anti-temporal", while its quality is "eternal, for in this state man and his environment are one unified whole" (ibid.), where the sense of
time is transcended. In this, YASUDA approaches the ideas
of BLYTH, who has influenced American haiku with his Zen-
Buddhistic interpretation more than anyone else except
probably SUZUKI Daisetsu (cf. SATŌ 1978). In the preface

to his voluminous *Haiku*, BLYTH states (1949: vii):
"Haiku is a kind of 'satori', or enlightenment, in
which we see into the life of things".

Donald KEENE, a popular scholar in Japan, emphasizes
the containment of "two elements", "usually divided by
a break" of kireji in his brief but influential *Japanese
Literature: An Introduction for Western Readers* (1955).
One of the elements may be "the general condition", such
as "the end of autumn, the stillness of the temple grounds,
the darkening sea", and the other "momentary perception"
(ibid., 40). KEENE declares that "it is absolutely necessary for haiku to be effective" that it should have
"two electric poles between which the spark will leap",
and that without this spark "it is no more than a brief
statement" (ibid.)[39]. Here again we find the emphasis on
two elements, as we have already seen in POUND's "super-
position", important points that will be discussed below. It is in the lack of these two "electric poles",
KEENE argues, that such Western "imitators of the haiku
form as Amy Lowell" have failed, though they recognized
the "brevity and suggestion" of haiku (ibid.). Earl MINER
(1958: 115) refers to this phenomenon as "discordia concors", explaining it as "metaphor which is all the more
pleasurable because of the gap which must be imaginative-
ly leaped between the statement and the vivid metaphor"
- a phenomenon MINER (1961, 1979) detects throughout the
poetic tradition in Japan.

While the earlier haiku experts were thus concerned with
introducing the "correct" notions of traditional haiku by
explaining its cultural background (BLYTH 1949, 1964,
STEWART 1960, YASUDA 1957) as well as its internal, i.e.,
deep, structure (HENDERSON 1934, 1965, KEENE 1955), recent scholars

are concerned more or less with "the form of English
haiku", a quest which was first initiated by YASUDA
(1957: 178ff.). I shall return to this theme later
(Ch. 6). Suffice it here to mention that such work
as that of Joan GIROUX (1974: 75-93) or Atsuo NAKAGAWA
(1976: 20-50) deal with the problem of how the
Japanese poetic 5-7-5 syllable-pattern can successfully be transplanted into the soil of the English-language
literary tradition. While both (GIROUX, 78, and
NAKAGAWA, 32) refer to YASUDA's (1957: 34) assertion that the number of syllables that can be uttered
in "one breath", during which the "state of ah-ness"
as an initial poetic inspiration occurs, must be "less
than eighteen", they differ in their solution to the
problem of finding an appropriate form for English
haiku. GIROUX (ibid., 79) suggests using an "approximation of the Japanese method of counting syllables"
in order to avoid "overly long" English haiku (80),
i.e., English haiku poets are advised to count "at least
consonant clusters and long accented vowels" as 2 syllables, punctuation as one, and "slowing consonants"
such as *pl* and long vowels such as *ow* as two, so that
"plow", e.g., has 4 syllables (80-1). In this way,
she believes, English poets could attain 17 syllables,
which is "the best length for English haiku" (81).
NAKAGAWA (ibid., 33) maintains that "the counterpart
of haiku or epic lines in the Japanese language
is the hexameter in English and other languages",
since such poetic forms include "sound groups" that can
be spoken in one breath (29). He bases his argumentation
on the laboratory experiments conducted by DOI (1970):
"We Japanese speak three to nine syllables in one sound
group (i.e., pause-groupe, breath-group, rhythm-unit,
or run), and two to four sound groups in one breath" (29).

NAKAGAWA (ibid., 30) thus offers three possible forms for English haiku: a three-line form with three "sound groups", a two-line form with two, and a one-line form with one. Although in reading such "recommendations" and "propositions", one cannot avoid the impression of excessive arbitrariness on the part of scholars ("plow" as 4 syllables, e.g.), they are nonetheless significant in that they show the attempts by non-Japanese to consolidate the surface structure, i.e., the "form", of English haiku, which hitherto had not existed.

In the above, we have seen that the poetry of haiku has been discussed, by both Japanese and American poet-analysts, in terms of three aspects: (i) poeticalness, (ii) morphology, and (iii) metaphor. We have also seen that the poeticalness of haiku has been described as consisting of three elements in the writings of Kiyosuke, Bashō, and POUND. Comparing the three, we can obtain the following table, though it demands further elucidation (cf. KOCH 1983: 282):

(12th c.) Kiyosuke	(17th c.) Bashō	(1928) Pound
eloquence	(prosodical intention)	melopoeia
clever parlance	kotoba	phanopoeia
oddity	kokoro	logopoeia

Fig. 33
The Trichotomy of Haiku-Poetics

It is perhaps surprising to find such correspondences
between the renga-scholar and the poets of the oriental
and the occidental world, who belong to such disparate
phases. On the other hand, the correspondences should
not be too startling, considering the fact that "the
basic aesthetic principles [...] are universal to all
poetry", as we have already seen in YASUDA's assumption
(1957: xx) or in Shiki's assertion (3.3.1).

Of the three elements of poeticalness, it should be
emphasized that the last, namely, kokoro - "oddity" or
"unconventionality", but also "sincerity, spirituality" -
has been most highly evaluated in haiku poetry, or for that
matter, in Japanese poetry in general. Moreover, the
assurance given by BLYTH, YASUDA, and HENDERSON that
haiku record "spots of moments" seems to relate to the
last kind of poeticalness because of its "eternal" nature,
as YASUDA argues: it can thus be restated that haiku moments are the moments in which the harmonization of the
"unerträgliche Opposition" takes place, that is, man
and nature are unified (1.4.1 and 2.2.5).

The second aspect mentioned in the brief scrutiny of
"the content" of haiku is the morphological characteristic
of haiku: "2-clauses, 1-statement" in Otsuji's terms,
or "super-position" in POUND's. While the three elements
mentioned above describe the poeticalness of haiku, this
morphology prescribes the text-format of haiku. The prerequisite, however, is not only that haiku contain two
"clauses" but also that these two must present a certain contrast - they must form "das Merkmal der Kontrapunktik zweier Ideen oder Bilder, aus deren Spannung ein
wesentlicher Reiz dieser Dichtung resultiert", as the
German Japanologist Bruno LEWIN writes (1969: 30). These
assertions that haiku manifests binary opposition confirm
the previous two chapters: the "curse of cognition", i.e.

the awareness that "man is mortal", is to be mediated.
This "myth-making", or "Neurotisierung" (KOCH 1978: 309),
i.e., the becoming conscious of the *dilemma* (KOCH ibid.,
81), must be "neutralized" (ibid.) by "motor activities",
as discussed in 2.2.4. This process is a matter of
"resorting to creativity", as in the examples by schizophrenics (2.3.2), or as in the fine arts of Zen. Haiku,
too, is a possible "neutralizer", to borrow KOCH's
parlance.

3.3.3 Semioticians

We can easily see that the third aspect, "metaphor" deals
a priori with the binary construction (REINHART 1976).
It seems, then, that clarification of this binary structure in its different dimensions can provide a clue to
the nature of haiku in particular, and of poetry in
general[40]. BLYTH states (1964: 8): "Zen and (European)
poetry and haiku and senryū have all a sameness, in that
two opposite things, or things of different categories
are united in one". BLYTH is apparently referring in
literary-critical terms to the same poetical phenomenon
which Roman JAKOBSON (1960: 358) describes in terms of
structuralism:

> The poetic function projects the principle of
> equivalence from the axis of selection onto
> the axis of combination.

This is one definition of the poetic function of language, and a second will presently be discussed.
JAKOBSON's oft-quoted assertion pinpoints the fundamental phenomenon of the "poetic function" of language, though, as we will see in the course of the discussion, it requires elaboration. Earlier (1.1.1) I
diagrammed what BARTHES (1974: 11) refers to as "naming"

and "metonymic labour" (Fig. 7). Using the same diagrammatic presentation of the two axes JAKOBSON refers to, Fig. 34 can be introduced below (cf. POSNER 1972: 150, HOLENSTEIN 1974: 152ff.):

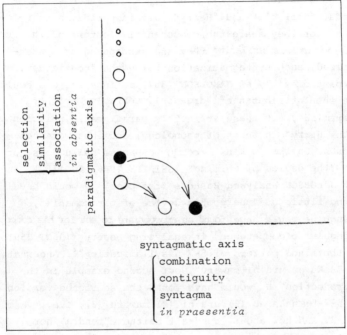

Fig. 34
The Poetic Function of Language: the Principle of Equivalence

JAKOBSON (ibid., 358) clarified that "in poetry the equation is used to build a sequence", i.e., paradigms are syntagmatized (cf. KOCH 1983: 457-60). In JAKOBSON's consideration, what dominates is phonological-metrical-syntactical parallelism[41], i.e., the "matrix" of texts,

in KOCH'S terms (0.3.2). Consequently he finds Gerard
Manley Hopkins one of the most interesting analytic objects because Hopkins "repeat[s] the same figure of
sounds" (ibid., 358-9). Following one of his examples,
let us consider "horrible Harry" (357). The two
words, "horrible" and "Harry", are in paradigmatic relation, for they share the consonantal clusters of /h...rr/,
and due to this similarity they are juxtaposed or syntagmatized, such syntagmatization being the "poetic device
of paranomasia", as JAKOBSON (357) defines it. One could
use such attributes as "dreadful, terrible, frightful,
disgusting", yet these are not in paradigmatic relation
with "Harry" in terms of phonology, and thus were not
chosen. Unlike Hopkins's poetry, Japanese haiku does not
use "the device of chiming" (SHIPLEY 1946: 1001ff.), and
had JAKOBSON analysed Bashō's frog poem, he would have
found little of "the poetic device of paranomasia",
though he would have found an appropriate object for his concept of
"linguistic competence" in analyzing poetry (1960: 359)
in the fixed pattern of 5-7-5 syllabication[42]. And what
of "Haka no ura ni mawaru", our second example in the
introduction? He would have found the shortened version
of 5-7-5: haka no (3) ura ni (3) mawaru (3), i.e.,
3-3-3. And how about "tundra"? Neither "tundra" nor
"the amount of the white space" includes "metrics".

What JAKOBSON dealt with in his consideration of the
"poetic function" of language was "the bundle of distinctive features" which each phoneme possesses (cf. JAKOBSON/
WAUGH 1979: 3-56). Yet language includes more than "matrix"
or "kotoba". It also manifests "mapping" or "kokoro" in
addition to the "situations" in which it is spoken, i.e.,
"semantics and pragmatics", in MORRIS's semiotic systems
(1946: 217-20)[43]. ECO (1976: 84ff.) clarifies this point.
In his semiotic investigation, he correlates what JAKOBSON

found on the phonological level to the level of semantics: Phonemes correspond to "sememes", whereas "the bundle of distinctive features" corresponds to "the same internal work of mutually opposed features" which governs "the differences between two sememes" (ibid.). In ECO's opinion semiotics is thus capable of explaining the "interrelationship of a bunch of formants" (1976: 49-50):

> ... semiotics gives us a sort of photomechanical explanation of semiosis, revealing that where we saw images there were only strategically arranged aggregations of black and white points, alternations of presence and absence, the insignificant basic features of a raster, sometimes differentiated in shape, position and chromatic intensity. Semiotics, like musical theory, states that where we recognize familiar melodies there is only a sophisticated intertwining of intervals and notes, and where we perceive notes there are only a bunch of formants.

ECO thus declares that analysis in terms of bundles of distinctive features - including connotations and denotations (54-7) - of a sememe promises us the clarification of rhetorical inventions thus far believed to be the product of an "intuitive perception, a sort of 'illumination' or a sudden revelation", which is nothing but the text-producer's "glimpse of the paths that the semantic organization entitled him to" (1976: 284). We are thus forced to turn to semiotics, but not linguistics, in our attempt to qualify such multi-dimensioned binary structures, especially when we are assured by the semiotician KOCH that "linguistische Theorien rechnen kaum mit einer informationellen Poetizität" (1978: 303).

3.3.4 The Poetics of Haiku and the Semiotics of Poetry

Anyone who reads the poetics of haiku, or *hairon* (3.3.1), old and new, will be surprised to discover so many correspondences between it and contemporary writings on the semiotics of poetry (JAKOBSON 1960, 1976, KOCH 1978, 1983, MATEJKA/TITUNIK 1976, SHUKMAN 1977, TODOROV 1977). The reason why hairon began, as early as the mid-seventeenth century, to deal with the question of *poeticalness* (JAKOBSON 1960: 359), or *poeticity* (JAKOBSON 1976: 174), "an element sui generis" (ibid.) which makes a piece of writing poetry, seems to be that haiku operates on the border line between the "practical functions" and the "poetic function" of language (MUKAŘOVSKÝ 1976a: 158ff., cf. BÜHLER 1934, JAKOBSON 1960). Stripped of any "artificial technique" of poetry (1.2.2), haiku, from the time of its origin, has been in a favourable position to confront the reader with the question as to what makes poetry poetry, while the European tradition of poetics had to wait for the exposition of the Russian Formalists beginning in the twenties of our century (HAWKES 1977: 62ff.). In the following I shall discuss four such correspondences which throw light on the general nature of haiku poetry: 1) the autotelic mechanism of poetic function; 2) the principle of the syntagmatization of paradigms; 3) the spatiality of poetry; and 4) trimodal poeticalness.

The first correspondence, the autotelic poetic function of language, concerns Bashō and the Russian Formalists and their followers. In HATTORI Dohō's *Sanzōshi* ("Three Booklets") (1776: 604), Bashō is recorded to have preached that[44]

the merit of haiku is to rectify non-poetic words. Be watchful about the materials [of poetry]. People

when a poetic function, as opposed to other functions of
language (JAKOBSON 1960: 357ff.), becomes dominant. The
manifestation of poeticity is observed, JAKOBSON (1976:
174) clarifies, when "the word is felt as a word" and
"words and their composition, their meaning, their external and internal form acquire a weight and value of
their own", as opposed to words "referring indifferently
to reality". MUKAŘOVSKÝ (1976a) argues in the same vein,
differentiating the "practical" functions of language on
the one hand and the "aesthetic" or "poetic" on the
other and designating the former functions of language as the
"informational" and "practical", and the latter functions as
the "aesthetic" and "poetic" (ibid., 158). He agrees with
BÜHLER (1934) on three practical functions that informational language possesses, *Darstellung*, *Ausdruck*, and *Appell*, to which JAKOBSON (1960) later added two more, the
phatic and the metalingual. The sentence "It's turning
dark" used by MUKAŘOVSKÝ as an example (ibid., 155), can
be spontaneously perceived as a piece of information in
which the attention of the perceiver is focused on the
relationship between the reference and the reality. The
same utterance, however, the Prague semiotician argues,
can be taken as a poetic citation, if attention is shifted
from practical to aesthetic function, i.e., if the
attention is attracted "not by its relationship to the
reality indicated, but by the way it is set into the verbal context" (156). It follows that "poetic reference"
differs from informational reference in that its relationship to reality is weakened in favor of its semantic linkage
with context (162, cf. "significance" as the formal and semantic unity of poetic discourse, and "meaning" as the literary representation of reality or "mimesis", in RIFFATERRE
1978: 2-22, and "poetic" and "normal" discourse in HAWKES
1977: 63). HAWKES (ibid., 63), following the argumentation

of Russian Formalism, clarifies that poetic discourse differs fundamentally from other discourses in its *modus operandi*, i.e., it "raises the activities of discourse to a much higher degree than 'normal' language does". In Bashō's poetics of haiku (*haikai* at the time), however, the signifier's relationship to reality was not intended to be "weakened" by any means, as our investigation into Zen semiotics in the previous chapter has made clear. What is involved is rather the simultaneous activation of two functions, the "poetic" and the "referential" in JAKOBSONian terminology.

Another of Bashō's writings, "An Essay of the Unreal Dwelling", shows his awareness of the *universality* of poetic function. He writes (UEDA 1970: 132, cf. PILGRIM 1977: 44ff.):

> One thing permeates Saigyo's tanka, Sōgi's linked verse, Sesshū's painting and Rikyū's tea ceremony. That is the spirit of the artist who follows nature and befriends the four seasons. Everything he sees becomes a flower, and everything he imagines turns into a moon.

The "*permeation* of one thing" through which "everything becomes a flower" is, in our terms, the *universality* of poeticalness (JAKOBSON 1960, KOCH 1983: 351), or deep structure. The surface structure expressing this "one thing" may in fact vary; poetry, painting, tea ceremony, and Bashō's haikai poetry. Towards the end of his life, Bashō's notion crystallized into *fueki-ryūkō* (MUKAI Kyorai, 490-7), which is translated by HAMMITZSCH (1954: 111) as "das Unwandelbare" and "der Wandel der Form". HAMMITZSCH (ibid.) elucidates that

> was aus seinen Werken spricht, ist das für alle Zeiten Unwandelbare (*fueki*), welches nicht Alt und

Neu kennt, welches sich am Strom des Werdens und
Vergehens niemals ändert ..., wenn auch die Form (ryūkō)
sich wandelt.

Although Bashō's notion of the universality of poeticalness is highly colored by its religious tone (PILGRIM 1977, UEDA 1962, 1970), which modern theories of poeticalness lack, it seems unquestionable that he was well aware of the "ubiquity" of poetic function through focalization (KOCH 1983: 368-451).

Deeply related to focalization or *Einstellung* in poetic discourse is what Formalists considered to be the central issue of poetic device, "making strange" (HAWKES, 62). Their representative Shklovsky (1917: 105 cit. in SHUKMAN, 41)[47] formulated the notion of *ostranenie* ("the device of making strange") as the "device of art", thus predating the "Brechtian concept of *alienation* (Verfremdung)", HAWKES (63) ascertains. According to Shklovsky, the aim of art is "to give the feeling of a thing as something seen, and not as something recognized" (cit. in SHUKMAN, 42, cf. FOUCAULT 1970):

> ... so it is in order to restore the feeling of life,
> to be aware of things, in order to make the stone
> stony, that there exists what is called art.

For Shklovsky, in SHUKMAN's opinion (41), the purpose of art was to "restore de-automatized perception", to "replace 'recognition' by 'seeing': in fact to see the 'thing in itself'", i.e., "to make the stone stoney[sic]".

Shklovsky's assertion sounds very like Bashō, who said[48], "Learn about a pine tree from a pine tree, and about a bamboo plant from a bamboo plant" in a "famous passage on the poet's creative process" (UEDA 1970: 167). Or BLYTH (1964: 7: cf. CASALIS 1979), who asserted that haiku makes one realize the coldness of a cold day[49], the heat of a hot day[50], the smoothness of a stone[51], the whiteness of a seagull[52], the distance of a far-off mountain[53], the smallness of a small flower[54], the dampness of the rainy season[55], the quivering of the hairs of a caterpillar in the breeze[56].

Bashō, then, while employing the 5-7-5 form as the *priem* for his poetry, came to recognize the existence of poetic function through which his poetry was capable of "rectifying" even vulgar expression. The previous chapter (2.3.2) has shown that Zen T in general are characterized by dyadic structure both in deep structure and surface structure. Similarly, haiku, according to Bashō's ideal, goes through *little transformation* as far as the signifier (matrix) is concerned, except that the *normal discourse* is required to coincide with the rhythm pattern. Our prototypical example (1) of the frog poem sufficiently proves this point in that it presents no *stylization* (3.4.1.2) in the surface structure. Fig. 35 diagrams the relationship between "normal, informational, mimetic discourse" and haiku discourse.

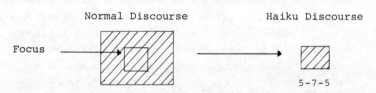

Fig. 35: The Autotelic Mechanism in Haiku Poetry

The second correspondence between *hairon* and the semiotics of poetry deals with the principle of the syntagmatization of paradigms. Again in Dohō (592) and Kyorai (498), Bashō is recorded to have said that "Hokku is made by combining things"[57] (cf. UEDA 1970: 165ff.). The contemporary semiotician LOTMAN (1964: 64 cit. in SHUKMAN, 54) elucidates

the notion of *povtor* ("repetition"), the realization of
the "principle of juxtaposition of elements":

> The *povtor* in the literary text is the traditional
> name given to the basic operation that determines
> the relationship of juxtaposition of elements in a
> literary structure and which may be realized as
> antithesis and as identification. Antithesis means
> the isolation of what is opposite in what is simi-
> lar (the correlative pair); identification means the
> coincidence at one point of that which seemed
> different.

LOTMAN's elucidation of *povtor* is quite compatible with
what HENDERSON (1934: 8) expounds as "the form of association of ideas" or "a comparison of two or more ideas
expressed in the poem itself", which he later termed an
"internal comparison" (1967) and the basic form of haiku
poetry. LOTMAN (1976: 51) declares, in his investigation
of the cinematic technique called "montage", that such
juxtapositions, or "the collision of elements from
different systems (they must be both contrastive and
comparable, i.e., unified on some more abstract level)",
is "the customary manner in which artistic meanings are
formed". Bashō's disciple Kyorai (498) also notes the
comment of a colleague concerning the methodology of
haiku: "In hokku composition, one should search for
materials outside of the (given) domain". According to
KURIYAMA (1973: 499), this statement means the "compari-
son-combination of the two unrelated elements" and, consequently, "a leap of association". Kyorai meant, in
KURIYAMA's opinion (ibid.), that this "leap" must be
moderate, since an excessive "leap" would simply culminate
in "sheer fantasy" (cf. UEDA 1970: 105).

As a matter of fact, the notion of *povtor* is a leitmotive of the following discussion, in which *povtor* on different linguistic levels will be discussed. Suffice it, therefore, to present here the following diagram, in which art in general from the points of view of P_{xs} and P_{xe}, is expounded. Fig. 36 presents the equivalent principle projected onto the axis of syntagmatization in the text-production by P_{xs} on the one hand, and its opposite operation by P_{xe} on the other; i.e., because of the syntagmatization (juxtaposition) of two (or more) elements (paradigms) presented to P_{xe} by P_{xs}, the former is forced to reconstruct, or "project", the paradigmatic relationship between the given "ideas" in a haiku. P_{xs} thus syntagmatizes paradigms, while P_{xe} "paradigmatizes" the given syntagma as haiku (cf. SHUKMAN, 55):

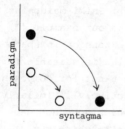
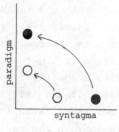

Fig. 36: Haiku Production (P_{xs}):   Haiku Reception (P_{xe}):
The Snytagmatization of   The Paradigmatization of
Paradigm   Syntagma

The third correspondence between *hairon* and the semiotics of poetry is closely related to the second correspondence just discussed above: the spatial nature of haiku manifests itself as the juxtaposition of paradigms.

LOTMAN (1975) divides all cultural texts into two major categories: the primary text (where the text is an integral sign, and thus primary), and the secondary text (where the text is a sequence of signs, and thus secondary). In discussing LOTMAN's theory

WINNER (1979: 112) explains primary texts as the texts
which "are associated with statics or with limited change
by transformation and thus with paradigmatic structures",
and which can be described as "plotless texts" emphasizing
"iconic, spatial and visual systems" (cf. LOTMAN 1976:
4-9). Distinguishing this type from secondary texts, which
can be "broken down into signs, and are associated with
the dynamics of change by addition of new elements",
LOTMAN (1975) divides primary texts further into two subtypes: Subtype 1, which is "continuous", and Subtype 2,
which is "not continuous" because it has "a form
of discreteness" to a greater extent (112-3). The sub-
type 1 includes among other texts, "the plotless lyric
poem" (ibid.), since "the unit in a poetic text is not
the word but the text as such" (LOTMAN 1975: 80).

LOTMAN is here in agreement with MASAOKA Shiki
(1893: 156) and YAMAMOTO (1946). Shiki maintains that
haiku, specifically referring to our example (1) of the
frog poem, "possesses neither extension in space nor
duration in time" and that "haiku is suitable for composing a spatial inspiration but not for composing 'time'"
(1896: 511 and 1899: 453 respectively). Similarly, YAMAMOTO
argues that "haiku is poetry which does not have temporal
duration; in the period of time in which the 31-syllabled
(tanka) became 17-syllabled, a violent jump, namely, the
effacement of time-ness was executed" (cit. in MATSUI 1965:
555). With its syllabic limitation, haiku seems in fact
to have established itself as an art of paradigm, in spite
of the "narrative" quality language usually possesses.
LOTMAN (1976: 7), divides signs into two groups, "conventional" and "pictorial", corresponding to "symbolic"
and "iconic" in PEIRCEian semiotics (2.3.4), and asserts that
conventional signs which "easily acquire a syntax" are
capable of "telling", of "creating narrative texts", where-

as pictorial, iconic signs are "restricted to the function of naming". In the previous chapter, we saw that the semiotics of Zen, of which haiku is an offspring, is characterized by indexicality and iconicity due to its essential rejection of "conventional", "conceptualizing" signs. As we will see in the next chapter, in the discussion of the development of this poetic genre, haiku had possessed that "narrative" quality, or "timeness" in YAMAMOTO's terms, prior to Bashō. But the introduction of Zen metageneticity totally erased narration from haiku, for narration requires "conceptualization" in that each concatenated event must be memorized. In the general trend of the proletarian literature of the Twenties, haiku, too, attempted to express Socialistic ideals, but proved to be unsuitable for such ideological writings (4.2.2.2, cf. BARTHES 1970: 94-115).

Because of this "naming" nature, as opposed to a "narrative", "telling" nature, the chronological order of two "ideas" is not so decisive as is the case in narrative structures (cf. "tension and relief" as opposed to "suspense and détente" in KOCH 1982c: 2-20). Significantly enough, both *hairon* and the semiotics of poetry refer to this essentially "state-oriented" mode of perception rather than to "process-orientation" (KOCH ibid., cf. TODOROV 1977: 111). HATTORI Dohō (592) comments that "the writing of a hokku consists of grasping the movement of the mind that goes and then returns"[58] (trans. by UEDA 1970: 165), and LOTMAN (1964: 63 cit. in SHUKMAN, 54) posits "the principle of return" as the structural principle of poetry.

Dohō (ibid.) uses the following hokku to make his point:

(10) 山里は 万歳遅し 梅の花
Yamazato wa / manzai oshoshi / ume no hana
In the mountain village/ Manzai dancers[59]
are late--/ plum blossoms

> The poet first declares that in a mountain
> village Manzai dancers are late, and then he
> goes on to observe that plum blossoms are
> in bloom. His mind goes, and then returns. This
> is what happens in writing a hokku. If he were
> merely to say that in a mountain village Manzai
> men are late, that would make only an ordinary
> verse, a verse more properly placed in the main
> body of a renku.
> (trans. by UEDA 1970: 165)

KURIYAMA (1973: 592) annotates the above passage by Dohō, which is presumably a restatement of Bashō (cf. UEDA, ibid.), by explaining that the method of this hokku is the "inversion of the initial flow of poet's consciousness", i.e., the chronological order of poet's experience, "Plum blossoms → in the mountain village → Manzai dancers are late", is inverted so that the initial trigger, "plum blossoms", is placed at the end. Thus haiku, too, deals to a certain degree with one of the main concerns of narratology, i.e., the difference between *histoire*, or what happened, and *narration* or how it is told (GENETTE 1980: 31-85), or the Russian Formalists' distinction between the *fable* (the story) and the *sujet* (the plot) (TODOROV 1977: 26), or *story*, "the signified or narrative content" and *narrative*, "the signifier, statement, discourse or narrative text itself" (GENETTE ibid., 27). The discrepancy between the *histoire* and the *narration*, or the signified and the signifier of (10) can be depicted as below:

histoire of (10): (signified)	I. Poet's surprise in discovering *plum blossoms* already blooming ↓
	II. His recognition of his being *in the mountain village* ↓
	III. His realization that *Manzai dancers have not yet arrived.*
narration of (10): (signifier)	II → III → I

In thus *narrating* (GENETTE, ibid.), i.e., in the "mediation of the *récit*" (GENETTE 1972: 74), the signifier forces the reconstruction of the signified, thus resulting in "the mind's going and returning":

récit of (10):   II → III → I

It is important to note that the trigger of the poet's composition of (10), "his discovering plum blossoms blooming in the very early time of the year" is placed at the end of the surface structure, i.e., a climax tends to be placed at the very end (BLYTH 1956: 24, COHEN 1965: 225).

Actually, this passage of Dohō directly precedes his recording of his master's precept that "Hokku is made by combining things", discussed above in terms of the second correspondence, and it seems plausible to consider, as KURIYAMA (1973: 592) suggests, that Dohō is here concerned more with the spatial nature of hokku. Hokku, and accordingly haiku (UEDA, ibid.), thus deals with a "static type of episode in a narrative" rather than a "dynamic type" describing "the passage from one state to the other", in TODOROV's parlance (ibid., 111, cf. KOCH 1982c). In a similar vein, LOTMAN (1964: 63 cit. in SHUKMAN, 54) characterizes poetry. SHUKMAN (ibid.) sums up LOTMAN thus: "While ordinary speech is perceived chronologically, in time, poetry is spatial, demanding a constant return by the reader to the text [...]" It is, continues SHUKMAN (ibid.)," this constant process of

return and comparison that reveals to the reader ever
new semantic content". Thus, the "universal structural
principle of poetry" is "the principle of return" (ibid.,
cf. RIFFATERRE 1978: 19ff.).

The fourth correspondence, the *trimodality* of poeticalness encompasses the previous three correspondences. It
deals with the first correspondence, the autotelic mechanism of poetic function, in that it recognizes three subdivisions of such an autotelic, or *focalizing*, mechanism:
the *aesthetic*, the *metalingual*, and the *informational
focus*[60]. It deals with the second correspondence, the equivalence principle, in that it analyses how this poetic
principle operates in each domain of the different foci.
And it deals with the third correspondence, the spatial
nature of haiku, in that it elucidates the "metaphorical"
or "metalingual" juxtaposition as the fundamental morphology of haiku. This last correspondence, observed in
hairon and the semiotics of poetry, preoccupies both
Bashō and the German semiotician Walter A. KOCH (1966,
1971, 1974, 1976, 1978, 1981a, 1983), and it is one of
the major topics of the present study.

3.4   The Trimodal Poeticalness of Haiku
3.4.1 The Theory of Trimodal Poeticalness of KOCH

In 1966 KOCH launched the *theory of poeticalness* in
Recurrence and a Three-Modal Approach to Poetry. This
theory detects "the three levels of *non-trivial*[61] recurrence
manifestation": *phonic*, *syntactic*, and *semantic* (ibid., 19).
Recurrences are *non-trivial* or "unusual" (KOCH 1983: 73),
if they motivate P_{xe} to "deflect from his normal decoding
attitude" (1966: 18). *Phonic recurrence* manifests itself
in such poetic conventions as stress, rhyme, meter, i.e.,

the "*aesthetic* side of the poem" (11) that can be appreciated even by "those who do not understand the language in which it is written" (19). Thus the syllabic pattern of haiku, 5-7-5, is the *aesthetic* manifestation of poeticalness. *Syntactic recurrence* occurs between *in praesentia* and *in absentia* (Fig. 34), i.e., between the signifier and the signified: a given text is analyzed, interpreted, or commented upon (15). It thus concerns itself with "the *cryptic* side of the poem" (11) as opposed to the first type of recurrence, the *aesthetic*^{62} one, and it therefore forces P_x to *discover* (ibid.) the meaning, i.e., to practise "naming" in the BARTHESian sense (1.1.1, specifically Fig. 7). Syntactic recurrence is the *stylistic* manifestation of poeticalness (24). *Semantic* recurrence, the third type, occurs in the "manifestation-level" (36) of *topic* or *information* (24). It deals with "semantic sames" (24), as most typically exemplified in Keats's *To Autumn*, in which two topics, i.e., "autumn" and "mature/fruitful" recur (21). This type, too, similar to the second type, is thus concerned with the discovery-side of the poem, and these two have hardly been approached by analysts traditionally, KOCH ascertains, presumably due to "premature analytical satisfaction" (20). Yet, very often, KOCH continues, the last two types of recurrence "supersede a primary phonic recurrence" (ibid.), as is indeed the case with haiku, as we will see below.

Poeticalness, as opposed to "poetry" (KOCH 1973: 24), refers to the "structural properties susceptible of being universally regarded as potentially pertaining to poetry" (1983: 45), while poetry's specific properties very much depend on "epoch and culture" (ibid., cf. fueki-ryūkō by Bashō: 3.3.4). KOCH's theory of trimodal poeticalness deals with *focus*, with which P_x *selects* or *structures* the sentence, the text (T), and indeed *every* experience

in the world (1973: 23, cf. KOCH 1971, 1972). As we
saw at the very beginning of the present study (0.3.4),
this *focal selection* of P_x occurs in the *communication situation*
Once in a communication situation, i.e., confronted with the
T, P_x is compelled to activate his language competence
as it is reflected in the three modes mentioned above.
The three modes, aesthetic, stylistic or *metalingual*
(1978: 298ff.), and informational, *correspond* to three
modern fields of study, aesthetics, linguistics, and
metaphysics, respectively (1978: 40, 1983: 75). The
three fields deal with each corresponding mode in the
abstract forms, whereas the theory of poeticalness does
so in the *concrete* forms, i.e., it elucidates each mode
as it is concretized and realized in poetry (1983: 67f.,
cf. BLYTH's assertion about the abstractness of Zen texts
and the concreteness of haiku discussed in 2.1). KOCH
surveys his proposition of trimodal poeticalness as
follows (1983: 75):

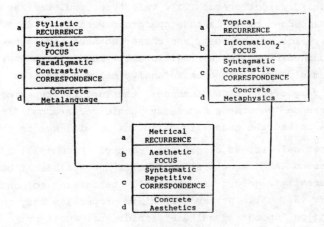

Fig. 37
The Theory of Correspondence
(from KOCH 1983)

As our earlier discussion of P_{xe}'s confronting the drawing of the Zen Temple Ryōanji (Illustr. 1) showed, to encounter a T means going through three phases, symmetry-asymmetry-integration, which can be restated "psychobiologically" as "attention-irritation-surprise/memory" (1983: 406). Further, this scheme of ontological procedure is to be found in each focalized field of poeticalness, starting with the symmetrical phase "◯◯", or *prosphory*, moving to the asymmetrical phase "◯●", or *diaphory*, and arriving at the integrational phase "◐", or *symphory* (383). The three modes of poeticalness, i.e., the *concretization* of the modes, and their respective three phases, can thus be related as below (386):

modes phases	concrete meta-aethetic	concrete meta-lingual	concrete meta-physical	complex
◯◯	recurrence	incompatibility	archetypal constellation	modal knot
◯●	counter-point	simile	opposition	modal dissonance
◐	tertium attractionis	tertium comparationis	tertium mediationis	tertium diversionis

Fig. 38
Three Poetical Modes and Three Phases
(from KOCH 1983)

What exactly do these *concretizations* look like? In
illustrating the point in concern, let us follow KOCH's
three examples which most prototypically exhibit each
mode of poeticalness:

A. *Concrete aesthetics*
(11) Zack hitti zopp
Hitti betzli betzli
Prusch kata
Fasch kitti bimm   (Hugo Ball)

B. *Concrete metalanguage*
(12) Anyone lived in a pretty how town

(e. e. cummings)

C. *Concrete metaphysics*
(13) If I should die, think only this of me:
That there's some corner of a foreign field
that is for ever England.

(Rupert Brooke)

Before we go into the analysis of poeticalness, however, let me introduce two sets of terms, which will be useful in this analysis: *sememes* as *cultural units* with regard to semantics or the signified, as ECO explains them (3.3.3), and *manifesta* as *sign-vehicles* with regard to the signifier (KOCH 1974a: 313, cf. ECO 1976: 23, also 2.1.1). Further, I shall use as graphic conventions slashes, as in /death/, to indicate a word as a sememe, and single quotation marks as in 'die' to indicate a manifestum.

3.4.1.1 Aesthetic Poeticalness

The first mode of poeticalness deals with phonological, morphological or syntactical *parallelism* appearing in manifesta (KOCH 1983: 54ff.). Ball's poem strikingly

exploits JAKOBSON's equivalence principle discussed as
"*Horrible Harry*" (3.3.3). The recurrences of sibilants,
stops, short interconsonantal vowels, rhythm, etc.,
characterize the poem due to their prominence, steering
P_{xe}'s aesthetic focus. Although the poem exhibits further poetical modes (1983: 62), if P_{xe} concentrates on
the semantics of each apparently nonsensical word, it
nonetheless predominantly presents aesthetic poeticalness (cf. ibid., also 227ff. for further examples).

KOCH (ibid., 76) attempts to trace this mode of
poeticalness in the human phylogenetic past. We, too,
have seen (2.2.4) the survival value of "repetitive
stimuli" functioning for both communication and "tuning"
(2.2.3). In discussing the *phylogeny of art*, SCHENK
(1982: 433) points out that artistic standards began,
for instance, with the "line formations" in caves, and
the "macaroni" (BIEDERMAN 1948: 65-8) or "rhythmical engravings on bones discovered in the Aurignacian (Paleolithic)
period (35,000 to 18,000 years ago) (SCHENK, 420). Ontogenetically
structures viewed as aesthetic formations dominate prepictorial drawings by children, as Rhoda KELLOG (1969:
208-25) shows in her stimulating analysis (cf. SCHENK,
424ff.).

3.4.1.2 Stylistic Poeticalness

The second poeticalness, the metalingual, lies in "finding a semantically and syntactically acceptable" understanding of the given text. In reading cumming's poem
(cf. KOCH 1972: 429-61 also 1983: 85-6 for further examples), P_{xe} is compelled to focus on the word "how",
which is inserted between "pretty" and "town". Taken as
it is, the sentence is "ungrammatical". P_{xe}'s focus is

thus steered to the *understanding* of "how", which is
incompatible (1983: 86) with the rest of the line. In
order to clarify this *deviation*, or *styleme* (86-9, cf.
128ff.), P_{xe} launches a "metalingual operation", i.e.,
the "five-step-procedure of stylistics" (KOCH 1971a: 557,
1972: 446, 1983: 89, cf. REINHART 1976):

1) P_{xe}'s *realization* of the incompatibility of the
   surface T with 'how' and "the rest of the
   poem".
2) The *determination* of a styleme: 'how' is a styleme,
   because the poem's context is obviously the description of a "town", i.e., "how" occurs in the
   "frame" (REINHART 1976: 386ff.) of a context.
3) The *search* for a *substitution* for 'how': What is
   the equivalence of 'how'?, i.e., the problem stated
   (1.4.1, 2.2.4, 2.2.5) as a *riddle* (KOCH 1966: 11,
   1983: 90ff.).
4) The *solution* of the problem: 'how' can be substituted for by such modifiers as "nameless",
   "unknown", or "nondescript" (1972), *because* "how"
   and "non-descript" *share a common core* of, say,
   /some kind of indeterminacy/" (cf. "non-literal" and
   "literal expression" in [REINHART 1976: 386ff.], or
   "vehicle" and "tenor" in RICHARDS [1936]).
5) The rechecking of the solution for *comprehensibility*,
   i.e., *translation* of the original T by *substituting*
   'nondescript' for 'how'[63].

The incompatibility in cumming's line occurs within a sentence. It can, however, also occur at various other syntactical levels (1983: 89). As REINHART's minute analysis of
metaphor clarifies (1976: 384ff.), this five-step-procedure
is exactly what happens in *understanding* a metaphorical expression. Further, she clarifies that as far as the proce-

dure of *understanding* a given expression goes, there is
no *difference in principle* between understanding a
metaphorical and a literal expression (cf.KOCH 1983:
86ff.), for in both cases the signifier, whether as a
styleme or a literal expression, triggers the *search*
for the signified. Thus, traditional rhetorical devices
such as metaphor, tropes, similes, etc., are said to be
the *stylization* of this fundamental language operation
(KOCH ibid., 96ff.), and they can be analysed in terms
of stylistic poeticalness.

The T which manifests stylistic poeticalness can be
described as the product of "matrix-orientation" on the
part of P_{xs}, or *kotoba*, to recall the Japanese poetological tradition (1.2.2). The matrix-orientation of the
poet can take various forms when concretized in a text.
KOCH points out that such *Einfache Formen* (JOLLES 1930)
as fairy-tale, nursery rhyme, riddle and joke are further
transformations of basically identical "metalingual operations" (90ff.): they all deal with "matching" between the
signifier and the signified. Phylogenetically and ontogenetically speaking, this *exploration of matrices* can be
found in the behavior called *play* (76ff.), in which both
innate and learned patterns of behavior are *tentatively*
tried out (76-7). In passing, the series of experiments
with primates in which attempts were made to teach them
"language" have clarified that they are well endowed with
the capability for "metalingual" or "naming" operations
(GARDNER/GARDNER 1969, 1971, 1975, HEWS 1973, 1976,
PREMACK 1976).

3.4.1.3 Informational Poeticalness

In the lines of the Georgian poet, "If I should die, think
only this of me:/That there's some corner of a foreign

field/that is for ever England", KOCH (83ff.) detects
the "curse of cognition" (2.2.4) *mediated* by reasoning
(2.2.5). The *unbearable opposition* of "death and life"
or "nature and man" is *harmonized* by Brooke's *identifying* "the clod of earth into which bacteria will have
transformed the body of the Englishman killed in action
during the First World War" with a "particular individual" (84). This *identification* of a handful of earth
with an individual is the *solution* to the problem, "the
panacea of the witch doctor ... the therapeutic ideas of
FREUD" (ibid.). If Zen monks have chosen to attain satori
(2.2.4), BOBON/MACCAGNANI's psychopathic patient to produce "fusions" of numerous items (Illustr. 2), and the
ancient Buddhist artist to make an image of Ashura (Illustr. 3), Brooke has chosen to use the "logic" (2.2.5)
of identifying "some corner of a foreign land" with /me/.
Similarly, Blake's line "To see a World in a Grain of
Sand", also offers a mediation, i.e., *metaphysical* poeticalness, in that it "harmonizes" the metaphysical conflict between the greatness of the world and the micro-
scopic nature of the individual (85; also 80-6, for
further examples). KOCH further analyses (80ff.) a poem
by Wang Wei (ca. 700), a Chinese poet with this scheme,
but in this case the results are less convincing. It
seems that Wang Wei's poem is based on a totally
different kind of mediation, as we will see in the
later discussion (3.5.3.4).

Informational or metaphysical poeticalness has something to do with the poet's *thinking process* (239), or
kokoro as opposed to kotoba (1.2.2), i.e., with *mapping*
(57-8) instead of matricizing. KOCH (462) points out
that there has hitherto been no place in linguistics or
semiotics for the informational *mode* of the poetic, for,

he reasons, linguistics deals "almost exclusively"
with matrix but not with mapping (cf. 281ff.). Linguistics,
then, has been dealing with "d[er] bezeichnend[en] Seite
(Lautung)" (matrix) that has to do with the left hemisphere,
while neglecting "d[ie] bezeichnete Seite" that has to do
with the right hemisphere, to refer to IVANOV's (1977: 34ff.)
correlation between the two brain hemispheres and semiotic
systems.

The mapping of world structures has been characterized
as "binary" in such studies as those of LÉVI-STRAUSS or
MARANDA/KÖNGÄS-MARANDA, as we saw in the previous chapter
(2.2.4). KOCH (237), too, ascertains that "through the
thousands of years certain *dilemmas* keep being passed on",
being "concretized" as "poeticalness". RIEDL (1979: 158ff.)
suggests that the archeological evidence from the Cave of
Shanidar in Irak, i.e., the great amount of pollen from
mallow, lychnis, and hyacinth found at the site of a
burial that took place 60,000 years ago, points out the
metaphysical motive of the Neanderthals still evident in
present-day funeral conventions. The potential of flowers
as a metaphysical motive seems to have come about through
the Neanderthals' observation that flowers return every
spring in spite of their apparent death in autumn. Thus,
it can be hypothesized that flowers easily became the
manifestation of immortality and presumably accompanied
the burial at Shanidar. It seems then that the Neanderthals in Shanidar activated the mental operation of the
axis of metaphor (Fig. 34), which underlies what the anthropologist Sir James Frazer termed imitative magic, as
opposed to contagious magic (JAKOBSON 1967: 158ff.): it
is the *identification* posited by these early men between
flowers and their metaphysical thought that motivated them
to put the flowers at the burial site (3.4.1.3).

In addition to the existence of informational poeticalness, KOCH (238ff.) further postulates the existence of
four modes of *conjecture*, i.e., conjecture as to how such
metaphysical mediation can be achieved. The four types of

"transfer of emotional and cognitive structures between *ego* and *world*" are: *projection, introjection, equijection,* and *nullijection.* Fig. 39 diagrams the four types of conjection (238):

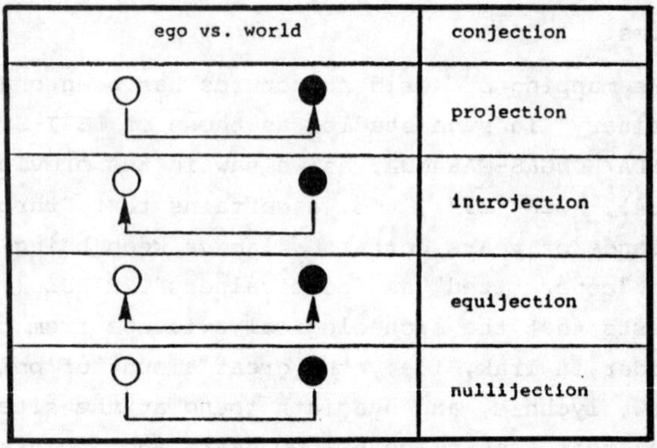

ego vs. world	conjection
○ ●↑	projection
○↑ ●	introjection
○↑ ●↑	equijection
○ ●	nullijection

Projection   : transferring structures from the ego to the world
Introjection: transferring structures from the world to the ego
Equijection : the mixture of the two modes above
Nullijection: "non-involvement" by the poet

Fig. 39
Four Types of Conjection (from KOCH 1983)

How such types of *conjection* or "thinking process" can be observed in haiku will be one of our major concerns.

3.4.2 The Three Haikai-Elements of Bashō

If KOCH feels rather alone in advocating the tripartite theory of poeticalness among the occidental scholars of linguistics and semiotics, he could easily ally himself

with Kiyosuke, the twelfth-century poet-theorist, and with
Bashō (3.3.2). By including informational poeticalness,
KOCH finds, however, a "protagonist of tripartition" in
POUND (281ff.). Yet POUND has "far less to say about
logopoeia than about melopoeia or phanopoeia", i.e.,
informational poeticalness was handled rather sparsely by
POUND (UEDA 1965: 113). UEDA (ibid.) infers the possible
reason for POUND's sparse treatment of "logopoeia" as
follows: "POUND thinks it the most tricky and *undependable*
mode". At any event, surveying KOCH's theory, we are now
able to obtain the following correspondences among four
scholars and poets: Kiyosuke, Bashō, Pound, and KOCH (cf.
KOCH 1983: 282):

	Kiyosuke	Bashō	Pound	Koch
1	eloquence	(prosodic intention)	melopoeia	aesthetic poeticalness
2	clever parlance	kotoba	phanopoeia	stylistic poeticalness
3	oddity	kokoro	logopoeia	informational poeticalness

Fig. 40: Four Advocates of Tripartite Poetics

Now let us inspect the three elements of haikai as
Bashō elucidates them (HATTORI Dohō, 524):

> [On some other occasion Master Bashō] explained the
> following: " 春雨の柳 " (a willow in the spring rain) is
> as a whole a renga. " 田螺取る烏 " (a crow picking up mud
> snails) is truly a haikai. " 五月雨に鳰の浮巣を見にゆかん "
> (In the early summer rain, I now feel like going to
> Biwa Lake to see the floating nest of the grebe):

in this poem, haikai-poeticalness does not lie in kotoba [words, diction] but in the kokoro [mind, spirit, feeling, heart] of the poet [Bashō] ... To the hokku " 霜月や 鴨のつくづく双び居て " (The month of the frost (i.e., November)!/ several ducks are detachedly / standing in a row), I appended the following "wakiku" (the second verse of renga and haikai), " 冬の朝日の あはれなりけり " (The winter morning sun/ is weak and touches our emotions. In this wakiku there is no haikai-poeticalness (" 俳 ") in either kotoba nor kokoro. Instead this haikai-poeticalness lies in the prosodic intention (" 作意 ") of providing wakiku with the characteristic of the second part of waka so that together with hokku, it produces the impression as though the whole were a complete waka. As you see in these examples, *haikai-poeticalness* (" 俳諧 ") lies in the *kotoba*, in the *kokoro*, and in the *prosodic intention*, as the example of this wakiku shows. You should not consider, therefore, that what haikai is based upon consists of one single element.

Bashō clearly observed, as Kiyosuke had done five centuries earlier, that there are three elements that constitute the poeticalness of haikai: (i) kotoba, (ii) kokoro, and (iii) prosodic intention. This trichotomy offered by Bashō has been re-interpreted by a contemporary haiku-scholar, KURIYAMA Riichi (1972: 15-6). The first element, i.e., "kotoba" is elucidated by KURIYAMA thus:

By naming kotoba, Bashō inherited the tradition of haikai, namely, the application of *haigon* (haikai diction) which includes the vocabulary rejected by the waka-renga tradition such as colloquialism, Sino-Japanese words[64], Buddhistic terminology, and so on.

His designation of *haigon* as one *part* of poeticalness can be regarded as his intention, which strove for the establishment of the aesthetics of ordinariness, opposing that of elegance in waka and renga. He does not, however, accept every single word without conditions. As he states that "It is haikai's virtue to correct colloquialism" or "to employ colloquialism with good taste", he demands a high criterion ...

The second element is "kokoro":

> In the second ... [Bashō recognized] the unconventional intention [as a form of haiku-poeticalness]. In such a nonconformist contemplation beyond any conventional scheme he attempted to find the satisfaction of human life.

The third element is the "prosodic intention":

> In the third, he exemplified an unusual technique of linking verse - to answer with an irregular wakiku to the unconventional hokku ... This is an example of Bashō's sharp sense of spontaneous witticism.

It is quite apparent, KURIYAMA affirms (ibid.), that this passage in *Sanzōshi* elucidates *the poeticalness of haikai* (haiku), and furthermore, the fact that it is a "refined variation" of Kiyosuke's trichotomy exposition unmistakably points to a close relationship between the trimodal poeticalness advocated by KOCH and that of Bashō:

KOCH	BASHŌ
aesthetic poeticalness	prosodic intention
stylistic poeticalness	kotoba (words, diction)
informational poeticalness	kokoro (mind, heart)

This rapport suggested above demands, however, further discussion, for Japanese conceptions nurtured in the long tradition of poetics overlap to some extent with one another. We will now examine this problem.

do not pay attention to this point; it is, however,
extremely important [for the learners of haikai to
bear it in mind].

What Bashō had in mind in this preachment seems to concern exactly what contemporary, especially Prague School semioticians have investigated under the rubric of "literariness", i.e., "that which makes of a given work a work of art (ERLICH 1965: 172, cf. MUKAŘOVSKY 1976: 4-9). KURIYAMA (1973: 604) explains that Bashō's poetics differed from that of his contemporaries in that he recognized that what makes poetry is not "poetic diction" (" 稚語 ") but its function "of elevating vulgar expressions to poetic expressions". It is "watchfulness", or "focalization" as we might say in the context of this study (0.3.5.3), that makes poetry poetry, or art art (cf. ERLICH, 81). Bashō's admonition, stated above, to ignore the difference between poetic and non-poetic diction and to "rectify" ordinary language, amply suggests his awareness of the "Einstellung" (JAKOBSON 1960: 356) that occurs in the composition of haiku. Along with the equivalent principle of poetic function discussed in the previous section, JAKOBSON (ibid.) offers us the following definition of "the poetic function of language", i.e., "poeticalness"[45]:

> The set (Einstellung) toward the MESSAGE as such,
> focus on the message for its own sake, is the POETIC
> function of language.

This autotelic mechanism of poetic function[46], which Bashō formulated in the same vein as the striving "to rectify non-poetic words", is JAKOBSON's elaboration of the Russian Formalists (HAWKES 1977: 62ff., cf. MATEJKA 1976: 267-84). JAKOBSON (1976: 174) emphasizes the "autonomy of the aesthetic function" operative in the domain of art. A verbal work "acquires poeticity", he ascertains (ibid.),

3.4.2.1 Aesthetic Poeticalness and Prosodic Intention

As was observed in connection with Ball's poem, in which phonological parallelism on the level of manifesta is explored to its extremes, the key notion of aesthetic poeticalness is the syntagmatization of paradigms in the level of manifesta (3.3.3). In his example, Bashō explains that he added a wakiku with abnormal character, that is, with the characteristic of waka, because the preceding verse, hokku, also had waka-like character. According to KURIYAMA (1972: 16), the waka-like feature of the two verses is the ending, '*keri*-stop' for the former and '*te*-stop' for the latter. The independence of hokku was fairly established by the time of Bashō: which is to say, hokku should stop, and not run on. '*Te*-stop', however, is the manifestum of so-called run-on lines and is, therefore, abnormal for hokku. To this '*te*-stop', Bashō juxtaposed a wakiku with '*keri*-stop' rendering the wakiku waka-like détente to the verse, which in its turn violates the normal haikai rule. Normally, wakiku would end with a noun-stop but not a 'keri-stop'. Thus, we observe the juxtaposition of two manifesta, '*te*-stop' and '*keri*-stop', on the ground that both share the identical cultural unit belonging to waka, i.e., both are paradigms as far as waka-features are concerned. Bashō's wakiku was thus syntagmatized to the hokku, since both constitute a paradigmatic relation because of their abnormality or deviation from the prescribed poetic norm.

It should be remembered, however, that Bashō's prosodic intention is meant more or less for haikai-poetry, and he is mainly concerned here with the witticism employed in a linkage technique, which is a slightly different matter from the aesthetic poeticalness of haiku per se (3.5.2).

3.4.2.2 Stylistic Poeticalness and Kotoba

Stylistic poeticalness is the provocation of a metalingual operation. The given signifier is matched to the appropriate, "culturally defined and distinguished" signified, i.e., to cultural units or sememes. Bashō assures us that

(i) "a willow in the spring rain" = renga (elegance) and
(ii) "a crow picking up mud-snails" = haikai (humor, unconventionality).

Bashō seemingly refers to the *incompatibility* observed in (ii), which is lacking in (i).

Let us first consider why (i) is "as a whole renga". (i) contains two manifesta 'willow' and 'spring rain', both of which share sememes such as /grace/, /elegance/, /melancholy/, /sensitivity/, etc. (cf. MIYAMORI 1956). Both belong to waka-diction, whose tradition aimed to be aristocratic and elegant (cf. BROWER/MINER 1961). The two are perfectly *compatible* in terms of the level of the signifier, as well as in terms of the level of the intertextual cultural unit, i.e., poetry equals /elegance/. (ii), on the other hand, is *incompatible* with both levels. The word "crow" could appear as a poetic subject, although the more common birds poetically dealt with were /nightingale/, /cuckoo/, /plover/, or /duck/ (MIYAMORI, ibid.). Thus, employing these conventional birds means on the one hand that an association, i.e., a metalingual operation is guaranteed, and on the other hand that the poetry is charged with informational poeticalness. Conversely, if a poet employs the manifestum 'karasu', juxtaposed to such unpoetic - in view of the poetic tradition - activities as "picking up mud-snails", this proves that the metalingual operation has taken place,

since such an unusual combination must be organized
into the network of cultural units (ECO 1976: 73ff.).
While the juxtaposition of one signifier less common
and the other absolutely new thus presents the *incompatibility* within the sentence, it simultaneously exhibits
the incompatibility between the sentence "crow picking
up mud-snails" and the concept of poetry. As Fig. 41
shows, "crow picking up mud-snails" is an asymmetrical
unit (●) against the background of the whole gamut of
traditional poetics (○), i.e., *kotoba* in haikai possesses a high potential for "innovation":

⎡○ traditional poetic diction   → cliché

⎣● non-poetic diction
    "crow-picking up mud-snails"   → innovation

Fig. 41: The Provocation of Asymmetry through Kotoba

At this point, however, a question arises: Why can such
expressions as "crow picking up mud-snails" acquire such
a positive potential, and why at the time of Bashō but
not before? This "innovation" is due to the general trend
of the poetogenesis (KOCH 1983: 281ff., also 4.2.1) of
Japan: at this point the metagenetic direction dominated
due to the influence of Zen Buddhism, i.e., poetry no
longer strove for symmetry but rather for asymmetry. As
we saw in the previous chapter, however, the innovation
of Bashō discussed here was brought about through his
Weltanschauung, which *focalized* the *particular* in nature.
Thus Bashō's kotoba as one of three haikai elements is
strongly imbued with informational poeticalness, though
metalingual poeticalness is, as shown above, dominant.

3.4.2.3 Informational Poeticalness and Kokoro

KURIYAMA's analysis (3.4.2) has already revealed that
Bashō found his satisfaction in being unconventional.
The literary critic KUBOTA Harutsugu (1968: 253-4) explains that Bashō was unsuccessful in the mundane world;
because of this, the poet turned to anti-pragmatism
(cf. PILGRIM 1977, UEDA 1970):

> For Bashō "fūga" (" 風雅 " = poetry) meant a faint
> light which was caught by the desperate eye of the
> person who had failed in becoming a social climber
> as a samurai (warrior), and in pursuing the then pre-
> vailing Zen Buddhism as a monk.

Bashō himself wrote about his being engaged in this "use-
less" poetry in "Saimon no Kotoba" (A Leavetaking
at Saimon) (1969: 542)[65]:

> My fūga is just like the stove in summer or a fan in
> winter (" 夏炉冬扇 "). It is exactly opposite to what
> normal people strive after, and it is of no use.

Bashō is quick, however, to encourage Kyoroku, to whom he
gave this writing, to pursue "the way of poetry"
(ibid.). This apparent paradox - his concession of
the uselessness of haikai poetry on the one hand, and his
simultaneous encouragement of its pursuit - is interpreted
by KUBOTA (ibid., 254) as the philosophy of life necessary
to succeed in an "exodus" from a world in which the paramount principle is "usefulness" or "serviceability":

> The attempt to live as a hermit or in seclusion in the
> forest or deep in the mountains is nothing but the exodus
> by those who no longer could endure the "ordinary life"
> in the mundane world whose principle is that of "pragmatism".

Let us quote once again the hokku which Bashō refers to as the poem of kokoro[66]:

(14) 五月雨に 鳰の浮巣を見にゆかん
Samidare ni / nio no ukisu o / mini-yukan
(In the early summer rain/ to see the floating nest of the grebe/ I will go)

"The floating nest of the grebe" was, affirms HORI (1972: 111), an often-used theme in waka as a symbol of /transitoriness/, /uncertainty/ or /instability/ of destiny[67]. The nests in the Biwa Lake in the vicinity of Kyōto were the most famous. The manifestum 'nio no ukisu', thus seems itself to retain a mediation, which was, however, not an innovation of Bashō. The tiny nest of the grebe survives in spite of the harshness of nature and thus became the potential for a *metaphysical identification* similar to the flowers of the Neanderthals in Shanidar, as mentioned above.

In addition to this mediation, we can observe two other mediations, which are expressed through "in the middle of early summer rain, I feel like going to Biwa Lake" to see the floating nest, the lake being located at a distance of over 500 kilometers. The "unerträgliche Oppositionen" encoded in the poem seem to be two-fold: (i) incessant rain[68] vs. poet's desire to go outside, and (ii) grebe's floating nest vs. travel on foot to see it, whereby the last sememe /travelling to see it/ functions as the mediations involved here: (1) /floating nest of the grebe/, (2) /travelling/ and (3) /travelling to go to the Biwa Lake to see the grebe's floating nest/:

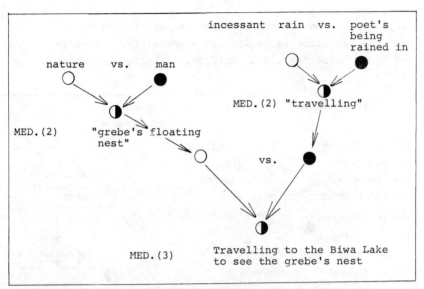

Fig. 42
Three mediations in the hokku (14)

In the following we will observe how each mediation originates. As has already been mentioned, 'nio no ukisu' was a well-versed theme in waka poetry. The reason why the "floating nest of the grebe" possesses such a symbolic value might be explained as in Fig. 43. Man observed the opposition of macrocosmic nature and a microcosmic floating nest of the grebe, the latter being at the mercy of the former. Nonetheless, the tiny, fragile thing on the lake survives, and co-exists with the macrocosm. This perception is organized semantically in the observer's mind as being *analogous*, or metaphorically identical, in JAKOBSON's sense (cf. HOLENSTEIN 1975: 152), to his own fragile existence in nature, and his existence despite this fragility is a consolation for his initial dilemma: nature vs. man. This mediatory mode, then, can be described as "introjection" in KOCH's classification (3.4.1.3), for the natural phenomenon is taken as such with little intervention of "I". This mode

of introjection is most frequent, especially in Zen-
infused classical haiku. It was a prevailing conception
of " 自得 " (self-satisfaction, self-fulfilment) (HORI
1972: 112).

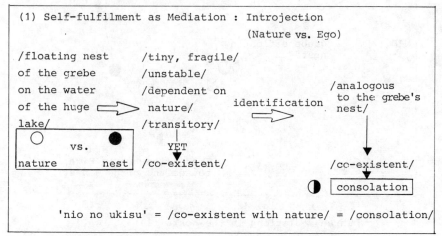

Fig. 43
The Mediation of Introjection

While the first mediation can be called an example of
"introjection", which differs radically from, say, Brooke's
"I"-insisting mediation (projection), the second mediation
can be called "projection" insofar as the poet's ego is
necessary for mediation, though not to the degree of
Brooke's projection. The mediation here, however, seems
to require a slight modification, for it involves the conversion of established cultural units, or, the reorganisation
of them, which Bashō denoted as "oddity" or "craziness"
(1687: 311). The incessant rainfall during the rainy season (from May to the beginning of July) was a traditional
poetic theme for /depression/, /melancholy/, /resigned des-
pair/, etc.[69] The traditional poet, then, at any rate, stayed
indoors, philosophizing on his inner emotion. On this conven-

tion, Bashō, so to speak, turns the tables, thinking
about exactly the opposite, i.e., going out in the
middle of the rain. Thus, cultural units of /samidare/
including the poetical convention (/inactive/, melancholic/
etc.) as well as social convention (/indoors/, /avoiding
getting wet/, etc.) are invalidated or converted so that
the opposite (the principle of antipragmatism) becomes a
valid credo. This transfiguration, however, is frequently seen as a "return to nature", as ICHIKAWA (NGS 1958:
xiv) asserts:

> [For Bashō, to travel meant to] seek relief from the
> cares of the world and escape into solitude, which
> enabled him to devote himself to the contemplation of
> nature and the pursuit of beauty.

One of his five travel diaries *Oku no Hosomichi* ("The
Narrow Path in the Northern Provinces": 1694), testifies to
his inclination for travelling (NGS 1958: xiv):

> Many ancient bards died during their travels. In years
> past I wanted to wander like a cloud blown by the
> wind ... I wander through distant provinces, having
> no thought for my life and meditating upon the
> evanescence of all things. If I die by the roadside,
> I shall consider it to be the will of Heaven.

/Travelling/, accordingly, is a projectional mediation,
which, as in this case, is often coupled with the conversion
of conventional cultural units: instead of /being at home,
staying comfortably dry/, Bashō values /going out, getting
wet/, which is in its turn the unification with nature.
Let us call this specific type of projective mediation,
fūkyō-mediation, "poetry-crazed"-mediation (cf. HAMMITZCH
1953: 5). Fig. 44 shows why Bashō's unconventionality is
characterized as the projectional mediation resulting in
the conversion of cultural units.

The third mediation (cf. Fig. 62) takes place between the
two above-mentioned mediatory sememes: /grebe-nest/ on
the one hand, and /travelling/ on the other, at the same
time that "early summer rain" reinforces the constellation of
"Nature": Nature would be consoling, for it presents
the poet with the scenery of the floating nest (Mediation 1), but it is now raining. The poet reacts to this
by travelling not to the near-by lake but to the far-
distant famous Biwa Lake, whose grebe's nests are also
famous. Therefore, the mediation here is quite similar
to the mediation (2), whose conversion is this time
"walking over 500 kilometers" in addition to "travelling".
As a matter of fact, this type of mediation, i.e., projection with the conversion of cultural conventions, plays
quite an important role. As is seen above, to be "odd",
"crazy", "unconventional", is one of his attempts not to
"collapse totally", as KUBOTA puts it (1968: 208ff.).

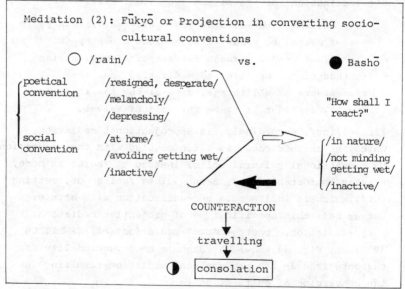

Fig. 44: The Mediation of Fūkyō in Projection

Bashō's haiku poetry is no doubt the product of the
mentality which he inherited: from native Shintōism, he
received animism and simplicity; from mingled Taoism and
Buddhism, the oneness of all natural life; from Confucianism, "sobriety, reserve, brevity and pithiness", as
BLYTH expounds (1949)[70]. BROWER/MINER observe that the
lack of "dualism" is in fact the definite point that
differentiates the oriental culture from the occidental (1961: 8):

> [A sophisticated and philosophical concept of the
> oneness of all natural life] gives what we call
> eternal nature a closeness and relevance to human
> nature that is not found in Western cultures, shaped
> as they are by various dualisms between spirit and
> matter, man and nature, and life and death.

KUBOTA (163ff.) also argues along this line in his study
of Satō Haruo (1892-1964), a poet-novelist of the Meiji
and Taishō Eras:

> Fūryū [similar to fūga: in the broader sense, poetry]
> is characterized by adoring [the pathetic sorrow
> for the minuteness of human beings in contrast to the
> infinity of nature], instead of rationalizing it ...
> [This] means that our ancestors attempted to turn
> back to the bosom of the Infinite, contrary to other
> nations that attempted to confront it with the very
> recognition of the minuteness of man ... [To try to
> be embraced in the arm of nature] was understood
> as a return to nature ... Thus even death was interpreted as going back to the place where one came from.
> Consequently, nature became a dear domicile ... instead of threatening.

3.5 Dyads in Classical Haiku

The foregoing discussion has emphasized the relevance of a trifocal approach in haiku analysis. One of the recurring themes concerning the structure of haiku is the *principle* of *dyad*, or *paradigm*, or *povtor* (3.3.4). LOTMAN states (cited in SHUKMAN, 54): "Juxtaposition (opposing and identifying), while being the principle of the structure's organization, is also the operational principle for its analysis". In what follows, I shall scrutinize the poetic principle of *dyad* as it is concretized in the classical haiku of Bashō. The text-corpus for this discussion is Bashō's haiku for two reasons: first, his poetry presents the widest spectrum out of which later haiku evolved, and second, several versions for one and the same haiku are often recorded, which provides useful insights into the process of gradual improvement through repeated production.

3.5.1 The Aesthetic Poeticalness of Classical Haiku

The aesthetic poeticalness of haiku can be analysed in terms of five major points: (i) rhythm, (ii) phonology, (iii) onomatopoeia, (iv) orthography, and (v) presentation. We will examine these aspects in this order.

3.5.1.1 Rhythm

As is often stated, haiku takes the syllabic pattern of 5-7-5 as its standard form. The long-lived existence of this pattern has been shown with regard to the historical accounts in Fig. 32. It is a challenging question as to why this form, but not some other - e.g., 5-7-7, or 5-7, or 7-7, all of which were being composed during the

Nara Period, though in longer concatenations - was
adopted for haiku form. It would be expedient for us to
say that Bashō, who purged haiku of every obvious arti-
ficialness[71], saw no artificial element in the form
of 5-7-5, because by the time of Bashō this pattern had
a millenium of tradition behind it, and in fact YASUDA
(1957: 108) asserts this. Yet, the deep-rootedness of
the "poetic instinct of man and the inner necessity of
realizing it aesthetically" (ibid.) is, as we saw
(3.4.1.1), far "deeper" than the ancient tradition. To
use the specific rhythm of the alternation of 5- and
7-syllable lines is, BROWER/MINER (1961: 58) assure us
actually "the later [type of] composition or revisions"
of the compilers of Man'yōshū (ca. 759). Indeed, at the
beginning of this century, 200 years after Bashō, the so-
called avant-garde haiku poets discarded this pattern as
a "man-made rule" (UEDA 1976: 9).

In seeking an answer to this question, KURIYAMA (1972:
10) turns to the "theory of walking rhythm"[72]. His assertion is quite suggestive in that it points out "the deep-
rootedness" of the rhythm - the rhythm for bipeds. His
proposition that haiku has the rhythm of "4-beats, 3 measures"[73] demands, however, a further investigation which
is beyond the scope of the present study. Suffice it to
mention that semiotics has been quite successful in discovering aesthetic instincts - pictorial, musical, architectural - embedded in animals in general (SEBEOK 1979:
35-60). In the light of such zoosemiotic investigations,
it is hard to believe that the ancient language of Japan
prior to Man'yōshū might have lacked a "prosodic sense",
as BROWER/MINER (ibid.) suggest[74]. We have practically
no means of answering this question, since no records
exist.

One of the faint clues available, however, may be
the fact that the bulk of the basic vocabulary of
the Japanese language is bisyllabic, as the German
Japanologist, Bruno LEWIN (1959: 33) affirms. LEWIN
also affirms that "die japanischen Postpositionen sind
in ihrer Mehrzahl ein- oder zweisilbige Enklitika (z.B.,
no, wo, ka, made, namu)" (ibid., 102). Thus, the most
frequent syllabic combination results in three or four
syllables, and it is therefore in accordance with the
assertion made by BROWER/MINER (ibid.) that the "shorter
lines [are] made up of as few as three syllables". The
combination of two such phrases would result in either
six or seven, which would approximate the middle line.
It is, however, no more than a guess: at this point it
should suffice to note that this rhythm may be focussed
upon in future semiotic research.

The Japanese language does not play with rhyme-schemes
or metric schemes as much as European languages do. This
is due to the fact that the language has no consonantal
clusters, which is a prerequisite for rhyme-schemes, nor
does it have stress accent, a prerequisite for metric
systems. Although it possesses a system of tonal accent[75],
it seems to have been too weak to constitute a definite
pattern. Accordingly, the minimal prosodic unit is a
mora, consisting either of (i) one vowel, (ii) one consonant with a short vowel, or (iii) one nasal consonant
/n/ (LEWIN ibid.: 33). The number of morae is the sole
feature in prosody. BROWER/MINER (ibid.), too, assert
that the "two groupings of line" can be detected in
"amorphous" primitive songs. We can obtain the following
alternatives haiku could have had from the prevailing form
of renga:

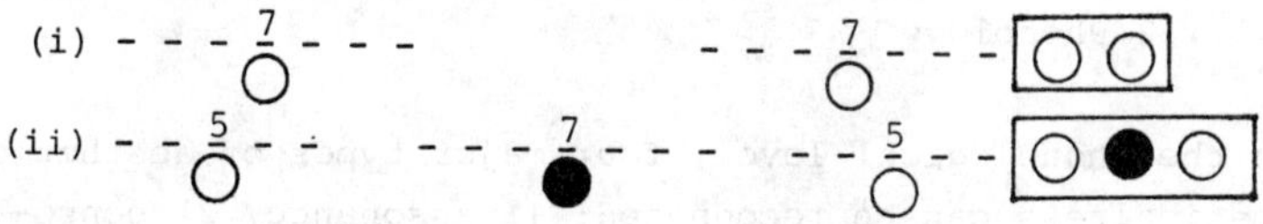

(i) - - - $\frac{7}{\text{O}}$ - - -   - - - $\frac{7}{\text{O}}$ - - - $\boxed{\text{O O}}$

(ii) - - $\frac{5}{\text{O}}$ - -   - - - $\frac{7}{\bullet}$ - - -   - - $\frac{5}{\text{O}}$ - - $\boxed{\text{O} \bullet \text{O}}$

Haiku decided in favor of (ii) perhaps for two major reasons. Firstly, it can thus present a most reduced narrative structure, as is exemplified in the notion "subject, theme, predicate" (" 序破急 ") elucidated by ASANO (1962: 173ff.). Similarly, William H. COHEN (1965: 224) perceived in haiku a structure of three steps: the first element, then an opposing element, and the last line as a "punch line". BLYTH (1956: 23-5), too, detects some "syllogistic" nature in this tertiary structure, though he emphasizes the absence of discursive reasoning in it. Ian REID (1977: 6), in his study of the structure of the short story, remarks that the frequency of a tripartite sequence, which is most prototypically manifested in Aristotele's "beginning - middle - end" as a plot, "seems to support the idea that a deep-rooted aesthetic preference is behind it" (4.2.3). Secondly, the principle of informational asymmetry seems to govern the form: instead of even numbers of syllables, there are odd numbers; instead of an even number of lines, there is an odd number. The standard form of haiku, then, presents a *triad*, which indeed seems to be internally motivated, i.e., the process of /symmetry-asymmetry-integration/ is reflected[76].

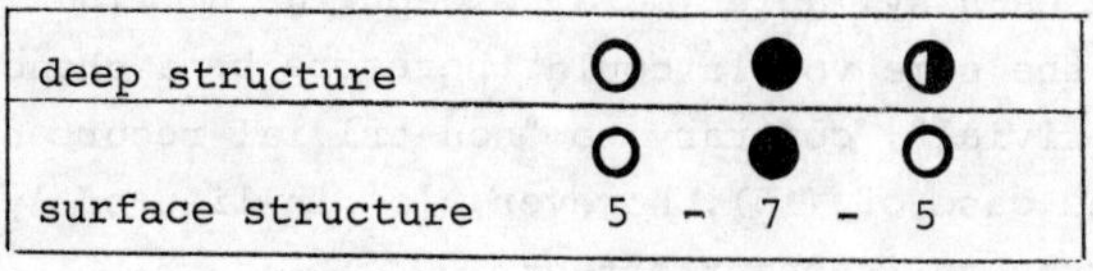

deep structure	O	●	O
surface structure	5	- 7 -	5

Fig. 45: The Triadic Structure of Haiku Form

3.5.1.2 Phonology

On the phonological level, four major types of aesthetic poeticalness can be recognized: 1) assonance, 2) conscnance, 3) rhyme, and 4) alliteration.

The poems (15) and (16) are variants, the difference being the postposition: (15), 'yuku haru *ya*' and (16), 'yuku haru *o*'. The two can exemplify the *assonance* of haiku.

(15) 行春や近江の人とおしみける   (A 333)
Yuku haru ya / Ōmi no hito to / oshimikeru
(The departing spring!/ the people in Ōmi as well as/ I regretted)

(16) 行春を近江の人とおしみける
Yuku haru o / Ōmi no hito to / oshimikeru
(The departing spring/ the people in Ōmi as well as/ I regretted

IMOTO (1972: 199) recounts that Bashō changed the kireji 'ya' of the first version (15) into 'o', which changes the syntax: in the first version, "the departing spring" is separated from the rest of the poem, while in the second version it is the direct object of the verb "regret". In addition to the structural change mentioned above, the change seems due to the assonant effect produced by 'o'. As is already mentioned, Japanese has only five vowels which occur in each syllable (mora) except in "n". The recurrence of the same vowels could therefore be a chance product, or "trivial", contrary to "non-trivial recurrences" (3.4.1). In the case of (15), however, 'o' in lieu of 'ya' definitely causes an assonant effect.

The next haiku (17) exemplifies *consonance*.

(17) ひばりなく 中の拍子や 雉子の声   (A 256)
    Hibari na<u>k</u>u / na<u>k</u>a no hyōshi ya /<u>k</u>iji no <u>k</u>oe
    (Among the singing larks/keeps good time/the
    call of the pheasant

Dohō (ibid., 564) explains that Bashō finally decided on the present version after many attempts to "express the call of the pheasant in the middle of the skylark's singing, as if it were keeping good time with the music – similar to the orchestra of Nō-theater". The call of the pheasant is heard as [ke:n][77], and the recurring /k/ seems to represent the scene Bashō attempted to express. Concerning the cry of the pheasant, we can find the "non-trivial recurrence" of this voiceless linguavelar in other haiku as well[78], and we can thus see that the poem has an onomatopoeic effect.

The haiku (18) is an example of a haiku by Bashō with a rhyme-scheme:

(18) 能なしの寝たし我をぎょうぎょうし   (A 378)
    Nōna<u>shi</u> no / numeta<u>shi</u> ware o / gyōgyō<u>shi</u>
    (I, a good-for-nothing/ and just sleepy/ yet, that
    noisy bird!)

According to conventional grammar, 'nemuta<u>shi</u>' ought to be 'nemuta<u>ki</u>', but because of the two other 'shi's, the ungrammatical 'nemuta<u>shi</u>' is employed (IMOTO in NKBS 1972: 220).

The next three haiku, (19), (20), (21), all present alliteration, the syntagma of /*ishi*/ and /*ishi*/.

(19) 石山の石より白し 秋の風   (A 304)
    <u>Ishi</u>yama no/ <u>ishi</u> yori shiroshi /aki no kaze
    (Whiter than the stones of Ishiyama-temple!/
    the autumn wind)
                        Ishiyama=lit. stone-mountain

(20) 石山の石にたばしるあられ哉 (A 358)
Ishiyama no/ ishi ni tabashiru /arare kana
(On the stones of Ishiyama-temple are hammering/
hailstones!)

(21) 菊の花 咲や石屋の石の間 (A 425)
Kiku no hana / saku ya ishiya no / ishi no ai
(The chrysanthemum/ is blooming: between the stones
of a stone-shop)

By the repetition of the sibilant /ʃ/, the signifier emphasizes the harshness of the stone ("*ishi*"). At the same time, however, this alliteration is linked with informational poeticalness. In (21), e.g., we find Bashō's awe at discovering the chrysanthemum among the lifeless "stones of a stone-shop". The expression "*ishiya*(ma) no *ishi*" is an example of what KOCH (1983: 241ff.) terms a *modal knot*. A modal knot is a *coordination of different poetical modes* (ibid.). Obviously, the manifesta realized in the alliteration of '*ishi*' combine aesthetic and informational poeticalness in that the coldness ([19]), hardness ([20]), or lifelessness ([21]) of stones as natural objects can be expressed more effectively.

As has already been mentioned, Bashō rather limited this type of poeticalness. In fact it seems that Bashō would rather have preferred "Awful Harry" or "I vote for Eisenhower" to "Horrible Harry" or "I like Ike", the famous examples of JAKOBSONian poeticalness (1960: 356). "Akazōshi" (Red Booklet), the second of *Sanzōshi* (Three Booklets), relates that Bashō changed the second segment of one haiku "*zan*mu *zan*getsu" (" 残夢残月 " = residual dream, residual moon) to "*zan*mu tsukitoshi" (" 残夢月遠し " = residual dream, the moon afar) on the ground that there was too much "chiming", to borrow Hopkin's parlance, in the first version, "which is not good" (Dohō, 554). Numerous other accounts[79] make us suppose that this change is due to his credo: poetry must

be free from any artificiality. Some prosodical devices
that can be regarded as prerequisites for occidental
poetry, such as rhyme or excessive alliteration, should
be avoided, according to Bashō: when the poet focuses his
attention on the external features of the words - which
Jakobson was eager to analyse - "artificiality" sets in,
destroying the poetry. His avoidance of the repetition of
'*zan*' seems due to the foreignness of the voiced sound
in the initial position of a word. As LEWIN asserts, the
native Japanese language did not have voiced consonants
in initial position (1959: 32). Due to the influence of
Chinese phonology, however, an adaption began to take
place during the Heian Period. At the time of Bashō, some
seven centuries later, the voiceless sound still seems
to have been preferred to the voiced, as *Sanzōshi* reports:
"Concerning the 'clean and muddy sounds' [i.e., the voiceless and the voiced, respectively], to pronounce the muddy
as the clean is accepted: to pronounce the clean as the
muddy is vulgar" (Dohō; 611).

Although Bashō thus rejected too much "chiming", he
was by no means unaware of haiku-cadence. Kyorai testifies
(ibid., 502):

> As for versification, there is "sound effect" ("語路").
> It denotes "verse-flow" ("句走リ"). It is somehow ana-
> logous to a ball rolling on the board; that is to say,
> sound effect is at its best when there is no stagnation.
> It is also analogous to a willow-tree being gently blown
> by a breeze. To possess such gentleness or elegance ("優")
> is also valuable ...

Akutagawa Ryūnosuke (1892-1927), a literary genius, finds
haiku euphony in the following haiku by Bashō (KUBOTA, 241):

(22) 秋深き 隣は何をする人ぞ　　　　　　　　470)
Aki fukaki / tonari wa nani o / suru hito zo
(The autumn is deep/ how is the neighbor/ making
a living?)

In Akutagawa's opinion, Bashō is the "sole figure capable
of procuring such a solemn euphony in the three hundred
years of haiku history" (KUBOTA 1968: 241). "Musical elements" heard by Akutagawa, then, seem far more subtle than
obvious "syntagmatized paradigms"; Akutagawa must have
fully activated his aesthetic poeticalness in recognizing
this.

3.5.1.3 Onomatopoeic *Gion-go* and Mimetic *Gitai-go*

In addition to the rhythmic pattern and the phonological
repetition, haiku often employs "*lautmalende Wörter*"
(LEWIN 1959: 4) or onomatopoeic expressions that can be
described as the manifestation of aesthetic as well as
stylistic poeticalness. The onomatopoeic expressions of
Japanese can be categorized into two groups: *gion-go*
("sound-imitating words") and *gitai-go* ("state-expressing
words"). Gitai-go, or mimetic words, are a kind of expression in which "things or events which do not result
in sound are expressed through sound" (ASANO/KINDAICHI
1979: 19ff.). Gion-go, the onomatopoeia proper, can most
typically be exemplified in the repetition of the linguavelar stop /k/, imitating the pheasant cry heard as /ke:n/
in the poem (17) discussed above. According to ECO (1976:
227), "full onomatopoeias", i.e., "realistic reproductions of a given sound by a human voice or other instrument", can be categorized in terms of sign-production as
the combination of "ostention" and "replicas". ECO (ibid.)
thus terms the English example of "/thunder/" as "onomatopoeic stylization".

Gitai-go mimics "things or events" which do not have
any sound through verbal sounds. For instance, if a
Japanese wishes to depict the way a firefly flies, i.e.,
"waveringly", "unsteadily", "unpredictably", "discon-
tinuously", "fluctuatingly", "vibratingly", "unquietly",
etc., he uses "*yurari yurari to*", to cite SUZUKI's
(1959: 234) example. As is seen in translation, where
English employs an adverb, which is based on the more
"abstract way of thinking", both the Chinese and the
Japanese use sounds which "appeal more to the feeling
than to the intellect" - a fact leading SUZUKI to
assert that "the Easterners live closer to the pristine
experiences of reality" than the Westeners who are
used to their "systems of analysis and abstractions"
(SUZUKI ibid.). Gitai-go, then , is an onomatopoeic mimesis.
Let us now take the following example from Bashō:

(20) ほろほろと 山吹ちるか 滝の音　　　　　　　(A 214)
　　　Horo-horo to / yamabuki chiruka / taki no oto
　　　(Continuously/ the yellow-rose is falling!/the
　　　roar of the water-fall.)

"*Horo-horo to*" is a gitai-go: it describes the way the
petals of the yellow rose are falling, i.e., in succession,
quietly, slowly, etc. It is "onomatopoeic stylization", since
it belongs to the Japanese language, just as the word "thunder" belongs to the repertoire of English. The signified
of this manifestum '*horo-horo*' is explained by ASANO (ASANO/
KINDAICHI ibid., 629) as

   the states in which small and feathery things are
   noiselessly falling one by one [...] When only one piece
   falls, "horo" [instead of the reduplicative "horo-horo"]
   is used. A similar expression is "hara-hara".

It is very illuminating to note that the manifesta of
this type of onomatopoeia, gitai-go, are evidently moti-

vated by the impressions that certain sounds can elicit.
KINDAICHI (ibid., 20), a noted Japanologist, demonstrates
the correlation between the manifesta and the signified
of gitai-go. Some of the examples are as follows:

(i)   /i/ : things with velocity, opposed to /a/ or /o/
(ii) voiced as /g/, /z/, /d/, /b/: something blunt,
      heavy, big, dirty
(iii) voiceless: something sharp, light, tiny, beautiful
(iv) /h/: sophisticated and noble
(v)   /p/: vulgar and unrefined

Significantly enough, the opposition of the negative and
the positive connotation observed in (ii) and (iii) is
mirrored in the phonological opposition of the voiced and
the voiceless. This might very well be related to the
Japanese unfamiliarity[80] with the voiced, as we saw in
Bashō's avoiding the repetition of /zan/. It should also
be noted that onto- and phylogenetically the voiced is
marked against the voiceless, i.e., the voiceless is the
primum ($\bigcirc$) over the voiced ($\bullet$), as JAKOBSON clarifies
(1941: 95ff., 1.2).

Japanese onomatopoeic expressions can be either a single
tone, as in "*horo*", "*niko*", or "*nita*" when the occurrence
takes place only once, or they can be "reduplicative" (cf.
SUZUKI 1959: 234), as in "*horo-horo*", "*niya-niya*", or
"*hāhaha*", when the occurrence is repeated. Although in
the former the aesthetic poeticalness fails to be a non-
trivial recurrence, in both cases the P_{xe} is forced to recapitulate the immediateness between the manifestum and
the signified. The employment of gitai-go and gion-go in
haiku poetry thus becomes autometically a *styleme*. In
poem (23), therefore, "*horo-horo*" and "the roar of the
water-fall" are opposed to each other.

Hirose Izen (?-1711), a friend and disciple of Bashō, seems to have exploited the potential of onomatopoeia to an excessive degree. Take the following two haiku dealing with the theme of water-birds:

(24) 水鳥や むかふの岸へ つういつうい (B 403)
    Mizutori ya / mukō no kishi e /tsūi-tsūi
    (Water-bird!/to the bank beyond /gliding)

(25) 水さっと 鳥よふはふは ふうはふは
    Mizu satto / tori yo fuwa-fuwa / fūwa-fuwa
    (Water's flash / a bird! buoyantly/ buoyantly)

The last segment of the first haiku describes the water-bird gliding on the surface of the water towards the other side of the shore. In the second, the onomatopoeia dominates the whole poem: there are only two nouns, "water" and "bird", and the rest is onomatopoeia. Understandably enough, Izen was accused of "lacking kokoro" by his contemporaries (KURIYAMA 1972: 186)[81] and enjoyed little renown (MUKAI: 471). Kyorai reproached Izen for his extremeness which "is not haikai-poetry at all" (ibid.). The haiku Kyorai gave as an example is the following:

(26) うめの花 赤いは赤いはあかいはな (B 396)
    Ume no hana / akai wa akai wa / akai wa na
    (The plum-blossoms!/ oh, how red, how red/ how red!)

The non-trivial recurrence of (23) is quite conspicuous: "akai wa" (they are red) is repeated three times! Presumably, Izen was too avant-gardistic for his contemporaries. Had Izen composed the same hokku two centuries later, he might have been recognized more. At least he would have found an ally in Hara Gesshū (1919), who composed the following haiku consisting of only one noun and the rest gion-go, mimicking an autumn insect:

(27) リリリリリ チチリリリチチ リリと虫   (Gesshū)
Ri ri ri ri ri / chi chi ri ri ri chi chi / ri ri to mushi
(Ri-ri-ri-ri-ri/chi-chi-ri-ri-ri-ri-chi-chi/ ri-ri, thus an insect)[82]

3.5.1.4 Orthography

The orthographical uniqueness of Japanese also plays an important role in terms of text-production and subsequently in aesthetic poeticalness. In emphasizing the importance of orthography BLYTH (1964: 7) states:

> Nowadays, most Japanese can with difficulty understand a spoken haiku. Written in Chinese and Japanese characters it is grasped by the eye rather than by the ear or mouth.

Japanese orthography knows three types of writing system: (1) ideographic "kanji" (Chinese characters); (ii) phonetic "hiragana" (cursive characters); and (iii) "katakana" (square-form characters). Every haiku poet - for the matter, every Japanese - meticulously chooses one of these alphabets in order to express himself most appropriately. IMOTO (1972: 165-6), e.g., gives an example in which Bashō chose to sign his name in hiragana, since hiragana is dominant in the poem. BLYTH's assertion, furthermore, supports the idea of the right-hemisphericity of haiku poetry: it emphasizes *visual* rather than phonic aesthetic poeticalness (1.3.2), i.e., when read aloud or when presented in roman script, the phonetic aspect becomes dominant, and thus reading as an act of phonological mediation (2.3.2) belongs to the domain of the left hemisphere, whereas a written haiku with its "hieroglyphic" nature is handled by the right hemisphere, as IVANOV (1977: 34ff.) clarifies (1.3.2).

Although the orthographical option thus manifests aesthetic poeticalness, it also shows stylistic poeticalness at the

same time in some cases, for in choosing one specific kanji,
or Chinese character, the poet can allude to a specific
well-known poem. It is a technique well-established
and practised in Japanese poetry, as we will see in the
discussion on stylistic poeticalness. Such is the case
with the *kanji* " 横 " appearing in the poem:

(28) 郭公 声横たふや水の上 (A 418)
    Hototogisu / koe yokotau ya / mizu no ue
    (A cuckoo!/ his voice still lingering/ on the
    surface of the water.)

Dohō (553) recounts Bashō's intention of alluding to a
well-known Chinese verse, which was to be represented
through the *kanji* " 横 " (side, sideways), explaining
that this letter is "the eye of the whole poem" (ibid.).

Although the peculiarities of Japanese orthography could
thus provide us with a rich field for the analysis of poeticalness, this problem will not be discussed in further
detail, since our concentration with transliterated haiku
precludes consideration of the poet's sign-production.

3.5.1.5 Presentation

In order to emphasize the importance for the P_{xe} of a poem
of seeking a "unified interpretation" so that the poem "makes
sense" to him, CULLER (1975, 161-88) points to "the work
of the signifier's typographical characteristics" observed
in poetry in general (183-4):

The most obvious feature of poetry's formal organization is the division into lines and stanzas. The break
at the end of a line or the space between stanzas must
be accorded some kind of value, and one strategy is
to take poetic form as a mimesis: breaks represent

spatial or temporal gaps which can be thematized and
integrated with the poem's meaning[...] To read is[..] to
assume that typographic space reproduces a space in the world
or at least a gap in the mental processes[...] Poetry
of this sort[...] assumes that such procedures form
part of the institution of poetry.

CULLER's notion can be eloquently supported by the presentation of haiku (29) (Illustr. 12: SUZUKI 1959: Plate 48).
Bashō writes the 17-syllables as four lines - rather strange,
considering the normal practice of writing it in three lines
of 5, 7, and 5. The poem reads:

(29) 蓑虫の音を聞に 来よ 艸の庵 (A 172)
　　 Minomushi no / ne o kiki ni/koyo / kusa no io
　　 (To listen.to the cry/of a bagworm/ Come!/ the
　　 hut of grasses)

The second segment is divided into two, of which the latter
is an imperative, "Come!" The imperative is foregrounded
in that it is placed in the third indentation, and preceding
indentations show the gradual fall, this being the last and
the lowest. The movement thus produced is balanced by the
fourth segment, "the grass hut", Bashō's dwelling, whose
object is iconically represented in the lower space of the
paper as $haiga^{83}$ (an accompanying sketch-like picture of
haikai-haiku poetry). The typographical as well as the calligraphic aspect of the presentation of haiku-poetry is
thus super-imposed on the rhythmic pattern, inviting P_{xe}
to focalize the two poetical modes, aesthetic and systlistic.

Haiga (cf. STEWART 1960) is a phenomenon that accompanies
haiku-haikai poetry. The juxtaposition of two types of
art, one with verbal signs and the other with pictorial
signs, is *metaphorical*, i.e., of stylistic poeticalness, in
sofar as it provokes P_{xe} to seek the "common core" between

Illustr. 12: The Presentation of Haiku

verbal and pictorial presentation. As far as *stylization* is concerned, however, each juxtaposition may vary, as BLYTH states (1964a: xxvii):

> The writing and the picture may be the same in subject, or different, or distantly connected. The third is the best.

BLYTH's assertion that "the third is the best" implies
the distance between the "two electric poles" between
which "the spark will leap", to refer to KEENE again
(3.3.2), and reflects the warning of Kyorai that this
"leap" ought to be "moderate" (3.3.4). Illustr. 12 thus
presents a rather moderate "leap", since the haiga depicts
the "grass hut" in which Bashō dwelled. The investigation
of the relationship between the two types of the signifier
is in fact an extremely challenging theme which deserves
future investigation.

3.5.2 The Stylistic Poeticalness of Classical Haiku

The aesthetic poeticalness of haiku is manifested in the
triad of the syllabic pattern, 5-7-5, and the *dyad* of
phonological manifestations. The stylistic poeticalness of
haiku, a fruitful subject for investigation, can be divided into two categories; *synonymy* and *polysemy*. TODOROV
(1977: 22), in his study of the relation between language
and literature, ascertains that the absence of a one-to-
one relation between the sounds and the meaning, one of
language's essential properties, "gives rise to two well-
known linguistic phenomena", synonymy and polysemy. Synonymy
can be characterized as "the existence of two forms for the
same content", he states (ibid., 23). By the same token,
then, polysemy can be denoted as the existence of one form
for the two contents. In order to avoid the confusion of
such terms as form or content, let us employ manifestum for
the former and sememe for the latter in the sense already
defined (3.4.1). As should be clear, the first belongs to
the domain of the signifier and the latter to the domain
of the signified. Synonymy is then, "one sememe and two
manifesta", while polysemy is "two sememes and one manifestum".

Fig. 46 diagrams the structural characteristics of the two:

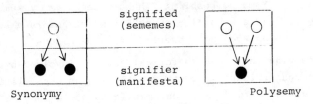

Fig. 46: Synonymy and Polysemy

Needless to say, the number of sememes or manifesta is not necessarily only two. Take, e.g., the sememe /improvement/ to illustrate synonymy. It has such manifesta as 'improvement', 'betterment', 'uplift', 'amelioration', 'good influence' etc., filling half a page in a thesaurus (DUTSCH 1962: 654). Polysemy, conversely, can be illustrated by the manifestum 'spring', a noun having at least five sememes; /a source of supply), /spring tide/, /one of the four seasons/, /an elastic body or device/, /the act of leaping/ (*Webster's* 1973: 1126).

The rhetorical figures of the Japanese poetic tradition which Bashō inherited and employed can be analysed in terms of the two well-known phenomena: 1) *engo* ("verbal association") and *hiyu* ("comparison") in terms of synonymy; and 2) *kigo* ("season word"), *kake-kotoba* ("pivot word"), and *honka-dori* ("allusive variations") in terms of polysemy (cf. BROWER/MINER 1957, 1961, MINER 1955, GIROUX 1974).

3.5.2.1 Synonymy: *Engo* or Verbal Associations

Verbal associations, *engo*, concatenate manifesta which stand in a metonymic relationship to their sememe within one poem. Let us take one poem by Matsunaga Teitoku (1571-1653), one of Bashō's precursors, for this technique was presumably too "artificial" for Bashō, and we can hardly find any illustrative examples in his anthology.

(30) 山の腰にはく夕だちや雲の帯 (B 18)
Yama no koshi ni / haku yūdachi ya / kumo no obi
(The mountain-around its waist/ wears a sword of
an evening shower!/ a sash of clouds!)

Ignoring the other rhetorical devices involved here[84], we
recognize four manifesta functioning as *engo*, literally,
"related words". All four manifesta are metonymically related to the sememe /the clothes of a samurai-warrior/:
'koshi' ("waist"), *'haku'* ("wear"), *'tachi'* ("sword")[85],
and *'obi'* ("sash"). The relationship between the sememe
and the four manifesta can thus be depicted:

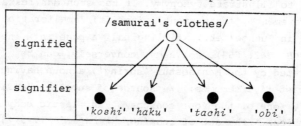

Fig. 47: *Engo* as Synonymy in (30)

In verbal associations, then, words belonging to a homogeneous field are syntagmatized, which effects a cluster
of imageries. This technique was found quite effective in
waka poetry as well as the Nō-play (FENOLLOSA/POUND 1916:
3-24, cf. POUND 1970: 94). The technique was, however,
doomed to lose its position in haiku poetry for two reasons: first, because it was considered to be too "artificial" (EBARA 1952: 68-81), and second, because haiku
chose, as we will see in the following section, polarization or *dyad*, as its guiding principle.

3.5.2.2 Synonymy: *Hiyu* or Comparison and *2-ku*, *1-shō*
through *Kireji*

The most typical morphology of haiku is *2-clauses and
1-statement* (ASANO 1962, 1963), as was mentioned in the

introduction to this study. We are now in a position to
scrutinize the morphology of haiku in terms of stylistic
poeticalness. Bashō's awareness of the importance of
juxtaposition has already been referred to: "Hokku is
made by combining things" (3.3.4). Let us consider the
haiku (31), which has been regarded as the landmark in
Bashō's establishment of this poetic genre[86]. It laid down
the standard for haiku in various respects, such as "allusive variation" (cf. NGS, 11) or "season word" (cf. YASUDA,
173). I shall concentrate on the structural properties
which constitute the essence of haiku.

(31) かれ朶に烏のとまりけり 秋の暮　　　　　　　　(A 43)
　　　Kare-eda ni / karasu no tomarikeri / a ki no kure
　　　(Upon a withered bough/ a crow has perched /
　　　autumn evening)

Kireji, literally "severing letter", designates either
the end of a haiku or a division within it (HENDERSON
1967: 18, cf. ASANO 1962, 1963). In this poem we have a
kireji, *keri*, at the end of the second segment. Still
another version of this haiku presenting another *kireji*,
ya, reads as follows (NKBZ 41: 61):

(32) 枯枝に烏のとまりたるや 秋の暮
　　　Kare-eda ni / karasu no tomaritaru ya / aki no kure

Such *keri* or *ya* is a linguistic manifestation whose regulation was recorded as early as the mid-thirteenth century
(ASANO 1939: 198). In emphasizing the function of kireji
or a caesura, ASANO (1962: 7ff.) classifies two types of
hokku which are cut by the practice of kireji: one,
1-ku, 1-shō ("one-verse, 1-statement"), and the other,
2-ku, 1-shō ("two-verses, one-statement"):

1) *1-ku, 1-shō*

$$\underbrace{\_\_5\_\_ \quad \_\_7\_\_ \quad \_\_5\_\_}_{\text{Independent Body}}\text{kireji} \qquad \begin{array}{c} 5+7+5 \\ \bigcirc \end{array}$$

2) $2-ku$, $1-sh\bar{o}$

a) $\underbrace{\underline{\quad 5\text{ kireji}}}_{\text{I.B.}}$ $\underbrace{\underline{\quad 7 \quad}\ \underline{\quad 5 \quad}}_{\text{I.B.}}$ $\quad$ 5 $\quad$ 7+5

$\qquad\qquad\qquad\qquad\qquad\qquad\qquad\quad\ \ $ ○ // ●

b) $\underbrace{\underline{\quad 5 \quad}\ \underline{\quad 7\text{ kireji}}}_{\text{I.B.}}$ $\underbrace{\underline{\quad 5 \quad}}_{\text{I.B.}}$ $\quad$ 5+7 $\quad$ 5

$\qquad\qquad\qquad\qquad\qquad\qquad\qquad\quad\ \ $ ○ $\quad$ ●

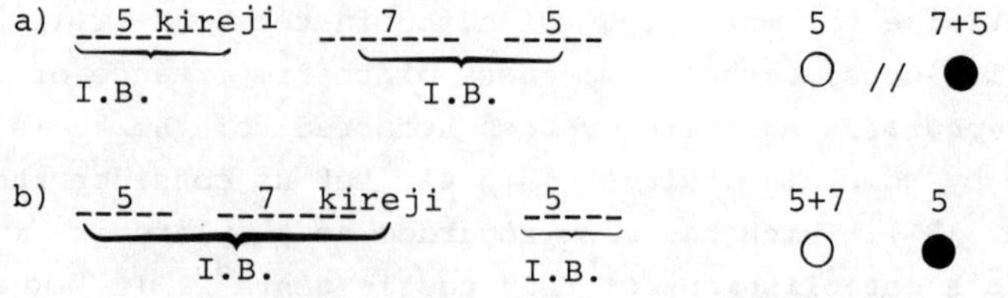

Fig. 48: The Morphological Classification
of Haiku in Terms of Kireji

"Independent-Body" is, ASANO expounds (ibid.), equal to
a "clause" in which "subject + verb" is expressed. In
order to clarify the meaning of "to cut" or "to sever",
ASANO (ibid.) annotates:

> To "cut" means the end of predication in a broad
> sense [...] i.e., the expression "The wind ... is
> cool" (subject + predicate) is cut at the end. This
> expression is normally called a "sentence". To use
> kireji means that one can express this "cutting"
> [without constructing a whole sentence]. "Akikaze
> ya" is equal to "Oh, the autumn wind is blowing!"

According to ASANO, then, the function of kireji lies in
the fact that it provides a poem with a structural separation while expressing simultaneously the poet's exuberant
feelings. Through the function of kireji, a poem which
expresses "one statement" as a whole is enabled to have
two "poles" in the most economical way. It should be
further emphasized that owing to this function even one
noun can convey the information which otherwise necessitates
the whole "clause", i.e., "subject + predicate".

In our crow poem (31), we thus have two "clauses"
severed by kireji, i.e., the Type 2-b in Fig. 48.(31)
is a typical example of $2-ku$, $1-sh\bar{o}$, which ASANO (ibid.,
9) explains as below:

2-*ku*, 1-*shō* is a succinct expression of the structural pattern of hokku. In general, hokku is "cut" by a kireji consisting of the upper *ku* ("verse") and the lower *ku* both of which together compose one body of hokku. The terminology "2-ku, 1-shō" clarifies this hokku notion.

The juxtaposition of two such "clauses" or "verses" produces "the poetical quality of hokku" which is "the poetical gravity of hokku", maintains ASANO (ibid., 11). It should also be mentioned that Bashō seems to have been aware of this structural function of kireji as the manifestum of "cutting" (MUKAI, 477-9; cf. ASANO 1963: 2-18).

How, then, are two *ku*, or clauses, related to each other? On this question, HORI (1972: 62) offers us a significant account of the genesis of this specific haiku:

> In order to emphasize [his endeavour to recognize the poetical in something most unpoetical], Bashō composed his first version thus:
>
> (32) 秋ノ暮とは 枯枝に烏のとまりたる
> *Aki no kure* to wa / kare-eda ni karasu no / tomaritaru
> (As for the autumn evening/-- it is the crow perching/ on a withered bough)
>
> In this first version recorded in *Azuma-nikki* (1681) it appears as if the whole were a light *mondō* (question-answer used in Zen-Buddhism). Later he revised it as a purely "descriptive verse" and the latter form was collected in *Arano* (1689), (a haikai-anthology by Bashō School poets).

HORI's exposition clarifies that the deep structure of (32) is an equation of the two *ku*, i.e.,

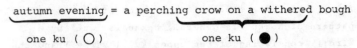

one ku (○)   one ku (●)

Thus, the juxtaposition of the two halves is a *hiyu* "comparison" which has the formula of "A = B", or ○ = ●, in our terms. The most typical linguistic manifestation of " = " is "is", which stimulates the metalinguistic operation.

According to ECO (1976: 168), this linguistic device of "is" *compares* "two semiotic objects, that is, the content of a linguistic expression with the content of a perceptual act". The "content of a perceptual act" in the poem (32) is obviously the whole landscape which Bashō had in front of him (ULENBROOK 1979: 167ff.), which we can express as the sememe of /the landscape of the autumn evening/. The "content of the expression" of (32) is both /autumn evening/ and /the crow perching on a withered bough/, which has *two* manifesta of 'aki no kure' and 'kare-eda ni karasu no tomaritaru', i.e., the poem (32) can be diagrammed in the format of synonymy:

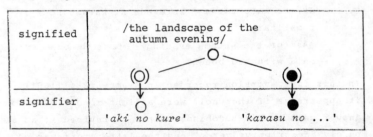

Fig. 49: The Haiku (32) as a Synonymy

In the original form of (32), i.e., "As for the autumn evening", it is "the autumn evening" which *manifests* the "frame" of the metaphor in which a metaphor occurs (REINHART 1976: 386ff.). Thus, the manifestum 'autumn evening' is a *comparandum* (cd), 'the crow perching ...', a "comparans" (cs) (KOCH ibid.), or, as HORI's elucidation indicates, "autumn evening" is a *question* that can be verbalized as "What is an autumn evening like?", to which the *answer* is, "It is *like* the crow perching ..." If Bashō had been asked the *reason* why he made this equation, he might have answered, "*Because* both *share* lonesomeness or the feeling of isolation" (ULENBROOK, ibid.).

The point under discussion might be illuminated by the more obvious example of such a metaphor as (33), discussed by REINHART (1976: 387):

(33) Man is a wolf.

REINHART (ibid.) explains that we can determine that "a wolf" is a metaphorical expression with the presumption that the subject "man" is referring to /humankind/; otherwise, the expression is literal (388). /Humankind/ is then the "frame", which is manifested as 'man', constituting the *cd*, while 'a wolf' the *cs*, or verhicle, in RICHARDS' terminology (cf. REINHART 1976), and "cruelty, harshness, etc.", the *reason*, or the *common core*, i.e., *tertium comparationis* (tc = ●) (cf. KOCH, 262ff.). Comparing the four items operating in the metaphor of (32) and (33), we arrive at the following:

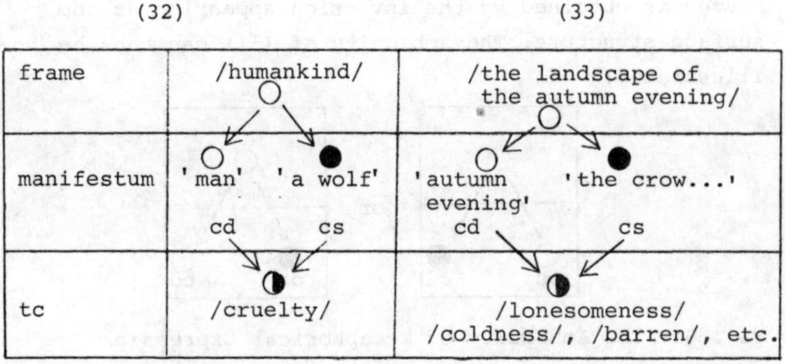

	(32)		(33)	
frame	/humankind/		/the landscape of the autumn evening/	
manifestum	'man' cd	'a wolf' cs	'autumn evening' cd	'the crow...' cs
tc	/cruelty/		/lonesomeness/ /coldness/, /barren/, etc.	

Fig. 50: The Structure of the Metaphor of (32) and (33)

Thus, as far as the original version of the crow poem is concerned, the form of "question-answer" is clearly recognizable, and P_{xe}'s task is to find the "solution", i.e., the tertium comparationis, on which the *riddle* is most prototypically based, as KOCH (1966:11) emphasizes: "The optimal poem [...] might be called a beautiful *riddle*" (3.4.1.2).

Having clarified the relationship between the two manifesta of (32), our last task in this section is to expound the reason why Bashō made the change from (32) to (31), i.e., eliminating the explanatory "*to wa*" (as for ...) in (32) and placing "the autumn evening" at the end of the poem. I submit that Bashō made the change because of his Zen-Buddhistic conviction that the ego, here manifested as intellectualization or conceptualization, should be abnegated (2.2.1): The logical connection of "first the question, and then the answer, and then the reason" discernable in (32) is *ambiguated* through the change (cf. KOCH 1983: 262ff.).

In 3.3.4 the example of (10), the poem about the plum blossoms and Manzai dancers, showed that the *inversion* of *histoire* in the *récit* intensifies the "mind's going and returning", i.e., the spatial quality of the juxtaposed *povtor* is obtained by the inversion appearing as the surface structure. The ambiguity of (31) can thus be illustrated:

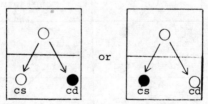

Fig. 51: The Ambiguity of Metaphorical Expression in Haiku (31)

The question of ambiguity between cd and cs is further
complicated by the fact that the two halves are often
statements describing nature without any apparent involvement of the poet's ego, i.e., such statements are "objective presentations", one of the two "text-forms", as Egon WERLICH
(1975: 48), a German text-theorist, categorizes. According to
WERLICH (ibid.), "Anwendung der Sprecherperspektive" is *subjective*, if P_{xs} relates himself to the expression, whereas it is *objective*, if he simply presents "einen exakt
verifizierbaren situativen Bezugsrahmen außerhalb seiner
selbst". BROWER/MINER point out the recurring characteristic in the poetic continuum of Japan of what they term
"impersonalism" (1957) or "objective symbolism" (ibid.).
If (32) discloses the poet's ego in the manifestum of
'*to wa*' as a questioning person, (31) completely hides
it: neither half, "perching crow" nor "autumn evening",
helps us to decide the cd or cs.

According to KOCH (1983: 263), the Imagists' poetic
innovation was to ambiguate between the cd and cs. POUND's
famous "*hokku-like sentence*" (1914: 89), (34), however,
"consists of a relatively straight-forward, unmetaphori-
cal statement ... [and] a sharply defined, metaphorical
image", as MINER (1958: 115) explains:

(34) *In a Station of the Metro*
The apparition of these faces in the crowd;
Petals on a wet, black bough.

Indeed, (34)'s title unambiguously defines the "frame",
and subsequently the first line as the cd, not mentioning
the deictic "these", which would never have appeared in
Japanese hokku-haiku poetry (2.3.4). We will return
to this haiku later (5.2.1).

The fact that both ku, or clauses, of (31) are "descriptive", as the previous chapter has clarified, is due to

Bashō's commitment to Zen Buddhism and thus has something
to do with informational poeticalness. We will, however,
return to this point later in discussing haiku's informational poeticalness (3.5.3.1). Here it is important
to mention that in haiku the distance between the cd and the
cs is of crucial importance. ASANO (1962: 19), a kireji-
expert, concurs, calling this distance "the poetical
gravity of hokku". Actually, the requirement of kireji
was felt to have become too conventionalized by the New Haiku poets
and many of them discarded it altogether. As it turned
out, haiku could possess "the poetical gravity of hokku"
without such manifesta of kireji as 'ya' or 'kana',
as long as the poem juxtaposed two elements. English-
language haiku, as we will see in Chapter 5, substitutes
a comma, a semicolon or simply a change of lines, for
the transference of kireji. To conclude the discussion
of *2-ku, 1-shō*, or the *montage* technique of haiku (3.3.1),
I quote Stephan ULLMANN (1962: 213-4), who assures us
that what Kyorai and KURIYAMA meant by the "leap", or
KEENE by "the spark", and what ULLMANN designates as "the
distance between tenor and vehicle in French Surrealist
poetics, are in fact identical:

> An important factor in the effectiveness of a meta-
> phor is the distance between tenor [i.e., cd] and
> vehicle [i.e., cs], or, as Dr. Sayce calls it, the
> "angle" of the image. If the two terms are very close
> to each other - if, for example, one flower is likened
> to another - the metaphor will be appropriate but with-
> out any expressive quality ... Modern writers are fond
> of producing surprise effects by drawing unexpected
> parallels between disparate objects. The French Sur-
> realist poet André Breton has unequivocally stated:
> "To compare two objects, as remote from one another in
> character as possible, or by any other method put them

together in a sudden and striking fashion, this
remains the highest task to which poetry can aspire".

The French Surrealists, ULLMANN, Bashō's disciple Kyorai,
KURIYAMA, and KEENE are all concerned with the "distance"
between the two manifesta in montage technique, *or* two
sememes. The difference among them is the amount of
distance they accept: while Kyorai preaches "modera-
tion", French Surrealists aim to be "shocking". Thus, as
far as our crow poem is concerned, the distance is minimum; both manifesta belong to a homogeneous field
But the distance in the plum-blossoms poem (10) is
considerably greater.

Concerning the frog poem, BLYTH (1949: 277-9) passes
on the account according to which Bashō opted for "the
old pond" as the first five syllables rather than "the
mountain rose" (cf. ULENBROOK 1961). The "distance" is
the issue in this story, which claims that in composing
(1), Bashō eliminated the stylistic focus resulting
from the "distance", which on other occassions he emphasized. Fig. 52 presents this shift in stylistic
poeticalness by comparing the examples of (1) and (31)
with the *homogeneous manifesta* on the one hand, and (10)
with the *contrastive manifesta* on the other. The latter
is charged with the *additional reinforcement* of the
"distance" or "leap" between the cd and cs (cf. KOCH
1983: 405):

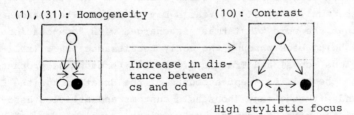

Fig. 52: The Shift of the Distance between the Comparandum and the Comparans

3.5.2.3 Polysemy: *Kigo* or Seasonal Words

Kigo, or seasonal words, are the manifesta of the sememes called *kidai* ("seasonal theme") (cf. HENDERSON 1934, 1965, YASUDA, 174ff.)[87]. Kigo functions in haiku as "a kind of poetic algebra or shorthand, enabling poets to speak to one another open secrets to [sic] which the unpoetical reader is not initiated" (BLYTH 1949: 382). Remaining with our crow poem, the kigo, 'aki no kure', "the autumn evening", taken as a manifestum of the whole gamut of the sememes relating to the ambience, i.e., as an instance of polysemy, can be expounded as thus:

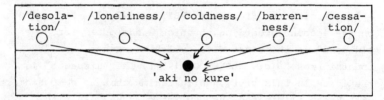

Fig. 53: Kigo as an Instance of Polysemy

Kigo, then, automatically becomes a *styleme* in that it triggers a metalingual operation to connect the specified event or phenomenon of the specific season and the "Stimmungsbild von schlichter Harmonie" (ULENBROOK 1979: 167). GIROUX (1974: 100), in her exploration of the "English season word", ascertains that Christmas, e.g., could be considered a "fifth season" in the West, like the equivalent of New Year's Day in Japan. She reasons that the word "Christmas" is charged with "connotations echoing back through the early Renaissance *lauda* (religious songs) and Francis of Assisi, through the prophets to the Old Testament accounts of the Creation and the Fall", and with the many "household customs and articles associated with Christmas - bells, trees, candles, carols".

Due to such backgrounds, the word "Christmas", not in the sense of "the modern commercialized abuses of the sacred season" but of "the traditional aspects", has "great allusive potentiality".

Kigo as the manifestum of the seasonal theme, or sememe, is thus an established technique based on the principle of polysemy: one manifestum and *innumerable* sememes. Further, kigo is a modal knot in that it coordinates stylistic as well as informational poeticalness: it triggers the metalingual operation discussed above, and at the same time it manifests the *Weltanschauung* of the poet.

3.5.2.4 Polysemy: *Kakekotoba* or Pivot Word

If a kigo provokes P_{xe} to recall a whole gamut of cultural units, the traditional poetic technique called *kakekotoba* focuses specifically upon *two* sememes which can be diagrammed as follows:

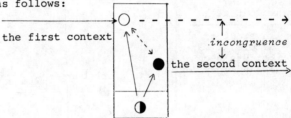

Pivot Word (Kakekotoba)

Fig. 54: Kakekotoba as an Instance of Polysemy

Let us consider the following haiku by Teitoku, the composer of (30), in order to see another typical technique of his school, kakekotoba:

(35) 門前に市も立花の盛哉 (B 17)
　　　Monzen ni / ichi mo tachi-bana no / sakari kana
　　　(Before the temple/ a market has been opened up:
　　　and wild oranges are/ now in full bloom!)

In this poem "tachi-bana" is a pivot word. BROWER/MINER (1961: 507) define this traditional rhetorical device as follows:

[A] Rhetorical scheme of word play in which a series of sounds is so employed as to mean two or more things at once by different parlance.

In (35), we have on the one hand "*ichi mo tatsu*" (a market comes into being), and on the other "*tachibana*" (the wild oranges). A pivot word, thus, can be compared to a door hinge[88]: like the hinge joining door to jamb, a pivot word joins one dimension of the deep structure, the first context, to the second dimension, the second context. It is a "word-play" which exploits the polysemic character of language. Fig. 55 presents the pivot word "*tachi*(bana)", functioning as a door hinge or an *abrupt switch of meaning*, i.e., kakekotoba is a symphony (◐) which mediates two contexts:

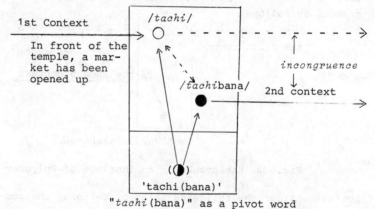

"*tachi*(bana)" as a pivot word
Fig. 55: The Function of a Pivot Word in (35)

Due to the introductory (first) context, P_{xe} is forced to attribute the first sememe /set up/ to the manifestum '*tachi*', which is a continuative form[89] of the verb

tatsu ("stand, set up") until he encounters the "*tachibana*"
("wild oranges"). There is a discrepancy, an *incompatibility*, between the sememe /set up/ and the manifestum
'*tachibana*', thus provoking P_{xe} to *find* the *solution*,
i.e., to activate a metalingual operation, going through
the *five-step-procedure of stylistics* (3.4.1.2), though
the procedure would occur within a second. P_{xe} will then
find the second sememe /wild orange/ with the help of
the manifestum '*tachibana*' and the rest of the T (second
context). The discrepancy between two sememes is the
fundament of the pivot word.

P_{xe} might admire the ingenuity of this *find* (◐) by
P_{xs}, as the haikai-audience prior to Bashō's crow poem
did, or reject it as an intellectual game, like Bashō and
all his followers. As far as the T-production is concerned, however, this *find* (KOCH 1983: 243ff.), the recognition of the two distinct sememes in one manifestum,
must first be carried out by P_{xs}.

TODOROV (1977: 23) takes *syllepsis*, i.e., the type of
pun just exemplified, as a typical example of polysemy,
which "has had a great extension in narrative", e.g.,
in Boccaccio's novellas. This potential in polysemy is
analysed by Arthur KOESTLER (1964) extensively as "the
logic of humor and its emotive dynamics". The potential
of polysemy practiced as kakekotoba or syllepsis is termed
by KOESTLER the "bisociation" of the two disparate dimensions (1964: 33):

> The pattern [...] is the perceiving of an idea, L, in
> two self-consistent but habitually incompatible frames
> of reference, M1 and M2. The event L, in which the two
> intersect, is made to vibrate simultaneously on two
> different wavelengths, as it were. While this situation
> lasts, L is not merely linked to one associative context,
> but "bisociated with two".

KOESTLER illustrates this bisociation as follows (ibid.):

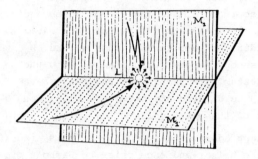

Fig. 56: Bisociation (from KOESTLER 1964)

Of the many examples KOESTLER analyses, that of the Chamfort anecdote suffices to clarify his thesis (cf. KOCH 1983: 98ff.). The anecdote, also discussed by FREUD (KOESTLER, 33), reads (ibid., 32):

> (36) Chamfort tells a story of a Marquis at the court of Louis XIV who, on entering his wife's boudoir and finding her in the arms of a bishop, walked calmly to the window and went through the motions of blessing the people in the street.
> "What are you doing?" cried the anguished wife.
> "Monseigneur is performing my functions", replied the Marquis, "so I am performing his".

The explanation KOESTLER attributes to this anecdote is worth quoting here, for it is applicable to the hokku we are concerned with (32-33):

> In the Chamfort anecdote [...] the tension mounts as the story progresses, but it never reaches its expected

climax. The ascending curve is brought to an abrupt
end by the Marquis' unexpected reaction, which debunks
our dramatic expectation; it comes like a bolt out of
the blue, which, so to speak, decapitates the logical
development of the situation. The narrative acted as
a channel directing the flow of emotion; when the
channel is punctured the emotion gushes out like a
liquid through a burst pipe; the tension is suddenly
relieved and exploded in laughter.

BROWER/MINER (1957: 509-10) point out that pivot words
were important rhetorical devices, which were major products of over a thousand years of endeavours to enrich a
poetic form limited in its number of syllables. They are
not *ipso facto* witty or comical, since they are also the
major tools in the "serious" poetry prior to haikai (ibid.).
Nonetheless, they possess a strong potential for the phenomenon called "humor", as KOESTLER makes clear: *bisociation*
causes the relief of tension which explodes as laughter.
Because of this potential, which was exploited directly
prior to Bashō as *suku* ("witty verse") (cf. NGS 1959),
this device, kakekotoba, was renounced as too contrived by
the Bashō school. The focalization of P_x is, as we saw above,
on the matrix of kotoba or versification but not on the
mapping or kokoro.

3.5.2.5 Polysemy: *Honka-dori* or Allusive Variations

Let us consider the hokku which became so famous in connection with POUND's Imagist movement. This poem has been attributed to Arakida Moritake (1473-1549), a Shintō priest and
one of the two major precursors of haikai-poetry (the other
being Yamazaki Sōkan (? -1539) (KURIYAMA 1972: 19 ff.).
KURIYAMA, however, demonstrates that the poem was actually
written by Arakita Takeari, who possessed the same family
name and also happened to be a Shintō priest.

(37) 落花枝にかへると見れば胡蝶哉 (B 10)
　　 Rakka eda ni / kaeru to mireba / kochō kana
　　 (Falling blossom - to the branch/ returning ...
　　 but looked at closely/ is a butterfly!)

KURIYAMA (ibid., 56) states that this haiku employs the
technique called *honka-dori*, literally, "taking out of
the original poem", i.e., the haiku explicitly refers
to some existent classical waka or to the kind of Chinese
poetry called *kanshi*. KURIYAMA (ibid.) cites two such
references for this poem:

> In "Denshōroku" we read "破鏡重ネテ照サズ、落花枝ニ上リ難シ"
> (the broken mirror does not reflect any longer: the
> fallen blossom does not return to the branch). Direct-
> ly, however, this (Moritake's) haiku seems to refer
> to the Noh-play "Yashima" in which it is sung:
> " 落花枝にかへらず、破鏡 再び照こず " (The fallen blossom
> does not go back to the branch: the broken mirror does
> not reflect any more).

In fact there is a technical difference depending on the
type of original: if the reference is to poetry, it is
called honka-dori, whereas if the reference is to the
parlance or diction of Nō-chant or some equivalent, it
is called *monku-dori* ("taking a parlance from the original"). Since (37) evidently refers to the Nō-chant, as
KURIYAMA suggests above, it should be categorized as the
latter, *monku-dori*. Structurally speaking, however, this
difference is unimportant: both function in an identical
way, i.e., one manifestum refers both to the first sememe,
within the given poem, and also to the second sememe, outside
the poem, the original referential T. Fig. 57 diagrams the
honka-dori, allusive variations, as a case of polysemy.
Honka-dori is, similarly to kakekotoba, or pivot word,
a stylistic mediation:

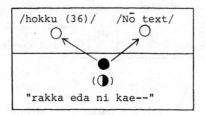

Fig. 57 Honka-dori as an Instance of Polysemy

Actually, (34) combines this device of allusive variation and the one we just discussed, the pivot word: the two sememes are contrasted so that the turn or the discrepany between the two could result in laughter, i.e., the structure is that of the joke.

In (37), what KOESTLER called "the progress of the story", i.e., the first context, is the first eight syllables "rakka eda ni kae--". The Nō text, well-known and often quoted, allows the P_{xe} to expect something religious, profound, reflective, and serious as the theme of this hokku. Tension amounts. The expectation is then diverted or surprised by the change of the original T, "*kaerazu*" ("not return"), to "*kaeru*" ("does return"). The phrase, well-known to the literati at the time is a Zen version of "No use crying over spilt milk". In the middle of the poem, then, this allusion is stood on its head: "the fallen blossom does go back". This breach of the initial expectation caused by the change of the negative to the affirmative is then followed by the first turning of the tables: "*to*" ("so I thought"). The next manifestum, '*mireba*' ("when looking closely"), turns the tables for a second time in that it confirms the Zen truth, "the fallen blossom does not return". But then, in a third turning of the tables, the poet sees a butterfly, rather than a blossom. The structure of the joke, re-

cognizable as bisociation in this hokku (37) can
be shown as below:

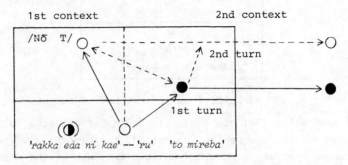

Fig. 53: The Structure of the Joke in (37)

As already noted (3.5.1.4, 3.5.2.2), Bashō did exploit
the potential of honka-dori: the character " 横 " in (28)
was "the eye of the whole poem" because of its allusion
to the Chinese poem, and the crow poem (31), too, had a
Chinese poem as a reference. The difference between
Bashō's way with honka-dori and that of his precursors
lies, then, in the fact Bashō used it *polysemically*, and
the latter *bisociatively*. Similarly to the usage of kigo,
Bashō's " 横 " alludes to the whole gamut of sememes which
enhance (28), i.e., the sememes are *homogeneous* (Fig. 47).
By contrast, both kakekotoba and (37)'s sememes are contrastive, demarcating two distinctive sememes attributed
to one manifestum. And it is the potential of the two
disparate sememes which Bashō's precursors played upon as
the "puns" or "wordplays" which the founder of haiku poetry
forever renounced.

3.5.3 The Informational Poeticalness of Classical Haiku

The modes of informational poeticalness in Bashō's work
can be categorized into four groups: (i) projection,

(ii) fūkyō or projection in converting social conventions, (iii) equijection, and (iv) introjection (cf. Fig. 28). The involvement of the poet's ego decreases from (i) through (iv). There is a gradual shift from the left-hemispheric mode of mediation to the right-hemispheric mode.

(i) Projection: structuring the world in terms of the poet's own frame of mind

(ii) Fūkyō or Projection in converting social conventions: re-organizing the world by transposing the existent conventions

(iii) Equijection: the ego and the structure of the world interpenetrate one another

(iv) Introjection: transferring structures from the world to the ego

As one might suppose, relatively few specimens of the first mode, projection, can be found. This fact is quite understandable considering the mentality which Bashō inherited, i.e., Zen Buddhism (cf. Ch. 2). It is the third and the fourth groups that are dominant not only in Japanese but also in American haiku. Furthermore, the first three modes can be characterized as "homeorhetic", while the last mode is "homeostatic": while the first three categories offer mediations which neutralize somehow "the curse of cognition" by activating the *logic of nature*, the fourth offers the specific Zen mediation, i.e., the acceptance of oppositions as such (2.3.2).

3.5.3.1 Projection

(38) 五月雨の降のこしてや 光堂　　　　　　　　　(A 477)
　　　Samidare no /furinokoshite ya / Hikari-dō
　　　(Has the early-summer rain/ spared you?! / Hikari-dō?)

During his journey to the Northern Provinces (3.4.2.3), Bashō came to the Hikari-dō ("Golden Hall") which preserved three mummified warriors[90] from a period five centuries earlier. Bashō was greatly moved when he contemplated their faces. Quite unusually for Bashō, his presence is here revealed in the first half, which is interrogative-interjectional. As HORI (1972: 274) comments, the poem proclaims the poet's sympathy towards human beings who "have been bravely challenging the pressure exerted by eternal, magnificent nature". Nature is here regarded as something destructive - "samidare" corroding human endeavour -, against which *Hikari-dō* has survived. Fig. 59 depicts the informational poeticalness of (38):

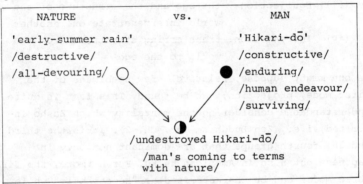

Fig. 59: The Informational Poeticalness, Projection, of (38)

Bashō interprets the survival of the Hikari-dō as a triumph of human endeavour and finds consolation in, as well as deep empathy with, the world-structure, although he customarily observes the ephemerality of human destiny. '*Hikari-dō*' is thus identified with /human beings/. This identification becomes a mediation with which Bashō overcomes the *unbearable opposition* which can be expressed as "human vs. nature".

Contrary to (1) or (31), in which the whole poem consists of *objective presentation* (3.5.2.2), (38) consists of two *ku* (clauses), one, *subjective* presentation and the other, *objective* presentation. Employing the broken underlining for the former and the solid underlining for the latter, we obtain the following presentation of (38). As noted, the subjective presentation manifests (38)'s homeorhetic mediation (◐):

Samidare no / furiyokoshite ya / Hikaridō
              O   ◐

(38), thus, differs from such total "objective symbolism", as BROWER/MINER calls it (3.5.2.2), for it discloses the poet's ego far more clearly. The voice of the poet, like that of Brooke in (13), appears in the surface structure. The homeorhesis in the deep structure is then realized as the juxtaposition of /nature/ "O" and /homeorhetic mediation/ "◐" in the surface structure, as Fig. 60 shows:

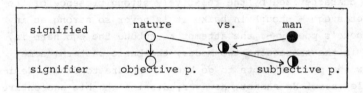

Fig. 60: Text-Production in Projection

Another haiku by Bashō which can be presented here as an example of projective mediation is the very last hokku he composed.

(39) 旅に病んで夢は枯野をかけ廻る   (A 471)
     Tabi ni yande / yume wa kareno o / kakemeguru
                         ◐   O

(Being ill on my journey/my dreams, on the withered moor/ hovering about)

Bashō had been on his death-bed for over ten days, and he
died four days after its composition. His confrontation
with his own impending death - probably the most "unbearable"
opposition a human being confronts - is mediated in that
his dream wanders around on the moors, just as he used to
do, while his real body is confined to his bed. It is, then,
the poet himself, or rather his mind, which leaves the
decaying body. It is the etherealized self (◐), which is
'kakemeguru' ("hovering about") here and there on the withered
moor. Although historical accounts state that Bashō was
rather ashamed of himself for still being attached to life
at the point of his death (HORI 1972: 269), his vitality in
pursuing "the way of poetry", as HORI (ibid.) puts it, is
certainly impressive.

3.5.3.2 Fūkyō or Projection in Converting Social Conventions

If the first mode of informational poeticalness, projection,
is characterized by the relatively strong presence of the
poet's ego - though in haiku it is never so strong as in
Brooke's poetry -, the attempt to subdue the ego here is,
as in the subsequent two modes, the basic pattern: somehow the poet attempts to go back to nature to find a domi-
cile there. He cannot, however, dissimilate his ego entirely, as can well be seen in the other two modes. *Fūkyō*, or
projection converting social conventions, is the second
type of informational poeticalness, which presents a homeorhetic mediation. Here we find Bashō's solution to a more
mundane conflict: the oppositions we observe are concerned
not so much with "life vs. death" as with "his personal failure in the mundane world vs. the society" in
which he lived, though in the broader sense it is of course
what KOCH designates as "world", namely, everything outside
of an individual (Fig. 39). As has already been mentioned
in the discussion of the haiku (14), Bashō failed both in

entering the monastic life as well as in achieving social
status; which is to say, he could not subjugate his personal desires entirely, nor could he satisfy them by becoming a social success. Instead, he remained a poet of
haikai, as UEDA (1962: 430) affirms: "For Bashō [...] the
haiku was a kind of religion. It was no wonder that he
did not enter the priesthood; he did not need to".

We have already seen (3.4.2.3) that "unconventionality"
was Bashō's reaction to coming to terms with the world, or,
the life of *fūga* (" 風雅 "), or *fūkyō* (" 風狂 "), both denoting anti-pragmatism, "craziness", "lack of restraint", etc.
Let us now inspect more closely this mode of conjection,
i.e., *fūkyō*, or projection in converting social conventions.

(40) 花にやどり 瓢箪斎と白いヘリ   (A 43)
    Hana ni yadori / Hyōtansai to/ mizukara ieri
    - - - - - - -   - - - - - - - - - - - - - -
                         ◐

    (Sleeping under cherry-blossoms,/"*Hyōtansai*"*/
    I call myself.)

                                    *Gourd-man

Except for the styleme "*Hyōtansai*" which alludes to a
legendary Chinese figure (" 頼淵 ") (HORI 1972: 60), the
poem can be translated word for word, presenting the poet's
life philosophy; while turning his back on the conventional
respectable life, he claims that he is totally contented
with the life of an outsider or a non-conformist. The poet
sleeps under the blossoms of cherry trees, and drinks and eats
just enough to stay alive, thus opposing the normal social
life. While his adopted pseudonym reveals his mocking attitude toward his own non-conformism, the whole poem demonstrates Bashō's solution: anti-pragmatism (◐) merged with
the return to nature. Fig. 61 depicts this projectional mode
of informational poeticalness, i.e., fūkyō:

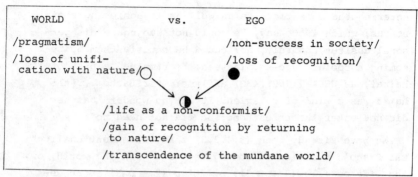

Fig. 61: The Informational Poeticalness of (40):
Fūkyō or Projection in Converting Social
Conventions

It is quite interesting to note that this type of mediation can be observed frequently in Bashō's transitional period, i.e., from the Danrin School (4.2.2) to his own style, and from his deep commitment to Zen-Buddhism to his new style. In the following we will read four such examples; (41), from the first transitional phase (1680); (42), from the post-Zen-commitment phase; and (43) and (44), composed in 1687 and 1690 respectively, from the mature phase.

(41) 富家喰肌肉、大夫喫菜根．予乏し (A 51)
 (The rich eat meat: the powerful taste vegetable-roots: I am poor.)
 雪の朝 独り干鮭を嚙得タリ
 Yuki no asa / hitori karasake o / kamietari
 ──────── ─ ─ ─ ─ ─ ─ ─ ─ ─ ─ ─ ─
   ○·   ◐
 (This snowy morning/ all alone, the dried salmon/ I am chewing)

As is seen in the preface and in the poem itself, the influence of Chinese poetry is conspicuous: he employs many

Chinese characters with *katakana* and includes a prefatory
comment which shows a typical "parallelism" (" 対句 ") of Chinese
poetry. The stylistic poeticalness is thus more foregrounded
than in (40), and the metaphysical opposition is also more
explicitly verbalized in a prefatory comment: "winner vs.
loser", "conformist vs. misfit", "rich vs. poor", etc.
Bashō's declaration, "I am poor", as well as his composing
on his chewing dried food all by himself in his seclusion,
juxtaposed with "the winter morning when it is snowing outside" is mediatory in that he thus places his existential
philosophy above the ordinary way of life. The amusing tone
we could detect in (40) is, however, subdued here.

(42) 霧しぐれ 富士をみぬ日ぞ 面白き   (A 78)
    Kirishigure / Fuji o munu hi zo / omoshiroki
    ―――――――――   ― ― ― ― ― ― ― ― ― ― ― ― ― ― ―
       ○   ◐

    (Misty rain / the day when Fuji cannot be seen/ is
    interesting)

Similar to (14), in which Bashō expresses his inclination
to travel to the Biwa Lake in the middle of the early summer
rain, this poem turns the tables in that it declares that
the day on which the beautiful sight of Mr. Fuji - traditionally a mediative object[91] - "cannot be viewed" from
the Barrier of Hakone is "interesting": it is quite the
opposite of the normal attitude of complaining about bad
weather. HORI (1972: 74) detects in this poem in our analytical terms the stylistic poeticalness effected by the
rather unusual parlance of "kirishigure" ("misty autumn
rain") - "kiri" alluding to traditional poetry which dealt
with it as "something that blocks the view" and thus of
negative value, while Bashō turns it into something
positive ((◐).

(43) 旅人と 我名よばれん 初しぐれ   (A 175)
　　 Tabibito to / wagana yobaren / hatsushigure
     ‒‒‒‒‒‒‒‒‒‒‒‒‒‒‒‒‒‒‒‒‒‒‒‒‒   ‒‒‒‒‒‒‒‒‒‒‒‒
                     ◐   ○

     ("Wanderer" -/I will have myself called / the first
     autumn rain)

As has been often mentioned, Bashō lived his life either in
seclusion or travelling. In a similar tone to that which we
encountered in (14), this poem declares that his life is
"fūkyō", "poetry-crazy". It is included in the opening
passage of one of his travelling diaries, *Oi-no-Obumi*
(1687-8), which is quite famous for his disclosure of his
fatal inclination towards *fūkyō*^{92}.

(44) うき我をさびしがらせよ かんことり   (A 376)
　　 Uki ware o / sabishi-garase yo / kanko-dori
     ‒‒‒‒‒‒‒‒‒‒‒‒‒‒‒‒‒‒‒‒‒‒‒‒‒‒   ‒‒‒‒‒‒‒‒‒‒
                 ◐   ○

     (Me, already distressed/ do sadden more!/ Oh bird
     of empty house [= cuckoo]!)

This hokku was written when he was 48, two years before
his death. The personification of the cuckoo and the
apostrophe, "*kanko-dori*", constitute stylistic poeticalness, while the metaphysical - the spirit of *fūkyō* - is
deepened in that the poet asks "the bird of empty house",
another name for a cuckoo, to sadden one who is "already
distressed". The cuckoo is one of the birds appearing most
frequently in Japanese poetry. The ancient poets sought to
hear its voice, which was supposed to be exceedingly rare.
To hear the voice of a cuckoo was then a way through which
the poets and the poetic convention attempted to be unified
with nature. In this hokku, however, Bashō breaks with this
poetic convention: instead of asking the cuckoo to "console"
him, he asks it to "sadden" him, to augment his desolation.

As is mentioned, the haiku that manifest this "$fūkyō$-mediation" constitute a fairly high percentage of his poetry. At one time, Bashō sang that he was "a man who eats his breakfast by looking at the morning glory"[93]. At another, he called to the people at the market that he would "sell his straw hat, on which the fallen snow lay so beautifully"[94]. When the moon was most beautiful in autumn, he would "stay up all night long just walking around and around the pond"[95]. When he received an overnight visitor, he treated his guest not with a big dinner but with the haiku: "At my hut/the mosquitoes are small--/ that is the treat for you"[96]. When the chilly winter-rain began to fall, instead of complaining about its unpleasantness, Bashō offered the following to the host of the poetry-meeting on that evening: "How interesting!/ soon it will turn to snow/ the winter-rain"[97].

3.5.3.3 Equijection

As opposed to the previous two modes of mediation, in equijection the poet's ego is discernibly repressed but not to the degree of total effacement, as in introjection. We can detect the poet's involvement in so far as he is willing to discover such consoling natural phenomena as "a blooming chrysanthemum among lifeless stones of a stone-shop", as mentioned in the discussion of (21) (3.5.1.2). The T-production of equijection presents a pattern identical with the first two modes of conjection, i.e., it too juxtaposes a homeorhetic mediation (◐) and an objective presentation:

(45) 艸菴雨　　起あがる菊ほのかせ　水のあと　　　　(A 173)
　　　　　　　The Rain on the Grass-Hut
　　Okiagaru / kiku honoka-nari / mizu no ato
　　---------------------------   ---------------
　　　　　　　　　　　◐　　　　　　　　　○
　　(Rising up delicately/ the chrysanthemum is a touching sight /
　　after the flood)

The mediatory quality in (45) is expounded as follows
by HORI (1972: 116):

> Because of the incessant rain fall, the garden of the
> grass hut had been all flooded, but it stopped raining,
> finally, and the water was at last gone. Then, the poet
> suddenly noticed the chrysanthemums that had fallen
> down due to the flood starting to rise up, though al-
> most imperceptibly, in the corner of the ruined garden.
> To a mind that had been made alert by the catastrophe of
> a flood, the faint change which the humble creations of
> nature showed must have been impressive.

The poet discloses his presence in his judgement that the
rising up of the chrysanthemum from the flood-covered earth
is "a touching sight". As HORI asserts, "the faint change which
the humble creations showed" impressed him and made him compose this hokku; which is to say, Bashō was ready to catch
such small natural dramas depending on *hopeful perception*
by the poet - accordingly, on the mutual influence between
ego and nature. The poet is here more conscious in viewing
and interpreting the significance of natural phenomena than
he was in composing the frog poem.

It seems that we can detect in this poem one of the religious notions that Bashō inherited (cf. BLYTH 1949:
3-160), i.e., the notion of *Taikyoku* ("Great Ultimate")
of Confucianism[98]: it assures the human being that there
is some eternal power, which transcends the evanescence
of this mundane world. While Mahayana Buddhism taught the
transience of the world - and subsequently offered a mediative credo of accepting all earthly events as karma - Chinese
optimism and pragmatism taught the existence of the Great
Ultimate, which is by definition, a mediation[99]. Bashō, in-
heriting both streams, also attempted to discover evidence
of the latter. The sight of a damaged chrysanthemum raising

its head in spite of the destructive flood can thus evince
the cosmic power that governs the whole universe: the sight
was, for Bashō, the evidence of the "unchangeable force" in
the world of ephemerality. This little drama of nature is
a point of contact, so to speak, in the eye of a searching
mind, where a willful soul and nature directly meet. The
contact point is a balanced one, for there is no manipulation demanding that "you should think this soil as part of
me", as in Brooke's words. It can thus be classified as
equijectional mediation.

    (46) よくみれば 薺花さく 垣ねかな   (137)
    Yoku mire-ba / nazuna hanasaku kakine kana
    ─ ─ ─ ─ ─ ─ ─ ─ ─ ─ ─ ─ ─ ─ ─ ───────────
              ◐   ○
    (Looking closely/ [I find] the shepherd's purses
    are blooming/ on the hedge!)

Bashō's searching eye focuses this time on a tiny, white,
insignificant flower which is normally considered an un-
interesting, unpoetical plant. HORI (ibid., 101) comments
thus: "the poem seems to show that every creature on the
earth has its own place and fulfills its fate".

Another interesting account concerning this poem
is offered by SUZUKI (1959: 263-5), clarifying the fundamental difference between an oriental and occidental
mediation. Comparing this hokku to one of Tennyson's most
famous poems, "Flower in the Crannied Wall", SUZUKI expounds as follows:

    (47) Flower in the crannied wall,
        I pluck you out of the crannies
        I hold you here, root and all, in my hand,
        Little flower - but *if* I could understand
        What you are, root and all, and all in all,
        I should know what God and man is.

Tennyson is here quite inquisitive, philosophically speaking. He thinks if he could know what he has in his hand - the little flower, root and all - he would also know what God and man is. Did Bashō have the same inquisitive mind? No, his mind was far from being so. In the first place, he would never think of mercilessly plucking the poor "nazuna" with its "root and all" and holding it in his hand and asking himself any question. Bashō knew better than Tennyson. He was no scientist bent on analysis and experiment, nor was he a philosopher. When he saw the white, flowered "nazuna", so humbly, so innocently, and yet with all its individuality, growing among other vegetation, he at once realized that the herb was no other than himself. If it is arrayed better than "Solomon in all his glory", Bashō is also glorified in the same style. If it is "alive today and tomorrow thrown into the oven", Bashō, too, has the same destiny. A Zen master declares that he can turn one blade of grass into the Buddha-body sixteen feet high and at the same time transform the Buddha-body into a blade of grass. This is the mystery of being-becoming and becoming-being. This is the mystery of self-identification and universal interpenetration or interfusion.

What SUZUKI designates "interpenetration" or "interfusion", as we might easily recognize, is in fact a mediation, by which the poet achieves his internal serenity. UEDA (1963: 430-1) also argues along this line in his discussion of Bashō's seven poetic principles, affirming that writing poetry was a kind of religion for Bashō:

> Bashō's aesthetic principles are, in the end, the principles of his religion. $Sabi^{100}$, $shiori^{101}$, and $hosomi^{102}$ are the principles by which man purges his tormenting passions and gains calm of mind: they enable man to live

in this world while transcending it. "Fragrance",
"reverberation", and "reflection" are the ideas by which
man unites opposites and resolves struggles; they help
man to see a correspondence between himself and nature.
Synesthesia is a mode by which man comes to recognize
the interrelatedness of all things; it is a principle
of assimilation and integrity, as against the method of
natural science which is analysis and dissociation ...
"Lightness" is a concept through which man perceives
a true value in common ways of life; it teaches man
how to endure hardship with a smile, how to accept
the fact of human imperfectibility.

Fig. 62 depicts this reciprocal mode of informational
poeticalness. On the one hand it is introjective insofar
as the human transfers the microcosmic natural phenomena
directly from the world into the ego, and it is projective,
on the other, insofar as the poet's frame of mind - here
the belief in cosmic power - structures the world, i.e.,
seeks such sights intensely. The discovery of the lives
of unrecognized, insignificant creatures is thus affirmed
as a consoling sight, in addition to having the function of
poetic innovation (Fig. 41):

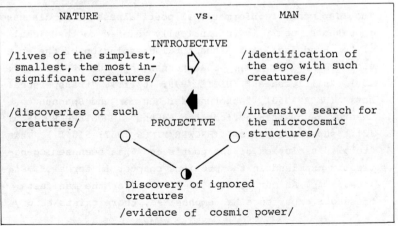

Fig. 62: The Informational Poeticalness of (46): Equijection

The following three haiku will further exemplify this
mode of informational poeticalness:

(48) さゞれ蟹 足はひのぼる清水哉　　　　　　　　(A 168)
　　Sazare-gani / ashi hainoboru / shimizu kana
　　━━━━━━━━━━━━━━━━　　━━━━━━━━━━━
　　　　　　　　◐　　　　　　○

　　(A tiny crab/ is climbing up my leg/a clear brook!)

(49) 痩ながらわりなき菊のつぼみ哉　　　　　　　(A 174)
　　Yasenagara / warinaki kiku no / tsubomi kana
　　━━━━━　　━━━━━━━━━━━━━━━━━━━━━━
　　　　　　　　◐　　　　　　○

　　(Though too slender/the unfathomable chrysanthemum
　　has/ its bud!)

(50) 桟や いのちをからむつたかづら　　　　　　(A 239)
　　Kakehashi ya / inochi o karamu / tsuta-kazura
　　━━━━━━━━━　　━━━━━━━━━━━━━━━━━━━
　　　　○　　　　　　　　◐

　　(Suspension bridge!/twining for existence around the
　　ropes/ vines)[103]

3.5.3.4 Introjection

The last mode of informational poeticalness to be discussed
in Bashō's poetry is intrinsically related to the ideal
of Zen Buddhism: it is "the total dissolution of the poet's
ego" (UEDA 1963: 424), "Selbstentsagung" (ULENBROOK 1979:
168), "selflessness" (BLYTH 1949: 163ff.), "transpersonal-
ness" (UEDA 1963), "Abtötung der Wünsche und Spannungen
unseres nach außen gerichteten Lebens" (MUNSTERBERG 1965:
12), "superpersonalism" (BROWER/MINER 1957: 515ff.). This
"total dissolution of the poet's ego" has been semiogenetically examined in the previous chapter in terms of *metageneticity*. As our discussion of Zen T as the manifesta
of satori experience has emphasized, there exists hardly

any manipulation for transforming the deep structure (Zen experience) into the surface structure (Zen fine arts). In terms of signs, Zen T resort to the employment of indexical-iconic signs. In terms of the text format, they manifest irreconcilable opposition as such, since to accept such opposition is the very nature of Zen *mediation*: instead of activating Aristotelian logic, like the Georgian poet Brooke (3.4.1.3), Zen resorts to the solution which results from the bio-physiological, right-hemispheric experience of zazen (2.2.4).

Let us cite once again the frog poem, which is the most prototypical haiku exhibiting "almost too much of Zen in it" (SUZUKI 1959: 229, cf. ULENBROOK 1961, 1979: 168ff.):

(1) *The old pond! / a frog jumps in / a sound of water.*

   objective p.   objective p.
        O   O

Contrary to the three modes of conjection discussed above, (1)'s surface T gives hardly any indication of the poet's presence except for the exclamatory kireji. This is the very characteristic of the mode of introjection, perfectly conforming to other non-verbal arts of Zen: the surface T lacks the obvious speaking voice of the poet, and the two manifesta are objectively presented.

Based on ECO's model of "code-making" (1976: 245-58), Fig. 63 presents the genesis of (1) as the T presenting the informational poeticalness of *introjection*:

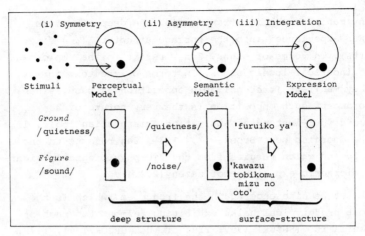

Fig. 63: The Genesis of (1) as Introjection

BLYTH (1949: 277-9) provides us with an interesting account concerning the genesis of (1) (cf. ULENBROOK 1961). The mode of introjection which is manifested in the surface structure as the simple objective presentation seems to be clarified by this account. The dramatis personae of BLYTH's account, which will now be quoted, are: Bucchō (Bashō's Zen master), Gohei (Bucchō's companion), and Bashō in the first half of the account, and, in addition, some of Bashō's disciples in the latter half. The first half of the account reads:

> Bucchō , 佛頂 , of Komponji Temple, 常州鹿島根本寺 , a monk of wide reading and profound enlightenment, became the teacher of Bashō. Moving to Chokeiji, 長慶寺 , at Fukagawa near Edo, he one day visited the poet, accompanied by a man called Rokusō Gohei, 六祖五兵衛 . The latter first entering into the hermitage, cried out, "How is it, the Buddhist Law in this quiet garden with its trees and grasses?" Bashō replied, "Large leaves are large, little ones are little." Bucchō then entering said, "Recently, what is your attainment?" Bashō replied, "The rain over, the green moss is fresh." Bucchō further asked him, "What is this Buddhist Law, *before* the green moss began to grow?"

At this moment, hearing the sound of a frog that lept
into the water, Bashō exclaimed, "The sound of the
frog jumping into the water."
      Kawazu tobikomu / mizu no oto

Responding to questions of "Buddhist Law" or "Buddha Nature"
thrown at him, Bashō simply verbalizes what his senses at
the given moment perceive. Note that this "question-answer"
corresponds to what we discussed in terms of the comparandum and the comparans (cf. the original version of the crow
poem, [32] in 3.5.2.2). What Bashō does here is verbal
"ostention", so to speak. "Ostention occurs", according to
ECO (1976: 225), "when a given object or event produced by
nature or human action (intentionally or unintentionally
and existing in a world of facts as a fact among facts) is
'picked up' by someone and shown as the expression of the
class of which it is a member" (cf. 2.3.4). The T Bashō utters upon the questions are then *reflexive* (KOCH 1982: 70):
they are "naming, referring, pointing, identifying, mapping
[...] mirroring" (2.3.3).

    The "capacity of naming" is based on the metaphorical
rather than the metonymic operation of semiotic activities, as JAKOBSON (1971: 62) clarifies in his study of
"Two Aspects of Language and Two Types of Aphasic Disturbances". The fact that the patient who suffers "similarity
disorder" (ibid., 56ff.) is not capable of metalingual
operation and accordingly cannot produce the subject of the
sentence proves that it is the substantives among the parts
of speech which are most independent of contexts. BLYTH's
account shows that the part of speech which dominates in
the interlocution between the dramatis personae is nouns.
The employment of substantives is, according to BROWER/
MINER (1957: 505, 1961: 109), one of major characteristics
of Japanese poetry. The preference for nouns in Japanese
poetry in general seems to be, as a matter of fact, one

manifestation of the general cultural inclination in
Japan towards the metaphorical operation (cf. JAKOBSON
1967: 158ff.). Furthermore it should be noted that nouns
are used very much in their primary sense, i.e., abstractness is avoided. As mentioned in the previous chapter
(2.3.3), the principle of the "First Correlate" with regard to the types of signs used in the fine arts of Zen
governs the poetry of haiku as well, in spite of the fact
that haiku is a verbal art: the words of haiku tend to be
qualisigns, indexical and rhematic.

In this connection, IVANOV (1977: 46ff.) offers us an
extremely interesting account; the correlation between
right-hemisphericity and the "nominal style" observed not
only in pathological cases of sensory aphasia, but also in
artistic works such as the films of Eisenstein, the Russian
lyric poetry of the nineteenth century, etc. (47-8). IVANOV,
ascertaining the onto- and phylogenetic primacy of the right
hemisphere (37, 103), explains that the right hemisphere,
"which is *not* dominant", *understands almost no verbs* while
it perfectly understands *nouns* (46-7). IVANOV (47) reasons
that this linguistic discrepancy between the two hemispheres
is due to their functional difference: "Visuelle und räumliche Muster, mit denen die rechte Hemisphäre zu tun hat,
sind vor allem Abbilder von Gegenständen. Eigenschaften und
Merkmale, aber auch Tätigkeiten, werden erst später bei der
Analyse der Bilder der Dinge separiert". Further (IVANOV,
[48]): "[I]n der modernen russischen Sprache werden Nominalsätze immer im Zuge des Präsens angewandt", assuming subsequently "eine konkrete raumzeitliche Lokalisierung der Rede"
in such practice, which is very often accompanied by the
deictic "dieser". The deictic nature of the fine arts of
Zen has been already discussed in the previous chapter
(2.3.3). The same principle is operative in haiku, as BLYTH
(1949: xiii) formulates: "Haiku [...] is the infinite grasped
in the hand, before the eyes, in the hammiering of a nail,
the touch of cold water, the smell of crysanthemums, the
smell of *this* crysanthemum".

IVANOV (37, 41, 43, 48, 57, 60, 82, 100, etc.) repeatedly emphasizes the *concrete* operation of the right hemisphere as opposed to the *abstract* operation of the left. One such passage (60) is of the greatest importance in supporting the idea of the right-hemisphericity of haiku:

> Wenn unter Elektroschock die linke Hemisphäre ausgeschaltet ist, verliert der Patient die Fähigkeit, abstrakte Begriffe zu verstehen wie Gesundheit, Bosheit, Freude, Religion usw., wobei aber das Verständnis konkreter Gegenstände völlig erhalten bleibt.

Now let us proceed to the latter half of BLYTH's account of the genesis of the frog poem:

> Bucchō was full of admiration at this answer, considering it [i.e., /a frog jumps in/ the splash of water/] as evidence of Bashō's state of enlightenment ... At this time Sampū, 杉風 , respectfully congratulated Bashō on having composed this verse, acknowledged by Bucchō, adding to art the glory of religion; Ransetsu, 嵐雪 , said, "This sentence of the sound of the water may be said to represent fully the meaning of haiku, yet the first part of the verse is missing. Please complete it." Bashō answered, "I was thinking about it myself, but I would like to hear your opinions first and then I will decide." Several of his pupils tried their hands at it;
> Sampū suggested
>   The evening twilight;
> as the first five syllables;
> Ransetsu,
>   In the loneliness;
> Kikaku,
>   The mountain rose.
> Bashō looking at these said, "You have each and all in your first line expressed an aspect of the matter and

composed a verse above the ordinary; especially Kikaku's
is brilliant and strong. However, not following the
conventional mode, just for this evening I will make it,
    The old pond.
While the above account eloquently expresses the significance
of the relationship between the two manifesta, i.e., "the
conventional mode" is contrastive while Bashō's option here
is homogeneous (Fig. 52), it also testifies that the first
five syllables, "furuike ya", are, similarly to the other
half of (1), a reflexive T. Thus, the two clauses of (1)
are the juxtaposition of two reflexive T which in turn
make up a *descriptive* T (KOCH 1982: 70). But the discussion
of the *typology of T* is the subject of the next chapter:
let it suffice at this point to mention that the T-production
motivated by introjection results in reflexive T.

In addition to the exposition of the T-type of the two
manifesta, BLYTH's account provides yet another important point in terms of narratology. In 3.3.4, we saw by the
example of (10) the difference between the *histoire* as the
deep structure and *narration* as the surface structure. We
also saw *récit*, the actual occurrence of reading, as the
mediation of the deep and surface structure, i.e., "the
mind goes and returns", due to the P_{xe}'s reconstruction of
the deep structure in a récit. In addition, BLYTH's account
supports our observation in (10) that the trigger of the
composition tends to be placed at the very end of the poem:
in the *histoire* it was the second half, "a frog jumps in/
a splash of water", which was composed first, while in
narration this latter part is placed at the end as the
"climax".

The difference between the homeorhetic T and the homeostatic T has already been discussed in terms of the pictorial sign (2.3.2). While the three modes of informational
poeticalness above discussed all reveal homeorhetic media-

tion in the surface structure, the mode of introjection lacks such mediation. *Asymmetry without the homeorhetic mediation* is manifested as the juxtaposition of the two reflexive T that are of objective presentation. (1) is a *homeostatic* T presupposing "the transcendence of any dichotomy". The surface structure simply presents the asymmetry as the "direct reflex of stimulus-response", and initial homeostasis is to be reinstated when the stimulation is over (Fig. 26). Fig. 64 depicts the introjective mediation observed in (1) in terms of T-production as well as in T-reception (1.1):

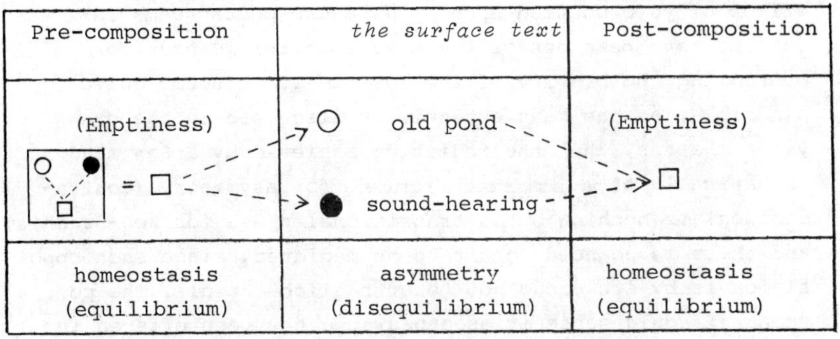

Pre-composition	the surface text	Post-composition
(Emptiness) ⟨diagram⟩ = □	⟶ ○ old pond ⟶ ● sound-hearing	(Emptiness) ⟶ □
homeostasis (equilibrium)	asymmetry (disequilibrium)	homeostasis (equilibrium)

Fig. 64: The Informational Poeticalness of (1): Introjection

Recalling such T of the fine arts of Zen as those in Illustr. 4, 5, 6, and 10, we can see that exactly the same principle of T-production underlies the haiku (1) and Zen T in terms of stylistic and informational poeticalness: as for stylistic poeticalness, both juxtapose "figure" and "ground", the syntagmatization of both of which is due to P_{xs}'s discovering the paradigmatic relationship between the two, and as to informational poeticalness, both present oppositions resulting from the Zen experience of "homeostasis - response - homeostasis". The only difference between them is in terms of the aesthetic: (1) as a verbal art employs the syllabic pattern, which is a triad, while Zen T, being mostly pictorial, iconic arts vary from case to case, though the most fundamental format seems to be a dyad, as seen in the case of chabana (Illustr. 10).

In confronting (1) as a *récit*, P_{xe} is supposed to experience the homeostasis as an "after-effect", so to speak in the phase of post-composition. This "after-effect" has been known as *yojō* in traditional poetological discussion in Japan[104]. The neurophysiological excitement aroused by the T is transmitted by the principle of "cascade connectives" and in fact "takes some time" (1.4). This lingering effect of yojō counted upon by Japanese poets seems in fact to have been one of the most powerful methods for overcoming the brevity of the surface T. It seems quite plausible, as has been extensively discussed in the previous chapter, that the mediation achieved by a Zen student is basically of a homeostatic nature, for asymmetry (contradiction) is nothing but a transitional phase for Zen-Buddhism, and there is no need for it to be mediated, since such opposition is by its credo not "unerträglich" at all. The poet's ego that could sense it as unbearable has been effaced in the first place: impending death, therefore, as confronted by Brooke, is no unbearable event for a Zen master, for he has transcended such relativity. This assertion finds strong support in a statement offered by a Chinese scholar of comparative literature, Pauline R. YU (1978). In her essay titled *Chinese and Symbolist Poetic Theories*, in which she compares Chinese theories of literature, which are "metaphysical", with those of Symbolists and Post-Symbolists, she concludes:

> Both regard poetry as the manifestation of a unitary principle and of the poet's intuitive or mystical union with [nature]. A crucial difference, of course, rests in the

fact that for the Chinese the Tao (Zen) already exists
as a given union that has only to be revealed, whereas
the Western poets must create their unifying myth (307).

YU's point that the "Tao already existed" for the Chinese
(and accordingly for the Japanese), whereas Western poets,
such as Brooke, have to create their own myth, or mediation, by themselves, can thus support our premise. It also
clarifies our suspicion that in Wang Wei's poem there might
be a totally different type of mediation (3.4.1.3). Wang
Wei's poem[105] reads:

(51) Man at leisure. Cassia flowers fall.
Quiet night. Spring mountains empty.
Moon rises. Startles - a mountain bird.
It sings at times in the spring stream.

The analogous feature between Bashō's frog poem and Wang
Wei's should by now be clear: both lack the homeorhetic
mediation. The only difference lies in the fact that in
Bashō's poem the two diaphoric, i.e., asymmetric paradigms
are juxtaposed, whereas in Wang Wei's the two diaphoric
paradigms are multiplied - the primum five-fold, and the
secundum two-fold[106]:

	Bashō's poem (1)			Wang Wei's poem (51)
perceptual quietness	/furuike ya/	◯	◯	◯/leisure/ ◯/flowers fall/ ◯/quiet night/ ◯/mountains are empty/ ◯/moon rises/
a temporal sound	/mizu no oto/	●	●	●/startles: a mountain bird/ ●/it sings/

Fig. 65: The Comparison between (1) and (51) as
Asymmetrical Texts

Another equally famous haiku of Bashō (52) presents an
identical structure with (1) and (51):

(52) 閑さや岩にしみ入る蟬の声   (A 280)
    Shizu̧kasa ya /   iwa ni shimiiru / semi no koe
          O   O
    (Quietness!/ penetrating into rocks/ voice of
    cicada)

On his journey to the Northern Provinces, Bashō visited an
old temple called *Yamadera* or *Ryūshakuji*-Temple, which was
known for the absolute tranquility of its sacred compound
(Bashō 1694: 367-8). This visit inspired the haiku. According
to AKABANE Manabu (1970), a Bashō-scholar, Bashō changed
the first two segments of this poem four times, as follows:

    (i)   Yamadera ya / ishi ni shimitsuku/ ...
           (At Yamadera!/ permeating the stone/...)

    (ii)   Sabishisa no / iwa ni shimikomu / ...
           (Loneliness / piercing into the rock/...)

    (iii) Sabishisa ya/ iwa ni shimikomu/ ...
           (Loneliness!/ piercing into the rock/...)

    (iv)   Shizukasa ya / iwa ni shimiiru / ...
           (Quietness! / penetrating into the rock/ ...)

Between the first version[107] and the last[108] lay a period
of five years. Interestingly enough, the whole process of
improvement, as we may easily discern, is concerned with
stylistic poeticalness, i.e., matrix-orientation, while
the informational poeticalness remains unaltered. This
refinement process by Bashō exemplifies beautifully what
Claude LÉVI-STRAUSS calls "the universality of myth" in
his *Structural Anthropology* (1958: 206) (cf. SCHOLES 1974: 60ff.):

> Myth is the part of language where the formula
> "traduttore, traditore" reaches its lowest truth
> value ... Poetry is a kind of speech which cannot

be translated except at the cost of serious distortions;
whereas the mythical value of the myth is preserved even
through the worst translation. Whatever our ignorance of
the language and the culture of the people where it originated, a myth is still felt as a myth by any reader
anywhere in the world. Its substance does not lie in its
style, its original music, or its syntax, but in the
"story" which it tells. Myth is language, functioning on
an especially high level where meaning succeeds practically "taking off" from the linguistic ground on which
it keeps on rolling.

The "myth", or the informational poeticalness of (52)
is, as in (1), introjective-homeostatic mediation, going
through the phases "symmetry-asymmetry-symmetry": instead
of the opposition of "the old pond vs. a splash of a
diving frog", we have here "tranquility vs. a cicada's
voice".

Thus, while Zen mediation can be characterized as the
introjective-homeostatic mode, there are a number of haiku
which can be characterized as "introjection", which transfer structures from the world to the ego, as we have already seen in the example of "the floating nest of the
grebe" (3.4.2.3). The poet simply discovers the fellow creatures that manifest *jitoku*, self-fulfillment. This introjective mode is in fact very close to equijection, insofar as
both modes concern the discovery of the natural phenomena
manifesting "Buddha Nature". The difference lies, however,
in the fact that in equijection the speaking poet is more
discernible, with his involvement appearing in the surface
T as subjective presentation, whereas in introjection his
ego is subdued so that the surface T contains only two manifesta of objective presentation.

Let us now consider the following haiku, which HORI
(1972: 108ff.) characterizes as a haiku presenting *kansō*

(" 観相 " literally, observing natural phenomena):

(53) 原中や 物にもつかず 鳴雲雀   (A 158)
　　　Haranaka ya / mono ni mo tsukazu / naku hibari
　　　　　　　　Ｏ　　　　　　　　　　　　　　　Ｏ
　　　(The middle of a field!/ holding onto / a singing
　　　syklark)

Bashō is standing in the middle of a field - the skylark being a kigo for spring - and watching the bird. It is flying high and low in the "Emptiness" of space as it merrily sings. The singing bird thus is a manifestation of a life which is free from any bondage and restriction, and it is "self-fulfilling", i.e., "every creature on the earth is satisfied with its existence and self-fulfilling according to its destiny" (ibid.). The sight of a singing bird that can move through space at will is thus transferred into Bashō's mind and reflected as a consolatory picture.

Introjection can also be Buddhistic in that ephemeral phenomena are accepted as such: this is again based on the effacement of the ego. The following two examples show this mode of mediation: both symbolize the transitoriness of the human world where events are eventually replaced by natural phenomena which are themselves transitory phenomena - "heat waves" in the first poem and "summer grass" in the second:

(54) 丈六に かげろふ高し 石の上   (A 207)
　　　Jō-roku ni / kagerō takashi / ishi no ue

　　　(As high as Jō-roku*/ are heat waves/ above the stone)

　　　*Jō-roku = the normal height for a statue of the
　　　　Buddha (ca. 4. 8 metres)

(55) 夏草や 兵共がゆめの跡   (A 275)
　　　Natsukusa ya / tsuwamono-domo ga / yume no ato

　　　(Summer grass!/ ancient warriors'/ dream's reminiscence.)

3.6 Summary

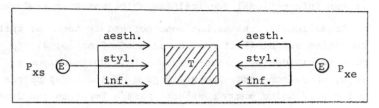

Fig. 66: The Three Foci in the Communication Situation

In confronting T, P_x (both partners in communication) structure the T according to the *focal energy* available to them. This energy is the sum of the three *modes* of focalization: *aesthetic focus, stylistic focus, informational focus*. Each focus selects its own analytical field: the aesthetic focus deals with the *unusual, non-trivial recurrences* on the level of the signifier or *manifesta*; the stylistic focus deals with the metalingual operation which clarifies the relationship between the signified and the signifier, i.e., between the *sememes* and manifesta; the informational focus selects the *mediation* mapped through the signifier, i.e., some kind of *solution* to overcome the *irreconcilable metaphysical opposition* expressed in the T. The three foci, due to their *autotelic* mechanism, make up *poeticalness* or *poeticity*. Accordingly, there are three modes of poeticalness: aesthetic, stylistic, and informational poeticalness.

Contrary to traditional linguistics, the semiotic approach thus provides us with a *tripartite* or *trimodal theory* of poeticalness. The poetics of haikai in Japan recognized trimodal poeticalness: prosodic intention, kotoba or diction, and kokoro or spirit or feelings. Haiku, evolved out of haikai poetry, exploits these three types of poeticalness, though the degree of exploitation was once and for all defined by the founder of the genre, Matsuo Bashō: it was informational poeticalness which was most explored.

Traditionally, haiku has been defined in terms of three normative rules: 1) it must consist of 17 morae; 2) it must be divided by a kire-ji; and 3) it must include a kigo, or season word. The *rigid form of the 5-7-5 pattern quarantees* haiku poetry *aesthetic poeticalness* on the level of the matrix or the signifier. This form in turn manifests the *internal necessity* of the tripartite structure: *symmetry-asymmetry-integration*. The second rule, the "cutting" of the poem by a caesura most prominently manifests the stylistic poeticalness of haiku: the *juxtaposition of two manifesta* provokes P_{xe} to *compare* the two sememes, i.e., to establish the paradigmatic relationship of the two syntagmatized elements (Fig. 34). The common core or the *tertium comparationis* is the *solution* to the *riddle* presented in poetry. Haiku's manifesta can thus be regarded as the realization of one sememe, the tc, and, for this reason, haiku is the exploitation of *synonymy*. The third rule, the inclusion of a kigo, results from the informational poeticalness of haiku defined by Bashō: the strong inclination toward the *effacement of the struggling ego* on the part of the poet, and towards a merging with nature. Kigo itself is the exploitation of *polysemy* caused by the specific property of language, i.e., the lack of a one-to-one relation between the signified and the signifier.

Fig. 67 summarizes the standard of the classical haiku as established by Bashō according to each mode of poeticalness and with regard to the morphology of haiku, i.e., *2-ku, 1-shō* [109]:

Mode of poeti-calness	characteristics	structural patterns	
		surface structure	deep structure
aesthetic poeticalness	1) 5 - 7 - 5 2) prosodic intension		
stylistic poeticalness	1) homogeneity 2) contrast		
informational poeticalness	1) projection 2) fūkyō 3) equijection 4) introjection		

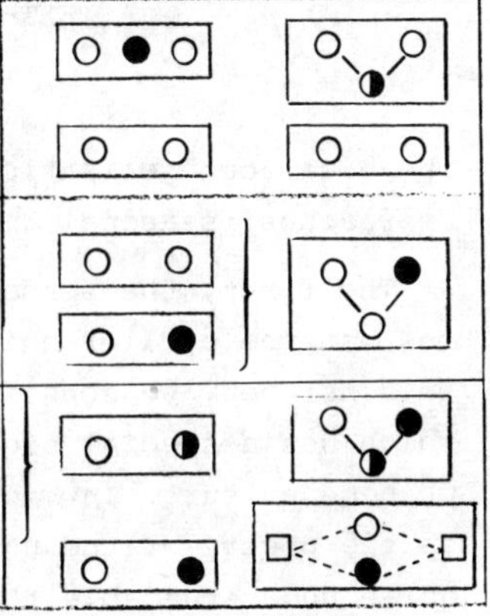

Fig. 67: *2-ku, 1-shō* as the Standard Format of Haiku

Comparing the most prototypical haiku, (1), and Zen T involving not verbal signs but pictorial signs as represented by Illustr. 10, we can further obtain the following:

mode of poeticalness	the haiku (1)	Zen T, Illustr. 10
aesthetic		
stylistic		
informational		

Fig. 67a: The Comparison between the Haiku (1) and Zen T.

CHAPTER 4

A TEXT-TYPOLOGY OF HAIKU

The usual categorizations of haiku take three major approaches: seasonal, morphological, and formal.

The first, the seasonal categorization, is applied in most of the earlier haiku anthologies. It consists of five seasons: four seasons in addition to the "New Year's Month", which has a special significance in Japanese as well as Chinese culture. In view of haiku's genetic development as the poetry of the unification of man and nature, it is quite understandable that this categorization has been most conventional in the classical haiku anthologies. The second categorization is primarily based on the study of kireji or "cutting" words (ASANO: 1962, 1963). ASANO advocates three typologies of haiku according to the morphological features, depending on the location of caesuras. If there is no caesura within a haiku, it is "1-clause, 1-statement"; if there is a caesura, severing the haiku into two, the poem is "2-clauses, 1-statement"; and if there appear more than one caesura, the poem is "3-clauses, 1-statement".

The third type of categorization is formal, i.e., criteria are based on the observation or non-observation of the three formative rules of haiku. Three established categories of contemporary haiku in Japan are the following: *Yūki-teikei* (including seasonal word, observing 5-7-5 pattern); *Muki-haiku* (no season word, yet with the pattern); and *Jiyūritsu* (haiku vers libre) (SHIODA 1969: 940-1). In addition to such categorization attempts, several other attempts have been made: Shiki, for instance, once classified haiku into 24 different styles according to criteria derived from the thematic inventory (MASAOKA, 1896). Many anthologies of

of modern-haiku classify the poems according to the factions
to which the poets belong such as "Season-Inclusive", "Season-Exclusive", "Romantic", "Realistic", "Humanity-searching",
"haiku vers libre"   each claiming its own creed (YOSHIDA
1962: 3-24).

Such categorizations depend entirely either on the "content" of haiku, as in the first, thematic categorization,
or on the "form" as in such criteria as the obeying-ignoring
of the 5-7-5 rule or the inclusion-exclusion of kigo. The two are,
however, inseparable, as the previous chapter has made clear,
since the signifier and the signified support and motivate
each other: the 5-7-5 is, e.g., not simply a neat form but
is motivated by deep-rooted "aesthetic feelings", as
YASUDA put it (3.5.1.1) as well as by the equally deep-rooted
"logic of nature" (1.4.1). In the following, I shall attempt
to categorize haiku according to its structural properties
based on the analytical tools used in the previous chapter.
The ontological and phylogenetic development of haiku poetry,
i.e., the *poetogenesis* of haiku thus will be the central issue
in this chapter. This investigation will yield to the *text-typological classification* of haiku.

4.1 The Seven Text-Types

In discussing the ontogeny and the phylogeny of semiotic
competence KOCH (1982: 69, 1983: 352) offers us the following
diagram. Fig. 68 exhibits *seven fundamental text-types*
along with their ontogenetic and phylogenetic order
(1982: 68):

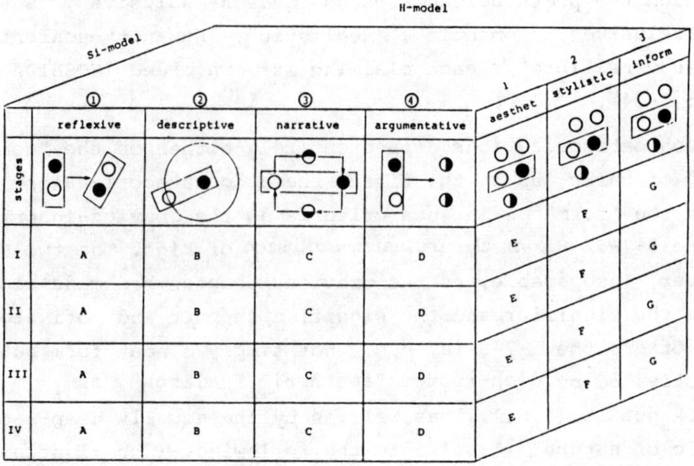

Fig. 68: Fundamental Text Types Derived from H- and
Si-Dimensions (from KOCH 1982)

The onset of lingual competence is seen in mapping or
naming (1982: 68), activities already discussed in terms
of deixis (2.3.4). This beginning is followed by three
further *psychogenic* structures: spatial, temporal, and
interactive structures (ibid., cf. MOERK 1977: 92ff.).
For both artistic and linguistic T-competence, KOCH (ibid.,
cf. 1983: 346-57) discerns the correlation of *psychogenic*
and *semiogenic* structures:

    mapping   -   reflexive
    spatial   -   descriptive
    temporal   -   narrative
    interactive - argumentative

These four structures are based on the "deepest-lying model",
i.e., the "Model of History", which deals with "space, time
structure, evolution" (ibid., cf. 1983: 346ff.). For this

reason, KOCH (1983: 353) maintains that four "H-model-
types" reflect the "universe", and these "universe-types"
may be "altogether prior to" the other three types, or
"brain-types", which are derived from the "Situation
Model" (Fig. 4). KOCH (1982: 70) characterizes the first
four of the "seven universal T-types" as follows (the first
has already been discussed in connection with Zen haiku,
[1] [3.5.3.4]):

    Reflexive text-type: "naming, referring, pointing,
identifying, mapping, transform-
ing, mirroring, self-analysing,
modelling, meta-structuring etc."

    Descriptive text-type: "spatial relations of objects,
'gestalts', figure-ground, geo-
metrical patterns, logical relations, 'sets', reversibilities,
parts and wholes, etc."

    Narrative text-type: "homeostasis and homeorhesis [...],
causal relationships, suspense,
irreversible structures, etc."

    Argumentative text-type: "the processual construction of
'truth', 'convention', 'common
sense' [...] settling disputes and
pacifying antagonism by referring
to a 'tertium quid'".

The other three "brain-types" are derived from the Si-Model.
The "ineluctable tripartition of the processual interaction"
between "brain: cortex" on the one hand and "ecosystem" on the
other results in the three further T-types: aesthetic, metalingual and metaphysical structures (1982: 68, cf. 1983: 350ff.).
As we have seen in the previous chapter, these three T-types
"make up what we call *poeticalness*" (1982: 70). Onto- and phylogenetically speaking, the three can be ordered as follows
(cf. SCHENK 1982, WENZEL 1982):

⎧ aesthetic T-type
⎨ stylistic T-type
⎩ informational T-type

Needless to say, there is "mutual translatability" among all of the seven T-types or between the two major groups, one mapping the universe and the other mapping the brain, as KOCH emphasizes (1983: 348). The very principle of evolution is, as we saw at the beginning of the present study, "order-on-order", (1.2), i.e., each new system builds on the precedent structure by "reduplicating" its precursor (cf. KOCH 1983: 350ff.). Thus, the more evolved structure exhibits simultaneously its preceding structures as well.

Nonetheless, it is possible to categorize a given T according to its "dominant" T-type, in the sense in which JAKOBSON speaks of the "dominance" of poetic function in poetry over the other five functions (1960: 353ff.). In the course of the following discussion of the T-typology of haiku, this "dominance" must be kept in mind.

4.2 The Diachronic Diversification of Haiku

The three-hundred-year history of haiku can be divided into five epochs. The haiku of each epoch tend to group themselves according to a specific T-type. The five epochs are:

(i)   Pre-Bashō Period (16th century - 1685): Genesis
(ii) Classical Haiku Period (1685-1896): First Metagenesis
(iii) Haiku-Reformation Period (1896-1 10): Second Metagenesis
(iv) New Haiku Period (1910-1940): Third Metagenesis and second Genesis
(v)   Contemporary Haiku

It goes without saying that there is some overlapping between the periods, and some tendencies are observable in each epoch, though they might not be predominant.

4.2.1 The Trajectory of Haiku Poetogenesis

Investigating European Modernism as manifested in science, art, poetry and poetics, KOCH (1983: 285) recognizes a cyclical pattern appearing as the *trajectory of poetogenesis*: the alternate direction of geneses (⇩) and metageneses (⇧) is observed repeatedly in the shift of the dominance in terms of the three modes of poetic structures. In the continuum of haiku poetry, spanning three centuries, a similar pattern can be detected, as shown below:

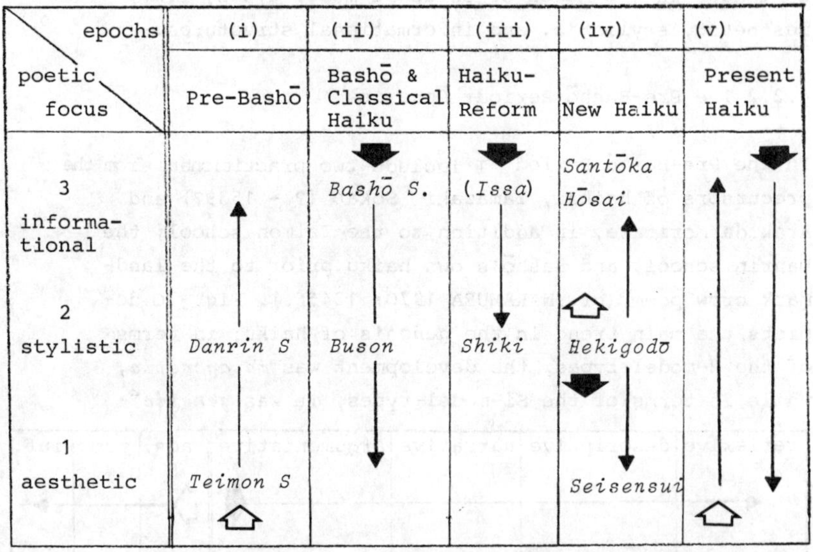

epochs poetic focus	(i) Pre-Bashō	(ii) Bashō & Classical Haiku	(iii) Haiku-Reform	(iv) New Haiku	(v) Present Haiku
3 informational	⬆	⬇ *Bashō S.*	⬇ (*Issa*)	*Santōka* *Hōsai* ⬆	⬇ ⬆
2 stylistic	*Danrin S*	*Buson*	*Shiki*	*Hekigodō* ⬇	
1 aesthetic	*Teimon S* ⬆			*Seisensui*	⬆ ⬇

Fig. 69: The Trajectory of Haiku Poetogenesis: the Shift of the Dominant Mode of Poeticalness

Of the two groups of the seven universal T-types, Fig. 69 deals with only the second group which is derived from the Si-Model. As will be shown, the first group, derived from the H-Model, concerns only the first epoch, (i), since the

haiku standard of Bashō with regard to the H-model-types
has not changed in the course of time.

As often mentioned, Bashō established the standard of
haiku in 1685 when he composed the crow poem, (31). As
far as the universe-types are concerned, Bashō's standard
has remained, i.e., "two clauses of reflexive T-type constituting a descriptive T-type", although, in addition to
this standard, a narrative T-type has also been in haiku's
repertoire, as we will presently see. The *poetogenesis of
haiku* can be thus discussed in terms of the shift of the
dominance in the modes of three Si-model-types, i.e.,
aesthetic, stylistic, and informational structures.

4.2.2 The Pre-Bashō Period: Genesis

In the Pre-Bashō Period[1] I include two practitioners from the
precursors of haikai, Yamazaki Sōkan (? - 1539?) and
Arakida Moritake, in addition to the Teimon school, the
Danrin school, and Bashō's own haiku prior to the landmark crow poem (cf. NAKAMURA 1970: 124ff.). Fig. 70 depicts the main trend in the genesis of haiku: in terms
of the H-model-types, the development was *metagenetic*,
while in terms of the Si-model-types, it was *genetic*[2]:

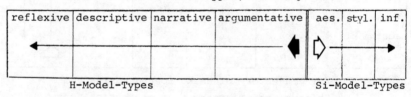

Fig. 70: The Genesis of Haiku

I shall demonstrate the metagenetic order with regard to the
H-model-types, beginning with argumentative T-types. The
genetic order in the Si-Model, which has been rather
extensively dealt with in the previous chapter with regard

to several traditional poetic devices (3.5.2.1, 3.5.2.4,
3.5.2.5), will also be considered in the course of the discussion.

4.2.2.1 Argumentative Text-Types

(56) 月にえをさしたらばよき団扇 (B 5)
Tsuki ni e o / sashitara ba / yoki uchiwa kana
(To the moon / if I give a handle/ it would
become a nice fan!)

Yamazaki Sōkan is regarded as the precursor of the haikai
poets due to his compilation *Shinsen Inu-Tsukuba-shū* (1632-
32). His poetry is mostly word-play based on kakekotoba
(KURIYAMA 1972: 25), i.e., the polysemic stylistic poeticalness was the central concern. The above hokku is, however,
nearly styleme-free: it exemplifies an argumentative T-type.
It is decisive, contrary to the spatial haiku such as (1)
or (31), that the two semantic groups here, /if I give a
handle to the moon/ and /it would become a nice fan/ are
logically connected: if A, then B. The manifestum, '*ba*',
realizes in the surface T this logical connection between
the two semantic groups. Understandably enough, (56)'s
kire-ji appears at the end, i.e., it belongs to the category of "one clause, one statement" in the traditional
categorization. "One clause" is, however, not appropriate,
since (56) consists of two "clauses" which are logically
ordered: they are needed here for "reasoning" (KOCH 1983:
354), or syllogism:

Syllogism in (56):
1) The full-moon is round. (○) = thesis
2) One could give it a handle (●)
   = antithesis
3) *Then* it would become a nice fan
   (◐) = synthesis

As would surely be expected, this T-type with its clear
logicality activating the left hemisphere of the brain
cortex was to be rejected as a result of the rise of
Zen metageneticity.

Another doomed argumentative T-type, which has a proverbial character, is the hokku (57) by Saikaku with a
"conceit" (cf. NGS, xff.), in which the manifestum 'sadame'
is a typical modal knot (3.5.1.2):

(57) 大晦日定めなき世の定め哉 (B 106)
Ōmisoka / sadame naki yo no / sadame kana
(New Year's Eve/ in a world of uncertainty/ comes,
but with certainty.)

Ihara Saikaku (1642-1693), Bashō's contemporary, was the
foremost advocate of the Danrin school and later became
known as a novelist. (57) presents a rather complicated deep
structure, which can be paraphrased as follows in the order
of manifesta:

1) We wish that *New Year's Eve*, when all debts must be
   paid, would not come.

2) We could have expected that it might not come, *since*
   Buddhism preaches that *this is a world of uncertainty*.

3) But that day will surely come as the only *certain
   thing* (in a world of uncertainty).

The deep structure of the logical connection seems to be:

2) Thesis: This is a world of uncertainty. (○)
3) Antithesis: But the arrival of New Year's Eve
   is certain. (●)
1) Synthesis: To hope that New Year's Eve would not
   come is therefore vain: we must accept its coming
   as fatidic. (◐)

(57) thus shows a typical argumentative T-type, i.e., "the
processual construction of *truth* or *common sense*" (4.1),

exhibiting simultaneously a strong overtone of the moral, as clarified above. This *proverbial nature* with a rather outspoken, as in (57), or latent accompanying moral lesson was to be observed even in Bashō's poetry. As a matter of fact, some haiku have survived as proverbs rather than as poems (cf. Excursus). Yet due again to strong logicality, i.e., to left hemisphericity, (57) represents the doomed argumentative hokku.

Furthermore, (57) is prominent in its aesthetic-stylistic structure manifested in the repetition of 'sadame', i.e., this manifestum is a modal knot. As is clear even in the transliterated text, the repetition of 'sadame' ("rule, fate, karma") is the predominant feature of the poem. The first 'sadame' combined with 'naki yo' constitutes a typical Buddhistic proverbial phrase "sadame naki yo" or /this world of no certainty/. The Buddhistic concept alluded to, is then juxtaposed to 'sadame kana', which discloses Saikaku's conceit, i.e., /in this world of uncertainty, New Year's Eve - the day of settling accounts - comes with definite certainty/. Since it was written by the novelist who repeatedly depicted the commercialism then current in Ōsaka, this hokku became famous as an exemplary specimen of his treatment of the theme of "money" (KURIYAMA 1972: 88). We may also notice that the manifestum 'Ōmisoka' designates no seasonal atmosphere - a sememe of nature - but denotes only /the day of balancing accounts/.

4.2.2.2 The Narrative-Joke Text-Type

(56), and (57) thus represent the argumentative T-types, and (57) further exemplifies the aesthetic-stylistic structure of the Pre-Bashō Period. (58), by the founder of the Danrin School, Nishiyama Sōin (1605-1682), represents the narrative T-type coupled with the structure of the joke (cf. 3.5.2.4):

(58) ながむとて花にもいたし頸の骨 (B 93)
Nagamu to te / hana ni mo itashi / kubi no hone
(Having watched [for such a long time]/ the cherry-
blossoms, I've gotten used to them - oh, it's got
sore/ my neck-bone!)

Structurally, (58) is almost identical with (37), which
we discussed as the example of honka-dori or allusive variations (3.5.2.5): this hokku, too, is "bisociative" in that
the whole T concentrates on the discrepancy between the two
sememes, /get used to/ and /get sore/, realized in the manifestum 'itashi'. KURIYAMA (1972: 84) cites the original waka
composed by Saigyō, the famous waka-poet of the late Heian
Period (Fig. 32) to which this hokku refers:

(59)

ながむとて	Nagamu to te	Looking up
花にもいたく	Hana ni mo itaku	I became quite used to
馴れぬれば	Narinureba	the cherry-blossoms; so,
ちるわかれこそ	Chiru wakare koso	to fall with their blossoms
かなしかりけれ	Kanashikarikere	is truly a sad matter.

(58) starts out with the traditional theme of "cherry-blossom
sentiment", channelling the P_{xe} into (59), Saigyō's waka - a
serious poem, laden with informational poeticalness. The con-
duction continues to the end of the second line, reinforcing
the effect of a sentimental atmosphere, when a reversal occurs
with the juxtaposition of the "neck-bone": the sentimental
course is abruptly transposed into the ungraceful, unroman-
tic event of straining one's neck because of an awkward posture held for too long. The twist lies in the permutation of
'*itaku*/naru' meaning /becoming very much attached to/, into
"*itashi*/kubi no hone", meaning / my neck-bone aches/. The
manifestum 'itashi' thus functions as a pivot word (●),
reinforcing the metalingual operation demanded here. It
should also be noted that this hokku presents "irreversibility" (4.1) in terms of narratology, i.e., in order to

establish a clash between the two planes of semantically incompatible nature (M1 and M2 in KOESTLER's analysis: 3.5.2.4), the first plane - here, the allusion to Saigyō's waka - must precede the second plane - hurting one's neck-bone. With regard to the potential for laughter, however, (58) has still greater potential than (37), since the discrepancy between the first and the second context of (58), i.e., /Saigyō's waka/ and /straining one's neck/, is far greater than the discrepancy between /falling blossoms are returning to the branch/ and /butterfly/. The irreversibility of a joke-like haiku, (58), is as follows (cf. 3.5.2.4):

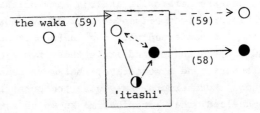

Fig. 71: The Irreversibility in the Joke-Like Hokku, (58)

In the previous chapter, we discussed the matrix-orientation of the Teimon school using the examples of (30) and (35). This school was mainly concerned with aesthetic as well as stylistic poeticalness, i.e., such traditional devices as engo (verbal associations) or kakekotoba (pivot-words) were the main issues in their composition. The Danrin school, as shown above, is a "transition" (NAKAMURA 1970: 124ff., HATTORI 1776: 522) from the Teimon school to the Bashō school, insofar as it emphasized the exploitation of *analogy*: it explored the free associations between the two paradigms (cf. YASUDA 1957: 166).

Saikaku, e.g., emphasized the manifestation of stylistic poeticalness, "hyperbolic analogy". In *Dokugin Hyakuin* (A Hundred Verses by Himself) Saikaku states:

In our School (Danrin) extraordinary prosody is regarded as the way of haikai: for instance, Mount Fuji with its volcanic smoke is compared to a tea pot, and the lake is likened to a pail ... (quoted by KURIYAMA 1972: 24).

The contribution of the Danrin School to its successor, the Bashō School, can accordingly be characterized as the exploitation of paradigm: while the Danrin school experimented with obvious and extreme "analogies", whose tertium comparationis can be logically recognized, Bashō moved to the more subtle "discordia concors". The underlying principle of what Saikaku here calls *analogy* and what HENDERSON refers to as "internal comparison" (3.5.2.2) is, however, identical: both are concerned with the juxtaposition of a comparans and a comparandum. And it is these types of T, the left hemispheric and bisociative, that were banned by the Bashō school. Furthermore, they were the ones, it should be emphasized, that later became known as *senryū* (3.3). The difference between haiku and senryū lies, therefore, not so much in their thematic concerns, since one deals with nature and the other with "human nature", as the Haiku Society of America maintains (3.3), but in their text-structural properties. Senryū, "humorous and satiric" (3.3), are based on argumentative, narrative-joke T-types, which haiku abandoned (left-hemisphericity!).

Haiku attempted in vain to be the poetry of socialistic ideology during the Twenties of the present century. It seems in fact too much to ask for a haiku of 17 syllables to express revolutionary ideas which could be convincingly presented only through the argumentative T-type, and there is no mystery as to why "proletarian haiku" could not have flourished.

4.2.3 The Classical Haiku Period: Metagenesis

Literary critics have taken either the frog poem (1) or the crow-perching poem (31) as the turning point (NGS 1958: 11, BLYTH 1949: 340). The poetry of haiku was established when informational poeticalness was foregrounded, as we have seen above, and these two can be represented as such, although in (31), stylistic poeticalness is also conspicuous (3.5.2.2). Not only did Bashō reach the focus of informational structure through the Danrin school's extreme emphasis on *stilization*, but so did some of his contemporaries (KURIYAMA 1972: 27). It is noteworthy that the drive toward informational structure occurred independently of Bashō's influence.

Uejima Onitsura (1661-1738) was one of them, declaring that "there is no haikai except *makoto* ('truthfulness, sincerity')" (quoted in KURIYAMA ibid., 112):

(60) 骸骨 のうへを粧ひて花見かな　　　　　　　　　　(B 185)
　　　Gaikotsu no / ue o yosoite / hanami kana
　　　(On the surface of the skull/ the decoration of
　　　make-up/ for flower-viewing!)

The ephemerality of the mundane world - a fundamental precept of Buddhism - is manifested with the styleme-free rendition. The juxtaposition of metaphysical premises is here outspoken: youth vs. old age, life vs. death, human endeavour vs. destructive nature, etc.

4.2.3.1 The Narrative Text-Type

Konishi Raizan (1654-1716) was another poet who outgrew witty word-play:

(61) 秋風を追へば我身に入りにけり   (B 158)
Akikaze o / oeba wagami ni / iri ni keri
(I followed the autumn wind/ into my body/ it
penetrated!)

(61) presents a morphology called "1-ku, 1-shō", namely
"1-clause, 1-statement", as we saw in (54). It seems that
"1-clause, 1-statement" concentrates on syntagma instead
of paradigm, i.e., it can be regarded as an elliptical
narrative text (4.1, cf. KOCH 1982c). Instead of the five-
fold structure of "the canonic minimum format of the
homeostatic cycle"[3] (KOCH 1983: 353ff., cf. BREMOND 1973,
PRINCE 1973, TODOROV 1969, CANISIUS 1982), haiku narrative
has a three-fold structure. Haiku narrative fulfills the
requirement of art   stated in "Aristotele's sage remark",
i.e., a plot must have beginning, middle, and end in order
to be a whole (REID 1977: 6):

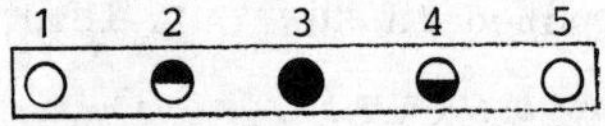

```
                       1    2    3    4    5
Narrative Cycle:      | O   ◐   ●   ◐   O |
```
  1) state of stability
  2) procedure of instabilization
  3) state of instability
  4) procedure of stabilization
  5) return to stability

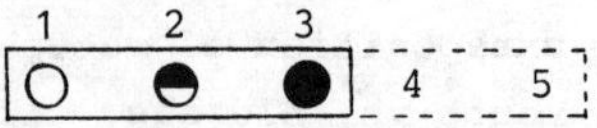

```
                       1    2    3
Haiku Narrative:      | O   ◐   ● |  4    5
```
  1) Beginning: (I was touched with) the *autumn wind*. (O)
  2) Exposition: I *followed it*. (◐)
  3) End: It has *penetrated into my body*! (●)

Fig. 72: The Narrative T-Type of Haiku (61)

Let us take another such "narrative" haiku by Bashō:

(62) 道のべの木槿は馬にくはれけり
  Michi-nobe no / mukuge wa   uma ni / kuware keri
  (At the road-side/ the marsh-mallow has been by
  my horse/ eaten up!)

1) *The marsh-mallow* (was blooming)
   at the road-side (◯)
2) *My horse* (then came by) (◐)
3) *It was eaten up by my horse* (●)

Significantly enough, both (61) and (62) are *1-ku*, *1-shō* with the kire-ji "keri", which is a verbal suffix denoting "den nachdrücklichen Abschluß einer Aussage" or "lyrische Emphase" (LEWIN 1959: 171). TODOROV (1977: 111) explains that there are "two types of episodes in a narrative: those which describe a state [...] and those which describe the passage from one state to the other". While the first type is "static" and "iterative", the second is "dynamic" and occurs "in principle once"[4] (ibid.). He then correlates these two types of narrative episodes with two parts of speech: the first to the adjective and the second to the verb (ibid., cf. 3.5.3.4)[4]. The narrativity of (61) and (62) is thus reinforced in the verbal manifesta of each poem as well: 'hairi-keri' and 'kuware-keri', respectively. Although not every *1 ku*, *1-shō* haiku, i.e., with the morphology of "1-clause, 1-statement" with the kire-ji at the end, is of the narrative T-type, it is often dominated by "the second, dynamic type of narrative episode". (61) or (62) are thus fundamentally different T-types from, say, (1), which is "static", "iterative", or "adjectival", as we will see in the next section. Before we proceed to examine the T-type of (1), however, it should be pointed out that (61) and (62) differ from (58), though they share the narrative characteristic of "irreversibility": while (58) is charged with the stylistic structure that makes up the "logic of humor", these two (61) and (62) are free of that structure.

4.2.3.2 The Descriptive Text-Type with Two Reflexive Texts

The Classical Period takes not only the narrative T-type,

charged with informational structure but free any obvious
stylization, but also the frog poem, (1), as its prototype.
The informational structure, imbued with Zen Buddhism, of
this prototypical haiku has been extensively discussed in
the previous chapter and in 3.5.3.4. The reflexivity of
(1) with regard to T-production has also been pointed out:
the two clauses, "the old pond" and "a frog jumps in/ the
sound of water", are both reflexive in that they simply
"name" or "point out" the phenomena (4.1). (1) consists,
thus, of the juxtaposition of the two reflexive T.

These two T of reflexivity are, however, antonymic in
that each points to two antithetical phenomena: they constitute
thus one descriptive T. Descriptive T deals with
such phenomena as spatial relations, gestalts, figure-ground-contrasts,
sets, reversibilities, parts, and wholes
(KOCH 1982: 70), to repeat the definition of this text-type
once again. The "part" or microcosm of /a frog jumping
into the water/ is thus juxtaposed to the "whole" or macrocosm
of /the old pond/, and together they designate the transcendence
of both spatial and temporal limitations. In terms of "figure-ground-contrasts",
/frog jumping .../ is a "figure", whereas
/the old pond/ constructs a "ground". With regard to
the "reversibility" of the two elements, the two could
theoretically be reversed - provided that the manifestum
'ya' be changed[5] -, as the first version and the final version
of the crow-perching poem eloquently demonstrate: they
do not involve any temporal feature, i.e., the two are not
related chronologically or causally (hence, this is no
"narrative text") or logically (hence, this is no "argumentative
text"). It seems that one of the crucial features
of haiku lies here, i.e., in the fact that haiku - or Bashō's
hokku, to be specific - became a poetic genre when it reached the
"reflexive text-type" in its kernel structure, which further
effected a "descriptive text", as Fig. 73 illustrates:

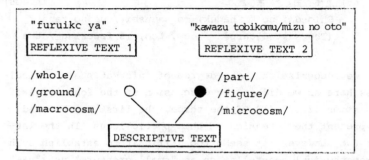

Fig. 73: The Descriptive T-Type Consisting of
Two Reflexive Texts

As mentioned, the "descriptive T-type consisting of "reflexive T" resulted from Bashō's commitment to Zen Buddhism: it is a *right-hemispheric* T presenting a fundamental dyadic structure. This type has remained to the present as the quintessential standard format of haiku.

4.2.3.3 The First Metagenesis

While Bashō and his contemporaries busied themselves with information poeticalness, an inevitable metagenesis had already set in. This tendency can even be detected in Bashō himself, who in his last five years advocated "lightness" instead of haiku laden with informational poeticalness. The following three examples typify this "lightness"[6].

(63) 木のもとに汁も膾も桜かな   (A 329)
    Ko no moto ni / shiru mo namasu mo / sakura kana
    (Under the tree [of cherry-blossoms]/both the soup
    and salad/ are covered with cherry-blossom!)

(64) 水仙や 白き障子のとも移り   (A 391)
    Suisen ya / shiroki shōji no / tomo-utsuri
    (Narcissi !/ the white-paper sliding-door/ is
    reflecting too.)

(65) 塩鯛の歯ぐきも寒し魚の店 (A 408)
　　　Shio-dai no / haguki mo samushi / uo no tana
　　　(The salted carp's / gum, too, is freezing / the
　　　fish-stand.)

Can we recognize the same degree of informational poeticalness here as we did in the discussion of the four types of mediation (3.3.3.4)? Of the three, the first may be said to present the retention of this poetic focus. In the latter two, however, it seems too difficult to establish such a metaphysical constellation as "small creature" vs. "nature", "the floating nest of the grebe" in (14) or "the singing skylark depending on nothing" in (53). Instead of concentrating on such a philosophy of life, these poems focus more or less on imageries as such, i.e., they focus on the *comparans* only (cf. KOCH 1983: 266). It is in a way the result of a certain tendency which we have already mentioned, namely, the increasing subtlety of a tertium comparationis. In Saikaku (Danrin School), we had "hyperbolic analogy", which is to say, the paradigmatic relationship between a cd and a cs is based on the tertium comparationis that can be easily inferred. In Bashō this relationship became more and more distant. In the last phase of his poetic activity, Bashō seems to have reached the stage in which one of the two constituents of this relationship, i.e., cd, is no longer discernible. This tendency is metagenetic insofar as it is more concerned with stylistic poeticalness than with informational poeticalness.

　　This metagenetic trajectory already observable in Bashō was crystallized in Yosa Buson (1717-1783), who is often compared to Bashō in terms like those used by ICHIKAWA (NGS 1958): "Being a painter, (Buson) naturally described impressions vividly through pictorial and visual imagery rather than by using lyrical effects, as in the case of

Bashō" (xxii). He further underlines the difference between Bashō and Buson as follows:

While Bashō was subjective and symbolistic and possessed something of the spiritual quality of the Kamakura-Muromachi period (1185-1603), Buson went back to the sensuousness of the Nara-Heian period (710-1185), adding to it the intense, bright and clear colouring of Chinese poetry and "nanga" (Southern school of brush painting). In his theories of haikai Buson never mentions, as Bashō did, the union of the individual with Nature, but advocates rather exploring and enjoying to the full the world of the imagination, irrespective of any philosophy of Nature.

This difference between the two most significant figures of classical haiku was to be inherited later by the American "haikuist" as the "most fundamental [of] questions raised about haiku", namely, as in VAN DEN HEUVEL's formulation: "Is it basically a religious or an aesthetic experience?" (V.D. HEUVEL 1974: xxx). Interestingly enough, this first metagenesis - which resulted in the production of a comparans stripped of its comparandum, as it were, and which focuses primarily on stylistic poeticalness - coincides with what KOCH terms "the most radical outcome of the Imagist's endeavour", "the focus is on the comparans as such, on a 'catalog of images' (Šeršenevič: *Katalog obrazov*)" (KOCH 1983: 268). The evolution of haiku is, however, homeorhetic (ibid., 286), as is any evolution for that matter, and the stylistic poeticalness of the pre-Bashō period and that of Buson and his contemporaries (the Tenmei School)[7] could never have been the same: the former concentrates on *paranomasia* or wordplay, but the latter on *comparantia*.

The following three haiku by Buson should clarify this point:

(66) 牡丹散りて 打ちかさなりぬ二三片   (B 637)
    Botan chirite / uchi-kasanarinu / ni-san-ben
    (The petals of peony are falling/ and lie one on
    top of the other/ two or three petals)

(67) 山蟻のあからさまなり 白牡丹   (B 635)
    Yama-ari no / akarasama nari / haku-botan
    (A mountain-ant* is/ quite conspicuous/ a white peony)
    *yama-ari = a large pitch-black ant

(68) 柳ちり 清水かれ 石ところどこ   (B 675)
    Yanagi chiri / shimizu kare / ishi tokoro-doko
    (The willow is barren/ the brook is dried up/ the stones
    here and there)

(66) is a look at a microcosmic natural phenomenon in which red
petals of the peony flower are spotlighted and presented. In
(67) the color contrast, a pitch-black spot on the surface of
brilliant white, is presented as such. (68) describes the desolate landscape of late autumn (KURIYAMA 1972: 276).

In contrast to (31), in which Bashō's stylistic focus selected the juxtaposition of "the autumn evening" and "the
perching crow", or "ground-figure", all three of Buson's haiku
present only "figures". This shift in stylistic structure can
be diagrammed as:

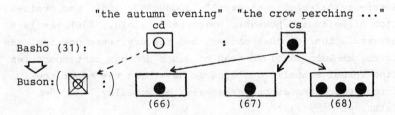

Fig. 74: From Bashō to Buson: from Comparison to
        Comparantia

Of the three, (68) presents the morphology that is called "3-ku, 1-$sh\bar{o}$", i.e., "3 clauses, 1-statement". As is clear by now, all three are the manifesta of one sememe, /autumnal desolation/. Although this concatenation of three or more paradigms is by no means Buson's patent - Bashō has a few famous ones, too[8] - Buson's general tendency to concentrate on comparantia is obvious. In fact, this tendency was to be continued and further reduced one and a half centuries after Buson as haiku vers libre, as we will see. With regard to the H-model-types, it should be pointed out that descriptivity remained. Both (66) and (67) consist of two reflexive texts, while (68) consists of three.

Buson's metagenetic endeavour went further: he explored the potential of phonological recurrences, i.e., aesthetic structure used with stylistic poeticalness. Buson's haiku, thus, frequently present modal knots.

(69) 春の海 終日 のたりのたり哉 (B 576)
Haru no umo / hinemosu notari-/notari kana
(The spring sea!/ all day long up and down/
up and down!)

(70) 日は日くれよ 夜は夜明けよと 啼く蛙 (B 582)
Hiwa hikure yo / yo wa yo akeyo to / naku kawazu
(In the day time, "be dusk"/ in the night, "be dawn"/ -
so croak frogs)

(71) をちこちをちこちと 打つ砧かな (NKBZ 42, 261)
Ochi-kochi / ochi-kochi to utsu /kinuta kana
(Here and there/ there and here - so beating/ fulling*!)
*to full = to shrink and thicken (woolen cloth) by moistening, heating and pressing.

(64) presents the onomatopoeic gitai-go (state-expressing word: 3.5.13), expressing the undulation of the spring sea. (70) plays with the onomatopoeia of the frog, "kero-kero"

(croak-croak) by superimposing Japanese imperative sentences
on it. (71) plays, similarly, with the onomatopoeia of beating the woolen cloth: "ochi-kochi" (over there - here).
The above three examples show, then, Buson's endeavour to exploit the matrix-level - the orientation that was subjugated
so radically by Bashō.

4.2.3.4 The Second Genesis in Issa

The first metagenesis seems to have reached its turning
point in the work of Kobayashi Issa (1763-1827), whose
haiku reveal the fusion of predominantly aesthetic and informational poeticalness. Issa employs a good deal of colloquialism (BLYTH 1949) and onomatopoeia as well:

> (72) 月ちらり 鶯ちらり 夜は明けぬ   (B 1023)
>   Tsuki chirari / uguisu chirari / yo wa akenu
>   (The moon flashing/ the cuckoo flashing/ the dawn
>   has come)
>
> (73) どんど焼き どんどと雪の降りにけり   (B 1024)
>   Dondo-yaki[9]/ dondodo yuki no/ furini-keri
>   (The dondo-festival/ the snow is falling/ unceasingly)

As opposed to Buson who enjoyed a successful life as a painter
and a haikai-poet, Issa's life was unhappy[10] with "the miseries which are told of in his poems" (NGS 1958: xxiii). ICHIKAWA
et al. (ibid., xxiii) affirm the following, testifying that the
informational poeticalness observed in Issa is far more outspoken than Bashō's:

> It might be said of him that he went a step further than
> Bashō in expressing in verse his attitude towards life.
> His feeling of compassion for defenceless creatures, such
> as sparrows, frogs, butterflies and mosquitoes, is used
> by him as a means of satirizing the heartlessness of
> human society [...] Issa could not accept the miseries of

life (contrary to Bashō), nor rise above them and attain
peace of mind, as Bashō did, but struggled with a grim
smile to escape from the web of circumstances by giving
them a comic turn.

While Bashō's mediation tends to be introjective, Issa's is
quite projective, with a strong empathy of the poet with
the solitary, undervalued creatures appearing in the surface structure.

(74) 夕燕 我には翌のあてはなき   (B 1010)
    Yū-tsubame / ware ni wa asu no / ate wa naki
    (Evening swallow/ for me there is no place / to
    go tomorrow)

(75) 痩蛙 まけるな一茶これにあり   (B 1022)
    Yase-gaeru / makeruna Issa / kore ni ari
    (Skinny frog!/ don't be defeated: Your Issa/ is here)

Although the variety in Issa's haiku is itself of the most
challenging nature, a comprehensive examination of it cannot be undertaken here. It should suffice to mention that
Issa did not rely on Zen Buddhism and that in order to
overcome his personal antagonism, he wrote haiku charged with
informational poeticalness quite similar in their nature to
that of Brooke's projective mediations. (74) and (75) present Issa's identification of himself with such solitary
figures as an "evening swallow" or a "wretched little frog".
Unlike Bashō's, Issa's poetry exhibits the speaking poet quite
overtly.

Although Issa deserves speial examination, he was no more
than "an obscure poet with no influence on the contemporary
poetic scene" (UEDA 1976: 5), with practically no good disciples, quite unlike Bashō or Buson (BLYTH 1964: 351). It
had been over 150 years since Bashō established informational-focus-laden haikai, and "poetry" was now in the hand of the
haikai professionals, whose concern was not the improvement

of poetry but the possibility of making a living with it.
In another half a century we will be confronted with
Masaoka Shiki, a young poet-critic, whose "hobby of painting" had such a fatal impact on the metaphysical side of
modern haiku (KANDA 1958: 426ff.) because of his "metagenetic"
reformation.

4.2.4 The Haiku Reformation

UEDA describes the background against which Shiki launched
his reformation as follows:

[The haikai-professionals] lacked the passion to write
good poetry [...] Consequently the haikai and hokku written
in the nineteenth century were, by and large, lifeless [...]
The poems that reached the reading public in the nineteenth century were trite, pretentious, and devoid of
emotional appeal.

Bashō's haiku had its fundamentality in metagenetic Zen
Buddhism, which purged the poetry of every cognitive "sedi-
ment", as we have already seen: it rejected intellectualism,
conceptualization, self-consciousness. As the previous section has made clear, however, the effacement of ego (introjective mediation) was not a prerequisite for every poet, and
most of the later generations including Buson did not experience the metagenesis of Zen-Buddhism and remained in the
progenetic order of the H-model. One typical "tsukinami"[11]-
haiku, the prefix signifying "conventional" or "trite",
will illustrate this point: it is by Sakurai Baishitsu (1769-
1852):

(76) 名月や 草木に劣る人のかげ   (B 1170)
    Meigetsu ya / kusaki ni otoru / hito no kage
    (The full moon!/ inferior to the shadow of grasses
    and trees/ is the shadow of a man)

This is "a haiku of reasoning" (MARUYAMA in NBKZ 42
1972: 451), for the poet measures the shadow of grasses
and trees against the shadow of man, who is considered to
be "generally superior to all the creatures on the earth"
(ibid.) and judges that the former is superior. BLYTH
(1949: 196), too, expounds upon "the failure, as poetry"
of this poem by quoting the proverb "Comparisons are
odious". This is an interesting specimen in that it has the
guise of a descriptive text - the juxtaposition of "the full
moon" and "the shadow of a man" - but in its deep structure, it is an argumentative text: it constructs "processually the *truth*" (4.1, also Fig. 82 in 5.5.1).

Against this literary scene the young Shiki and his
followers[12] revolted (UEDA 1976: 5). In his view the Japanese haiku of the nineteenth century were "trite in motif,
diffuse in style, pedantic in expression, restrictive in
vocabulary, and too conscious of poetic factions" (ibid., 6).
Shiki turned to Buson, instead of Bashō, praising the former's "objectivity" and rejecting the latter's "subjectivity" (BLYTH 1964: 21-32). Shiki explains his position
on this problem of haiku autobiographically (1896b: 467):

> At first I was quite subjective, but then I became
> more and more objective. To expound further: at first
> I attempted to depict the object which I felt was
> beautiful as well as the resulting feeling. Later,
> however, I came to realize the superfluity of adding
> my resulting feeling, and thus that triggered my
> aesthetic experience. For instance, I said at the
> beginning: "There is a mountain: there is a river:
> oh, how beautiful!"; but later, I discarded the sub-
> jective words, "how beautiful", and instead I merely
> delineated the beautiful spots of mountains and rivers
> and attempted to let the reader feel "beautiful" with-
> out my mentioning "how beautiful".

The logical consequence was Shiki's advocation of "shasei" (the delineation of nature) - an emphasis on the pictorial characteristic of haiku, as is most conspicuously observed in his assertion that "extreme objective beauty is equated with painting" (ibid.). The paramount credo of his haiku-revolution was thus "unblurred impression". The following two poems exemplify his credo, which can be rendered in our terms as Shiki's advocation of the descriptive T-type:

(77)　一つ落ちて二つ落ちたる椿かな　　　　　　(NKBT 16:61)[13]
　　　Hitotsu ochite / futatsu ochitaru / tsubaki kana
　　　(Falling one / and then two / camellias!)

(78)　一束の葉生姜ひたす 野川かな　　　　　　(NKBT 16:57)
　　　Hito-taba no / ha-shōga hitasu / no-gawa kana
　　　(A bundle of / ginger-root with leaves submerged/
　　　a brook in the field!)

According to MATSUI (in NKBT 16, 1972: 13-34), Shiki had been influenced by Herbert Spencer's theory as contained in *The Philosophy of Style*: he considered Bashō the founder of the "species" of haikai, and Shiki's school evolved out of this species (ibid., 23). This evolutionary process is "progenetic" in his opinion. It is worth quoting here as the forerunner of the present study, which applies the theory of *evolution* to the haiku's poetogenesis. Shiki states (1899: 346):

> Art and literature evolve from simplicity to complexity, from imperfection to refinement, from dispersion to coherence. Similarly, haiku have been evolving in this direction.

In discussing the difference between Bashō and Buson, Shiki (1897: 648) describes diachronic diversification thus: "Bashō thought that by composing [the frog poem] he reached

the essence of haiku and never in his life wrote complex
haiku, whereas "Buson caught the complex beauty and gave
haiku a new life" (ibid., 649). In emphasizing the complexity of Buson's haiku, which predict the further complexity of his own school, Shiki discovers two exceptional
haiku by Buson that show a narrative structure and are
hence "shōsetsu-teki" (novel-like), since they contain
"temporalness", and which accordingly contributed to the
increasing complexity of haiku:

(79) 御手討の夫婦なりしを 更衣　　　　　　　　(B 612)
Oteuchi no / fūfu narishi o / koromogae
(They were a couple/ supposed to have been exe-
cuted by their lord:/ the change of clothes)[14]

(80) 討ちはたす荒論つれだって 夏野かな　　　　　(B 615)
Uchihatasu / boro tsure datte / natsu-no kana
(Bound to have a duel/ two beggar-priests are
walking side by side/ on the summer moor)

He comments (1897: 642-3):

> The former depicts a human event that took place in
> the past, the latter a future event. The two are
> identical in that both deal with human events: the
> former with one in the past and the latter with one
> in the future. They are also identical in that their
> main events are complex ones.

Shiki thus detects the complication of haiku in Buson;
however, its maturation, Shiki argues, was first accom-
plished by his school, although "the value of the verses
is not necessarily [his] concern" (1899: 351). He clarifies this evolutionary process of increasing complexity
by citing examples from two leading disciples, Kawahigashi
Hekigodō (1873-1937) and Takahama Kyoshi (1874-1959):

(81) 箒木は皆伐られけり芙蓉咲く
Hokigi wa / mina kirare-keri / fuyō saku
(Broom-grasses/ have all been cut down/ hollyhocks are blooming)

(82) 枯葛を引き切りたりし葎かな
Kare-kuzu o/ hikikiritarishi / mugura kana
(Dried vines/ were cleared away/ but now mugura-vine everywhere!)

According to Shiki, the above two haiku possess "two temporally different scenes" and thus, "two center points" (1899: 352): "The first point lies in the first part - i.e., first "clause" -, and the second in the latter". Interestingly enough, however, Shiki admits that the fact that these haiku have two center points is due to "the syntax" and if the syntax were to be changed - that is, by employing the attributive form instead of the final form - the two would possess only once center point (ibid.). Although Shiki thus refers only to the surface text, or matrix-structure, these two haiku seem to have still deeper differences than the haiku which we have already discussed: these differences do not concern their spatial relationship to each other but rather their temporal relationship, i.e., the narrative structure which is, in its *histoire*, "irreversible". In (81) the two events - "broom-grasses had been cut down", *and now*, "hollyhocks are blooming" - are chronologically ordered, and one must precede the other: the poet's inspiration lies in the fact that at the place where broom-grasses were seen, "now hollyhocks are blooming". Similarly, (82) deals with two events that have a chronological sequence: first, the cleaning up of the dried vine, and then, the appearance of the mugura-vine. The difference between both (81) and (82) and the other poems, say, (31), in which "the autumn evening" and "the perching crow" are juxtaposed, is apparently more profound than Shiki assumed: it is the difference between the "suspense" of the *dynamic* T and the "tension" of the *static* T, as KOCH[15] and TODOROV explain this distinction. Shiki's discovery of the narrativity in Buson's (79) and (80) is, however, the discovery of the latent potential that haiku had inherited from the beginning, as we have seen.

Shiki's reformation of haiku thus concentrates on two major goals: (i) the depiction of "unblurred impressions", or "the delineation of nature", which corresponds to the Poundian "catalog of images", emphasizing "objective beauty" above everything else; and (ii), the complexification of haiku by the conscious employment of "two temporally different events", human and natural, thus enabling haiku to present a clear miniature narrative structure. Consequently, his reformation can be said to have contained three components which were by nature incompatible with the ideal of haiku established by Bashō: (i) it advocated the emphasis of stylistic structures above informational ones; (ii) it advocated the exploration of narrativity rather than descriptivity; and (iii) it advocated the expansion of the mapping of haiku from a rigid adherence to nature to a wider context of the "novel-like", that is, to a concern also with human affairs. Shiki's reformation is, then, metagenetic in its nature, as far as poeticalness is concerned, for it negates informational poeticalness (i), it prefers narrativity to descriptivity (ii), and it changes the mode of informational poeticalness - from introjective mediation to projective mediation (iii). It seems then quite understandable that BLYTH, who understands haiku from the Zen point of view (1949: iii), regrets Shiki's revolution, for it standardised "beauty" - the "same mistake Keats made" (1964: 104, cf. 5.1). BLYTH declares that

> the history of haiku would have been different if only Buson and Shiki had realised, as Issa (and Bashō) did,

that it is the nature of humanity and the humanity of
nature which is the important thing, not the beauty or
the harmony (ibid.).

BLYTH is aware of the fact that the society in which Shiki
"reformed" haiku was under the strong influence of Western
civilization, which rejected the ground of informational
poeticalness on which haiku grew:

> We may say then that Shiki was both the product of and
> the hastener of this tendency, a world-tendency indeed,
> toward irreligion, unpoeticalness, and mechanization
> (1964a: 103).

Shiki's credo, which contained some contradictory components, had an incredible impact on the poetic genre now labelled "haiku": On the one hand, he advocated the pictorial nature of haiku, that is, the "tension"-type of representation, and simultaneously he promoted narrative texts, that is, the "suspense"-type of presentation. It can be said that the succeeding evolution of haiku was an inevitable response to his advocacy. Against (i), the negation of informational poeticalness, there arose the poets who valued this metaphysical focus over the other two, such as Bōsha, Hōsai, and Kusatao. And the precept (ii), narrativity, caused the discarding of the traditional pattern of 5-7-5, for in order to gain complexity, the syllabic limitation must be overridden, triggering the rise of "vers libre" in haiku, as is seen representatively in Santōka and Hōsai. The treatment of human affairs in narrative form (iii) generated haiku without kigo, which in the course of time had become so conventionalized that they no longer possessed much poetic impact for some poets. In the next section, we will thus see two contradictory trajectories: one a reaction against Shiki's reformation, which is the second genesis, and the other an extension of

Shiki's credo, which is the further metagenetic evolution,
i.e., the third metagenesis.

4.2.5 New Haiku: The Third Metagenesis and the Second Genesis

Of the two leading disciples of Shiki, Hekigodō took the leadership when Shiki died, extending the reformation further. Hekigodō at first promoted Shiki's ideas, in particular "the delineation of nature", approximating more and more to a realistic style. At first he experimented with a poetic form of 5-5-3-5 or 5-5-5-3; i.e., instead of the tripartite syllabic structure, he used a tetradic structure (YOSHIDA 1962: 50). The experiment was, however, short-lived, and he then proceeded to the extremity of this tendency: he joined some of his students who had been writing *haiku vers libre*, discarding the syllabic pattern which "would damage the freshness of impression and kill the vitality of language" (UEDA 1976: 9). In the following discussion of the trends of New Haiku, we will examine Hekigodō, Ogiware Seisensui (1884-1970), Ozaki Hōsai (1885-1926), and Taneda Santōka (1882-1940). In their poetry, we will see the shift of dominant poeticalness: in Hekigodō, the mixed mode of aesthetic and informational poeticalness; in Seisensui, the dominance of the aesthetic and the stylistic; and in Hōsai and Santōka, almost pure informational poeticalness.

4.2.5.1 Vers-Libre Haiku

Let us begin with Hekigodō's New Haiku:

(83) 父はわかってゐた 黙ってゐた 庭芒   (C 71)
    Chichi wa wakatte ita damatte ita niwasusuki
    (Father knew; remained silent; pampas grass in the
    garden)[16]

(84) 草をぬく根の白さ深さに堪へぬ (C 71)
Kusa o nuku ne no shirosa fukasa ni taenu
(I pull out a stalk of grass; the root's whiteness
and depth; I bear with the sight)[17]

(85) 雲の峰 稲穂の走り (cit. in YOSHIDA 1962: 51)
Kumo no mine inaho no hashiri
(The ridge of cloud; the swiftness over the crop-ears)

Although Hekigodō no longer adheres to the syllabic pattern,
the cadence of 3-syllabled and 2-syllabled lines can be detected: in (83), 'chi-chi- wa' (3) /wakatte/ (4) 'ita' (2)
'damatte' (4) 'ita' (2) 'niwa-' (2) 'susuki' (3); in (84),
3-2 —2-3-3-1-3; and in (85), 3-2, 4-3. In addition, Hekigodō
exploited syntactic recurrences; in (83), the repetition
of 'wakatte ita damatte ita' and in (85) 'shirosa fukasa'.
Such recurrences present at the same time phonological parallelism.
While aesthetic poeticalness is principally exploited, the
informational can be also detected: the three provide evidence of introjective mediation. The poet's realistic attitude simply presents the natural scene: nonetheless, the
poet's deep identification with the vitality of nature, especially in (84) and (85), is conspicuous. In addition to
these two modes of poeticalness which Hekigodō explored, we
can note one more important feature in his poetry: the multiplying of paradigms, which we saw in Wang Wei's poem (51) and
Buson's (68).

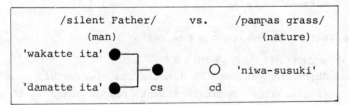

Fig. 75: The Multiplication of Paradigms in New Haiku

Ogiwara Seisensui wrote many haiku that resemble "lines
of a children's song" (BLYTH 1964: 199). Phonological recurrences characterize these haiku:

(86) たんぽぽたんぽぽ 砂浜に春が目を開く　　　　　　(C 76)
    Tanpopo tanpopo sunahama ni haru ga me o aku
    (Dandelions; dandelions; on the sandy shore spring
    opens its eye)

(87) 花があるのに花をさがしている蝶々　　　　　　(C 80)
    Hana ga arunoni hana o sagashite iru chōchō
    (Flowers are there; and yet, looking for flowers,
    a butterfly)

(88) 牡丹一弁一弁の動きつつ開きつつ姿ととのう　　(C 81)
    Botan ichiben ichiben no ugokitsutsu hirakitsutsu
    sugata totonou
    (Peony; one petal after another, moving, opening,
    gets in shape)

Seisensui discarded not only the syllabic pattern but also
kigo, for "the season word is a fetter fastened on the
living flesh" (UEDA 1976: 10). He attempted to "get a sensory perception of his subject matter within himself and to
express it in a rhythm unique to that perception" (UEDA
ibid., 11). It seems that Seisensui freed himself from the
sole realization of aesthetic poeticalness in traditional
haiku, namely, the syllabic pattern, and in lieu of that,
he chose Jakobsonian poeticalness: recurrence of sounds
accompanied by syntactic parallelism, which Hekigodō also
attempted. While Hekigodō's (85) with its reduced 12 syllables still reveals a dyadic deep-structure - the juxtaposition of "the ridge of cloud" and "the swiftness over
the crop-ears" -, (86), (87), and (88) comprise only one
event similar to Buson's (66). Seisensui is no longer concerned with "montage". In other words, he discards the most
fundamental structure for haiku, "2-clauses, 1-statement".
All three of these haiku focus on only one cultural unit,

or only "one half" of the "discordia consors", i.e., on comparantia, although, as far as the surface T is concerned, the form is extended: (8) and (87) have 20 morae, while (88) has 24!

In choosing a mono-structure in lieu of a dyad, Seisensui naturally focuses on syntagma - that is, his poem tends to narrativity. Interestingly enough, he attempts to apply paradigm not on the level of two "halves" but on the level of narrative components. Fig. 76 illustrates the point under discussion:

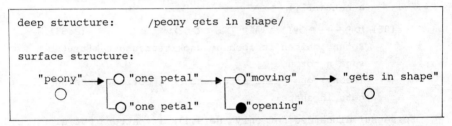

Fig. 76: The Narrative Text-Structure of the Poem

The deep structure, or *histoire*, of the poem is /peony gets in shape/, which could have been expressed by 'botan ... sugata-totonou' with only 10 syllables. A traditional haiku poet would have juxtaposed to this deep structure which is simultaneously surface structure, the other "half", so that two halves would make 2-ku, 1-$sh\bar{o}$. Instead, Seisensui enriches this deep structure by multiplying the transitional phases of narration: thus, "petals" is repeated (repetition "○-○"), and the next step of motion is multiplied (pairing "○-●"). This is in fact an innovation of Seisensui, and once he discovered this method, he exploited it more and more, rendering his poems "something inconceivable from the point of view of the traditional conception of haiku" (YOSHIDA 1962: 58). These two poets, Hekigodō and Seisensui, thus represent those who furthered Kyoshi's ideas. Their focus lay in matrix-production rather than in mapping-production and thus can be characterized as the continuation of metagenesis, whose tendency Shiki set in motion.

4.2.5.2 Tanritsu or Short Haiku

While the above-mentioned poets were concerned with the invention of new matrices, or surface texts, there were some more concerned with the "content" of haiku, while discarding the traditional form of it. Ozaki Hōsai, for instance, sought to liberate not only his poetry but also his entire life from the traditional haiku-rules (UEDA 1976: 10). If Seisensui was concerned solely with aesthetic poeticalness, paying scant attention to the informational, Hōsai works in the contrary direction to Seisensui by basing his work purely on the informational, though he seems to be conscious of the rhythm of this poem - (3). Let us return to (3) once again:

(3) H̲a̲k̲a̲ n̲o̲/ u̲r̲a̲ n̲i̲/ m̲a̲w̲a̲r̲u̲

    3   3   3

To the back of the tombstone I go around.

Similar to Seisensui's poetry, (3) no longer concerns the "montage-technique" of haiku, and yet in contrast to the examples by Seisensui, it does not present any phonological recurrences, except that it seemingly manifests the 3-morae rhythm, as is marked above. It seems that this haiku is as short as a Japanese haiku can be: it consists of only 9 syllables. It is thus called *tanritsu* ("shorter verse"). The text is quite free of stylistic as well as aesthetic poeticalness, at least, no Jakobsonian poeticalness is to be observed. What we witness in (3) is pure informational poeticalness. A question arises: can we still detect a metaphysical opposition? The answer is yes: /haka/ is normally a manifestation of /death/, which

is   opposed here to the "haka no ura", /the backside of
the tombstone/. The metaphysical opposition between "death
vs. life" thus is manifested in the first 5 syllables.
The back of the tombstone usually bears the name of the
deceased and the dates of his birth and death. The backside of the tombstone denotes not only the area behind the
tombstone, i.e., some mysterious zone behind the symbol of
death, but also the inscription through which a living man
can relate himself to the dead. "To this *haka no ura*", says
the poet, "I go around to this", or "into this" or "I step into this". The
whole manifestum then corresponds to the subjective presentation
we discussed concerning the informational poeticalness in
Bashō's haiku: it enacts a homeorhetic mediation (3.5.3).
(3) can be categorized as fūkyō-mediation, i.e., the projective mediation in converting social conventions, since
one normally does not care about the backside of the tombstone, let alone stepping around into it.

Similarly to Senseisui, (3) presents a mono-structure
in its morphology. This becomes clear if (3) is compared
to   Bashō's (41), in which Bashō chose a dyadic structure: "This snowy morning" and "all alone, the dried
salmon/ I am chewing" (3.5.3.2). Hōsai, however, excludes
the equivalent of "the snowy morning", thus ignoring the
traditional rule of seasonal themes. Another of Hōsai's
haiku consisting of 9 morae, (89), can be given as a further example of the informational T-type of fūkyō, although
the tone of the self-amusement observed in Bashō's (14) or
(40) is here totally subdued:

(89) 咳をしてもひとり   (GNBZ 91: 64)
Seki o shite mo hitori
(And even when I cough, I am alone)

While (3) and (89) typically exemplify the informational
structure of Hōsai, one more example of Hōsai, (90), will

make clear the T-type of his so-called *tanritsu* ("short haiku")

(90) 切られる花を病人見ている (C 129)
   Kirareru hana o byōnin miteiru
   (A flower being cut the ailing person is watching)

In principle such monostructures of the New Haiku poets concentrate on the syntagma. Though Seisensui and Hōsai differ both in the increase or reduction in the number of syllables, and in their emphasis on aesthetic-stylistic structure (Seisensui) or informational structure (Hōsai) with regard to the Si-model-types, both share one characteristic, namely the shift of dominance with regard to the H-model-types. They explored the syntagmatic potential of T, i.e., the narrative T-type. The point becomes clearer if we compare Seisensui and Hōsai on the one hand and Santōka on the other. While the first two opted for the monadic structure, Santōka preferred the dyadic structure in terms of informational opposition realized in the surface structure. Thus, Santōka approximates the old haiku masters, although as far as the surface text is concerned, his poems give the impression that his poetry and, say, Bashō's haiku had nothing in common. If we read the translated versions of his haiku, however, we do notice the similarities to Bashō, for once translated, such haiku manifesta as kireji or the 5-7-5 pattern disappear.

(91) ひとりすめば あおあおとして 草 (GBNZ 91: 59)
   Hitori sumeba ao-ao to shite kusa
   (Living all by myself; green are the grasses)

(92) こころ落ちつければ 水の音 (GBNZ 91: 59)
   Kokoro ochitsuke ba mizu no oto
   (My mind quiet, a sound of water)

(93) こうして生きてはいる 木の芽や草の芽や   (BNZ 91: 59)
    Kōshite ikite wa iru kino me ya kusa no me ya
    (Thus, I have been managing to live; the buds of
    trees and the buds of grasses)

The above mentioned haiku and their poets are among those
that dominated the period of the liberation of haiku. Their
endeavours were, however, inherited by the poets who followed
their doctrines. Their impact was great at that time and has
reached down to the present-day haiku world. The contribution of the haiku poets of this new trend is that they expanded the possibilities of haiku, not only in its thematic
fields - some even dared to compose "proletarian haiku"
in an attempt to charge haiku with ideological narrativity
(YOSHIDA 1962: 18) - but also in its exploration of poetic
foci as well as text-types, thus overwhelming the "tsukinami",
the professional composers of trite haikai (GBNZ 91, 1957:
430).

4.2.6 Present-Day Haiku: The Age of Diversification

The free verse movement triggered by Hekigodō, Seisensui, and
others alarmed the conservatives who adhered to classical
haiku. The most influential of these reactionary poets was
Kyoshi. As the editor of the haiku periodical *Hototogisu*
(The Cuckoo), founded by Shiki, he began to campaign for
traditional haiku, as UEDA explains:

> Kyoshi's defence of traditional haiku was based on the
> theory that haiku is a classical form of poetry ... "Haiku
> is a type of literature in which form is a pre-determined
> factor", Kyoshi observed. "Its life depends on its classical flavour. With its seventeen-syllable form and its
> sense of the season, haiku occupies a unique place in
> the realm of poetry" (UEDA 1976: 11).

4.2.6.1 Classicism

Thus, the trajectory of haiku evolution was turned for the second time in the genetic direction. Haiku was defined anew as the poetry of "flower-bird-wind-moon" (UEDA 1976: 12f.), a definition requiring adherence to the standard established by Bashō: the emphasis in ego-subdued informational poeticalness with the dyadic structure of the descriptive T-type. Of the new poets who were led by Kyoshi, the "most individual" was Murakami Kijō (1865-1938) (ibid.):

(94) 夏草を這い上がりたる捨蚕かな (C 86)
Natsu-kusa o / haiagaritaru / sute-go kana
(On the summer grass/ crawling up and up/ an abandoned silkworm!)

(95) 冬蜂の死にどころなく歩きけり (C 92)
Fuyu-bachi no / shini-dokoro naku / aruki-keri
(A winter hornet/ without a place to die/ staggers along)

(94) resembles (45): both focus on the small creature that affirms the vitality of life, thus presenting an equijective mediation. (95) seems more projective in that the unhappy poet, deaf and struggling with life[18], identifies himself with the winter hornet. The above two haiku also present the manifesta of traditional haiku: 'kana' and 'keri', on the one hand, and the syllable pattern and kigo on the other.

Kawabata Bōsha (1900-41) was another poet whose "Buddhism gave his work a background which most other haiku poets lacked" (BLYTH 1964a: 344). His haiku are "classical" in that two reflexive T-halves charged with informational poeticalness constitute a descriptive T:

(96) 水晶の念珠に映る若葉かな　　　　　　　　　　　(C 183)
　　 Suishō no / nenju ni utsuru / wakaba kana
　　 (In the crystal beads/ of my *juzu* rosary young
　　 leaves/ are mirrored!)

(97) 葱の花　ふと金色の仏かな　　　　　　　　　　　(C 188)
　　 Negi no hana/ futo konjiki no / hotoke kana
　　 (Green onions flowering/ for a moment golden/ Buddha
　　 was there)

(98) 我が魂のごとく朴咲き　病よし　　　　　　　　　(C 191)
　　 Waga tama no/ gotoku hō saki. / yamai yoshi
　　 (As if it were my soul/ a magnolia blooms out/
　　 ailing, I feel better)

Mizuhara Shūōshi (1892-) and Yamaguchi Seishi (1901-) can be named as two of the most influential figures in modern haiku. The former's "youthful lyricism" as opposed to the "passivity" of regressive classical haiku has had a great impact on modern readers, and the latter's "exploring [of] modernity in material and [of] intellectuality in the creative process" has contributed to the integration of haiku into modern technical society (UEDA 1976: 16ff.). Two haiku by each poet (99) and (100) by Shūōshi and (101) and (102) by Seishi are given below:

(99) 朝雲の故なくかなし　百日紅　　　　　　　　　　(C 153)
　　 Asagumo no / yue naku kanashi / sarusuberi
　　 (The morning clouds/make me sad, and I don't know
　　 why/ a crepe myrtle)

(100) 山の蛾はランプに舞はず月に舞ふ　　　　　　　　(C 152)
　　 Yama no ga wa /rampu ni mawazu /tsuki ni mau
　　 (Mountain moths/do not dance around a lamp/ they
　　 dance around the moon)

(101) 夏草に汽関車の車輪来て止る　　　　　　　　　　(C 159)
　　 Natsukusa ni / kikansha no sharin /kite tomaru
　　 (To the summer grass/the wheels of a steam engine/
　　 come and halt)

(102) 夏の河赤き鉄鎖のはし浸る (C 160)
Natsu no kawa / akaki tessa no / hashi hitaru
(Summer's river/ a red iron chain, its end/ is under the water)

In spite of the alleged modernity attributed to these famous poets, they are, structurally speaking, working with the descriptive T-type based on the exploitation of paradigm. The principle of *discordia concors* applies here, too. (99) juxtaposes 'asagumo' and 'sarusuberi'. The resulting /make me sad for no specific reason/ can be characterized as "modern", in that such an emotion should have been subdued according to the traditional poetics of "descriptive symbolism". (100) similarly presents two paradigmatic cultural units: /(city moths) dance around a lamp/ whereas /mountain moths dance around the moon/. Here, two beautiful images are concatenated. (101) more pronouncedly shows the pattern: /the greenness of summer grass/ representing /natural vitality/ is combined with /black moving object/ representing /the power of human civilization/. (102) likewise discloses two sememes that are juxtaposed, producing a montage effect. In discussing these two poets, UEDA (1976: 18) emphasizes their modernity, correlating it with Eliot's use of themes in the *Waste Land*[19].

Their popularity was apparently due to the fact that their haiku were based on precisely the principles that were developed for this poetic form, i.e., those associated with a dyadic structure; their themes, or matrices, on the other hand, began to deal not only with "flower-moon-viewing" but also with such modern items as "a red iron chain", "locomotives", or "rampu" (the Japanese loan-word for "lamp"). By and large their position can be termed constructivistic, in that they advocated more "the imaginative truth" as opposed to "the factual truth" sought by the traditionalists. It can thus be said that "intellec-

tualism" was introduced into haiku and that this brought
about another reactionary phase.

4.2.6.2 Modernism

The intellectualism thus infused triggered the rise of
the so-called "humanists" represented by Nakamura Kusatao
(1901-), who valued "life over art", as UEDA explains (1976:
21). Kusatao's focus, as might be imagined, is on informational poeticalness - tending to projective mediation.

    (103) 永久に生きたし女の声と蟬の声と   (C 197)
        Towa ni ikitashi onna no koe to semi no ne to
        (I wish to live forever! the woman's voice and
        the cicada's cry)

    (104) 万緑の中や吾子の歯生え初むる   (C 195)
        Banryoku no naka ya a-ko no ha hae-somuru
        (Myriad green leaves - in their midst! / the
        teeth of my child beginning to grow)

    (105) 耕せばうごき憩えばしづかな 土   (C 196)
        Tagayase ba ugoki ikoeba shizukana tsuchi
        (When I plough, it moves; when I rest, it is
        still: the earth)

The poets of classical haiku would never have dared to express the unification of man and nature so explicitly and
projectively, or to permit such a pronounced, obvious, and
foregrounded appearance of the poet's ego.

Saitō Sanki (1900-62) is known for his non-typical
Japanese mentality: he is "a spiritual foreigner", as
UEDA (1976: 21) affirms, who feels little affinity to the
Japanese poetic tradition. In his poetry, we recognize,
for the first time in haiku history, an example of *nullijection* - the fourth type of mediation according to KOCH's
category (3.4.1.3):

(106) 機関銃　眉間に赤き　花が咲く　　　　　　　　(YOSHIDA: 44)
Kikanjū / miken ni akaki / hana ga saku/
(Machine-gun:/ in the middle of the forehead/
a red flower blooms)

(107) 年新し　狂院鉄の門開く　　　　　　　　　　(GNBZ 91: 201)
Toshi atarashi/kyōin tetsu no / mon hiraku
(A new year has come/ lunatic asylum - it opens/ its
iron door)

"Chilling nihilism" is an attribute often used to describe
Sanki (UEDA 1976: 21). KOCH's (1983: 238-9) definition
states that "nullijection is a label that may be attached
to a poet who neither projects his psychic states into the
world or the text nor introjects particular relationships
of the world or the universe of discourse into himself".
KOCH cites Ernest Hemingway as an example of such a *nullijective* informational structure of "non-involvement" (ibid.).
Although Sanki can be characterized as a poet of informational poeticalness employing the mode of projection, we
are here witnessing rare cases of nullijective mediation.

Tomizawa Kakio (1902-62) advocated the separation of
haiku as art from the poet's life. His poetry is known
for its "surrealistic images" (UEDA 1976: 21), and his
poetry, understandably enough, reveals a dominance of a
combination of stylistic and aesthetic poeticalness, reminding us of Bashō's unrecognized   contemporary, Izen,
who was accused of being too artificial (3.5.1.3):

(108) ひとの瞳のなかの　蟻蟻蟻蟻蟻　　　　　　　(C 250)
Hito no me no naka no ari ari ari ari ari
(In the eyes of a person; ant, ant, ant, ant,
ant)

(109) 雲にあるあかるさ　葦にあるくらさ　　　　　(C 249)
Kumo ni aru akrusa ashi ni aru kurasa
(Brightness that lies in the clouds; darkness
that lies in the reeds)

While (108) and (109) show the further metagenetic development of the previous period, the following poem, (110), also by Kakio, exemplifies geneticity with reference to H-model-types in modern times: it has the structure of the argumentative T-type and seemingly exemplifies the mentality of modern man in suggesting the isolation of urban society:

(110) 善意？ どこまでつづく零の環よ　　　(C 251)
　　　 Zen'i? Dokomade tsuzuki zero no wa yo
　　　 (Good will? How far do the rings of zeros extend?)

4.2.6.3 The Various Haiku Factions

The Museum of Haiku Literature estimates that the practitioners of haiku in present-day Japan number over one million (3.1.1). The spectrum of this enormous production ranges from haiku vers libre to classical haiku, roughly categorized into such factions as "season-inclusive", "season-exclusive", "romantic", "realistic", "humanity-seeking", "haiku vers libre" (YOSHIDA 1962: 3-24), each group claiming its own creed. The prediction Shiki (1892: 141ff.) made ca. 100 years ago, based on his calculation according to the rule of "permutation", that haiku would sooner or later be doomed because of its syllabic limitation, has so far proved incorrect. This wide spectrum, however, makes it difficult to establish a definite trajectory of poetogenesis for contemporary haiku.

With regard to the Si-model-types, the aesthetic poeticalness of phonological recurrence which was rejected by Bashō has drawn the attention of such poets as Seisensui or Shuōshi, whereas the aesthetic poeticalness of morae-construction is no longer a priori "poetic", but is rather considered to be clichéd by the haiku poets of vers libre. The fundamental dyadic structure of "montage" realized through kireji no longer plays a decisive role for many of the modern haiku poets, irrespective of the forms they employ. Kigo, the seasonal elements which were the predetermined condition for Japanese poetry in general, have also been questioned, bringing a profound change in the deep structure of haiku. The mode of informational poeticalness has shifted from an introjective to a projective mediatory type, closely related to the fundamental question as to whether haiku is primarily "religious or aesthetic", or, in our terms, "informational or stylistic". It is also noteworthy that the former kind of poeticalness can be detected in the poets who led a hard life - voluntarily or involuntarily - such as Bashō, Issa, Santoka, Hōsai, or Bōsha; whereas the latter kind is crowned by those poets whose main concern was not "how to live", poets such as Buson, Shiki, Hekigodō in his earlier stage, or Kakio. However, the stylistic poeticalness manifested in paronomasia was purged by Bashō once and for all, though haiku poets may still employ some ambiguity of a syntactic nature[20].

With regard to the H-model-types, their geneticity, i.e., their tendency towards the argumentative T-type, is observable, as is seen in Kakio's modern suspicion of "good will" in (109). Yet this remains the exception, and the general tendency seems to be towards haiku's settlement on the descriptive T-type as an authentic stream while accepting the narrative T-type as well.

4.3 The Diachrony of Condensation and Expansion

This survey of the diachronic development of haiku so far presents us with another interesting pehnomenon in terms

of the semiotics of literature: textual condensation
and expansion. RIMER/MORRELL (1976: 16) point out the
general tendency that is observed in the literary history
of Japan: "The shortening was accompanied by procedures
for organizing these basic units into larger complexes".
Although a scrutiny of this phenomenon is beyond the
scope of the present study, the general drive for condensation or "shortening" (ibid., 17), and expansion or
"integration of short units into longer forms" (ibid.)
should be clarified by the table (Fig. 82) already presented (3.2). An interesting observation on this point
is made by POUND (1970: 94), who considers haiku as condensation and Nō as expansion, both of which express, however, "one image": "The Japanese, who evolved the hokku,
evolved also the Noh play. In the best 'Noh' the whole
play may consist of one image. I mean it is gathered about
one image: Its unity consists in one image, enforced by
movement and music".

Haiku's attempt to expand in this century can be seen
in the practice called *rensaku* ("concatenated verse"),
i.e., a group of several haiku is composed by one author
with one main theme. The practice can be characzerized
in our analytical terms as the multiplication of paradigms
through haiku. This new practice has been, however, controversial: for one thing, it weakens the impact of a
17-syllable, succinct form, and for another, it generates
"season-exclusive haiku", for once produced as a sequence,
each haiku depends upon the others, so that a season word can
appear only once among the serialized haiku-group. This
opposing impulse towards expansion will also be observed
in American haiku.

Another challenging theme emerging from this survey of
diachronic diversification is the question of the relationship among the other genres showing a close affinity

to haiku. We saw proverbial haiku ([57], [110]);
we saw joke-like haiku ([35], [37], [58]); we saw a
riddle-like haiku ([32]); and we saw miniature-narrative haiku ([61], [62], [79], [80], [81], [82]). As mentioned, there are several haiku that were originally made
as poems but have become known as proverbs or as epigrams.
Haiku was in fact first translated as "epigram", so that in
1934, HENDERSON (1934: 2) felt it necessary to emphasize
the point that haiku is "primarily a poem; and being a
poem it is intended to express and to evoke emotion".
Senryū has the same syllabic pattern as haiku, i.e.,
the 5-7-5 pattern, yet it is "primarily concerned with
human nature", as the definition of the Haiku Society
of America states (3.3). I suggest that the difference
between haiku and senryū lies not so much in their thematic concerns as in their T-typology. The former deals with
descriptivity and narrativity, the latter with argumentativity. We will later (7.1) look at the problem of haiku
as one type of *Simple Forms*, the quest for the understanding of which was first launched by the Dutch literary
scholar André JOLLES (1930).

4.4 Summary

Morphostructurally, haiku can be categorized into three
groups: 1) *one-paradigm haiku*; 2) *two-paradigm haiku*,
and 3) *multi-paradigm haiku*. One-paradigm haiku tends to
be *narrative*, as in:

(61) ① ② ③
Akikaze o / oeba wagami ni / hairikeri
(When I followed the autumn wind/ into my body/ it
penetrated!)

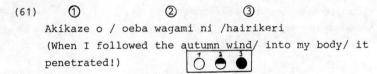

Two-paradigm haiku, the most frequent type, employs the

principle of montage: the *juxtaposition* of two disparate sememes or cultural units. It often juxtaposes two *reflexive* T which constitute as a whole a *descriptive* T, depicting "figure and ground" as in:

(111) 菊の香や ならには古き仏達   Bashō (A 462)
Kiku no ka ya / Nara ni wa furuki / hotoke-tachi
(The scent of chrysanthemum!/ in Nara, ancient/ Buddhist images)

        clause 1   *clause 2*
/the scent of chrysanthemum/ : /ancient Buddhist images in Nara/

                    ◯ : ●

Multi-paradigm haiku concatenate three or more sememes, presenting thus a descriptive T, as in:

(112) 奈良七重七堂伽藍八重ざくら   Bashō (A 251)
Nara nanae / shichi-dō-garan / yae-zakura
(In Nara things are seven-fold:/ seven halls of the cathedrals/ eight-fold cherry-blossoms)

   clause 1 :   *clause 2*   :   *clause 3*
  "Nara nanae" "shichi-dō-garan" "yae-zakura"
            ◯ : ◯ : ◯

Fig. 77 shows the relationship among the morphology of haiku, its T-typological nature based on the H-model, and the *place of caesura* through either *kire-ji* or its equivalent. It also presents some prototypical examples for each category.

Similarly, Fig. 78 shows the T-typology of haiku based on the Si-Model. The three modes of poeticalness are often *coordinated* or compressed, appearing in the surface structure as a *modal knot*.

	category	format	T-Typology of the H-model	the frequent place of a caesura	typical examples
1)	one-paradigm haiku	○ ○ ◐ ●	narrative T-type	5 —7— 5 |* //	3 61 62
2)	two-paradigm haiku	○ ○ ○ ●	two reflexive texts in one descriptive T-type	O // ● 5 7 | // ⌈5 5⌋ ⌊7 5⌋	1 85
3)	multi-paradigm haiku	○○○ ○ ○ ○	descriptive T-type	O //O //O	68 112

* " $\overline{5}$ —$\overline{7}$— $\overline{5}$" for traditional haiku and "———" for vers-libri haiku

Fig. 77: The Morphology and Text-Typology of Haiku Based on the History-Model

Lastly, Fig. 79 presents the *trajectory* of *haiku's evolution* according to the seven *universal T-types*. As mentioned at the very beginning of this chapter, the categorization is based on the *dominance* of a certain T-type which does not exclude the presence of other structures in one and the same poem, as our discussion of *modal knots* has made clear. The last poem, (112), can be categorized as a poem of stylistic structure, i.e., (112) is dominated by that mode of poeticalness. As is clear from the surface T, however, it is also dominated by aesthetic structure, while the T-type on the H-model-level is evidently descriptive. Furthermore, each poem can be categorized in terms of both the H-model-types *and* the Si-model-types: (112) is *predominantly* both of the descriptive T-type and of the stylistic T-type. Yet, as for the first four T-types of the H-model, the standard of haiku has remained very much unchanged since its establishment as a *descriptive T-type* and a *narrative T-type*, though the former is more frequent. Concerning the H-model-types, then, only the most representative of the specimens we discussed are classified.

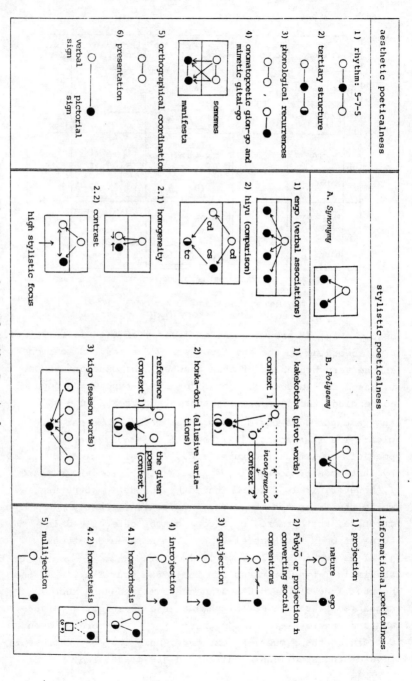

Fig. 78: The Typology of Haiku Poeticalness

text-type / epoch	reflexive	descriptive	narrative	argumentative	aesthetic	stylistic	informational
(i) Pre-Bashō	↑	111	37,58,61	56,57	⇧	30,32,35	31
(ii) Bashō & Classical Haiku	⇩ (1)	1,63,64,65,67,68	62,66	⇩	16,17,18,19,20,21,23,24,25,26,27,29,69,70,71,72,73	4,5,10,28	14,38,39,40,41,42,43,44,45,46,47,48,49,50,52,53,54,55
(iii) Haiku Reformation	↑	77,78	79,80,81,82	⬆	83,84,85,86,87	77,78	76
(iv) New Haiku	⇩		3,89,90		⇩		90,91,92,93
(v) Present Haiku	⇩	99,100,101,102		110	108,109	99,100	94,95,96,97,98,106,107
	HISTORY MODEL				SITUATION MODEL		

Fig. 79: The Trajectory of Haiku's Evolution

353

CHAPTER 5

A TEXT-TYPOLOGY OF HAIKU IN ENGLISH

Let us recall Fig. 6, which presents the analytical framework of the present study:

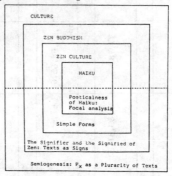

Haiku is a cultural product which came into being in Japan. The first chapter thus dealt with P_x, who constructs this verbal art as a plurality of texts. P_x is provided with culture, i.e., with the "stored information" which has been phylogenetically as well as ontogenetically acquired. In confronting the *world*, P_x mobilizes this sum of stored information and structures or *selects* the T with the *energy* thus available to him.

The second chapter concentrated upon the specific culture that gave birth to haiku: both the signified of Zen culture, i.e., Zen experience in general and *satori* or Enlightenment in particular, and the signifier of Zen T were semiogenetically inspected. Zen T differ from normal artistic works in their deep structure: in breaking free of "the curse of cognition", human awareness of inevitable death, Zen resorts to the method which is onto- and phylogenetically an older form, i.e., problem-solving through motor activity enhancing the *right-hemispheric mode* of

cognition, as opposed to the left-hemispheric
mode of Aristotelian logic. In conveying this signified of
Zen, one manifestation of Zen, the signifiers of Zen T
employ signs which are indexical and iconic as a necessary
result of Zen's principle of *metageneticity*. Haiku as the
verbal art of Zen inherited this fundamental characteristic
of Zen culture, i.e., "the effacement of the ego".

The third chapter then dealt with the P_x's focalization
in selecting the T. The focalization is trimodal in that
it consists of three separable analytical fields; *aesthetic*
and *stylistic foci* defining the *matrix* of haiku, and
informational focus, the *mapping*. The most prototypical haiku, the frog poem, (1), exhibits predominantly
informational poeticalness, although the other two modes
are by no means excluded, since the poem has a definite
rhythm of the mora-pattern, 5-7-5, (aesthetic mode), and
two sememes, /the old pond/ and /the sound of splashing
made by the frog's jumping into the pond/, are juxtaposed
in order to be *compared* (stylistic mode). The informational
poeticalness of (1),in which Zen's mode of cognition is
mapped, is introjective: the human mind simply *reflects* the
outer world's stimulation without any semiotization. Characteristically, the surface T simply maps two antinomous
sememes indicating *Zen's mediation*, and accepting *oppositions*
as such. (1) is thus a *homeostatic* T, as opposed to a
homeorhetic T, which summons P_{xe} to *reinstate* the initial
homeostasis achieved by Zen practice.

Comparing then the haiku created by the metageneticity
of Zen Buddhism and this metageneticity's other manifestations, the Zen
fine arts discussed in the second chapter, we can obtain
the following diagram showing the homologous nature of the
two-paradigm haiku as the representative of the genre, and of
the fine arts of Zen in general:

models	surface structure / T-types	Zen fine arts	haiku
Si-Model T-Types	aesthetic structure	○ ○ (dyad)	○ - ● - ○ (5 - 7 - 5)
Si-Model T-Types	stylistic structure	○ : ● (juxtaposition)	∪ : ● or ○ : ○
Si-Model T-Types	informational structure	○ ● (asymmetry)	○ ●
H-Model T-Types	Descriptive T-type	○ reflexive T	● reflexive T

Fig. 80 : The Homologue Observed in a Typical Haiku
and the Fine Arts of Zen

Yet, as a verbal art, haiku possesses two variations
that cannot be found in the Zen fine arts: one-paradigm
haiku based on the narrative T-type, and multi-paradigm
haiku, which specifically explore stylistic poeticalness
by concatenating more than three paradigms:

models	structures / types of haiku	one-p. haiku	multi-p. haiku
Si-Model T-Types	aesthetic structure	○ ● ○	○ ● ○
Si-Model T-Types	stylistic structure	○ : ●	● ● ●
Si-Model T-Types	informational structure	○ ●	○ ●
H-Model T-Types	Descriptive T-Type		○ ●
H-Model T-Types	Narrative T-Type	○ ● ●	

Fig.81 :   Two Variations of Haiku

Yet, haiku has been written for approximately 300 years
since its creation by Bashō and has diversified to a great
extent. The fourth chapter thus dealt with the diachronic
diversification of haiku in terms of *seven universal text-
types* which are derived from onto- and phylogenetic concerns
(the Model of History) and from the P_x's focalization within
a context of communication (the Situation Model), the last
of which corresponds to the three focal modes of poeticalness discussed in the previous chapter. Haiku can be, according to these T-typologies, both descriptive and narrative, though the former is more frequent than the latter,
conforming to LOTMAN's notion of *povtor* as the principle of
art.

The present chapter shifts to another cultural environment, to the American culture into which Haiku has been
transplanted. We will see that haiku's basic characteristic,
prominent information structures consisting of descriptive
and narrative T-types, was successfully taken over, though at
the very beginning of the transplantation, which was carried out
by the group of poets known as the Imagists, only the stylistic structures of haiku were recognized. We will see that
haiku has crossed the Pacific "hand in hand" with Zen,
defining *American haiku* with its metageneticity.

5.1 The Epitome of the Development of Haiku in English

Although V. D. HEUVEL rejects the notion that the Imagist
movement seriously influenced the genesis of haiku in English, or to be more specific, American haiku, it seems
nonetheless undeniable that such "hokku-like sentences"
as POUND's "In a Station of the Metro" possess the stylistic poeticalness developed in haiku poetry (3.5.2.2). First
led by T. E. Hulme and later by Ezra POUND, the poets associated with this movement utilized their "pan-Impressionist

heritage", to quote MINER (1958: 180), which consisted
chiefly of "French painting and poetry, James McNeill
Whistler (who was fascinated by Japanese woodblock
prints) , and Japanese art and poetry". In discussing
the change of artistic and poetic modes from the nineteenth
to the twentieth century, MINER locates the origin of Impressionism in Felix Bracquemond's discovery of "a volume
of Katsushika Hokusai's *manga*"("drawings", but the term
also refers to prints) (ibid., 68). Hokusai's block prints
as well as other collections of Japanese art offered the
"justification" of a technical background for the theory of
Impressionism (ibid., 69): in such prints the Impressionists
found "a liberation from academic formalism". The "strange
perspectives and frequently unbalanced compositions" opened
up new formal possibilities, and they found an "excuse for
their own many-hued palettes" in the brilliant and unusual
colors and color-combinations of the Japanese artists (60-
70). The emphasis on the expression of one's personal impressions and reality was then adapted from art to literature, a process upon which Whistler's painting exerted a
strong influence (ibid., 79). MINER notes the "synthetic
aspect" of this movement: an intermingling of the arts -
"aims, techniques", and "critical vocabularies of art,
music, and literature" - made it possible "for Japanese
art at first and Japanese literature later, to interpenetrate art and poetry to a degree which probably would not
otherwise have been possible" (ibid.).

It seems then natural that the Imagists concentrated on
the stylistic poeticalness of haiku: they first encountered
this poetic form through its pictorial quality. In particular, they focussed on the juxtaposition of two images, as
in (25), attributed to Moritake, with its "returning-flower-butterfly" (POUND 1914: 89). Supported by such "popularizers of
Japan" (MINER 1958: 76) as Whistler[1], Lafcadio Hearn (an

American journalist residing in Japan, who rewrote in
English the Japanese stories he heard [ibid., 90]),
Basil Hall Chamberlain, and A. G. Aston, the Imagists
launched their search for "The New Verse", "The Poetic
Renaissance", or "The New Poetry" (ibid., 98). MINER (99)
designates "with some confidence" 1907 or 1908 as the
year of the discovery of Japanese poetry by English poets,
for by then the Poet's Club, led by T. E. Hulme, had been
meeting once a week at a café in London or at their friends'
houses to discuss poetry, art, and philosophy (cf. SATŌ
1978: 11). They were very much influenced by "Biblical,
Symbolist, Japanese poetry, and vers libre", which they
took as their stimuli for literary activities (MINER, 101).
F. S. Flint, one of the leading poets at these gatherings,
wrote about their activities thus (cit. in MINER, ibid.,
101):

> We proposed at various times to replace (Victorian
> poetry) by pure vers libre; by the Japanese tanka and
> the haikai (i.e., haiku); we all wrote dozens of the
> latter as an amusement.

MINER (ibid.) lists three qualities regarded by these poets
as essential to haiku: (i) concision or economy of style;
(ii) precise imagery, usually taken from nature; and (iii)
avoidance of moralizing or didacticism. In these credoes
and in Shiki's appeal, made some ten years prior to, and
independently of, the European enthusiasm for haiku, we recognize a common reaction against excessive informational
poeticalness: Shiki, too, rejected didacticism in the haiku
written by his contemporary haikai-professionals (UEDA
1976: 7). Just as Shiki looked to Buson instead of Bashō as
his poetic ideal, the rejection of moralism or didacticism in poetry by the Poet's Club inevitably led the poetic
trend into the metagenetic order (4.2.1).

POUND became associated with the Poet's Club and then became its leader, acquiring a knowledge of Japanese poetry from Flint (MINER, cf. POUND 1970: 89). Hilda Doolittle ("H.D.") joined the group in 1910, and Richard Aldington in 1911. "By the time Amy Lowell, John Gould Fletcher, and such other diverse figures as Ford Madox Ford and D. H. Lawrence" became associated with Imagism, "Pound was leader of the group in every way, including the study of Japanese poetry"[2]. Although POUND dissociated himself later from what he termed "Amygism", i.e., Imagism "degenerated" into sentimentality (ELLMAN/O'CLAIR 1973: 331), his poetic principles remained unchanged, even when he labelled them "Vorticism" instead of "Imagism" (MINER ibid., 126ff.)[3]. One of the most succinct, precise accounts of his literary theory can be observed in the three principles he published in *Poetry* (March 1913) under the title "A Few Don'ts for an Imagist", or "the tenets of the Imagiste faith" (POUND 1914: 83):

(i) Direct treatment of the "thing", whether subjective or objective.
(ii) To use absolutely no word that does not contribute to presentation.
(iii) As regarding rhythm: to compose in the sequence of the musical phrase, not in the sequence of the metronome.

These precepts "sound as if he were lecturing on the way to compose haiku", writes SATŌ (1978: 18). "Concision, separation of imagery from abstract statement, and an emphasis upon natural images", according to MINER (ibid., 123), are POUND's prescriptions - the very qualities which haiku evidently brought to French poetry (ibid.).

POUND's emphasis on "imagery", subsequently inherited by T. S. ELIOT (1933) as his famous notion of the "objective correlative"[4], proceeded further along the metagenetic axis: Amy LOWELL and Adelaide Crapsey attempted to adapt the syllabic forms of haiku and tanka, respectively, into English. LOWELL experimented[5] with the 5-7-5 syllable pattern in her "Twenty-Four Hokku on a Modern Theme" which appear in *What's O'Clock* (1925), while Crapsey developed her "cinquain" stanzas, consisting of five lines in a pattern of 2-4-6-8-2, although this pattern was more likely influenced by tanka rather than by haiku (MINER 1958: 188).

If these two poets experimented with the potential of Japanese syllabic patterns in English poetry, it was Fletcher who probably came closest to the haiku informed with Bashō's kind of informational focus, as MINER affirms (ibid., 177): "[Fletcher] sees three meanings in haiku: a statement of fact", and "emotion deduced from that", and "a sort of spiritual allegory". MINER believes (ibid.) that Fletcher expresses the "chief relevance of haiku for English poetry" in his exhortation: "Let us universalize our emotions as much as possible, let us become as impersonal as Shakespeare or Bashō was". Fletcher seems to get even closer to the Zen mode of informational poeticalness in his foreword to Kenneth YASUDA's *A Pepper Pod* (1947). Fletcher states, namely, that haiku might "lead some of the more intelligent moderns to cast off the burden of too-conscious intellectualism that they carry". Fletcher's summary of the "indebtedness of the whole Imagist movement to Japanese poetry" is of great interest, although in MINER's opinion (ibid., 179), he never practiced what he preached:

> I should say that the influence of haiku on the Imagists was much more considerable than almost anyone has suspected. It helped them make their poems short, concise, full of direct feeling for nature (Fletcher 1947 cit. in YASUDA 1957: ix-x).

MINER (ibid., 184ff.) detects the influence of Imagism in terms of "superposition" in such major poets as Conrad Aiken, William Carlos Williams, Wallace Stevens, William Butler Yeats, and T. S. Eliot. Although the initial enthusiasm for Japanese poetry, and especially haiku, was subsequently diluted by the main stream of American poetry, the original impact of haiku seems to have remained: even VAN DEN HEUVEL (1974: xxvii) admits that "all modern poetry owes [the Imagist poets] a debt for their call for concision and clarity in language".

If this first phase of the impact of haiku on Western poetry was primarily concerned with stylistic poeticalness, the second phase beginning during the post-World War II period was concerned with informational poeticalness, as SATŌ points out (1978: 38):

> The most characteristic feature of the popularity of haiku in the U. S. after World War II is that Zen and haiku entered America hand in hand [...] The American reception of haiku in post-war America was concerned with "the quest for 'how to live'".

The pioneer work documenting this impact, as V. D. HEUVEL assures us, was "the extraordinary four-volumes of haiku" ([edited] between 1949 and 1952) by R. H. BLYTH, YASUDA's *The Japanese Haiku* (1957), and HENDERSON's *An Introduction to Haiku* (1934, 1965), to all of which reference has been made in this study. This second discovery of haiku, including its informational poeticalness, was due to the socio-psychological needs of post-war America, as V. D. HEUVEL assumes (ibid., xxviii):

> Haiku in English got its real start in the fifties, when an avid interest in Japanese culture and religion swept the post-war United States. Growing out of the increased contacts with Japan through the Occupa-

tion and a spiritual thirst for religious and artistic fulfillment, this interest centered on art, literature, and Zen Buddhism. Allan Watts, Donald Keene, D. T. Suzuki, the Beats, and others all contributed to both arousing and feeding this interest.

For the first time, American poets possessed "the solid foundation necessary for the creation of haiku in English" (ibid.). In 1965 HENDERSON writes that haiku in English is "still in its infancy", ascertaining that its criteria have not yet been established (1965: 28):

> There are as yet no generally accepted criteria for what haiku in English are, or should be. What kind of poems they will eventually turn out to be will depend primarily on the poets who write them. It seems obvious that they cannot be exactly the same as Japanese haiku - if only because of the difference in language. At the same time, they cannot differ *too* much and still be haiku.

Possessing from the outset of its history the ideals set up by classical haiku poets, specifically Bashō, haiku in English had kept oscillating between this ideal haiku and variations on it, aside from the poems made by those who have abandoned "the standards [for classical haiku] without knowing anything of them" (HENDERSON 1965: 29). One decade after the publication of HENDERSON's book, V. D. HEUVEL (ibid., xxx) writes that "haiku in English is still in the process of finding its 'way'" and claims that one of the most fundamental questions concerning haiku has been whether it is "basically a religious or an aesthetic experience" (ibid.). What V. D. HEUVEL here refers to is, as should be clear by now, the difference in the dominant poeticalness: he designates the predominance of informational poeticalness as "religious" and that of stylistic

poeticalness as "aesthetic". His assertion indicates that he has
directly inherited BLYTH's regret over Shiki's haiku reformation, since it was Shiki and Buson who over-emphasized
"the beauty or the harmony" in haiku instead of "the nature
of humanity and the humanity of nature" of Bashō and Issa,
to quote BLYTH again (4.2.4).

In addition to this "fundamental question", this editor-
poet (xxvii) cites two other disputes over haiku in English: (i) the controversy about the form, opinions being
divided into three groups, i.e., the "5-7-5-ers", the
"shorter-formers", and the advocates of haiku vers libre
(cf. GIROUX 1974, NAKAGAWA 1976); and (ii) the involvement
of "subjectivity" and to what degree it is permissible.
In addition to these arguments, noted by V. D. HEUVEL,
one more point of controversy, discussed by HENDERSON
(1965: 66), can be added: the inclusion of kigo (cf.
GIROUX, 94-117). While *The Haiku Anthology*, edited by
V. D. HEUVEL, exemplifies a wide spectrum of American
haiku and evidently accepts each deviation, there are
other groups of poets who strictly adhere to the standards
of classical haiku (*Haiku Journal* 1978-1980; and *Borrowed
Water*, publ. by the Los Altos Writers Roundtable 1966).
In the following, we will first examine the diachronic
diversification of haiku in English, dividing the years
from 1910 to the present, into four periods: (i) Ezra Pound
and Imagism; (ii) Amy Lowell and Adelaide Crapsey; (iii)
Kenneth Yasuda and his contemporaries; and (iv) American
haiku.

5.1.1 The Trajectory of the Poetogenesis of Haiku in English

Fig. 82 shows the shift of the dominant mode of poeticalness
in the course of approximately 70 years, a shift comparable
to the trajectory of haiku poetogenesis in Japan.

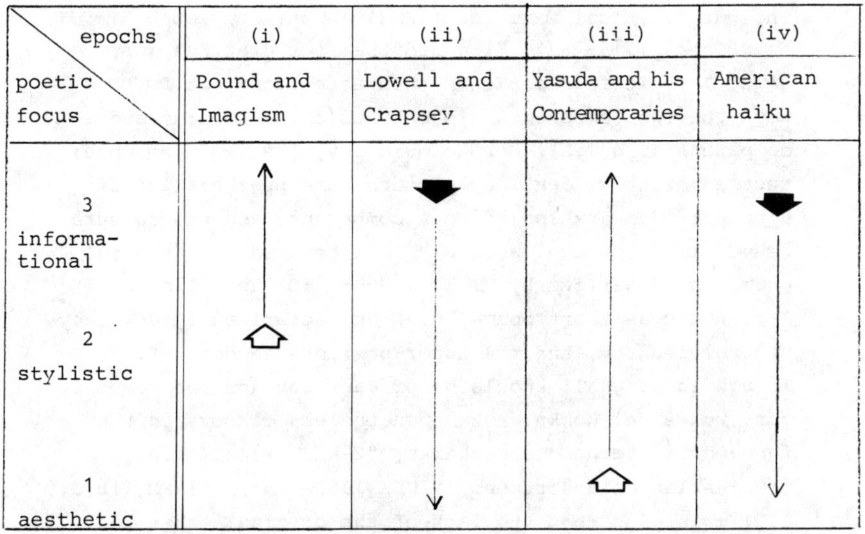

epochs poetic focus	(i) Pound and Imagism	(ii) Lowell and Crapsey	(iii) Yasuda and his Contemporaries	(iv) American haiku
3 informational	↑	▼	↑	▼
2 stylistic	⇧	│	│	│
1 aesthetic	│	↓	⇧	↓

Fig. 82: The Trajectory of the Poetogenesis of Haiku in English

5.2 Pound and Imagism: Genesis

5.2.1 Ezra Pound and His Metro Poem

In his association with the Poet's Club, POUND learned the following two hokku: the original version (37) of the first (113) is attributed to Moritake, and the second (114) is by "a Japanese naval officer" (POUND 1914: 8), who was stationed in London (cf. SATŌ 1978: 9ff.):

(113) The fallen blossom flies back to its branch:
  A butterfly (cf. our ex. [37]).

(114) The footsteps of the cat upon the snow:
  (are like) plum-blossoms.

The parenthetical insertion of (114) was added by POUND himself, as
he writes (1914: 89): "I added them for clarity" (cf.
SATŌ, 10). It is clear from this assertion that POUND
took the two components of hokku as a comparandum and
comparans (3.4.1.2). Morphologically, the two poems present an exactly identical pattern: the presentation of
a comparandum juxtaposed to a comparans, and the caesura
"sundering" the two. What POUND discovered in these two
poems is summarized by MINER (1958: 160) as follows:
"... haiku as short poems [are] characterized by delicacy,
natural imagery, and the super-pository technique".
Though lacking all knowledge of Japanese and the compository rules for hokku, POUND nonetheless discovered the
fundamental technique of haiku, "2-ku, 1-shō", i.e.,
combination or assortment (MINER 1958: 151). MINER (ibid.,
115) maintains that the lack of the original texts led
him to believe that haiku does not have any definite form,
i.e., he took it for granted that haiku is *vers libre*.
The two texts he was confronted with also lacked the informational poeticalness which haiku, at least in Bashō's
school, was based upon. The dominance of stylistic poeticalness in POUND's adaption of Japanese poetry seems, therefore, to have been preordained. In addition, the lack of
the cultural unit, namely, the Buddhistic text referred
to, which allows Moritake's hokku to function as honka-dori
or as an allusive variation (3.5.2.5) on the part of the P_{xe},
led POUND to consider this poem a sheer juxtaposition without any further rhetorical devices. What he received, then,
can be illustrated in terms of the formula of metaphor,
"A is B" (3.4.1.2, 3.5.2.2):

	COMPARANDUM	*caesura*	COMPARANS
(113)	"the fallen blossom flies back to its branch"	○ : ●	"a butterfly"
(114)	"the footsteps of the cat"	○ : ● (are like)	"plum blossoms upon the snow"

Fig. 82$_a$: Pound's Understanding of Hokku as a Comparison

Now let us quote again POUND's famous metro-poem
(34):

(34)   In a Station of the Metro
   The apparition of these faces in the crowd:
   Petals on a wet, black bough.

POUND's (1914: 86-9) description of the genesis of (34), this "*hokku-like* sentence" (ibid., 89), is quite revealing on two points: first, it exemplifies the procedure of *condensation* (4.3), the last topic of the previous chapter, and second, it makes it clear that (34) deals with "an equation" (87) or "a short metaphor" (88):

   Three years ago in Paris I got out of a "metro" train
   at La Concorde, and saw suddenly a beautiful face and
   then another beautiful woman, and I tried all that
   day to find words for what this had meant to me, and I
   could not find any words that seemed to me worthy, or
   as lovely as that sudden emotion. And that evening ...
   I was still trying and I found, suddenly, the expression. I do not mean that I found words, but there
   came an equation ... not in speech, but in little splotches
   of colour.

This passage, with its explicit notion of "an equation", shows that the two components of the poem - one, /the experience at La Concorde/, and the other, /little splotches of colour/ - are in a paradigmatic relationship. It should be also pointed out the POUND's "Ah-experience" was thus, from the beginning, of a stylistic nature, in that it compares one event to another, i. e., it was a metaphorical operation. Comparing this "language in color" (87) to Kandinsky's notion of "the language of form and color" (ibid.), POUND states that his experience in Paris "should have gone into paint" (88). He goes on to call this experience of colour the "primary pigment" or *image* (ibid.). The image of *Imagisme*, POUND clarifies (1970: 88), has been defined as "that which presents an intellectual and emotional complex in an instant of time": it is "the word beyond formulated language" (1914: 88) differing thus from "images *as ornaments*" (ibid.), dealt with by "the professional student of symbology" (ibid., 86).

The "primary pigment" or "the first adequate equation that [comes] into consciousness" in language is, POUND (88) assures us, "poetic language" or "the language of exploration". He then introduces *hokku*[6] to support his argument (ibid.):

> The Japanese have had the sense of exploration. They have understood the beauty of this sort of knowing. A Chinaman said long ago that if a man can't say what he has to say in twelve lines he had better keep quiet. The Japanese have evolved the still shorter form of the *hokku*.

The two Japanese hokku cited by POUND (88-9) are (113) and (114). He elucidates his understanding of hokku further:

> The "one image poem" is a form of super-position, that is to say, it is one idea set on top of another. I found it useful in getting out of the impasse in which I had been left by my metro emotion. I wrote a thirty-line poem, and destroyed it because it was what we call work of "second intensity". Six months later I made a poem half that length; a year later I made the following *hokku*-like sentence.

It seems undeniable that POUND discovered the principle formative technique of this poetic genre. Bashō's "*toriawase*" (combining things), ASANO's "2-ku, 1-shō", LOTMAN's "povtor",

and JAKOBSON's "metaphor", is here expressed as "a form
of super-position" constituting the "one-image poem".
Whether or not "the two electric poles" (KEENE 1955: 40)
of POUND's two-line poem create a beautiful "spark" or
fall flat is another matter[7]. Comparing the metro poem
to the two haiku POUND modelled it after, we can see
exactly how he adapted the structural principle of this
genre (cf. KOCH 1983: 266ff.):

	CD ○ (is like)	CS ●	◐
signified	/the experience at La Concorde/	= /little splotches of color/	/beautiful faces/ /sud- den emotion/
signifier	'the apparition ':' of these faces in the crowd'	'petals on a wet, black bough'	

Fig. 83 : Pound's Adaptation of the Haiku Principle
in (34)

POUND (89) characterizes this type of Imagist poetry,
or "Vorticism", as the attempt to "record the precise instant when a thing outward and objective transforms itself,
or darts into a thing inward and subjective". Interestingly
enough, he seems to have been aware of the "descriptivity"
of such hokku-like poetry when he speaks of "an intensive
art" as opposed to "a spreading, or surface art", the
second of which can best be manifested in "cinematograph"[sic]
(89-90). Although he of course does not use our T-typological terminologies, his assertion that "the logical end of
impressionist art is cinematograph" (89) strongly suggests
his awareness of the difference between a paradigmatic art
as hokku-like "poetic language" on the one hand and a syntagmatic art such as cinematography on the other.

Once discovered, the super-pository method became almost
"a tour de force" for POUND, as MINER asserts (1958: 117).
Yet, as a man with the slogan "Make it new" (ELLMANN/O'CLAIR
1973: 329), POUND attempted to develop his discovery further.

His elaboration on this hokku-like sentence can be described
as three-fold: 1) the exploration of a metalingual operation,
as KOCH (1983: 263ff.) terms it, which eventuated in the
"finding of as yet unrelated potential images" (ibid., 268);
2) the "clarity of imagery" as the consequence of 1), or
the discipline of the *mot juste* (cf. NILSSON 1970: 17, KOCH
ibid.); and 3) the textual expansion of the syntagmatization of paradigms.

5.2.2 Pound's Exploration of Stylistic Poeticalness

Having learned the effectiveness of the technique of super-
position, POUND soon began to reverse the order of cd and
cs. MINER (1958: 117) presumes this change to have been
due to POUND's inclination for "variety as much as [to] anything else". This change is most clearly seen in "Alba",
where the cs appears as an explicit simile (MINER ibid.):

(115) As cool as the pale wet leaves
of lily-of-the-valley
She lay beside me in the dawn.

The description of the situation, or cd, is located at the
end, whereas the image, or cs, as a simile precedes it.
This shift from the order of cd-cs to that of cs-cd reminds
us of what we observed in Bashō's improvement of his "crow-
perching poem": in changing the initial (32), in which the
equation "cd is cs" is explicit, into (31), in which the
ambiguity, or "indeterminacy" (KOCH ibid., 263), becomes
greater, Bashō invented a more challenging haiku format. In
fact, this correspondence between Bashō and POUND with regard to the "ascension of indeterminacy" (KOCH ibid., 265)
seems worth exploring. Bashō's inclination to "lightness"
toward the end of his life has been mentioned (4.2.3.3):
instead of concentrating on the philosophy of life, Bashō's
later poems focus more on the imagery as such, i.e., on comparantia in which the subtlety of the tertium comparationis
reaches an extremity, as exemplified in (64) and (65). We
have also seen that this focalization of the poet, the search

for images, was to be inherited by Buson, as in (66), (67), and (68), 70 years after Bashō's poetic activity, then by Shiki, as in (77) and (78), 200 years later, and was then taken over by the one of the two camps of American haiku which considers haiku to be "basically an aesthetic experience", to quote V. D. HEUVEL again (5.1).

Similarly to the poetogenesis observed in Japan, the culmination of this indeterminacy can be observed in the following poem titled "Ts'ai Chi'h". KOCH (ibid., 266) ascertains that (116) presents only "the pure potential cs":

(116) The petals fall in the fountain,
      the orange-coloured rose-leaves,
   Their ochre clings to the stone.

As Busons's three haiku, (66), (67), and (68), lacked the cd (Fig. 74), (116) also lacks the "pretext" (KOCH, 267) or the "frame" in which metaphor occurs (3.5.2.2).

Fig. 84 compares the poetogenetic shift within the stylistic poeticalness to the POUNDian elaboration on the super-pository technique (4.2.3.3, cf. KOCH, 263ff.):

	the poetogenesis of Japan	Pound's elaboration on the super-position
Phase 1 comparison	Bashō (32): question answer cd = cs ○ ● /autumn evening/ /crow .../	(34): A (is like) B cd = cs ○ ● 'the apparition...' 'petals'
Phase 2 indeterminacy	Bashō (31): juxtaposition cd : cs cs cd ● ○ 'kare-eda ni...ya' 'aki...'	(115): inversion cd = cs cs ●⤢ ○ cd 'As cool as...' 'she...'
Phase 3 katalog obrazov	Buson (66),(67): image cs ● (68): ●●●	(116): image cs ● 'The petals...'

Fig. 84: The Exploration of Stylistic Poeticalness by the Japanese Haiku Poets and Pound

5.2.3 The Image of Imagism

POUND's understanding of (113) and (114), however, possessed another dimension, namely, "imagery", which seems to have had more enduring impact than the superpository technique[8]. "The clarity of imagery" (MINER 1958: 261) became the paramount goal for him as well as for such poets as H. D., T. S. Eliot, W. C. Williams, Wallace Stevens, and R. Frost, to name but a few representative figures[9]. In the metro poem, he employs 'petals on a wet, black bough' to express his perceptory /little splotches of colour/. As REINHART (1974: 392) in her essay "On Understanding Poetic Metaphor" states, it is a "double perception" involving "the apparition of the faces" seen in a Metro station and "petals on a wet, black bough" at the same time. In "Gentildonna", 'grey olive leaves beneath a rain-cold sky' should be perceived simultaneously with the notion of a /noble lady/ ([117]): in "Liu Ch'e", 'a wet leaf clinging to the threshold' must be apprehended at the same time as an unlucky lady beneath the leaves ([118]), just to mention two examples of such "double perception" of the imagery aspect of Imagism. The significant factor here is the concomitance of the two images, or two fields on a ground of a purely pictorial nature - colour, perspective, and position. In other words, there is little attention paid to informational focus - as opposed to Bashō's haiku in which "a floating nest of the grebe", for instance, embodies not the pictorial feature of the comparandum but the informational mediation - a small, insignificant creature as a manifestation of consolation. Thus, lacking informational poeticalness at the beginning of his exploration of the hokku style, it seems natural that POUND and his followers further developed their credo so that they tended simply to present the concatenation of comparantia, much as Shiki and his followers

were led to do - at least at the beginning of their haiku
reformation. Yet this total lack of informational poeticalness inevitably triggered a reaction among the followers
of Imagism. The reaction has two aspects; "a long imagiste
or vorticist poem" (POUND 1970: 94), which coincides with
POUND's own elaboration on the metro poem, as will be discussed in 5.2.4, and the shift towards informational
poeticalness, as will be discussed in 5.2.5 and 5.2.6.

5.2.4 The Expansion of the Form of Super-Position

POUND's endeavour to develop his discovery of Japanese
hokku exhibits precisely the opposite impulse to what he described as the genesis of (34), i.e., textual expansion
instead of condensation. Let us consider two examples,
(117)[10] and (118), which present the impulse for expansion:

   (117)   Gentildonna
        She passed and left no quiver in the veins, who now
        Moving among the trees, and clinging in the air she
        severed,
        Fanning the grasses she walked on then, endures:
        Grey olive leaves beneath a rain-cold sky.

Although the first three lines present a narrative structure in that the concatenation of activities is predominant,
the poem as a whole can be presented as follows: the first
half is multiplied, similar to Wang Wei's (51) and Hekigodō's
(83) and (84), in which one of the two paradigms is multiplied. Here the first half is five-fold, while the caesura
of (117) appears as the space between the first half and
the second instead of as a colon:

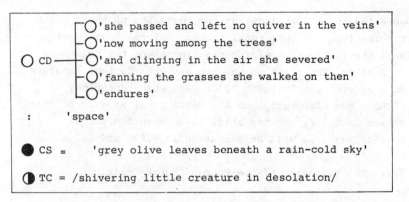

Fig. 85: The Multiplication of one of the Two Paradigms in (117)

Similarly, (118), another famous "Chinese" poem, "Liu Ch'e", manifests the identical structure:

(118) The rustling of the silk is discontinued,
Dust drifts over the court-yard,
There is no sound of foot-fall, and the leaves
scurry into heaps and lie still,
and she the rejoycer of the heart is beneath them:

A wet leaf that clings to the threshold.

In both cases, and similar to the earlier examples by Buson and Hekigodō, it is the first half of the two juxtaposed elements that is multiplied, whereas the latter half remains unexpanded as a "punch line". Recalling KOESTLER's "bisociative" function of the turning point, we can safely assume that only the first part can be expanded so that the effect of the "punch line", a surprise ending, would be greater in terms of narrative technique. Obviously, we are dealing here with exactly the opposite impulse of condensation, i.e., *expansion*.

In discussing the structure of the short story before
O. Henry, Boris EICHENBAUM (1971), the Russian formalist critic, remarks that the short story tends to amass
its weight towards the end[11], towards the "maximal unexpec-
tedness of a finale concentrating around itself all that
has preceded it". Although modern short stories have gone
through various transformations, as REID (1977: 59ff.)
ascertains, it is the first half that is predestined to
be expanded, while "a finale" remains unexpanded (cf.
HENDRICKS 1977: 294). Earlier (3.2, 4.3), RIMER/MORRELL's
explanation of the tendency towards "the integration of
short units into longer forms", a tendency which has always been present in the literary continuum of Japan, was
cited. One of haiku's methods of compensating for its
brevity, pioneered by Bashō, was to precede the hokku with
a *haibun*, a piece of prose (cf. MATSUO 1974). POUND's textual expansion[12] and that of Bashō, both of which may occur
in the structure of short stories, can be presented as
follows:

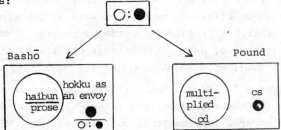

Fig. 86: The Textual Expansion of Haiku and the *Hokku-
Like* Sentence (34)

5 2.5 From Stylistic Poeticalness to Informational Poeticalness

The super-pository technique affected other poets who
followed this doctrine: F. S. Flint, Richard Aldington,

Hilda Doolittle (H. D.), to name but a few of the immediate associates (POUND 1970: 89). If H. D. in her "Oread" "express[es] much stronger emotions than that in [my own] lines here given", as POUND assures us (ibid.), Flint seems to suggest in his *The Beggar* the limitation of the "form of super-position" (cf. MINER 1958: 158):

(119) Hark! the strange quality
of his sorrowful music,
wind from an empty belly
wrought magically
into the wind, -

Pattern of silver on bronze

While the poems of POUND cited here tend to do away with any "adjective which does not mean something", in accordance with his own advocation of "Don'ts" for verse-writers[13], Flint uses adjectives generously, such as "strange", "sorrowful", "empty", not to mention the adverb, "magically". The poem thus exemplifies the tendency toward a "longer imagiste poem". Further, it reveals the tendency towards a more informational structure, as in "the strange quality of his sorrowful music" the poet's empathy with the "beggar" is shown.

Aldington's "R. V. and Another" also reveals an obvious affinity with the super-pository technique as well as with the shift towards informational poeticalness (cf. MINER, 161):

(120) You are delicate strangers
In a gloomy town,
Stared at and hated -

Gold crocus blossoms in a drab lane.

Aldington, though affiliated with the Imagist movement, was almost "unique in being able to retain a refreshing sense of humour amidst all the solemn business of getting the 'New Poetry' set in motion". MINER (160) states that

Aldington wrote a parody of POUND's metro poem (cit. in
MINER, ibid.):

(121) The apparition of these poems in a crowd:
White faces in a black dead faint:

We can recognize in passing that exactly the same mechanism of the joke - here in the form of an allusive variation
(3.5.2.5) - is operating between POUND's metro poem
and Aldington's parody of it.

5.2.6 Post-Imagism and Informational Poeticalness

It would take a number of encyclopedic studies to encompass POUND's influence on modern poetry: concerning the
metro poem alone, there are at least three points which had an
immediate impact on his contemporaries; 1) the superpository technique, which manifests, as we saw, the most
fundamental artistic impulse; 2) the clarity of imagery;
and 3) textual expansion. Let us therefore limit ouselves
to a glance at a few poems of William Carlos Williams and
Wallace Stevens as typical examples of POUND's impact.
While the super-pository technique turned out to be
short-lived, the influence of the second and third points
was to be more enduring.

In discussing the difference between the "most persistent of imagistic poets", W. C. Williams, and Bashō,
YASUDA (1957: 5) ascertains that this American poet "would
not excape censure by Japanese critics", even though he
has maintained that "'all art is necessarily objective.
It doesn't declaim or explain; it presents'". YASUDA
(ibid.) considers the first line of the following "beautiful poem" to be "primarily explanatory":

(122)   so much depends
             upon

             a red wheel
             barrow

             glazed with rain
             water

             beside the white
             chickens   (D 292)

Indeed, Japanese haiku poets could not afford the first
line in the limited form of 17 syllables. Further, haiku
would count on the speech act of composition itself, i.e.,
indexicality as we saw in the previous chapter (2.3.4),
instead of verbalizing 'so much depends upon' as in (122):
for them, it would be a superfluous statement. Aside from
this "primary explanatory line", however, (122) could be
accepted as a well-composed haiku: it consists of vivid
images, as if "objects in the world should be allowed to
retain their nature without being conceptualized into abstract schemas" (ELLMAN/O'CLAIR 1973: 7). In Williams,
such concrete "images" seem to have gained informational
poeticalness.

While the "images" - "red wheel barrow" and "white
chickens" - first draw our attention (stylistic focus),
in that the colour contrast is so vivid, they also manifest the dependence of beings, animate or non-animate,
on the earth, since both are equally "glazed" - or spotlighted - under the rain. The macrocosm (rain, i.e., nature) and microcosm are compatible and dependent on each
other. Both the typography and the orthography of the poem
seem to support this informational poeticalness - an
introjective mediation (3.5.3.4). A similar attitude
can also be observed in another short poem written two
years before (122), "The Great Figure", a poem lacking any

"Explanatory statement":

(123)   The Great Figure

Among the rain
and lights
I saw the figure 5
in gold
on a red
firetruck
moving
tense
unheeded
to gong clangs
siren howls
and wheels rumbling
through the dark city   (D 290)

Similar to (122), the poem (123) presents the interdependence of the macrocosm and the microcosm, and the poet simply presents the "particulars" without any overt intervention of his ego, except in the title of the poem, which evaluates his experience as "great" or meaningful. To a certain degree, Williams also seems to have retrograded on the scale of the H-model, i.e., he rejects "conceptualization" or "intellectualism". In his "Manifesto" for the magazine *Contact* - the name itself is quite suggestive - which he edited during the 1920s, he declares:

> I take contact to mean: man without the syllogism, without the parody, without Spinoza's ethics, man with nothing but the thing and feeling of that thing (cit. in KOCH, V. 1950: 38).

Vivienne KOCH, therefore, characterizes Williams as "one of the most distinguished Neanderthal men" (ibid.), affirming that "Williams [...] must go back to the source: and the process has undeniably its beauties" (ibid.). It seems

natural then that Williams only "points out" objects
i. e., he approximates reflexive texts, as he himself
maintains: "The particular thing offers a finality that
sends us spinning through space" (ROSENTHAL 1966: 109).
His credo was still clear some thirty years later when
he composed "From Paterson". He described the genesis
of this long poem thus (cit. in ELLMANN/O'CLAIR, 303):

> I realized that the isolated observations and ex-
> periences (among the details of my life) needed
> pulling together to gain "profundity" [...] I wanted [...]
> to know in detail, minutely, what I was talking about
> [...] That is the poet's business. Not to talk in vague
> categories but to write particularly, upon the thing
> before him, in the particular to discover the uni-
> versal.

The poem "From Paterson" thus sets out "to make a start/
out of particulars/ and make them general, rolling/
up the sum, by defective means - /Sniffling the trees,
just another dog among a lot of dogs. What/ else is
there? And to do?", an attitude similar to that of the
Japanese haiku poets whose focalization was aimed at the
microcosm. Williams seems thus to have reached the domain of haiku when he exhorts: "Say it, no ideas but
in things" - a famous line appearing in "From Paterson".

If Williams was more concerned with introjective mediations in his compositions, Stevens seems to have been
occupied with projective mediations. He writes about the
creation of "myth" in his book *The Necessary Angel* thus
(STEVENS 1951: 31):

> What makes the poet the potent figure that he is, or
> was, or ought to be, is that he creates the world to
> which we turn incessantly and without knowing it and
> that he gives to life the supreme fictions without
> which we are unable to conceive of it.

At another time he writes in the same vein (cit. in
STEVENS, H. 1966: 370):

> If one no longer believes in God (as truth) [...] it is
> not possible merely to disbelieve; it becomes necessary
> to believe in something else. Logically, I ought to
> believe in essential imagination, but that has its diffi-
> culties. It is easier to believe in a thing created by
> the imagination. A good deal of my poetry recently has con-
> cerned an identity for that thing.

We are reminded of YU's argumentation that the "Western
poets must create their unifying myth" (3.5.3.4), while
for the Chinese (and accordingly Japanese) poets "Tao",
or mediation, already existed. We are also reminded that
Bashō had to create his own myth in order to overcome his
dilemma as a misfit in his society (3.5.3.2). Stevens was
very much aware that such "myth-creation" is crucial for
the poet. He upholds, according to ELLMANN/O'CLAIR (244),
"the poet's 'instinctive integrations' as means of establishing value, of emerging from a personal world of mere
chaos". In terms of "myth-creation", "Anecdote of the Jar"
(1923) appears to be the most pertinent example. While
Williams self-effacingly lets the objects spell out their
significance, Stevens creates "a thing" which one can believe in "as truth" by "plac[ing] a jar in Tennessee":

(124)   Anecdote of the Jar

I placed a jar in Tennessee,
And round it was, upon a hill.
It made the slovenly wilderness
Surround that hill.

The wilderness rose up to it,
And sprawled around, no longer wild.
The jar was round upon the ground
And tall and of a port in air.

It took dominion everywhere.
The jar was gray and bare.
It did not give of bird or bush,
Like nothing else in Tennessee. (D 249)

Another of Stevens's poems from this period, "Thirteen Ways of Looking at a Blackbird", seems to point out its affinity to haiku more overtly (FUKUDA 1962, ŌTAKE 1965). Stevens writes the following about the collection which includes this poem: "This group of poems is not meant to be a collection of epigrams or of ideas, but of sensations" (cit. in STEVENS, H. 1966: 251). MINER (1958: 190-1) points out the observable influence of Japanese block prints as well as poetry on this poem:

> [The] most Impressionistic and most nearly Japanese poems are those which give a series of several quasi-Impressionaistic pictures, apprehensions, or impressions of one subject[...]The titles of such poems (as "Six Significant Landscapes", "Study of Two Pears" and "Variations on a Summer Day" in addition to the poem in concern) recall such series of Japanese prints as Hiroshige's "Eight Views of Ōmi", Hokusai's "Thirty-Six views of Fuji", or Utamaro's "Seasons". These poems are also closest to the Imagist method and haiku technique, and are especially reminiscent of Amy Lowell's "Twenty-Four Hokku on a Modern Theme".

We have seen that modern haiku poets attempted to overcome the brevity of haiku by serializing several haiku, the practice called *rensaku* (4.3). Similar to rensaku, Stevens' "Thirteen Ways" is a multiplication of paradigms. Let us here cite the part of the poem most clearly "haiku-like in spirit" (MINER ibid., 195):

(125)   Thirteen Ways of Looking at a Blackbird

                    I

        Among twenty snowy mountains,
        The only moving thing
        Was the eye of the blackbird.

                   III

        The blackbird whirled in the autumn winds.
        It was a small part of the pantomime.

                   IV

        A man and a woman
        Are one.
        A man and a woman and a blackbird
        Are one.

                  XIII

        It was evening all afternoon.
        It was snowing
        And it was going to snow.
        The blackbird sat
        In the cedar-limbs.   (D 249-50)

Let us compare the first stanza with a haiku by Naitō Jōsō (1662-1704), one of Bashō's disciples, whose commitment to Zen Buddhism pervaded his life:

(126) 鷹の目の枯野に居るあらしかな   (B 300)
       Taka no me no/ kareno ni suwaru/ arashi kana
       (The eyes of the hawk/ are glaring on the withered
          moor/ a storm!)

The juxtaposition of natural phenomena with a focalized "particular" in both poems is quite obvious.

In the third stanza, the interdependence between the macrocosm and the microcosm is expressed in more abstract

terms, "small part of the pantomime". For haiku poets in
Japan, it was self-evident that any insignificant creatures
could carry the message of Buddha-Nature, as we have seen
(3.5.3.4). Thus, the second line of the third stanza would
have been rejected by YASUDA as "primarily explanatory":
It is a comparandum that should be not verbalized.

The fourth stanza presents a mixed mode of aesthetic
and informational poeticalness; the repetitive structures
of the manifesta reflect the "supreme fiction" of belief
in the oneness of all creatures, i.e., projective, informational poeticalness. This stanza echoes the second stanza
in which we see the treble-ness of an 'I' who is 'of three
minds', a 'tree' in which 'there are three blackbirds',
and 'three blackbirds'.

The last stanza XIII, reminds us of Bashō's (31).
ŌTAKE (1965: 161) compares this stanza to Kawabata Bōsha's

(127) しんしんと雪降る空に鳶の笛
Shin-shin to/ yuki furu sora ni /tobi no fue
(Snow is falling and falling/ in the sky remains/
the whistling of the black kite)[14]

As should be clear, the images Williams and Stevens employ
differ fundamentally from those of the Imagists, for the
former are loaded with informational poeticalness; Williams's
images, introjectively, and Stevens's more projectively.
POUNDian influences on the two are nonetheless unmistakable
in that both contribute to the enhancement of "paradigms",
Williams more pictorially, and Stevens with his "series"
of different aspects of one image or sememe, to use our
analytical terms. Among the poets who did not know anything about the religious background of the hokku-like
sentence, the super-pository technique was bound to cause
divergence from the original models, as (117), (118), (119),
and (125) eloquently demonstrate. In the first three poems

the juxtaposition of cd and cs is no longer based on the
ratio of "one cd to one cs" as in the case of haiku, but
on "five-to-one" in (117) and (118), and on "two-to-one"
in (119). (125) illustrates still another method of textual expansion, i.e., the multiplication of paradigms,
rather as in the work of such modernist painters as the
Cubo-Futurists who depicted on canvas "slightly different,
paradigmatic perspectives" in a "simultaneous way", as
KOCH (1983: 291) expresses it. This fundamental operation
of the collecting of paradigms has been discussed in
connection with Japanese rhetorical devices, i.e., *engo*,
or verbal associations (3.5.2.1) based on *synonymy*. The
synonymy of engo occurs on the level of words, whereas
that of (125) occurs on the level of T, i.e., each constitutes its own closed structure of "○:●". Fig. 87
presents the specific method of the textual expansion
developed by the Imagist poets, as well as the general
expansion observed in (122) and (123):

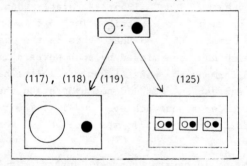

Fig. 87: Two Types of Textual Expansion used
by the Imagists

It is worth noting that throughout the period of the
first transplantation the T-type of Imagist poems remained
descriptive, as our examples show, except for (123) and (124),
in which some kind of "anecdote" is told, i.e., which are

of the narrative T-type. The essential descriptivity of
the Imagist poems is, as we can safely assume, due precisely to POUND's technique of "super-position" applied to
the "one-image poem".

However, interest in the technique POUND discovered
in the hokku (113) and (114) faded away, as its advocate
moved on to other poetic experiments. Although POUND in his
later works still valued this technique (MINER 1958: 115),
the longer the poems became, the less effective the impact
of "2-ku, 1-shō" turned out to be, and the first phase of
the transplantation of haiku into Western poetry thus
came to an end.

5.3 Lowell and Crapsey: Metagenesis

5.3.1 Lowell's Adaptation of Hokku

In discussing haiku, KEENE (1955: 44) states that if a
haiku does not have "two electric poles", it is "no more
than a brief statement", and that "this is the exactly
the point which has been missed by such Western imitators
of the haiku form as Amy LOWELL, who saw in the haiku its
brevity and suggestion, but did not understand the methods
by which the effects were achieved" (44)[15]. The two haiku
of LOWELL KEENE (ibid.) criticizes are:

(128)   A Lover
   If I could cater the green lantern of the firefly
   I could see to write you a letter.

(129)   To a Husband
   Brighter than the fireflies upon the Uji River
   are your words in the dark, Beloved.

We have seen in the previous chapter (4.4, also Fig. 77)
that a "one-paradigm haiku" is perfectly legitimate, and

that it tends to be narrative rather than descriptive.
The problem with (128) and (129) is, therefore, not so
much the fact that they are one-paradigm hokku, but that
they are of the argumentative T-type. Similarly to
(56), in which Sōkan argued, "*If* I gave a handle to the
moon, *then* it would become a nice fan!", (128) argues, "If A,
then B" (4.2.2). (129), too, is comparable to (76),
in which Baishitsu argued that "the shadow of a man is
inferior to the shadow of grasses and trees". In addition
to the fundamental difference between Japanese hokku according to Bashō's and LOWELL's metageneticity in terms
of T-typology, she is evidently guilty of using "imageries"
as a mere decoration, which POUND, as we saw (5.2.1), ab-
horred. 'The green lantern of the firefly' and 'the fireflies upon the Uji River' are not "imagistic" in the
Imagistic sense, nor do they possess an adequate "objective correlative". In her later phase, however, she
appears to have carried out her aim, "to keep the brevity
and suggestion of the hokku and [to preserve] it within
its natural sphere", more successfully, though her poems
are evidently more direct translations of originals than
they are her own creation (MINER 1958: 168). Two of these
"more successful hokku" are:

(130) Even the iris bends
When a butterfly lights on it.

(131) Perched upon the muzzle of a cannon
A yellow butterfly is slowly opening and shutting
its wings.

The originals she might have been reading[16] are, according
to MINER (1958: 168ff.):

(132) The first snow fall
is just enough to bend
The jonquil leaves   (Bashō)

(133) A tiny butterfly is settled
A flower returns; returning I see
It is a butterfly.   (Cf. our ex. [37])

While LOWELL thus experimented with "imageries" from the
Japanese literature and block prints she found in the books
her brother Percivall Lowell, who spent some time in Japan[17],
sent her, she also attempted to "naturalize Japanese prosody to English verse" (MINER 1958: 170). In "Twenty-Four
Hokku on a Modern Theme", appearing in *What's O'Clock*,
LOWELL thus "emulated" the pattern of haiku - the first
attempt at what was later carried out more successfully
by YASUDA (1957):

(137)   VI
This then is morning   (5)
Have you no comfort for me,   (7)
Cold-coloured flowers?   (5)

LOWELL, then, attempted to realize the aesthetic poeticalness manifested in the rhythmical pattern. Her efforts were
soon dropped, presumably for the reason that these prosodic units, i.e., morae, which were adopted by a language
which lacks stress accents as well as consonantal clusters
(3.5.1.1), cannot be transplanted mechanically into English
(MINER 1958: 170). If she failed to establish the form of
English haiku and was accused by POUND of having misguided
the Imagist movement with her "Amygism" (ELLMANN/O'CLAIR,
331), credit is still due her for establishing a definite
form for haiku in English.

5.3.2 Crapsey and the Cinquain

If LOWELL's attempt was finally rather superficial, Crapsey's
attempts to naturalize Japanese prosody appear to have been
more considered. She adapted the five-line scheme presumably

from tanka-form, reducing, however, the syllables to
2-4-6-8-2 in iambic meter (MINER 1958: 188). With this
scheme, termed a *cinquain*, she wrote poems that echo
either an orginal tanka or haiku.

(135) Keep though   (2)
      Thy tearless watch   (4)
      All night but when blue-dawn   (6)
      Breathes on the silver moon, then weep!   (8)
      Then weep!   (2)

MINER (ibid.) points out that (135) echoes William Porter's
translation of a tanka by Mibu no Tadamine, a Heian poet:

(136) I hate the cold unfriendly moon
      That shines at early morn
      And Nothing seems so sad and grey
      When I am left forlorn
      At day's returning dawn.

Though Crapsey attempted thus to adapt the prosodic features of Japanese poetry, she seems to have failed to reach the point where haiku begins, i.e., the avoidance of "explanatory" lines. Just as Williams put the line "so much depends upon" into his (122), Crapsey added the initial lines which would have been eliminated, had she had only three lines available instead of five. Another of Crapsey's cinquains is also guilty of superfluous lines:

(137) These be
      Three silent things:
      The falling snow ... the hour
      Before the dawn ... the mouth of one
      Just dead.

The juxtaposition of not two but three paradigms has been discussed above: Bashō in (112) syntagmatized "three praiseworthy things in Nara" without telling us "these be three things"; Buson in (68) syntagmatized "three desolate things" in an autumn landscape without saying that "these be".

Although Crapsey's cinquain as well as LOWELL's experimentation can thus be associated with haiku, their endeavours were primarily oriented to the form, or, to aesthetic poeticalness, which should play the least significant role, as we have already seen. The haiku form in Japanese prosody was the result of a process of condensation, which was completed by Bashō's infusion of Zen Buddhism. Since such a genetic process was totally lacking in their tradition, it is understandable that neither LOWELL nor Crapsey could win further followers for the form they artificially constructed. While POUND's adaptation of the stylistic poeticalness of haiku had a more enduring impact on the Western poetic tradition, their adaptation of the aesthetic poeticalness of haiku was bound to be a short-lived experiment.

5.4 Yasuda as a Poet-Analyst and His Contemporaries: The Second Genesis

5.4.1 Kenneth Yasuda and The Second Genesis

Although there were some poets who travelled to Japan after the fading of the Imagist movement in order to obtain first-hand experience - Arthur Davidson Ficke and Witter Bynner, to name two representative figures (cf. MINER 1958: 197-202) - their voices did not carry far, and "the real start for American haiku" had to wait for the post-war period (V. D. HEUVEL 1974: xxvii). In YASUDA (1957), we find evidence of the first American haiku poet proper. Having studied Japanese literature in Japan and written a dissertation about haiku, which was later published and became one of the classic books on haiku in English, YASUDA,

an American of Japanese descent, appears to have successfully
established standards for haiku in American English. His
haiku embody the concomitancy of the three modes of poeticalness which we observed in classical haiku. With respect to
aesthetic poeticalness, YASUDA urged the necessity of the
17-syllable form with the 5-7-5 division (1957: 79-90) as
well as phonological recurrences, including rhyme (90-97),
alliteration (98-104), and assonance (104-6). With respect
to stylistic poeticalness, he gives "three elements", "where,
what and when", which should be clearly stated and organi-
cally unified (11-60), and whose totality is in turn related
to informational poeticalness. YASUDA emphasizes above all
the significance of the "seasonal element" (142-77), whose
function, as discussed (3.5.2.3), lies in its contribution
to stylistic poeticalness. With respect to informational
poeticalness, he models himself after Bashō (69-78): "Haiku
[...] is a vehicle for rendering a clearly realized image just
as the image appears at the moment of aesthetic realization,
with its insight and meaning, with its power to seize and
obliterate our consciousness of ourselves" (31). This passage indicates that YASUDA is not concerned with "image
for image's sake" but with its "meaning and insight" (ibid.).
YASUDA's inclination towards informational poeticalness is
further specified in terms of the mode of mediation (introjection), for he, too, is concerned with the effacement of
the "consciousness of ourselves" (ibid.).

Let us now follow his analysis of his own haiku, especially with regard to the general genesis of a haiku, or the
encoding process in haiku composition. YASUDA maintains that
haiku begins with a "haiku moment", which we can equate with
our analytical term, the "symphorical phase of informational
focus" (30ff., cf. 3.4.1):

I know that when one happens to see a beautiful sunset
or lovely flowers, for instance, he is often so de-
lighted that he merely stands still. This state of
mind might be called "ah-ness" for the beholder can
only give one breathlong exclamation of delight [...]
In a brief moment he sees a pattern, a significance
he had not seen before in, let us say, a rye field and a
crimson dragonfly.
(138) A crimson dragonfly,
    As it lights, sways together
    With a leaf of rye

Calling this the "aesthetic moment", YASUDA (31) quotes
Ōsuga Otsuji, a Japanese poet-theorist (3.3.1), who ascertains that such moment is "a true haiku moment":

At the instant when our mental activity almost merges
into an unconscious state - i.e., when the relationship between the subject and object is forgotten - we
can experience the most aesthetic moment. This is what
is implied when it is said that one goes into the heart
of created things and becomes one with nature.

Otsuji's statement echoes Bashō's famous statement about
"becoming" instead of "making"[18] (HATTORI 1776: 574). Furthermore, it suggests that in the encoding process, the
perception of a symphony of informational poeticalness is
a primary occurrence (1.5.3). Metaphysical oppositions
such as "subject and object", in Otsuji's elucidation, or
"man vs. nature", "microcosm vs. macrocosm", "individual
vs. world", are, as already discussed, integrated, neutralized, harmonized, or mediated (1.1) in such "haiku moments".

5.4.1.1 The Aesthetic Poeticalness of Yasuda

YASUDA (ibid., 31) goes on to theorize why haiku should
be 17-syllabled. First, he points out that the "ah-ness"-

experience coincides with the duration of a breath, for
"as the poet exhales, that in itself draws the haiku
moment to its close", thus completing his vision (31).
He then counts several lines of English poetry[19], noting
that the number of syllables that "can easily be read
in the span of one breath" varies from sixteen to eighteen (34), and he concludes (ibid., cf. NAKAGAWA 1976:
33ff.):
> Therefore we can say that the number of syllables
> that can be uttered in a breath makes the natural
> length of haiku. This is why it is written in seventeen syllalbes, matching the length of the experience.

For YASUDA, haiku's 17-syllable form "has its raison
d'être", and he maintains that English haiku ought to have
the same syllable count. We have already seen, however,
that such "haiku moments" are independent of syllable
counting, as the discussion of the genesis of the frog
poem emphasized: the "haiku moment" of (1) consisted of
12 syllables rather than 17 (4.2.3.2).

In addition, there is the admonition given by BLYTH
(1964a: 349ff.) that the English language, in which a
syllabic duration, i.e., mora, plays a minor role, cannot
transplant the 17 syllable-pattern mechanically (5.6.1).
Seventeen syllables might have been a "raison d'être"
for japanese haiku but not for the English version of
this form. At any rate, later haiku poets tend to compose
shorter lines - in accordance with BLYTH's suggestion, as
we will see presently.

Another aspect of the syllable count for YASUDA (33)
is the "simultaneity" of "the words and the experience",
in contrast to novels, or even to "the sonnet or quatrain",

where words "contribute" to the total meaning but are not
themselves "experience" (ibid.). His notion is clearly related to the "atemporalness" of haiku (3.3.1): he quotes
(32) YAMAMOTO's assertion that "in its inner nature a
haiku tends to deny in itself the temporal element inherent in its poetic form".

As for the 5-7-5 pattern, YASUDA (61) detects an inherent "sense of harmony and balance": the ratio between
5 and 7 is approximately "two-to-three", whose proportion
is "almost that of the golden section" (ibid.), aided by
the concluding line of 5, which gives the poem "symmetry"
(ibid.). Haiku experience is an "organized experience"
(ibid.), in which "the art of synthesis rather than of
analysis, of intimation, rather than realism" (62) is
realized. He continues:

> The insight into felt objects at the haiku moment can
> be grasped only through a unified, well-ordered whole
> corresponding with the insight. For this reason, a
> formalistic structure, of which balance, harmony,
> and symmetry are qualities, seems best suited for
> realizing a haiku moment [...] The 5-7-5 pattern is
> such a formalistic structure.

YASUDA attempts to introduce a rhyme scheme in addition
to transplanting the syllabic pattern. He justifies his
use of rhyme in haiku thus (90):

> The definite repetition of the accented vowel and
> subsequent sounds produces a synchronous vibration
> when two words rhyme with each other, which can create
> a frame, as it were, around a haiku, so that its edges
> are sharp and concrete.

Precisely for this reason, the tendency of rhyme to enclose
a poem, later haiku poets would discard rhyme, for haiku
should be "open-ended" (HENDERSON 1965: 34ff.). YASUDA's

employment of a rhyme-scheme was, however, probably due
to the historical background: most of his predecessors
had translated haiku with rhyme, conforming to one Western
tradition of poetry[20]. It was BLYTH who declared that
haiku should be unrhymed (1964: 351). In all the haiku of
YASUDA cited here we observe rhyme, however: in the first
and third lines of (138), for example. In addition, we
witness the alliteration of /w/ in (142), the assonance
of /æ/ in (144), the chiming of the liquid /l/ in (143),
which echoes the title,'lizard'. With regard to rhythm,
YASUDA (80) develops a "haiku measure", which is "the
rhythm of thought [...] measured or counted by the number
of syllables in accordance with the flow of thought in
each line, or from one line to another" (80). YASUDA (81)
thus allies himself with the Imagists, especially with
POUND, whose pronouncement on the desirability of rhythm
composed in the sequence of the musical phrase, rather than in the
sequence of a metronome, he quotes with approval. Though
he analyses painstakingly according to this haiku measure,
it seems rather arbitrary[21]. His haiku certainly show more
cadence than the ticking of a metronome.

5.4.1.2 The Stylistic Poeticalness of Yasuda

In terms of stylistic poeticalness, YASUDA seems to have
inherited only kigo, the seasonal element, but not the
montage-technique, although he refers to Otsuji's "2-ku,
2-shō" briefly[22]. KEENE's criticism of LOWELL's haiku
would apply equally to YASUDA's. YASUDA either did not
perceive this fundamental structure - though it seems most
unlikely - or did not consider it fundamental. At any rate,
he composes his haiku exclusively in what is called "1-ku,
1-shō"; one-clause, one-statement. This is easily seen in
his translation of Japanese haiku which typify "2-clauses,
1-statement". Let us take Bashō's famous haiku (139), which

ASANO (1963: 3) cites as a prototypical specimen of the
morphological as well as structural characteristic of
classical haiku, i.e., 2-ku, 1-shō. A literal translation by the present author is given in the parentheses
directly under the haiku . (140) is the translation by ICHIKAWA
et al. (NGS 1958: 6) and (141) that of YASUDA (1957:
184):

(139) 草臥て宿かる比や 藤の花   (A 221)
Kutabirete / yado karu koro ya / fuji no hana
(Being tired/ it is the time for asking for an
overnight lodging!/ blossoms of wisteria)

(140) Worn out,
Seeking a lodging for the night -
Wisteria in flower!

(141) As I seek a bower,
Weary from travel, I find
A wisteria flower.

Both (139) and (140) clearly present two "independent clauses"
(3.5.2.2) severed by an exclamation mark in (139) and by a
dash in (141). The two are juxtaposed by the caesura of the
kireji 'ya' in the original: /The time when Bashō, worn
out, asks for a lodging/ on the one hand, and /wisteria in
flower/ on the other. (141), however, constitute one complex sentence in which an originally "independent clause",
'wisteria in flower!', becomes an accusative object of
the agent 'I', which does not appear in the original. More decisively, YASUDA translates the two paradigmatic halves - or cultural units - of the original into a
syntagmatic sequence through the subordinator "as". Thus
the deep structure of (139), "his being worn out from his
travel on foot at dusk" (cd) and "a whitish wisteria flower
in the evening" (cs), is transformed into the single event
of "I find a wisteria flower", whereas (139) and (140) retain

the deep structure in the surface structure. The "sparks"
between these two poles observed in the original, as well
as in the translation of (139) and (140), are totally lacking in (141). Similarly to (141), YASUDA's own haiku (138)
manifests only one "event" or "independent clause", namely,
"crimson dragonfly sways together with a leaf of rye".
YASUDA's haiku can thus be categorized in morphotypological terms
as a "one-paradigm haiku with narrativity" (Fig. 77). Two
more examples of his haiku will suffice as evidence of
YASUDA's tendency to make one-paradigm haiku:

(142)   THE MISSISSIPPI RIVER

Under the low grey
Winter skies water pushes
Water on its way.   (E 204)

(143)   THE LIZARD

A lizard flicks over
The undulating ripples
Of sunlit clover   (E 202)

With regard to stylistic poeticalness, one more important
feature of YASUDA's haiku should be mentioned. As in
the four examples cited above, YASUDA titles his haiku.
This can make a world of difference. The P_{xe}'s reception
of (142) would be totally different without the title.
The extra line of the title, the manifestum 'the Mississippi
River', provides the poem with the whole gamut of sememes
attached to this cultural unit. He always titles both his
own haiku and as his translations of Japanese classical
haiku, an often superfluous step which spoils the desired
effect of condensation.

5.4.1.3 The Informational Poeticalness of Yasuda

As mentioned, YASUDA states that the length of the "ah-ness-experience" and the length of haiku coincide. The T-production of haiku, in his view, begins with this "ah-ness". Let us recall again his haiku (138). There is another YASUDA haiku on the same theme of the "crimson dragonfly" (144), which we can discuss here:

(138) CRIMSON DRAGONFLY - I

   A crimson dragonfly,
   As it lights, sways together
   With a leaf of rye. (E 203)

(144) CRIMSON DRAGONFLY - II

   A crimson dragonfly,
   Glancing the water, casts rings
   As it passes by. (E 203)

The haiku-experience, or the starting point for composing these haiku seems to be "ah-ness", in which the microcosmic view presents an interrelatedness of the particulars and the whole: similar to "the floating nest of the grebe", such a view offers the poet a consolation, in that the minute coexists with macrocosmic nature. The existence of the poet's ego is apparently totally effaced, and the surface text presents a sheer "objective statement".
Can this poem be called a "catalogue of images", just like the extremes of Imagism which produced such a poem as, say, (116), which also presents a sheer "objective statement"? As far as the surface text is concerned, there is a great deal of resemblance in that both simply present their comparantia. The question, then, is whether or not we can perceive the hidden comparanda. In the case of Imagism, we have seen that poetic striving can lead to the rejection of cd altogether. In the case of classical haiku, we have

also seen that this rejection was due to informational poeticalness, a concept which comprehends the Buddhistic, Zen-Buddhistic, or Confucian *Weltanschauung* upon which haiku is based, or "objective symbolism", as BROWER/MINER term it (3.5.3.4). YASUDA's two poems about a crimson dragonfly offer us, like the classical haiku of Japan, the poet's "ah-ness" - experience in terms not only of the beauty of the scene but also of "its significance" - the significance of the interrelatedness of microcosm and macrocosm, which is the cd of the poem. In terms of informational poeticalness, YASUDA thus can be said to have directly inherited the Japanese haiku tradition. Fig. 88 depicts the informational poeticalness of (138), introjection:

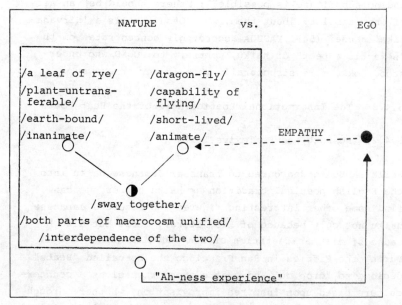

Fig. 88: The Informational Poeticalness of the American Haiku, (138): Introjection

Similarly, the introjective mediation of (139) presupposes
the opposition of /the water/ vs. /dragonfly/, mediated
into /cast rings/ on the water.

YASUDA clarifies the "content", which he defines in
terms of "what, when, and where", or "objects located
in time and space" (41): in the example of (138), what
= "a crimson dragon-fly"; when = "that single moment
when the dragonfly lights and sways" and at the same time,
"by implication", "autumn, since the dragonfly suggests
the autumn in which it lives" (47); and where = "with a leaf
of rye", adding to the poem "harmony as well as the seasonal element" (ibid.). He emphasizes that these three
elements should be "so unified that they are immovable
and no substitute is possible[23]: [there should be] an air
of inevitability about them, what Otsuji calls a 'Nirvana-
like' sense" (54). YASUDA accordingly concentrates on the
"semantic aspect" of haiku, contrary to POUND, who understood hokku more structurally than in any other way.

5.4.2   The Informational Poeticalness of the Beat Poets

5.4.2.1 Rexroth and Reflexive Texts

While YASUDA endeavoured to transfer Japanese haiku into
the English poetical tradition as haiku proper, we can
find some other interesting figures who absorbed Japanese
haiku not only because of its literary merit but also because of its manifestation of Zen Buddhism (WATTS 1958).
During the Fifties in San Francisco the so-called "Beats"
decided to "drop out and create among themselves a counter-
culture based upon inspired improvisation, whether through
jazz, drugs, or transcendence by way of oriental mysticism"
(ELLMANN/O'CLAIR 1973: 14). Kenneth REXROTH, the "doyen of
the San Francisco poets", encouraged such poets as Allen
Ginsberg, Gregory Corso, and Lawrence Ferlinghetti - three

exiles from New York - along with William Everson (Brother Antoninus) and Gary SNYDER, the last of whom went to Japan to study Zen Buddhism in a monastery (ibid.). Although they did not attempt to transplant haiku proper in the sense that YASUDA did[24], their poetry nonetheless reflects the influence of "oriental mysticism". Kenneth REXROTH, who has translated Japanese poetry, both haiku and tanka (1964), wrote, e.g., "The Wheel Revolves" (1963), in which a "haiku-like" quality can already be abundantly observed.

In this poem (145), REXROTH describes his joy in wandering "among mountains of snow and granite" with his daughter. He compares her to the "You" in the lines of Po Chu I, a famous Chinese poet of the T'ang Dynasty (9th century A. D.), which read: "You were a girl of satin and gauze/ Now you are my mountain and waterfall companion". The excerpt from "The wheel Revolves", in which haiku-like features can be observed, is given below:

(145) [...]
        The earth turns towards the sun.
        Summer comes to the mountains.
        Blue grouse drum in the red fir woods
        All the bright long days.   15
        You put blue jay and flicker feathers
        In your hat.
        Two and two violet green swallows
        Play over the lake.
        The blue birds have come back   20
        To nest on the little island.
        [...]   (D 704-5)

In spite of the length of the poem and its narrativity as a whole, (145) nonetheless exhibits a true component of haiku in terms of T-typology, i.e., reflexive T constituting descriptive T. While the concatenation of short sentences expressing objective natural phenomena contributes to the paradigmatic character of the composition, the 14th and 15th lines would make a perfect haiku, in the sense of KEENE's definition: the unification of microcosm and macorocosm. Introjective mediation seems to predominate in his poetry, as the other lines indicate. REXROTH elsewhere confesses his affinity to Imagism in terms of the "direct treatment of objects" (cit. in ELLMANN/O'CLAIR, 699):

> Imagism was a revolt against rhetoric and symbolism in poetry, a return to direct statement, simple clear images, unpretentious themes, fidelity to objectively verifiable experience, strict avoidance of sentimentality. I suppose this is the actual "programme" of all good poetry anywhere.

REXROTH is not, however, "solely a nature poet" but rather "a highly civilized and political man" (ibid.). Yet the influence of haiku as the literary manifestation of Zen Buddhism is unmistakable in his literary activity (cf. REXROTH 1964).

5.4.2.2 Snyder and Haiku Components

If the influence of oriental religion and culture was subtle in the case of REXROTH, Gary SNYDER, whom REXROTH has called "a Buddhist monk" (ELLMANN/O'CLAIR, 1261) is another matter: he does not have merely a "superficial acquaintance" with these influences (ibid.). Just as Bashō did, he metagenetically retrograded in the realm of human cognitive development - a far more through-going process than that undergone by the "Neanderthal" Williams (5.2.6) - in his commitment to Zen Buddhism. SNYDER duly grants that the poet faces in two directions at once:

> [...] one is to the world of people and language and society, and the other is to the nonhuman, nonverbal world, which is nature as nature itself; and the world of human nature

- the inner world - as it is itself, before language, before custom, before culture. There's no words in that world. There aren't any rules that we know and that's the area that Buddhism studies (cit. in KHERDIAN 1969: 35).

It is then his intention (ibid.) to

hold the most archaic values on earth: they go back to late Paleolithic: the fertility of the soil, the magic of animals, the power-vision in solitude, the terrifying initiation and re-birth, the love and ecstasy of the dance, the common work of the tribe.

Significantly enough, SNYDER assures us that a student of Zen attempts to return to the stage "before language, before custom, before culture", or in KOCH's terminology (0.3.1), before "semiogenesis", before "sociogenesis", before "psycho-affective genesis", that is to say, to "biogenesis", the stage where "all sediments" of cognitive development are purged (2.2.4). What BROWER/MINER term "neo-classicism" - returning to the past for superpersonal order - is thus inherited by SNYDER, and thus it is not surprising to find his poetry full of Zen mediation - the acceptance of "contradiction" or "opposition" as such (2.3.2).

In a poem titled "A Walk", SNYDER writes about his walk one Sunday to "Benson Lake", beginning the poem, "Sunday the only day we don't work: /Mules farting around the meadow/ Murphy fishing", and continuing the elliptical, "nominal" or "averbal" style, the style characteristic of Zen verbalism (Cf. IVANOV 1977: 47ff., also 2.4, 3.5.3.4):

(140) Goodbye. Hopping on creekbed boulders
     Up the rock throat three miles
                   Piute Creek -
In steep gorge glacier-slick rattlesnake country

>   Jump, land by a pool, trout skitter,
>   The clear sky. Deer tracks.
>   Bad place by a falls, boulders big as houses,
>   Lunch tied to belt,
>   [...]

It seems that if YASUDA can be compared to the classical haiku poets in Japan because of the narrativity of his poems, SNYDER can be compared to Bashō in respect to the creation of (1) because of the reflexivity of his poems. The 13th line is, e.g., nothing but an ostensive text juxtaposing two primal experiences: "The clear sky. Deer tracks". It is a "pairing" (○—●) in that two juxtaposed halves manifest two spheres which constitute one of the most fundamental oppositions in human cognition, "the sky and the earth", as IVANOV/TOPOROV (1982: 61ff.) explain. It should be noted that in such an extremely retrogressed perceptory composition, a dyadic structure, which consists of merely "sky and earth" or "above and below", is retained (IVANOV/TOPOROV 1982) when "all intellectual sediments" are taken away (metageneticity!). In "A Walk" line 13 is echoed in the 25th line: "A lone duck in a gunsightpass step side hill".

Similarly to the prototypical haiku (1), (140)'s reflexivity is the realization of its introjective mediation. In "Meeting the Mountains", to give another typical example, we read only the concatenation of the actions of the poet's son Kai; nonetheless, the vitality or "the archaic value" of the "nonverbal world" can be expressed:

>   (147)   Meeting the Mountains
>   He crawls to the edge of the foaming creek
>   He backs up the slab ledge
>   He puts a finger in the water
>   He turns to a trapped pool
>   Puts both hands in the water

Puts one foot in the pool
Drops pebbles in the pool
He slaps the water surface with both hands
He cries out, rises up and stands
Facing toward the torrent and the mountain
Raises up both hands and shouts three times!   (D 1267)

5.4.3 The Haiku of Two Black American Poets: Wright and Knight

The Black American writer Richard Wright "discovered the haiku form" in the last month of his life, when he was living in Paris, and he wrote "more than two thousand of these tiny, elliptical poems" (ELLMANN/O'CLAIR, 785). A Haiku anthology he aspired to compile was not completed, however; his haiku offer an interesting specimen for our research in that he was probably introduced to haiku not by American literary circles but by French Existentialists (ibid.), where owing to the Imagists' influence it had long been established[25]. The following "Four Haiku" closely resemble those by YASUDA in that they more or less record "1-clause, 1-statement", concentrating more than anything else on informational poeticalness, though differing in mediational mode: his mediation can be characterized as equijection rather than introjection, in that the voice of a poet who is willing to let himself be influenced by Nature is discernible in each haiku. It should also be pointed out that Wright's haiku conform to the 5-7-5 pattern:

(148)   Four Haiku

A balmy spring wind
Reminding me of something
I cannot recall.

The green cockleburrs
Caught in the thick wooly hair
Of the black boy's head.

Standing in the field
I hear the whispering of
Snowflake to snowflake.

It is September
The month in which I was born,
And I have no thoughts.   (D 788)

If Wright resembles YASUDA in his application of haiku
principles, Etheridge Knight, another Black American poet,
writes a short poem with the seventeen-syllable pattern.
He writes "pastorals of prison life" (ELLMANN/O'CLAIR, 1304)
by concatenating ten examples of this "tiny Oriental form"
(ibid.). It seems that Knight avoids the use of
articles in his attempt to conform to the syllabic pattern.
Curiously enough, the first four include an explicit as
well as an implicit simile:

(149)   Haiku
            1
Eastern guard tower
glints in sunset: convicts rest
like lizards on rocks.

            2
The piano man
is sting at 3 am
his songs drop like plum.

            3
Morning sun slants cell.
Drunks stagger like cripple flies
On jailhouse floor.

            4
to write a blues song
is to regiment riots
and pluck gems from graves.   (D 1305)

Knight's first haiku presents a two-fold structure: on
the one hand there is a juxtaposition of 'guard tower'
and 'convicts [resting] like lizards', and on the other,
there is a simile comparing [resting] convicts to 'lizards
on rocks'. The second haiku has a three-fold structure;
1) the first implicit simile or metaphor in which 'the
piano man' is compared to a 'sting'; 2) the second simile
in which the way his songs are sung is compared to the
way the plums drop; and 3) the juxtaposition of the first
simile and the second simile. The third haiku shows an identical structure to the first: a juxtaposition of 'morning
sun' and 'drunks', and the simile of staggering 'drunks'
to 'cripple flies'. The fourth is an almost proverb-like
implicit simile: to do A is to do B, whereby the second
part B is doubled so that A equals B' and B''.

In Knight's poem, (149), consisting of "pastorals of prison life"
as a series of haiku, the poetry of haiku seems to have
reached the border line in which haiku as poetry should be
differentiated from, say, epigram or proverb. When we compare
Knight's fourth haiku with SNYDER's line "The clear sky.
Dèer tracks.", this point becomes clear. As BLYTH assures
us, poetry is "sensation", not intellectualism. "A is B'
and B''" is an intellectual concept such as SUZUKI denounced. It could be argued, however, that Knight simply
turns the deep structure into the surface structure, thus
retaining a copula "is" or "like" instead of employing a
semi-colon or exclamation mark - the equivalent to the
Japanese kireji, or cutting word. As our discussion has made
clear, however, such a comparison normally takes place between microcosm and macrocosm, reflecting metaphysical
oppositions. Knight evidently deals with more material
than haiku is capable of managing: we have already seen
that the fundamental structure of haiku is a *dyad* which
consists of two "cultural units", often manifesting a comparandum and a comparans (3.5.2.2), whereas Knight's com-

parison often involves more than three sememes, of which
his second haiku provides an eloquent example. It seems
natural, then, that Knight concludes his series of "Haiku"
with a "meta-poetic" comment consisting of 17 syllables,
which, as we will see presently, would have been labelled
a non-haiku by HENDERSON:

(150) Making jazz swing in
 Seventeen syllables AIN'T
 No square poet's job.

5.5 American Haiku: Metagenesis

During the Sixties the term "American haiku" came into
vogue. The semi-annual magazine bearing that name began
to circulate, and haiku contests began to be held. Both
aspects of haiku, "form" and "content", had now been
understood by the Americans, and were evident in the
haiku they composed.

The following discussion is divided into two main parts:
the establishment of American haiku, and its diversification: The first part includes three aspects which seem to
represent the phenomenon: 1) the misunderstood informational
poeticalness of the classical haiku of Japan which is observed in *Borrowed Water*; 2) the American haiku of
James William HACKETT; and 3) the haiku contests conducted
by *American Haiku*. The second part discusses the contemporary haiku scene in terms of its diversification, which
can be observed in *The Haiku Anthology*, edited by V. D.
HEUVEL. The *Anthology* will provide the present study with
examples of the metagenetic tendencies corresponding to
the second phase we observed in Japan, in which the establishment of haiku by Bashō was metagenetically diversified,
primarily by Buson (4.2.3.3).

5.5.1 The Misunderstood Informational Poeticalness of the Classical Haiku of Japan

In 1956 the Writers Roundtable of Los Altos, California, was organized by Helen Stiles CHENOWETH "to further creative writing among adults who were interested in publishing their writings" (CHENOWETH 1966: 9). After the "creating of three rhymeless lines of 5, 7, and 5 syllables, a total of 17", and then of trying the cinquain (5.3.2), some of the poets "intensively studied" Japanese classical haiku and became "fascinated with composing their own haiku" (ibid., 10). They studied the "four most prominent Japanese poets" - Bashō, Buson, Issa, and Shiki - and decided to devote themselves to the composition of American haiku (ibid.). They received advice from Clement Hoyt, then the editor of *American Haiku*, which had been founded in 1963. Hoyt's guidelines are worth quoting here for his comparison of the transplantation of haiku to that of the sonnet (ibid., 11):

> There is no authority on the haiku in English unless you accept, as I do, the haiku to be a definite form (and to be followed in a like manner) as the sonnet, which was introduced successfully into English from Italian and which has just as definite a restriction of CONTENT as the haiku. Its seventeen syllables, 5, 7, 5 in three lines, with its restrictions on content, its seasonal implication, its balancing images, its naturalness of expression, its dependence on "effect" rather than intellectual "point" is nowhere near as difficult as sonnet's structural and internal restrictions and look how long the sonnet has been part of our literary heritage!

In addition to this guiding principle, Hoyt further gave them three "important lessons"(ibid.):

(i) The beauty and delicacy of Bashō's "let your haiku
    resemble a willow branch struck by a little shower
    and trembling a little in the wind".
(ii) The Japanese masters of haiku produced their best
    work through observation and meditation.
(iii) The corollary or contrast, often "far out", which
    flows from the major thought.
The first lesson for the Roundtable poets in our terms
refers to the "cadence of haiku", aesthetic poeticalness;
the second, to "the unification of man and nature", by implication, informational poeticalness; the third, to "two
contra-points", stylistic poeticalness. With this credo in
mind, the thirteen poets wrote American haiku which were then
compiled according to the four seasons, except for those
which do not include a seasonal element and are therefore
compiled under "miscellaneous". As for rhyme, they "preferred" the 3-line unrhymed form, thus differing from YASUDA
as well as HENDERSON (1934), and allying themselves with
BLYTH (1949) (cf. SEEGAL 1977).

Their haiku, in spite of Hoyt's guidelines for the composition of haiku, seem to have tended towards the triviality
of "tsukinami" - "trite haiku" - against which Shiki
launched a reformation, as discussed in 4.2.4. Curiously
enough, the haiku of this group with the fanciful name
"The Los Altos Writers Roundtable", very much resemble
a poem by Baishitsu, (76), which we categorized as an argumentative T in the guise of descriptive T (4.2.4): in the
surface structure, it juxtaposes "the full moon" and "the
shadow of a man" but in the deep structue, it evaluates
"the shadow of grasses" as superior to "the shadow of a man".
(76) thus constructs "processually the *truth*" in that
the alleged superiority of a man is subverted by the real
superiority of the natural objects. Let us consider the
following four typical specimens of this group of poets:

(151) Gay kite in the sky
      tugs against tethering string -
         birds boast their freedom   (G 18: Peggy Card)

(152) Spider-woven trap
      is caught in a web of wind -
         butterflies go free   (G 20: Rosemary
                                            Jeffords)

(153) Hollowed charred tree stumps
      denied their part of living -
         new bees make honey   (G 61: Helen S.
                                            Chenoweth)

(154) In our old oak tree
      the parasitic starlings
         scold the mistletoe   (G 89: Georgian
                                            Tashjian)

It is clear that these four examples all include an overt didacticism: (151) and (152) contrast imprisonment and freedom; (153) preaches the amazing vitality of nature, and (154) presents the irony of one parasite scolding another. Their didactic character is due to the argumentative T-type in the deep structure.

The argumentative T in the deep structure of the four haiku by the writers of Roundtable can be depicted as below:

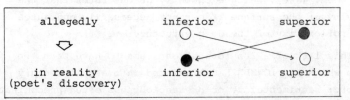

Fig. 89: The Argumentative T-type of the Haiku Composed
        by the Writers Roundtable

The inversion of the value of two culturally evaluated entities is the key notion of the above haiku: In (151), the apparent gaiety of the kite is subordinated to the "freedom" of birds; in (152), the predator is caught in his own trap, while the intended prey, the butterflies, "go free", and are thus superior; in (153), the dead tree stumps (negative) are compensated for (positive) by honey-bees; and in (154), the alleged superiority of "the starlings" which "scold the mistletoe" is subverted by the fact that they are themselves "parasites", i.e., the starlings are made to seem ridiculous and inferior.

According to KÖNGÄS-MARANDA/MARANDA (1971: 70) in their study *Structural Models in Folklore*, this type of narrative, i.e., the "permutation-of-authority", most typically underlies the *Schwank* (the funny tale). They found that the fundamental structure of *Schwänke* is the "negation of authority", e.g., the *socially inferior* "servant" outwits his superior, "the farmer", by being *intellectually superior* (ibid.). They (70-1) maintain that this narrative kind can also be presented as a riddle, "What is socially inferior and yet superior? - Intellectually superior", and thus conclude: "riddles and narratives are transformations of identical basic structures" (71). One could presume, then, that Western poets without the experience of Zen metageneticity tend to produce haiku with the left-hemisphere, resulting in the logical, argumentative T-type. We are reminded of SNYDER's reflexivity in spite of the apparent length of the poem, (146), which eloquently demonstrates that the brevity of the surface T does not necessarily guarantee the reflexivity of the deep structure.

This lack of a Zen foundation seems to have been the trap which Amy LOWELL had blundered into a half century before: sentimentality or pretentiousness often predominate, in spite of their handy recipe for writing haiku:

(155) What sound when a plant
      bursts through the soil, what song
          if a flower dies?   (G 30: H. S. Chenoweth)

(156) Here by the seaside
          sea gulls promenade with me ...
                footprints tell the tale.   (G 44: Margot Bollock)

(157) Lilies of the water,
          like white gifts on green trays,
                beg to be received.   (G 52: Joy Shieman)

(158) Silver teas of rain -
          do you weep for dusty earth
                or for rainbows?   (G 60: P. Card)

(159) Twin pomegranates
          for my ancient bronze pitcher -
                how cross the jays are.   (G 72: Catherine N. Paton)

(160) The tree seems lifeless
          yet the mistletoe prospers -
                a kiss for Christmas?   (G 94: H.S.Chenoweth)

(161) Moan of wind in trees
          tongue, court-jester of the mind,
                do not speak of it!   (G 90: M. Bollock)

The Roundtable poets also employed the "contrast"-technique according to Hoyt's advice, and their contrasts indeed seem "far out", as the following examples indicate:

(162) Baled hay in a neat row
          still smells wild and sweet:
                my book is finished.   (G 18: Hilda Aarons)

(163) The toes of her shoes
          are worn out - wild hyacinths
                were lovely this year.   (G 35: Anne Rutherford)

(164) Tin can of daisies,
          on an old scratched table -
                garbage cans below.   (G 57: Jerri Spinelli)

(165) White calla lilies -
          you can surely tease a croak
                from this plastic frog.   (G 29: Tashjian)

The haiku compiled in *Borrowed Water*, written by the Roundtablers, also make us wonder whether 17 syllables might not be in fact too many for American haiku, especially when we encounter such specimens as:
(166) At early sunrise
     the ancient charred tree trunks flow -
         moment of deceit.   (G 45: Chenoweth)

(167) Two leaning tombstones
     took seventy years to touch -
         mist and peace dwell here. (G 79: Shieman)
(168) This monk loves rain
     as well as sun and hence does not
         mend his umbrella.   (G 106: Tashjian)
(166) can do without the explanatory manifestum of 'moment of deceit': (167) should drop 'mist and peace dwell here'; (168) could be accused of "discursive reasoning" which is realized in 'as well as sun and hence'.

The examples by the Roundtablers and Knight make clear the danger of verbosity for American haiku. As a matter of fact, haiku has been called "the wordless poem" by Alan WATTS (V.D. HEUVEL, xxx: cf. also AMANN 1969): the few words employed in haiku "have such an ontological immediacy that the sensitive reader can almost reach out and touch the things they describe" (ibid.). Our discussion of the immediate relationship between a refereme and a manifestum is pertinent here: those phrases we labelled as either "didactic" or "superfluous" refer to something abstract, i.e., they do not refer to any concrete objects[26]. Thus, such manifesta as 'go free', 'denied their part of living' in (153), 'parasitic' in (154), 'moment of deceit' in (166), 'took seventy years' and 'mist and peace' in (167), or 'as well as' and 'hence' in (163) - all depend upon abstract sememes. IVANOV (1977: 60) makes it clear that the understanding of abstract nouns depends, contrary to that of concrete nouns, on the left hemisphere - an assertion that supports the left-hemisphericity of these poets (3.5.3.4).

James W. HACKETT, whose haiku will next be discussed
also warned against this danger of verbosity: in listing
20 "suggestions for beginners and others" for haiku composition, HACKETT states:

> Express your experience in syntax natural to English.
> Don't write everything in the Japanese 5, 7, 5 form,
> since in English this often causes padding and contri-
> vance (cit. in HENDERSON 1965: 61).

The problem of the 17 syllables will be discussed once
again in connection with the definition of haiku in English. Suffice it here to mention that even 17 syllables
can be too long to record "haiku moments". This fact sheds
light on the question as to how short a haiku can be. In
fact English haiku tend to become shorter than 17 syllables,
as the Haiku Society of America affirms: "Though 17 syllables
is still the norm in English language haiku, it is more and
more common for a haiku to consist of 'fewer' syllables"
(V. D. HEUVEL 1974: 250).

5.5.2 Hackett and Informational Poeticalness

Of the individual poets who contributed to establish "American Haiku" during the Sixties, James W. HACKETT[27] seems to
be the most noted (V. D. HEUVEL 1974; BLYTH 1964; HENDERSON
1967). He is the author of *Haiku Poetry* (1965), and he "represents what may loosely be called the Bashō School" (HEN-
DERSON 1967: 60). HACKETT himself writes the following, emphasizing the symphorical phase of informational poeticalness (cit. in BLYTH 1964: 351-2):

> I regard haiku as "fundamentally" existential, rather
> than a form of poetry. Bashō's statement that: "Haiku
> is simply what is happening in this place at this
> moment", shows that he regarded intuitive experience
> to be the "basic" of Haiku. And now, his criterion is

my own [...] It seems clear that the whole matter of
syllables and lines is an arbitrary one, and should be.
For haiku is ultimately more than a form (or even a
kind) of poetry: it is a Way - one of living awareness.
Haiku's real treasure is its touchstone of the present.
This, together with its rendering of the suchness of
things, gives Haiku a supra-literary mission, one of
moment.

HACKETT, unlike the Roundtable Writers, appears in fact
to have successfully avoided "padding", as in the following
examples which do not conform to the syllabic pattern of
5-7-5:

(169) Bitter Morning:
    Sparrows sitting
        Without necks   (F 355)

(170)   Ever lingering
    In the taste of the walnut:
    Deep Autumn.   (F 356)

Like Bashō's crow poem, (31), both (169) and (170) juxtapose
two manifesta, each of which can be categorized as belonging
to the reflexive T-type. The two manifesta constitute as a
whole the descriptive T-type of haiku. In both poems, kigo,
season words, play an integral part: in (169), the manifestum 'bitter morning' is polysemic in that it indicates
the whole gamut of sememes connected to /a chilling winter
morning/, whereas in (170), 'deep autumn' indicates /the
contemplative mood of the transitional season prior to the
desolate winter/.

While HACKETT writes such two-paradigm-haiku, he also
composes one-paradigm haiku, comparable to Bashō's (62),
"the marshmallow at the road-side is eaten up by my horse":

(171)   The kitten
    So calmly chews
    The fly's buzzing misery   (F 359)

Such natural phenomena as in (62), or in (171), with its
predator and victim, in fact offer either an introjective
mediation or moralization, depending on how P_x maps such
phenomena: they can offer him an introjective mediation
in that in the Buddhistic *Weltanschauung*, everything has
its karma or fate, or they can offer a moral lesson, e.g.,
that the strong never learns the misery of the weak. If
Bashō's (62) does not reveal any personal involvement in
the surface T, (171) does so because of the manifesta,
'calmly' and 'misery'. This exposure of the poet's emotional involvement could suggest a moralizing stance. (171),
however, differs from the haiku of the Writers of the Roundtable in that there is no inversion of the evaluation in
the deep structure. HACKETT seems indeed to revive the momentum of haiku composition in English language, i.e., the
specific informational poeticalness that established the
classical haiku in Japan. HACKETT's haiku will be discussed further in the following section, for he was the
winner of the first prize in the first haiku contest held
by *American Haiku*.

5.5.3 Haiku Contests

In addition to the composition of haiku by the Writers
Roundtable and by HACKETT, the third event which contributed to the establishment of American haiku during the
Sixties was the haiku contests conducted by, among
other sponsors, *American Haiku* and Japan Air Lines (HENDER-
SON 1965: 30). In 1965 HENDERSON writes that "Haiku - and
attempts at haiku - are now being written in English by the
hundred thousands", and notes that 41,000 haiku were submitted to Japan Air Line's National Haiku Contest in 1964
(ibid., 28). He (29-31) then lists the six haiku which
"won the first prizes in *American Haiku*'s and Japan Air
Line's Contests" (from 1963 to 1966) in order to give "some idea of what
American poets are doing" in terms of haiku. Of the six haiku

HENDERSON lists, the last one, the first-prize winner of the 1964 Japan Air Lines Contest, is our (169), already discussed in connection with its informational poeticalness. We will therefore examine the five remaining haiku according to our analytical scheme.

(172) Searching on the wind,
    the hawk's cry
        is the shape of its beak.   (1963: J. W. Hackett)

The same haiku is re-written as follows when it appears in V. D. HEUVEL's anthology (ibid., 25):

(173) Searching on the wind,
    the hawk's cry ...
        is the shape of its beak.

HACKETT snapshots the "heightened moment" in which the sharp cry of the hawk is heard, and his spontaneous perception of the resemblance between the sharpness of the cry and the sharpness of the hawk's beak is realized. At first, the gliding movement of the hawk in the void is introduced, much in the same way Bashō employed 'furuike ya' in his frog poem.

    This perceptory quiescence is then juxtaposed to the short line, presenting the sharp cry of the hawk. In the latter version (173), the juxtaposition is more accentuated because of the three dots added to the end of the second line: the dots emphasize the brief echoing of the hawk's cry in the air. This lingering effect then is followed by the poet's realization of the resemblance between auditory and visual perception.

    In (173) we witness a rather complicated deep structure: in the initial part, there is a Zen-type of mediation, which proceeds through the phases of "symmetry-asymmetry-symmetry". In the phase of asymmetry "the difference" made by some kind of movement is perceived, as was the "sound of water" in the frog-poem. In (172), the initial perceptory

quiescence, corresponding to "the old pond" in (1), is
broken by the sound and a difference is perceived, i.e.,
the /void/ surrounding 'searching on the wind' is
juxtaposed to 'the hawk's cry'. The restoration of the
initial equilibrium is expressed by three dots, which
HACKETT presumably added in the later version in order to
emphasize this reinstatement of the initial quietness.
In the course of this reinstatement, however, there occurs
the poet's perception, in which the auditory and visual
identity of the hawk is felt. Thus the deep structure of
(173), i.e., the initial experience, is two-fold: it is
the typical Zen experience of "symmetry-asymmetry-symmetry"
and also the poet's sudden realization of the identical
features of the hawk's cry and shape of its beak. Fig. 90
depicts the two-fold deep structure of (173):

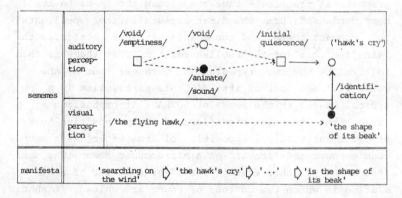

Fig. 90: The Two-fold Deep Structure of (173)

The next haiku discussed by HENDERSON is by Nicholas
Virgilio:

(174) Lily:
    out of the water ...
        out of itself.   (1963: N. Virgilio)

Although Virgilio is usually associated with Buson [28] rather than Bashō, which is to say, he stresses "poetic value" rather than "spiritual value" - i.e., stylistic rather than informational poeticalness -, here he concentrates on his admiration for the vitality manifested in a blooming lily. The way the lily blooms impressed him - with all its vitality and selffulfilment (3.5.3.4).

In an extremely condensed form (it only has 2, 5, and 4 syllables), Virgilio's haiku first mentions the manifestum 'Lily:' without any article - the otherwise obligatory grammatical practice - thus compacting the theme to its most condensed form. The first caesura further spotlights this compact theme, and the change of lines reinforces the "kireji-effect" of the English version. This theme is then followed by the two prepositional phrases; 'out of the water ...' and 'out of itself'. This parallelism is a typical *povtor* in the sense of LOTMAN: it emphasizes through the identical signifiers of the preposition 'out of', the antithetical opposition of 'the water' as a macrocosmic power and 'itself' as a microcosmic power. The manifestum 'Lily:' thus reveals itself as a bearer of a mediation in which two sources of power are united. It should be mentioned that this manifestum is placed at the very top of the orthographical arrangement of (174), whose conspicuous position reinforces the importance of the manifestum.

The mode of mediation can be characterized as "equijective", for the poet is overwhelmed by the vitality of the lily on the one hand (introjection) and at the same time he "interprets" the way it blooms (projection): the 'Lily' is nurtured by 'the water' which synechdochally manifests /the fertility of of nature/, but at the same time it grows 'out of itself', /out of its own vitality/. Fig. 91 depicts the analysis of the equijectional informational structure of (174):

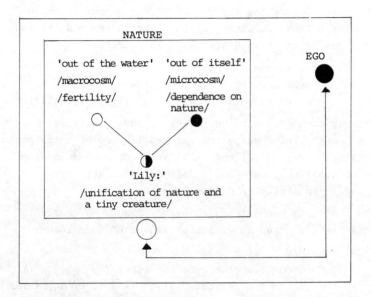

Fig. 91: The Equijectional Informational Poeticalness of (174)

The third poem which HENDERSON discusses is about "aesthetic experience" rather than about "religious experience" in V. D. HEUVEL's parlance (5.1):

(175)   Sunset: carrying
            a red balloon, he looks back ...
                a child leaves the zoo.   (1964:W.F.O'Rourke)

Similarly to (31), Bashō's poem about the perching crow, we witness in (175) one of the specific modes of stylistic poeticalness: a *montage* technique, since the appearance of the huge red sinking sun is superimposed on the red balloon the child is carrying; both are juxtaposed on the base of

the similarity of being /round/, /huge/, /red/, which
provide the poem with an appropriate decor of day's end.

The fourth poem (176), also by Virgilio, shows an outspoken resemblance to YASUDA's haiku: it is a "one-paradigm haiku" describing the moment of the sunset in which the natural light remaining in the western sky and the manmade light of the town clock exist in harmony:

(176) The town clock's face
       adds another shade of yellow
       to the afterglow.   (1964: Virgilio)

Similarly to YASUDA's haiku, (176) employs "1-clause, 1-statement", reinforcing the unified imagery with its hue of yellow. While (172) and (174) are more concerned with informational poeticalness, (175) and (176) are more interested in stylistic poeticalness.

In the fifth poem discussed by HENDERSON, we confront a haiku that strikes us with its "Japanese" impression:

(177) The old rooster crows -
       out of the mist come the rocks
       and the twisted pine.   (1965: O.M.B. Southard)

While (175) and (176) concentrate on two rather homogeneous or "concordant" pictures, (177) concentrates on the heterogeneous - "incompatible", "discordant" - pictures. The poem begins with an opening "fanfare" conducted by 'the rooster' which is 'old'. The sememe /ancient/ manifested in the first line as 'old' permeates the rest of the poem as well: 'the rock' and 'the twisted pine', are the traditional manifesta of Japanese poetry for the expression of ancientness. The comparison realized in (177) is threefold: 1) /sound/ vs. /quiescence/; 2) /animate/ vs. /inanimate/; and 3) /the transitoriness of the mist/ vs. /eternity of the rocks and the pine/. This threefold comparison, however, makes this haiku somewhat overcrowded. Southard conforms to the

5-7-5 syllabic rule, and (177) could thus be taken as another example
of "padding". At any rate, however, the dominance of
informational poeticalness is evident: the effacement of
the poet's ego simply mirrors the significant moment - the
moment of the unification of the animate and the inanimate.

A survey of the American haiku that gained a secure footing
during the sixties indicates the successful transplantation of
classical haiku from its native country to the U. S. In
terms of aesthetic poeticalness, the undisputed 5-7-5
of the Japanese classical form was first imitated almost
mechanically (5.3, 5.5.1). Then the poems became shorter and shorter, as exemplified by some of the
prize-winning poems. Such phonological recurrences as
rhyme are quite subdued, though there are occasional recurrences, as in "yellow" and "afterglow" in (176). In
terms of stylistic poeticalness, American haiku also
adapted the montage-technique, the juxtaposition of two
"compatible" homogeneous sememes or of two "incompatible",
contrastive sememes (FRANK 1968)[29]. American haiku also
adapted seasonal elements, though not invariably. The haiku
manifestum "kireji", the cutting word, was also taken
over and domesticated in American haiku: the American
poets replaced it by a semicolon, or by dots, or sometimes by simply changing lines. More importantly, the
fusion of stylistic poeticalness and informational poeticalness predominates in American haiku - in an environement where
aesthetic poeticalness manifested in rhyme and metrics
had been dominant. The informational poeticalness of
haiku in English is introjective, as was the case in
classical haiku in Japan.

5.5.4 The Diversity of American Haiku: Metagenesis

The spectrum of American haiku is wider than that of

Japanese haiku. To encompass all the trends of American
haiku is, as we also experienced in considering Japanese
haiku,   an impossible task. We will instead limit ourselves to a survey of *The Haiku Anthology*, for
its introduction assures us that "a great diversity lies
in the pages ahead" (V. D. HEUVEL: xxxiii). It was our
point of departure not to be prescriptive but to be
descriptive, and thus it is not our purpose here to
select "real" haiku but to examine the underlying structure of the poems which are labelled "haiku" by the poets.
Some standard specimens, in the sense of conforming to the
Japanese classical haiku, such as YASUDA's, HACKETT's,
AMANN's, and Virgilio's have already been mentioned in the
previous section. They present characteristics of aesthetic
poeticalness: either 5-7-5 or some shorter version, though
not a definite rhythmic pattern. They also present certain
aspects of stylistic poeticalness, a montage-like construction. The surface text can be a one-paradigm haiku, i.e.,
of the one-complex-sentence-type, or a two-paradigm haiku
of the juxtaposition-type with the caesura marked by a semi-
colon, comma, or simply a line change. In addition, the
seasonal element also plays an integral part. With regard
to informational poeticalness, they present mostly introjective mediation, which in turn determines the subject
of these haiku, namely, the interrelationship between man
and nature. In the following discussion, we will examine
specimens that differ from such standard haiku with respect
to trimodal poeticalness. Two specific questions that arise
in this context will be: (i) how short a haiku can be; and
(ii) whether or not a haiku can remain a haiku without
dealing with the interrelationship between nature and man.

5.5.4.1 A Search for Greater Brevity?

One of the controversial points regarding haiku in English
is its form (5.6.1). Anthony SURACI (1979: 46-51) argues

that haiku seems to need a certain length in order to
render not only the circumstance that triggered its composition in the first place, but also its cadence as poetry,
which, as JAKOBSON (1960) and KOCH (1978) assure us, plays
a definite role. We have seen in Japanese vers libre, however, that an extreme brevity of nine syllables was reached
([3], e.g.). In haiku in English, this tendency goes even
further: as our "tundra" (2) shows, brevity can attain the
extreme of a single word. Let us now examine some specimens spotlighting this aspect:

(178)   an empty elevator
          opens
          closes   (H 9: Jack Cain)

(179)   beyond
          stars beyond
             star   (H 13: l. a. davidson)

Interestingly enough, where the syllable count is no longer
observed, the trifold structure is still maintained. (178)
is a reflexive text in that it consists of purely ostensive
manifesta. (179) presents a somewhat more complex deep-
structure, while the surface structure consists of only
four manifesta, showing a dominance of aesthetic poeticalness: the repetition of 'beyond star(s)'. On the one hand
there are /stars beyond star/, and on the other, there are
/millions of stars/ which transcend the numerical manifestations of 's' and become simply 'star' beyond 'stars'.
Neither (178) nor (179) includes seasonal elements: what is
left is a sheer juxtaposition of two cultural units "○:●".

The following by Hotham is a distich, the only specimen
of a dyadic presentation in the entire collection of 280
haiku.

(180)   Deserted tennis court.
          wind through the net.   (H 45: Gary Hotham)

A comparison of (178) and (180) indicates a deep-rooted justification for the tertiary structure of haiku, formulated thus by BLYTH: "a rise, suspense, and fall" (cf. 3.5.1.1). (178) presents a "fall" contrasted to the preceding two lines through the manifestum 'closes', indicating /the motion of an empty elevator/ which "closes" at the same time as the poem. (180) merely demonstrates a juxtaposition of two cultural units taken from one scene depicting a lonely tennis court.

This tertiary structure indeed appears to be what characterizes haiku in English as well. The question arises, however, as to whether such a tertiary structure depends on the typography or on the deep-structure that underlies the poem. Suppose that we rewrite (180) as follows:

(181) Deserted tennis court.
  wind
   through the net.

We have a haiku comparable to this, composed by Larry Wiggin:

(182) dreaming ...
  dust
   on the window   (H 207: Wiggin)

As far as the deep structure of (182) is concerned, it seems to be identical to that of (180): it consists of two counterpoints, one 'dreaming' and the other 'dust on the window'. By being placed in the middle alone, however, the manifestum 'dust' gains more independence than when it is written in one line, and for this reason the surface structure of (182) becomes tertiary. Let us now consider the following monostich, also a unique specimen, by Michael Segers:

(183) in the eggshell after the chick has hatched
             (H 131: Segers)

It consists of 11 syllables, but its statement seems less clear than, say, (182) which consists of seven. The prepo-

is experienced as a "détente" (KOCH 1982c), stimulation must exist. For this purpose, Japanese haiku is equipped with the rhythm of the 5-7-5. The tertiary structure, which seems indeed deep-rooted, coupled with some kind of repetitive stimulation can thus be taken as the necessary element for American haiku.

5.5.4.2 Can Haiku Deal with Other than the Nature-Human Relationship?

Another aspect of the diversification of haiku in English is related to the question of whether or not haiku is capable of dealing solely with human affairs instead of referring to the mapping of the human within a natural setting, the informational poeticalness most typical of haiku. Let us consider the following:

(185)   the fat lady
        bends over the tomatoes
        a full moon   (H 122: Alan
                                                        Pizzarelli)

(185) is obviously a two-paradigm haiku in which 'the fat lady bends over the tomatoes' is juxtaposed to 'a full moon'. To that extent, (185) could be compared to, say, HACKETT's (169), in which 'bitter morning' and 'sparrows sitting without necks' are juxtaposed. Yet the problem of (185) is that it arouses the impression that (185) is more senryū, haiku's sibling (4.2.2.1), than haiku[30].

Let us consider Fig. 92, which compares (185) and Saikaku's "hyperbolical analogy", in which Mt. Fuji with its volcanic smoke is compared to a "tea pot", cited earlier as typical of the compository method of pre-Bashō haikai (4.2.2):

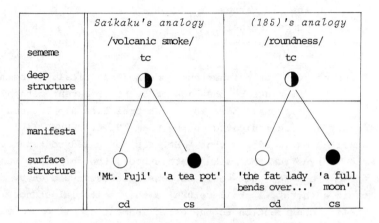

Fig. 92: Comparable Analogies in Saikaku's
Hyperbolic Analogy and Haiku (185)

Although the comparison of (185) is by no means "hyperbolic" in the sense of Saikaku's, the structural similarity is clear. In Saikaku's analogy, the sememe which is selected from Mt. Fuji is /its volcanic smoke/ and not such metaphysical sememes as /the mediation between the earth and heaven/ or /the symbol of eternity/, such as the ancient poets used to select. Similarly, the sememe of the presumable kigo, or season word, 'a full moon', in Japan a well-established kigo for the autumnal evening, is /its roundness/ and not its seasonal implication. To put it another way, the 'full moon' does not function polysemically to indicate the whole gamut of the autumnal atmosphere but as a bisociation of /a full moon/ and /its roundness/.

If (185) exemplifies a border-line case between haiku and senryū, another "haiku" from the anthology lacks seasonal references altogether:

(186)
      the old barber
      sweeping hair
      into the giant bag   (H 159: James
                                                                             Timpton)

Although (186) is neither humorous nor satirical, it seems to be a senryū due to the lack of overt or latent metaphysical oppositions. There is no interrelationship between nature and man indicated in the poem. V. D. HEUVEL (ibid., xxxii) himself admits that "[He] has not tried to separate the senryū from the haiku in this book, though [he] is sure there are a few that would be considered senryū even by their authors". I shall return to this editorial stance, for its contribution to the establishment of the genres both of haiku and of senryū merits comment.

The theme of love is another field which traditional haiku had avoided but which entered into senryū, as BLYTH (1949a: 38) summarizes in his book *Senryū*:

> Nothing brings out the difference between senryū and haiku more clearly than their relation to the subject of sex. To haiku sex hardly exists; to senryū, it is all-pervading. There are, it is true, a few semi-love verses by Kikaku, Ransetsu, Buson, Kyoshi, but they amount to nothing. Senryū is concerned above all things with the vital relation of man to man, and man to woman ... [Sex] is tragic, it is comic, it is so, - there is nothing more to be said than this concerning any phase of life. These three elements, the grievous, the humorous, and the inevitable, enter into all the best senryū on this subject.

Now, let us consider the following sequence of four haiku[31] by McClintock. It seems that these four concatenated haiku have indeed transgressed the realm of haiku not only thematically but also by their excessive narrativity:

(187) pushing
            inside ... until
                her teeth shine
                                    she leaves -
                                    warm pillow scent
                                    remaining
                    the first melt ...
                        her eyes gone
                            under their lids

            while we wait
            to do it again
            the rains of spring
                                        (H 92-3)

McClintock seems to be familiar with the endeavours undertaken by the Japanese poets during the Thirties to compensate for the brevity of haiku (4.3) by rensaku, the serialization of haiku. As we have seen, these attempts at the serialization of haiku were two-edged: on the one hand, they enabled haiku to express "suspense" in addition to "tension", but on the other, the concentration of the single haiku was blurred. Of the four poems of McClintock's serialization only the fourth includes the seasonal element, 'the rains of spring', while the other three depict the subject of sex directly. Whether or not McClintock's direction, which tends thematically towards "senryū", but still retains some aspects of haiku in the practice furthered in American haiku, will be carried on remains to be seen. Suffice it to say that in the process of genre-establishment such contradictory diversification of the domination of condensation and expansion has appeared both in Japan and in the U. S.

5.6 Towards the Definition of American Haiku

In editing *The Haiku Anthology*, V. D. HEUVEL declares that he is aware that he is helping "to work out Americans' own standard" of haiku (xxxii). He is at the same time indiscriminate, for he includes poems in what is nominally a haiku anthology even if they are senryū, in spite of the emphatic assertion made by the Haiku Society of America that the two are fundamentally different (3.3). In our own discussion, we have also seen that the two genres differ from each other with respect not only to their themes but also to their poetic foci and their text-types: haiku is concerned primarily with informational poeticalness coupled with stylistic poeticalness, and its text-type is characterized as "descriptive" instead of "argumentative". On the other hand, V. D. HEUVEL is quite intolerant of the Imagists on the grounds that the poets of this group had no knowledge of haiku at all. Imagist poems, however, as we have seen, do share common ground with haiku in specific points - in their stylistic poeticalness (POUND) as well as in their informational poeticalness (W. C. Williams). As HENDERSON affirms, what haiku in English will become "will depend primarily on the poets who write them" (1965: 28), and, we can add to HENDERSON's affirmation, "on the editors who compile haiku anthologies". Setting up standards of haiku in English, HENDERSON maintains that haiku in English cannot be "exactly the same [as] with classical haiku in Japan", but at the same time, they "cannot differ too much" with respect to Japanese haiku (ibid.). Let us now survey the debates on the "form and content" of American haiku.

5.6.1 Debates on the Form of Haiku

In considering the form of haiku, American haiku poets fall into three major groups: (i) those who adhere to the

5-7-5 pattern, whose voice can be most characteristically heard in the Yūki-Teikei-Haiku Society (*Haiku Journal* 1978, 79, 80); (ii) those who prefer shorter lines; and (iii) those who reject syllable-counting completely, composing "liberated haiku" (V. D. HEUVEL, xxxiii). A brief chronology suggests that Haiku in English tend to become shorter (cf. GIROUX 1974, NAKAGAWA 1976):

(i) Imagists (1910-25): Japanese tanka and haiku meant for them "vers libre" (5.2.1).
(ii) Lowell and Crapsey (1915-25): 5-7-5 and cinquain 2-4-6-8-2 (5.3.1, 5.3).
(iii) YASUDA (1957): 5-7-5 (5.4.1.1).
(iv) BLYTH (1964): "Three short lines, the second a little longer than the other two".
(v) HENDERSON (1965): "an approximation to a 5-7-5 syllable count"[32].
(vi) Haiku Society of America (1974): The assertion that it is "more and more common for haiku to consist of 'fewer' syllables" (quoted in V. D. HEUVEL, 252).
(vii) Yūki-Teikei-Haiku Society (Season-inclusive-formal haiku): 5-7-5.

Of the seven parties, the last, the Yūki-Teikei-Haiku Society, is the most outspoken advocate not only of the 5-7-5 form but also of a direct transplanting of Japanese classical haiku: they propose *Yūki-Teikei* haiku, i.e., "season-including and rigidly formed" haiku, employing the Japanese terminologies for classical haiku (TOKUTOMI 1979: 10-1). They maintain that "the spirit of haiku is lost when the seventeen syllable count is reduced ... just as when the rules of baseball are changed, the game is no longer 'baseball'" (TOKUTOMI 1980: 10). Although they state that "the spirit is more important than the syllable count", they conclude by somewhat contradictorily reasoning that "the traditional 5-7-5 syllable count is basic to the

spirit of haiku" (11). The haiku which appear in these
periodicals are thus exclusively formal. Let us take some
examples of those which won the "Grand Prize" in the annual contests in 1978, '79, and '80 respectively:

(188) The names of the dead (5)
sinking deeper and deeper (7)
into the red leaves (5) (1978: Eric
 Amann, Toronto,
 Canada: 23)

(189) A small child napping (5)
beside toys in the sand pile ... (7)
the afternoon shade ... (5) (1979: Jerald
 T. Ball, Livermore,
 CA: 39)

(190) Campfire extinguished (5)
the woman washing dishes (7)
in a pan of stars (5) (1980: Raymond
 Roseliep, Dubuque,
 IA: 39)

One of the contributors to the *Haiku Journal*, Anthony SURACI
(1979: 46-51), supports this formalism on the grounds that
"most, if not all, of the greatest haiku by Bashō, Buson,
Issa, and Shiki contain two to four images (rarely five),
and they needed no less than seventeen *jion* to create the
haiku-moment in most cases". He discounts such poems as our
example (2) thus (49):

> Mere brevity is not haiku - true brevity stems from
> quality and not mere quantity. Yet, some are using a
> single word and calling it haiku, with all due respect,
> but they are presuming to improve on Bashō, Buson, Issa,
> and Shiki, which is the same as any of us trying to improve
> on Shakespeare, Wordsworth, Bach, or Rodin.

As for the three-lined structure, another contributor,
June E. LAMSON (1979: 66-68), refers to BLYTH's affirmation:

> This 5-7-5 has a wave-like character of flow, suspense
> and ebb; it is symmetrical, yet in odd numbers. Further,

there is a kind of syllogistic nature about the form
which gives it the utmost clarity while actually containing no logical elements, often no intellectual connections between parts - there is a rise, suspense, and
fall of poetical meaning [BLYTH 1949: 373].

As is seen above, their arguments for this credo are
more or less based on the fact that this form is found in
the prototype of haiku. They do not, however, offer any
explicit reason why it should not be otherwise. Although
the poets in this group indeed seem to have succeeded in
practising the form, as the three poems above evidence,
without falling into the trap of "padding and contrivance",
like the Roundtablers, the question of the difference between the two languages still needs to be answered.

Opposing the rigid stand of the Yūki-Teikei-haikuists,
the Haiku Society of America grants[33] "latitude for variations in syllable count and in number of lines or other
external aspects of 'form'" providing that they meet "the
primary stringent requirements - haiku recording the essence
of a moment keenly perceived, in which Nature is linked to
human nature" (3.3). They thus affirm that it is more common now to use fewer syllables. Robert Spiess (cit. in
V. D. HEUVEL, 268), whose haiku are compiled in *The Haiku
Anthology* (1974: 134-49), explains that he "prefers to
think of the haiku in English as a POEM that, as a norm,
has about nine to thirteen simple words aesthetically
structured in three lines (deriving from the poetically
perfected, seventeen-syllable Japanese haiku's division
into three parts)". Spiess's poetry includes beautiful
haiku with fewer than seventeen syllables:

(191) Winter moon;   (4)
    a beaver lodge in the marsh, (7)
        mounded with snow   (4) (H 135)

(192) Misting rain;   (3)
      in a red bud on the bank (7)
         a yellow warbler   (5) (H 137)

While poets like Spiess write within the "latitude" granted by the Haiku Society, it is interesting to note that there is an alternative form offered by Japanese haiku poets for "haikuists overseas". The *Haiku Journal* (1979: 44) introduces Shugyō TAKAHA, an "eminent haiku poet in Japan", who proposes the following:

> Understanding and appreciation of this 17-syllable pattern cannot be forced and decisions by haikuists overseas as to whether they choose to use the 5-7-5 syllable count (or the shorter 3-4-3 form) will grow out of individual decisions, experience and new understandings.

Eric AMANN, a noted Canadian haiku poet, provides examples of the "shorter form":

(193) Snow falling   (3)
         on the empty parking-lot: (7)
             Christmas Eve ...   (3)   (H 5)

(194) The circus tent   (4)
         all folded up: (4)
             October mist ...   (4)   (H 7)

V. D. HEUVEL (ibid., xxxii) cites Michael McClintock as a writer of "liberated haiku", who discards not only the syllable pattern but also the seasonal element:

(195) dead cat ...
      open-mouthed
      to the pouring rain   (H 83)

(196) peering out
      the scarecrow's ear -
      two glittering eyes   (H 84)

Syllable counting, therefore, is one of the major concerns in establishing haiku in English. It seems, however, more important to have a haiku cadence, which is not the product of a mechanical 5-7-5 count but more necessarily the result of the expression of a "haiku-moment". Let us consider another haiku by McClintock[34]:

(197)   a poppy ...
          a field of poppies!
       the hills blowing with poppies!   (H 101)

This experience seems to be appropriately expressed only in this form: the poet's discovery of one poppy, then the extension of his sight to include the field, finally the climax in the perception of the whole hill "blowing with poppies". The augmentation of the syllable count is thus more effective than anything else. The rhythmical pattern, not metronomic but musical, also seems to be concomitant with haiku in English, as the following example, already mentioned, clearly evinces:

(194) The circus tent
         all folded up:
            October mist ...

The first iambic line is followed by the accented 'all' and 'folded', and is then echoed by the iambs of the last line. A detailed analysis of such rhythmical manifestations is not possible here - suffice it to say that English haiku seem bound to possess the effect of metrics, which Japanese haiku lack totally.

In this connection, BLYTH offers us an important argument (1964a: 349ff.). In admonishing English-language haikuists not to adhere strictly to the Japanese syllable regulation, BLYTH quotes some "odd translations" of Japanese haiku: our very first haiku (1), which he translates quite literally, and is similar to the present author's translation, was translated by the Monograph Committee, Los Angeles (1964) thus:

(198) Old pond, ancient pool: (5)
      A frog jumping plunges in: (7)
      Waterish splash-splcsh   (5)

BLYTH comments: "This is 5, 7, 5 but the last line suggests that Bashō himself fell in, and (as was probably actually the case) could not swim" (1964a: 350). We can add to BLYTH's admonition that the poetic focus of the translation is totally different from the original version: where there was hardly any stylistic as well as aesthetic poeticalness, there appear the recurrences of the two foci. The first line syntagmatizes the two manifesta referring to 'furuike ya' - only one manifestum in the original. The last segment, 'splash-splosh', manifests aesthetic poeticalness. In addition, the morphology of the original, "2-ku, 1-shō", is changed into a three-fold structure in that the two caesurae of colons sunder the poem into three parts.

BLYTH's (ibid.) other example of "odd translation" due to strict adherence to the syllable pattern is the translation of poem (31), the crow-perching poem:

(199) Bare barren branch on   (5)
      which a crow has alighted: autumn   (7)
      Nightfall darkening.   (5)

BLYTH's comment: "This is a line of 17 syllables, sliced arbitrarily into 5, 7, 5". BLYTH (ibid.) goes on to clarify the fact that "syllable" does not have the same meaning "for the Japanese, the Romans and Greeks", stating that for English-speaking people both "a" and "clothes" are syllables (cf. GIROUX 1974: 794; also 3.3.2). He then presents an example of 5-7-5 to "eye and ear", asserting that "to the sense of counting", which is the dominant feature of the Japanese prosodic units, or morae, it has no meaning whatever:

(200) In a potato,   (5)
      Those groans whose forced prayers change nought,   (7)
      can never occur.   (5)

BLYTH admits, however, the merit of the triplex structure, which gives us "the feeling of ascent, attainment, and resolution of experience" (ibid.), ascertaining that the "ideal haiku form" for English poetry would be "three short lines, the second a little longer than the other two": "a two-three-two rhythm, but not regularly iambic or anapestic", while rhyme should be avoided "even if felicitous and accidental" (351). Significantly enough, BLYTH, for whom haiku is the Zen way of life, accepts vers libre without conditions (1964a: 173-203), subordinating thus the fixed form of haiku to vers libre. His concept of shorter haiku has proved to be quite influential, as we have seen in the foregoing section.

Another manifestation of aesthetic poeticalness relating to the question of form is phonological recurrence. BLYTH's firm stand (1964: 351) that rhyme should be avoided, "even if felicitous and accidental", appears to have made its way, as can be observed in the definition of haiku put forth by the Haiku Society: an "unrhymed poem". Although occasional supporters of rhyme in haiku can be found, such as Raymond ROSELIEP (1979: 3o-3), their voices remain unheard. In *The Haiku Anthology*, YASUDA is the sole poet among the 38 contributors employing an overt rhyme scheme whose haiku were written prior to World War II. This credo depends, as already mentioned, on the phase of haiku genesis in Japan, when all kinds of artificiality were rejected. Whether or not rhyme-schemes in English poetry are analogously "artificial" seems to be rarely questioned. American poets nonetheless have evidently followed this restriction in that they explore sound quality, instead of employing a mechanical rhyme-scheme, in much the same way as Japanese poets explored the field of onomatopoeia (3.5.1.3). Let us consider, e.g., Foster Jewell (V. D. HEUVEL, 56-66), who seems to be quite aware of this syntagmatic manifestation of phonological paradigms:

(201) Cliff dweller ruins,
    and the silence of swallows
        encircling silence.   (H 57)

The predominant voiced and voiceless sibilants govern
the poem, lending it the additional aura of "hush". Assonance can also play a role, and it predominates in
AMANN's (188), effectively combined with the voiced
stop /d/:

(188) The names of the dead
    sinking deeper and deeper
    into the red leaves

The dominance of high vowels, /i/ and /i:/, characterizes
the incessant falling of leaves, appropriate to the scene.

5.6.2 Debates on the Content of Haiku

If the debates on the form of haiku in English present a
spectrum equivalent to that between advocates of classical and New Haiku observed in Japan, so do the debates
on the content of haiku. Although such controversies normally boil down to the question of the inclusion of the
kigo, i.e., whether or not a haiku has the seasonal element(s),
this question is actually more a matter of informational
and stylistic poeticalness than that of the actual presence of kigo. As our survey of American works
significant for the establishment of haiku in English
has emphasized, haiku record a heightened moment, a "haiku-
moment", in which the unification of nature and man is felt
by the poet. Therefore haiku inevitably record the
interrelationship between the two - hence the definition
of haiku by the Haiku Society (3.3). Such a standpoint
is clearly voiced in the *Haiku Journal* (1979: 47):

   In English or Japanese, the subject of haiku is the
   hidden unity contained in the suchness of things and

conditions existing in a universe infinitely mysterious,
paradoxical, and diverse, as interpenetrated by Man in the
here-and-now.

5.6.2.1 The Bashō School and Informational poeticalness

The informational poeticalness of haiku, according to such
precepts as the above, presents, by implication, the introjective mode of mediation in which "objective symbolism" is
textualized. HACKETT and AMANN are considered to be the two
most outstanding poets of the school loosely termed the
Bashō school (5.1).

We have already encountered their haiku in examples (169), (170), (171), (172) by HACKETT, and (188), (193),
(194) by AMANN. Three further prototypical haiku by HACKETT
cited below are evidently based solely on information poeticalness (introjective mediation), yet they appear to be
didactic, similar to (171) and Bashō's (62), in which a moral
lesson could be inferred due to the narrative structure:

(202) Time after time
caterpillar climbs this broken stem
then probes beyond (H 28)

(203) Deep within the stream
the huge fish lie motionless
facing the current (H 31)

(204) The fleeing sandpipers
turn about suddenly
and chase back the sea! (H 27)

Though HACKETT declares that he writes "in the conviction
that the best haiku are created from direct and immediate
experience with nature, and that this intuitive experience
can be expressed in any language", thus relating his principles to the philosophy of Zen (V. D. HEUVEL: xxxi), he nonetheless stays in the realm where his epistemology is

active, i.e., some subtle didacticism remains: the
vain but unceasing effort of such an "insignificant"
creature to explore "the unknown" in (202); the cryptic
significance of attitudes toward life observed in the
"motionlessness" of the fish which swim against the
current (203); and the sudden alternation of roles between
pursuer and pursued in (204). Shiki, who rejected any
didacticism whatsoever, criticized Bashō's poem (62) for
its touch of didacticism, which he felt degraded it
to "the worst kind of literature" (MASAOKA 1893: 178).
Had Shiki criticized these three haiku by HACKETT, he would
have rejected them on the same grounds. BLYTH (1964a: 362)
also criticizes HACKETT's poems - while recognizing them
in general as "excellent verses" - stating that "occasion-
ally there is too much ostensive, that is, overt thought".
Though HACKETT never adds such "explanatory" lines as "so
much depends on" (5.2.6) or "moment of deceit" or "mist
and peace dwell here" (5.5.1), his informational poeticalness nonetheless tends to "a good moral verse" but
not "a good literary haiku" (MASAOKA ibid., 178). It seems
that such "didacticism" results from the text-type of
the haiku, i.e., the narrative T-type, which is genetically the direct precursor of the argumentative T-type (4.1),
and thus likely to slip into the realm of the argumentative
T-type. It should be noted that the six haiku that won first
prize in the haiku contests discussed in 5.5.3 lack such
didacticism, presumably due to their descriptivity. We also
note in passing that it has been recently reported that
HACKETT "cannot write [haiku] any more" and is now writing
"sonnets and rhymed poetry" (YAMAGATA 1979: 37).

5.6.2.2 The Buson School and Stylistic Poeticalness

If the poets of the Bashō school are primarily concerned
with informational poeticalness, the poets of the Buson

(and Shiki) school are concerned with stylistic poeticalness. While the former take the "here and now" as the principle credo of their "existential and experiential" haiku (HACKETT 1969), the latter emphasize "imaginative creation, that is, the artistic role of the poet as a maker of imagined scenes as well as experienced ones" (V. D. HEUVEL, xxxi). Virgilio offers us, in addition to such poems as (174) and (176), the following typical examples of the Buson school:

(205) Lone red-winged blackbird
         riding a reed in high tide -
              billowing clouds.   (H 189)

(206) The cathedral bell
         is shaking a few snowflakes
              from the morning air.   (H 195)

(207) Now the swing is still:
         a suspended tire
              centers the autumn moon   (H 190)

While the effacement of the poet's ego still characterizes these examples, they are in fact pictorial in the construction of their images. The morphological feature of "2-clauses, 1-statement", most fundamental to haiku composition, is also present. Spiess, another haiku poet who can be considered a member of the Buson school, elucidates his use of this technique (cit. in V:D:HEUVEL, 268):

In my own often "highly objective" haiku I frequently
use multiple-sense imagery (juxtaposition of two or
more sense perceptions) to intimate the interrelations
within the natural world and between that world and
perceiving man (again, no exposition of man as part
of the natural world, etc.). Also, I try to make a haiku
be a creative unity through, among other associations,
a certain calm tension, or else a correspondence, between the thematic elements.

Spiess accordingly offers us such poems with "a certain
calm tension": (208), with its "montage"-like technique,
due to the juxtaposition of two "corresponding thematic
elements" (cd vs. cs) which are similar to or compatible
with each other; and (209) and (210), with their more
"collage"-like technique due to two "incompatible" elements (cf. FRANK 1968):

(208) Marsh marigold
    on a low island of grass;
      the warmth of the sun   (H 142)

(209) A long wedge of geese;
    straw-gold needles of the larch
      on the flowing stream   (H 149)

(210) Blue jays in the pines:
    the northern river's ledge
      cased with melting snow   (H 136)

5.6.2.3 The Problem of Kigo

The two schools described above are not mutually exclusive,
and they have a common ground in that they deal with nature manifested as objective symbolism. About the presence
of kigo, a norm in classical Japanese haiku (cf. *Zusetsu Haiku Daisaijiki* 1970), the American haiku poets appear to be less fastidious,
except for those whose position accords with that of the
Yuki-Teikei haikuists, who have been aspiring to compile
an English "saijiki", or compendium of kigo (TOKUTOMI
1978: 32). As HENDERSON argues (1965: 36), Americans
"cannot just take over the Japanese season-words, because
[their] seasons, flowers, animals, customs, etc., are very
different from Japanese". HENDERSON is also aware of the
danger of an "overdependence" on kigo, for it can lead
to "artificiality". Criticizing the common attitude of
Japanese conservatives towards haiku-composition, HENDERSON
(ibid.) makes his point clear:

There is certainly something wrong when a Japanese
book, purporting to show "How to Write Haiku" can
consist of practically nothing but a long list of
conventionally acceptable season-words. And artificiality is anathema in haiku.

The question of kigo and the related question of
the saijiki cited above offer us an interesting perspective
on genre-expectation. Proponents of kigo assert that
"kigo is definitely necessary in traditional Yūki-Teikei
haiku" (MOTOYAMA 1978: 34), arguing that

> saijiki is an essential requisite for Haikuists and we
> cannot live without it, because it includes all the
> information about kigo, classifying them into groups
> like Astronomy, Geography, Life, Annual Events, Ani-
> mals, Plants, and so forth, and it also indicates a
> direction for composing Haiku by citing some good
> Haiku examples using each kigo.

It can be affirmed then that to possess such a kigo-col-
lection is to establish conventions. The usage of these conventions inevitably functions in the decoding process as
a manifestum for the genre of haiku.

The *Haiku Journal* records a curious instance of Hawaiian
saijiki in this connection. Hawaii is a land where there
"seem to be no clear differences in the four seasons", but
"strictly speaking", there are "subtle distinctions" among
them, and therefore Hawaiian haikuists established four
seasons of "the land of eternal summer" (MOTOYAMA 1978: 35).

> Spring: January through April
> Summer: May through August
> Autumn: September through November
> Winter: December

This classification, MOTOYAMA, the editor of *Hawai SAIJIKI*,
writes (ibid.), was "approved by the founder" of their

mother organization, who resides in Japan, and has been
adopted in the *Hawaii SAIJIKI*. Furthermore, the editor
MOTOYAMA "ardently wishes" that American saijiki be
compiled, since there are "clear distinctions among the
four seasons on the U.S. mainland even though they vary
slightly from state to state" (ibid.). The approach of
establishing four seasons for the subtropical zone or
describing the climatic differences in the vast U. S. as
"slight" seems somewhat arbitrary; and, except as an aid
to the fulfillment of genre-expectation, the compilation
of such saijiki seems fruitless: after all, if such a work
does not gain a wide readership it can be suspected of
artificiality, the conventions cannot be established,
and hence genre-expectation also fails. The question of
kigo seems to have been modified to the point that American
haiku poets are satisfied to deal with nature without any
such collection (cf. GIROUX 1974: 94-117).

5.6.3 The Definition of American Haiku

In his book *Haiku in English* (1965), HENDERSON surveys some
contemporary haiku, and summarizes the results of his analysis as follows (ibid., 42-3):

(i) There is as yet no complete unanimity among American
poets (or editors) as to what constitutes a haiku in
English - how it differs from other poems which may
be equally short. In other words, haiku in English
are still in their infancy.

(ii) There is increasing agreement on certain basic points.
The vast majority of haiku in English, whatever their
form, do treat nature, or some aspect of nature, as
an integral part of the poem. Most express an emotion aroused by some one particular event, and try to
convey it to the reader as simply as possible.

(iii) The majority of American poets do not seem to be
familiar with the techniques developed by the
Japanese haiku-masters. It is not suggested that
these techniques must be adopted, but it does seem
obvious that some knowledge of them would be useful [...]

HENDERSON's first point, the demarcation between haiku and other short genres, is in fact difficult to define. We have seen, however, that some alleged haiku possess in their deep structure not the fundamental T-type of reflexivity as their constituents, but the more narrative-argumentative T-type of the riddle, joke (*Schwank*) or proverb, or meta-haiku. It is interesting to note that in Japan it was the poets of the pre-Bashō period, i.e., those prior to Zen metageneticity, and in the U. S. the poets not associated with Zen Buddhism who above all transgressed the demarcation. The metageneticity of Zen experience, then, as our second chapter has emphasized, seems in fact to play a decisive role in the composition of haiku: in terms of the H-model-types, it motivates P_{xs} to realize the initial perception as the two reflexive T which then constitute the descriptive T, and in terms of the Si-model-types, it thus defines the informational poeticalness as introjection.

The above assertion corresponds to HENDERSON's second point that haiku "treat nature [...] as an integral part of the poem". The third point includes the preceding two points. In fact the Western poets tend to produce left-hemispheric T, as our discussion of the Writers of the Roundtable, who claimed to have studied the classical haiku intensively, has indicated.

HENDERSON's (43-9) further discussion is in fact quite revealing in this respect in that he gives examples of four alleged haiku that in his opinion cannot be called haiku:

(211) by Sam Bryan, which appeared in "Color in Haiku" in
American Haiku;   (212) by J. M. Dusmore; (213) by A. R.
King; and (214) taken from a "school publication":

(211) Egocentrical
 influentiality
 unsymmetrical

HENDERSON (43) assures us that this is "obviously not haiku, not only because it does not follow the haiku rules but also because it does not convey emotion, and hence is not a poem of any kind".

Recalling the indexicality and iconicity of Zen fine arts in general, one of the characteristic features of classical haiku, as well, we can understand HENDERSON's reproach. The three terms concatenated by Bryan are, so to speak, "meta-haiku", a statement about "how a haiku should be".

(212) "I'm here, Dad!" I said,
 answering, waking in joy -
 but he was still dead!

HENDERSON gives three reasons why this cannot be haiku: (i) nature is not an integral part of it; (ii) it has the "senryū quality" of "the crack at the end"; (iii) it lacks the haiku quality of growth - no further emotion can be produced than is "obtained by the first great stab" (44). As we have already discussed, the depictions of natural phenomena obligatory for haiku are actually the manifestation of informational poeticalness. The haiku not dealing with nature thus tends to lack the haiku quality, as HENDERSON here points out. Lacking thus the metaphysical opposition presupposed in haiku in general, the interpretation of a poem such as (211) does not need to be carried on further. "The crack at the end" is due to the narrative structure, in this case the joke structure we have discussed in connection with, e.g., Moritake's poem on the butterfly returning to the branch, that is, to a *bisociative* function.

(213) Out they go again,
   the snakes - east, south, west, north.
   Hear that drumming-rain!

HENDERSON accepts this as haiku provided "the reference to forked lightning and thunder is intended and gets across": if it is "simply a description of a rain-dance, it is not haiku" (ibid.). His comment corresponds in our analytical terms to "focal selection". The surface T of haiku is at the mercy of trimodal foci in the specific communicative situation. The non-immanence of the sign-vehicle can thus conspicuously be observed in this genre.

(214) Just five, seven, five
   Having emotion and thought
   It makes a Haiku.

HENDERSON declares: "This of course is not a haiku. It is not even a poem. It is a statement, in rhythmic prose, about haiku. It may be informative, but it conveys no sense of emotion at all" (49). Like E. Knight's last haiku (150) discussed above, "Making jazz swing in/Seventeen syllables AIN'T / No square poet's job", and Bryan's (211), (214) is a "meta-text" which comments on "how to make haiku". The signifier of (214) is an abstract conception of "how-to" and not a concrete object such as /rooster/ or /rocks/.

Arguing from the above examples, HENDERSON considers a short poem a haiku when (i) it follows the haiku rules; (ii) it conveys emotion; (iii) it integrates nature; (iv) it does not have the "crack at the end"; (v) it possesses the quality of "growth" - presumably "lingering effect" or "totality". He thus emphasizes that haiku should be defined not only in terms of its 5-7-5 form but also in terms of its content, as is clearly stated in (ii), (iii), and (v). His term "emotion", however, is rather vague:

what he is referring to may be expressed as informational poeticalness fused with stylistic poeticalness, as we have so often observed in both Japanese as well as English haiku. The exclusion of "cracks at the end" points to the avoidance of the joke structure, i.e., not bisociation but polysemy must underlie haiku poetry. His admonition to exclude "cracks at the end" further suggests the descriptivity, as opposed to narrativity, of the genre.

5.7 Summary

In accordance with the trajectory of the poetogenesis of *haiku in English* depicted at the very beginning of this chapter (5.1.1), Fig. 93 summarizes the dominant poeticalness of the major poets discussed here as well as the general trend of the genesis and metagenesis. Vertically, the diagram presents the poetogenetic tendency of the specific poet(s), and horizontally it presents the typologies of each specific T-type according to the *seven universal T-types*:

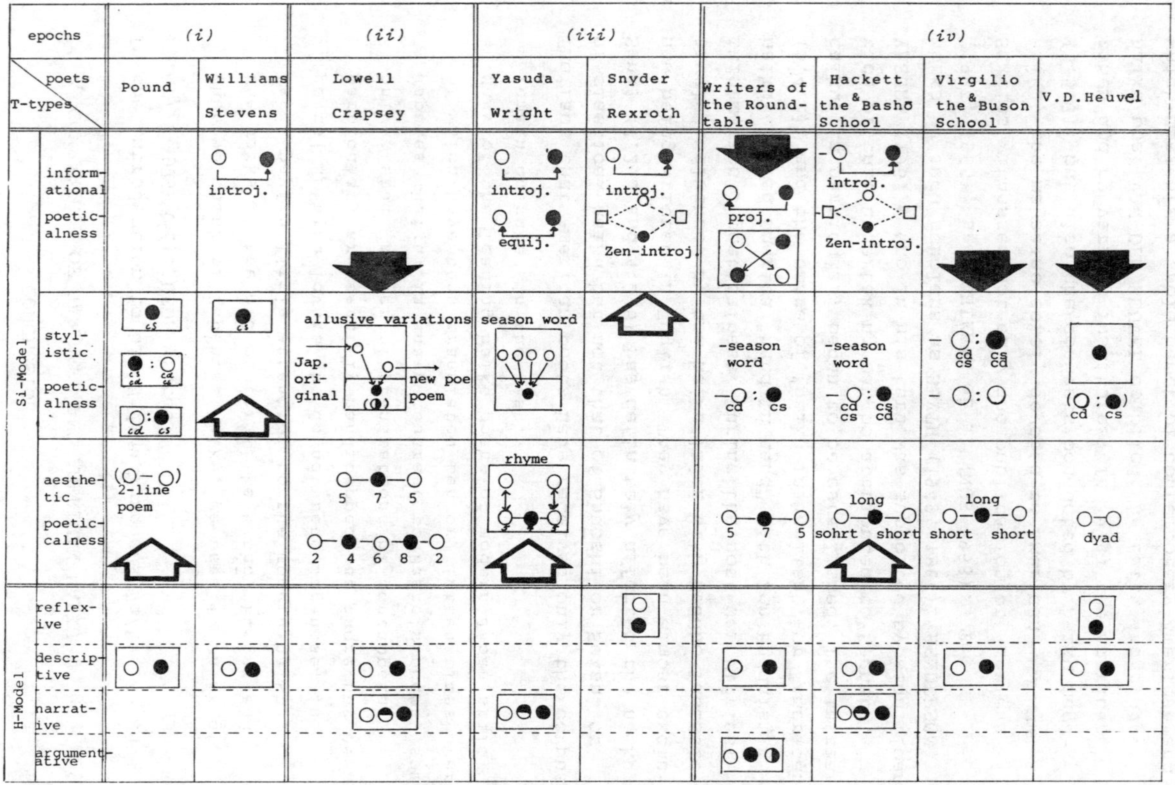

Fig. 93: The Text-Typology of Haiku in English

CHAPTER 6

CONCLUSION

A COMPARISON OF JAPANESE AND AMERICAN HAIKU

In the introduction to his *Modern Japanese Haiku: An Anthology* (1976: vii), UEDA writes:

> When we think of Japanese haiku, we usually think of the works of the old masters like Bashō, Buson, and Issa, paying little attention to the modern haiku poets [...] Haiku lovers who do not read Japanese, in particular, are severely handicapped, as there has been only a small number of translations of contemporary Japanese haiku, in sharp contrast to Bashō's poems, some of which have been translated ten or fifteen times over. Many of the leading haiku poets of modern Japan still remain obscure in the West.

The fact that American poets have received only the corpus of classical haiku, but not that of Shūoshi or Seishi or Sanki (4.2.5 and 4.2.6), has definitely affected the haiku now being written in English. They have been almost exclusively influenced by the haiku laden with Buddho-Taoistic informational poeticalness. During the post-war Fifties, haiku entered America "hand in hand" with Zen Buddhism (5.4.2), and the genre of "haiku in English", or "American haiku" in particular, began to be established. The initiation of this undertaking can be attributed to Kenneth YASUDA (1957), who in his turn was supported by significant works by such scholars as BLYTH (1949, 1964), HENDERSON (1934, 1965), and ICHIKAWA et al. (NGS 1958). The Sixties witnessed not only the publication of *American Haiku*, the magazine solely devoted to American efforts (5.5.3), but also the contests conducted by haiku magazines and by various institutes. In 1974, the American haiku poet VAN DEN HEUVEL compiled *The Haiku Anthology*, which presents a whole gamut of contemporary American and

Canadian efforts: from YASUDA's English version of Japanese classical haiku to the editor's one-word poem, all of which are labelled haiku.

This chapter summarily compares the prototypical haiku in both languages, using the analytical models discussed in this study with regard to the following three points: 1) poetical foci; 2) text-types; and 3) poetogenesis. In spite of the differences in language and culture, the haiku in Japanese and English will exhibit comparable features to a great extent.

6.1   The Poetical Foci of Haiku in Japanese and in English

6.1.1 The Trimodal Poeticalness of Japanese Haiku

In 1694, in the last autumn of his life, Bashō composed this haiku:

(215)   所 思   (Reflection)
此の道や 行く人なしに 秋の暮
Kono michi ya /   yuku hito nashi ni / aki no kure
(This road! / no wayfarer   treads / autumn evening)[1]

For a Japanese P_{xe}, the first segment, 'kono michi ya' ("this road!"), will suffice to recognize that (215) is a haiku. It consists of five syllables and ends with the typical kireji, "ya". The other two segments consist of seven and five syllables, as he would expect. In addition, the *sine qua non* of classical haiku, kigo, is there as the manifestum of 'aki no kure', "autumn evening". While *selecting* such formal aspects of (215), the syllable pattern of 5-7-5, the caesura through "ya", and the seasonal element of "autumn evening", this P_{xe} would visualize the possible circumstances in which (215) was written as somewhat similar to what IMOTO (1972: 266) depicts as follows:

There lies a long country road, as far as the eye can

see. The treetops all around are colored by the weak
light of the setting sun. On the earth, however, the
dusk has settled, and there is not a soul to be
seen on the road. All is still.

In reading the first segment, the P_{xe} would visualize a
foot-path which is then specified by the second segment,
"no one is walking on it". He then reads the third segment,
"the autumn evening", which completes the setting of the
poem described. Similar to the poem about the crow perching
(31), the picture of the /loneliness/, /desolation/,
/stillness/, etc., of the autumn evening would be imagined
by the P_{xe}. Whether or not he stops contemplating the poem
at this point depends on his interpretation of the title
of (212), "Reflection". If he felt summoned to "reflect"
on the title, he would attempt to integrate it in order
to find what CULLER (1975: 171) terms "the organic whole"
of the poem, or its "totality". He would thus move on to find
the metaphorical meaning of the poem (NGS 1958: 11; cf.
MIYAMORI 1932: 211, IMOTO 1972: 266): "The lonely country
road [...] appears to him to be a symbol of the path of
poetry, which he must follow alone if he is to realize
his ideal". The manifestum 'michi' in the first segment
triggered this metalingual operation, for it can signify
literally "country road", and metaphorically "way" or
"-ism" in many Japanese idioms (AITKEN 1978: 81). The
manifestum 'michi' thus becomes the *styleme* which polysemically represents the cultural units or sememes connected
to it, similarly to the other manifestum 'aki no kure' as
a kigo. "This road! No wayfarer treads" can accordingly
be interpreted as "The way of haikai! [which] no one is
following" (NGS ibid.).

IMOTO (1972: 266) explains that (215) presents Bashō's
awareness of isolation and solitude as an artist even in
the midst of his disciples. It appears then that Bashō

consoled himself and relieved his agonizing solitude by perceiving the similarity between his internal feeling of isolation and the solitude before his eyes, i.e., Bashō mediates his inner anguish, "the endlessness of the way of haikai poetry vs. his awareness of his own mortality", by accepting it as a phenomenon similar to another phenomenon in the world he perceives. Although the non-involvement of the poet's ego is prominent in (215), the title, "Reflection", suggests Bashō's agony, however subtle, which was totally absent in introjective poems such as (1), and the poem can thus be characterized as "equijective" in terms of informational poeticalness.

Fig. 94 diagrams the analysis of (215) in terms of the T-recipient, i.e., his focal selection:

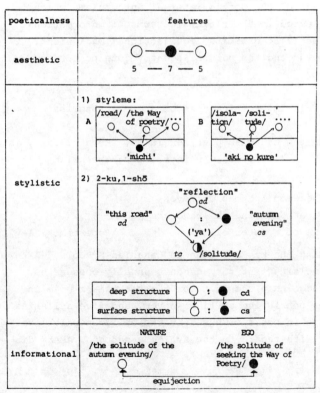

Fig. 94: The Trimodal Poeticalness in (215)

The tertiary structure with the syllable counts of
5-7-5 presents aesthetic poeticalness. The kigo 'aki
no kure' and the manifestum 'michi' function as stylemes
manifesting stylistic poeticalness as well as informational poeticalness, i.e., they are *modal knots*. In terms
of stylistic poeticalness (215) examplifies *2-ku, 1-shō*
severed by the caesura 'ya', after the first five syllables.
This kireji 'ya' triggers the comparison between the two
manifesta, 'this road!' and 'in this autumn evening not a
soul is treading'. The title, "Reflection", determines
the comparandum of the poem in a similar way to the title of
POUND's metro-poem, (34), (5.2.1): 'kono michi ya' is the first
comparandum of the two manifesta in which the *Way* of
poetry is reflected upon. Furthermore, the whole poem is
the comparans of the poet's internal antagonism, which is
the cd reflected in the title. In terms of informational
poeticalness (215) exhibits "equijectional mediation":
the poet's ego and the natural scenery interpenetrate
one another.

6.1.2 The Trimodal Poeticalness of Haiku in English

Eric AMANN, the Canadian poet, exclaims, "Here at last, is
a true haiku!" (1979: 35), in introducing the haiku (216):

(216)   The deep red maple leaves
        float down the quiet waters
            of a waterfall   (Robert McKinley)

In discussing "Haiku Education in Canadian Schools", AMANN
(ibid.) complains that the teachers usually possess no
more knowledge than the fact that "a haiku is a poem in
three lines consisting of five, seven, and five syllables".
This results in poems composed by the children which are
haiku only with regard to the syllable pattern. AMANN dis-

covers, however, "that this misconception regarding haiku is not universal" in all Canadian schools, giving as an example a school contest in which the task was to write haiku poems on the "specific theme of maple leaves in autumn" (ibid.). The winner of this contest was a ten-year-old boy. The poem is "a true haiku", AMANN (ibid.) assures us, for two reasons: 1) it is composed in the pattern of the traditional haiku poem, i.e., 5-7-5, and 2) the central image is shaped by a "season-word", "red maple leaves", which has a "special meaning for all Canadians". About the specific significance of the maple leaves for Canadians, AMANN (35-6) writes the following:

> We are all familiar with the particularly splendid colours of the maples in the late fall, but the anticipation of our long and bitter winter which we feel at their quiet falling evokes a specially deep emotion, mingling admiration for their beauty and sadness for their slow fading away. To add still another dimension to this particular kigo, it must be remembered that the maple leaf is also the national symbol and is carried on every flag of Canada from coast to coast (35-6).

Although the rhythm produced by the syllabic pattern of (216) is by no means identical with the rhythm of morae resulting from the regular measure of (215), the concatenation of the five short words in the first line followed by the further pattern of seven and five seems to guarantee the manifestation of aesthetic poeticalness. The manifestum 'the deep red maple leaves', similarly to the styleme observed in (215), evokes a "mingling [of] admiration for their beauty and sadness for their slow fading away", as well as the association with /national symbol/, presenting the stylistic poeticalness of (216). While (215) and (216) thus present identical features in terms of the syllable pattern as the manifestation of aesthetic poeticalness, and in terms of the styleme as that of stylistic poeticalness (Fig. 94), they differ in terms of their T-production: while (215), as discussed, is strongly oriented toward informational poeticalness, (216) concentrates on the picture of *how* the autumnal "maple leaves float down the river", quite similarly to Buson's pictorial haiku such as (66), (67), (68) or POUND's (116), in which a *katalog obrazov* or "catalog of images" is explored (4.2.3.3). It should also be noted that (216) consists of "one clause", i.e., it is a "one-paradigm haiku" which tends to narrate the event rather than to compare the two disparate sememes.

It seems that American haiku poets tend to compose this type of haiku, or that of "aesthetic experience", to refer to V. D. HEUVEL again (5.1), more often than haiku with a strong emphasis on informational poeticalness. As our previous discussion has emphasized, modern poets without the background of the right-hemispheric mode of cognition of Zen Buddhism, both in Japan and in the U. S., must either make their own "myth", as YU pointed out (3.5.3.4), or resort to looking for a comparans, as (216) typically exemplifies. In making a myth, however, American poets are prone to "argue", as the Writers of the Roundtable did (5.5.1), thus breaking out of the realm of haiku. The struggle not to fall into the trap of left-hemispheric, logical, intellectual poetry on the one hand, while conforming to the regulation not to use traditional prosodic devices on the other, seems to lead American poets and modern Japanese poets inevitably to seek such moments of "aesthetic experience"[1].

6.2 The Text-Types of Haiku in Japanese and English

The above discussion shows the validity of the trifocal approach in analyzing haiku in Japanese and English. It

simultaneously provides the present investigation with the
three T-types derived from the Situation-Model (Fig. 4
in O.3.2). In the following, we will thus concentrate on
the four of the seven universal T-types (4.1) derived from
the History-Model (Fig. 2 in O.3.1). In the genesis of
haiku in Japan, we saw that the four fundamental T-types
were realized metagenetically, i.e., starting from the
argumentative T-type and reaching to the reflexive T-type.
The major T-type of Japanese haiku is descriptive, consisting of two reflexive T, though the narrative T-type
is equally employed. In the poetogenesis of haiku in English we saw the identical general tendency, although its
trajectory was somewhat different from its Japanese counterpart: Haiku in English began to be descriptive in the en-
deavor of the Imagists, arriving at the point from which
Japanese haiku departed, i.e., the argumentative T-type.
Let us now consider the different T-types by comparing in each case
two haiku, one in Japanese and the other in English.

6.2.1 The Reflexive Text-Type

(217) お祭り 赤ん坊寝ている (C 128: Hōsai)
Omatsuri akanbō neteiru
(Festival: the baby is sleeping)

(218) wind:
the long hairs
on my neck (H 206: Larry
Wiggin)

The reflexive T-type "names, refers, points, identifies,
etc."[2] (4.1). (217) simply "points" out two apparently disparate phenomena in the world, and (218) refers to "the
wind" and "the long hairs on my neck" without describing
any causality between the two phenomena. It should be
noted, however, that both (217) and (218) adumbrate the
inevitable descriptivity of the "2-clause-1-statement" formula

due to the juxtaposition of two sememes. It is a matter
of degree whether a given haiku should be categorized as
reflexive or descriptive: recall that even the most reduced haiku, (2), is reflexive in that it only "names"
"tundra", and yet it contains descriptivity in that it consists of two disparate sememes[3]. In addition, the two sememes
employed in haiku possess the potential to be realized
in the surface structure as two "independent clauses", as
ASANO pointed out (3.5.2.2), though very often they appear
rather elliptically, as in "festival" or "wind", in the examples
cited above. The two haiku are *tanritsu*, shorter haiku
which do not conform to the syllable pattern of 5-7-5.
Nonetheless, there is certain rhythmicity in both manifested as the tertiary structure: 4-5-4 in (217) and 1-3-3
in (218).

6.2.2 The Descriptive Text-Type

(219) 菜の花や　月は東に日は西に
Na-no-hana ya / tsuki wa higashi ni / hi wa nishi ni
(Rape-flowers!/ the moon in the east/ the sun in the west)
(B 594: Buson)

(220) At the bottom
Of the rocky mountain slope
A pile of pebbles   (H 78: David Lloyd)

The descriptive T-type most typically deals with phenomena
of "spatial relationships" as well as with "figure-ground
contrasts" (4.1). (219) places the fields full of yellow rape
flowers in the middle of the picture and the rising moon and
the setting sun on either side of the fields. Not only this
spatial relationship of the three figures, rape-flower-fields,
the moon, and the sun, but also the three foregrounding figures are placed against the background of the atmosphere
of a hazy spring evening. (220) concentrates on the spatial
relationship between two gestalts: first, the vertical axis

of the 'rocky mountain' and its base or the 'bottom', and
second, the contrast of the geometrical patterns, i.e.,
/the hugeness of the mountain/ vs./the minuteness of a pile
of pebbles/ which resembles in its turn the figure of the
mountain. Characteristically, both are "two-paradigm haiku",
consisting of two reflexive texts juxtaposed.

6.2.3 The Narrative Text-Type

The tertiary structure of the syllable pattern is also
appropriate to manifest the Aristotelian notion of a plot,
beginning, middle, and end (4.2.3.1). The narrative T of
haiku is due to its syllabic limitation a triad rather than
a pentad, which is a complete narrative cycle.

(221) おもしろうてやがて悲しき鵜舟哉
Omoshirō te/yagate kanashiki/ ubune kana (A 230: Bashō)
(Amusing and/ then pathetic/ the cormorant-boats
fishing*)[4]

*ubune = boats devoted to $ukai$, the technique of
fishing with cormorants. The birds, on leashes,
are trained to catch fish in their beaks and
then disgorge them into the boat.

(222) My snow down her neck
my sister laughs, and shudders,
and kisses my mouth   (H 110: McClintock)

Fig. 95 presents the three-fold structure of each poem:

phases poems	Beginning ◯	Exposition ◐	End ●
(221)	/How amusing!/ ◯	"*And then*, /How pathetic!/" ◐	/on the boat of cormorant-fishing/ ●
(222)	/throwing snow down her neck/ ◯	{ /she laughs/ ◐ /she sudders/ ◐	/*then*, she kisses my mouth/ ●

Fig. 95: The Narrative of Haiku (221) and (222)

Characteristically, both are "one-paradigm haiku":
(221) with the kireji "kana" at the end, describing one
event, while (222) concatenates a series of events. To a
certain degree, the third segment of each poem functions
as a "punch line". In (221) tension mounts in the juxtaposition of two contradictory statements, "How amusing!" and "How pathetic!".
(221) resembles in this respect those types of riddle which DUNDES/GEORGES
(1963: 98), the American anlysts of folklore, term *oppositional
riddles*, i.e., questions containing "the antithetical
contradictive opposition" (98) such as in the riddle,
"What turns and never moves?" (the answer: "a road", ibid.,
99). Although it is clear that (221) is not meant to be
a riddle, but rather shows Bashō's empathy with the plight
of the cormorants, the third segment, structurally speaking,
"the cormorant-boats fishing", is, like "a road", the answer
to the preceding oppositional riddle. In (222), there are
four *ku* or clauses, two of which are paradigms constituting
the middle part. Tension amounts in observing the reaction
of "my sister", who at the end "kisses" him. The rather unexpected ending, instead of her resorting to some kind of
retaliation, suggests that (222)'s *narration* must be in
this order for the poem to be effective (3.3.4).

6.2.4 The Argumentative Text-Type

The last T-type of KOCH's seven universal T-types is argumentative: it processually constructs "truth", "convention", "common sense", by referring to a "tertium quid"
(4.1). Two typical examples are the following
by Takarai Kikaku, one of Bashō's disciples, and
by a writer of the Roundtable in Los Altos:

(223) 我が雪とおもへば軽し傘の上　　　　(B 241: Kikaku)
Waga yuki to / omoeba karoshi / kasa no ue
(This is my snow/so I think, and therefore the
snow is light/ on my hat)

(224) Monkey in a tree
man on a telegraph pole -
of human progress   (G 123: Chenoweth)

(223) implies that if a person is willing to consider the
snow on his hat as a part of his personal belongings, then
it is no longer a heavy burden. The logical connection stated in (223) can be depicted as

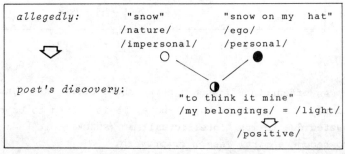

Fig. 96: The Argumentation of (223)

Actually, (223) has had a peculiar fate: though it was composed as a hokku, it has become a proverb with a slight textual change, and appears in most Japanese proverb collections (cf. Excursus). Shiki (1895: 325) harshly criticizes this hokku, stating that "the laity values this hokku because it is nothing but vulgar". It is an interesting specimen, and we will come back to it presently.

(224) compares "monkey" and "man" and mocks man's alleged superiority, similarly to (76) by Baishitsu or some poems by the Roundtable poets discussed in 5.5.1, in which the value of two culturally evaluated entities is inverted (Fig. 89). The manifestum 'monkey' stands for the /animal/ in general as opposed to /humankind/. The tertium quid which the poet has discovered is the fact that both entities are climbing up vertically:

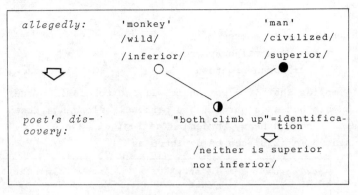

Fig. 97: The Argumentation of (224)

As often stated, when a haiku shows overt "argumentation", as in the examples above, it is doomed to be rejected due to its "intellectualism" (SUZUKI): it then tends to become a moral lesson or proverb.

6.2.5 The Frog Poem and Its English Versions

Although haiku both in Japanese and English present all four of the T-types of the H-Model, the second type, i.e., the "descriptive T-type consisting of two reflexive T", is certainly a dominant formula. To illustrate this point and to emphasize the strong influence of Bashō's haiku in the English-speaking countries, the following five specimens, all taken from *The Haiku Anthology*, can be presented. Similarly to the frog poem, (1), and the cicada poem, (52), the description of "parts and wholes" or "figure and ground" in terms of auditory perception predominates:

(225) Across the still lake
    through upcurls of morning mist -
        the cry of a loon!   (H 112: Mabelsson Norway)

(226)   A small noise ...
    papers uncrumpling.
        stillness again   (H 215: Rod Willmot)

(227) At the window, sleet ...
      Here in the darkening hut -
      sudden squeaks of mice   (H 109: McClintock)

(228) Lonely night:--
      the elephant tugs at his chain (H 153: Jan S. Streif)

(229) Heat before the storm:
      a fly disturbs the quiet
      of the empty store.   (H 188: Virgilio)

6.3. The Poetogenesis of Haiku in Japanese and in English

In Japan, as we saw in Chapter 4, haiku evolved *metagenetically* on the scale of the T-type derived from the H-Model, but *genetically* on the scale of the T-types derived from the S-Model. Let us cite Fig. 70 once again:

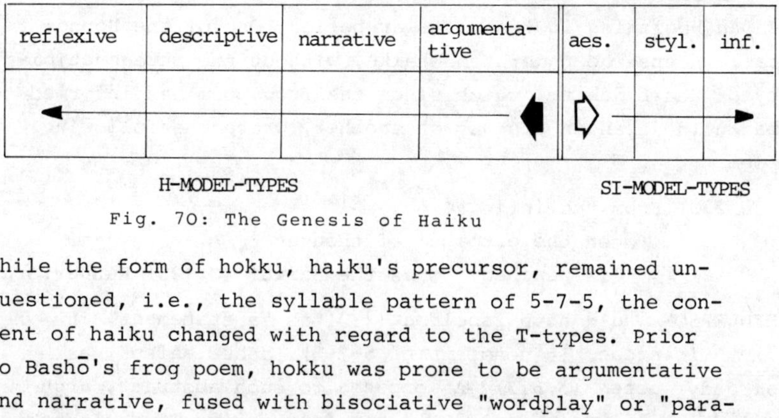

reflexive	descriptive	narrative	argumenta-tive	aes.	styl.	inf.
←			◀ ⇨		→	

H-MODEL-TYPES   SI-MODEL-TYPES

Fig. 70: The Genesis of Haiku

While the form of hokku, haiku's precursor, remained unquestioned, i.e., the syllable pattern of 5-7-5, the content of haiku changed with regard to the T-types. Prior to Bashō's frog poem, hokku was prone to be argumentative and narrative, fused with bisociative "wordplay" or "paranomasia". Yet Bashō's commitment to Zen Buddhism enabled him to compose "kawazu tobikomu mizu no oto" ("a frog jumps in/ the sound of water") which is a reflexive T, simply by *pointing out* the phenomenon of the world. It is a verbalization of Bashō's deixis, affecting thus the vocabulary used in the poem: the manifesta of the reflexive T refer to

concrete objects[5] which are mostly represented as nouns (3.5.3.4).
The metageneticity of Zen Buddhism thus forced haiku to be
phylo- and ontogenetically primary in terms of the H-model-
types extending to the reflexive T. Placing another equally
reflexive T, 'furuike ya' ("Old pond!") on top of the
first reflexive T, Bashō perfected the prototype of haiku:
a juxtaposition of two reflexive T which produce the effect
of descriptivity. With regard to the Si-model-types, however, haiku evolved genetically, i.e., purging traditional
poetic devices that are based on aesthetic and stylistic
poeticalness. The hokku prior to (1) oriented itself to a
matrix of puns and verbal conceits, proceeding to the "extravagant analogy" which is the transition between the matrix and mapping, and then reaching to the absolute orientation of
mapping, i.e., informational poeticalness.

This genesis of haiku seems to have been recapitulated
in the U. S. after the introduction of classical haiku from
Japan beginning in the post-war period. One of the Roundtable poets who understood haiku, without the metageneticity of Zen Buddhism, which since the frog poem has informed
haiku in Japan in one way or another, wrote the following
poem:

(230) From the infinite -
    when the estoppel of thought
        is reached, comes the haiku? (G 125: Rutherford)

HENDERSON would have labelled (230) as "a statement, in
rhythmic prose [it consists of 5-7-5], about haiku", as
already quoted (5.6.3). As opposed to such abstract, argumentative haiku   as (230), the descriptive T resulting
from two reflexive T, the haiku recipe, was more successfully transplanted by such poets as HACKETT or Virgilio.
It is worth noting that these poets have observed that
17 syllables in English can contain more sememes than
17 syllables in Japanese. GIROUX (1974: 79) writes, e.g.,

that "the average Japanese haiku contains only 5 or 6 words, [whereas] the average English haiku runs to 12 or 13, omitting articles". It was thus a rational and necessary step for the American haiku poets to reduce the syllable counts to whatever the content of haiku demanded. In a way it is a metagenetic development of haiku presumably immanent in the genre: in Japan, the syllabic reduction was carried out by the poets who opted for the haiku vers libre (4.2.5.2), and in America by the poets who understood the metageneticity of Zen Buddhism, like HACKETT or SNYDER, to name just two representative figures. The atemporality of haiku, which is the art of paradigms rather than that of syntagmas seems indeed to be spoiled if the surface T is too long.

In terms of the Si-model-types, the superiority of informational structure over others was unquestioned from the outset. The most controversial point in the adoption of haiku was a question of aesthetic poeticalness, i. e., whether or not the rhyme scheme should be assimilated. At the beginning it was natural for translators such as MIYAMORI (1932), HENDERSON (1934), and YASUDA (1949, 1957) to translate haiku with a rhyme scheme. From the perspective of Zen Buddhism most emphatically represented by BLYTH, however, any artificiality ought to be rejected. He writes that haiku "are not the cream of a western verse" (1949: 298), and he (ibid., 272) goes even further to assert that

> a haiku is not a poem, it is not literature; it is a hand beckoning, a door half-opened, a mirror wiped clean [...] It is a silent language because it only beckons to a certain region and does not explain why and where and how.

BLYTH's position that haiku "are not these peaks of strenuous poetic effort", i.e., lack aesthetic poeticalness, and that "poetry is not the words written in a book, but the mode of activity of the mind of the poet", i.e., consists in informational poeticalness, has been supported by the contemporary haiku poets in the U. S.

While BLYTH thus definitely advocates the dominance of informational poeticalness in haiku in English, he further specifies the type of informational structure, i.e., the Zen-homeostatic mode of mediation, introjection (ibid., 211):

> Paradox is the life of haiku, for in each verse some particular thing is seen, and at the same time, without loss of its individuality and separateness, its distinctive difference from all other things, it is seen as a no-thing, as all things, as an all-thing.

6.4 Poetry as Problem-Solving

BLYTH (1949: 318) writes:

> Poetry, or rather, haiku is a perception and expression of unity, even though it is at its highest, particular, concrete; an enumeration of differences, the slightest of infinite importance. The differences must be expressed directly, with no vagueness or ambiguity. The unity, on the other hand, must never be expressed; it must be overheard, seen in a glass darkly, felt like a breath of wandering air.

"Unity" provides humans as well as phylogenetically lower animals with the *Solution* for overcoming antagonism. Zen resorted to motor activity in order to obtain this "unity" by affecting the limbic system rather than the neocortex, a phylogenetically primary method. The logic of Zen is *abductive* in that it lets the human being be guided by *il lume naturale* as PEIRCE explains (2.2.5). The "unity" the psychopath works out is the *fusion* of initially totally unrelated entities (Illustr. 2), resulting from the activation of "paleologic". That "unity" is in the realm of "creativity". We saw that when this creativity or paleologic is overwhelmed by Aristotelian logic, such as in the hokku of the Danrin school or the haiku by the Writers of the Roundtable, haiku ceases to be haiku, i.e., the argumentative haiku transgressess not only the boundary of haiku but that of poetry in general. The "unity" the poet perceives, especially in the genre of haiku, must be of the kind "seen in a glass darkly", but must not be so overt as the unity between the "monkey on the tree" and the "man on a telegraph pole". The unity of the Georgian poet, Brooke, who substitutes a piece of foreign land which is immortal for his mortality, is, from the haiku point of view, too discursive: it is not paleological enough.

Let us recall Fig. 25, in which the genetic relationship of the various methods of problem-solving is presented:

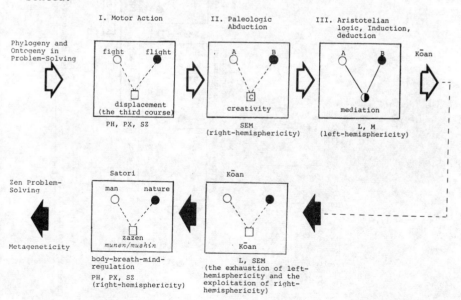

As Fig. 25 clarifies, the polarization of the various methods is seen in the onto- and phylogenetically primary "Motor Action" on the one hand and Aristotelian logic on the other, with *creative* "Paleologic" in between. Haiku poetry as the verbal art of Zen can be placed in this spectrum: it occupies the area of paleologic as presented in Fig. 98:

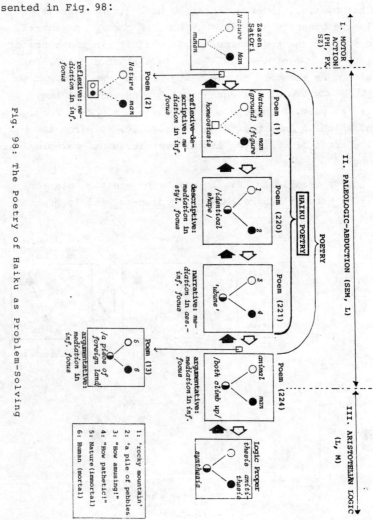

Fig. 98: The Poetry of Haiku as Problem-Solving

We can see that the very fundamental pattern of "the logic of Nature", i.e., "symmetry-asymmetry-integration", is ubiquitous, while it is the logical connection of the tripartite which increases as left-hemisphericity is augmented: the closer to the left-hemispheric extremity, the more logical the synthesis, or integration, or mediation, of the initial opposition becomes. *Poetry* evidently covers a wider range than haiku: it includes such "concrete poetry" as (2) as well as Brooke's (13), which are too logical from the haiku point of view. Haiku's lower threshold is thus located in such poems as (217) and (218) of *tanritsu*, shorter haiku, in which both *sememes are verbalized with a certain rhythmicity*, which guarantees aesthetic poeticalness. Conversely, the higher threshold is located in narrative T such as (221) or (222), in which the tripartite narrative unit, beginning-middle-end, is realized. The descriptive T such that as in (219) or (210) is most dominant in haiku poetry. The *tertium quid* or *tertium comparationis* of haiku resulting from the juxtaposition of two sememes is very delicate, as BLYTH's above assertion makes clear: if the juxtaposition defies P_{xe} and motivates him to "find the answer", as in a riddle, like the *hyperbolical analogy* between "Mt. Fuji and a tea pot" in Saikaku's example, or "man on the telegraph pole and monkey on a tree" in (224), it becomes too "intellectual" and is rejected; on the other hand, if the juxtaposition is too "far-out", as we saw in some of the haiku written by the Writers of the Roundtable, it is also likely to be rejected as too "fantastic" (Fig. 52 and 3.5.2.2) or self-complacent. The "leap" must be "moderate", though it must be there, as Kyorai and KEENE insisted.

6.5. The Poetic Principle of Haiku

From Bashō's frog poem to V. D. HEUVEL's "tundra", haiku has come a long way. Despite the surface difference of

the two poems, we have recognized that the two share a
common feature: they syntagmatize two paradigmatic sememes.
It is P_{xs}, the poet, who first perceives the "unity" between two cultural units which hitherto nobody has related.
He discovers the paradigmatic relationship between the two,
projecting then onto the syntagmatic axis as the surface T:

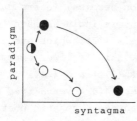

Fig. 99: The Text-Production of Haiku

Bashō thus syntagmatized "the old pond" and "a frog jumps
in/ the sound of water" in what IVANOV calls "nominal
style" (3.5.3.4), and V. D. HEUVEL did the same with
"tundra" and "the amount of the white space".

It is then P_{xe}, the reader, who receives the two syntagmatized sememes. In confronting this surface structure, he is called upon to *recapitulate* the initial *unity*,
which triggered P_{xs} to compose the poem in the first place.
P_{xe} encounters thus a *beautiful riddle*, to repeat KOCH's
parlance (3.5.2.2):

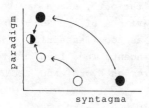

Fig. 100: The Text-Reception of Haiku

P_{xe} as a haiku reader is not supposed to be logical or
inductive. He is not expected to find the solution of this

problem by activating his left-hemispheric, discursive mental capacity, which he has acquired quite recently in terms of phylogenesis and ontogenesis. He is supposed to "overhear and see" the poet's initial experience of unity and to "feel" it "like a breath of wandering air", as BLYTH assures us. The *beautiful riddle* designated haiku exists in the realm of right-hemisphericity. To subjugate neocortical neural connections as much as possible is the fundamental rule for the "twin arts of reading and writing" haiku. Zen Buddhism has effected this regulation, demarcating this genre ever since Bashō composed the frog poem.

EXCURSUS

HAIKU AS ONE TYPE OF SIMPLE FORM:
DIRECTIONS FOR FURTHER RESEARCH

7.1 Haiku as a Simple Form

André JOLLES, the Dutch literary scholar, published in 1930 *Einfache Formen*, or "Simple Forms". In this influential work (cf. RANKE 1965: 184), JOLLES attempts to clarify "den Weg [...], der von Sprache zu Litterature führt" (ibid., 9, cf. BAUSINGER 1968: 53). The two poles of this "way" are, JOLLES explains (222-6), simple forms and artistic forms, a polarization about which JOLLES's precursors[1], approximately one century earlier, had disputed in terms of *Naturpoesie* and *Kunstpoesie*. JOLLES (222) differentiates the two poles in referring to Jakob Grimm, one of the two parties to the debate and the compiler of the famous *Märchen*-collection, who insisted that *Naturpoesie* is "ein *Sichvonselbstmachen*" whereas *Kunstpoesie* is "*eine Zubereitung*". This dichotomy exactly corresponds to Bashō's idea of poetic composition: he, too, differentiated "becoming" and "making" (HATTORI, 547-8, cf. UEDA 1970: 167ff.). UEDA (ibid., 168) explains this difference as follows:

> A good poet does not "make" a poem; he keeps contemplating his subject until it "becomes" a poem. A poem forms itself spontaneously. If the poet labors to compose a poem out of his own self, it will impair the "soul" of his subject. He should enter into the external object (the subject of his poem), instead of forcing it to come to him.

The second chapter of the present study elucidated the

specific source of this attitude in Bashō's case: it was his commitment to Zen Buddhism, which purged him of his ego, which would have caused the poet merely to "make" a poem, i.e., "*eine Zubereitung*". The very nature of Zen Buddhism, metageneticity, is, as extensively discussed, to return to the *mental frame* in which only "*Sichvonselbstmachen*", or "becoming" or "forming itself spontaneously" dominates. We have seen that Zen is a conscious attempt to return to the mental frame which is onto- and phylogenetically primary, as one of Zen's kōan most axiomatically formulates: "Show me your face before you were born" (2.2.4). We have also seen that this specific mental frame attained through Zen meditation results in the specific T which invariably show the common feature, "the manifestation of asymmetry" (2.3.1). There is an immediate realization from the deep structure to the surface structure, i.e., two cultural units often belonging to the macrocosm and microcosm are juxtaposed, and so appear in the surface structure as "juxtaposition" [2].

In the verbal art of haiku, we have observed this governing princple of T-production resulting from the *Zen mental frame*, which manifests itself as the preference for a diction which is iconic and indexical (2.3.3), consisting mostly of *concrete* substantives, which exist in the world as *objects* in the PEIRCEian sense (6.3). Haiku exhibits what IVANOV terms the "averbal" or "nominal" style, which in its turn points to the right-hemispheric T-production of this genre. We have observed in the present study how closely haiku, at least at the time of its establishment as one genre of poetry, stands to what Grimm called *Naturpoesie* and *Sichvonselbstmachen* and JOLLES *Einfache Formen* or *simple forms*.

What exactly are "simple forms"? What is meant by "simple"? What is meant by "forms"? According to JOLLES there are limited numbers of "mental frames" with which humans *unconsciously* operate and which *inevitably* result

in specific types of "linguistic formulation" (1930: 19-20).
In defining the genesis of the simple form, JOLLES writes
(ibid., 45):

> Wo also unter Herrschaft einer *Geistesbeschäftigung* die
> Vielheit und Mannigfaltigkeit des Seins und des Geschehens sich verdichtet und gestaltet, wo dieses von der
> Sprache in seinen letzten, nicht teilbaren Einheiten
> ergriffen, in *sprachlichen Gebilden* wiederum Sein und
> Geschehen zugleich meint und bedeutet, da reden wir von
> der Entstehung der *Einfachen Form*. (my italics)

"Geistesbeschäftigung" is a mental disposition, "a particular frame of mind" (SCHOLES 1974: 43) which results in an "Aktuelle oder Gegenwärtige Einfache Form" through "Sprachgebärde" (JOLLES, 457), i.e., "verbal formulations" (BEN-AMOS 1969: 282ff.).

For JOLLES, then, a simple form is "a kind of structuring principle of human thought as it takes shape in language", as SCHOLES (ibid., 42) explains. JOLLES (10) counts *nine* types of such *Geistesbeschäftigung* which result in corresponding simple forms; the *legend*, the *saga*, the *myth*, the *riddle*, the *proverb*, the *case*, *memorabilia*, the *Märchen*, the *joke* (cf. BAUSINGER 1968: 51-64, BEN-AMOS 1969: 281-4, MOHR 1958: 321-3, PETSCH 1932: 335-69, DUNDES 1962: 95-105, RANKE 1965: 184-200, KÖNGÄS-MARANDA/MARANDA 1971). JOLLES's monograph, which deals with "ontological archetypes of various genres" (RANKE 1965: 185) is indeed quite illuminating. The scrutiny of his theory is, however, beyond the scope of the present study. Let us content ourselves with the following diagram, Fig. 101, which schematically presents the relationship between the nine types of "mental frame" which create the nine simple forms (cf. BEN-AMOS, 282):

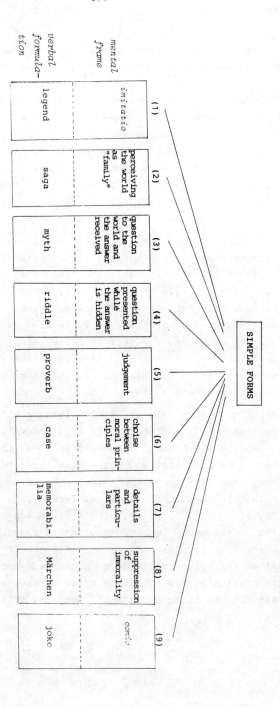

Fig. 101: Nine Types of Simple Forms According to JOLLES

Three and a half decades later, Kurt RANKE (ibid., 184) supported JOLLES's approach in stating that "die Forschung der letzten Jahre hat [...] die wesentlichen Kategorien der Einfachen Formen anerkannt". RANKE (185) also pointed out the correction made by JOLLES's successors: what JOLLES had thought of as "unconscious mental frames" was displaced by the notion of the "momentum generativum", i.e., of humans actively constructing the world according to the mental impulses which result from psychic and functional necessity (cf. BAUSINGER, 59). RANKE (ibid.) reduced such fundamental *Willensakte* from JOLLES's nine to three:

> Es gibt [...] eine Art, die Welt märchenhaft, d. h. in mythisch-heroischer Erhöhung zu bewältigen, seit es dem Menschen gegeben ist, so zu hoffen und zu denken; es gibt eine Art, die Welt sagenhaft, d. h. in erschütternder Ungelöstheit und Tragik zu erleben, seit es dem Menschen gegeben ist, so zu leiden und zu denken; es gibt eine Art, der Welt lächelnd, d. h. im erlösenden Gelächter über ihre Anfälligkeiten zu widerstehen, seit es dem Menschen gegeben ist, sich so zu behaupten und zu denken.

In RANKE's opinion (ibid.), simple forms are *Urformen* of human statement, which come into life through "dreams and affection", through "magic and rational thought processes" and through "play and cult". The three *Willensakte* create, according to RANKE (ibid.), the three categories of folkloristic genres; 1) "saga, legends, *Märchen*"; 2) "myth"; and 3) "*Schwank*, simple dance songs, lamentation". Each genre generates with its own *energeia* the corresponding form and statement (186). RANKE (200) emphasized the universality of such genres, supporting his argumentation by his amazingly exact investigations into cross-cultural distributions of identical motives (RANKE 1978).

Various criticisms[4] have been raised to the works of
JOLLES or RANKE which employ this approach, which BEN-AMOS
(1969: 281) terms "archetypal". SCHOLES (ibid., 43), in
discussing JOLLES's "postulation of universal structuring
entities", e.g., asks "why these nine and no others? [...]
[JOLLES] discusses nine forms but nowhere faces the problem
of the completeness of this grouping". BAUSINGER (ibid.,
61), too, in discussing JOLLES and RANKE, points out, among
other dangers that of immediately equating these genres with
"archetypes". Aside from such questions and criticism, however, the validity of JOLLES's essential point, i.e., the
recognition of the specific mental frames which manifest
themselves in the oral-literal tradition, seems to be unquestionable, as RANKE stated above.

In the course of our discussion, we have seen that haiku
is well-qualified to be called *one type of simple form*,
despite the fact that it is a form of "Litteratur", since
it too presents the precise procedure through which a
simple form comes into life, as JOLLES's quotation above
clarifies: haiku's manifesta as surface structures are
the "letzten, nicht teilbaren Einheiten" of the mental
frame as the deep structure.

The *Geistesbeschäftigung*, the mental frame, i.e., the
"field" of classical haiku (JOLLES 1930: 46, cf. BAUSINGER,
57) in which haiku crystallizes, is the one I have depicted as
follows (Fig. 27):

Homeostatic Zen Texts

	phase	term	symbol	
The Signified based on "the Logic of Zen Semiotics"	1	pre-homeo-stasis		
	2	asymmetry		Signifier with little transformation
	3	post-homeo-stasis		

The *Sprachgebärde* or verbal formulation of haiku is the
surface structure which has been analysed in terms of trimodal poeticalness and universal T-types. The three major
variations of this verbal formulation we have observed
are (cf. Fig. 80 and 81):

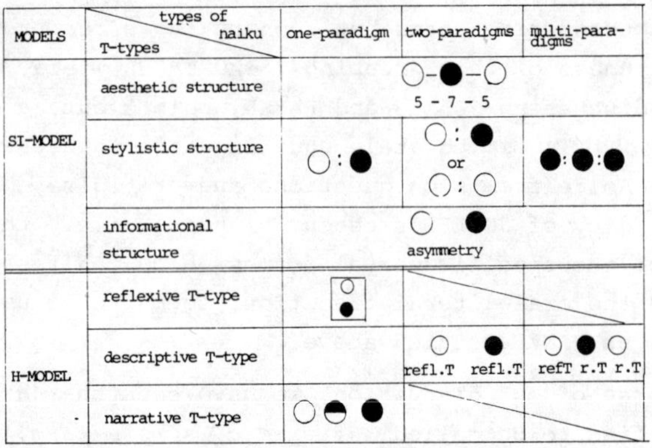

MODELS	types of haiku / T-types	one-paradigm	two-paradigms	multi-paradigms
SI-MODEL	aesthetic structure		○-●-○ 5-7-5	
	stylistic structure	○ : ●	○ : ● or ○ : ○	● : ● : ●
	informational structure		○ ● asymmetry	
H-MODEL	reflexive T-type	○ / ●		
	descriptive T-type		○ ● refl.T refl.T	○ ● ○ refT r.T r.T
	narrative T-type	○ ● ●		

Fig. 102: Three Major Variations of Haiku

7.2 The Affinity of Haiku to Other Simple Forms

In 1691 Bashō wrote a haiku with a short preface which
reads as follows:

(231)　座右の銘　　人の短をいふ事なかれ　　　　　(A 492)
　　　　　　　　　己が長をとく事なかれ
(The Motto: Speak not of other's weak points:
Boast not your strong points)

物いへば　唇寒し　秋の風
Mono iebe / kuchibiru samushi / aki no kaze
(When speaking / my lips feel chill: the autumn wind)

On several occasions Bashō wrote this haiku on a *shikishi*-
paper (a special paper for poem-writing) and presented it
to his acquaintances, sometimes leaving out the aphoristic
preface or just adding "the Motto" instead (IMOTO 1972: 280ff.).
This poem, originally meant to be a hokku, was to survive
through the following centuries, and contemporary Japanese
society is still well acquainted with it as a proverb rather

than a haiku. Accordingly, it has been included in most
of the proverb-collections in Japan. In a book *Japanese
Proverbs* (1955: 107) OKADA, e.g., comments thus:

> The mere act of speaking makes one's lips feel a cold
> autumn wind. Here is [an] instance of haiku, or
> 17-syllable verse, by Bashō, becoming a proverb. The
> suggestion conveyed is that there are times when it
> is wise to refrain from talking. "Silence is golden".

Still another collection, *Kotowaza, Koji, Kingen Shōjiten*
(Small Encyclopedia of Proverbs, Historical Allusions,
Aphorisms) (ETŌ/KAKO 1968: 395) explains (231) as follows:

> One talks too much or speaks about what he does not
> need to say, and as a consequence he invites misfor-
> tunes, or his relationship to others suffers. This
> proverb, Bashō's verse, expresses such a disastrous
> feeling. It resembles the proverb, "Kuchi wa wazawai
> no kado" (The mouth is a gate of hell).

Sometimes (231) appears as a reduced form, i.e., "mono
ieba/ kuchibiru samushi" in which the last five syllables,
"aki no kaze", are dropped (YODA 1962: 106, cf. REINIRKENS
1955: 58).

In 1693, shortly after Bashō wrote his proverbial hokku,
Kikaku composed poem (223), which as mentioned has had a
similar fate. With a slight textual change, this haiku began
to be sung as a popular song, surviving up to the present
day as a proverb. The juxtaposition of the original version and the later one makes it clear that the argumentative
mediation of /to think of the snow on my hat as among my personal
belongings/ (Fig. 96) appears in the new version as 'waga
nono to' ("as my belongings"):

(223) 我が雪とおもへば軽し笠のうへ
Waga yuki to / omoeba karoshi / kasa no ue
(This is my snow/ so I think, and therefore the snow is
light/ on my hat)

(232) 我がものと思えば軽し笠の雪
Waga mono to / omoeba karoshi / kasa no yuki
(These are my belongings / so I think, and therefore
it is light/ the snow on my imbrella)

OKADA (ibid., 177) comments that

> Whether the snow lying thick on the umbrella is felt
> to be heavy or not depends, according to the proverb,
> on the attitude of mind of the person under it.

ETŌ/KAKO compare it to an English proverb (ibid., 437):

(233) A burden of one's own choice is not felt.

The significance of these two examples by Bashō and
Kikaku is clear: they point out the strong affinity between
haiku, as one form of poetry, and the genre of the proverb.
Such affinity is exactly what W. A. MERWIN (1973), the
American poet-critic, refers to in his "Foreword" to *Asian
Figures*, a collection of "Asian proverbs, short poems, and
riddles":

> There is an affinity which everyone must have noticed
> between poetry - certain kinds and moments of it - on
> the one hand, and such succinct forms as the proverb,
> the aphorism, the riddle, on the other. Poetry, on many
> occasions, gathers the latter under its name. But it
> seems to me likely that the proverb and its sisters are
> often poetry on their own, without the claim being made
> for them.

MERWIN (ibid.) affirms that what he intends in this collection is "to try to give voice and form to something that
these other genres, and what [he] take[s] to be poetry,
share". MERWIN (ibid.) characterizes this "something"
as "an urge to finality of utterance [...], to be irreducible and unchangeable" in addition to "the urge to brevity".
These "qualities" MERWIN mentions have been elucidated in
the present study. "Finality" or "to be self-contained, to

be whole" (MERWIN, ibid.) refers precisely to the "unity", in BLYTH's terms, or "mediation" in our analytical terms, which results from the reconciliation of the initial opposition. To put it another way: those succinct forms, however "succinct" they may be, invariably deal with the formula, "symmetry-asymmetry-integration", i.e., an *initial dyad* is resolved into a *monad*, as diagrammed by Fig. 98 in the previous chapter. What MERWIN terms "finality" is thus based on some kind of "problem" and its "solution".

We are now reminded of the very first premise of the human problem, "the curse of cognition" (2.2.4). Humans must come to terms with this ontological problem and have attempted various "solutions"; verbal, as in poetry or narratives; non-verbal, as in painting or sculpture; or actional, as in zazen or dance. It can thus be proposed that the "logic of Nature" is the very origin of any simple forms, as Fig.103 depicts (cf. Fig. 27). V. V. IVANOV/V. N. TOPOROV (1982: 61), the two Russian semioticians, in their extensive investigations into the archetypal schemes of the arts in various semiotic systems, clarify that "die verschiedenen Entwicklungsstufen der Kunst können durch den unterschiedlichen Grad charakterisiert werden, wie sich ein [oppositioneller] Binarismus und - entsprechend - die Deutlichkeit der symmetrischen und antisymmetrischen Aufbauformen in der Kunst herauskristallisiert hat".

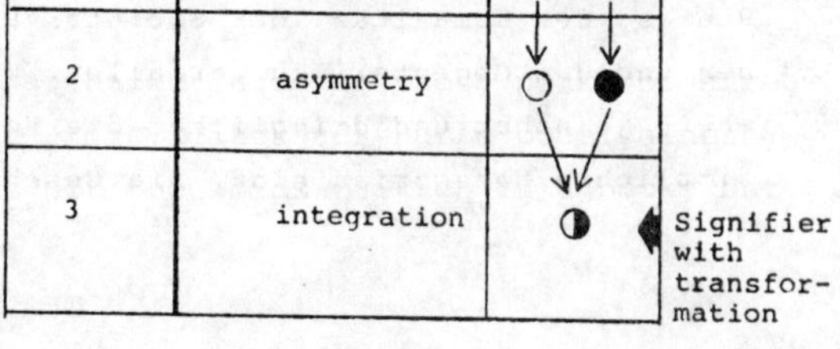

Fig. 103:

The Origin of Simple Forms

	phase	term	symbol	
		Homeorhetic Texts		
	1a	symmetry	○ ○	
	1b	antisymmetry	◐ ◑	
	2	asymmetry	○ ●	
	3	integration	◐	Signifier with transformation

It is hardly necessary to mention that there are numerous
transformations and differentiated *Geistesbeschäftigungen*
between this cradle of simple forms and the realizations of
the genres. But the point is that haiku
without the "field" of Zen, without its mental frame, as
shown in Fig. 27, invariably tends to crystallize into the
homeorhetic mental frame, out of which the genres such as
the proverb, riddle, joke are evolved. It departs as a result from the domain of haiku into other types of simple
forms closely related to haiku. We have seen that many
specimens subsumed under the genre of haiku are more riddle,
proverb, joke, or other types of poetry. Haiku, the genuine
type in the sense of (1), is an evolutionary latecomer: it
presupposes the metageneticity of Zen Buddhism. In order to
be established as the poetry of the simple form, haiku had
to hold its ground on its specific type of *Geistesbeschäftigung*, and it will have to maintain its "field", if it wishes
to avoid losing its position among the simple forms which
are more universal and thus more resistant.

7.3 Haiku and Senryū

RANKE (1955: 41), in discussing the *Schwank* and witticism, assures us of the universality of the joke, suggesting that the genre of the joke is deeply ingrained
in our existential necessities:

> Ganz offensichtlich stehen wir vor einem Komplex
> negativer Tendenzen, vor einem Grundtrieb unseres
> Wesens: der Mensch kann auf die Dauer das Getragene
> nicht ertragen. Es liegt ihm, sich von Zeit zu Zeit
> den zwingenden Gewalten der Religion etwa, oder der
> Pietas, der Humanitas, der Societas usw. zu entziehen und dem Gegenteil zu verfallen. Und das um so
> eher, je höher und dringlicher die Forderung dieser
> sittlichen Kategorien sind. Die Geschichte der Völker

aller Zeiten und Gegenden beweist das, nicht nur
die jüngstvergangene unseres Volkes. Anscheinend
handelt es sich also um einen tief im Menschlichen
begründeten psychischen Vorgang, der vielleicht sogar
von einer gewissen Notwendigkeit im Haushalt unserer
Existenz sein mag. Und der daher ebenso unzeitlich
wie gemeingültig sein wird.

KOESTLER (1978: 141) explains the phenomenon of humor,
the process of "bisociation", neurophysiologically: we
laugh because our emotions are more sluggish and obsti-
nate than our processes of reasoning. Emotion results from
the apparatus of our sympathetic nervous system, which is
phylogenetically older and sluggish and is not able to
"change course" as quickly as the phylogenetic latecomer,
the neocortex, which governs human language and intellect
(141-2). KOESTLER maintains, agreeing with Aldous Huxley
(142-3), that human beings are still in possession of an
apparatus which was quite appropriate for the life of
paleolithic times, since in those times it was absolutely
necessary for the survival of humans to react to any emergency as quickly as possible, but which became more and
more irrelevant due to the increasing security of life.
Humans thus tend to overproduce the adrenalin which can
literally poison our mood as well as our bodily organs
(ibid.). Our species accordingly, KOESTLER (143) explains,
began to release such superfluous hormones through the
new vent: laughter, a "present of nature" which is part of
our inborn equipment (142), was adopted as such a vent
(143). This vent, the alternative to the releasing of
hormones, consists in laughing at people (142), incorporating
aggression, which in its turn has found other acceptable
vents such as sporting matches or literary criticism
(ibid., cf. KOCH 1982c: 25-31). JOLLES (ibid., 260), too,
recognized the two streams that are combined in the joke:
"*Spott und Scherz*", or "mockery and fun", or "a negative

world and a positive world": "Die Welt des Komischen
ist eine Welt, in der die Dinge in ihrer Lösung oder in
ihrer Entbindung bündig werden".

The literary-cultural tradition of Japan can only
corroborate the correctness of the assertion of the
universality and dual nature, negative-positive, of
the joke. Senryū, the travesty of haiku, is but the
"Gegenteil" of "zwingenden Gewalten der Religio etwa,
oder der Pietas, der Humanitas, der Societas", as in RANKE's
comment cited above. Japan had (Fig. 32) the opposition of
serious *waka* and the playful *waka* called *haikai*; when *renga*
developed out of waka, then *haikai no renga*, or humorous renga,
also evolved; when *haikai no renga*, originally meant to
be humorous, aspired to be artistic and poetic and became
"serious" in the hands of the Teimon school, there arose
the Danrin school, which aimed to be humorous and friv-
olous; when *haikai no renga* definitely became an art
in the hand of Bashō, and haiku was born, the travesties
of Bashō's haiku, of classical literature, and of the
social phenomena under the pressure of the rigid caste
system, came into vogue, and both senryū, which shared its form
with haiku, and *kyōka* (crazy waka), which shared its form
with waka, were born. In this connection it should be mentioned that serious Nō theater is coupled with humorous
kyōgen, like the Tragedy and Comedy of the Greek Theater [5].
One of the major elements of senryū, along with kyōgen
(HARADA 1980: 150), is the mockery of the feudal lords,
priests, samurai, and the historical heroes, i.e., the higher
classes of the caste system were satirized (BLYTH 1949a,
SUGIMOTO 1958: 13-4).

Let us glance at the simple form of senryū. Though a
minute analysis cannot be made here, the principle of
"bisociation", the juxtaposition of two incongruous do-
mains, charged with the "aggressive-defensive tendency"
(KOESTLER 1978: 155), should be quite obvious (cf. DUNDES
1975: 192-225, BAUSINGER 1968: 142-153, KÖNGÄS-MARANDA/

MARANDA 1971: 68-71, RÖHRICH 1977: 2ff.).

(234) is a parody of Bashō's (62), "The marsh-mallow at the road side has been eaten up by my horse!":

(234) 煮うり屋の 柱は馬に喰はれけり   (BLYTH 1949a: 22)
Niuri-ya no / hashira wa uma ni / kuwarekeri
(The post of the cheap eating-house/ by the horse/ was eaten)

(235) travesties Bashō's composition of the frog poem, (1):

(235) 芭蕉翁 ぼちゃんといふと立ち止まり   (SHIODA/YOSHIDA 1965: 640)
Bashō-ō / *botchan* to iuto / tachi-domari
(Master Bashō,/ hearing "Splash!"/ stopped walking)

The following (236), one of the most famous specimens, jeers at the government officials:

(236) 役人の子はにぎにぎを能覚   (NKBZ 57 1958: 33)
Yaku-nin no / ko wa nigi-nigi o / yoku oboe
(The baby of the government official / very proficiently / learns how to close his hand)

(236) mocks the officials who were well known for taking bribes, by "closing their hand". "The typical hand-movement of a new born baby" on the one hand and its metaphorical application to the "reception of a bribe" by the government officials in the feudal society on the other are two "incongruous" spheres that are juxtaposed. The principle of this bisociation is realized in the next two senryū within the T: (237), the making merry of the flower-viewing vs. the house's incineration and (238), the sorrowful crematory funeral vs. the greed of the survivors sifting the ashes for the deceased's false teeth:

(237) 花見から踊れば家は焼けている   (BLYTH 1949a: 182)
Hanami kara / kaereba ie wa / yakete iru
(Back from the flower-viewing /the house / is burned to the ground!)

(238) 骨揚げに泣き泣き金歯探して居   (BLYTH 1949a: 205)
Kotsu-age ni / naki-naki kinba / sagashite i
(Gathering the ashes of the dead/ weeping
weeping/ looking for the gold teeth)

7.4 The Genealogy of Haiku as a Simple Form

BAUSINGER (1968: 60) examines three "hindering" points implied in JOLLES's work: "die Annahme der *Ubiquität* der Einfachen Formen, ihre Gleichsetzung mit genetischen *Urformen* und im Zusammenhang damit die Hypothese einer eindeutigen Hierarchie der Formen". Yet precisely these three points seem to offer us the most challenging fields for further investigation: 1) the question of the universality of simple forms; 2) the number of such forms, which SCHOLES wonders about; and 3) the question of the hierarchic order of simple forms, i.e., the genetic relationship among such known *simple* forms.

Analyzing visual arts diachronically as well as crossculturally, IVANOV/TOPOROV (1982) ascertain that the various stages of the evolution of art can be characterized as the different degrees of the *transformation* of "binary opposition", which is *universal* (60-1). In fact, any simple form deals with some kind of *dyad*, as DUNDES (1970: 109) in his analysis of the proverb thus affirms: "The minimum structural definition of a proverb is one descriptive element (consisting of one topic and one comment)[and] it is theoretically impossible to have a one word proverb". Haiku, too, confirms the ubiquity of "binary opposition", yet in a very specific way: instead of elaborating such binarism, haiku as one manifestation of Zen metagenetically manifested binary opposition in the most pristine sense.

While the first field for further investigation has seemingly gathered enough concrete data, the second field,

the determination of the number of simple forms is still
open. The third field, the genetic relationship of the
forms, depends on the number of such forms. In the case of
haiku, however, which is a recent member of the family of
simple forms, the genetic relationship is rather obvious:
haiku essentially grew out of the *comparison* and the
catechetical *riddle*, both of which are based on one of the
two linguistic phenomena caused by the lack of a one-to-one
relationship in language (3.5.2).

Haiku *compares* two sememes, i.e., it is *synonymic*.
Haiku as a comparison has its precursor, known as "*mono-
wa-zuke*", the "matching game", which was most prominently
manifested in *Makura no sōshi* ("The Pillow Book" completed
ca. 1000 A.D., NKBT 19, 1958). In this collection of
"essays" the author, *Sei Shōnagon*, exploited the synonymic
comparison (cf. NKBT 19, 6). The opening phase reads as follows
(NKBT 19, 43):

(239) 春はあけぼの
Haru wa akebono
(As for the spring, the dawn is the best)

We can clearly recognize the similar formulation of the
original version of the crow poem, (32): A = B. This
form in its turn is very close to the form of the riddle,
as we saw (cf. DUNDES/GEORGES 1963). If we relate the two
linguistic phenomena caused by language's lack of a
"one-to-one relation", as TODOROV points out (3.5.2),
we can construct the following genealogy of haiku (Fig.
104), though it is extremely skeletal and tentative. Haiku
is based on the synonymic operation of language, while the
polysemic operation entered into haiku in the form of kigo, the
seasonal words:

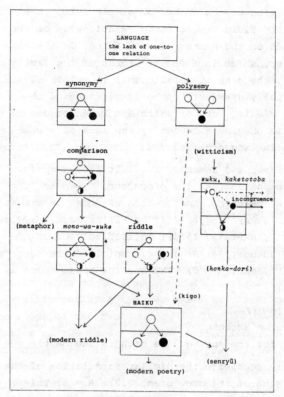

Fig. 104: The Genealogy of Haiku

In the investigation of simple forms, however, there must be included their pragmatics, along with their semantics and syntax. Roger D. ABRAHAMS (1969: 109-10) points out the hitherto neglected aspect of structural analyses of folklore forms, i.e., he shows that such study must include "the structure of context" in which "performance-audience relations" should be focused upon. As pointed out by JAKOBSON/BOGATYREV (1929) more than a half century ago, and Dell HYMES (1962), two decades ago, the generic categories of such simple forms quite often depend on the actual context in which they are uttered. According to the "ethnography of speaking folklore", to borrow DUNDES/AREWA's parlance (1964: 70), haiku, too, can become another simple form.

Pages 1-9   NOTES

0.0 INTRODUCTORY REMARKS: THE DOMAIN OF THE PRESENT
    STUDY

[1] In the prewent study, the corpus of haiku is presented
as follows:
   1) 古池や ...   (original text)
   2) Furuike ya/.../...   (transliteration with the divisions
                                    according to the 5-7-5 syllable
                                    pattern marked)
   3) (The old pond/.../...)   (translation)
The translation attempts to be quite literal and
to retain as far as possible the characteristics of the
original texts. Translations both of haiku and of secondary
works are mine unless otherwise specified.

[2] A *mora* is the smallest prosodic unit in Japanese poetry.
In the course of the discussion, I shall use the term
"syllable" for the sake of clarity.

[3] Cf. HENDERSON 1934:2, SUZUKI 1959: 228, YASUDA 1957: 24ff.

[4] VAN DEN HEUVEL, Cor 1974: 163.

[5] "自由律". In his declaration of independence from the
traditional haiku pattern 5-7-5, Kawahigashi Hekigodō
writes: "Any arbitrary attempt to mould a poem into the
5-7-5 syllable pattern would damage the freshness of impression and kill the vitality of language. We sought
to be direct in expression, since we valued our fresh impressions and wanted our language to be vital. This soon
led us to destroy the fixed verse form and to gain utmost
freedom of expression" (cit. and trans. by UEDA 1976: 9).

[6] This haiku belongs to so-called "tanritsu" (short verse),
a sub-type of haiku vers libre.

[7] Cf. UEDA 1976: 131. Trans. by UEDA.

[8] Examples (4) and (5) are cit. and trans. by BLYTH (1949: 98).

[9] "Haikai" was the term current at that time for the poetic
genre out of which haiku evolved. Cf. 3.2.

[10] SAUSSURE 1960: 65ff. Cf. 2.1.1, especially, Fig. 17.

[11] Cf. ECO 1976: 22-4, and 151-90. Also, cf. Note 8 to Ch.2.

[12] "Hokku" was the "opening verse" of haikai and the current
term at that time for the verse which later was called
"haiku". Cf. 3.2.

INTRODUCTION

O. SEMIOTICS: THE THEORETICAL BACKGROUND

[1] AARSLEFF 1982, COSERIU 1970, DEELY 1982, ESCHBACH 1979: 14-29, HOLENSTEIN 1978: 43-67, TODOROV 1978.

[2] DEELY (1982: 197) lists, in addition to PEIRCE and SAUSSURE, six "neglected figures": Bühler, Collingwood, Lieber, Poinsot, Smart, von Uexküll.

[3] For the introductory works of semiotics, see BAILEY et al. 1978, ECO 1976, ESCHBACH/RADER 1980, HAWKES 1977, JAKOBSON 1980, NÖTH 1975, BUSSE/RIEMENSCHNEIDER 1979, SCHOLES 1982, TRABANT 1976, WINNER 1981.

[4] PEIRCE writes in his letter to Lady Welby of December 23, 1908: "In a paper of 1867 May 14 [...], I defined logic as the doctrine of the formal conditions of the truth of symbols; i.e., of the reference of symbols to their objects" (HARDWICK 1977: 79).

[5] PEIRCE's comment: "The man who makes researches into the reference of symbols to their objects will be forced to make original studies into all branches of the general theory of signs, and so I should certainly give the logic-book that I am writing the title 'Logic, considered as Semeiotic', if it were not that I foresee that everybody would suppose *that* to be a translation of 'Logik, als Semeiotik dargestellt', which would not comport with my disagreement (bordering closely upon contempt) from German logic" (HARDWICK 1977: 80; see also DEELY 1982: 11, FISCH 1977: 21-37).

[6] The fields which semiotics covers are linguistics, logic and philosophy, social sciences and their subfields, psychology, the verbal arts, music, the visual arts, the dramatic arts, applied semiotics, metasemiotics, biological and physical sciences (WINNER 1981: 22). See also ECO 1976: 9-14, PEIRCE's letter dated on Dec. 23, 1908 in HARDWICK 1977: 85, and CHATMAN et al. 1974.

[7] PEIRCE (5.484): "[By] 'semiosis' I mean [...] an action, or influence, which is, or involves, a coöperation [sic] of *three* subjects, such as a sign, its object, and its interpretant, this tri-relative influence not being in any way resolvable into actions between pairs". Cf. BENSE/WALTHER 1973: 91.

[8] BENSE 1975, MORRIS 1946, POSNER/REINECKE 1977, WALTHER 1974.

Pages 12-13

9 JAKOBSON/WAUGH 1979, KOCH 1982, 1983, LENNEBERG/LENNEBERG 1975, NÖTH 1980.

10 Systemtheorie: "Theorie der Systeme, Kerngebiet der allgemeinen liegenden Gemeinsamkeiten order Isomorphien;'Die Formulierung und Ableitung jener Prinzipien, die für Systeme im allgemeinen gelten' (Bertalanffy), die Theorie wirklicher und möglicher Systeme, die Klassifizierung von Systemen, Allsystemen" (LEWANDOWSKI 1980: 958). Cf. BERTALANFFY 1968, LASZLO 1972, MESAROVIĆ 1968.

11 ARDREY 1966, CRANACH et al. 1979, LORENZ 1965, 1973, RIEDL 1979, SEBEOK 1968, 1972, 1979.

The term "human ethology" has been introduced by the participants of the "Colloquium Sponsored by the Werner-Reimers-Stiftung" to designate "the Biology of Human Behaviour" (CRANACH et al. 1979: xiii).

12 BOGEN 1969, GAZZANIGA 1970, GESCHWIND 1974, LENNEBERG 1967, MILNER 1976, POPPER/ECCLES 1977, PRIBRAM 1971.

13 LENNEBERG/LENNEBERG 1975, PIAGET 1945, 1954, 1967, 1969, PIAGET/INHELDER 1966.

14 For an excellent overview of the state of the art of the new discipline, semiotics, see WINNER 1981.

15 "Die Zusammenfassung, Ordnung, Distribution bzw. Komposition von Mitteln, die Bildung von Superzeichen aus Elementarzeichen [...] ist der eigentliche semiotische Prozeß, der in der Erzeugung von Kunstobjekten die wichtigste Rolle spielt" (WALTHER 1974: 134).

16 Cf. "Superzeichen, Superisation, Superzeichenbildung" in LEWANDOWSKI 1980: 936. "Superisation: das aus Phonemen/ Graphemen zusammengesetzte Wort, der aus Untereinheiten konstituierte Text" (ibid.).

17 The word "syllable" here means the smallest prosodic unit of Japanese *jion* (syllable-sound), which can be equated with the term "mora". LEWIN (1959: 33) explains as follows: "Silben mit kurzem Vokal sind einmorig zu werten, Silben mit langem Vokal oder Diphthong (dgl. Nasaldiphthong) zweimorig (als zweimorig gelten auch die Positionslängen vor langen Konsonanten). Cf. V. D. HEUVEL 1974: 249.

18 The foremost advocate of this standpoint is BLYTH (1949, 1964): "Historically speaking, haiku is the flower of all the pre-Buddhist religious speculation, Mahayana Buddhism, Chinese and Japanese Zen, Taoism and Confucianism (BLYTH 1949: ix). See also AITKEN (1978).

Pages 13-14

[19] YASUDA (1957: 41) emphasizes that "the 'where, what, and when' [...] are the properties which constitute that experience , the necessities to make that experience meaningful and alive. Without them the experience cannot be fully realized, nor can a haiku moment be created completely". Haiku anthologies are quite often accompanied by the elucidation of these three properties.

[20] Cf. NKBZ 41 1972, NKBZ 42 1972.

[21] Cf. HENDERSON 1934: 2-5, YASUDA 1957: 4-7.

[22] See Note 18 in INTRODUCTION.

[23] "It is impossible to speak of Japanese culture apart from Buddhism, for in every phase of its development we recognize the presence of Buddhist feeling in one way or another. There are, in fact, no departments of Japanese culture which have not undergone the baptism of Buddhist influence, an influence so pervasive, indeed, that we who are living in its midst are not at all conscious of it" (SUZUKI 1959: 217).

[24] The term "languages" is used in the sense of the Moscow-Tartu School, i.e., "individual sign systems" which are autonomous yet embedded in the macrocosmic structure of a culture. See LOTMAN et al. 1975: 1.0.0, also SHUKMAN 1977:

[25] The Moscow-Tartu School defines the natural language as the "primary system" and other sign systems as "secondary modelling systems", both of which are *hierarchically* ordered (LOTMAN et al. 1975: 6.1.3). This notion that the verbal sign system upon which other sign systems are based is most *primary* is clearly reflected in KOCH's assertion (1983: 63), too: "World structures may nowhere be *mapped* more efficiently than in language - in abstract science or concrete literature or everyday aphorisms". Such views sound indeed "glottocentric", as WINNER in discussing the Moscow-Tartu School rightly points out (1981: 14, cf. SHUKMAN 1977: 120-6). WINNER (ibid., 15) postulates that the natural language and other sign systems sould be considered to be parallel rather than hierarchical. SHUKMAN (1977: 24) quotes "the warning by Piatigorsky" that the notion of a secondary modelling system "should be understood as a working concept rather than a real entity". In the case of the fine arts of Zen, such modification of glottocentrism is an essential analytical premise. The verbal manifestation of Zen, haiku, is even called a "wordless" poem by Alan WATTS (cit. in V.D.HEUVEL 1974: xxx), one of the American popularizers of Zen. What is emphasized in the arts of Zen is, as we will see in Ch. 2, the *mapping of metageneticity*, i.e., the human acquisition of language and the resulting intellect are to be subdued. In mapping

this ideal of Zen Buddhism, the Zen fine arts inevitably
resort to "signs in a lesser degree" (LOTMAN 1976: 7),
i.e., signs which are "pictorial, depictive, visual,
iconic" as opposed to "conventional, more arbitrary, linguistic"
signs, i.e., language (LOTMAN ibid., 4-7). LOTMAN (ibid., 7)
quotes "the oriental proverb", "Better to see it once than
hear about it a hundred times", which is obviously the
Japanese proverb, "百聞は一見に如かず", in order to emphasize
the advantageous point of non-verbal signs.

[26] "None of the sign systems possesses a mechanism which would
enable it to function culturally in isolation" (LOTMAN
et al. 1975: 1.o.o).

[27] Cf. Note 5, also BERTALANFFY 1958: 38ff.

[28] Cf. The book title, *A Perfusion of Signs* (SEBEOK 1977).

[29] On PEIRCE's notion of signs, see 2.3.3 and 2.3.4. Cf.
also BENSE 1967, 1969, 1971, FEIBLEMAN 1946: 81-143,
JAKOBSON 1980: 31-8, WEISS/BURKS 1945: 383-8.

[30] PEIRCE, 8.332.

[31] "Any organism for which something is a sign will be called
an *interpreter*. The disposition in an interpreter to respond, because of a sign, by response-sequences of some
behavior-family will be called an interpretant" (MORRIS
1946: 17). SEBEOK (1975: 85), in referring to PEIRCE's
notion of "the perfusion of signs" (Note 28), comments:
"Peirce refused to draw a sharp distinction between animal
and human sign-processes. His heir, Charles Morris, cast
his net equally widely".

[32] BENSE/WALTHER (1973: 121) formulate the triadic relation
of signs as "Z = R (M, O, I)": "Ein Zeichen ist [...]
eine dreigliedrige oder triadische Relation, die aus dem
Zeichen als Mittel (Mittelbezug M), dem bezeichneten
Objekt (Objektbezug O) und dem interpretierenden Zeichen
(Interpretantenbezug I) besteht". Their formulation is
based on PEIRCE's definition of signs (2.228): "A sign
[...] is something which stands to somebody for something
in some respect or capacity. It addresses somebody, that
is, creates in the mind of that person an equivalent sign,
or perhaps a more developed sign. That sign which it
creates I call the *interpretant* of the first sign. The
sign stands for something, its *object*". Cf. MORRIS's
behavioristic formulation of signs in Note 31, and also
2.3.3.

[33] "To Peirce, all the sciences, and even mathematics, are
observational. Signs as such are products of abstraction;
and 'as to that process of abstraction, it is itself a
sort of observation' (2.227)" (FEIBLEMAN 1946: 89).

Pages 15-18

[34] "[The] science of Phenomenology, then, must be taken as the basis upon which normative science is to be erected, and accordingly must claim our first attention" (PEIRCE 5.39). Cf. FEIBLEMAN 1946: 144-83.

[35] Cf. FEIBLEMAN 1946: 196-214.

[36] In the "Epistemological Prolegomena" of LORENZ's *Behind the Mirror* (1977: 1). This translation of the German original *Die Rückseite des Spiegels* (1973) is by Roland Taylor.

[37] Cf. RIEDL 1979: 35-7.

[38] "Classical empiricist philosophy sees the human mind as a *tabula rasa*, an empty blackboard, or an empty sheet, empty until sense perception makes an entry ('there is nothing in our intellect which has not entered it through our senses'). This idea is not merely mistaken, but grotesquely mistaken: we have only to remember the ten million neurons of our cerebral cortex, some of them (the cortical pyramidal cells) each with 'an estimated total of ten thousand' synaptic links [...] These may be said to represent the material (World 1) traces of our inherited and almost entirely unconscious knowledge, selected by evolution" (POPPER 1977: 121). Cf. LORENZ 1967: 8, 44, and also RIEDL 1979: 54ff. For ethological accounts, see EIBL-EIBESFELDT 1970.

[39] "A life of emancipation which results from the experience of enlightenment means that one is free from the bondage of karmic causation, or that one has crossed the stream of birth-and-death (*samsāra*) to the other side, to nirvana" (SUZUKI 1958: 4).

[40] Cf. ARIETI 1976, BINDRA 1980, SCHNELLE, 1981.

[41] Cf. HOLENSTEIN 1975, 1978.

[42] "Peirce's ideas on abduction were rather vague, and his suggestion that biologically given structure plays a basic role in the selection of scientific hypotheses seems to have had very little influence. To my knowledge, almost no one has tried to develop these ideas further, although similar notions have been developed independently on various occasions" (CHOMSKY 1979: 71). Cf. SEBEOK 1980: 23.

[43] In reviewing *A Semiotic Landscape*, Mihai NADIN (1981: 373) questions the "discipline's identity": "Not just the diversity of methods and perspectives is alarming but moreover, the impossibility of stating what the object of semiotics is". As NADIN (ibid.) points out, in integrating such diversified disciplines, there must be "the epistemological viewpoint". It is precisely this epistemological

Pages 19-22

condition which KOCH's theory is based upon.

44 In incorporating "Systems Theory" KOCH (1982: 16) writes: "We, ideally, proceed from the conviction that no system - and no science, for that matter - 'is an island in itself'. Ultimately, then, the most satisfactory view will be to embrace a 'system of all systems'. Systems Theory is, as is well known, among those branches of the theory of science which dedicate themselves to a comparable holistic integration".

45 Cf. NÖTH 1980: 16, RIEDL 1979: 163.

46 Cf. NÖTH's (1980: 15-6) modification and simplification of KOCH's "Rahmenmodell" (KOCH 1973, 1974).

47 Cf. RIEDL's exposition of the homologous features of "creative learning of the universe" (1979: 106):

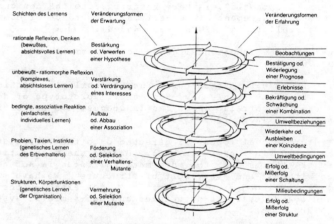

Die evolutiven Schichten des schöpferischen Lernens. Rechts steht jeweils die gemachte Erfahrung aus der jüngsten Vergangenheit, links die daraus gewandelte Erwartung für die unmittelbare Zukunft. Die Formen der Erwartung und Erfahrung wandeln sich von Schicht zu Schicht. Das Prinzip des Algorithmus bleibt unverändert, da die Entstehung jeder Schicht den Erfolg der vorhergehenden voraussetzt.

48 PEIRCE (2.334) assumes in every "assertion" a speaker and a listener, although the latter "need have only a problematical existence", as in the case of a letter in the bottle thrown upon the water; or the listener and speaker exist in one person, as "when we mentally register a judgement, to be remembered later".

[49] KOCH (1983: 218ff.), in his elaboration of the difference between the "poetic and scientific varieties of these foci", introduces new terms: "meta-aesthetic", "meta-lingual", and "metaphysical" are substituted for our "aesthetic", "stylistic", and "informational", respectively.

[50] Habituation is a phylogenetically acquired capacity that enables an organism to distinguish the alarming situation from the familiar, safe situation. See ORNSTEIN (1972: 130-1) for the interesting account of "non-habituation" cultivated in Zen meditation. Cf. 2.3.1.

[51] For the parameters of focalization, see KOCH 1971: 341ff.

[52] The materials used for the fine arts of Zen such as gardening or ikebana (flower arrangement) are very often "found objects", whose artistic values lie solely in the focalization of the text-participant (P_x). Cf. KOCH 1971: 361.

[53] The term, "aesthetic", is here restricted to the designation of the "phenomena of non-trivial recurrence or comparable constellations" (KOCH 1983: 453-4).

[54] "Focus" is "the fundamental generator of structures" (KOCH 1983: 18).

[55] "Style" is used for "structural incompatibilities within texts" which invariably have "as their prototype of deep structure the correlation of two languages, two codes or two subcodes" (KOCH 1983: 233).

[56] The "informational focus" is directed onto the "structuring of the world via a semiotic code. Unlike the mathematical Theory of Information, the informational focus is not concerned with all and every sort of structure. We have pointedly excluded from 'information', for example, the aesthetic and stylistic structures and non-semiotic systems" (KOCH 1983: 235).

[57] Cf. KOCH 1966.

[58] "Stylemes" have to do with deviation: "'Deviation', 'ostranenie', *foregrounding, actualisace* are widely accepted concepts for comparable features of style" (KOCH 1983: 65). Also, cf. KOCH 1972.

[59] "For JAKOBSON, poeticalness consists only of *aesthetic* structures - to use [KOCH's] own terminology -, not of *stylistic* structures, and least of all, of *informational* structures" (KOCH 1983: 61). Cf. also KOCH ibid., 65ff.

[60] The composer(s) is(are) unknown (HENNIG 1980: 81).

Pages 28-39

61 "P_{an} is, strictly speaking, the *meta-analyst*. His position is an ideal one. It is determined by the fact that P_{an} transcends the natural limits of situational or cultural partiality in analysis. Ideally, P_{an} knows everything that can be known from the viewpoint of the sum total of all the variant positions of P_x. P_{an}, then, is some sort of secular rendition of individualized omniscience or the 'religion *in germine*' of our basic ontology" (KOCH 1983: 153).

62 The role of the author of the book *Japanische Gertenkunst* in which this illustration appears is not considered here. Though HENNIG is a mediational person who passes the illustration onto us and possesses a certain amount of influence on our T-reception insofar as he selects and arranges Illustr. 1 editorially, his role is nonetheless minor.

63 Cf. PEIRCE 2.92.

64 Cf. Note 48 in INTRODUCTION.

65 On Kristevian semiotics oticians in general, see SCHIWY 1973, STURROCK 1979. Cf. YOUNG 1981.

CHAPTER 1

1 "I believe Richard Miller [the translator of BARTHES's *S/Z*] has been both plausible and adroit in his translation of *lisible* and *scriptible*; the dilemma is characteristic of the problem any translator of Barthes confronts, and the solution is characteristic of Mr. Miller, properly concerned with his reader's comprehension, not his comfort" (in the Preface to BARTHES's *S/Z* by Richard Howard: 1974: x-xi). Cf. JOHNSON 1981.

2 Cf. HOLENSTEIN 1975: 142-57, JAKOBSON 1971: 49-63, SAUSSURE 1960: 122-34, SHOLL 1982: 204ff.

3 On the relationship between this language operation of "naming" and its resulting T-type, see 4.1.

4 *Aristocratic reading* is, according to BARTHES (1975: 12-3), the "leisure of bygone readings": "it skips nothing; it weighs, it sticks to the text, it reads, so to speak, with application and transport, grasps at every point in the text the asyndeton which cuts the various languages - and not the anecdote [...]". Cf. BARTHES 1970:100-4.

5 *"Jouissance"*. Cf. ROUDIEZ 1980: 15.

Pages 39-40

6 BARTHES 1975: 21.

7 Ibid., 22.

8 "The French have a vocabulary of eroticism, an amorous discourse which smells neither of the laboratory nor of the sewer, which just -attentively, scrupulously - puts the facts. In English [...] by tradition our words for our pleasures, even for the intimate parts of our bodies where we may take those pleasures, come awkwardly when they come at all. So that if we wish to speak of the kind of pleasure we take - the supreme pleasure, say, associated with sexuality at its most abrupt and ruthless pitch - we lack the terms acknowledged and allowed in polite French utterance; we lack *jouissance* and *jouir* as Barthes uses them here [...] Roland Barthes's translator, Richard Miller, in translating *jouissance* as 'bliss', cannot come up with 'coming', which precisely translates what the original text can afford. The Bible they [the translators of the King James Bible] translated calls it 'knowing', while the Stuarts called it 'dying', the Victorians called it 'spending', and we call it 'coming'; a hard look at the horizon of our literary culture suggests that it will not be long before we come to a new word for orgasm proper - we shall call it 'being'" (Richard Howard in the Preface to BARTHES's [1976] *The Pleasure of the Text*).

9 "Roland Barthes is an incomparable enlivener of the literary mind. He is as adventurous in the formulation of new principles for the understanding of literature as he is provocative in dispatching the old ones. To read him is to be led to think more intelligently and enjoyably about what literature is; about both the practice of writing and its function" (STURROCK 1979a:52). Cf. KRISTEVA 1980: 92ff.

10 BARTHES 1981.

11 Cf. "The mechanism of various reader- perception modes that seem typical of poetry" by RIFFATERRE 1978: 115-66, and also TODOROV 1977: 234-46.

12 "Seit $3,5 \cdot 10^9$ Jahren wird von Structuren mit einem Alter von $1,2 \cdot 10^{10}$ Jahren gelernt" (RIEDL 1979: 177). Cf. also CULLER 1981: 102-3.

13 *Intertextualité*: "This French word was originally introduced by Kristeva and met with immediate success; it has since been much used and abused on both sides of the Atlantic. The concept, however, has been generally misunderstood. It has nothing to do with matters of influence by one writer upon another, or with the sources of a literary work; it does, on the other hand, involve the components of a *textual*

system such as the novel, for instance. It is defined in *La Révolution du language poétique* as the transposition of one or more *systems* of signs into another, accompanied by a new articulation of the enunciative and denotative position" (ROUDIEZ 1980: 15).

[14] Cf. ROUDIEZ 1980: 6-7.

[15] For the criticism of JAKOBSON's theory, see OKSAAR 1977: 170ff.

[16] Cf. JAKOBSON 1971: 49-125.

[17] Cf. FURGASON/GARNICA 1975, KOCH 1974: 280ff. SARNO 1972.

[18] The oppositons between /a/ and /p/ are; vowel vs. consonant, voiced vs. voiceless, open vs. closed: cf. JAKOBSON 1941: 68ff., and also JAKOBSON/WAUGH 1979.

[19] JAKOBSON (1941: 50) cites Bühler, "In the beginning our children articulate neither German nor Caucasian sounds", modifying further that the child possesses in the beginning "only those sounds which are common to all the languages of the world, while those phonemes which distinguish the mother tongue from the other languages of the world appear only later".

[20] "Appeal has been made especially to the biogenetic law of Häckel, according to which every individual passes through the evolution of the species in an abridged manner: ontogeny recapitulates phylogeny" (JAKOBSON 1941: 65); cf. KOCH 1982: 80.

[21] "Oppositions which occur in the languages of the world comparatively rarely are among the latest phonological acquisitions of the child" (JAKOBSON 1941: 57).

[22] Cf. KOCH 1982: 19.

[23] Cf. Note 20 in CHAPTER 1.

[24] Cf. Hughlings JACKSON's (1884: 46) discussion of "evolution and dissolution" cited and discussed by MILNER (1976: 49).

[25] Cf. LORENZ 1967.

[26] "Es steht, wie schon der chinesische Weise sagte, keineswegs aller Mensch im Tiere, wohl aber alles Tier im Menschen" (LORENZ 1971: 9).

[27] Cf. PIAGET 1976.

[28] PIAGET's developmental psychology can be characterized as an interactionistic approach. Cf. PIAGET 1977: xviiiff.

Pages 49-51

[29] Cf. PIAGET 1976: xiiiff., also "Phenotext" by KRISTEVA 1980.

[30] Cf. PIAGET 1976: 56ff.

[31] PIAGET (1972: 56ff.) condemns LORENZ's "too restricted biology", which PIAGET believes is due to LORENZ's innatism. Nevertheless, LORENZ's interactionist position seems to be incontestable (LORENZ 1967: 5, 44).

[32] In designating the "genetically primary value" as the "genetic primum" and indicating it by the sign " O", I follow KOCH (1983: 426).

[33] Cf. PIAGET 1976: 69ff.

[34] Cf. PIAGET 1972: 56ff., 1976: 41ff.

[35] "Die höhere Struktur schafft auf der neidrigeren größere Ordnung, *aber nur vorläufig*. Die niedrigere Struktur, 'Herd der Unordnung', gibt immer neuen Anlaß zu weiteren höheren Ordnungsversuchen" (KOCH 1974: 200).

[36] The acquisition of new structures by integrating the older ones is often diagrammed as helicoidal, as RIEDL's model of "Der Kreislauf des Erkenntnisgewinns" (1979: 10) cited below exemplifies. Cf. also the helicoidal model presented by KÖNGÄS-MARANDA/MARANDA (1971: 29) as the mythological structure.

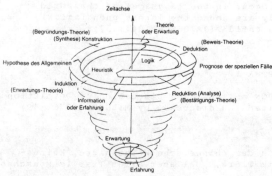

Der Kreislauf des Erkenntnisgewinns.

(from RIEDL 1979)

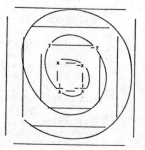

(from KÖNGÄS-MARANDA/MARANDA 1971)

sitions, particles, and a conjunction "clarify" the relationship between /eggshell/ and /chicken has hatched/ but the monostich, as one manifestum, does not seem to suffice as a haiku. This leads to the hypothesis that even in very reduced haiku, there are two prerequisites: (i) the tertiary structure and (ii) two counterpoints. Let us take the following which consists of 5 syllables or 3 words:

(184) crickets ...
      then
      thunder   (H 205: Wiggin)

It still fulfills the prerequisites stated above. How about the shortest of all the 280 haiku appearing in the anthology *The Haiku Anthology*? It is (2), by the editor of this book. Needless to say, here the tertiary structure has vanished, and the last prerequisite remaining is that of two counterpoints - the most fundamental text format of "pairing": 'tundra' on the one hand, and 'the amount of white space' on the other. In this most reduced "haiku", we still recognize the fusion of stylistic poeticalness and informational poeticalness: a black printed 'tundra' juxtaposed with, or rather surrounded by, the 'white space', thus signifying the poet's identification of the word with himself as a perceiver of this vast snow-covered area. Yet (2) seems to be more appropriately categorized as "concrete poetry", in which iconicity plays an important role (KOCH 1971: 432-58).

The above examination of the potential brevity of haiku has shown that the haiku (184) can be regarded as exemplifying the most reduced form of the principles of haiku, whereas (2) assures us of the persistency, and subsequently, the fundamentality of the text-format of "pairing".

Yet, whether these reduced haiku can legitimately be called haiku is, as mentioned, another question. In order for the brain cells to be excited so that the final relief

[37] See PIAGET's (1972: 60ff.) discussion of "self-regulative systems".

[38] In the very recurrence of the same sound observed in children's utterances such as /papa/, KOCH (1983: 286) detects the incipient structure of poetry as the manifestation of aesthetic poeticalness. Cf. his stimulating elucidation of *Dadaism* as well as *Modernism* (1983: 285ff.).

[39] JAKOBSON (1941: 62-4) explains partial speech disturbances, which occur in our daily life. In the dream JAKOBSON cites from his own experience, the Czech word *zemřel* ("dead") was pronounced as *seme*: the liquids were dropped, and the voiced sounds became, as in typical aphasic impairment, the voiceless. Another example JAKOBSON gives of aphasic-like language disturbance is the occasion when one cannot recall the name of another person. In those cases, phonemic combinations will be simplified, and phonemic differences will be ignored. Therefore, chances are that the genetically unmarked tend to be more resistant and substitute for the marked, i.e., the prima are more resistant than the secunda.

[40] Cf. BROWN 1977, JAKOBSON/WAUGH 1979, LENNEBERG/LENNEBERG 1975, SARNO 1972, SHOLL 1982.

[41] Cf. LORENZ 1973: 1-19.

[42] "Der Glaube reinen Unsinns ist ein Privileg des Menschen" (stated by K. LORENZ in his lecture at the University of Vienna during the Winter Semester 1976, and cit. in RIEDL 1979: 29, 172). Cf. RIEDL 1979: 29ff., KOESTLER 1978, KOCH 1974: 341.

[43] Cf. RIEDL (1979: 176ff.).

[44] Cf. Note 12 in INTRODUCTION.

[45] "Meta-ieren": KOCH 1974: 341.

[46] Actually the term "haiku" was not used until the end of the nineteenth century. Prior to that time, the term *hokku* was used in designating "the opening verse of long poems in linked stanzs" (3.2). In the course of the discussion, I shall use mainly the term "haiku", even though the word was not in circulation in the earlier times, in order to avoid unnecessary terminological confusion. Sometimes, however, a distinction between the two is called for.

[47] BROWER/MINER (1961: 507) define *kotoba* as follows: "Materials, diction. With 'kokoro', one of two most important critical terms used by Japanese Court poetics. Used in many senses depending on context, but may be translated 'materials' in contrast to kokoro 'spirit'. "Materials' included

poetic diction, imagery, prosody, rhetoric, syntax, and beauty and elegance of phrasing and sound". *Kotoba* can thus be equated with the surface structure, i.e., *matrix*. *Kokoro* is defined by the two Japanologists (ibid.) as: "Spirit, feeling, conception. Together with 'kotoba', one of the two basic critical terms of Japanese Court poetics. Kokoro has a wide range of meanings depending on the context, but may be translated 'spirit' as opposed to 'kotoba' (materials). Thus kokoro embraces all aspects of tone and treatment, including theme, conception, atmosphere, emotion, meaning, personalism, technique, and originality or conventionality of treatment". *Kokoro*, including thus semantics, can be equated with *mapping*.

In *Sanzoshi*, Dohō (HATTORI 1776: 521ff.) records the chronology of the development of haikai in terms of the dichotomy of *kotoba* and *makoto* ("genuineness in kokoro"): "Ever since the poetry of haikai began, all the precursors [of this poetic practice] had, generation upon generation, been concerned solely with witty paronomasia ("利口") and had never understood the poetry of *makoto* [truth, sincerity, essentiality]. Prior to Master Bashō, Nishiyama Sōin from Naniwa [the founder of the Danrin school] began to break with the fetters of traditionalism and compose haikai with a great deal of freedom. Although his style became widely practised, it was a style below the average. His fame was only due to his manipulation of kotoba. But then, my late Master Bashō began to write haikai, and after practising them more than 30 years, he wrote for the first time real haikai. Though my Master's haikai share their name with the older haikai, they are no longer the same: they are the haikai of *makoto*". Cf. MUKAI 1776: 430, 439, 454, 468.

[48] HATTORI (1776: 523): "A verse is superior, when kotoba is not vulgar and kokoro is playful, and it is inferior when kotoba is vulgar and kokoro is not playful".

[49] In his study of *Formen der "Volkspoesie"*, BAUSINGER (1968: 75) points out that in such forkloristic *Sprachformeln* (verbal formulas) as the *Kultformel*, which includes the blessing, exorcism, charm, laud, or spell, what is indispensable is the "poetisches Sagen", i.e., "gebundene, feierlichgefaßte Worte (verba concepta)". Recurrent rhyme schemes and metrics are thus essential in such traditional, forkloristic formulas, indicating, as BAUSINGER convincingly submits, the deep-rootedness of the rhythmic, recurrent features of aesthetic poeticalness.

[50] Cf. ECCLES 1977: 274.

[51] "Biogenetic structuralism is an amalgamation of evolutionary, biological, neurophysiological, and structuralist theories" (D'AQUILI et al. 1979: 4).

Pages 57-62

52 "Es ist für uns aber gerade entscheidend, die vom religiösen Glauben, der nicht Voraussetzung unserer Analyse sein kann und darf, unabhängig und tatsächlich eintretenden seelischen Veränderungen herauszufinden. Religiöse Erlebnisse sind nun einmal auch psychologische Vörgänge. Wir maßen uns jedoch nicht an, über transzendente Dinge etwas auszusagen. Für die Religionspsychologie ist Mystik nur Forschungsgegenstand, insofern sie als Erlebnis den psychophysischen Bedingungen unterworfen und psychologischer bzw. psychopathologischer Methodik zugänglich ist" (SCHÜTTLER 1974: 83).

53 Cf. HIRAI 1974.

54 See ORNSTEIN 1972: 30, 130-1, also 2.3.1.

55 "Was in der Seele beim Satori vorgeht, kann nicht völlig psychologiert werden, ohne den Boden einer wissenschaftlichen Betrachtung zu verlassen" (SCHÜTTLER 1974: 140).

56 "Im Grunde genommen ist diese Frage [des Satori] eine metaphysische. Wer nach metaphysischen Wahrheiten strebt, wird zu immer neuen Fragen aufgerufen. Bei redlichem Bemühen dürfte er seine eigenen Auffassungen immer wieder in Frage stellen. Auf der Suche nach Vervollständigung des Bildes vom Menschen wird stets ein ungeklärter Rest zurückbleiben" (SCHÜTTLER 1974: 140-1).

57 Cf. CURTIS et al. 1972:, SCHMITT et al. 1974.

58 Many scientists point out the irrelevance of the terms "dominant" or "major" for the left hemisphere and "minor" for the right hemisphere, since both hemispheres work complementarily (cf. BROWN 1977: 52, BOGEN 1972, A. KOCH 1982: 157, Note 6).

59 Cf. HARNAD et al. 1977.

60 BOGEN 1969, GAZANNIGA 1970, SPERRY 1974.

61 SCHNELLE 1981_a: 13.

62 JAKOBSON/WAUGH 1979: 30ff.

63 Cf. TSUNODA 1978, also 1.3.2.

64 There are languages, however, such as "a polytonic language like Thai", in which "pitch is used linguistically to distinguish one lexical item from another", i.e., tonality belongs to the "distinctive features" of languages. Accordingly, "word tones" are more "readily perceived by the right ear", i.e., they are handled by the linguistic, left hemisphere, contrary to the European languages (JAKOBSON/WAUGH 1979: 45).

Pages 62-64

[65] "The principle that the CNS is structured in a complex lowest-center reduplicative fashion, with the highest centers functionally dominant over the lower centers, has been a basic assumption of biologists such as Weiss and Tinbergen, and neurophysiologists such as Fulton and Himwich for some time" (A. KOCH 1982: 151). Cf. LORENZ 1973: 120.

[66] Cf. MILNER 1967, 1976.

[67] The genetic direction in the maturation of the human brain is diagrammed by KOCH (1981: 165-6) as follows:

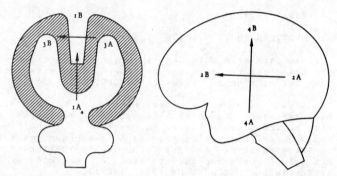

Hintere Frontansicht des Gehirns   Seitenquerschnitt des Gehirns (links)

IVANOV (1977: 37) also points out the genetic primacy of the right hemisphere.

[68] Cf. KOCH 1982: 33ff.

[69] Cf. ECCLES 1977: 352, ORNSTEIN 1972. For bibliographical information, see LEX 1979: 124.

[70] In the debate over the relationship between brain and mind, ECCLES belongs to those who advocate the "dualist-interactionist" position (1977: 374ff.) instead of the position of "psychophysical monism" (BUNGE 1980: 3).

[71] ECCLES (1977: 327, 375) diagrams the "liaison" between the left hemisphere and human consciousness as follows:

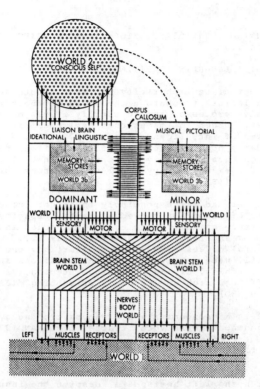

[72] Cf. BERLUCCHI 1974, SPERRY 1974, TEUBER 1974.

[73] Speech areas of the dominant hemisphere:

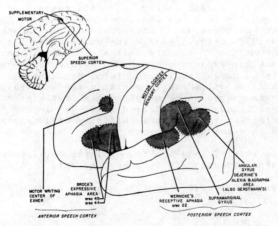

(from Penfield/Roberts 1959: 201, cit. in MARCUS 1972: 525)

Pages 65-71

[74] Cf. GESCHWIND 1974: 92ff., "TOP-area" by ARIETI (1976: 393), also 1.4.

[75] Cf. D'AQUILI/LAUGHLIN 1979: 162, also 2.2.4.

[76] "The concept of hemisphericity may enable both anthropologists and psychologists to sharpen the focus of their research on cognitive processes and to clarify issues of cognitive capacities. Bogen intimates that hemisphericity may bias the outcome of intelligence tests (1972: 51), and the same tendency possibly accounts for assertions that primitive thought qualitatively differs from that of civilized peoples (for example, Levy-Bruhl's concept of 'prelogical mentality')" (LEX 1979: 129).

[77] "The left ear and correspondingly the right (nondominant) hemisphere of the brain showed a greater capacity for all other auditory stimuli, such as musical tones and melodies (both unknown and familiar), sonar signals [...] , and environmental noises such as a car starting, the sharpening of a pencil, water running, and oral emissions apart from speech - coughing, crying, laughing, humming, yawning, snoring, sniffling, sighing, panting, or sobbing" (JAKOBSON/WAUGH 1979: 30).

[78] A *formant* is a "concentration of acousitic energy representing a resonance of the vocal tract" (LIBERMAN 1974: 47).

[79] "純音". Cf. *A Dictionary of Phonetics* 1976: 237.

[80] TSUNODA's discovery that the Polynesian languages handle vowels with the left hemisphere, despite the insufficiency of the number of samples, seems to contribute to the support of MURAYAMA Shichirō's position in the age-old debate over the genealogy of the Japanese language: one of the "Mehrschichten der japanischen Sprache" is Austronesian (1978: 51). Traditionally, the relationship of the Japanese language to other languages has remained "umstritten", like to the question of the origin of the Japanese people (LEWIN 1959: 6-13). "Eine Reihe von Idizien", however, "spricht für eine Urverwandtschaft sowohl des Koreanischen als auch des Japanischen mit den Altaischen Sprachen (Turkisch, Mongolisch, Tungusisch, Mandschu)" (ibid., 10). MURAYAMA (1978), while recognizing the substratum of the Altaic languages in terms of syntax, believes that the Japanese language is a "mixed language" in its origin: he emphasizes the unmistakable affinity of Japanese to Austronesian in terms of phonology.

[81] For the role of language in cognitive development, cf. LENNEBERG/LENNEBERG 1975, SCHNELLE 1981.

[82] IKEGAMI (1981: 284ff.) points out the genetic primacy of

Pages 72-76

"BECOME-BE-languages" when he states: "It seems that originally only such a rudimentary mode of perception, i.e., to perceive everything as 'the change of a state', existed and later it evolved, through increasing human awareness, to the more self-oriented mode of perception, i.e., to cognize the self as an individual which opposes to a situation [...] It can thus be hypothesized that 'BECOME-BE-languages' exhibit primordial features of human language more than 'DO-HAVE-languages' do. Conversely, it can be stated, it belongs to the newer evolutionary phases to provide the concept of the 'agent' with a superior position and to construct a sentence in accordance with it. The hominids, who were at first at the mercy of supernatural powers which lay far beyond their control, gradually became metamorphosed into human beings, who began to conquer nature with their own might. This awareness of their existence as humans may well have triggered the introduction of certain changes in linguistic expressions as well. This is a very attractive speculation. In this regard, English, which in this respect is obviously like German, can be said to be a language which has evolved to the extremity of one direction, and in this sense, one can say, English is a very special language. In comparison with English, then, Japanese seems to have retained a great deal more of the 'primordial features' of human language" (290-1).

[83] Cf. A very similar notion by Erich FROMM (1979), "To have or to be".

[84] Cf. Cf. GAZZANIGA /SPERRY 1972.

[85] Cf. 3.5.1.3.

[86] Cf. KOCH 1981, 1982, 1983, 1983b, ECCLES 1977: 458ff.

[87] "Biological evolution, in its innumerable creative aspects comes closer to our understanding: at this stage in our knowledge we can recognize, in the long course of evolution, developmental processes similar to those found in human creativity. Obviously it is not evolution that follows man but man who follows evolution - or who follows something related to evolution in his civilization" (ARIETI 1976: 401). Cf. also MESAROVIĆ 1968.

[88] Cf. MARCUS 1972: 516ff.

[89] ARIETI's "creative areas" are correlated to PENFIELD's *uncommitted cortex*. In comparing "functional diagrams of the cerebral cortex of some mammals", PENFIELD (1975: 20) shows how extensive this "uncommited cortex" in the human brain is:

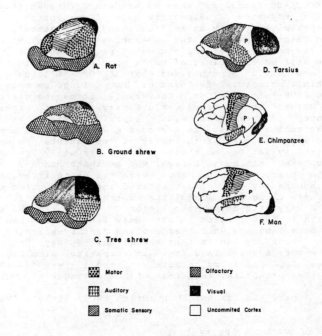

"The blank areas suggest the approximate extent of gray matter that is not committed to motor or sensory function at birth. In man, for example, the auditory sensory-cortex has really been crowded off the external surface of the brain into the fissure of Sylvius" (PENFIELD 1975: 20).

[90] For the "cross-modal associations", see ECCLES 1977: 306-7, 328-9.

[91] For the function of the prefrontal cortex, see MARCUS 1972: 494ff.

[92] ECCLES (1977: 281) presents the "pathway (the pyramidal tract) from the motor cortex of the cerebral hemisphere to the motor neurons" as follows:

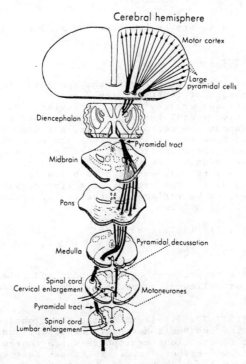

[93] According to ARIETI (1976: 15ff.), this was the first theory attempting to understand the creative process of humans and has been functioning as the foundation of this inquiry ever since it was advanced by Joseph Wallas in 1926.

Wallas believed, ARIETI summarizes, that the "creative process consists of four stages: preparation, incubation, illumination, and verification". The four stages of Wallas are explained by ARIETI as follows: "Preparation is the phase during which the creative person does all the preliminary work. He thinks in a sort of free way, he collects, he searches, listens to suggestions, lets his mind wander. The stage of incubation is inferred from the fact that a certain period of time, ranging from a few minutes to months or years, elapses between the period of preparation and that of illumination [...] The illumination occurs when the creative person sees the solution to his problem. It is at times a sudden intuition, or a clear insight, or a feeling - something between a 'hunch' and a 'solution' and at other times the result of a sustained effort. In any case it has to pass the stage of verification in order to be definitely accepted by the critical evaluation of the innovator". For the further elaboration of Wallas's theory by his successors, see ARIETI 1976: 14-34.

94 RIEDL 1979: 128ff.

95 "[The] structure of the cortical apparatus is consistent with a margin of indeterminacy concerning mental processes in general and creativity in particular. Not everything about a high mental function can be predicted from what we know about the cerebral cortex, nor can everything be predicted from the experiences of the external world that bring about the formation of specific engrams. That is, the indeterminacy principle of Heisenberg, or something similar, may to some extent be applicable to the cerebral cortex as well. The concept of strict causality has to be abandoned, to be replaced by the law of probability" (ARIETI 1976: 390).

96 Cf. KOCH 1981, 1982, 1983, 1983b.

97 Cf. KOCH 1982: 409.

98 Cf. KOCH's "hypotheses on the dyadic and triadic organization of neurolingual connections" in *Semiogenesis* 1982: 33ff.

99 IVANOV (1977:37ff.) clarifies the functional difference between the two hemispheres of the brain, according to which it is the right hemisphere which controls the movement of human beings "in der konkreten Zeit und im konkreten Raume", while the left hemisphere "benennt die linke und die rechte Seite des Raumes mit Wörtern". It can thus be hypothesized that PEIRCE's "firstness" is perceived by the right hemisphere. His "secondness" can be correlated with the analytical function of the left hemisphere, whereas "thirdness" corresponds to the synthetic function of the both hemispheres. Cf. IVANOV's presentation of the analogous model of a "Zweimaschinenkomplex" made after the cerebral interaction of the two hemispheres (Fig. 12b): also, "Schema der Reihenfolge, in der taubstummblinde Kinder Zeichensysteme erlernen" (ibid., 73):

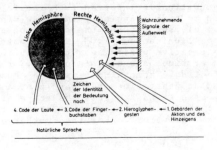

Pages 83-87

Cf. also the presentation of "the Asymmetry of Eisenstein's Brain" (ibid., 82), which is based on the autopsy of the film director:

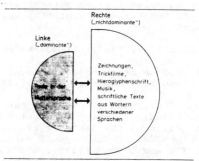

IVANOV (ibid.) writes: "Ich war erstaunt, daß man in der angeführten Äußerung Eisensteins gewissermaßen eine Projektion dieser Asymmetrie auf die verschiedenen Aspekte seiner Tätigkeit sehen konnte. Jene Auffassung, wonach die rechte Hemisphäre mit ungegliederten globalen Ganzheiten zu tun hat, könnte eine indirekte Besätigung darin finden, wie Eisenstein seine Vorliebe für die kontinuierliche Linie (daunter auch in der analytischen Geometrie, die ihn in der Jugend gereizt hatte) mehrfach beschrieben hat".

[100] "Es erscheint unzweifelhaft, daß durch die Experimente die deutliche Verwandtschaft einiger Besonderheiten der rechten Hemisphäre des heutigen Menschen mit dem Gehirn seiner frühen Ahnen bewiesen ist" (IVANOV 1977: 103).

[101] The term "discretic" is used by KOCH 1982: 50ff. Cf. also IVANOV's elucidation of the correspondences between the two cerebral hemispheres and the different types of languages: "Die Beziehung der Sprache der Hieroglyphengesten ('mimischgestikulatorischen Rede') zur rechten Hemisphäre und die des Fingeralphabets zur linken Hemisphäre kann erhärtet werden durch den Fall, daß die Sprache der hieroglyphischen Gesten erhalten bleibt bei Schädigung der linken Hemisphäre, die den Verlust des Fingeralphabets zur Folge hat" (ibid., 75).

[102] See 2.1.1 for the triadic relation of signs.

[103] Cf. Note 25 in INTRODUCTION.

CHAPTER 2

[1] Cf. KOCH 1983: 68.

² Cf. MATEJKA 1978: 148ff., SHUKMAN 1977: 26.

³ *Ritual trance* is the term employed by LEX (1979: 117) to designate "unusual behavior by participants in rituals" induced through "patterned, repetitive acts on the human nervous system".

⁴ Cf. LEVI-STRAUSS 1958, 1963, KÖNGÄS-MARANDA/MARANDA 1971.

⁵ "Daß der PEIRCE'sche Zeichenbegriff triadischer Natur ist, kann als erwiesen vorausgesetzt werden" (STETTER 1979: 124).

⁶ In naming both PEIRCE and SAUSSURE as the pioneers of the notion of the triadic relation in signification, contrary to the usual notion of the latter's dyadic relation (*signifiant* and *signifié*), I base myself on the contributions of ENGLER (1973) and STETTER (1979). STETTER (1979: 126) writes: "Beginnen wir beim begriff des zeichens selbst, so lautet Saussures these nicht, daß das 'signe linguistique' aus der 'opposition' von 'signifiant' und 'signifié' bestehe, sondern vielmehr, daß dieser begriff in drei aspekte zu analysieren sei, nämlich in den der materialität des 'image acoustique' als die, in der zeit sich linear erstreckender qualität, den der intentionalität des 'concept' und den, daß keiner von beiden unabhängig vom anderen gedacht werden könne. Diese ist klarerweise eine triadische relation im sinne Peirces".

⁷ Cf. FEIBLEMAN 1946: 156-69, ECO 1976: 59-62.

⁸ BUSSE/RIEMENSCHNEIDER (1979: 32) present the following diagram summarizing the various terminologies offered by the numerous scholars, old and new, in designating the triadic relation in signification:

Inhalt des Bewußtseins (Aristoteles)
Mentales Bild (Peirce, Saussure)
Bewußtseinszustand (Buyssens)
Signifikation (Morris 1946)
Designation (Morris 1938)
Referenz (Ogden/Richards)
Semainomenon (Stoiker)
Vorstellungen (Hegel)
Interpretant (Peirce)
Bedeutung (Husserl)
Intension (Carnap)
Begriff (Saussure)
Konnotation (Mill)
Inhalt (Hjelmslev)
Abbilder (Klaus)
Ideen (Locke)
Sinn (Frege)

Sem (Buyssens)
Zeichen (Peirce)
Semainon (Stoiker)
Ausdruck (Hjelmslev)
Mittelbezug (Walther)
Representamen (Peirce)
Signifikant (Saussure)
Symbol (Ogden/Richards)
Zeichenhaftes Vehikel (Morris)

pragma (Stoiker)
Bedeutung (Frege)
Extension (Carnap)
Denotatum (Morris)
Signifikat (Frege)
Denotation (Russell)
Bezeichnung (Husserl)
Objektbezug (Walther)
Gegenstand (Peirce-Frege)

[9] Cf. BUSSE/RIEMENSCHNEIDER 1979: 52, TRABANT 1976: 39-41.

[10] ECO (1976: 59ff.) points out that the notion of *object* in semiotic investigation can make sense only when it is conceived as a semioticized, *cultural unit*. The actual, physical existence of an *object* is thus unimportant as far as the "theory of codes" is concerned (ibid., 61). In discussing the semiotics of Zen culture, however, it is absolutely necessary to include the notion of "object" as an actual entity, since Zen, as we will see later, is concerned precisely with the notion of the "actual existence" of physical entities but not with "conceptualized, cultural units".

[11] Cf. The criticism raised by MORRIS (1946: 290) to the inclusion of the notion of infinite semiosis in defining "sign".

[12] "This concept of cognitive imperative refers to the drive in man, other mammals, and birds to order their world by

Pages 93-98

differentiation of adaptively significant sensory elements
and events, and to the unification of these elements into
a systemic, cognitive whole" (LAUGHLIN/MCMANUS/D'AQUILI
1979: 10).

13 Cf. PEIRCE's (1.303) description of *firstness*, "purely
monadic state of feeling" in which "unobjectified, still
less unsubjectified" sense is merely felt. Zen Buddhism
trains its aspirants to remain in this state, inhibiting
their "understanding" or "organizing" the world, i.e.,
the aim is to subjugate the cognitive imperative itself.

14 "Like all other animals, man attempts to master the environmental situation by means of motor behavior. The
motor behavior man chooses goes far back into his phylogenetic past. It usually takes the form of a repetitive
motor, visual, or auditory driving stimulus, which strongly
activates the ergotoropic system" (D'AQUILI/LAUGHLIN 1979:
177).

15 Cf. AKISHIGE 1977, DÜRKHEIM 1974, OGATA 1959, SEKIGUCHI
1970, SUZUKI 1958, UCHIYAMA 1973.

16 Cf. AKISHIGE 1977: 50-1, CHIHARA 1977: 364.

17 "No reflecting whatever. When you want to see, see immediately . As soon as you tarry, (that is, as soon as
an intellectual interpretation or mediation takes place),
the whole thing goes awry [...] The door of enlightenment-
experience opens by itself as one finally faces the dead-
lock of intellectualization" (SUZUKI 1959: 15).

18 "We humans all aspire to perfect communication, but every
form of communication implies some kind of medium. And
as soon as we appeal to a medium the original experience
is lost or at least loses its personal value. The retention of this value, which makes up the reality or vitality or intimacy of the experience, is possible only where
the recipient himself has the same experience" (SUZUKI
1958 : 49).

19 *Semiotic function*, also symbolic function: "Bei Piaget
die Fähigkeit des sich entwickelnden Kindes, vom zweiten
Lebensjahr an etwas durch ein Zeichen (bzw. durch irgendein
Objekt) zu repräsentieren. Die semiotische Funktion kann
durch Sprache, durch Gesten u. a. Systeme realisiert
werden (z.B. Taubstummensprache)" (LEWANDOWSKI 1980: 777).

20 Cf. PEIRCE 5.66, 5.105.

21 PIAGET (1945: 63) gives the famous example: "At [the age of one
year and four months]J. had a visit from a little boy of [one

and a half], whom she used to see from time to time, and who, in the course of the afternoon got into a terrible temper. He screamed as he tried to get out of the play-pen and pushed it backwards, stamping his feet. J. stood watching him in amazement, never having witnessed such a scene before. The next day she herself screamed in her play-pen and tried to move it, stamping her foot lightly several times in succession. The imitation of the whole scene was most striking. Had it been immediate, it would naturally not have involved representation, but coming as it did after an interval of more than twelve hours, it must have involved some representative or pre-representative element". Cf. BOYLE 1969: 39ff.

22
Significantly enough, one of the most famous kōan for beginners is,"Show me your face before you were born" (2.2.4).
  HISAMATSU (1971: 12) terms what we called the "meta-geneticity of Zen" as "the 'prior to form' quality" of Zen, giving such examples from Zen writings as follows: "when not one thing is brought forth", "where not one particle of dust is raised", "prior to the separation of heaven and earth", "prior to the birth of one's father and mother", "utterance before voice", "not one word spoken", etc.

23
Cf. a very interesting account in "Vergleich der Zen-Erlebnisse mit der Mystik des Abendlandes: ärztlich-psychologische Analyse" by SCHÜTTLER 1974: 83-125.

24
Cf. ECCLES 1977: 243ff., TANIGUCHI 1977: 296.

25
"It is a fundamental premise [...] that all functions of the body, mental and emotional as well as the more obvious 'physical' functions, depend on alterations in the patterns of materials of which the body is built" (E. GELLHORN/ G. N. LOOFBOURROW cit. in LEX 1979: 117).

26
Cf. modern versions of raptus in Zen experiences (KAPLEAU 1966: 204-67).

27
Cf. SCHÜTTLER 1974: 107-14.

28
AKISHIGE 1977: 49ff.

29
For the differences of the various schools of Zen, see SUZUKI 1958: 36-61.

30
For a more minute accout, see MILNER 1967.

31
The major categories of brain waves are classified according to frequency:

Delta waves (the lowest waves) (1-4 cycles/sec): deep
sleep.
Theta waves (4-8 cycles/sec): emotionally charged or
creative imagery, reverie, daydreaming, presleep stages of arousal.
Alpha waves (8-13): relaxed, alert state of consciousness.
Beta waves (above 13): critical attitude, tense concentration, mental effort - narrow focus of attention.
(FEHMI 1978: 165).

32 "A 'marked' increase in alpha activity was reported to
have occurred in four subjects practicitng Raja Yoga [...]
Two of the yogis were exposed to external stimuli (visual,
auditory, thermal, and vibratory). None of these stimuli
produced any blocking of the alpha waves when the yogis
were meditating" (KANELLAKOS/LUKAS 1974: 10). Cf. also
AKISHIGE 1977: 50-1.

33 "What is kōan? A kōan means 'a public document setting
up a standard of judgement', whereby one's Zen understanding is tested for correctness. A kōan is generally
some statement by a Zen master, or some answer given to
a questioner" (OGATA 1959: 71). Kōan, then, is a *riddle*
which is given to the Zen aspirant by his master from the
answer of which the master will know how far his learner
has advanced. In this sense kōan-practice is a *catechism*,
about which JOLLES states (1930: 140) that: "Wenn das, was
verrätselt wird, von dem Sinn des Abgeschlossenen, von
der Heimlichkeit des Bundes bedingt und bestimmt wird, so
muß es vor allem in der Sprache des Bundes abgefaßt sein -
man könnte also sagen: die Prüfung besteht an erster Stel-
le darin, zu ergründen, ob der Fremde die Sprache des
Eingeweihten versteht. Erinnern wir uns noch einmal an
den Begriff Katechismus. Katechismus [...] ist dem
Rätsel verwandt, unterscheidet sich aber dadurch, daß hier
die Spontaneität des Rätsels fehlt" (Cf. ibid., 131, also
KAPLEAU 1966: 335-6).

34 Cf. CARRINGTON 1978, KANELLAKOS/LUKAS 1974.

35 A common form of yogic mediation practice involves the use
of mantra. Mantra are "often words of significance such
as names of the deity but for the psychology of consciousness the important element is that the technique uses a
word as the focus of awareness, just as the first Zen
excercises make use of breathing. Similarly mantra have
analogous sounds such as *Ayn* or *Hum*, somewhat similar in
sound to *Mu* in the first Zen kōan. The instructions are
to repeat the mantram over and over again, either aloud
or silently [...] Mantra are sonorous, flowing words, which
repeat easily" (ORNSTEIN 1972: 113-4). Cf. KAPLEAU 1966:
16ff.

36 GLUECK/STROEBEL (1978: 121ff.) point out that a number

of mantra show that they have "a value of 6-7Hz, which is
in the high theta EEG range and also approximates the
optimal processing of the basic language unit, the phoneme,
by the auditory system".

[37] Cf. BLYTH 1966: 17-38, KAPLEAU 1966: 63-82.

[38] BLYTH 1960, 1964, 1966.

[39] Cf. SCHÜTTLER 1974: 43ff., KAPLEAU 1966: 192ff.

[40] Investigations have been made, however, on the effect of
zazen on the "hemispheric symmetry of the EEG" by DOI 1977:
237ff., or on the effect of Transcendental Meditation on
the "interhemispheric synchrony" by GLUECK/STROEBEL 1978.

[41] SUZUKI 1958: 47-53, KAPLEAU 1966: 189-294.

[42] In all seven subsequent examples of the experience of satori, the movement of a "bursting into laughter" is recorded,
except for the fourth account. Such descriptions are in accordance with one of the typical themes of Zen paintings,
the laughing sages (HISAMATSU 1971: Plate 40, 42, 44, 47,
SUZUKI 1959: Plate 30, 58). KOESTLER (1978: 139) explains
the phenomenon of laughter as the dénouement of excessive tension. The physiological process of the satori
moment, however, awaits closer investigation.

[43] "As to incommunicableness, nothing that enters into the
very constitution of our being can be transmitted to
others - which means that what is at all communicable
is the result of intellection or conceptualization"
(SUZUKI 1958: 49). Cf. IVANOV's elucidation: "Beim normalen
erwachsenen Menschen (mit nicht getrennten Hemisphären)
kann die rechte Hemisphäre (oder das 'rechte Gehirn')
als fast völlig stumm gelten: sie kann nur unartikulierte
Laute hervorbringen, wie Brüllen und Winseln" (1977: 33).

[44] "It is by no means certain that ryhthmicity evolved first
in the service of signaling and only secondarily developed
its function of affective arousal. One may just as well
maintain that the affective arousal is primary and that
signaling became grafted onto the already present rhythmicity,
using those very patterns of rhythmicity as signals. Whether signaling or affective arousal was first in the evolutionary sequence, however, is relatively unimportant. What
is important is that we can distinguish two aspects of
ritual behavior, one involving affective arousal as a result of rhythmic stimuli, and the other involving non-
affective communication using patterns of rhythmic stimuli,
although both elements in fact seem inextricably woven
together" (D'AQUILI/LAUGHLIN 1979: 159). It should be
noted that in the ontogeny of language acquisition, the

Pages 115-125

first phonemic manifestion is the reduplication of the same sound such as /papa/ or /pipi/ (1.2).

45 Biogenetic structuralists define "ritual behavior" as "a sequence of behavior" with four characteristics: "1) it is sequentially structured (patterned); 2) it is repetitive and rhythmic (to some degree at least) - that is, it tends to recur in the same or nearly the same form with some regularity; 3) it acts to coordinate affective, perceptual processes (cognitive in man and other higher vertebrates); and most particularly, 4) it coordinates and synchronizes these processes among the various individual participants" (D'AQUILI/LAUGHLIN 1979: 156). For examples of animal ritual behavior, see EIBL-EIBESFELDT 1970, 1979, FRISCH 1967, TINBERGEN 1965.

46 Cf. LEVI-STRAUSS 1963: 226.

47 Cf. ECCLES 1977: 233ff.

48 D'AQUILI/LAUGHLIN (1979: 167) mentions the possibility that *Homo erectus* might have existed ca. 2.5 million years ago, "if the East Rudolf skull [found by Leaky] represents the genus Homo". Cf. LEAKY 1981.

49 "*Australopithecus* shows minimal development of the inferior frontal convolution, where Broca's area is located in the genus *Homo*, as well as minimal development of the middle temporal convolution, where Wernicke's area is located in *Homo*" (D'AQUILI/LAUGHLIN 1979: 167).

50 Cf. Note 22 in CHAPTER 2.

51 For a more minute account of this kōan, see OGATA 1959: 111-2.

52 Cf. SCHÜTTLER 1974: 29.

53 "本来面目" (BLYTH 1966: 169-74).

54 "Die rechte Hemisphäre lenkt die Bewegungen des Menschen in der konkreten Zeit und im konkreten Raume. In kybernetischer Analogie zu einem Doppelmaschinen komplex könnte man sagen, daß die rechte Hemisphäre an denjenigen Rechner gemahnt, der in Echtzeit arbeitet [...] Untersuchungen der letzten Jahre berechtigen zu der Annahme, daß diese Fähigkeit der rechten Hemisphäre auf den allerfrühesten Stufen der Evolution der Vorfahren des Menschen entstanden ist" (IVANOV 1977: 37). Cf. Note 89 in CHAPTER 1.

55 Cf. HERRIGEL 1958: 33ff., KAPLEAU 1966: 228.

56 Cf. SUZUKI 1958: 45, Illust. 8 in the present study.

Pages 125-135

57 Cf. SUZUKI 1959: 8ff.

58 Cf. KOCH 1982a: 458ff.

59 Ibid., 460.

60 Cf. KOCH ibid., 447-73, SCHENK 1982: 435-8, SEBEOK 1979.

61 Cf. PEIRCE 1.65-8, 2.96-7, 2.100, 5.145, 7.97, 7.202-7.

62 Abduction is also called *Hypothesis* or *Retroduction* by PEIRCE. See Editor's Note 21 by Arthur W. BURKS in Vol. 7 (1958: 61).

63 In discussing "retroduction", Maryann AYIM (1974: 36) writes that instinctive activities "have this feature in common - the activity caters to the survival and well-being of the species as a whole by enabling species members to react appropriately to environmental conditions". Cf. IVANOV's assertion concerning the difference between the two hemispheres of the brain: "Für die rechte Hemisphäre müssen all ihre Ausagen wahr sein; falsch können nur Behauptungen der linken Hemisphäre sein" (1977: 41). Cf. also "Vernunft und Unvernunft von Erb-Programmen" in RIEDL 1979: 78.

64 "Wie wunderbar vernünftig leitet uns also noch immer der ratiomorphe Apparat; leitet jener angeborene Lehrmeister, der gesunde Hausverstand die Heuristik unseres Erkenntnisprozesses, da wir von Entdeckung zu Entdeckung eilen" (RIEDL 1979: 70).

65 "*Konkrete Sinn-Information* über die Außenwelt, wie sie in erklärenden Wörterbüchern der natürlichen Sprachen (und analogen 'Thesauren' der Informationsmaschinen) enthalten ist, wird in der rechten Hemisphäre gespeichert und verarbeitet (IVANOV 1977: 42).

66 SUZUKI (1959: 11) explains that the *Tao*, yet another designation of the Buddha Nature, is "really very much more than mere animal instinct and social usage, though those elements are also included in it. It is something deeply imbedded in every one of us, indeed in all beings sentient and nonsentient, and it requires something altogether different from the so-called scientific analysis. It defies our intellectual pursuit because of being too concrete, too familiar, hence beyond definability". His elucidation clearly points out Zen's recognition of the existence of *il lume naturale*.

67 See Note 62 to this chapter.

68 See Note 25 to this chapter.

Pages 137-154

69 IVANOV (1977: 45) makes it clear that the memory of human beings can be stored in two distinct forms in accordance with the functional difference of the two hemispheres; "in der linken Hemisphäre, in der die Wörter in ihren phonetischen Hüllen aufbewahrt werden, und der rechten Hemisphäre mit ihrem Vorrat an bildlichen Darstellungen".

70 SUZUKI (1959: 117-20) also gives the example of the "Bull Fighter" in Spain. Cf. also HERRIGEL's description of the art of archery, 1948.

71 See ARIETI (1976: 200-16) for further examples of extreme interest presenting the various types of "fusion".

72 Cf. ARIETI's (ibid., 224-32) discussion of Chagall's and Dali's painting.

773 Cf. FISCHER's cartography (Fig. 21) in 2.2.2.

74 "The 'one-corner' style is psychologically associated with the Japanese painters' 'thrifty brush' tradition of retaining the least possible number of lines or strokes which go to represent forms on silk or paper" (SUZUKI 1959: 22).

75 Cf. UEDA's (1970:30ff.) explanation of *sabi* in terms of Bashō's aesthetics: "Bashō's life was based on the idea of 'sabi', the concept that one attains perfect spiritual serenity by immersing oneself in the ego-less, impersonal life of nature. The complete absorption of one's petty ego into the vast, powerful, magnificent universe - this was the underlying theme of many poems by Bashō". Cf. also EBARA 1952: 86ff.

76 Cf. "The seven characteristics" of Zen aesthetics defined by HISAMATSU 1971: 28ff.: 1) asymmetry; 2) simplicity; 3) austere sublimity or lofty dryness; 4) naturalness; 5) subtle profundity or profound subtlety; 6) freedom from attachment; and 7) tranquility. Also cf. the similar elucidation by BLYTH (1949: 163-269), who lists 13 traits of Zen as "the state of mind for haiku".

77 Cf. NÖTH's criticism of BENSE's attempt to elucidate the PEIRCEian sign system (1975: 18).

78 NÖTH (1975: 19) asserts that indexical signs are the only type of signs that occur in animal communication. It has been reported, however, that in animal communication "arbitrary signs" can also be observed in, e.g., bee dances.

79 Cf. HARTSHORNE/WEISS's Note to PEIRCE's 2.243 (1931: 142). According to their annotation, PEIRCE discovered "ten trichotomies and sixty-six classes of signs", whose analysis was, however, "never satisfactorily completed". Cf.

SANDERS 1970, WEISS/BURKS 1945, ZEMAN 1978: 34ff.

[80] Cf. PEIRCE 1.558, 2.230-43, 2.247-9, 2.274-308.

[81] Cf. ZEMAN 1978: 36-8.

[82] ECO (1976: 218) formulates a new typology of "modes of sign production" refuting the "untenability" of the "naive notion of index and icon". Yet he himself (ibid., 178) concedes the usefulness of the trichtomy of "symbols, icons, and indices" with regard to the discrimination "between different kinds of mentions". Though his postulation of "modes of sign production" is very elaborate and challenging, I shall refer only to his formulation of "type-token-ratio" as relevant to the present study.

[83] Cf. HRDLIČKOVÁ 1969.

CHAPTER 3

[1] According to a letter to the present writer from SATŌ Kazuo, author of a comparative work on the theme of the Western reception of haiku, *Na no hana wa ishoku dekiru ka* (Can Rape-Flowers Be Transplanted?) (1978), and head of the Museum of Haiku Literature in Tokyo.

[2] Edited and commented upon by IMOTO Nōichi/HORI Nobuo/MURAMATSU Tomotsugu. In the course of this discussion, when references to their comments are made, the name is specified. Poems from this source are referred to as "A" plus the number assigned them in the comilation (e.g., "A 142").

[3] Edited with commentaries by KURIYAMA Riichi/ YAMASHITA Kazumi/ MARUYAMA Kazuhiko/ MATSUO Yasuaki. When references to their comments are made, the name is specified. See Note 2 directly above.

[4] The work will be referred to henceforward as "C" with the page number indicated after it.

[5] Edited by Chikuma Publication and including the works of 73 poets.

[6] According to the letter by Satō (see Note 1 above): (i) *Frogpond* published by The Haiku Society of America in New York; (ii) *Haiku Highlights*; (iii) *Modern Haiku* in Madison, WI; (iv) *Cicada* in Tronto, Ontario; (v) *Dragonfly* in Portland, ORE; (vi) *Haiku Journal* in San Jose, CA.

[7] Subtitled *Its Essential Nature, History, and Possibilities in English.* "This work deals with both Japanese and English-language haiku, though it primarily considers the latter through (and not in addition to) the Japanese form" (BROWER 1972: 9).

Pages 173-175

8 "The following thirty verses are chosen, not altogether at random, from a forthcoming book of haiku by J. W.HACKETT of San Francisco. They are in no way mere imitations of Japanese haiku, nor literary diversions. They are [aimed at] the Zen experience, the realising, the making real in oneself of the thing-in-itself, impossible to rational thought, but possible, all poets believe, in experience" (BLYTH 1964: 351).

9 "The book is a selection of some 300 poems, chosen from more than 700 haiku submitted by the Group in Writers Roundtable. The haiku have been read, discussed, criticized, and in some cases, annotated by every member of the Group". In "Introduction" by the editor, Helen Stiles CHENOWETH (13).

10 "A great diversity lies in the pages ahead. But though these poets are all moving along individual paths, they are all following the haiku 'way'. The variety of their voices should delight us as much as the oneness they reveal enlightens us. For the joy of life is to be able to see it anew each moment. These haiku moments await only your contribution of awareness". In "Introduction" by V.D. HEUVEL (xxxiii).

11 "YŪKI TEIKEI haikuists beyond Japan may be understandably proud that YUKI TEIKEI HAIKU is being recognized by leading haiku poets and scholars in Japan. With the development of common ground through understanding and appreciation of haiku as written in Japan, YUKI TEIKEI HAIKU appears to be developing strong roots in the United States and Canada" (TOKUTOMI 1979: 11).

12 YASUDA's work was "originally submitted to Tokyo University as a doctoral theses in 1955 under the title *On the Essential Nature and Poetic Intent of Haiku*" (YASUDA 1957: xi).

13 "Borrowing the concept from the Japanese, a Group of writers from Los Altos, California, have come up with something distinctively new - a book of American haiku" (cover blurb).

14 Cf. MATSUI 1972: 14.

15 It is customary to refer to Japanese poets by their first names.

16 About the terminologies: Cf. V.D. HEUVEL 1974: 248-51. For *renga* and *haikai*, see BENL 1954, HIBBETT 1960/61.

17 Shiki(1893: 177) discarded the practice of writing long poems by more than two poets and declared that only *hokku* can be qualified as the work of art: "Hokku is a kind of

Pages 177-186

literature. 'Renpai' i.e., haikai composed by more than two poets in a poetic gathering is not any kind of literature. Therefore, I even don't bother arguing about it. Although 'renpai' needless to say possesses the elements of literature, at the same time it possesses something *unliterary*. For this reason, when I discuss the elements of literature, only hokku will do".

18 "Katauta is a poem of three lines in which the first two lines consist of one short and one long one; and the last line is the same length as the second line, which is added as a prop to help harmonize the rhythm. This is the unit of ancient poetry" (YASUDA 1957: 111).

19 The diagram is based on the elucidation by Nihon Gakujutsu Shinkōkai (ICHIKAWA et al. 1958) and RIMER/MORRELL 1975. Cf. KURIYAMA 1963.

20 "談笑のうちに風諭すること".

21 Cf. KOMIYA/OGATA/YOKOZAWA 1959.

22 "火をも水にいいなす".

23 See Note 47 in CHAPTER 1.

24 Ibid.

25 The comment on "makoto" by BROWER/MINER (1961: 507): "An important ideal of Court poetry, primarily in the late classical period". Cf. HATTORI 1776: 522 (Note 47 in CHAPTER 1).

26 Author's translation.

27 Cf. UEDA 1962,1970.

28 Shiki was a prolific writer. BLYTH (1964 B.II: 21) notes: "In the 25th year of Meiji, 1892, he entered the Nippon Newspaper Company, and established a new school of haikai. He published several books, many articles on haikai, and a periodical, *Hototogisu*".

29 "It was the 11th year of Meiji [i.e., 1878] when the theory of evolution was brought to Japan: An American natural scientist, Morse, was invited to the University of Tokyo, and then E. Fenollosa came to Japan. The former lectured upon the evolutionary theory of Darwin in connection with zoology, whereas the second lectured on, in addition to Darwin's theory, Spencer's social evolutionary theory" (MATSUI 1972: 14).

30 Cf. Shiki in *Shiki-Zenshū(1897): Vol. 11-3*, also *Vol. 13:* 96-8.

Pages 186-198

[31] Author's translation.

[32] The present author could not consult Ōtsuji's essay. The following discussion is based on the explication by MATSUI 1965: 174-82.

[33] The concept of "2-ku,1-shō" was first advocated by Harada Kyokusai during the Edo Period, according to ASANO 1962: 10.

[34] MATSUI (1965: 179) expounds: "Concerning the terminology '暗示' [suggestion, metaphor], Seisensui states that he was lecturing on Hermann Paul, the German linguist, and his book *Principien der Sprachgeschichte* [at that time]. He thought, he continues, that the thesis stating that 'language is nothing but suggestions' was quite interesting; accordingly, he told Otsuji, who was quite impressed and wrote about ["スゲスチオン "=suggestion]".

[35] The Japanese loan-word for "montage".

[36] Cf. MATSUI 1965: 572.

[37] Cf. QANBER 1974: 37-58.

[38] The terminology "internal comparison" is first employed in his *Haiku in English* (1965). In 1934, he simply states: "comparison of two or more ideas" (ibid., 8).

[39] KEENE in this statement criticises A. LOWELL, but he does not mention POUND's super-pository technique at all - the principle that his leader of the Imagist group had perceived.

[40] Cf. EHRLICH 1965: 252ff., SHUKMAN 1977: 38-68.

[41] JAKOBSON (1960: 358): "In poetry one syllable is equalized with any other syllable of the same sequence; word stress is assumed to equal word stress, as unstress equals unstress; prosodic long is matched with long, and short with short; word boundary equals word boundary, no boundary equals no boundary; syntactic pause equals syntactic pause, no pause equals no pause. Syllables are converted into units of measure, and so are morae or stresses".

[42] LOTMAN (*Lektii*: 65 cit. in SHUKMAN 1977: 55) defines the rhythm of poetry as "the cyclical repetition of different elements in similar positions in order to equate the unequal and to reveal similarity in what is different, or the repetition of what is similar in order to reveal the imaginary character of this similarity and to show difference in what is similar". In haiku poetry, the repetition of the lines of five morae interrupted by the line of seven morae is the sole arrangement that carries out the mechanism of the LOTMAN's notion of the *povtor* (cf. SHUKMAN 1977: 55).

Pages 198-205

[43] Cf. SHUKMAN 1977: 61ff.

[44] "師の曰く「俳諧の益は、俗語を正すなり。つねにものをおろそかにすべからず。この事は人の知らぬ所なり。大切の所なり。」と伝えられ侍るなり。"

[45] Later JAKOBSON (1976: 174) employs the terminology "poeticity" instead of "poeticalness".

[46] Cf. KOCH's criticism of JAKOBSON's definition of the poetic function (1983: 59ff.).

[47] Cf. SHUKMAN 1977: 40-2.

[48] HATTORI 1776: 547: "「松の事は松に習へ、竹の事は竹に習へ」"

[49] Cf. "寒き田や　馬上にすくむ影法師" (Bashō)
Samukita ya/ bajō ni sukumu / kageboshi
(The cold rice-rields; / On horse-back, / My shadow creeps below) (BLYTH 1964a: 123).

[50] BLYTH concatenates "ninety-six haiku on heat", affirming that "in Shiki's *Bunrui Haiku Zenshū*, 12 Volumes, under 'atsusa' (heat) we are given 533 verses [...]" (1964a: xxxi-lii). Two such examples of "haiku, the poetry of sensation" (ibid.) are:
a) "大蟻の畳を歩く暑さかな" (Shirō)
Ōari no / tatami wo aruku / atsusa kana
(A huge ant/ walks over the tatami; / Ah, the heat!) (BLYTH 1964a: xxxix).
b) "暑き日や無言禅師のにらみあひ" (Seibi)
Atsuki hi ya / mugon zenshi no / nirami-ai
(A hot day; / With a silent Zen master, / Glaring at each other) (BLYTH 1964a: li).

[51] Cf. "石のまろさ　雪になる" (Seisensui)
Ishi no marosa yuki ni naru
(Stone's / plumpness / turns into snow) (UEDA 1976: 80).

[52] I was unable to find the corresponding haiku. The following haiku by Bashō, however, can be cited as a possible candidate:
"海くれて鴨のこゑほのかに白し" (Bashō)
Umi kurete / kamo no koe / honoka ni shiroshi
(It is getting dark on the sea: / (and) the cry of seagulls / is faintly white).

[53] Cf. "遅き日や鉦きこゆる京のすみ" (Bashō)
Osoki hi ya / kodama kikoyuru / Kyō no shumi
(Slow days passing / In a corner of Kyōto /Echoings are heard) (BLYTH 1964: 271).

Pages 205-230

54 Cf. "二もとの 梅に遅速を愛すかな " (Buson)
   Futamoto no / ume ni chisoku o / aisu kana
   (The two plum trees; / I love their blooming; One
   early, one later) (BLYTH 1942: 2).

55 Cf. "五月雨や 桶の輪切るる夜の声 " (Bashō)
   Samidare ya/ oke no wa kiruru / yoru no koe
   (Early summer rain! / the rings of a tub tearing up /
   the voice of the night) (A 111).

56 Cf. "朝風に毛を吹かれ居る毛虫かな " (Buson)
   Asakaze ni / ke o fukare-oru / kemushi kana
   (The morning breez / Ruffles the hairs / Of the
   caterpillar) (ICHIKAWA et al. 1958: 46).

57 MUKAI 1776: 498: "先師曰く「発句は物を合すれば出来せり…」"

58 HATTORI 1776: 592: "発句の事は、行きて帰る心の味はひなり。"

59 Manzai dancers: "a troupe who visited one house after
   another with congratulatory messages in the New Year's
   season" (UEDA 1970: 166).

60 On the three terms, see Notes 53, 55, and 56 in the
   INTRODUCTION.

61 KOCH 1966: 13-6.

62 "Der auf Ästhetik gerichtete Fokus erzeugt Strukturen -
   und damit schränken wir die Bedeutungsstreuung von 'Ästhetik' für unsere Zwecke terminologisch ein -, die auf einer
   nicht-trivialen, inrgendwie regelmäßigen Wiederkehr (Re-
   kurrenz) von sprachlichen Einheiten beruhen" (KOCH 1973:
   27-8).

63 "Stylistics without deep structure translation ('Klartext')
   is like scratching oneself in mid-air without touching
   one's skin" (KOCH 1983: 468).

64 "Der sinojapanische Wortschatz, d.h. die lexikalischen
   Entlehnungen aus dem Chinesischen, übertrifft den japanischen
   Grundwortschatz um mehr als das Doppelte an Umfang und ist
   seiner Ausgangsposition entsprechend nominaler Natur"
   (LEWIN 1959: 4).

65 Cf. HAMMITZSCH 1953: 7-8, 1954: 117-9, 1957.

66 Cf. KOCH's analysis of the same poem,1983: 239-41.

67 The nest of the grebe is made of twigs, fallen leaves,
   water grasses, etc., located among reeds. The nest is
   constructed to move up and down according to the rise and
   fall of the waterlevel of lagoons, lakes, ponds, or rivers.
   One traditional example of waka on the floating nest of

Pages 230-237

the grebe cited by HORI (1972: 111) is : "Karasaki!/How does the floating nest of the grebe/ manage to live on/ in the world of aimless wandering?".

68 The rainy season in Japan is from the end of May till the beginning of July. During this season, it rains three or four days in a row with intervals of one or two clear days.

69 One typical example offered by BROWER/MINER (1961: 217) is by Ono-no-Komachi in *Kokinshū* (II 113):

"花の色は	Hana no iro wa	"The color of these flowers
うつりにけりな	utsuri ni keri na	No longer has allure, I am
いたづらに	itazura ni	left to ponder unavailingly:
我がみよにふる	waga mi yo ni furu	The desire that may beauty once aroused
ながめせしまに"	nagame seshima ni	Before it fell in this long rain of time"

70 According to BLYTH (1949: 3), "the spiritual origins of haiku" can be diagrammed as follows:

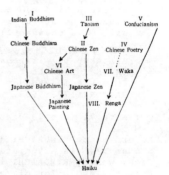

71 Bashō's advocation of non-artificiality is all-pervasive. In his own sayings, we find such expressions as "get a three-feet child to write haikai" (Cf.BLYTH 1949: 241) recorded in HATTORI (1776: 548), or "Things about pine-trees, learn from a pine-tree: things about bamboos, learn from a bamboo" also recorded in HATTORI (ibid., 547). Cf. also MUKAI 1776: 438, 456, 462, and EBARA 1952: 68-81.

72 The theory KURIYAMA is referring to could not be found. Mention of it is made here, however, because the theory may shed light on the "deep-rootedness" of haiku-rhythm.

73 KURIYAMA (1972: 10) elucidates: "According to the 'theory of walking rhythm', the smallest unit of measure is one-mora or two-morae, and in the form of hokku, the construction of '4-beats, 3-measures' is established".

Pages 237-250

[74] "[The] irregular length of these songs and the lack of fixed prosody are symptoms either of an absence of a prosodic sense or of a close tie to certain melodies in which they might acquire regularity through extension or elision of sounds. Such amorphousness often makes division into verse or line units a difficult matter [...]" (BROWER/MINER 1961: 57).

[75] Cf. LEWIN 1959: 33.

[76] Alan DUNDES (1968: 206) in his study "The Number Three in American Culture" notes that "no one has questioned the importance of the number three in Greek and Roman culture" ever since H. USENER (1903) published "Dreiheit". The trichotomic structure, though "three" is not necessarily a universal pattern number (ibid.), seems quite pronouncedly operative in Japanese culture as well.

[77] *Nihon Kokugo Daijiten: katsuma-kinin* 5 1973: 557

[78] Cf. "美しき顔かく雉の距かな." (Kikaku)
Utsukushiki / kao kaku kiji no / kezume kana Kikaku)
(Such a beautiful face/ and scratching it/ a fingernail of a pheasant!)

"蛇くふと聞けば恐し雉子の声" (Bashō)
Hebi kuu to / kireba osoroshi/kiji no koe
(When I hear that a pheasant eats a snake, / it makes me shudder / the cry of a pheasant). Cf. HATTORI 1776: 565.

[79] Cf. Note 71 in this chapter.

[80] According to KINDAICHI (ASANO/KINDAICHI 1979: 20), the phoneme /e/ is associated with something vulgar and tasteless, which, KINDAICHI infers, might be due to the fact that the evolution of /e/ in Japanese set in in the relatively late phase of the language development". In addition, palatalization, which set in in the Heian Period (LEWIN 1959: 18) is also considered to be "inelegant" (KINDAICHI ibid.). Cf. SEKO 1965.

[81] KURIYAMA (1972: 186) cites a letter from Kyoroku to Kyorai, both Bashō's best disciples and friends, in which Kyoroku writes: "[Izen] composes only through colloquialism [vulgar expression] and there has been no single haiku of 'makoto' [sincerity] in [Izen's] poetry".

[82] Cf. MATSUI 1965: 274.

[83] "'Haiga' seems to be quite a modern word. Even Shiki did not use it apparently" (BLYTH 1964a: xxvii). Cf. *Zusetsu Nihon no Koten 14: Bashō, Buson* 1978.

[84] Obviously the poem involves kake-kotoba (3.5.2.2): 'haku'= /wears/ and /sweeps/; 'yūdachi ' = /evening shower/ and /sword/ (tachi). See 3.5.2.4.

[85] "Tachi" becomes the voiced "-dachi" due to the preceding "yū", a long vowel. See the regulation of rendaku (voiceless becomes voiced after a nasal or long vowel) in LEWIN 1959: 19.

[86] Cf. ICHIKAWA et al.(NGS) 1958: 11, HENDERSON 1965: 21ff. ULENBROOK 1979: 167ff., YASUDA 1957: 169.

[87] YASUDA (1957: 142-77) defines in Kokinshū (905) the prototypical concept of seasonal words, for this imperial anthology includes "for the first time categories for the four seasons". By the time of renga, to encapsulate seasonal words in hokku was "obligatory", as KURIYAMA (1972: 11) also elucidates. Nijō Yoshimoto maintained in his renga-poetics Renri Hishō (ca. 1349) that "it is truly unpardonable that some hokku do not conform to the ambient of the season in which they are composed [...]" (cit. in KURIYAMA ibid.). Nijō listed (ibid.), e.g., "chilling, unmelted snow, plum-tree, cuckoos" for the "New Year", while listing further such seasonal elements for each month. Turning to the haikai-period, the number of such season-words increased, eventually being compiled as saijiki (cf. Z. Haiku Daisaijiki 1970), i.e., "collections of seasonal themes which were usually used in haiku being classified into certain pre-determined seasons" (ibid.). Cf. GIROUX 1974: 94-117.

[88] "Türangelwort", the term suggested by Professor Bruno LEWIN in his lecture in the summer term of 1979 at the University of Bochum, West Germany.

[89] On the flection of Japanese verbs, see LEWIN 1959: 118-33. Cf. McCLAIN 1981: 5ff.

[90] "Three warriors": Fujiwara Kiyohira, Motohira, and Hidehira in the late Heian Period. "Konjiki-dō" or "Hikaridō" was built in 1124 (IMOTO 1972: 365). Cf. MATSUO 1974: 56-8.

[91] The mediatory aspect of Mt. Fuji can be most eloquently evidenced by the fact that this highest mountain in Japan has been regarded as a sacred object. Its height, beauty, and vulcanism seem to have contributed to its becoming a mediation proper: man projected his wish to reach the sky onto this mountain, which was, in spite of its height, earthbound.

[92] In one of his travel-diaries Oi no kobumi or Yoshino-kikō (1687-8), Bashō writes: "In a hundred bones and nine holes, i.e., a human body, 'one thing' exists, and it is provisionally called 'Fūrabō' [a ragamuffin like a thin cloth

that flaps in the wind]. He must be named so, because
a thin cloth can be easily ripped and torn off by the wind.
It has been quite some time since this ragamuffin started
enjoying 'kyōku' [crazy verse = haikai]. Eventually, it
became his life-long activity" (Bashō in NKBZ 41, 1972:
311). Cf. PILGRIM 1977: 38ff.

93
"あさがほに我は食くふおとこかな" (A 68)
Asagao ni/ware wa meshi-kuu / otoko kana
(While viewing morning-glories/ I eat my rice [I take
my meal] / such a man I am!).

94
"市人よ比笠うらふ雪の傘" (A 104)
Ichi-bito yo / kono kasa urō / yuki no kasa
(Town-people! / I will sell you this hat / a hat full
of snow!).

95
"名月や池をめぐりて夜もすがら" (A 145)
Meigetsu ya/ ike o megurite / yomosugara
(A beautiful moon! / around the pond I have been walking/
all night long).

96
"我が宿は蚊のちいさきを馳走かな" (A 339)
Wa ga yado wa / ka no chiisaki o / chisō kana
(At my bower/ mosquitoes are small / and that is
my treat for you!).

97
"面白し 雪にやならん 冬の雨" (A 185)
Omoshiroshi / yuki ni ya naran / fuyu no ame
(How interesting! / would it turn to snow? / the rain of
winter).

98
KONISHI Jun'ichi (1960) in his *Bashō to Gūgensetsu*
(Bashō and the Theory of Allegory) explains the interpre-
tation of the cosmos as follows:

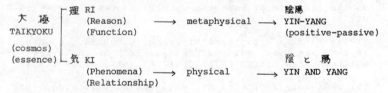

The word "Taikyoku", literally, "the ultimate greatest pole", is
interpreted by AKABANE Manabu (1970: 163) thus: "Taikyoku
is then the Existence itself that lies in the innermost
essence of the creation of the earth".

99
Cf. HAMMITZSCH's (1954: 111ff.) discussion of Bashō's notion
of *fueki-ryūkō*, the notion Bashō advocated in his later

years concerning the poetics of haikai (MUKAI 1776: 490-6, HATTORI 1776: 545-6). *Fueki* ("the unchangeable") is "das für alle Zeiten Unwandelbare, welches nicht Alt und Neu kennt, welches sich im Strom des Werdens und Vergehens niemals ändert. Dies Unwandelbare kann man erkennen, wenn man nicht seinem Ich verhaftet ist, sondern dieses aufgibt und sich eins fühlt mit dem All, wenn man in das Wesen der Dinge eindringt. Nur auf diese Weise kann der Dichter wahre Werte schaffen und keine bloßen Machwerke. Dann enthält sein Werk *makoto*, Wahrheit, wenn auch die Form (*ryūkō*) sich wandelt". *Ryūkō* is "der Wandel der Form", in accordance with the cosmic principle that "everything changes" (HATTORI, 545). To a certain degree, this notion corresponds to JAKBOSON's dichotomy of *poeticity* as a universal component, on the one hand, and *poetry* as its realization, which varies from time to time, on the other (cf. JAKOBSON 1979, KOCH 1983: 45ff.). See 3.3.4.

[100] "さび". Cf. MUKAI 1776: 512, EBARA 1952: 69ff., MINER 1979, UEDA 1970: 51ff.

[101] "粋". MUKAI 1776: 513-4. Cf. EBARA 1952: 70ff.

[102] "細み". MUKAI 1776: 513-4. Cf. EBARA 1952: 70, PILGRIM 1977: 47ff.

[103] In analying this poem, HENDERSON (1934: 23) states: "The association of ideas which connects the hanging bridge with the rest of the poem is mundane as well as metaphysical, for rustic suspension bridges of this type actually were made with ropes of twisted vines".

[104] "余情". "[Yojō] might be literally translated as 'surplus-meaning'. 'Surplus meaning' is a term age-old in Japanese literary criticism, dating back long before Bashō's time. Ordinarily, it was used to describe a poem that means more than its words say; there is a 'suggested' meaning as well as 'stated' meaning" (UEDA 1970: 161).

[105] The poem appears in *Hiding the Universe: Poems by Wang Wei* (1972). Cf. KOCH 1978: 309, 1983: 80.

[106] Cf. "The textual expansion" of POUND's elaboration on the "superpository technique" in 5.2.4.

[107] The first version was jotted down by Kawai Sora, Bashō's traveling companion, in Sora's travel diary (AKABANE 1969).

[108] The last version is compiled in his journey accounts, *Oku no hosomichi* (1694). Cf. MATSUO 1974: 61-2.

[109] According to ASANO (1963: 3), "haiku normally take the structure of '2-ku,1-shō'; there are, however, '1-ku,1-shō', or '3-ku,1-shō', in addition to the rare case of '4-ku,1-shō'".

CHAPTER 4

[1] Cf. KURIYAMA 1972: 17-26; for a more detailed account of the history of haikai, see KURIYAMA 1963.

[2] If we were to include the waka-tradition in this cyclic pattern, the period of such precurosors of haikai as Sōkan or Moritake would be characterized as "metagenetic", for in waka as well as its direct successor, renga, informational poeticalness was indispensable, as is explained by BROWER/MINER (1957, 1961). With regard to haiku-poetry, however, the period prior to Bashō, which includes different types of precursors, can be considered to make up one trend leading up to the establishment of haikai by Bashō.

[3] See some samples of spontaneous child narrative in LEONDAR (1977: 180ff.): these samples clearly show the five-fold homeostatic cycle. The following sample, e.g., was narrated by the 3 1/2-year-old boy:
Once there was a funny bird (○). He lived in a tree (◐). And he fell down (●). The mommy bird came and made him fly (◑). Then he went back in the tree (○).

[4] "'Spannung' as a typically process-like structure may be projected on space or onto time and will accordingly be split into two types: *tension* or *suspense* (KOCH 1982c: 1). "Tension" is thus *static* in TODOROV's sense, while "suspense" is *dynamic* (ibid., 10). Furthermore, the static "tension" is correlated to the axis of paradigm while "suspense" is correlated to that of syntagma (ibid., 6).

[5] The kireji "ya" must be changed into "kana". "Ya" appears in the middle of the poem but not at the end, whereas "kana" is employed at the end.

[6] HATTORI Dohō records: "When Master Bashō composed this poem, he said; 'I understood a few interesting points in the poem on flower-viewing, and so I attempted to express 'lightness'"(KURIYAMA 1973: 565). On "lightness", see UEDA 1970: 66-8, 158-62.

[7] For the poets contemporary with Buson, see ICHIKAWA et al. (NGS) 1958: xxii, and also 39-65.

[8] One of the most famous specimens of multi-paradigm haiku by Bashō is the following:
"奈良七重 七堂伽藍 八重ざくら" (A 251)
Nara nanae / shichidō garan / yae-zakura
(In Nara things are seven-fold/ seven halls of the cathedrals/ eight-folded cherry-blossoms)

PARADIGM ─┬─ ○ 'In Nara things are seven-fold'
          ├─ ○ 'seven halls'
          └─ ○ 'eight-folded cherry-blossoms'

Pages 324-329

Cf. also; A 365, B 208.

9 Also called "Sagichō". "Ornaments for the New Year's month are gathered from each household, put in the center of a village, and burnt. It is a kind of fire-festival, which takes place in the center of the village. In the middle of collected ornaments, people put wood which is called 'the Sacred Wood' ... In the rural area, they tell their fortune, according to the intensity of the fire, for the harvest of the following year. When the flame gets high, they are pleased to regard it as a promise for a rich harvest" (MARUYAMA 1972: 385).

左義長(難波鑑)

10 "[Issa] stands in striking contrast with Bashō, whose works have the smile of a man who has trancended sufferings. Bashō willingly accepted a life of solitary desolation and left his home at an early age, and sought a haven in solitude. Issa, on the contrary, though having lost his mother in childhood and being persecuted by his step-mother and half-brother, never could bring himself to abandon completely the place where he was born and bred. After wandering many years he returned to his native village and settled down there. But his wife and children died, his house was burnt down, and he finally ended his life in the storehouse, mocking his own sufferings" (ICHIKAWA et al. NGS: xxiii).

11 "Tsukinami" means, literally, "monthly-like" (conventional, static) referring to the monthly meetings of haikai-professionals. It thus implies "conventional", or "static". Cf. BYLTH 1964: 102.

12 They were called "Nihon-ha", the Nihon School. After Shiki began to edit a haiku-periodical, *Hototogisu* (cuckoo) - incidentally, his name connotes also "cuckoo" as does the name of this periodical -, the poets associated with him were called "Hototogisu-ha", the Hototogisu School. Cf. YOSHIDA 1962.

13 The number shows the pages on which the poems appear.

14 Translation by BLYTH (1964a: 31). BLYTH elucidates this poem as follows: "Illicit intercourse was banned, but they were saved by the mercy of the lord, and had now become man and wife, and changed their clothes to summer ones, living peacefully" (ibid., 31-2).

Pages 331-347

15 See Note 4 to this chapter.

16 Haiku vers libre cannot be divided by the segment-markers, "/", which have been employed in the present study up to this point, since they do not conform to the syllabic pattern. Caesurae appear, nonetheless, as in the case of (83):
   Chichi wa waktte ita ∥ damatte ita ∥ niwasusuki
In order to make this point clear, I shall use colons or semi-colons in English translation in accordance with the convention of translating Japanese haiku into European languages.

17 Poems from (84) to (110) are translated by UEDA (1976), except for (85), (89), (91), (92), (93), (106), and (107). While "C" refers to the haiku anthology translated with commentary by UEDA (1976), the numbers after "C" show the pages on which the poems appear in the anthology.

18 "[Kijō] was poor, and had to struggle desperately to support his family of ten children. At one time his house was burnt down in a fire and he lost the few things he had owned. At another time he was dismissed from his job, and regained it only after his friends, who knew his reputation as a poet, intervened on his behalf" (UEDA 1976: 13).

19 Another famous poet influencing the trend at that time was Hino Sōjō, about whom UEDA writes (1976: 15-6): "A young college student, he soon developed a distaste for the kind of traditionalist attitude underlying the majority of poems published in *Hototogisu*. More than anything else he valued the free expansion of the poet's fancy [...] He therefore advocated venturing into areas of life hitherto unexplored by haiku poets, especially the area of youthful, romantic love. What he advocated he put into practice: once he shocked his readers by writing a series of haiku depicting the first night of the bride and groom after their wedding". Cf. GNBZ 91: 165.

   UEDA (ibid., 18) further stresses the "modernity" of such haiku writers as Sōjō, Shūōshi and Seishi by comparing them to T. S. ELIOT.

20 Cf. e.g., "空をあゆむ 朗々と 月ひとり"   (C 77: Seisensui)
       Sora o ayumu   rōrō to tsuki hitori
       (In the sky/ walk/ serenely - /the moon alone) (UEDA 1976: 77).
UEDA (ibid.) comments: "Ayumu can mean either '(I) walk' or '(the moon) walks'. No doubt the ambiguity is intentional". Haiku seem to tend to be ultimately ambiguous by discarding postpositions, a fact which supports our argumentation that haiku is paradigmatic rather than syntagmatic, since postpositions clarify syntagmatic, i.e., grammatical, relationships.

Pages 358-375

CHAPTER 5

[1] Cf. also MINER 1958: 68ff.

[2] After Hulme "comes a genius from Idaho, Ezra Pound. Late in 1913 or early in 1914, Pound became literary executor for the estate of Ernest Fenollosa. Mrs. Fenollosa's choice of Pound was a propitious one, and one that also brought incidentally, William Butler Yeats closer to the Japanese Noh" (ŌTAKE 1965: 163). Cf. STOCK 1970, also FENOLLOSA/POUND 1916. For Yeats's relationship to the Nō theatre, see QANBER 1974.

[3] "Vorticism was an excuse to join more capable fellow artists to fight the old cause of Imagism more effectively. Since the poetry shows no sudden change at this period which can be attributed to Wyndham Lewis or Gaudier-Brzeska, it is wrong to say that Vorticism represented more than a change of name and scene" (MINER 1958: 127).

[4] Cf. YASUDA 1957: xviii. Also, his comment appearing on page 45: "I feel that some aspects of T. S. Eliot's concept of 'the objective correlative' are too much a product of a conscious method; his use of nature symbols such as gulls, hyacinths, etc., seems overly conscious and thin".

[5] When the work of a poet is not cited in the bibliography as his/her own book, the last name remains uncapitalized.

[6] The term "haiku" was first used by MASAOKA Shiki, whose literary activities in terms of haiku took place one decade prior to the Imagist movement, in his endeavour to differentiate his poetry from the potry of "tsukinami"-haikai-professionals (3.3.1, 4.2.4. Cf. also ICHIKAWA et al, NGS, 1958: xvii). The Imagist poets were evidently acquainted with only the original term, *hokku*, which had been introduced to the Western world earlier. In Paris, the term *haikai* was preferred due to the translations of Japanese poetry by Marcel Revon (MINER 1958: 75., LEWIN 1969: 30ff.).

[7] Cf. YASUDA's criticism of POUND's poem (34): "The unrelatedness [between the two points of interest] is a disintegrating force and the experience is not unified" (1957: 65).

[8] Cf. MINER 1958: 123-7.

[9] Cf. POUND 1970: 89.

[10] Cf. MINER 1958: 116.

[11] Cf. REID 1977: 62ff.

[12] In 1914, after the presentation of the metro poem (34),

POUND writes (1914: 89): "I dare say it is meaningless unless one has drifted into a certain vein of thought. In a poem of this [i.e., *hokku-like*] sort one is trying to record the precise instant when a thing outward and objective transforms itself, or darts into a thing inward and subjective". This passage evinces POUND's recognition that once "a poem of this sort" is expanded, it could well be prone to lose its intensity. Cf. SMITH 1965.

[13] Cf. MINER 1958: 123, KOCH 1983: 266, also his Note 277 (ibid., 507).

[14] ŌTAKE 1965: 161. Translation by ŌTAKE.

[15] As MINER (1958: 115) rightly points out, KEENE does not refer to POUND's super-pository technique at all.

[16] Cf. SATŌ 1978: 28.

[17] MINER (1958: 162) points out that Amy LOWELL was familiar with Japanese art and culture at a much earlier age than any other poet of the Imagist group.

[18] In composing haikai, HATTORI Dohō (1776: 574) explains, there are two ways: "'becoming' and 'making'. When a poet who has always been assiduous in pursuit of his aim applies himself to an external object, the color of his mind naturally becomes a poem. In the case of a poet who has done so, nothing in him becomes a poem; consequently he has to make up a poem through the act of his personal will" (translated by UEDA 1963: 424). Cf. also UEDA 1970: 168.

[19] The lines that "can eaily be read in the span of one breath" are, according to YASUDA (1957: 34):
   A) More precious was the light in your eyes than the roses in the world.
   B) It was many and many a year ago
      In a kingdom of the sea.
   C) I must go down to the sea again, to the lonely sea and the sky.

[20] Cf. HENDERSON 1934, MIYAMORI 1932.

[21] E.g.: <u>Brushing</u> <u>the leaves</u>, <u>fell</u>
           2   2   1

   <u>A white</u> <u>camellia</u> <u>blossom</u>
      2   3   2

   <u>Into</u> <u>the</u> <u>dark well</u>
      2   1   2
                                    (YASUDA 1957: 83)

YASUDA (ibid.) puts the article in the first line with "leaves" so that the two constitute 2 syllables, whereas in the third line he separates "the" from the succeeding words, "dark well", when he should have put them together to make a line with the pattern of "2+3" instead of his "2+1+2".

[22] YASUDA translates "2-ku,1-shō" as "two parts make one whole" (1957: 40, 82).

[23] Whether a word in a haiku can be substituted for or not is an age-old issue. MUKAI Kyorai (1776: 422) records, e.g., a controversy over "furu-furanu" (movable or immovable). See also MUKAI ibid., 440, 463.

[24] Gary SNYDER, however, wrote many good haiku. STEUDING (1976: 57) states: "like Bashō [...] Snyder has used the haiku extensively. The haiku is found in his short poetic essays, in larger poems as interludes, and in the travel journals, such as those found in *Earth House Hold*. The poet Allen Ginsberg has stated that Snyder is one of the few American poets capable of writing genuine haiku. And Thomas Lyon has even gone so far as to state that the haiku is "the guiding principle of Snyder's poetics, whatever the length of the application".

[25] In 1910 Marcel Revon published his *Anthologie de la Littérature japonaise*, which "almost immediately, and for the next fifteen years" motivated French poets to imitate the techniques of Japanese poetry and "even [to adapt] the five-seven-five syllabic arrangements of haiku" (MINER 1958: 75). In 1916 Paul-Louis Couchoud published his essay "Epigrammes lyriques au Japon", which has been quite influential in the French literary world (75-6).

[26] "Wenn unter Elektroshock die linke Hemisphäre ausgeschaltet ist, verliert der Patient die Fähigkeit, abstrakte Begriffe zu verstehen wie Gesundheit, Bosheit, Freude, Religion usw., wobei aber das Verständnis konkreter Gegenstände völlig erhalten bleibt" (IVANOV 1977: 60).

[27] Cf. HACKETT 1965-68, *Haiku Poetry: Original Verse in English Vol. 1-4*.

[28] Cf. HENDERSON 1965: 62-3.

[29] "In der Geschichte des Haiku wechseln Perioden u. Geschmacksrichtungen, die ein homogenes Bild bevorzugen, mit solchen, die sogar recht eklatante Bildkontraste akzeptieren" (FRANK 1968: 182).

[30] My American colleague, Mr. William Walker, has suggested to me that poem (185) alludes to the phenomenon of "mooning" (showing one's naked buttocks), which was popular among American college students in the sixties. Whether "a full moon" in (185) is taken as /the fully exposed buttocks/ or

Pages 430-459

31 not surely depends on the cultural backgound of P_{xe}. If he selects this sememe, (185) automatically becomes a senryū.

31 I take the liberty of interpreting the four poems printed on two pages of the *Anthology* as a haiku sequence because of their thematic coherence as well as their narrative character.

32 Cf. HENDERSON 1965: 43.

33 "There is a growing tendency to approximate a 5-7-5 syllable form but so far no experienced poet or editor has advocated an absolutely strict adherence to it. In the Japan Air Lines Contest, 13 of the 100 published (as the best of 41,000 submitted) are not in the 5-7-5 form. The 1963 *American Haiku* has a somewhat larger variation in its published poems; the 1964 *American Haiku* considerably less" (HENDERSON 1965: 31).

34 In analyzing haiku (our example [1] and [52]), KOCH (1983: 269) ascertains that the "overall information" that we receive from the "concrete-metaphysical" of the two poems can be depicted as follows:

Lines	Focus-zooming	○ Nature (immortal, quiet)	vs.	● Man, Animal (mortal, quick and loud)
1		○		
2				●
3				●
after 3		○		

McClintock's poppy-poem can be characterized as the exact opposite of such "zooming".

CHAPTER 6

1 Ann ATWOOD (1977), e.g., explores the photographic nature of haiku. In her work *Haiku-Vision*, the juxtaposition of two semems is demonstrated especially in terms of iconic signs.

2 Cf. IVANOV 1977: 37ff.

Pages 460-486

³ Cf. IVANOV/TOPOROV 1982.

⁴
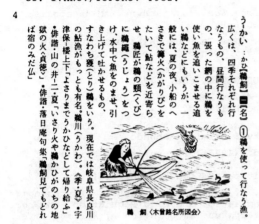

うーかい…かひ【鵜飼】□【名】① 鵜を使って行なう漁。広くは、四季それぞれ行なうものの、昼間行なうも、張った網の中に鵜を使い魚を追いこませる追い鵜などにもいうが、一般には、夏の夜、小舟のへさきで篝火（かがりび）をたいて鮎などを近寄らせ、鵜匠が鵜の頸（くび）に鵜縄（うじょう）をつけ、水中で魚をのませ、引き上げて吐かせるものをいう。現在では岐阜県長良川の鮎漁がもっとも有名。鵜川（うかわ）。《季・夏》・字津保・楼上下「よさりまでうかひなどして帰り給ふ」・俳諧・山の井二・夏「いさり火や鵜かひがのちの地獄の火〈貞徳〉」・俳諧・落日庵句集「鵜飼見てもどれば宿のみだ仏」

鵜　飼〈木曽路名所図会〉

(*Nihon Kokugo Daijiten:*
Vol. 2, 1973, 508.)

⁵ Cf. The "nominal style" or "averbal style" affected by right-hemisphericity (IVANOV 1977: 47ff.).

EXCURSUS

¹ Jakob Grimm and Jürgen von Arnim. Cf. BAUSINGER 1968: 53.

² On "binary opposition" in the various types of sign systems (natural languages, artificial languages, literature, folklore, music, dance, myths, rituals, architechture, visual arts, etc.), see IVANOV/TOPOROV 1982.

³ In RANKE's assertion, however, the *Willensakte* and their resulting *genres* do not seem to conincide exactly, especially, in the first two categories.

⁴ Cf. BAUSINGER 1968: 51-64, BEN-AMOS 1968: 281-3, SCHOLES 1974: 42-50.

⁵ Cf. KEENE 1966, KOYAMA et al. 1980.

BIBLIOGRAPHY

AASLEFF, Hans (1982), *From Lock to Saussure*. Minneapolis: University of Minnesota P.

ABRAHAMS, Roger (1969), "The Complex Relations of Simple Forms" in *Genre* (1969), 104-28.

ABRAHAMS, Roger (1976), "Vibrations and the Realization of Form" in JANTSCH/WADDINGTON, eds. (1976).

AITKEN, Robert (1978), *A Zen Wave: Bashō's Haiku and Zen*. New York: John Weatherhill Inc.

AKABANE, Manabu (1970), *Bashō Haikai no Seishin* (The Spirit of Bashō's Haikai). Tokyo: Shimizu-Kōbundō.

AKISHIGE, Yoshiharu, ed. (1977), *Psychological Studies of Zen: Bulletin of the Zen Institute of Komazawa University Nr. 1*. Tokyo: The Zen Institute of Komazawa University.

AKISHIGE, Y./ NAKAMURA, S./ YAMAOKA, T. (1962), "Psychological Studies on Breath Regulation and Mind Regulation" in *Proc. 29th Convention of Japanese Association of Applied Psychology*.

AMANN, Eric (1969), *The Wordless Poem: A Study of Zen in Haiku*. Toronto, Canada: Haiku Publications.

AMANN, Eric (1979), "Haiku Education in Canadian Schools" in *Haiku Journal* (1979), 34-6.

ANDŌ, Suehiro (1977), "A Psychological Study on the Effects of Breath Regulation to Mental Self-Control" in AKISHIGE, ed. (1977), 160-207.

D'AQUILI, Eugene G./LAUGHLIN, Charles D. (1974): see LAUGHLIN/ D'AQUILI (1974).

D'AQUILI, Eugene G./LAUGHLIN, Charles D. Jr. (1979), "The Neurobilogy of Myth and Ritual" in D'AQUILI et al., eds. (1979), 152-82.

D'AQUILI, Eugene G./LAUGHLIN, Charles D., Jr./McMANUS, John, eds. (1979), *The Spectrum of Ritual: A Biogenetic Structural Analysis*. New York: Columbia U. P.

ARDREY, Robert (1966), *The Territorial Imperative: A Personal Inquiry into the Animal Origins of Property and Nations*. New York: Dell Pub. Co.Inc.

ARIETI, Silvano (1976), *Creativity: The Magic Synthesis*. New York: Basic Books.

ARNHEIM, Rudolf (1971), *Entropy and Art*. Trans. into German by the author: *Entropie und Kunst: ein Versuch über Unordnung und Ordnung*. Köln: Du Mont, 1978.

ASANO, Shin (1939), *Haiku Zenshi no Kenkyū* (A Study of Pre-Haiku History). Tokyo: Chūbunkan.

ASANO, Shin (1962), *Kireji no Kenkyū* (A Study of Kireji). Tokyo: Ōfūsha.

ASANO, Shin (1963), *Kireji no Kenkyū* (A Study of Kireji). Tokyo: Ōfūsha.

ASANO, Tsuruko/KINDAICHI, Haruhiko (1979), *Giongo Gitaigo Jiten* (A Dictionary of Giongo and Gitaigo). Tokyo: Kadokawa.

ATWOOD, Ann (1977), *Haiku Vision: in Poetry and Photography*. New York: Charles Scribners' Sons.

AYIM, Maryann (1974), "Retroduction: The Rational Instinct" in *Transactions of the Charles S. Peirce society* Vol. 10, No. 1, 33-43.

BAILEY, Richard W./MATEJKA, Ladislav /STEINER, P.,eds.(1978), *The Sign: Semiotics around the World*. Ann Arbor: Michigan Slavic Pub.

BALLMER, Thomas (in print), *Linguistic Dynamics*. Berlin: De Gruyter.

BALONOV, L. J./DEGLIN, V. L. (1976), *Slux i reč dominantnogo i nedominantnogo polušarij*. Leningrad.

BARTHES, Roland (1970), *L'empire des signes*. Trans. by Michael Bischoff: *Das Reich der Zeichen*. Frankfurt a.M.: Suhrkamp.

BARTHES, Roland (1974), *S/Z*. Trans. by Richard Miller. New York: Hill and Wang.

BARTHES, Roland (1975), *The Pleasure of the Text*. Trans. by Richard Miller. New York: Hill and Wang.

BARTHES, Roland (1981), "Theory of the Text" in YOUNG, ed. (1981), 31-47.

Bashō: see MATSUO.

BASSO, A./DE RENZI, P./FAGLIONI, L./SCOTTI, G./SPINNLER,H. (1973), "Neuropsychological Evidence for the Existence of Cerebral Area Critical to the Performance of Intelligence Tasks" in *Brain* 96 (1973), 715-28.

BAUSINGER, Hermann (1968), *Formen der "Volkspoesie"*. Berlin: Erich Schmidt.

BECKER, E. (1973), *The Denial of Death*.New York: Free P.

BEN-AMOS, Dan (1969), "Analytical Categories and Ethnic Genres" in *Genre* 2 (1969), 275-301.

BENL, Oscar (1954), "Das japanische Kettengedicht" in *Zeitschrift der Deutschen Morgenländischen Gesellschaft* (Wiesbaden) 104 (1954), 432-50.

BENSE, Max (1967), *Semiotik. Internationale Reihe Kybernetik und Information 4*. Baden-Baden: Agis.

BENSE, Max (1969), *Einführung in die informationstheoretische Ästhetik*. Reinbek: Rowohlt.

BENSE, Max (1971), *Zeichen und Design: Semiotische Ästhetik*. Baden-Baden: Agis.

BENSE, Max (1975), *Semiotische Prozesse und Systeme*. Baden-Baden: Agis.

BENSE, Max/WALTHER, Elizabeth (1973), *Wörterbuch der Semiotik.*
Köln: Kiepenheuer & Witsch.

BENSON, H.(1975), *The Relaxation Response.* New York: Marrow.

BENZ, Ernst (1962), *Zen in westlicher Sicht: Zen-Buddhism - Zen-Snobismus.* Weilheim: Otto Wilhelm Barth.

BERLUCCHI, G. (1974), "Cerebral Dominance and Interhemispheric Communication in Normal Man" in SCHMITT et al., eds. (1974), 65-71.

BERTALANFFY, Ludwig von (1955), "General System Theory" in *Main Currents in Modern Thought* 11 (1955), 75-83.

BERTALANFFY, Ludwig von (1968), *General System Theory.* New York: George Braziller.

BIEDERMAN, Charles (1948), *Art as the Evolution of Visual Knowledge.* Redwing, Minn.: Biedermann.

BILLOW, Richard M. (1975), "A Cognitive Developmental Study of Metaphor Comprehension" in *Developmental Psychology* 11 (1975), 415-23.

BINDRA, Dalbir, ed. (1980), *The Brain's Mind: A Neuroscience Perspective on the Mind-Body Problem.* New York: Gardner P.

BLACK, J. B./BOWER, G. H. (1980), "Story Understanding as Problem Solving" in *Poetics* 9 (1980), 223-50.

BLYTH, R. H. (1949), *Haiku,*Four Vols. Tokyo: Hokuseido P.

BLYTH, R. H. (1949a), *Senryū.* Tokyo: Hokuseido P.

BLYTH, R. H. (1956), "The Sturucture of Haiku" in *Bulletin of the Japan Society,* London, 2 (1956), 18, 23-5.

BLYTH, R. H. (1960), *Zen and Zen Classics: Vol. One.* Tokyo: Hokuseido P.

BLYTH, R. H. (1964), *A History of Haiku,* Two Vols. Tokyo:Hokuseido.

BYLTH, R. H. (1964a), *Zen and Zen Classics: Vol. Two.* Tokyo: Hokuseido P.

BLYTH, R. H. (1966), *Zen and Zen Classics: Vol. Four: Mumonkan.* Tokyo: Hokuseido P.

BOBON, J./MACCAGNANI, G. (1962), "Contributo Allo Studio della Communicazione non-verbale in psicopatologia" in *Riviste Sperimentale di Fremiatria* 86 (1962), 1097-173.

BOGEN, J. E. (1969), "The Other Side of the Brain: An Appositional Mind" in *Bulletin Los Angels Neurological Societies* 34 (1969), 135-62.

BOGEN, J. E. (1972), "The Other Side of the Brain IV: The A/P Ratio" in *Bulletin of the Los Angels Neurological Society* 37 (1972), 49-61.

BOYLE, D. G. (1969), *A Student's Guide to Piaget.* Oxford: Pergamon.

BREKLE, H. E. (1971), "Einige Bemerkungen zur Graphematik-Diskussion" in *Linguistische Berichte* 16 (1971), 53-9.

BREMOND, Claude (1973), *Logique du récit.* Paris: Seuil.

BROWER, Gary (1972), *Haiku in Western Languages: An Annotated Bibliography.* Methuen, NJ.: Scarecrow P.

BROWER, Robert H./MINER, Earl Roy (1957), "Formative Elements in the Japanese Poetic Tradition" in *Journal of Asian Studies* 16 (1957), 503-27.

BROWER, Robert H./MINER, Earl Roy (1961), *Japanese Court Poetry.* Stanford: Stanford U. P.

BROWN , Jason (1977), *Mind, Brain, and Consciousness: the Neuropsychology of Cognition.* New York: Academic P.

BRUNER, Jerome S. (1979), "Von der Kommunikation zur Sprache: Überlegungen aus psychologischer Sicht" in MARTENS, ed., (1979), 9-60.

BRUNSWIK, Egon (1955), "Ratiomorphic Models of Perception and Thinking" in *Acta Psychologica* 11 (1955), 108-9.

BUDZYNSKY, Thomas H. (1977), "Clinical Implications of Electromyographic Training" in SCHWARZ/BEATLEY, eds. (1977), 433-45.

BÜHLER, Karl (1934), *Sprachtheorie.* Stuttgart: Fischer, 1965.

BUNGE, Mario (1980), "Introduction: the Mind-Body Problem" in BINDRA , ed. (1980), 1-5.

BUSSE, Hans-Peter/RIEMENSCHNEIDER, Hartmut (1979), *Grundlagen semiotischer Ästhetik.* Düsseldorf: Pädagogischer Verlag Schwann.

CANISIUS, Peter (1982), "Narrative Competence in Children" in KOCH, ed. (1982), 322-56.

CARRINGTON, Patricia (1978), "The Use of Meditation in Psychotherapy" in SUGERMAN/TARTER, eds. (1978), 81-98.

CASALIS, Matthieu (1979), "Semiology and Semiotics of Haiku" in *Semiotica* 25 (1979), 3/4, 243-55.

CHANG, G. C. C (1971), *The Buddhist Teaching of Totality.* University Park: Pennsylvania State U. P.

CHAPPEL, E. D. (1970), *Culture and Biological Man.* New York: Holt, Rinehart & Winston.

CHATMAN, Seymour/ECO, Umberto/KLINKENBERG, Jean Marie (1979), *Panorama Sémiotique/A Semiotic Landscape: Proceedings of the International Association for Semiotic Studies. Milan, June 1974.* The Hague: Mouton.

CHENOWETH, Helen Stiles (1966), "Introduction" in THE LOS ALTOS WIRTERS ROUNDTABLE, 9-13, 1973 .

CHIHARA, Tadashi (1977), "Psychological Studies on Zen Meditation and Time-Experience" in AKISHIGE, ed. (1977), 361-98.

CHOMSKY, Noam (1957), *Syntactic Structures*. The Hague: Mouton.

CHOMSKY, Noam (1970), *Sprache und Geist*. Frankfurt: Suhrkamp.

CHOMSKY, Noam (1973), *Über Erkenntnis und Freiheit*. Frankfurt a. M.: Suhrkamp.

CHOMSKY, Noam (1979), *Language and Responsibility*. New York: Pantheon Books.

COHEN, H.D./ROSEN, R.C./GOLDSTEIN, L. (1976), "Electroencephalographic Laterality Changes during Human Sex and Orgasm" in *Archives of Sexual Behaviour* 5 (1976), 189-99.

COHEN, William H. (1965), "The Calligraphy of the Cosmos: the Essence of Haiku" in *Literature East and West* 9 (1965), 224-7.

COSERIU, Eugenio (1970), *Die Geschichte der Sprachphilosophie von der Antike bis zur Gegenwart* Vol. 1. Tübingen: TBL.

CRANACH, Mario von/FOPPA, Klaus/LEPENIES, Wold/PLOOG, Detlef (1979), *Human Ethology: Claims and Limits of a New Discipline*. Cambridge: Cambridge U. P.

CULLER, Jonathan (1975), *Structural Poetics*. London: Routledge & Kegan Paul.

CULLER, Jonathan (1981), *The Pursuit of Signs: Semiotics, Literature, Deconstruction*. London: Routledge & Kegan Paul.

CURTIS, Brian A./JACOBSON, Stanley/MARCUS, Elliot M. (1972), *An Introduction to the Neurosciences*. Philadelphia: W.B. Saunders.

DEELY, John (1982), *Introducing Semiotic: Its History and Doctrine*. Bloomington: Indiana U. P.

DEIKMAN, Arthur (1966), "Deautomatization and the Mystic Experience" in *Psychiatry* 29 (1966), 329-43.

A Dictionary of Phonetics (1976). Tokyo: Sansūsha.

Dohō, HATTORI: see HATTORI.

DOI, Masayuki (1977), "Psychological Study of the Relation between Resparatory Function and Mental Self-Control" in AKISHIGE, ed. (1977), 233-91.

DOMURUS, Eilhard von (1944), "The Specific Laws of Logic in Schizophrenia" in KASANIN, ed. (1944), 104-14.

DÜRCKHEIM, Karlfried Graf (1974), *Zen und Wir*. Frankfurt a. M.: Fischer.

DUNDES, Alan (1962), "From Etic to Emic Units in the Structural Study of Folktales" in the *Journal of American Folklore* (1962), 95-105: reprinted in DUNDES (1975), 61-72.

DUNDES, Alan (1968), "The Number Three in American Culture" in *Every Man His Way: Readings in Cultural Anthropology*. A. DUNDES, ed. (1968), Englewood Cliffs: Prentice-Hall, 401-24: reprinted in DUNDES (1975), 206-25.

DUNDES, Alan (1970), "On the Structure of the Proverb" in *Strutture E Generi Della Letteratura Etnica*: reprinted in DUNDES (1975), 103- 18.

DUNDES, Alan (1975), *Analytic Essays in Folklore*. The Hague-Paris: Mouton.

DUNDES, Alan/AREWA Ojo E. (1964), "Proverbs and the Ethnography of Speaking Folklore" in *American Anthroplogist* 66.6, Part 2 (1964), 70-85.

DUNDES, Alan/GEORGES, Robert A (1963), "Toward a Structural Definition of the Riddle" in the *Journal of American Folklore* 76 (1963), 111-8: reprinted in DUNDES (1975), 95-102.

DUSKIN (1974), *Psychology '73/'74*. Guilford: The Duskin Publishing Group Inc.

DUTSCH, Robert A. (1962), *Roget's Thesaurus on English Words and Phrases: New Edition completely revised, modernized and abridged*. Harmondsworth: Penguin books.

EBARA, Taizō (1952), *Haikaibungaku* (The Literature of Haikai). Tokyo: Kawade-shobō.

ECCLES, John C. ed. (1966), *Brain and Conscious Experience*. New York: Springer.

ECCLES, John C. (1977), *The Self and Its Brain: Part II*. in POPPER/ECCLES (1977), 227-421.

ECO, Umberto (1972), *Einführung in die Smiotik*. (UTB 105). München: Fink.

ECO, Umberto (1976), *A Theory of Semiotics*. Bloomington: Indiana U. P.

ECO, Umberto (1979), *The Role of the Reader: Explorations in the Semiotics of Texts*. London: Hutchinson, 1983.

EHLICH, K., ed. (1980), *Erzählen im Alltag*. Frankfurt a.M.:Suhrkamp.

EIBL-EIBESFELDT, Irenäus (1970), *Ethology: The Biology of Behaviour*. New York: Holt, Reinehart and Winstcn.

EIBL-EIBESFELDT, Irenäus (1979), "Ritual and Ritualization from a Biological Perspective" in CRANACH et al. eds. (1979), 3-93.

EICHENBAUM, Boris (1971), "O. Henry and the Theory of the Short Story" in MATEJKA/POMORSKA eds. (1971), 227-70.

ELIOT, T. S. (1933), *The Use of Poetry and the Use of Criticism*. London: Faber and Faber.

ELIOT, T. S. ed. (1954), *Literary Essays of Ezra Pound*. Norfolk, Conn.: A New Directions Book.

ELLMANN, Richard/O'CLAIR, Robert, eds. (1973), *The Norton Anthology of Modern Poetry*. New York: W. W. Norton & Co.

ELMORE, Andrew M./TURSKY, Bernard (1978), "The Biofeedback Hypothesis: An Idea in Search of a Theory and Method" in SUGERMAN/TARTER, eds. (1978), 130-54.

Encyclopedia Japonica Vol. 1 (1967). Tokyo: Shōgakukan.

ENGLER, R. (1973), "Rôle et place d'une sémantique dans une linguistique sassurienne" in *Cahiers Ferdinand de Saussure* 28 (1973), 35-51.

ERLICH, Victor (1965), *Russian Formalism: history-doctrine*. 2nd revised edition. The Hague: Mouton.

ESCHBACH, Achim (1979), *Pragmasemiotik und Theater: Eine Beitrag zur Theorie und Praxis einer pragmatisch orientierten Zeichenanalyse*. Tübingen: Günter Narr.

ESCHBACH, Achim/RADER, Wendelin, eds. (1980), *Literature-Semiotik I, II: Methoden-Analsen-Tendenzen*. Tübingen: Günter Narr.

ETŌ, Hiroko/KAKO, Saburō (1968), *Kotowaza, Koji, Kingen-Shōjiten* (A Small Dictionary of Proverbs, Sayings, and Aphorisms). Tokyo: Fukuinkan.

FEHMI, Lester G. (1978), "EEG Biofeedback, Multichaneel Synchrony Training, and Attension" in SUGERMAN/TARTER eds. (1978), 155-82.

FEIBLEMAN, James K. (1946), *An Introduction to the Philosophy of Charles S. Peirce*. Cambridge: The MIT P., 1970.

FENOLLOSA, Earnest (1964), *The Chinese Written Character as a Medium for Poetry*, edited by Ezra Pound. San Francisco: City Lights Books, 1968.

FENOLLOSA, Earnest/POUND, Ezra, eds. (1916), *The Classic Noh Theatre of Japan*. London: MacMillan & Co.

FISCH, Max H. (1977), "Peirce's Place in American Thought" in *Semiotica* 1/2 (1977), 21-37.

FISCHER, Roland (1978), "Cartography of Conscious States: Integration of East and West" in SUGERMAN/TARTER eds. (1978), 24-57.

FOUCAULT, Michael (1970), "The Order of Discourse" in YOUNG, ed. (1981), 48-78.

FRANK, Armin Paul (1968), "Das Bild in imagistischer Theorie und Praxis" in *Jahrbuch für Ameikastudien* 13, (1968), 174-95.

FRANK, P. (1957), *Philosophy of Science*. Englewood Cliffs: Prentice Hall.

FREGE, Gottlob (1892), "Über sinn und Bedeutung" in *Zeitschrift für Philosphie und Philosophische Kritik* 100 (1892).

FREUD, Sigmund (1901), *The Interpretation of Dreams*. New York: Basic Books, 1960.

FRIEDRICH, Wolf-Hartmut/KILLEY, Walther (1965), *Das Fischer Lexikon: Literatur II/1*. Frankfurt a.M.: Friedrich & Killey.

FRISCH, Karl von (1967), *The Dance Language and Orientation of Bees*. Cambridge: Harvard U. P.

FRISCH, Karl von (1974), *Animal Architecture*. New York: Harcout Brace Jovanovich.

FROMM, Erich (1956), *Die Kunst des Liebens*. Trans. by Liselotte and Ernst Mickel. Frankfurt a. M.: Ullstein-Materialien, 1980.

FROMM, Erich (1979), *To Have or To BE?*. Trans. by Brigitte Stein and edited by Rainer Fink: *Haben oder Sein*. Stuttgart: Deutscher Taschenbuch.

FUKUDA, Rikutarō (1962), "Japanese Elements in Western Literature" in *Yearbook of Comparative and General Literature* 11 (1962), 204-11.

FURGASON, Charles A./GARNICA, Olga K. (1975), "Theories of Phonological Development" in LENNEBERG/LENNEBERG eds. (1975), Vol. 1, 153-80.

GARDNER, Beatrice T./GARDNER, R. Allen (1971), "Two-Way Communication with an Infant Chimpanzee" in SCHRIER/STOLINITZ, eds., (1971), 117-84.

GARDNER, R. Allen/GARDNER, Beatrice T. (1969), "Teaching Sign Language to a Chimpanzee" in *Science* 165 (1969), 664-72.

GARDNER, R. Allen/Gardner, Beatrice T. (1975), "Early Signs of Language in Child and Chimpanzee" in *Science* 187 (1975), 752-3.

GAZZANIGA, M. S. (1970), *The Bisected Brain*. New York: Appleton.

GAZZANIGA, M. S./SPERRY, Roger (1967), "Language after Section of the Cerebral Commissures" in *Brain* 90 (1967), 131-48.

GELLHORN, E. (1970), "The Emotions and the Ergotropic and Trophotropic Systems" in *Psychologische Forschung* 34. (1970), 48-94.

GELLHORN, E./KIELY, W.F.(1972), "Mystical States of Consciousness: Neurophysiology and Clinical Aspects" in *Journal of Nervous and Mental Disease* 154 (1972), 399-405.

GELLHORN, E./KIELY, W. F. (1973), "Autonomic Nervous System in Psychiatric Disorder" in MENDELS ed. (1973).

GELLHORN, E./LOOFBOURROW, G. N. (1963), *Emotions and Emotional Disorders: A Neurophysiological Study*. New York: Harper & Row.

Gendai Nihon Bungaku Zenshū 91: *Gendai Haiku-shū* (1958). Tokyo: Chikuma-shobō.

GENETTE, Gérard (1972), *Figures III*. Paris: Seuil.

GENETTE, Gérard (1980), *Narrative Discourse*. Trans. by Jane E. Lewin with 'Forword' by Jonathan Culler. Oxford: Basil Blackwell.

GESCHWIND, Norman (1965), "Disconnection Syndromes in Animal and Man" in *Brain* 88 (1965), 237-94.

GESCHWIND, Norman/LEVITSKY, W. (1968), "Human Brain: Left-Right Asymmetries in Temporal Speech Regions" in *Schience* 161, (1968), 186-7.

GESCHWIND, Norman (1974), "The Development of the Brain and the Evolution of Language" in GESCHWIND (1974), 86-104.

GESCHWIND, Norman (1974), *Selected Papers on Language and the Brain.* Amsterdam: Reidel.

GIROUX, Joan (1974), *The Haiku Form.* Rutland: Charles E. Tuttle.

GLADWIN, Thomas/STURTEVANT, W. C., eds. (1962), *Anthropology and Human Behaviour.* Washington: Anthropological Society of Washington.

GLASS, Arnold L., ed. (1979), *Cognition.* Cambridge: Addison-Wesley.

GLUECK, Bernard/STROEBEL, Charles F. (1978), "Psychophysiological Correlates of Relaxation" in SUGERMAN/TARTER, eds. (1978), 99-129.

GOLDSTEIN, L./STOLTZFUS, N. W. (1973), "Psychoactive Drug-Induced Changes of Interhemispheric EEG Amplitude Relationships" in *Agents and Actions* 3 (1973), 124-32.

GRZYBEK, Peter (1983), *Neurolinguistik und Fremdsprachenerwerb: Argumente für eine Aufwertung der rechten Gehirnhälfte des Lehrners im Fremdsprachenunterricht.* Wiesbaden: Grzybek.

GUR, Raquel/GUR, Ruben (1977), "Correlates of Conjugate Lateral Eye Movements in Man" in HARNAD et al., eds. (1977), 261-81.

HACKETT James (1965-68), *Haiku Poetry: Original Verse in English,* Vol. *1-4.* Vol. 1-2: Tokyo: Hokuseido P. Vol. 3-4: Tokyo: Japan Publications.

HAHN, Martin E./SIMMEL, Edward C., eds. (1976), *Communicative Behaviour and Evolution.* New York: Academic P.

Haiku Journal (1978-80). San Jose: Yuki Teikei Haiku Society of U. S. A. and Canada.

HALL, R. A. (1960), "A Theory of Graphemics" in *Acta Linguistica* 8 (1960), 13-20.

HAMMITZSCH, Horst (1953), "Ein Reisetagebuch von Matsuo Bashō" in *Nachrichten der Deutschen Gesellschaft für Natur- und Völkerkunde Ostasiens* 75 (1953), 3-24.

HAMMITZSCH, Horst (1954), "Vier Haibun des Matsuo Bashō" in *Sinologica* 4 (1954), 2, 102-22.

HAMMITZSCH, Horst (1957), "Zum Begriff 'Weg' im Rahmen der japanischen Künste" in *Nachrichten der Deutschen Gesellschaft für Natur- und Völkerkunde Ostasiens* 82 (1957), 5-14.

HARADA, Tomohiko (1980), "Nō, Kyōgen no keisei to sono shakai-teki kaikei" (The Formation of Nō and Kyōgen and Its Social Backgrounds) in KOYAMA et al., eds. (1980), 144-52.

HARDWICK, Charles S., ed. (1977), *Semiotics and Significs: the Correspondence between charles S. Peirce and victoria Lady Welby.* Bloomington: Indiana U. P.

HARNAD, Stevan/DOTY, Robert W. (1977), "Introductory Overview" in HARNAD et al., eds. (1977), xvii-xLviii.

HARNAD, Stevan/DOTY, Robert W./GOLDSTEIN, Leonide/JAYNES, Julian/KRAUTHAMER, George, eds. (1977), *Lateralization in the Nervous System.* New York: Academic P.

HARNAD, Stevan R/STEKLIS, Horst D./LANCASTER, Jane, eds. (1976), *Origins and Evolution of Language and Speech*. New York: The New York Academy of Science.

HARTSHORNE, Charles/WEISS, Paul, eds. (1931), *Collected Papers of Charles Sanders Peirce*, Vol. 1-2. Cambridge: Harvard U. P., 1965.

HATTORI, Dohō (1776), *Sanzōshi*: reprinted in *Nihon Koten Bungaku Zenshū (NKBZ) 51: Rengaron-shū, Nōgakuron-shū, Haironshū* (1973), 519-624.

HAWKES, Terence (1977), *Structuralism and Semiotics*. London: Methuen & Co.

HAYASHIYA; Tatsusaburō/NAKAMURA, Masao/HAYASHIYA, Seizō (1974), *Japanese Arts and the Tea Ceremony*. New York: Weatherhill.

HEIN, Norbert (1976), "Ansatz zur strukturellen Dramenanalyse" in KOCH, ed. (1976), 119-213.

HELMERS, Hermann (1967), "Die Entwicklung von Sprache und Humor" in *Schule und Psychologie* 14 (1967), 186-96: reprinted in HELMERS, ed. (1969), 479-95.

HELMERS, Hermann, ed. (1969), *Zur Sprache des Kindes: Wege der Forschung. 42.* Darmstadt: Wissenschaftliche Buchgesellschaft.

HENDERSON, Harold Gould (1934), *The Bamboo Broom: An Introduction to Japanese Haiku*. Boston: Houghton Mifflin Co.

HENDERSON, Harold Gould (1965), *Haiku in English*. Rutland: Charles E. Tuttle, 1967.

HENDRICKS, William O. (1977), "'A Rose for Emily': A Syntagmatic Analysis" in *A Journal for Descriptive Poetics and Theory of Literature* 2 (1977), 257-95.

HENNIG, Karl (1980), *Japanische Gartenkunst: Form-Geschichte-Geisteswelt*. Köln: Du Mont.

HERRIGEL, Eugen (1953), *Zen in the Art of Archery*. New York: Pantheon.

HERRIGEL, Eugen (1958), *Der Zen-Weg*. München: Otto-Wilhelm-Barth.

HEUVEL, Cor VAN DEN: see VAN DEN HEUVEL.

HEWES, Gordon H. (1973), "Primate Communication and the Gestural Origin of Languaguage" in *Current Anthropology* 14 (1973), 1-12.

HEWES, Gordon H. (1974), "Language in Early Hominids" in WESCOTT, ed. (1974), 1-34.

HEWES, Gordon H. (1976), "The Current Status of the Gestural Theory of Language Origin" in HARNAD et al., eds. (1976), 482-504.

HIBBET, Howard S. (1960/61), "The Japanese Comic Linked Verse Tradition" in *Harvard Journal of Asiatic Studies* 23 (1960/61), 76-92.

HIRAI, T. (1960), "Electroencephalographic Study on Zen Meditation (zazen): EEG Changes during the Concentrated Relaxation" in *Psychiatria et Neurologica* 62 (1960), 76-105.

HIRAI, T. (1974), *Psychophysiology of Zen*. Tokyo: Igaku Shoin.

HISAMATSU, Shin'ichi (1971), *Zen and the Fine Arts*. Tokyo: Kōdansha International.

HJELMSLEV, Louis (1943), *Prolegomena to a Theory of Language*.
Madison: U. of Wisconsin, 1961.

HJELMSLEV, Louis (1959), *Essais linguistiques (Travaux du Cercle Linguistic de Copenhague)*. Copenhagen: Nordisk Sprogog Kultur.

HOLENSTEIN, Elmar (1974), "A New Essay Concerning the Basic Relations of Language in *Semiotica* 12 (1974), 97-128.

HOLENSTEIN, Elmar (1975), *Roman Jakobsons phänomenologischer Strukturalismus*. Frankfurt a. M.: Suhrkamp.

HOLENSTEIN, Elmar (1978), "Semiotic Philogsophy" in BAILEY et al., eds. (1978), 43-67.

HORI, Nobuo (1972), *Annotations to Bashō's Haiku* in *NKBZ 41, Matsuo Bashō-shū* (1972), 45-156.

HRDLIČKOVÁ, V. (1969), "Japanese Professional Storytellers" in *Genre* 2 (1969), 179-210.

HULLET, E. J. Jr. (1966), "A Symbolic Interactionist Model of Human Communication" in *AV-Communication Review* 14 (1966), 5-33.

HYMES, Dell (1962), "The Ethnography of Speaking" in GLADWIN et al., eds. (1962), 13-53.

ICHIKAWA, Sanki et al.; see The Nippon Gakujutsu Shinkōkai.

IHWE, Jens, ed. (1972), *Literaturwissenschaft und Linguistik*, 2 Vols. Frankfurt a. M.: Ihwe.

IKEGAMI, Yoshihiko (1981), *"Suru" to "Naru" no gengogaku: Gengo to Bunka no taiporojī e no shiron* (A Linguistic Study of "Do" and "BECOME" : Hypotheses of a Typology of Language and Culture). Tokyo: Taishūkan.

IMOTO, Nōichi (1972), *Annotations to Bashō's Haiku* in *NKBZ 41, Matsuo Bashō-shū* (1972), 156-270, 272-4, 280-2.

IVANOV, Vjačeslav Vsevolodovič (1977), *Gerade und Ungerade: Die Asymmetrie des Gehirns und der Zeichensysteme*. Trans. by Winfried Petri. Stuttgart: Hirzel, 1983.

IVANOV, Vjačeslav Vsevolodovič /TOPOLOV, Vladimir Nikolaevič (1982), "Die Struktur-typologischer Vorgehensweise in der semantischen Interpretation von Werken der bildenden Kunst unter diachronem Aspekt" in *Zeitschrift für Semiotik* 4 (1982), 55-92.

JACOBSON, Stanley (1972), "Cranial Nerves" in CURTIS et al. (1972), 236-59.

JACOBSON, Stanley (1972), "Hypothalamus and Autonomic Nervous System" in CURTIS et al. (1972), 386-95.

JAKOBSON, Roman (1941), *Kindersprache, Aphasie und allgemeine Lautgesetze*. Trans. by Allan R. Eiler: *Child Language, Aphasia, and Phonological Universals*. The Hague: Mouton, 1968.

JAKOBSON, Roman (1960), "Closing Statement: Linguistics and Poetics" in SEBEOK, ed. (1960), 350-77.

JAKOBSON, Roman (1967), "Conversazione sul cinema con Roman Jakobson a cura di Adriano Aprâe Luigi Faccini" in *Cinema e Film* 2 (1967), 154-62.

JAKOBSON, Roman (1971), *Studies on Child Language and Aphasia*. The Hague-Paris: Mouton.

JAKOBSON, Roman (1976), "What is Poetry?" in MATEJKA/TITUNIK, eds. (1976), 164-75.

JAKOBSON, Roman (1978), *Sound and Meaning*. Hassocks: The Harvester P.

JAKOBSON, Roman (1980), *The Framework of Language*. Michigan Studies in the Humanities.

JAKOBSON, Roman/BOGATYREV, Petr (1929), "Die Folklore als besondere Form des Schaffens" in *Donum Natalicium Schrijnen: Verzameling van Opstellen door Oud-leerlingen en Bevriende Vakgenooten opgedragen aan Mgr. Prof. Dr. Jos. Schrijnen.* Nijmegen-Utrecht: Dekker, 900-13.

JAKOBSON, Roman/WAUGH, Linda (1979), *The Sound Shape of Language*. Bloomington: Indiana U.P.

JANTSCH, E. /WADDINGTON, C. H., eds. (1976), *Education and Consciousness: Human Systems in Transition*. Reading: Addison-Wesley.

Japanese-English Buddhist Dictionary (1965). Tokyo: Daitō.

JEKOSCH, Ute (1982), "Syncretism and Gestalt in Psychogenesis" in KOCH, ed. (1982b), 252-73.

JOHNSON, Barbara (1981), "The Critical Difference: Balzac's 'Sarrasine' and 'Barthes's 'S/Z'" in YOUNG, ed. (1981), 162-74.

JOHNSTON, W. (1971), *The Still Point*. New York: Perennial Library, Forham U.P, Haper & Row.

JOLLES, André (1930), *Einfache Formen*. Tübingen: Max Niemeyer, 1974.

KANDA,Hideo (1958), "Gendai Haiku Shōshi" (A Brief History of Modern Haiku) in *Gendai Haiku-shū, Gendai Nihon Bungaku Zenshū 91* (1958), 424-38.

KANNELLAKOS, Demetri P./LUCAS, Jerome S. (1974), *The Psychobiology of Transcendental Meditation: A Literature Review*. Menlo Park: Benjamin.

KAPLEAU, Philip (1966), *The Three Pillars of Zen*. New York: Harper & Row.

KASAMATSU, A. (1957), "Electroencephalography and East Meditation" in *Psychosomatic* (1957), 73-88.

KASAMATSU, A./HIRAI T. (1966), "An Electroencephalographic Study on the Zen Meditation (zazen)" in *Folia Psychiatrica et Neurologica Japonica* 20 (1966), 49-52.

KASAMATSU, A./HIRAI T./IZAWA, H. (1962), "Medical and Psychological Studies on Zen" in *Proceedings of the 26th Convention of Japanese Psychological Assoication* 33 (1962).

KASAMATSU, A./HIRAI,T./IZAWA,H. (1963), "Medical and Psychological Study of Zen" in *Proceedings of the 27th Convention of Japanese Psychological Association* 34 (1963).

KASANIN, J. S., ed.(1944), *Language and Thought in Schizophrenia: Collected Papers*. Barkley: U. of California P., 104-14.

KEENE, Donald (1955), *Japanese Literature: An Introduction for Western Readers*. Rutland: Charles E. Tuttle.

KEENE, Donald (1966), *Nō: The Classical Theatre of Japan*. Tokyo: Kōdansha International.

KELLOG, Rhoda (1969), *Analyzing Children's Art*. Palo Alto: Mayfield.

KHERDIAN, David (1969), *Six San Francisco Poets*. Fresno:

KIMURA, Doreen (1967), "Functional Asymmetry of the Brain in Dichotic Listening" in *Cortex* 3 (1967), 163-78.

KIMURA, Doreen (1976), "The Neural Basis of Language Qua Gesture" in WHITAKER/WHITAKER, eds. (1976), 145-56.

KINDAICHI, Haruhiko (1979), "Introductory Comments" in ASANO/ KINDAICHI (1979), 1-23.

KIRSHENBLATT-GIMBLETT, Barbara, ed. (1976), *Speech Play: Research and Resources for Studying Linguistic Creativity*. Philadelphia: U. of Pennsylvania.

KLAUS, G. (1966), *Kybernetik und Erkenntnistheorie*. Berlin: Deutscher Verlag der Wissenschaften.

KLEIN, K. P. (1980), "Erzählen im Unterricht. Erzähltheoretische Aspekte einer Erzähldidaktik" in EHLICH, ed. (1980), 263-95.

KOCH, Annemarie (1982), "Brain and Language" in KOCH, ed. (1982b), 141-60.

KOCH, Vivienne (1950), *William Carlos Williams: The Maker of Modern Literature*. Norfork: new Direction.

KOCH, Walter A. (1966), *Recurrence and a Three-Modal Approach to Poetry*. The Hague: Mouton.

KOCH, Walter A. (1971), *Varia Semiotica*. Hildesheim: Olms.

KOCH, Walter A. (1971a), *Taxologie des Englischen*. München: Fink.

KOCH, Walter A. (1972), *Strukturelle Textanalyse*. Hildesheim: Olms.

KOCH, Walter A. (1973), *Das Textem*. Hildesheim: Olms.

KOCH, Walter A. ed. (1973a), *Perspektiven der Linguistik I*. Stuttgart: Kröner.

KOCH, Walter A. (1974), "Tendenzen der Linguistik" in KOCH, ed. (1974b), 190-311.

KOCH, Walter A. (1974a), "Semiotik und Sprachgenese" in KOCH, ed. (1974b), 312-46.

KOCH, Walter A., ed. (1974b), *Perspektiven der Linguistik II*. Stuttgart: Kröner.

KOCH, Walter A., ed. (1976), *Textsemiotik und strukturelle Rezeptionstheorie*. Hildesheim: Olms.

KOCH, Walter A. (1978), "Poetizität zwischen Metaphysik und Metasprache" in *Poetica* 10 (1978), 285-341.

KOCH, Walter A. (1981), "Evolution des Kreativen: Symmetrie, Asymmetrie, Integration - Hypothesen zum gegenseitigen Verständnis von Welt, Gehirn und Kreativität" in SCHNELLE, ed. (1981), 158-73.

KOCH, Walter A. (1981a), "Poetizität: das Triviale des Triadischen" in *Poetica* 14 (1982), 250-69.

KOCH, Walter A.(1982), "Semiogenesis: Some Perspectives for Its Analysis" in KOCH, ed. (1982b), 15-104.

KOCH, Walter A . (1982a), "The Biogenesis of Language, Literature, and Art: some Principles for Its Reconstructuon" in KOCH, ed. (1982b), 447-80.

KOCH, Walter A. ed. (1982b), *Semiogenesis: Essays on the Analysis of the Genesis of Language, Art, and Literature*. Bern: Peter Lang.

KOCH, Walter A. (1982c), "Tension and Suspense: On the Biogenesis and the Semiogenesis of the Detective Novel, Soccer, and Art" in BALLMER, ed. (in print).

KOCH, Walter A. (1983), *Poetry and Science: Semiogenetic Twins -- Towards an Integrated Correspondence Theory of Poetic Structures*. Tübingen: Günter Narr.

KOCH, Walter A. (1983a), "The Poetics of Evolution and the Evolution of Poetics: Ten Hypotheses on an Integrated Correspondence Theory of Poetry and Science" in MS.

KÖHLER, Wolfgang (1947), *Gestalt Psychology: An Introduction to New Concepts in Modern Psychology*. New York: Liverlight.

KÖLLER, Wilhelm (1980), "Der Peircesche Denkansatz als Grundlage für die Literatursemiotik" in ESCHBACH/RADER, eds. (1980), 39-64.

KÖNGÄS-MARANDA, Elli/MARANDA, Pierre (1971), *Structural Models in Folklore and Transformational Essays*. The Hague: Mouton.

KÖNGÄS-MARANDA, Elli (1972), *Theory and Practices of Riddle Analysis*. Urbino: Centro Internazionale di Semiotica e di Linguistica - Documents de travail, No. 11.

KOENIG, Otto (1970), *Kultur und Verhaltensforschung: Einführung in die Kulturethology*. München: Deutscher Tschenbuch Verlag.

KOESTLER, Arthur (1964), *The Act of Creation*. London: Pan Books.

KOESTLER, Arthur (1978), *Der Mensch - Irrläufer der Evolution (Janus: A Summing-up)*. München: Scherz.

KOFFKA, K. (1935), *Principles of Gestalt Psychology*. London: Routledge & Kegan Paul.

KOHEN, Alfred (1935), *The Way of Japanese Flower Arrangement*. London: Kegan Paul, Trench, Trubner, Co.

KOMIYA, Toyotaka/YOKOZAWA Saburō/OGATA, Tsutomu, eds. (1959), *Haiku·Hairon: Nihon Koten Kanshō Kōza 19*. Tokyo: Kadokawa.

KONISHI, Jin'ichi (1960), *Bashō to Gūgensetsu (Bashō and the Theory of Allegory)*. Tokyo: Nihon Gakushiin Kiyō.

KŌNO, Rokurō (1981), *Kōno Rokurō chosaku-shū 3: Mojiron. Zassan*. Tokyo: Heibonsha.

KŌNOSU, Hayao (1971), *The Edition and Annotation of Kayō in NKBZ 1: Kojiki, Jōdai-kayō* (1971), 371-509.

KOYAMA, Hiroshi/KIRIHATA, Takeshi/HARADA, Tomohiko, eds. (1980), *Zusetsu Nihon no Koten: Nō· Kyōgen*. Tokyo: Shūeisha.

KREITLER, Hans/KREITLER, Shulamith (1972), *Psycholgy of the Arts*. Durham: Duke U. P.

KRISTEVA, Julia (1974), *La Révolution du language poetique*. Paris: Seuil.

KRISTEVA, Julia (1980), *Desire in Language: A Semioitc Approach to Literature and Art*. Trans. by Thomas Gora/ Alice Jardine/Leon S. Roudiez and edited by Leon S. Roudiez. Oxford: Basil Blackwell.

KROEPSCH, Rainer A. (1976), "Zur strukturellen Theorie der Massenkommunikation" in KOCH, ed. (1976), 214-355.

KUBOTA, Harutsugu (1968), *Dasshutsu no Bungaku: Bashō o meguru Kindai-sakka-tachi* (The Literature of Exodus: Modern Writers around Bashō). Tokyo: Ōfūsha.

KURIYAMA, Riichi (1963), *Haikai-shi* (A History of Haikai). Tokyo: Haniwa, 1978.

KURIYAMA, Riichi (1972), "Kaisetsu" (Elucidation) in *NKBZ 42: Kinsei Haiku-Haibun-shū* (1972), 9-42.

KURIYAMA, Riichi (1973), "Kaisetsu" (Elucidation) in *NKBZ 51: Rengaron-shū· Nōgakuron-shū· Hairon-shū* (1973), 409-18.

KURIYAMA, Riichi (1973), *The Annotation and Translation of Hairon-shū* in *NKBZ 51* (1973), 419-629.

KURIYAMA, Riichi/MARUYAMA, Kazuhiko/YAMASHITA, Kazumi, eds. (1972), *Kinsei Haiku·Haibun-shū: NKBZ 42* (1972), 49-452.

LAMSON, June E. (1979), "Yuki Teikei: Freedom in 'Discipline'" in *Haiku Journal* (1979), 66-68.

LASZLO, Ervin (1972), *Introduction to Systems Philosophy*. New York: Gordon and Breach.

LAUGHLIN, C./D'AQUILI, Eugene (1974), *Biogenetic Structuralism*. New York: Columbia U. P.

LAUGHLIN, Charles D./McMANUS, John (1979), "Mamalian Ritual" in D'AQUILI et al., eds. (1979), 80-116.

LAUGHLIN, Charles D. Jr.,/McMANUS, John/D'AQUILI, Eugene G. (1979), "Introduction" in D'AQUILI et al., eds. (1979), 1-50.

LEAKY, Richard E. (1981), *Die Suche nach den Menschen: Wie wir wurden, was wir sind*. Frankfurt a. M.: Umschau.

LENNEBERG, Erich H. (1967), *Biological Foundations of Language*. New York: Wiley.

LENNEBERG, Erich H. (1975), "The Concept of Language Differentiation" in LENNEBERG/LENNEBERG, eds. (1975), 17-33.

LENNEBERG, Erich H. /LENNEBERG, Elizabeth, eds. (1975), *Foundations of Language Developement: A Multidisciplinary Approach. 2 Vols*. New York: Academic P.

LEONDAR, Barbara (1977), "Hatching Plots: Genesis of Story-making" in PERKINS/LEONDAR, eds. (1977), 172-91.

LEVI-AGRESTI, JERRY/SPERRY, Roger (1968), "Differential Perceptual Capacities in Major and Minor Hemispheres" in *Proceedings of the National Academy of Science* 61 (1968).

LEVI-STRAUSS, Claude (1958), *Anthropologie structurale*. Trans. into English: *Structural Anthropology*. New York: Basic Books, 1963.

LEVI-STRAUSS, Claude (1962), *Le Totémisme aujourd'hui*. Trans. into English: *Totemism*. London-Chicago: U. of Chicago P., 1964.

LEVI-STRAUSS, Claude (1962a), *La Pensée sauvage*. Trans. into English: *The Savage Mind*. London-Chicago: U.of Chicago P., 1966.

LEVI-STRAUSS, Claude (1964), *Le Cru et le cuit: Mythologiques I*. Trans. into English:*The Raw and the Cooked*. London-New York: Cape, 1970.

LEVI-STRAUSS, Claude (1967), *Du miel aux cendres: Mythologigues II*. Trans. into English: *From Honey to Ashes*. London-New York: Cape, 1973.

LEVI-STRAUSS, Claude (1968), *L'Origine des manieres de table Mythologiques III*. Trans. into English: *The Origin of Table Manners*. London-New York: Cape, 1978.

LEVI-STRAUSS, Claude (1971), *L'Homme nu: Mythologiques IV*. Trans. into German: *Der nackte Mensch 1-2*. Frankfurt a. M.: Suhrkamp.

LEVI-STRAUSS, Claude (1973), *Anthropologie structurale deux*. Trans. into German: *Strukturale Anthropologie II*. Frankfurt: Suhrkamp.

LEWANDOWSKI, Theodor (1979), *Linguistiches Wörterbuch*. Heidelberg: Quelle & Meyer.

LEWIN, Bruno (1959), *Abriss der japanischen Grammatik: zweite, verbesserte Auflage*. Wiesbaden: Harrassowitz, 1975.

LEWIN, Bruno (1969), "Literarische Begegnung zwischen Amerika und Japan" in *Jahrbuch für Amerikastudien* 14 (1969), 25-39.

LEWIS, Philip, E. (1974), "Revolutionary Semiotics" in *Diacritics*. Fall (1974), 28-32.

LEX, Barbara W. (1979), "The Neurobiology of Ritual Trance" in D'AQUILI et al., eds. (1979), 117-51.

LIBERMAN, A. M. (1974), "The Specialization of the Language Hemisphere" in SCHMITT et al., eds. (1974), 43-56.

LINDEN, Eugene (1980), *Die Kolonie der sprechenden Schimpansen*. Wien: Meyster.

LINDSLEY, D. B. (1952), "Psychological Phenomena and the Electroencephalogram" in *Electroencephalography and Clinical Neurophysiology* 4 (1952), 443-56.

LIVANOV, M. N./GAVRILOVA, N. A./ASLANOV, A. S. (1973), "Correlations of Biopotentials in the Frontal Parts of the Human Brain" in PRIBRAM/LURIA, eds. (1973), 91-108.

LORENZ, Konrad (1959), "Gestaltwahrnehmung als Quelle wissenschaftlicher Erkenntnis" in *Zeitschrift für experimentelle und angewandte Psychologie* 4 (1959), 118-65: reprinted in LORENZ (1965), 2. Vol., 255-300.

LORENZ, Konrad (1965), *Über tierisches und menschliches Verhalten: Aus dem Werdegang der Verhaltenslehre, 2 Vols.* München: Piper.

LORENZ, Konrad (1966), *On Aggression*. London: Methuen.

LORENZ, Konrad (1967), "Biologie von Ausdruck und Eindruck" in LORENZ/LEYHAUSEN (1971), 292-407.

LORENZ, Konrad (1973), *Die Rückseite des Spiegels: Versuch einer Naturgeschichte menschlichen Erkennens* München: Piper: Trans. into English: *Behind the Mirror: A Search for a Natural History of Human Knowledge.* New York: A. Helen and Kurt Wolff Book, 1977.

LORENZ, Konrad/LEYHAUSEN, Paul (1971), *Antriebe tierischen und menschlichen Verhaltens: Gesammelte Abhandlungen.* München: Piper.

THE LOS ALTOS WRITERS ROUNDTABLE (1966), *Borrowed Water: A Book of American Haiku.* Rutland: Charles E. Tuttle, 1973.

LOTMAN, Jurij M. (1964), *Lektsii po struktural'noy poetike.* Tartu.

LOTMAN, Jurij M. (1970), "Observations on the Structure of the Narrative Text" in *Soviet Studies in Literature.* IASP X, 4 (1974), 75-81.

LOTMAN, Jurij M. (1975), "On the Metalanguage of a Typological Description of Culture" in *Semiotica* 14/2 (1975), 97-123.

LOTMAN, Jurij M. (1976), *Semiotics of Cinema.* Trnas. from Russian and forworded by Mark E. Suino. Ann Arbor: U. of Mischigan, Dep. of Slavic Languages and Literature.

LOTMAN, Jurij M. (1976a), *Analysis of the Poetic Text.* Ann Arbor: Ardis.

LOTMAN, Jurij M./USPENSKIJ, B. A./IVANOV, V. V./TOPOROV, V. N./PJATIGORSKIJ, A. M. (1975), *Theses on the Semiotics Study of Culture (as Applied to Slavic Texts).* Lisse: de Ridder.

LOWELL, Amy (1925), *What's O'Clock?* New York: Houghton Mifflin.

LUCE, G. G. (1971), *Biological Rhythms in Human and Animal Psychology.* New York: Dover Pub.

LUDWIG, A. M. (1966), "Altered State of Consciousness" in *Archieves of General Psychiatry* 15 (1966), 225-34.

LURIA, A. R. (1966), *Higher Cortical Fucntions in Man.* New York: Basic Books.

LURIA, A. R. (1973), "The Frontal Lobes and the Regulation of Behaviour" in PRIBRAM/LURIA, eds. (1973), 3-28.

LUTHE, W. ed. (1965), *Autogenic Training: International Edition.* New York: Grune and Stratton.

McCLAIN, Yoko (1981), *Handbook of Modern Japanese Grammer.* Tokyo: The Hokuseido P.

MÄLL, L. (1964), "K rekonstruktsii pervonachal'nogo Buddhizma" in *Programma i tezisy dokladov v letney shkole po vtorichnym modeliruyushchim sistemam* (1964), 29.

MÄLL, L. (1965), "Nulevoy put" in *Trudy po znakovym sistemam* II (1965), 189-91.

MÄLL, L. (1968), "Dharma i znak" in *III letnyaya shkola po vtorichnym modeliruyushchim sistemam: tezisy* (1968), 6-7.

MÄLL, L. (1968a), "K osnovam liziologii" in *III letnyaya shkola po vtorichnym modeliruyushchim sistemam: tezisy* (1968), 249.

MÄLL, L. (1968b), "Une approche possible du Sunyavada" in *Tel Quel* 32 (1968), 54-62.

MAHARISHI MAHESH Yogi (1966), *The Science of Being and the Art of Living*. London: SRM Publications.

MAKI, S. (1972), *A Pschological Study on the Posture during Zen Meditation: A Master's Thesis in the Komazawa University*. Tokyo: Komazawa University.

MALTESE, Corrado (1970), *Semiologia del messagio oggettuale*. Milano:Mursia.

Man'yōshū (759?): see *Nihon Koten Bungaku Zenshū* 2.

MARANDA, Pierre (1974), *French Kinship: Structure and History*. The Hague-Paris: Mouton.

MARCUS, Elliott M. (1972), "Cerebral Cortex: Functional Localization" in CURTIS et al. (1972), 483-535.

MARCUS, Elliott M. (1972a), "Cerebral Cortex: Cytoarchitecture and Electrophysiology" in CURTIS et al. (1972), 447-82.

MARUYAMA, Kazuhiko (1972), *Annotations to Haiku* in *Kinsei Haiku-shū: NKBZ 42* (1972), 347-452.

MARTENS, Karin, ed. (1979), *Kindliche Kommunikation: Theoretische Perspektiven, empirische Analysen, methodologische Grundlagen*. Frankfurt a. M.: Suhrkamp.

MASAOKA, Shiki (1892), *Dassai-Shooku Haiwa* (Discussions on Haiku in Dassai-Shooku): reprinted in *Nihon Kindai Bungaku Taikei (NKBT) 16: Masaoka Shiki-shū* (1972), 138-43.

MASAOKA, Shiki (1893), "Bashō-zatsudan" (Colloquy on Bashō): reprinted in *NKBT 16: Masaoka Shiki-shū* (1972), 146-89.

MASAOKA, Shiki (1894), "Waka to Haiku" (Waka and Haiku): reprinted in *NKBT 16: Masaoka Shiki-shū* (1972), 213-8.

MASAOKA, Shiki (1895), "Haikai-taiyō" (A Survey of Haikai) in *Shiki-zenshū Vol. 4* (1925), 301-91.

MASAOKA, Shiki (1896), "Haiku 24-tai" (The 24 Categories of Haiku) in *Shiki-zenshū*

MASAOKA, Shiki (1896a), "Meiji 29-nen no haiku-kai" (The Haiku-World of the 29th Year of Meiji" in *Shiki-zenshū Vol. 4*, (1925), 511-49.

MASAOKA, Shiki (1896b), "Waga Haiku" (My Haiku) in *Shiki-zenshū Vol. 4* (1925), 456-76.

MASAOKA, Shiki (1897), "Haijin Buson" (Buson, a Haiku Poet) in *Shiki-zenshū Vol. 4* (1925), 624-99.

MASAOKA, Shiki (1897a), "Haiku Bunrui" (A Classification of Haiku) in *Shiki-zenshū, Vol 11-13* (1925).

MASAOKA, Shiki (1899), "Haiku Shimpa no Keikō" (New Trends in the New School of Haiku) in *NKBT 16:M. Shikishū* (1972),346-60.

MASAOKA, Shiki (1892-99), *Shiki zenshū: 14 Vols.* Tokyo: Arusu, 1925.

MASAOKA, Shiki (1972), *Nihon Kindai Bungaku Taikei 16: Masaoka Shiki-shū*. Tokyo: Kadokawa.

MATEJKA, Ladislav (1976), "Postscript: Prague School Semiotics" in MATEJKA/TITUNIK, eds. (1976), 265-90.

MATEJKA, Ladislav (1978), "The Roots of Russian Semiotics of Art" in BAILEY et al., eds. (1978), 146-72.

MATEJKA, Ladislav/POMORSKA, Krystyna, eds. (1971), *Readings in Russian Poetics: Formalist and Structuralist Views:* Cambridge: The MIT P.

MATEJKA, Ladislav/TITUNIK, Irwin R., eds. (1976), *Semiotics of Art: Prague School Contributions:* Cambridge: The MIT P.

MATSUI, Toshihiko (1965), *Kindai Hairon-shi*. Tokyo: Ōfūsha.

MATSUI, Toshihiko (1972), "Masaoka Shiki-shū Kaisetsu" (An Introduction to the Collection of Masaoka Shiki) in *NKBT 16: Masaoka Shiki-shū* (1972), 7-34.

MATSUO, Bashō (1693),"Kyoriku ribetsu no kotoba"/"Saimon no Kotoba" (A Farewell to Kyoriku/ A Farewell at the Gate of Saimon) in *Nihon Koten Bungaku Zenshū 41: Matsuo Basho-shū* (1972), 541-2.

MATSUO, Bashō (1694), *Oku no hosomichi* (The Narrow Path in the Northern Provinces) in *NKBZ 41: Matsuo Bashō-shū* (1972), 341-68.

MATSUO, Bashō (1709), *Oi no kobumi* (The Records of a Travel Worn Satchel) in *NKBZ 41: Matsuo Bashō-shū* (1972), 309-33.

MATSUO, Bashō (1972), *Nihon Koten Bungaku Zenshū 41: Matsuo Bashō-shū* (A Selection of Bashō's Prose and Poetry): edited and annotated by HORI, Nobuo/IMOTO, Nōichi/MURAMATSU, Tomotsugu). Tokyo: Shōgakukan.

MATSUO, Bashō (1974), *A Haiku Journey:"Bashō's Narrow Road to the Far North"and Selected Haiku*. Trans. by Dorothy Britton. Tokyo: Kōdansha, 1980.

MENDELS, J. ed. (1973), *Biological Psychiatry*. New York: Wiley.

MENIG-PETERSON, C. L./McCABE, A. (1978), "Children's Orientation of a Listener to the Context of Their Narratives" in *Developmental Psychology* 14. 6 (1978), 582-92.

MERWIN, W. S. (1973), *Asian Figures*. New York: Atheneum.

MESAROVIČ, Mihajlo D. ed. (1968), *Systems Theory and Biology*. Berlin: Springer.

MILNER, Esther (1967), *Human Neural and Behavioral Development: A Relational Inquiry, with Implications for Personality*. Springfield: Charles C. Thomas.

MILNER, Esther (1976), "CNS Maturation and Language Acquistion" in WHITAKER/WHITAKER, eds. (1976), 31-102.

MINER, Earl Roy (1955), "The Technique of Japanese Poetry" in *Hudson Review* 8 (1955), 350-66.

MINER, Earl Roy (1958), *The Japanese Tradition in British and American Literature.* Westport: Greenwood P., 1976.

MINER, Earl Roy (1979), *Japanese Linked Poetry: An Account with Translations of Renga and Haikai Sequences.* Princeton: Princeton U. P.

MIYAMORI, Asatarō (1932), *Anthology of Haiku: Ancient and Modern.* Tokyo: Maruzen.

MIYAMORI, Asatarō (1956), *Masterpieces of Japanese Poetry: Ancient and Modern.* Tokyo: Taiseidō.

MOERK, Ernst L. (1977), *Pragmatic and Semantic Aspects of Early Language Development.* Baltimore: University Park P.

MOHR, Wolfgang (1958), "Einfache Formen" in *Reallexikon der deutschen Literaturgeschichte.* Established by Paul Merker/Wolgang Stammler. 2. edition. Vol. 1. Berlin: Kohlschmidt & Mohr.

MOLES, Abraham (1977), "Superzeichenbildung und Problemlösung in der künstlerischen Kommunkation" in POSNER/REINECKE, eds. (1977), 69-106.

MONTAGU, Ashley (1972), "Sociogenic Brain Damage" in *American Anthropologist* 74 (1972), 1045-61.

MORRIS, Charles (1932), *Six theories of Mind.* Chicago: U. of Chicago P.

MORRIS, Charles (1946), *Signs, Language, and Behavior.* New York: George Braziller, 1955.

MOTOYAMA, Gyokushu (1978), "Regional Saijiki" in *Haiku Journal* (1978), 34-5.

MUKAI, Kyorai (1776), *Kyoraishō in Nihon Koten Bungaku Zenshū 51: Rengaron-shū. Nōgakuron-shū. Hairon-shū* (1973),421-515.

MUKAŘOVSKÝ, Jan (1976), "Art as Semiotic Fact" in MATEJKA/ TITUNIK, eds. (1976), 3-10.

MUKAŘOVSKÝ, Jan (1976a), "Poetic Reference" in MATEJKA/TITUNIK, eds. (1976), 155-63.

MUKAŘOVSKÝ, Jan (1976b), "The Essence of the Visual Arts" in MATEJKA/TITUNIK, eds. (1976), 229-44.

MUNSTERBERG, Hugo (1965), *Zen Kunst.* Köln: Du Mont, 1978.

MURAYAMA, Shichirō (1978), *Nihongo keitō no tankyū* (The Quest of the Genealogy of the Japanese Language).Tokyo: Taishūkan.

NADIN, Mihai (1981), "Book Review" of *A Semiotic Landscape/ Panorama Sémiotique*, CHATMAN et al. (1979), The Hague: Mouton, in *Kodikas/Code* 3/4 (1981), 373-5.

NAGASHIMA, Chosetsu (1977), "The Physiological Considerations on the Relationship among Extracellular Fluid of Cerebral Cortex, Hypo- or Hyperventilation and PaCO^2 from the View point of Zazen" in AKISHIGE, ed. (1977), 156-9.

NAGASHIMA, Chosetsu/IKAWA, Yukio/AKISHIGE, Yoshiharu (1977), "Studies on 'Jōsoku'" in AKISHIGE, ed. (1977), 153-5.

NAKAGAWA, Atsuo (1976), *Studies on English Haiku*. Tokyo: The Hokuseido P.

NAKAMURA, Shunyō (1970), *Haikai-shi no shomondai* (Various Aspects of Haikai). Tokyo: Kasama-shoin.

NAKAMURA, T. (1972), "Psychological Study on the Problems of Self-Regulation". *Proceedings of the 39th Convention of JAAP* (1972), 75-6.

NEHER, A. (1962), "A Physiological Explanation of Unusual Behaviour in Ceremonies Involving Drums" in *Human Biology*, 34 (1962), 151-61.

Nihon Kindai Bungaku Taikei 16: see MASAOKA (1972).

Nihon Kokugo Daijiten (1973). Tokyo: Shōgakukan.

Nihon Koten Bungaku Zenshū 1: Kojiki·Jōdai-kayō (712). Edited and annotated by OGIWARA, A./KŌNOSU H. Tokyo: Shōgakukan, 1972.

Nihon Koten Bungaku Zenshū 2: Man'yōshū (759?). Edited and annotated by KOJIMA, Noriyuki/KONOSHITA, Masatoshi/SATAKE, Akihiro. Tokyo: Shōgakukan, 1972.

Nihon Koten Bungaku Zenshū 41: see MATSUO (1972).

Nihon Koten Bungaku Zenshū 42: Kinsei Haiku·Haibun-shū (ca. 1550-1850). Edited and annotated by KURIYAMA, Riichi/YAMASHITA, Kazumi/MARUYAMA, Kazuhiko/MATSUO, Yasuaki. Tokyo: Shōgakukan, 1972

Nihon Koten Bungaku Zenshū 51: Rengaron-shū·Nōgakuron-shū· Hairon-shū (1345-1776). Edited and annotated by IJICHI, Tetsuo/ OMOTE, Akira/KURIYAMA, Riichi. Tokyo: Shōgakukan, 1973.

NILSON, Nils Ake (1970), *The Russian Imagists*. Uppsala: Alnigvist.

THE NIPPON GAKUJUTSU SHINKŌKAI (NGS) (1958), *Haikai and Haiku*. Tokyo: The Nippon Gakujutsu Shinkokai.

NISHIKAWA, Isshōtei (1964), *Floral Art of Japan*. Tokyo: Japan Travel Bereau.

NOBAK, C. R. (1967), *The Human Nervous System*. New York: McGraw-Hill.

NÖTH, Winfried (1975), *Semiotik: Eine Einführung mit Beispielen für Reklameanalysen*. Tübingen: Max Niemeyer.

NÖTH, Winfried (1980), *Literatursemiotische Analysen: Zu Lews Carrolls Alice-Büchern*. Tübingen: Gunter Narr.

NÖTH, Winfried (1980a), "Linguistische, semiotische u. interdisziplinäre Literaturanalyse - am Beispiel von Lewis Carrols Alice-Büchern" in ESCHBACH/RADER, eds. (1980), 29-54.

OGATA, Sohaku (1959), *Zen for the West*. Westport: Greenwood P.

OGATA, Tsutomu (1959), "Hairon-monogatari" (On Hairon), in KOMIYA et al. (1959), 199-214.

OGDEN, C. K. /RICHARDS, I. A. (1923), *The Meaning of Meaning*. London: Routledge & Kegan Paul.

OKADA, Rokuo (1955), *Japanese Proverbs*. Tokyo: Japan Travel Bureau.

OKSAAR, Els (1977), *Spracherwerb im Vorschulalter: Einführung in die Pädolinguistik*. Stuttgart: Kohlhammer.

ONDA, A. (1965), "Autogenic Training and Zen" in LUTHE, ed. (1965), 251-8.

ORME-JOHNSON, E. W. (1971), "Autonomic Stability and Transcendental Meditation" in *Proceedings of the First International Symposium on the Science of Creative Intelligence*. Humbolt State C.

ORNSTEIN, Robert (1972), *The Psychology of Consciousness*. San Francisco: W. H. Freeman.

ŌTAKE, Masaru (1965), "The Haiku Touch in Wallace Stevens and Some Imagists" in *East West Review*, Kyōto: Dōshisha U. P., (1965), 152-64.

PEIRCE, Charles Sanders (1931-35, 1958-60), *Collected Papers of Charles Sanders Peirce*. Edited by Charles Hartshorne, Paul Weiss, and Arthur W. Burks. Eight Vols. Cambridge: Harvard U. P.

PEIRCE, Charles Sanders (1929), "Guessing" in *Hound and Horn* Vol. 2, No. 3 (1929), 267-82.

PENFIELD, Wilder (1966), "Speech, Perception and the Uncommited Cortex" in ECCLES, ed. (1966), 217-37.

PENFIELD, Wilder (1975), *The Mystery of the Mind: A Critical Study of Consciousness and the Human Brain*. Princeton: Princeton U. P.

PENFIELD, W./ROBERTS, L. (1959), *Speech and Brain Mechanisms*. Princeton: Princeton U. P.

PERKINS, David/LEONDAR, Barbara, eds. (1977), *The Arts and Cognition*. Baltimore: The Johns Hopkins U. P.

PETSCH, Robert (1932), "Die Lehre von den 'Einfachen Formen'" in *Deutsche Vierteljahresschrift für Literaturwissenschaft und Geistesgeschichte* 10 (1932), 335-69.

PIAGET, Jean (1945), *La formation du symbole chez l'enfant*. Trans. into English by C. Gattegno/F. M. Hodson: *Play, Dreams and Imitation in Childhood*. New York: Norton, 1962.

PIAGET, Jean (1954), "Sprechen und Denken in genetischer Sicht" in PIAGET (1972), 269-80.

PIAGET, Jean (1959), *The Language and Throught of the Child*. London: Routledge & Kegan Paul, 1967.

PIAGET, Jean (1967), *Biology and Knowledge*. Trans. of *Biologie et Connaissance*, Paris: Gallimard. Chicago: U. of Chicago P., 1971.

PIAGET, Jean (1968), *Le structuralisme*. Trans. and edited by Chaninah Maschler: *Structuralism*. London: Routledge & Kegan Paul, 1971.

PIAGET, Jean (1969), *The Early Growth of Logic in the Child: Classification and Seriation*. London: Routledge& Kegan Paul.

PIAGET, Jean (1970), *Genetic Epistemology*. Trans. by Eleanor Duckworth. New York: Columbia U. P.

PIAGET, Jean (1972), *The Principle of Genetic Epistemology*. New York: Basic Books.

PIAGET, Jean (1972a), *Psychologie et pédagogie. Six études de psychologie*. Trans. into German: *Theorien und Methoden der modernen Erziehung*. Wien: Molden.

PIAGET, Jean (1974), *La prise de conscience*. Trans. into English by Susan Wedgwood: *The Grasp of Consciousness*. Cambridge, Mass: Harvard U. P., 1976.

PIAGET, Jean (1976), *Behaviour and Evolution*. New York: Pantheon Books, 1978.

PIAGET, Jean (1977), *The Devleopment of Thought: Equilibration of Cognitive Structure*. New York: Viking P.

PIAGET, Jean/INHELDER, Bärbel (1966), *La Psychologie de l'enfant*. Trans. by Helen Weaver: *The Psycholgy of the Child*. New York: Basic Books, 1969.

PIIRAINEN, I. T. (1968), *Graphematische Untersuchungen zum Früherenhochdeutschen*. Berlin: De Gruyter.

PIIRAINEN, I. T. (1971), "Grapheme als quantitative Größen" in *Linguistische Berichte* 13 (1971), 81-2.

PILGRIM, Richard B. (1977), "The Religio-Aesthetic of Matsuo Bashō" in *Eastern Buddhist* 10 (1977), 35-53.

POPPER, Karl R. (1973), *Objektive Erkenntnis. Ein Evolutionärer Entwurf*. Hamburg: Hoffmann und Campe.

POPPER, Karl R./ECCLES, John C. (1977), *The Self and Its Brain*. Berlin: Springer International.

POSNER, Roland (1972), "Strukturalismus in der Gedichtinterpretation" in IHWE, ed. (1972), 136-76.

POSNER, Roland/REINECKE, Hans-Peter (1977), *Zeichenprozesse: semiotische Forschung in den Einzelwissenschaften*. Wiesbaden: Athenaion.

POUND, Ezra (1914), "Vorticism" in *Fortnightly Review*: reprinted in POUND (1970), 81-94.

POUND, Ezra (1928), "How to Read" in ELIOT, ed. (1954), 15-40.

POUND, Ezra (1970), *Gaudier-Brzeska: A Memoir*. New York: A New Direction Book.

POUND, Ezra/FENOLLOSA, Ernest (1916): see FENOLLOSA/POUND (1916).

PREMACK, David (1976), *Intelligence in Ape and Man*. Hillsdale: Erlbaum.

PRIBRAM,Karl H.(1969), "The Neurophysiology of Remembering" in *Scientific American* Jan. (1969), 73-86. Offprint: 520.

PRIBRAM,Karl H.(1971), *Languages of the Brain: Experimental Paradoxes and Principles in Neuropsychology*. Englewood Cliffs: Prentice-Hall.

PRIBRAM, Karl H. (1973), "The Primate Frontal Cortex - Executive of the Brain" in PRIBRAM/LIRIA, eds. (1973),293-314.

PRINCE, Gerald (1973), *A Grammer of Stories*. The Hague: Mouton.

QAMBER, Akhtar (1974), *Yeats and the Noh*. New York: Weatherhill.

RADO, S. (1969), *Adaptational Psychodynamics: Motivation and Control*. New York: Science House.

RANKE, Kurt (1955), "Schwank und Witz als Schwundstufe" in *Festschrift für Will-Wrich-Penckert zum 60. Geburtstag*, publ. by H. Dölker (1955), 41-59: reprinted in RANKE (1978), 61-78.

RANKE, Kurt (1965), "Einfache Formen" in FRIEDRICH/KILLY (1965), 184-200.

RANKE, Kurt (1978), *Die Welt der Einfachen Formen*. Berlin: De Gruyter.

RAPPAPORT, Roy A. (1967), *Pigs for the Ancestors: Ritual in the Ecology of a New Guinea People*. London: Yale U. P.

REICHENBACH, H. (1951), *The Rise of Scientific Philosophy*. Berkeley: U.of California P.

REID, Ian (1977), *The Short Story*. London: Methuen.

REINHART, Tanya (1976), "On Understanding Poetic Metaphor" in *Poetics* 5 (1976), 383-402.

REINIRKENS, Hubert (1955), *Sprichwörter und Redensarten. Deutsch-Japanisch: Kotowaza to Seigo*. Tokyo: Deutsche Gesellschaft für Natur- und Völkerkunde Ostasiens.

REXROTH, Kenneth (1964), *One Hundred Poems from the Japanese*. New York: A New Directions Book.

RICHARDS, I. A. (1936), "'Metaphor' and 'the Command of Metaphor'" in RICHARDS.I. A., ed. (1936), *The Philosophy of Rhetoric*. London: Oxford U. P.

RICHTER, Hans Günther (1976), *Anfang und Entwicklung der zeichnerischen Symbolik: Eine Gegenüberstellung der Theorien über den Ursprung und Verlauf der bildhaft-symbolischen Aktivitäten im Kinder- und Jugendalter*. Kastellaun: Aloys Henn.

RIEDL, Rupert (1976), *Die Strategie der Genesis: Naturgeschichte der realen Welt*. München: Piper.

RIEDL, Rupert (1979), *Biologie der Erkenntnis*. Berlin: Paul Parey.

RIFFARTERRE, Michael (1978), *Semiotics of Poetry*. Bloomington: Indiana U. P.

RIMER, Thomas J./MORRELL, Robert E. (1975),*(Guide to)Japanese Poetry*. Boston: G. K. Hall.

RÖHRICH, Lutz (1977), *Der Witz: Figuren, Formen, Funktionen.*
Stuttgart: Metzler.

ROSELIEP, Raymond (1979), "On a Rhyming Planet" in *Haiku Journal*
(1979), 30-3.

ROSENTHAL, M. L., ed. (1966), *The William Carlos Williams:
Reader.* New York:

ROTHENBERG, Albert (1971), "The Process of Janusian Thinking
in Creativity" in *Am M. A. Archives of General Psychiatry*
24 (1971), 195-205.

ROUDIEZ, Leon S. (1980), "Introduction" in KRISTEVA (1980),1-20.

SANDERS, Gary (1970), "Peirce's Sixty-six Signs?" in *Transactions of the C. S. Peirce Society* 6 (1970), 3-16.

SARNO, Martha Taylor, ed. (1972), *Aphasia: Selected Readings.*
New York: Appleton-Century-Crafts.

SASANUMA, S. (1975), "Kana and Kanji Processing in Japanese
Aphasics" in *Brain and Language* 1/2 (1975), 369-83.

SASANUMA, S./FUJIMURA, O. (1971), "Selective Impairment
of Phonetic and Non-phonetic Transcriptions of Words in
Japanese Aphasic Patients: Kana vs. Kanji in Visual Recognition and Writing" in *Cortex* 7 (1971), 1-18.

SASANUMA, S./FUJIMURA, O. (1972), "An Analysis of Writing
Errors in Japanese Aphasic Patients: Kanji vs. Kana Words"
in *Cortex* 8 (1972), 265-82.

SATŌ, Kazuo (1978), *Na-no-hana wa ishoku dekiru ka: Hikaku-bungaku-teki haikuron* (Can Rape-flowers Be Transplanted?:
Discussion on Haiku from the Viewpoint of Comparative Literature). Tokyo: Ōfūsha.

SATŌ, Nobushige (1977), "Psychophysiological Study on 'Zenjō'--
with Microvibration of Fingertip as a Guide" in AKISHIGE,
ed. (1977), 342-60.

SAUSSURE, Ferdinand de (1960), *Course in General Linguistics.*
Edited by Charles Bally/Albert Sechehaye in collabroation
with Albert Reidlinger: trans. by Wade Baskin. London: Peter
Owen.

SCHENK, Brigitte (1982), "The Phylogeny of Art: Aspects of
the Development of Prehistoric Art" in KOCH, ed. (1982b),
417-46.

SCHIWY, Günther (1973), *Strukturalismus und Zeichensysteme.*
München: C. H. Beck.

SCHMITT, Rancis O./WORDEN, Frederic G., Editors-in-Chef, (1974),
The Neuroschiences: Third Study Program. Cambridge: The
MIT P.

SCHNELLE, Helmut, ed. (1981), *Sprache und Gehrin.* Frankfurt
a. M.: Suhrkamp.

SCHNELLE, Helmut (1981a), "Einführung" in SCHNELLE, ed. (1981),
7-17.

SCHNITZER, Marc L (1976), "The Role of Phonology in Linguistic Communication: some Neurolinguistic Considerations" in WHITAKER/WHITAKER, eds. (1976), 139-60.

SCHOLES, Robert (1974), *Structuralism in Literature*. New Haven: Yale U. P.

SCHOLES, Robert (1982), *Semiotics and Interpretation*. New Haven: Yale U. P.

SCHRIER, Allan M./STOLLNITZ, Fred, eds. (1971), *Behaviour of Non-Human Primates*. New York: Academic P.

SCHÜTTLER, Günter (1974): *Die Erleuchtung im Zen-Buddhismus: Gespräche mit Zen-Meistern und Psychopathologische Analyse*. München: Karl Alber Freiburg.

SCHWARTZ, Gary E./BEATTY, Jackson (1977), *Biofeedback: Theory and Research*. New York: Academic P.

SEBEOK, Thomas A., ed. (1960),*Style in Language*. New York: Sebeok.

SEBEOK, Thomas A., ed. (1968), *Animal Communication*. Bloomington: U. of Indiana P.

SEBEOK, Thomas A. (1972), *Perspectives in Zoosemiotics*. The Hague: Mouton.

SEBEOK, Thomas A. (1975), "Zoosemiotics: at the Intersection of Nature and Culture" in SEBEOK, ed. (1975), 85-95.

SEBEOK, Thomas A., ed. (1975a),*The Tell-Tale Sign: A Survey of Semiotics*. Lisse: De Ridder.

SEBEOK, Thomas A., ed. (1977), *How Animals Communicate*. Bloomington: Indiana U. P.

SEBEOK, Thomas A., ed. (1977a), *A Perfusion of Signs*. Bloomington: Indiana U. P.

SEBEOK, Thomas A. (1979),"Prefigurements of Art" in WINNER/ UNIKER-SEBEOK, eds. (1979), 3-74.

SEBEOK, Thomas A. (1979a), *The Sign and Its Masters*. Austin: U. of Texas P.

SEBEOK, Thomas A./UMIKER-SEBEOK, Jean (1980), *"You Know My Method": A Juxtaposition of Charles S. Peirce and Sherlock Homes*. Bloomington: Gaslight Pub.

SEBEOK, Thomas A./UMIKER-SEBEOK, Jean,eds. (1980a), *Speaking of Apes*. New York: Plenum P.

SEEGAL, David (1977), *Victories and Foibles: Some Western Haiku*. Rutland: Charles E. Tuttle.

Sei Shōnagon (ca. 1,000 A.D.), *Makura no sōshi* (The Pillow-Book) in *Nihon Koten Bungaku Taikei 19: Makura no sōshi· Murasaki-shikibu Nikki*, Tokyo: Iwanami, 1958.

SEKIGUCHI, Shindai (1970), *Zen: A Manual for Westerners*. Tokyo: Japan Publications.

SEKO, Suwa (1965), "On the Phonology of Japanese Modern Haiku and japanese Language" in *Haiku Bungaku Jiten*, Tokyo: Wakakusa-shoten.

SHANNON, C./WEAVER, W. (1949), *The Mathematical Theory of Communication*. Urbana: U. of Illinois P.

Shiki, MASAOKA: see MASAOKA.

SHIODA, Ryōhei/YOSHIDA, Seiichi (1969), *Hyōjun Kokugo Jiten*. Tokyo: Ōbunsha.

SHIPLEY, Joseph T. (1946), *Encyclopedia of Literature*. New York: Philosophical Library.

SHOLL, Cornelia (1982), "Language Acquisiton and Loss" in KOCH, ed. (1982b), 195-216.

SHUKMAN, Ann (1977), *Literature and Semiotics: A Study of Yu. M. Lotman*. Amsterdam: North-Holland Pub. Co.

SMITH, Richard Eugene (1965), "Ezra Pound and the Haiku" in *College English* 26 (1965), 522-7.

SNYDER, Gary (1969), *Earth House Hold*. New York: New Directions.

SOKOLOF, E. N. (1958), *Perception and Conditioned Reflex*. New York: MacMillan.

SPERRY, Roger W. (1974), "Lateral Specialization in the Surgically Separated Hemispheres" in SCHMITT et al. eds. (1974), 5-19.

STETTER, Christian (1979), "Peirce und Saussure" in *Kodikas/Code* 1/2 (1979), 124-49.

STEUDING, Bob (1976), *Gary Snyder*. Boston: Twayne.

STEVENS, Holly (1966), *Letters of Wallace Stevens*. London: Farber, 1967.

STEVENS, Wallace (1951), *The Necessary Angel*. London: Farber, 1960.

STEWART, Harold (1960), *A Net of Fireflies: Japanese Haiku and Haiku Painting*. Tokyo: Charles E. Tuttle.

STOCK, Noel (1970), *The Life of Ezra Pound*. London: Routledge Kegan Paul.

STURROCK, John, ed. (1979), *Structuralism and Since: From Lévi-Strauss to Derrida*. Oxford: Oxford U. P.

STURROCK, John, (1979a), "Roland Barthes" in STURROCK, ed. (1979), 52-80.

SUEDFELD, Peter E./BORRIE, Roderick (1978), "Altering States of Consciousness through Sensory Deprivation" in SUGERMAN/TARTER, eds. (1978), 226-52.

SUGERMAN, A. Arthur/TARTER, Ralph E., eds. (1978), *Expanding Dimensions of Consciousness*. New York: Springer.

SUGI, Y./AKUTSU, K. (1964), "Studies on Respiration and Energy-Metabolism during Sitting in Zazen" in *Reserach Journal of Physical Education* 12/3 (1964).

SUGI, Y./AKUTSU, K. (1968), "On the Respiration and Resparatory Change in Zen Practice" in *Japanese Journal of Physiology* 26 (1968), 72-3.

SUGIMOTO, Nagashige (1958), *Senryū-shū* in *Nihon Koten Bungaku Taikei 57: Senryū·Kyōka-shū*, Tokyo: Iwanami.

SURACI, Anthony (1979), "A Haiku is a Haiku: Dedicated to James W. Hackett" in *Haiku Journal* (1979), 46-51.

SUZUKI, Daisetsu Teitarō (1953), *Essays in Zen Buddhism, Series III*. London: Luzac.

SUZUKI, Daisetsu Teitarō (1958), *Zen and Japanese Buddhism.* Tokyo: Japan Travel Bereau, 1961.

SUZUKI, Daisetsu Teitarō (1958a), *Die große Befreiung: Einführung in den Zen-Buddhism.* Frankfurt a.M.: Fischer, 1975.

SUZUKI, Daisetsu Teitarō (1959), *Zen and Japanese Culture.* Princeton: Princeton U. P.

SUZUKI, Daisetsu Teitarō (1982), *Leben aus Zen: Mit einer Einführung in die Texte von Wei-Lang (Hui-neng).* Frankfurt a.M.: Suhrkamp.

SUZUKI, Shunryū (1970), *Zen Mind, Biginner's Mind.* New York: Weatherhill.

TAKAHA, Shugyō (1979), "Effective Expression in Haiku" in *Haiku Journal* (1979), 43-5.

TAKEDA, Shin'ichi (1977), "A Psychological Study on 'Zenjō' and Breath Regulation" in AKISHIGE, ed. (1977), 208-32.

TANIGUCHI, Yasutomi (1977), "Psychological Studies on Concentration and Non-Contrievance" in AKISHIGE, ed. (1977), 292-319.

TEUBER, Hans-Lukas (1974), "Why Two Brains?" in SCHMITT et al. (1974), 71-5.

TINBERGEN, Niko (1940), "Die Übersprungewegung" in *Zeitschrift für Tierpsychologie* 4 (1940), 1-40.

TINBERGEN, Niko (1965), *Animal Behaviour (Life Nature Library).* Time-Live International (Nederland) B. V.

TODOROV, Tzvetan (1969), *Grammaire du Décaméron.* The Hague: Mouton.

TODOROV, Tzvetan (1977), *The Poetics of Prose.* Trans. by Richard Howard. Oxford: Basil Blackwell.

TODOROV, Tzvetan (1978), "The Birth of Occidental Semiotics" in BAILEY et al. (1978), 1-42.

TOKUTOMI, Kiyoshi/TOKUTOMI, Kiyoko (1978), "Saijiki" in *Haiku Journal* (1978), 32-3.

TOKUTOMI, Kiyoshi/TOKUTOMI, Kiyoko (1979), "Editor's Overview 1975-1979" in *Haiku Journal* (1979), 3-12.

TOKUTOMI, Kiyoshi/TOKUTOMI, Kiyoko (1980), "The Spirit of Seventeen Syllable Count in Haiku" in *Haiku Journal* (1980), 9-12.

TRABANT, Jürgen (1976), *Elemente der Semiotik*. München: C.H.BECK.

TSUNODA, Tadanobu (1975), "Functional Differences between Right and Left Cerebral Hemispheres Detected by the Key-Tapping Method" in *Brain and Language* 2 (1975),

TSUNODA, Tadanobu (1978), *Nihonjin no Nō* (The Brain of the Japanese). Tokyo: Taishūkan, 1980.

UCHIYAMA, Kosho (1973), *Approach to Zen*. Tokyo: Japan Publications.

UEDA, Daisuke (1963), *Zen and Science: A Treatise on Casuality and Freedom*. Tokyo: Risōsha.

UEDA, Makoto (1962), "Bashō and the Poetics of 'Haiku'" in *Journal of Aesthetics and Art Criticism* 21 (1962), 423-31.

UEDA, Makoto (1965), *Zeami, Bashō, Yeats, Pound*. London: Mouton.

UEDA, Makoto (1970), *Matsuo Bashō*. New York: Twayne Pub.

UEDA, Makoto (1976), *Modern Japanese Haiku: An Anthology*. Tokyo: U. of Tokyo P.

ULENBROOK, Jan (1961), "Ein Haiku entsteht" in *Insel-Almanach* (1961), 59-62.

ULENBROOK, Jan (1979), *Haiku: Japanische Dreizeiler*. München: Wilhelm Heyne.

ULLMANN, Stephen (1962), *Semantics*. Oxford: Blackwell.

UMIKER-SEBEOK, D. J. (1979), "Preschool Children's Intraconversational Narratives" in *Journal of Child Language* 6 (1979), 91-109.

USENER, H. (1903), "Dreiheit" in *Rheinisches Museum für Philologie* 58 (1903), 1-47.

VAN DEN HEUVEL, Cor, ed. (1974), *The Haiku Anthology: English Language Haiku by Contemporary American and Canadian Poets*. Garden City: Anchor Books.

VYGOTSKY, Lev Semenovich (1971), *The Psychology of Art*. Cambridge: The MIT P.

WADDINGTON, C. H. (1957), *The Strategy of the Genes*. London: Allen and Urwin.

WALLACE, R. K./BENSON, H. (1971), "The Physiology of Meditation" in *Altered States of Awareness: Readings from Scientific American*, San Francisco: Freeman, 125-31.

WALLACE, R. K./BENSON, H./WILSON, A. F. (1971), "A Wakeful Hypometabolic Physiologic State" in *American Journal of Physiology* 221 (1971), 795-9.

WALTER, V. J./WALTER, W. G. (1949), "The Central Effects of Rhythmic Sensory Stimulation" in *Electroencephalography and Clinical Neurology* 1 (1949), 57-85.

WALTER, W. G. (1973), "Human Frontal Lobe Functions in Sensory-Motor Association" in PRIBRAM/LURIA, eds. (1973), 109-24.

WALTHER, Elizabeth (1974), *Allgemeine Zeichenlehre. Einführung in die Grundlagen der Semiotik*. Stuttgart:

WANG WEI (ca.750), *Hiding the Universe: Poems by Wang Wei*. Trans. by Wai-lin Yip. New York: Grossman, 1972.

WATTS, Allan (1958), *The Spirit of Zen: A Way of Life, Work, and Art in the Far East*. New York: Grove, 1980.

Webster's New Collegiate Dictionary (1973). Springfield: G.& C. Merriam.

WEISS, Paul/BURKS, A. W. (1945), "Peirce's Sixty-Six Signs" in the *Journal of Philosophy* 42 (1945), 383-8.

WENZEL, Peter (1982), "'From Form to Function': Poetic Competence in Children" in KOCH, ed. (1982b), 370-96.

WERLICH, Egon (1975), *Typologie der Texte: Entwurf eines textlinguistischen Modells zur Grundlegung einen Textgrammatik*. Heidelberg: Quelle & Meyer.

WERTHEIMER, Max (1967), *Drei Abhandlungen zur Gestalttheorie*. Darmstadt: Wiss. Buchgesellschaft.

WESCOTT, R. W. ed. (1974), *Language Origins*. Maryland: Silver Spring.

WHITAKER, Haigonnosh/WHITAKER, Harry A., eds. (1976), *Studies in Neurolinguistics*. New York: Academic P.

WINNER, Eleen/ROSENSTIEL, Anne K./GARDNER, Howard (1976), "The Development of Metaphoric Understanding" in *Developmental Psychology* 12 (1976), 289-97.

WINNER, Irene Portis (1979), "Ethnicity, Modernity, and Theory of Culture Texts" in WINNER/UMIKER-SEBEOK, eds. (1979), 103-47.

WINNER, Irene Portis (1981), *Semiotics of Culture: The State of the Art*. Brown University Center for Research in Semiotics.

WINNER, Irene Portis/UMIKER-SEBEOK, Jean (1979), *Semiotics of Culture*. The Hague: Mouton.

YAMAGATA, Teruo (1979), "An Unforgettable Impression on Visiting Mr. James W. Hackett" in *Haiku Journal* (1978), 37-8.

YAMAMOTO, Kenkichi (1946), "Aisatsu to Kokkei" (Greetings and Humour) in *Hihyō* (1946).

YASHIRO, Yukio/SWANN, Peter C. (1958), *Japanische Kunst*. München: Droemersche Verlagsanstalt.

YASUDA, Kenneth (1947), *A Pepper Pod*. New York: Alfred A. Knopf: reprinted, Rutland: Charles E. Tuttle, 1976.

YASUDA, Kenneth (1957), *The Japanese Haiku: Its Essential Nature, History, and Possibilities in English, with Selected Examples*. Rutland: Charles E. Tuttle.

YODA, Fumito (1967), *Shimpen Kotowaza, Meigen, Kogo* (Proverbs, Aphorisms, Sayings: New Edition). Tokyo: Ikeda Shoten.

YOSHIDA, Seiichi (1962), "Sakka·Sakuhin no kanshō to kenkyū" (Appriciation and Study of Haiku Poets and Their Works) in *Gendai Nihon Bungaku Kōza: Tanka·Haiku*, Tokyo: Sanseidō, 25-175.

YOUNG, Robert, ed. (1981), *A Post-Structuralist Reader*. Boston: Routledge & Kegan Paul.

YU, Pauline R. (1978), "Chinese and Symbolist Poetic Theories" in *Comparative Literature* 30 (1978), 291-312.

ZANGWILL, O. L. (1975), "The Ontogeny of Cerebral Dominance in Man" in LENNEBERG/LENNEBERG, eds. (1975), Vol. 1, 137-48.

ZEMAN, J. Jay (1977), "Peirce's Theory of Signs" in SEBEOK, ed.(1977a), 22-39.

Zusetsu Haiku Daisaijiki, 5 Vols. (1970). Tokyo: Kadokawa.

Zusetsu Nihon no koten 12: Nō·Kyōgen (1980). Tokyo: Shūeisha.

Zusetsu Nihon no koten 14: Bashō·Buson (1978). Tokyo: Shūeisha.

INDEX OF NAMES

A

AARONS, Hilda, 413
AARSLEFF, Hans, 492
ABRAHAMS, Roger, 115, 490
AIKEN, Conrad, 362
AITKEN, Robert, 454, 493
AKABANE, Manabu, 296, 532-3
AKISHIGE, Yoshiharu, 7, 88, 97, 99-106, 114, 126, 151, 516-8
AKUTAGAWA, Ryūnosuke, 243-4
AKUTSU, K., 102
ALDINGTON, Richard, 360, 375-6
AMANN, Eric, 414, 424,434-6, 440-1, 456-7
ANDŌ, Suehiro, 100,102
D'AQUILI, Eugene G., 12, 17, 54, 57-8, 88, 90, 92-3, 112, 115-8, 121-3, 126, 504, 508, 516, 519-20
ARAKIDA, Moritake (see Moritake)
ARAKIDA, Takeari, 269
ARDREY, Robert, 127, 493
AREWA, Ojo E., 490
ARIETI, Silvano, 26, 75-9, 126, 128-30, 133, 141, 143-4, 496, 508-9, 511-2, 522
ARNHEIM, Rudolf, 84
ASANO, Shin, 187, 239, 254-7, 262, 302, 368, 396, 460, 526, 533
ASANO, Tsuruko, 72, 244-5, 530
ASTON, A. G., 359
ATWOOD, Ann, 540
AYIM, Maryann, 521

B

BAILEY, Richard W., 492
Baishitsu, SAKURAI, 326, 410
BALL, Hugo, 216, 226
BALL, Jerald T., 434
BALNOV, L. J., 62
BARTHES, Roland, 29, 36-41,88,

105, 129, 196, 209, 213, 499, 500,
Basho, MATSUO (see also MATSUO, B.), 1-5, 9, 48, 56, 179, 180, 183-9, 191, 194, 200-37, 240-54, 257-63, 267, 269, 272-289, 291-2, 295-6, 298, 300, 306-31, 338-41, 345-7, 357, 359, 361-4, 368, 370-2, 375, 377, 381-4, 387-92, 395-6, 402, 404, 408-9, 415-8, 420-1, 428, 434, 438, 441-2, 447, 451-5, 461-2, 464-6, 471-5, 480-2, 486-7, 522, 527-34
BASSO, A., 117
BAUSINGER, Hermann, 474, 476, 478, 486, 488, 504, 541
BEATTY, Jackson, 150
BECKER, E., 118
BEN-AMOS, Dan, 476, 479, 541
BENL, Oscar, 524
BENSE, Max, 153-4, 159-60, 162, 492, 495, 522
BENSON, H. 114, 127
BENZ, Ernst, 57
BERLUCCHI, G., 507
BERTALANFFY, Ludwig Von, 75, 493, 495
BIEDERMAN, Charles, 217
BILLOW, Richard M., 48
BINDRA, Dalbir, 496
BLACK, J. B., 48
BLAKE, William, 220
BLYTH, R. H., 2, 3, 5, 6, 9, 13, 56, 58, 72, 87, 110, 128, 172-6, 182, 191-2, 195-6, 204, 211, 214, 235, 239, 248, 251-2, 263-4, 282, 286-9, 291-2, 315, 324-5, 327, 331-2, 335, 341, 362, 364, 393, 395, 407, 410, 415, 426, 430, 4 433-9, 442, 452, 467-8, 471, 473, 483, 486-7, 491, 493, 519-22, 524-5, 527-30, 535

BOBON, J. 143, 220
BOGATYREV, Petr, 490
BOGEN, J. E., 8, 64-5, 493, 505, 508
BOLLOCK, Margot, 413
BORRIE, Roderick, 101
Bōsha, KAWABATA, 332, 341, 347, 384
BOWER, G. H., 48
BOYLE, D. G., 517
BRACQUEMOND, Felix, 358
BREKLE, H. E., 70
BREMOND, Claude, 316
BROOKE, Rupert, 216, 220, 232, 276, 283, 287, 294-5, 325, 469, 471
BROWER, Gary, 523
BROWER, Robert, 2, 175, 177, 188, 227, 235, 237-8, 253, 261, 266, 269, 275, 286, 289, 399, 403, 503, 525, 529-30, 534
BROWN, Jason, 59, 503, 505
BRUNER, Jerome S., 153, 163
BRUNSWIK, Egon, 16, 43
BRYAN, Sam, 448-9
Bucchō, Priest, 288, 291
BUDZYNSKI, Thomas, H., 151
BÜHLER, Karl, 22, 26, 79, 200, 202, 492, 501
BUNGE, Mario, 506
BURKS, A. W., 495, 521, 523
Buson, YOSA, 5, 6, 186, 307, 320-5, 327-9, 331, 334-5, 347, 359, 364, 371, 374, 390, 408-9, 420, 430, 434, 442-3, 451-2, 458, 460, 528, 530, 534
BUSSE, Hans-Peter, 492, 514-5
BYNNER, Witter, 390

C

CAIN, Jack, 425
CANISIUS, Peter, 48, 316
CARD, Peggy, 411, 413
CARRINGTON, Patricia, 99, 518
CASALIS, Matthieu, 204
CHAGALL, Marc,522
CHAMBERLAIN, Basil Hall, 359
CHANG, G. C. C., 97

CHAPPEL, E. D., 101
CHATMAN, Seymour, 18, 492
CHENOWETH, Helen Stiles, 409, 411-4, 463, 524
CHIHARA, Tadashi, 97, 516
CHOMSKY, Noam, 18, 47-9, 53, 83, 496
COHEN, H. D., 107-8, 112
COHEN, William H., 211, 239
COLLINGWOOD, R. G., 492
CORSO, Gregory, 400
COSERIU, Eugenio, 492
CRANACH, Mario Von, 56, 115, 493
CRAPSEY, Adelaide, 361, 364, 388-90, 433, 451
CULLER, Jonathan, 13-4, 29, 36, 39-40, 249, 250, 454, 500
CUMMINGS, E. E., 216-8
CURTIS, Brian A., 505

D

DALI, Salvador, 522
DAVIDSON, L. A., 425
DEELY, John, 492
DEGLIN, V. L., 62
DEIKMAN, Arthur, 125
DIMMET, Earnest, 191
Dohō, HATTORI (see HATTORI)
DOI, Masayuki, 193
DOMURUS, Eilhard Von, 128
DOOLITTLE, Hilda (H. D.), 360, 372, 376
DÜRCKHEIM, Karlfried Graf, 57, 516
DUNDES, Alan, 462, 476, 486, 488-9, 530
DUSKIN, 64, 150
DUSMORE, J. M., 448
DUTSCH, Robert A., 253

E

EBARA, Taizō, 254, 522, 529, 533
ECCLES, John C., 8, 17, 43, 54, 59, 62-3, 65-6, 77-80, 108, 113, 117, 493, 504, 506, 509-10, 517, 520
ECO, Umberto, 13, 22, 29, 34,

(ECO continued), 36, 38, 40, 55, 89, 91-2, 156, 165-6, 168, 198-9, 216, 228, 244, 258, 287, 289-92, 515, 523
EIBL-EIBESFELDT, Irenäus, 98, 496, 520
EICHENBAUM, Boris, 375
ELIOT, Thomas S., 177, 360, 362, 372, 536
ELLMANN, Richard, 173, 360, 369, 378, 380-1, 388, 400, 402, 405-6
ELMORE, Andrew M., 150
ENGLER, R., 514
ERLICH, Victor, 201, 526
ESCHBACH, Achim, 492
ETŌ, Hiroko, 481-2
EVERSON, William (Brother Anthoninus), 401

F

FEHMI, Lester G., 107, 150, 518
FEIBLEMAN, James K., 83, 91, 130-1, 152, 155, 160, 495-6, 514
FENOLLOSA, Ernest, 70, 189, 254, 525, 537
FERLINGHETTI, Lawrence, 400
FICKE, Arthur Davidson, 390
FISCH, Max H., 492
FISCHER, Roland, 88, 97, 100-1, 103-8, 111, 139, 149, 522
FLETSCHER, John Gould, 360-1
FLINT, F. S., 359-60, 375
FORD, Madox Ford, 360
FOUCAULT, Michael, 204
FRANK, Armin Paul, 423, 444, 539
FRANK, P., 131
FRAZER, John, 221
FREGE, Gottlob, 89
FREUD, Sigmund, 128, 220, 268
FRISCH, Karl von, 127, 520
FROMM, Erich, 509
FROST, Robert, 372
FUJIMURA, O., 70-1
FUJIWARA, Kiyohira/Motohira/Hidehira, 531

FUJIWARA, Teika, 178
FUKUDA, Rikutarō, 382
FURGASON, Charles A., 501

G

GARDNER, Beatrice T., 48, 219
GARDNER, Howard, 48
GARDNER, R. Allen, 48, 219
GARNICA, Olga K., 501
GAUDIER-BRZESKA, 537
GAZZANIGA, M. S., 493, 505, 509
GELLHORN, E., 100, 109, 111-2, 115, 123, 517
GENETTE, Gérard, 210-1
GEORGES, Robert A., 462, 489
GESCHWIND, Norman, 59, 70, 117, 125, 493, 508
Gesshū, HARA, 247, 278
GINSBERG, Allen, 400
GIROUX, Joan, 193, 253, 264, 364, 433, 438, 446, 531
GLASS, Arnold L., 84
GLUECK, Bernard, 109, 114, 123, 518-9
Gohei, 288
GOLDSTEIN, L., 107-8, 112, GRIMM, Jakob, 474, 541
GRZYBEK, Peter, 61
GUR, Raquel, 63
GUR, Ruben

H

HACKETT, James W., 173-4, 408, 415-9, 424, 428, 441-3, 451, 467, 524, 539
HÄCKEL, Ernst, 46, 501
HAHN, Martin E., 48
HALL, R. A., 70
HAMMITZSCH, Horst, 203, 233, 528, 532
HARADA, Hokusai, 526
HARADA, Tomohiko, 486
HARDWICK, Charles S., 15, 492
HARNAD, Stevan, 60, 505
HARTSHORNE, Charles, 522
HATTORI, Dohō, 48, 185, 188,

(HATTORI continued), 200,
205, 209-11, 223, 241, 243,
249, 313, 392, 474, 504,
525, 527-30, 533-4, 538
HAWKS, Terence, 12, 200-2,
204, 492
HAYASHIYA, Tatsusabrō, 162
HEARN, Lafcadio, 358
HEIN, Norbert, 25
Hekigodō, KAWAHIGASHI, 307,
329, 333-6, 340, 347, 373-4
HELMERS, Hermann, 48
HEMINGWAY, Ernest, 345
HENDERSON, Harold Gould, 4, 6,
35-6, 181, 186, 190-2, 195,
206, 255, 264, 314, 349,
362-4, 394, 408, 410, 415,
417-8, 420-2, 432-3, 444,
446-9, 452, 466-7, 491,
494, 531, 533, 538-40
HENDRICKS, William O., 375
HENNIG, Karl, 27-8, 32, 49,
89, 148, 498-9
HENRY, O., 375
HERRIGEL, Eugen, 57, 97, 134,
520, 522
HEUVEL, Cor VAN DEN, 4, 6,
181, 189, 321, 357, 362-4,
371, 390, 408, 414-5, 418,
421, 424, 430, 432-3, 435-
6, 439, 441, 443, 451-2,
458, 471-2, 491, 493-4,524
HEWES, Gordon H., 48, 55, 98-
9, 219
HIBBET, Howard S., 524
HIRAI, T., 99, 107, 138, 505
Hiroshige, ANDŌ, 382
HISAMATSU, Shin'ichi, 14, 27-
9, 49, 146, 148, 157-8,
162-3, 166-7, 517, 519,522
Hitomaro, KAKINOMOTO, 178
HJELMSLEV, Louis, 91
Hokusai, KATSUSHIKA, 358, 382
HOLENSTEIN, Elmar, 37, 197,
231, 492, 496, 499
HOPKINS, Gerard Manley, 198,
242
HORI, Nobuo, 1, 230, 232, 257,
259, 274, 276-7, 279, 282-
3, 297, 523, 529
Hōsai, OZAKI, 5, 6, 307, 332-
3, 337-9, 347, 459
HOTHAM, Gary, 425

HOWARD, Richard, 499-500
HOYT, Clement, 174, 409,413
HRDLIČKOVÁ, V., 523
HULLET, E. J. Jr., 22
HULME, T. E., 357, 359, 537
HUXLEY, Aldous, 485
HYMES, Dell, 490

I

ICHIKAWA, Sanki (see also
the Nippon Gakujutsu Shinkōkai), 5, 176, 233, 324,
396, 452, 525, 527, 531,
534-5, 537
Ichū, OKANISHI, 184
IKAWA, Yukio, 102-3
IKEGAMI, Yoshihiko, 71-2,508
IMOTO, Nōichi, 188-9, 240-
1, 248, 453-4, 480, 523,
531
INHELDER, Bärbel, 98, 493
Issa, KOBAYASHI, 307, 324-5,
331, 347, 364, 409, 434,
535
IVANOV, Vjačeslav V., 22, 46,
48, 61, 64-5, 70-2, 84, 99,
108, 118, 121, 125, 128,
164, 169-70, 221, 248, 290-
1, 403-4, 414, 472, 475,483,
488, 506, 512-3, 519-22,
539-41
IZAWA, H., 106
Izen, HIROSE, 247, 345, 530

J

JACOBSON, Stanley, 101
JAKOBSON, Roman, 6, 9, 22-4,
26, 37, 44, 46-52, 59, 61-
2, 68, 74, 93, 188, 196-8,
200-3, 217, 221, 231, 242,
246, 289-90, 306, 336-7,
369, 425, 490, 492-3, 495,
498-9, 501-3, 505, 508,
526-7, 533
JEFFORDS, Rosemary, 411
JEKOSCH, Ute, 84
JEWELL, Foster, 439
JOHNSON, Barbara, 499
JOHNSTON, W., 111
JOLLES, André, 219, 349, 474-
9, 485, 488, 518
Jōsō, NAITŌ, 383

K

Kakio, TOMIZAWA, 345-7
KAKO, Saburō, 481-2
KANDA, Hideo, 326
KANDINSKY, Vasili, 367
KANELLAKOS, Demetri P., 88, 99, 138, 518
KAPLEAU, Philip, 99, 109, 112, 126, 517-20
KASAMATSU, A., 106-7, 138
KEENE, Donald, 167, 192, 252, 262-3, 363, 369, 386, 395, 402, 471, 526, 538, 541
KELLOG, Rhoda, 48, 217
KHERDIAN, David, 403
KI no Tsurayuki, 178
KIELY, W. F., 100, 109, 111, 112, 115, 123
Kijō, MURAKAMI, 341, 536
Kikaku, TAKARAI, 291-2, 430, 462, 481-2, 530
KIMURA, Doreen, 59
KINDAICHI, Haruhiko, 72, 244-6, 530, 542
KIRSHENBLATT-GIMBLETT, Barbara, 48
Kiyosuke, FUJIWARA, 183-5,189, 194, 223-4
KLAUS, G., 22
KLEIN, K. P., 48
KLINKENBERG, Jean Marie, 18
KNIGHT, Etheridge, 173, 405-8, 414, 449
KOCH, Annemarie, 505-6
KOCH, Vivienne, 379
KOCH, Walter A., 3, 6, 9, 13, 18-27, 43-53, 55, 63-4,72-3, 78-83, 93, 108, 118-9, 127, 137, 146, 177, 184, 187-8, 194, 196-200, 203-4, 209, 211-23, 225, 228, 231, 242, 259-63, 267-8, 276, 289, 292, 303-7, 309, 316, 318, 320-1, 331, 344-5, 369-71, 385, 403, 425, 427-8, 462, 472, 485, 493, 497-9, 501-3, 506, 509, 512-3, 521, 526-8, 533-4, 538, 540
KÖHLER, Wolfgang, 84
KÖLLER, Wilhelm, 130-1
KÖNGÄS-MARANDA, Elli, 116,119, 221, 412, 476, 486,502, 514

KOENIG, Otto, 47
KOESTLER, Arthur, 81, 116, 267-9, 271, 313, 374, 485-6, 503, 519
KOFFKA, K., 84
KOHEN, Alfred, 162
KOMIYA, Toyotaka, 176, 525
KONISHI, Jin'ichi, 532
KONO, Rokurō, 70
KŌNOSU, Hayao, 176
KOYAMA, Hiroshi, 541
KREITLER, Hans, 25, 63, 74-5
KREITLER, Shulamith, 25, 63, 74-5
KRISTEVA, Julia, 29, 39-41, 88, 129, 499, 500
KROEPSCH, Rainer A., 22, 25
KUBOTA, Harutsugu, 118, 229, 234-5, 243-4
KURIYAMA, Riichi, 183, 201, 206, 210, 224-6, 229, 237, 247, 262-3, 269-70, 309, 311-2, 314-5, 322, 523, 525, 529-31, 534
Kusatao, NAKAMURA, 332, 344
kyorai, MUKAI (see MUKAI)
Kyoroku,MORIKAWA, 229, 530
Kyoshi, TAKAHAMA, 329, 336, 340-1, 430

L

LAMSON, June E., 434
Lao-tze, 87
LASZLO, Ervin, 493
LAUGHLIN, C., 35, 88, 92-3, 112, 115-8, 121-3, 126, 508, 516, 519-20, 542
LAWRENCE, D. H., 360
LEAKEY, Richard E., 520
LENNEBERG, Elizabeth, 47,493, 503, 508
LENNEBERG, Erich H., 47-8,70, 73, 93, 96, 493, 503, 508
LEONDAR, Barbara, 534
LEVI-AGRESTI, Jerry, 113
LEVI-STRAUSS, Claude, 26, 115-6, 119, 221, 296, 514, 520
LEVITSKY, W., 59
LEWANDOWSKI, Theodor, 493, 516
LEWIN, Bruno, 1, 72, 195, 238, 243-4, 317, 493, 508, 528, 530-1, 537
LEWIS, Wyndham, 537

LEX, Barbara W., 58, 64, 88, 101, 1o9, 112, 127, 508, 514, 517
LIBERMAN, A. M., 508
LIEBER, Francis, 492
LINDEN, Eugene, 55
LINDSLEY, D. B., 107
LIVANOV, M. N., 117
LLOYD, David, 460
LOOFBOURROW, G. N., 109, 517
LORENZ, Konrad, 16-7, 24, 30, 41-3, 48-9, 53-4, 74, 79-81, 84, 88, 115, 127, 130, 132-4, 493, 496, 501-3, 506
LOTMAN, Jurij, 14, 25, 85, 205-9, 211, 236, 357, 368, 420, 494-5, 526
LOWELL, Amy, 192, 360-1, 364, 382, 386-8, 390, 395, 412, 433, 451, 526, 538
LOWELL, Parcivall, 388
LUCE, G. G., 101
LUDWIG, A. M., 101
LUKAS, Jerome S., 88, 99, 138, 518
LURIA, A. R., 117
MACCAGNANI, G., 143, 220
MCCAGE, A., 48
MCCLAIN, Yoko, 531
MCCLINTOCK, Michael, 430-1, 436-7, 461, 465, 540
MCKINLEY, Robert, 456
MCMANUS, J., 116, 121, 516, 542
MÄLL, L., 88, 96-7
MAHARISHI MAHESH YOGI, 114
MAKI, S., 100
MALTESE, Corrado, 165
MARANDA, Pierre, 116, 119, 221, 412, 476, 486, 502, 514
MARCUS, Elliot M., 25, 59, 77, 109, 117, 507, 509-10
MARUYAMA, Kazuhiko, 327, 508, 523, 535
MARUYAMA, Shichirō, 508
MASAOKA, Shiki, 5, 175-6, 178-9, 185-7, 189, 195, 208, 302, 307, 325, 327-33, 340, 346-7, 359, 364, 371-2, 409-10, 434, 442-3, 463, 524-5, 530, 535, 537
MATEJKA, Ladislav, 200-1, 514

MATSUI, Toshihiko, 175, 187-8, 208, 328, 524-6, 530
MATSUO, Bashō (see also Bashō), 375, 531, 533
MATSUO, Yasuaki, 523
MENIG-PETERSON, C. L., 48
MERWIN, W. A., 482-3
MESAROVIC, Mihajlo, 493, 509
MIBU no Tadamine, 389
MILLER, Richard, 499
MILNER, Esther, 48, 62, 77-8, 106-7, 117, 493, 501, 506, 517
MINER, Earl Roy, 2, 173, 175, 177, 180, 188-80, 192, 227, 235, 237-8, 253, 261, 266, 269, 275, 286, 289, 358-62, 366, 369-70, 372, 376-7, 382, 386-90, 399, 403, 503, 525, 529-30, 533-4, 537-9
MIYAMORI, Asatarō, 227, 454, 467, 538
MOERK, Ernst L., 304
MOHR, Wolfgang, 476
MOLES, Abraham, 13
MONTAGU, Ashley, 72
Moritake, ARAKIDA, 178, 269, 308, 358, 365-6, 448, 534
MORRELL, Robert E., 179-80, 348, 375, 525
MORRIS, Charles, 14, 17, 22, 198, 492, 495, 515
MOTOYAMA, Gyokushu, 445-6
MUKAI, Kyorai, 48, 185, 203, 205-6, 243, 247, 257, 262-3, 471, 504, 528-30, 533, 538
MUKAŘOVSKY, Jan, 200-2
MUNSTERBERG, Hugo, 49, 148, 286
MURAMATSU, Tomotsugu, 523

N

NADIN, Mihai, 496
NAGASHIMA, Chosetsu, 102-3
NAKAGAWA, Atsuo, 173, 193-4, 364, 393, 433
NAKAMURA, T., 100, 106, 308, 313, 542
NEHER, A., 101
NILSSON, Nils Ake, 370
THE NIPPON GAKUJUTSU SHINKŌ-KAI, 176, 233, 254, 269,

(NGS continued), 301, 315, 320, 324, 396, 452, 454, 525, 531, 534-5, 537
NISHIKAWA, Isshōtei, 162
NÖTH, Winfried, 18, 152-3, 492-3, 497, 522
NORWAY, Mabelsson, 464

O

O'CLAIR, Robert, 173, 360, 369, 378, 380-1, 388, 400, 402, 405-6
OGATA, Sohaku, 57, 94, 110, 120-1, 516-7, 520
OGATA, Tsutomu, 176, 184-5, 188, 525
OGDEN, C. K., 89
OKADA, Rokuo, 481-2
OKSAAR, Els, 47, 501
ONDA, A., 138
Onitsura, UEJIMA, 184-5, 315
ONO no Komachi, 529
ORME-JOHNSON, E. W., 99
ORNSTEIN, Robert, 63-5, 72, 110, 113, 138, 498, 505, 518
O'ROURKE, W. F., 421
ŌTAKE, Masaru, 382, 384, 537-8
Otsuji, ŌSUGA, 187, 392, 526
OZAKI, Hōsai (see Hosai)

P

PATON, Catherine N., 413
PAUL, Hermann, 526
PEIRCE, Charles Sanders, 12, 15-8, 22, 24, 53, 74, 79, 83-5, 89, 91, 96, 126, 130-5, 152, 154-6, 159-67, 208, 468, 475, 492, 495-9, 512, 514, 516, 521-3
PENFIELD, Wilder, 59-60, 64, 76, 507, 509-10
PETSCH, Robert, 476
PIAGET, Jean, 43, 47-9, 51, 55, 81, 93, 98, 153, 493, 501-3, 516
PIIRAINEN, I. T., 70
PILGRIM, Richard B., 203-4, 229, 532-3
PIZZARELLI, Alan, 428
POINSOT, John, 492
POPPER, Karl, 17, 54, 74, 493,

(POPPER continued), 496
PORTER, William, 389
POSNER, Roland, 197, 492
POUND, Ezra, 4, 173, 189, 192, 194-5, 223, 254, 269, 348, 360, 364-73, 375-7, 384, 386-90, 395, 400, 432, 451-6, 458, 526, 533, 537
PREMACK, David, 219
PRIBRAM, Karl H., 117, 138, 493
PRINCE, Gerald, 316

Q

QAMBER, Akhtar, 526, 537

R

RADER, Wendelin, 492
RADO, S., 114
Rizan, KONISHI, 315
RANKE, Kurt, 474, 476, 478-9, 484, 486, 541
Ransetsu, HATTORI, 291, 430
RAPPAPORT, Roy A., 90
REICHENBACH, H., 131
REID, Ian, 239, 316, 375, 537
REINHART, Tanya, 196, 218, 258-9, 372
REINECKE, Hans-Peter, 492
REINIRKENS, Hubert, 481
REVON, Marcel, 537-8
REXROTH, Kenneth, 173, 400, 401-2, 451
RICHARDS, I. A., 89, 218, 259
RICHTER, Hans Günther, 48
RIEDL, Rupert, 16-7, 21, 47, 51, 54, 74, 81, 221, 493, 496-7, 500, 502-3, 512, 521
RIEMENSCHNEIDER, Hartmut, 492, 514-5
RIFFATERRE, Michael, 13, 25, 202, 500
RIMER, Thomas, J., 179-80, 348, 375, 525
ROBERTS, L, 59
RÖHRLICH, Lutz, 487
ROSELIEP, Raymond, 434, 439
ROSEN, R. C., 107
ROSENSTIEL, A. K., 48
ROSENTHAL, M. L., 380
ROTHENBERG, Albert, 81
ROUDIEZ, Leion S., 499, 501
RUTHERFORD, Anne, 413, 466

S

Saigyō, Priest, 312-3
Saikaku, IHARA, 310-4, 320, 428-9, 471
Sampū, SUGIYAMA, 291
SANDERS, Gary, 523
Sanki, SAITŌ, 344-5
Santōka, TANEDA, 307, 332-3, 338, 347
SARNO, Martha Taylor, 47, 501, 503
SASANUMA, S., 70-1
SATŌ, Haruo, 235
SATŌ, Kazuo, 100, 189, 191, 359-60, 362, 365-6, 523, 538
SAUSSURE, Ferdinand de, 12,14, 19, 37, 74, 89-91, 491-2, 499, 514
SCHENK, Brigitte, 48, 217,305, 521
SCHIWY, Günther, 499
SCHMITT, Rancis, 505
SCHNELLE, Helmut, 54, 59, 496, 505, 508
SCHNITZER, Marc L., 71
SCHOLES, Robert, 25, 296, 476, 479, 488, 492, 541
SCHÜTTLER, Günter, 7, 57-8, 107, 111, 138, 505, 517, 519-20
SCHWARTZ, Gary E., 150
SEBEOCK, Thomas, 17, 85, 127, 132, 237, 493, 495-6, 521
SEEGAL, David, 410
SEGERS, Michael, 426
SEI Shōnagon, 489
Seibi, NATSUME, 527
Seisensui, OGIWARA, 307, 333, 335-40, 346, 526, 536
Seishi, YAMAGUCHI, 188, 342, 452, 536
SEKIGUCHI, Shindai, 57, 109, 111, 126, 151, 516
SEKO, Suwa, 530
SHANNON, C., 22
SHIEMAN, Joy 413-4
Shiki, MASAOKA (see MASAOKA)
SHIODA, Ryōhei, 302, 487
SHIPLEY, Joseph T., 198
Shirō, INOUE, 527
SHKLOVSKY, Viktor, 204
SHOLL, Cornelia, 499, 503

SHUKMAN, Ann, 85, 96, 200,204-5, 207, 209, 211, 236, 494, 514, 526-7
Shūōshi, MIZUHARA, 342, 346, 452, 536
SIMMEL, Edward C., 48
SMART, Benjamin Humphrey, 492
SMITH, Richard Eugene, 538
SNYDER, Gary, 173, 401-4, 407, 412, 451, 467, 538
Sōgi, 110, 178, 184
Sōin, NISHIYAMA, 178, 311
Sōjō, HINO, 536
Sōkan, YAMAZAKI, 178, 269,308-9, 387
SOKOLOV, E. N., 25
Sora, KAWAI, 533
SOUTHARD, O. M. B., 422
SPENCER, Herbert, 328
SPERRY, Roger W., 59-60, 64, 113, 505, 507, 509,
SPIESS, Robert, 435-6, 443-4
SPINELLI, Jerri, 413
STETTER, Christian, 514
STEUDING, Bob, 538
STEVENS, Holly, 381-2
STEVENS, Wallace, 173, 362, 372, 380, 382, 384, 451
STEWART, Harold, 192, 250
STOCK, Noel, 537
STOLZFUS, N. W., 108, 112
STREIF, Jan S., 465
STROEBEL, Charles F., 109, 114, 123, 518-9
STURROCK, John, 499, 500
SUEDFELD, Peter E., 101
SUGERMAN, A. Arthur, 58
SUGI, Y., 102
SUGIMOTO, Nagashige, 486
SURACI, Anthony, 424, 434
SUZUKI, Daisetsu Teitarō, 2, 3, 8, 14, 29, 49, 57-8, 72,94, 97-8, 105-6, 108, 110-1,113-4, 118, 121, 126, 128, 134, 137, 139-40, 146, 148-51, 156, 158, 164, 166, 191,245-6, 250, 283-4, 287, 363, 407, 464, 491, 496, 516-7, 519-22
SUZUKI, Shunryu, 57
SWANN, Peter C., 144, 146

T

TAKAHA, Shugyō, 436

TAKEDA, Shin'ichi, 103
TANIGUCHI, Yasutomi, 107, 517
TARTER, Ralph E., 58
TASHJIAN, Georgian, 411,413-4
TAYLOR, Roland, 496
Teitoku, MATSUNAGA, 178, 184, 253, 265
TENNYSON, Alfred Lord, 283-4
TEUBER, Hans-Lukas, 507
TIMPTON, James, 430
TINBERGEN, Niko, 127, 520
TITUNIK, Irwin R., 200
TODOROV, Tzvetan, 200, 209-11, 252, 267, 316-7, 331, 489, 492, 500, 534
TOKUTOMI, Kiyoshi/Kiyoko, 174, 433, 444, 524
TOPOROV, Vladimir Nikolaevič, 118, 404, 483, 488, 541
TRABANT, Jürgen, 492, 515
TSUNODA, Tadanobu, 65-73, 505, 508
TURSKY, Bernard, 150

U

UCHIYAMA, Kosho, 57, 95-6, 99, 102, 105, 516
UEDA, Daisaku, 97
UEDA, Makoto, 9, 172, 179,185, 189, 203-6, 209-11, 223, 229, 237, 277, 284, 286, 325-7, 333, 335, 337, 340-5, 359, 452, 474, 491, 522, 525, 527-8, 533-4,536, 538
VON UEXKÜLL, Jakob, 492
ULENBROOK, Jan, 56, 176, 258-9, 263-4, 286-8, 531
ULLMANN, Stephen, 262-3
UMIKER-SEBEOK, D. J., 17, 48
USENER, H. 530
Utamaro, KITAGAWA, 382

V

VIRGILIO, Nicholas, 174, 420, 422, 424, 443, 451, 465
VYGOTSKY, Lev Semenovich, 127

W

WADDINGTON, C. H., 51
WALKER, William, 539
WALLACE, R. K., 99, 127

WALLAS, Joseph, 511-2
WALTER, V. J., 115
WALTER, W. G., 115, 117
WALTHER, Elizabeth, 153-4, 160, 162, 492-3, 495
WANG WEI,220, 295,334,373,533
WAUGH, Linda, 24, 59, 61-2,68, 198, 493, 502-3,505, 508
WATTS, Allan, 363,400,414,494
WEAVER, W., 22
WEISS, Paul, 495, 522-3
WENZEL, Peter, 48, 56, 305
WERLICH, Egon, 261
WERTHEIMER, Max, 84
WHISTLER, James McNeill, 358
WIGGIN, Larry, 426-7, 459
WILLIAMS, William Carlos,173, 362, 372, 377-80,384, 402, 432, 451
WILLMOT, Rod, 464
WINNER, Eleen, 48
WINNER, Irene Portis, 14,208, 492-4
WRIGHT, Richard,173,405-6,451
THE WRITERS ROUNDTABLE OF LOS ANGELS, 174, 409-11, 414-7, 447,451,458,462,469,471,524

Y, Z

YAMAGATA, Teruo, 442
YAMAMOTO, Kenkichi,187,208-9, 394
YAMAOKA, T., 106
YAMASHITA, Kazumi, 523
YASHIRO, Yukio, 144, 146
YASUDA, Kenneth, 172-9, 191-5, 237,255,264,303,313,361,364, 377,384,387,390-401,404-6, 410,422-4,433,439,451-3,467, 491,494,524-5,531,537-8
YEATS, William Butler, 362,537
YODA, Fumito, 481
YOKOZAWA, Saburō, 176, 525
YOSHIDA, Seiichi, 303, 334-6, 340, 345-6, 487, 535
YOUNG, Robert, 499
YU, Pauline R., 294-5, 381
THE YUKI-TEIKEI-HAIKU SOCIETY OF U.S.A. AND CANADA, 174, 433, 435, 444-5, 524
ZANGWILL, O. L., 72
ZEMAN, J. Jay, 159, 523

REIHE "ANGEWANDTE SEMIOTIK"
HERAUSGEGEBEN VON DER ÖSTERREICHISCHEN
GESELLSCHAFT FÜR SEMIOTIK

AS 1:
Tasso BORBÉ, Martin KRAMPEN (Hrsg.):
Angewandte Semiotik, Wien 1978, öS 200.—
AS 1 zu beziehen über: Verlag H. Egermann
                      Hernalser Hauptstraße 196
                      A-117o Wien

AS 2:
Jeff BERNARD (Hrsg.):
Didaktische Umsetzung der Zeichentheorie,
Wien/Baden b.W. 1983, öS 200.—

AS 3:
Jeff BERNARD (Hrsg.):
Kunstsemiotik – Semiotische Kunst,
Wien/Baden b.W. 1984 (ersch. in Kürze), öS 200.—

AS 4:
Haimo L. HANDL (Hrsg.):
WERBUNG – Zeichencharakter, Rollenklischees,
Produktkultur, Wien 1985 (erscheint in
Kürze), öS 15o.— (Subskription bis 31.12.84:
öS 12o.—)
AS 2,3,4 und folgende zu beziehen über:
         I.N.K.-Sekretariat
         Simmeringer Hauptstr. 185/11
         A-111o Wien

AS 5:
Sammelband mit mehreren längeren Arbeiten von
J. Bernard, H. Bühler, R. Ganser, W. Schiebel u.a.
geplant für Mitte 1985

AS 6:
"ZEICHEN/MANIPULATION" – Akten des 5. Symposiums
der ÖGS, Klagenfurt 1984, geplant bis spätestens
Ende 1985

disPositio
Revista Hispánica de Semiótica Literaria

Vol. VI, No. 17-18; Summer-Fall, 1981

SEMIOTICS AND POETICS IN BRASIL

Guest Editor: Lucia Santaella Braga

Forword, Lucia Santaella Braga; *The Open Work of Art*, Haroldo de Campos; *Poetic Function and Ideogram, the Sinological Argument*, Haroldo de Campos; *Montage, Colage, Bricolage or: Mixture is the Spirit*, Decio Pignatari; *Reflections of and on Theories of Translation*, Julio Plaza; *Semiotics: Science or Method?*, Lucia Santaella Braga; *Semiotics on the U.S.S.R.*, Boris Schnaiderman; *Design-Re-Sign*, Lucricia D'Allessio Ferraro; *Narrating the Narrative*, Miriam Schnaiderman; *Eisenstein: A Radical Dialogism*,Arlindo Machado; *Meaning and Sense, Speech and Language*, Marcio Travares D'Amaral; *Contribution to the Concept of Person and Self in Lowland South American Societies*, Lux Vidal.

Vol. VII, No. 19-21; Winter-Spring, 1982

THE ART AND SCIENCE OF TRANSLATION

Guest Editors: André Lefevere and Kenneth David Jackson

Literary Theory and Translated Literature, André Lefevere; *A Rationale for Descriptive Translation Studies*, Gideon Toury; *The Conflict of Translation Models in France (end of 18th-Beginning 19th Century)*, Lieven D'hulst; *How Emile Deschamps Translated Shakespeare's MacBeth, or Theatre System and Translational System in French*, Jose Lambert; *The Tradition of a Translation and its Implications: 'The Vicar of Wakefield' in French Translation*, Katrin Van Bragt; *Cesare Pavese and America: The Myth of Translation and the Translation of Myth*, Cristina Bacchilega; *The Zodiac:* Hendrick Marsman, Adriaan Barnouw, James Dickey *(A Case Study in Interliterary Communication)*, Romy Heylen; *P. C. Hooft: The Sonnets and the Tragedy*, Theo Hermans; *Texts and Contexts of Translation: A Dutch Classic in English*, Ria Vanderauwera; *Strategies for Integrating Irish Epics into European Literature*, Maria Tymoczko; *Translator as Refractor. Towards a Re-reading of James Clarence Mangan as Translator*, David Lloyd; *Walter Benjamin as Translation Theorist: A Reconsideration*, Marilyn Gaddis Rose; *Review: Gideon Toury In Search of a Theory of Translation*, Ria Vanderauwera; *Mephistofaustian Transluciferation (Contribution to the semiotics of poetic translation)*, Haroldo de Campos; *On Translating Haroldo de Campos*, Jean R. Longland; *The Pleasure of Subverting the Text: Oswald de Andrade's Seraphim Grosse Pointe*, Kenneth David Jackson; *In the Wake of the Word: Translating Guimaraes Rosa*, Stephanie Merrim; *On Translation and the Art of Repetition*, Alicia Borinsky; *Palimpsests, Trans-forms, and the Presence of the Original*, Fritz Hensey; *Two Ways of Translating Oral Poetry*, Hans C. ten Berg.

Subscription, Manuscripts and Information:

Dispositio
Department of Romance Languages
University of Michigan
Ann Arbor, Michigan 48109

Feuillets

Groupe de travail en sciences du langage de l'Université de Fribourg

Analyse de divers types de discours

(volume publié
en collaboration avec l'Association Suisse de Sémiotique)

Table des matières

Claude Calame (Université de Lausanne)
Introduction

Jean-Luc Alber (Centre de Linguistique Appliquée de l'Université de Neuchâtel)
«Bonjour de Neuchâtel où il fait beau et chaud». Essai d'interprétation d'un corpus de cartes postales de vacances.

François-Xavier Amherdt (Faculté de Théologie de l'Université de Fribourg)
«Le songe de Jacob», (Gn 28, 10-15). Essai d'exégèse structurale et linguistique.

Peter Auer (Universität Konstanz)
Eine konversationsanalytische Fingerübung zum Thema «Namen».

Jean-Paul Bronckart (Section des Sciences de l'éducation de l'Université de Genève)
Théorie ou efficacité conjoncturelle? La voie éditoriale.

François Genuyt (Centre d'analyse du discours religieux. Université de Lyon)
«Le retour en Galilée et la guérison du fils d'un officier royal».

Albert Levy (Ecole d'architecture de l'Université de Genève)
Structures discursives de l'espace sacré: l'église de la Madeleine.

Georges Lüdi (Universität Basel)
«Das letzte Wort»: Funktionen des Titels bei der Bedeutungskonstitution im Diskurs.

Catherine Péquegnat (Centre de Recherches Sémiologiques. Université de Neuchâtel)
Logique naturelle, raisonnement non formel et analyse du discours. Un exemple: l'éditorial.

Henry Queré (Université de Lille III et Centre de Recherches Sémio-linguistiques (EHESS – CNRS, Paris)
Pour une sémio-stylistique: le thématique et le narratif dans «The Lilly» de William Blake.

Eddy Roulet (Université de Genève)
Actes de langage, connecteurs pragmatiques et structure du discours.
A propos de textes de presse.

Joëlle Tamine (Université de Provence)
Sur «L'Albatros» de Charles Baudelaire.

Luis Vélez Serrano (Faculté des Lettres de l'Université de Fribourg)
«Yo el Supremo»: analyse sémiotique d'un microtexte romanesque.

Uli Windisch et Bernard Plancherel (Département de Sociologie de l'Université de Genève)
Types idéologiques et types énonciatifs. (Analyse des «lettres ouvertes».)

Jean Widmer (Institut de Journalisme de l'Université de Fribourg)
Thème et maintien de l'ordre. (Analyse d'une émission télévisée.)

Feuillets - Case Postale 442 - CH 1701 Fribourg (Suisse)

Feuillets

Juillet 85   Groupe de travail en sciences du langage de l'Université de Fribourg   N°8

Literature and History

Conseiller scientifique: Prof. Anthony Mortimer, Doyen de la Fac. des Lettres de l'Université de Fribourg.
Directeur de ce numéro: Prof. Ass. Dimiter Daphinoff.
Conseiller en relations publiques: Willy Kaufmann, Lic. iur.
Directeur de la revue: Luis Vélez-Serrano, Lic. Phil.

Table des matières

- Préface, Dr. Dimiter Daphinoff.

- Literature and History, Prof. Anthony Mortimer (Université de Fribourg).

- The First Reader of Romantic Prose, Prof. Peter Hugues (Universität Zürich).

- The Intellectual milieu of Thomas Traherne, Prof. Christopher Hill (Oxford University).

- Romola Revisited, Prof. Robert Fricker (Universität Bern).

- Songs as Illustrations of Historical Processes in Walter Scott's Fiction, Prof. Georges Denis Zimmermann (Université de Neuchâtel).

- Metamorphose historischer und literarischer Stoffe in Doctorows 'Ragtime', Dr. Ingeborg Boltz (Universität München).

- Histoire et Littérature. Quelques réflexions, Dr. Alain Faudemay (Université de Fribourg).

- *Comptes rendus.*

- *Sommaires de revues.*

Adresse: FEUILLETS, c/o L. Vélez, Case Postale 442
CH-1701 FRIBOURG - Suisse

Correspondants: Prof. Eric Landowski (EHESC, Paris).
Prof. Renato Prada Oropeza (Univ. Veracruzana, Mexico).
Prof. Carlos Reis (Univ. de Coimbra, Portugal).
Prof. José Romera Castillo (Univ. Nacional, Madrid).

Zeitschrift für
Semiotik

Organ der Deutschen Gesellschaft für Semiotik e. V. (DGS)
in Kooperation mit der Österreichischen Gesellschaft für Semiotik (ÖGS)
und der Schweizerischen Gesellschaft für Semiotik (SGS/ASS)

Herausgegeben von **Roland Posner** (Berlin)
in Verbindung mit **Tasso Borbé** (Wien), **Annemarie Lange-Seidl** (München),
Martin Krampen (Ulm), **Klaus Oehler** (Hamburg)

Themenübersicht

Heft 1, 1979:	Semiotische Klassiker des 20. Jahrhunderts
Heft 2/3, 1979:	Verhaltenspartituren: Notation und Transkription
Heft 4, 1979:	Semiotik als philosophische Propädeutik – Die Zeichentheorie der deutschen Aufklärung
Heft 1/2, 1980:	Ikonismus in den natürlichen Sprachen
Heft 3, 1980:	Der Kode – Geheimsprache einer Institution
Heft 4, 1980:	Vom Piktogramm zum Alphabet: Semiotik der Schrift
Heft 1, 1981:	Probleme der theoretischen Semiotik
Heft 2/3, 1981:	Wahrnehmung und Gesellschaft
Heft 4, 1981:	Experimentelle Psychosemiotik: Wahrnehmung – Vostellung – Begriff
Heft 1/2, 1982:	Fragestellungen sowjetischer Semiotik
Heft 3, 1982:	Die Aktualität der altgriechischen Semiotik
Heft 4, 1982:	Kulinarische Semiotik
Heft 1/2, 1983:	Kodewandel
Heft 3, 1983:	Kunst und Wirklichkeit
Heft 4, 1983:	Sprache – Schriftsprache – Plansprache
Heft 1/2, 1984:	Semiotik und Medizin
Heft 3, 1984:	Und in alle Ewigkeit ... Kommunikation über 10 000 Jahre
Heft 4, 1984:	Europäische Semiotiker der Zwischenkriegzeit

Bestellcoupon
Zeitschrift für Semiotik

...... Jahresabonnement à DM 68,–
○ ab Heft 1, 1984   ○ ab Heft 1, 1981
○ ab Heft 1, 1983   ○ ab Heft 1, 1980
○ ab Heft 1, 1982   ○ ab Heft 1, 1979
...... Heft Nr. .... à DM 19,–
...... Studentenabonnement DM 34,80
(Fotokopie des Studentenausweises)
Die Preise gelten zuzüglich Porto.
Name ....
Anschrift ....
....
Datum/Unterschrift ....

Stauffenburg verlag
Postfach 2567 · D 7400 Tübingen

Publications Received

ECO, Umberto (1976), *A Theory of Semiotics*, transl. by Yoshihiko IKEGAMI: *Kigôron I + II*. Tokyo: Iwanami (Iwanami Gendai-sensho), 1980.

ESCHBACH, Achim (ed.) (1984), *Bühler Studien* (Studies on Bühler), Vol. I and II. Frankfurt a.M.: Suhrkamp.

HOLUB, Robert C. (1984), *Reception Theory: A Critical Introduction*. London: Methuen.

IKEGAMI, Yoshihiko (1984), *Kigôgaku e no shôtai* (Invitation to Semiotics). Tokyo: Iwanami.

SUERBAUM, Ulrich (1984), *Krimi: Analyse einer Gattung* (The Criminal Story: The Analysis of a Genre). Stuttgart: Reclam.

BBs

BOCHUMER BEITRÄGE ZUR SEMIOTIK

Ziele: Interdisziplinäre Beiträge zu praktischen und theoretischen Themen der Semiotik.
Erscheinungsweise: Unregelmäßige Abstände, ca. 5 bis 10 Bände pro Jahr. Monographien, Aufsatzsammlungen zu festgesetzten Themen, Kolloquiumsakten usw.
Herausgeber: Walter A. Koch (Bochum)
Herausgeberbeirat: Karl Eimermacher (Bochum), Achim Eschbach (Essen), Udo L. Figge (Bochum), Roland Harweg (Bochum), Elmar Holenstein (Bochum), Werner Hüllen (Essen), Frithjof Rodi (Bochum).

Bände: lieferbar und in Vorbereitung (bis Frühjahr 1986):
Bd. 1: HOLENSTEIN, Elmar, Sprachliche Universalien. Ca. 230 S., paperbound ca. DM 39.80, hardbound ca. DM 54.80, ISBN 3-88339-419-X
Bd. 2: ZHOU, Hengxiang, Determination und Determinantien: Eine Untersuchung am Beispiel neuhochdeutscher Nominalsyntagmen. Ca. 280 S., paperbound ca. DM 44.80, ISBN 3-88339-412-2
Bd. 3: KOCH, Walter A., Philosophie der Philologie und Semiotik. Ca. 270 S., paperbound ca. DM 44.80, hardbound ca. DM 59.80, ISBN 3-88339-413-0
Bd. 4: KOCH, Walter A. (ed.), Für eine Semiotik der Emotion. Ca. 180 S., paperbound ca. DM 29.80, hardbound ca. DM 44.80, ISBN 3-88339-415-7
Bd. 5: ESCHBACH, Achim (ed.), Perspektiven des Verstehens. Ca. 400 S., paperbound ca. DM 69.80, hardbound ca. DM 84.80, ISBN 3-88339-414-9
Bd. 6: CANISIUS, Peter (ed.), Perspektivität in Sprache und Text. Ca. 230 S., paperbound ca. DM 39.80, ISBN 3-88339-416-5
Bd. 7: EISMANN, Wolfgang, GRZYBEK, Peter (eds.), Semiotische Studien zum Rätsel. Ca. 280 S., paperbound ca. DM 44.80, ISBN 3-88339-417-3
Bd. 8: KOCH, Walter A. (ed.), Semiotik in den Einzelwissenschaften. Ca. 530 S., paperbound ca. DM 89.80, hardbound ca. DM 104.80, ISBN 3-88339-418-1

Neuere und detailliertere Informationen zur Reihe (z.B. aktuelle Preisliste) sowie Bestellungen (Reihe oder Einzelbände) beim Verlag:
Studienverlag Dr. Norbert Brockmeyer, Querenburger Höhe 281, D-4630-Bochum-Querenburg. Tel. (0234) 701360 oder 701383.

BOCHUM PUBLICATIONS in
EVOLUTIONARY CULTURAL SEMIOTICS

Aim and Scope: Transdisciplinary contributions to the analysis of sign processes and accompanying events from the perspective of the evolution of culture.
Modes of Publication: Irregular intervals, approximately 5 to 10 volumes per year. Monographs, collections of papers on topical issues, proceedings of colloquies etc.
General Editor: Walter A. Koch (Bochum).
Advisory Editors: Karl Eimermacher (Bochum), Achim Eschbach (Essen).
Advisory Board: Yoshihiko Ikegami (Tokyo), Rolf Kloepfer (Mannheim), Roland Posner (Berlin), Thomas A. Sebeok (Bloomington), Irene P. Winner (Cambridge, Mass.), Thomas G. Winner (Cambridge, Mass.).

Volumes: Available and in preparation (up to spring 1986):

Vol. 1: YAMADA-BOCHYNEK, Yoriko, Haiku East and West: A Semiogenetic Approach. Ca. 605 pp., pb (paperbound) ca. DM 94.80, hb (hardbound) ca. DM 109.80, ISBN 3-88339-404-1

Vol. 2: ESCHBACH, Achim, KOCH, Walter A. (eds.), A Plea for Cultural Semiotics. Ca. 320 pp., pb ca. DM 59.80, ISBN 3-88339-405-X

Vol. 3: KOCH, Walter A., Cultures: Universals and Specifics. Ca. 170 pp., pb ca. DM 34.80, ISBN 3-88339-407-6

Vol. 4: KOCH, Walter A. (ed.), Simple Forms: An Encyclopaedia of Simple Text-Types in Lore and Literature. Ca. 700 pp., pb ca. DM 129.80, hb ca. DM 144.80, ISBN 3-88339-406-8

Vol. 5: WINNER, Irene P., Cultural Semiotics: A State of the Art. Ca. 130 pp., pb ca. DM 24.80, ISBN 3-88339-408-4

Vol. 6: KOCH, Walter A., Evolutionary Cultural Semiotics. Ca. 370 pp., pb ca. DM 69.80, hb ca. DM 84.80, ISBN 3-88339-409-2

Vol. 7: KOCH, Walter A. (ed.), Culture and Semiotics. Ca. 220 pp., pb ca. DM 44.80, hb ca. DM 59.80, ISBN 3-88339-421-1

Vol. 8: EIMERMACHER, Karl (ed.), Cultural Semiotics in the Soviet Union. Ca. 270 pp., pb ca. DM 49.80, ISBN 3-88339-410-6

Vol. 9: VOGEL, Susan, Children's Humour: A Semiogenetic Approach. Ca. 270 pp., pb ca. DM 49.80, ISBN 3-88339-411-4

For more recent and more detailed information on the series (e.g. the current price-list) and for orders for the whole series or individual volumes please contact the publisher: Studienverlag Dr. Norbert Brockmeyer, Querenburger Höhe 281, D-4630 Bochum-Querenburg, Fed. Rep. Germany. Tel. (0234) 701360 or 701383.

Vita

Yoriko Yamada-Bochynek, born on March 4, 1946, in Numazu, Shizuoka, Japan. After the college education (1964-66), she became a teacher first at the Heda Elementary School, Shizuoka (1967-70) and then at the Katahama Jr. High School in Numazu (1970-73). In 1973 she crossed the Pacific Ocean in order to resume her studies in English. From 1973 to 1975 she studied at San Joaquin Delta College in Stockton, California, and then transferred in 1975 to California State University, Sacramento from which she graduated with a B. A. in English in 1977. Then she moved on crossing this time the Atlantic Ocean. Arriving in West Germany, she began to study Linguistics, American Literature, and Japanology at the Ruhr-Universität Bochum. In January 1983 she received a M. A. in the above-mentioned subjects. The present study was accepted as her doctoral dissertation by the Department of Philology at the Ruhr-Universität Bochum in December 1984.

Abstract

In analyzing human semiotic systems, the *semiogenetic approach* integrates both psycho-introspective ("mind") and neurophysiological data ("body"). Haiku poetry, as the semiotic product of the philosophy of Zen Buddhism, offers us challenging material: the extremely reduced format and the pictoriality of this poetic genre is dictated by the "right-hemisphericity" of Zen practices, i.e., by the neuro-physiological dominance of the right hemisphere of the brain cortex. In contrast to traditional works concerning haiku, most of which merely comment on individual poems, *Haiku East and West* elucidates the segmental structures, *isomorphies,* manifested not only in haiku but also in other semiotic fields of Zen culture (ikebana, calligraphy, gardening, etc.). This study applies a simple but fruitful analytical method: the exposition of *trimodal poeticalness* - the aesthetic, stylistic, and informational. It thus expounds on the creative process of poetry and its diachronic transformations including its transplantation into foreign soil, i.e., the *poetogenesis* of haiku.

Хайку на востоке и на западе: Семиогенетический подход.
Анализируя человеческие семиотические системы, семиогенетический подход объединяет психо-интроспективные ("душа") и нейрофизиологические данные ("тело"). Поэзия хайку как семиотический продукт восточной философии дзэн-буддизма дает нам интереснейший материал: крайне редуцированный формат и образность этого поэтического жанра диктуется "право-полушарностью" практик дзэн, т.е. нейрофизиологической доминантностью правого полушария мозговой коры. В отличие от традиционных работ о хайку, большинство которых более или менее комментирует каждое стихотворение, Хайку на востоке и на западе выясняет сегментальные структуры, изоморфизмы, проявленные не только в поэзии хайку, но и в других областях культуры дзэн (икебана, каллиграфия, садоводство и т.д.). Настоящее исследование применяет простой, но плодотворный аналитический метод: изложение трёхмодальной поэтичности - эстетической, стилистической и информационной. Итак, предлагаемая вниманию читателей книга объясняет творческий процесс поэзии и диахронические трансформации (включая и трансплантации на чужую землю), т.е. поэтогенезис хайку.   (Перевод: Петер Л. В. Кох)

「東洋と西洋の俳句：記号現象発生学的考察」
人間の記号現象体系を分析するに当たり記号現象発生学的理論は、心理的・自省的データ（「精神面」）と脳生理学的データ（「身体面」）との双方を統合する。この意味に於いて、東洋思想禅仏教の記号現象的結実としての俳句詩学は絶好の分析材料を提するものである。このジャンル特有の極端に圧縮化された形態及びその絵画性は禅に於ける「右脳性」(right-hemisphericity)、即ち脳両半球のうちの右側脳作用の優勢支配によって不可避に決定づけられている。これまでの俳句研究が多かれ少なかれ個々の俳句の説明に終始しているのに対し「東洋と西洋の俳句」は俳句のみにだけでなく禅文化一般（生け花、書道、造園等）に現象化されている類質同像(isomorphies)の特徴的構造を描写している。本研究は非常にシンプルではあるが有効な分析方法、即ち三様態――美的、語法的、及び思考的――に表する詩質(trimodal poeticalness)の分析方法を俳詩学に応用し、このジャンルに表われている詩質を詳述している。俳詩分析の実践を通して本書は俳詩創造過程を描き出し、又、同ジャンルの海外への移植を含めた通時的な変成、即ち俳詩の発生を解明するものである。